Nov. 4, 1974

For Richard E. Su

with best wishes y

Emil W. Knittner

AN INTELLECTUAL PROPERTY
LAW PRIMER

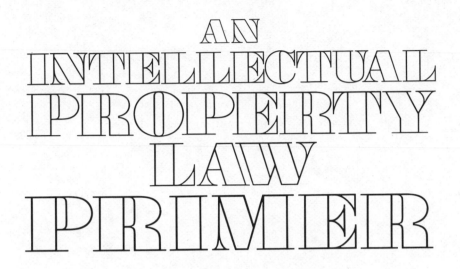

AN INTELLECTUAL PROPERTY LAW PRIMER

A Survey of the Law of Patents, Trade Secrets,
Trademarks, Franchises, Copyrights, and
Personality and Entertainment Rights

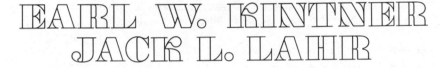

EARL W. KINTNER
JACK L. LAHR

Macmillan Publishing Co., Inc.
New York
Collier Macmillan Publishers
London

The authors gratefully acknowledge permission to reprint
"Reflection on Babies," from Verses from 1929 On, copyright 1940 by
Ogden Nash, appearing at page 327, by permission of
Little, Brown and Co.

Macmillan Publishing Co., Inc.
866 Third Avenue, New York, New York 10022

Collier-Macmillan Canada, Ltd.

Library of Congress Cataloging in Publication Data

Kintner, Earl W
  An intellectual property law primer.

  Bibliography: p.
  1. Intellectual property—United States. I. Lahr,
Jack L., joint author. II. Title.
KF2979.K56   346'.73'048   74–85
ISBN 0-02-364460-5

Printing: 1 2 3 4 5 6 7 8   Year: 5 6 7 8 9 0

FOREWORD

This sixth and final book in my series of Macmillan Publishing Co., Inc., primers for businessmen, lawyers, and students on the antitrust and trade regulation laws is coauthored by my law partner Jack L. Lahr. He and my law partner Mark R. Joelson, who is coauthor of the fifth book in this series, have agreed to share with me the burden of future revisions of all of the books as such become necessary.

E. W. K.

PREFACE

The U.S. commerce of making and selling products and services to the public carries with it a wide range of legal rights and duties, powers, and obligations. Product liability and quality laws, antitrust laws, tax and trade regulation laws, and the Uniform Commercial Code are but examples of the myriad laws affecting distribution and competition.

This book deals with products and services in a nonconventional and, to our knowledge, novel way. Our approach is one of providing for the nonspecialist an appreciation of the way in which so-called intellectual or intangible property rights work in the fabric of U.S. commerce— what they are and are not, how they are gained and lost, and what can and cannot be done with them. We survey the field of patent law, trade secret law, trademark law, copyright law, rights of publicity and privacy and related areas, in a way, we hope, that will provide the reader with a solid survey of the field in intellectual and intangible property rights in the United States. The general legal practitioner, the business executive, the technical administrator, and the student will gain a basic understanding of these relationships from this book if we have done our job.

E. W. K.
J. L. L.

ACKNOWLEDGMENTS

The authors have enjoyed the good fortune of having the benefit of excellent research, editorial, and typing assistance in the preparation of this book. Joseph A. Scafetta, Jr., made valuable research and editorial contributions to the patent chapter as did Jack Waddey in the patent–antitrust area. Thomas D. Lohrentz made valuable research and editorial contributions to the trade secrets chapter. Ruth P. Roland made important research and editorial contributions to the trademark chapter. David L. Cohen made comparably significant research and editorial contributions to the copyright area of the book, as did Rick E. Buell and William R. Charyk with respect to the chapter dealing with taxation. We also had the benefit of excellent research by Douglas G. Green, James L. Sandman, Jack M. Campbell, John C. Filippini, and Joseph P. Griffin. Matthew S. Perlman's comments and guidance with respect to government contracting areas were of great value. To each we express our deepest appreciation.

E. W. K.
J. L. L.

CONTENTS

Trade Secrets, Know-how, and Unsolicited Disclosures

4

Trademarks and Franchising

Copyrights

Rights of Privacy, Public Performances, and Publicity in Commerce

Federal Tax Aspects of Intellectual Property

Intellectual and Intangible Property Rights: The World of Ideas, Know-how, Writings, and Personalities

This is a book about commerce stemming from products of people's minds—ideas—that are translated into writings, communications, documents, and tangible things. These ideas commonly find their way into our society in the form of information, writings, as often as not on a piece of paper or book, a blueprint, a film, an advertisement, a label, a product, or whatever. These "products of the mind," as it were, touch on wide areas of commerce in our industrial society.

Where do we begin? A good way to start is to define the metes and bounds of the commercial acreage of creative (and not so creative) thinking. An individual's idea in a vacuum, kept silent from all, is something like the tree that falls in a forest where no one is present—no one hears what happened. For all you know the pleasant chap who sat next to you in the airplane just might have an undisclosed idea on how to solve the world's energy crisis while enhancing the environment at a fraction of what Congress is appropriating next year, one beneficial by-product of his genius being a cheap and sure cure for cancer. Assuming he has no contractual duty to disclose these ideas and he maintains his silence, the world will plod along spending billions to find his answers. Even if this pleasant chap is an M.D., Ph.D. in biochemistry, with a heavy background in physics, under a contractual duty to Goliath Corporation to disclose his ideas (in confidence and all that), if he chooses not to disclose, Goliath Corporation will never know.

Only if ideas and information are communicated is there a way for legal rights and duties to arise. This might be described as an area of a person's "information" in contrast to a person's "being" or personality, which involves a different notion of rights and duties, grounded more in the principles of the right of privacy or the right of publicity.

CONSTITUTIONAL AND COMMON LAW SOURCES OF INTELLECTUAL PROPERTY LAW

There are three basic touchstones of the law of intellectual property.

Federal Law

First, we have the U.S. Constitution and congressional legislation enacted under this authority. Article I, Section 8, Clause 8, of the U.S. Constitution authorizes Congress to grant to authors and inventors for a limited time the exclusive right to their writings and discoveries. Under this grant of power Congress has enacted the copyright and patent laws of the United States, dealing generally with writings and inventions. Although this legislation is seemingly intricate, complex, and obscure—"a subject for specialists"—its common denominator is simply that of Congress providing a detailed set of standards for (1) what does and does not qualify as a "writing" or "invention" to justify the monopoly grant conferred by the federal government, (2) what the owner of this right must do to preserve this right, and (3) the procedures to be followed in order to secure the right.

Related to this category of congressional legislation is other congressional legislation enacted under the Commerce Clause of the U.S. Constitution. Article I, Section 8, Clause 3, simply provides that: "The Congress shall have Power to regulate Commerce with foreign Nations, and among the several States, and with the Indian Tribes." Under the power of the Commerce Clause, Congress enacted the U.S. trademark laws, but unlike the field of patent law, there is a considerable body of state law in the field that complements the federal legislation in the field of trademarks.

State Law

Whereas federal law exclusively occupies the field of patents, principally the field of copyrights, and partially the field of trademarks and closely related areas of unfair competition, there are fifty states in the United States, each with their own body of law, legislative and judicial, civil and criminal, developed and undeveloped, sophisticated and unsophisticated, that deal with such subjects as trade secrets, trademarks, unfair competition, business and property values, right of publicity, and protection of personalities. Although the law in this field is not all that different between the various states, subtle nuances sometimes exist and may become important to settle a threshold issue of "which state law applies" to a given controversy.

Foreign Law

Ideas, writings, and information know no territorial boundaries and the issues arising under foreign law are resolved, like state law questions, by deciding which law is applied to any particular controversy of international dimensions. American corporations, for example, have learned to their chagrin that the laws of some foreign countries permit, even encourage, conduct that would be stopped immediately in the United States. For instance, some foreign countries provide for trademark registration rights without first using that trademark in the country. Thus, theoretically, if the owners of "Seven-Up" or "Chevrolet" decided to enter that country to sell their products, they might have to deal with the enterprising "trademark owner" of "Seven-Up" or "Chevrolet" for that country if they want to export these trademarked products into that country. On the other hand, in the field of patents and copyrights there are treaties between most of the industrial countries of the world that provide reciprocal protection of rights, subject to complying with the laws of the countries involved.

Then, too, there are revolutions and coups that may cast doubts on legal rights that were thought secure in a foreign country, as well as situations in such industrial countries as Russia and China where inadequate legal remedies currently exist for appropriation of inventions, information, and writings.

THE FEDERAL–STATE LAW QUESTION: WHICH TAKES PRECEDENCE?

With Congress having power under the U.S. Constitution to grant patents on inventions, copyrights on writings, and trademarks on commercial names and slogans, what happens if a state law seeks to grant rights in this area? The short answer is that it depends on the scope of protection sought to be granted in the particular area.

In 1973 the U.S. Supreme Court answered the question in the copyright area in *Goldstein* v. *California*. A state statute made it a criminal offense to retape or to re-record musical performances from commercially sold recordings without the permission of the owner of the master tape or record. The defendant was convicted as a "tape pirate" and appealed. The Supreme Court upheld the conviction saying that the Copyright Clause of the Constitution does not expressly or by inference vest all power to grant protection exclusively in the federal government. A state may grant copyright protection as long as it does not clash with federal law or prejudice the interests of other states.

In 1974 the Supreme Court was again faced with the task of resolving a federal–state law question, this time in the trade secret and patent area in *Kewanee Oil Co.* v. *Bicron Corp.* A federal district court had, in accordance with Ohio trade secret law, permanently enjoined Bicron employees from using trade secret information relating to the growth of synthetic crystals that they had formerly learned as employees of Kewanee. The Sixth Circuit Court of Appeals reversed the district court's decision on the grounds that Ohio's trade secret law was in conflict with the federal patent laws and therefore pre-empted. The Supreme Court disagreed and ordered reinstatement of the district court's judgment, saying that Ohio's trade secret law was not pre-empted by or in conflict with the federal patent laws. The Court ruled that just as states may regulate writings within the holding of its *Goldstein* decision, so may they "regulate with respect to discoveries" through the grant of protection to trade secrets. States may regulate in the area of patents so long as "they do not conflict with the operation of the laws in this area passed by Congress. . . ."

In the patent area in two 1964 companion cases the Supreme Court struck down under the Supremacy Clause certain state unfair competition laws that granted protection to articles the federal patent laws had declared to be unprotectable. In these cases, *Sears, Roebuck & Co.* v. *Stiffel Co.* and *Compco Corp.* v. *Day-Brite Lighting, Inc.*, the facts were quite simple: In the *Sears, Roebuck* case an unpatented Stiffel table lamp design was copied and sold by Sears. Sears did not create the impression it was selling a Stiffel lamp—it simply made a "Chinese" copy and sold it as a Sears lamp. (The facts were similar in the *Compco* case except that an overhead fluorescent lamp fixture was involved.) Stiffel sued Sears under an Illinois law, charging Sears with unfair competition in copying the Stiffel design, which was available in the marketplace. The Supreme Court ruled in favor of Sears' right to copy the Stiffel lamp, for to do otherwise would be to give Stiffel a monopoly on its lamp design based on Illinois state law, whereas congressionally enacted patent law had declared such designs to be in the public domain.

In the trademark area a declaration was made by the Supreme Court in 1879 that concurrent protection by both federal and state law was permissible. The federal authority is derived from the Commerce Clause to protect so-called interstate use. State laws supplement federal law by protecting purely local use.

Thus it follows as a general proposition that writings and technology "in general circulation" may be copied and commercially exploited without consent if the following criteria are met:

1. There is no infringement of a valid patent, copyright, or trademark.
2. There is no "palming off" of a product or service as coming from the copied source, such as would have been the case if Sears had misrepresented the copied lamp as a Stiffel lamp.
3. The writing or technology is "in general circulation" and is copied at arms length, without breach of any contractual or fiduciary duty to the aggrieved party, such as might be involved in misappropriating a technical trade secret.

In a significant way this book deals with these topics—what these rights are, where they begin and end, and what can be done with them. We thus develop this book topically in the areas of patents, trade secrets, trademarks, copyrights, and miscellaneous related rights, from the standpoint of: What are these rights? How are they acquired? What can be done with them? How are they lost?

AREAS UNEXPLORED BY THIS BOOK

This book focuses on the commerce of intellectual or intangible property. We pass over such issues as the flow of information to and from government, be it in the form of subpoena process of the courts, Fifth Amendment privilege against self-incrimination, executive privilege, or governmental secrecy. Commerce, to be sure, can be involved: *The New York Times* and *The Washington Post* published the "Pentagon Papers" without consent of the federal government and presumably enhanced their circulation commensurately. But these issues are not reviewed by us on the rationale that their central focus is the conflict between the First Amendment and the government's needs for secrecy. We also do not include the fields of pornography law, libel, and slander.

Patents

OVERVIEW OF THE U.S. PATENT SYSTEM

The framers of the U.S. Constitution provided in Article I, Section 8, Clause 8, that: "Congress shall have the Power . . . To promote the Progress of Science and useful Arts, by securing for limited Times to Authors and Inventors the exclusive Right to their respective Writings and Discoveries." This early industrial revolution impetus for fostering literary and technical progress is the underlying basis for the copyright and patent systems in the United States. Commencing with the Patent Act of 1790, subsequent legislation of ever-increasing complexity and sophistication has resulted in the present form of protection for intellectual property of an inventive nature.

What, exactly, is a patent and how does it operate to foster the "progress of the useful arts"? In its simplest terms a patent is an agreement between an inventor and the public, represented by the federal government: in return for a full public disclosure of the invention the inventor is granted the right for a period of seventeen years to exclude others from making, using, or selling the defined invention in the United States. It is a limited monopoly, designed not primarily to reward

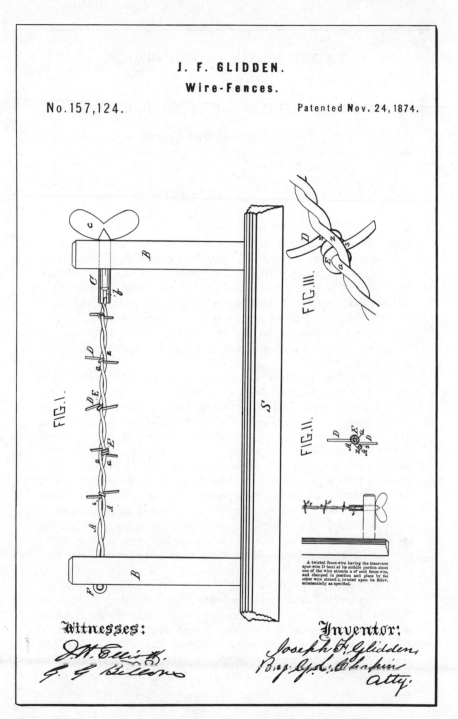

J. F. GLIDDEN.
Wire-Fences.

No. 157,124.

Patented Nov. 24, 1874.

Figure 1.

UNITED STATES PATENT OFFICE

JOSEPH F. GLIDDEN, OF DE KALB, ILLINOIS.

Improvement in Wire-Fences.

Specification forming part of Letters Patent No. **157,124**, dated November 24, 1874; application filed October 27, 1873.

To all whom it may concern:

Be it known that I, JOSEPH F. GLIDDEN, of De Kalb, in the county of De Kalb and State of Illinois, have invented a new and valuable Improvement in Wire-Fences; and that the following is a full, clear, and exact description of the construction and operation of the same, reference being had to the accompanying drawings, in which—

Figure 1 represents a side view of a section of fence exhibiting my invention. Fig. 2 is a sectional view, and Fig. 3 is a perspective view, of the same.

This invention has relation to means for preventing cattle from breaking through wire-fences; and it consists in combining, with the twisted fence-wires, a short transverse wire, coiled or bent at its central portion about one of the wire strands of the twist, with its free ends projecting in opposite directions, the other wire strand serving to bind the spur-wire firmly to its place, and in position, with its spur ends perpendicular to the direction of the fence-wire, lateral movement, as well as vibration, being prevented. It also consists in the construction and novel arrangement, in connection with such a twisted fence-wire, and its spur-wires, connected and arranged as above described, of a twisting-key or head-piece passing through the fencepost, carrying the ends of the fence-wires, and serving, when the spurs become loose, to tighten the twist of the wires, and thus render them rigid and firm in position.

In the accompanying drawings, the letter B designates the fence-posts, the twisted fence-wire connecting the same being indicated by the letter A. C represents the twisting-key, the shank of which passes through the fence-post, and is provided at its end with an eye, *b*, to which the fence-wire is attached. The outer end of said key is provided with a transverse thumb-piece, *c*, which serves for its manipulation, and at the same time, abutting against the post, forms a shoulder or stop, which prevents the contraction of the wire from drawing the key through its perforation in said post.

The fence-wire is composed at least of two strands, *a* and *z*, which are designed to be twisted together after the spur-wires have been arranged in place.

The letter D indicates the spur-wires. Each of these is formed of a short piece of wire, which is bent at its middle portion, as at E, around one only of the wire strands, this strand being designated by the letter *a*. In forming this middle bend or coil several turns are taken in the wire, so that it will extend along the strand-wire for a distance several times the breadth of its diameter, and thereby form a solid and substantial bearing-head for the spurs, which will effectually prevent them from vibrating laterally or being pushed down by cattle against the fence-wire. Although these spur-wires may be turned at once around the wire strand, it is preferred to form the central bend first, and to then slip them on the wire strand, arranging them at suitable distances apart. The spurs having thus been arranged on one of the wire strands are fixed in position and place by approaching the other wire strands *z* on the side of the bend from which the spurs extend, and then twisting the two strands *a z* together by means of the wire key above mentioned or otherwise. This operation locks each spur wire at its allotted place, and prevents it from moving therefrom in either direction. It clamps the bend of the spur-wire upon the wire *a*, thereby holding it against rotary vibration. Finally, the spur ends extending out between the strands on each side, and where the wires are more closely approximated in the twist, form shoulders or stops, *s*, which effectually prevent such rotation in either direction.

Should the spurs, from the untwisting of the strands, become loose and easily movable on their bearings, a few turns of the twisting-key will make them firm, besides straightening up the fence-wire.

What I claim as my invention, and desire to secure by Letters Patent, is—

A twisted fence-wire having the transverse spur-wire D bent at its middle portion about one of the wire strands *a* of said fence-wire, and clamped in position and place by the other wire strand *z*, twisted upon its fellow, substantially as specified.

JOSEPH F. GLIDDEN.

Witnesses:
    G. L. CHAPIN,
    J. H. ELLIOTT.

the inventor (this may or may not follow), but to encourage a public disclosure of inventions so that after the monopoly expires, the public is free to take unrestricted advantage of the invention. Because there exists no duty to disclose inventions, an incentive to disclose is embodied in the patent laws of the United States and most other industrial countries of the world.

The federal patent laws define the terms and conditions that must be met in order to take advantage of this contract offer, and both the federal patent laws and the federal antitrust laws define what can and cannot be done with this patent grant.

It was not until the advent of the industrial revolution of the 1800's that the U.S. patent system started to function in the mainstream of promoting technological progress. Over the past century the story of inventions that have been the subject of patents is the story of progress from an agrarian society to a sophisticated industrial society.

The invention of barbed wire (see Figure 1) was the forerunner of settling the West and producing a cattle-raising economy. Samuel Morse's telegraph, George Westinghouse's air brake, and Thomas Edison's incandescent light bulb were developments of yesteryear; Shockley's invention of the transistor, Carlson's electrostatic copying patents forming the basis of Xerox machines, and Land's instant-film-developing patents, forming the basis of Polaroid cameras, typify major inventions that foreshadowed the development of giant corporate enterprises since World War II.

Not all inventions are landmarks, of course. Each month the U.S. Patent Office issues more than 5,000 patents on inventions, most of which constitute modest, even minor, advances or refinements in the state of highly developed technologies. In order to define with precision the scope and limitations of the inventor's contract with the public a full disclosure of the invention is accompanied by "claims." These claims are carefully framed sentences defining the metes and bounds of the seventeen-year monopoly.

As we shall see shortly, the process of obtaining a patent involves the steps of deciding whether there is sufficient utility, novelty, and unobviousness to justify efforts to obtain a patent, developing a full and complete disclosure of the invention in the form of a patent application required by the U.S. Patent Office, and then negotiating with the Patent Office over the precise language of the "claims." Once the patent issues, whether it proves profitable depends on its commercial exploitation, either by the patent owner or by others under a license arrangement with the patent owner.

A U.S. patent necessarily confines its right to exclude to the United States, its territories, and possessions. If the inventor desires to extend this exclusionary right to foreign countries, corresponding patent applications must be filed in each of the countries of choice followed by compliance with the laws of such countries.

Issuance of the U.S. patent does no more than confer a patent right that is "presumed" valid. A third party who practices the invention without permission may be sued to enjoin the infringement, but that infringer has the right to prove that the patent is invalid and therefore should not have been issued in the first place or, for other reasons, should not be enforced.

Moreover, the patent owner is limited in a number of ways through a highly developed body of "patent misuse" law and the federal antitrust laws. With this introduction let us turn to a more detailed review of the field.

PATENTABLE SUBJECT MATTER

The Patent Act spells out what can be the subject of a U.S. patent in the context of patentable inventions being "any new and useful process, machine, manufacture, or composition of matter, or any new and useful improvement thereof." If something sought to be patented falls into one of these categories, it is patentable if it also satisfies the requirements of utility, novelty, and nonobviousness. Note that something sought to be patented may be useful, novel, and nonobvious yet not be patentable because it is not statutory subject matter.

Technical Process

The first statutory category is *process.* A process has been summarized in a judicial decision as a "means devised for the production of a given result. Its essence . . . may be more clearly ascertained by studying the result accomplished than by examining the means itself in actual operation; but as an art or process it is complete, apart from any end which it achieves. . . ." Thus it is clear that a process is not limited to any particular apparatus. Although at first impression one might think that a process would involve only a chemical operation, a mechanical process is also patentable.

A hundred years before the present Patent Act became effective, the Supreme Court said that a process that described the functioning of a machine is not patentable. Thus until 1968 the Patent Office routinely rejected process claims if they merely recited the inherent function of a machine. However, in that year the Court of Customs and Patent Appeals abolished this rule. In the pertinent case an applicant sought a patent on a process for sorting and counting electrical pulses. One of the claims recited only the steps of the machine that carried out the process. The Patent Office rejected this claim because it merely described the function of a machine. The CCPA reversed, saying that a rejection on such grounds is unwarranted in that the 1952 Patent Act specifically requires an inventor to point out and distinctly claim that which he considers his invention. The Patent Office has acquiesced in this decision and therefore a patent claim for a process may now describe the inherent function of the machine that carries out the process. A patentable process does not embrace the resulting product. If the product itself is useful, new, and unobvious, it is patentable separately as either a "manufacture" or a "composition of matter."

Before the present Patent Act was passed in 1952, a new use for an old process, machine, article of manufacture, or composition of matter was not patentable. However, the new code now permits a new use to be patentable as a process. For example, in one case a clothing manufacturer used a procedure for impressing designs on fabrics by passing them through rollers. The fabric was first passed through a solution that, unfortunately, deposited a resin on the rollers. After several hours it was necessary to stop the operation in order to clean the rollers. The manufacturer found that an old composition of matter, cyclic urea, could be used as the solution without depositing a resin on the rollers. Patents on the new use as a process and on the composition of matter itself were sought. The court ordered the Patent Office to issue a process patent because the new patent code now allows a new use for an old composition of matter to be patentable.

Machine

The second statutory category is *machine*. A machine is a distinctive means for accomplishing a certain result. Thus a machine, unlike a process, is limited to a particular apparatus. A combination of old apparatuses used to obtain a new result is a patentable machine, even though each of the components taken separately would not be patentable. Again, the combination itself must satisfy the conditions of patentability.

Two caveats should be observed about patents for machines. If a machine is claimed instead of a process and the claim is rejected by the Patent Office, a reviewing court will not change the nature of the claim to grant a patent even if there is a patentable process but not a patentable machine. The second caveat is that if an operation of a machine involves human interaction, that operation cannot be included as a machine claim because a human being cannot be a part

of a machine. However, if a step of a process involves human interaction, that step can be included in a process claim. Thus human action
can be a part of a process claim.

By way of illustration, an inventor obtained both machine and
process claims in a patent for sealing waxed milk cartons. The claims
covered a single machine that successively dewaxed cartons, applied
glue, folded the cartons, brought the glued edges together, and held
them until the glue set. The patentee sued another carton manufacturer
for infringement. The defendant dewaxed cartons by one machine.
Workers then trucked them to another room where another machine
glued, folded, and fastened the cartons. The court found that the
machine claims were not infringed because the patent could not cover
the human operations. However, the process claims were infringed
because the patented process could be performed by human interaction.

Manufacture

The third statutory category is *manufacture*. A manufacture is
an article or product. Shortly before the present Patent Act became
effective, the Supreme Court said that the patentability of a claim
for an article of manufacture must be found in its structural elements
and not in its function. However, after the passage of the present Patent
Act, the CCPA said the opposite. The patentability of an article of
manufacture no longer depends on its structural relationship but rather
on its functional relationship. This distinction is important. It can be
more clearly understood by examining the facts of a case decided by the
CCPA.

Cooks often have a problem measuring out the correct amount of
ingredients when they want to make only a fractional part of a cook-
book recipe. The inventor devised a set of measuring cups and table-
spoons marked in such a way as to solve this problem. For example, if
a cook wanted to make one third of a recipe, he used the measuring
cup and tablespoon marked "one third recipe." When the full recipe
called for one half of a certain ingredient, the cook would fill the "one
third recipe" measuring cup up to the line marked "one half." Because
the cup and tablespoon being used were actually one third of a cup
and tablespoon, the cook was able to use the correct amount for a
fractional recipe without making any mental conversions. The inventor's patent application was denied by the Patent Office on the
grounds that the structural elements for such an article of manufacture
were not patentable. The CCPA reversed the Patent Office and
ordered a patent to be granted on the grounds that the function of the
article of manufacture controlled its patentability, not its structure.

Composition of Matter

The fourth statutory category is *composition of matter*. A composition of matter is usually defined by its nature, that is, the elements in combination that make up the compound. However, for the compound to be patentable as a composition of matter, there must be a new result from the new combination of elements that constitute the new compound. This new result must be materially different from the properties the several elements possess individually. Thus a new chemical molecule, not found in nature, may be patentable. In one case a solution of a new chemical molecule administered orally and used to show up the gall bladder in X-rays was found patentable as a composition of matter. A new metal alloy may be patentable. The new combination of elements that constitutes the new metal alloy must have new and materially different properties than pre-existing alloys. A mere difference in proportions of elements is insufficient to make the new alloy patentable. A new food may also be patentable as a composition of matter. However, it is difficult to obtain a patent on a new food product because the recipe must be "unobvious." Clearly a new food would satisfy the other two patentability requirements of newness and usefulness. One such new food product that was patented was the first cured soft cheese. Before this discovery, cheese was of two types: soft and uncured or hard and cured. The cheese industry had considered the two incapable of being blended. Nevertheless the inventor was able to do this by combining cream cheese and Roquefort cheese in a special process that he devised. The result was a new cheese that was both cured and soft.

Note that a composition of matter is patentable separately from the process used for making it. In the case just discussed, the inventor was granted two patents, one for the composition of matter itself and another for the process of making the compound.

Improvement

The fifth statutory category is *improvement*. The improvement may be on an already patented process, machine, manufacture, or composition of matter. In order to be patentable the improvement itself must meet all three requirements of novelty, utility, and nonobviousness. Those that involve only changes in design or proportions are not patentable. Also, a more beneficial result from the improvement does not by itself make the improvement patentable.

Practical complications can occur for the owner of a basic patent if an improvement patent is granted to another party. The owner of the basic patent cannot use the improvement itself without the consent of the owner of the improvement and the improver cannot use the basic invention without the consent of its owner. The problem is alleviated by a cross-licensing agreement between the parties or a sale of one of the patents by one of the parties to the other. However, difficulties arise for both parties where the parties fail to agree on a cross-licensing arrangement. If no agreement can be reached, the public may be effectively denied the benefits of the improvement during the period of the basic patent.

Besides these five statutory categories, there are two other statutory categories that have been established in separate sections of the Patent Act. They cover designs and plants. Design patents will be discussed first.

Designs

The federal statute states: "Whoever invents any new, original and ornamental design for an article of manufacture may obtain a patent therefor . . ." 35 U.S.C. §171. The conditions for patentability of designs are not novelty, utility, and nonobviousness but novelty, originality, and ornamentality. The design patent is concerned only with how the article of manufacture looks, not with how it was made and not with what it constitutes. Many design patents are granted for product housings and other industrial designs.

Designs are also protectable under the Copyright Act. However, the type of protection differs. The copyright law protects creative and original designs for works of art; the patent law protects new, original, and ornamental designs for articles of manufacture. Thus some designs are only copyrightable and others are only patentable. Furthermore some designs may be both copyrightable and patentable. In such a situation the designer must elect to seek protection under only one of the two laws because the terms of protection are different; the patent term for designs is 3.5, 7, or 14 years, depending on the fee that the patentee pays. Also, if protection has already been obtained under one of the statutes, some courts have ruled that protection cannot be later sought under the other statute. There is said to be a public interest in having the constitutional grant pass into the public domain as soon as possible.

Plants

The second statutory category that has been established in a separate section of the Patent Act covers plants. "Whoever invents or discovers and asexually reproduces any distinct and new variety of plant, including cultivated sports, mutants, hybrids, and newly found seedlings, other than a tuberpropogated plant or a plant found in an uncultivated state, may obtain a patent therefor . . ." 35 U.S.C. §161.

Not many plant patents are issued. An average of only about 100 such patents have been issued each year since 1952. As a result there is not much litigation in this area. However, several clarifications of this statute have been made.

The inventor or, perhaps more appropriately, the grower of a specific variety of plant must have initially produced it by means of asexual reproduction, that is, by grafting, budding, cuttings, layering, division, and so on, but not by seeds, for such means is not asexual. There is only one means of asexual reproduction of plants for which a plant patent will not be granted. That is tuberpropagation, i.e., growth from roots.

In order to be patented, the plant must be distinct and new, i.e., having "characteristics thereof that distinguish the same over related known varieties, and its antecedents." The discoverer of a distinct and new plant, not previously known to exist in nature, cannot obtain a patent on the newly found plant because one cannot claim a monopoly on a phenomenon of nature, even if hitherto unknown. The plant must be cultivated or domesticated, i.e., grown and developed by human care. As implied earlier, wild plants are not patentable. These include those found in nature but commonly grown by humans. A plant patent cannot be obtained by a developer of a new strain of bacteria even though, scientifically speaking, bacteria are microscopic plants that reproduce asexually. Courts have interpreted the word *plant* to refer only to its popular meaning and not to its scientific meaning.

An interesting sidelight on plant patents is the nature of the drawings submitted to the Patent Office. These drawings are not mechanical drawings like all others submitted, but artistic works. Color drawings may be filed in oil paint or permanent water colors. Also, color photographs may be submitted.

SUBJECT MATTER EXEMPTED FROM PATENTABILITY

Implied Judicial Exemptions

The courts have denied patents to several classes of subject matter on the grounds that they are implicitly nonpatentable from a reading of the applicable federal statute. Thus subject matter in such classes, even though new, useful, and unobvious, may still be unpatentable.

There appear to be six types of nonpatentable subject matter: first, printed matter; second, naturally occurring substances; third, methods of doing business; fourth, ideas; fifth, scientific principles; and sixth, mental processes. Although some of these were previously mentioned, they will be discussed in detail here.

Printed Matter. The first judicially implied exemption is printed matter. Neither mere printed matter itself nor a process that involves nothing more than the use of printed matter is patentable. In one case a party applied for a process patent directed to a system of writing sheet music. The claim stated that the notes on the paper sheet were given different colors according to the volume of sound to be produced by the note. This information aided the beginner in learning to play a musical instrument. The court found that the claim was not patentable because it was directed to mere printed matter. Nevertheless, design patents have been issued on type fonts for letter styles and musical notes that have been found to be new, original, and ornamental. The printed matter itself is not patentable, only the printing style, such as block, fanciful, or Old English.

Naturally Occurring Substances. The second judicially implied exemption is naturally occurring substances. Such substances would include the elements, natural chemical compounds, bacteria, and other articles that are found in nature. Although a patent for a composition of matter or for an article of manufacture cannot be obtained, a patent for a process for artificial production of any naturally occurring substance can be obtained. Thus Glenn Seaborg, the Nobel Prize winner, was granted a patent on a process for the synthetic production of the transuranium elements. Even though the transuranium elements are not found in a natural state on Earth, it is theoretically possible that they may be found to exist naturally elsewhere in the universe.

In another case a party had obtained two patents, one on an article of manufacture consisting of a fresh fruit with skin impregnated with borax and the other on the process of impregnation for preventing decay. The Supreme Court found the patent on the article of manufacture invalid because the fresh fruit was patented in the form in which it appeared in nature.

Another illustration of this rule appears in the case of an inventor who sought two patents, one on a process of deveining shrimp and another on an article of manufacture consisting of the decapitated and deveined shrimp. A patent on the process was granted but a patent was denied on the shrimp as an article of manufacture. The Patent Office Board of Appeals said that even though the whole shrimp was not claimed, the part claimed was still in its natural state and therefore non-patentable.

Methods of Doing Business. The third implied judicial exemption is methods of doing business. This includes management procedures for saving time or labor. Thus any system of transacting business, regardless of how important or ingenious, is not patentable. For example, a mode of bookkeeping, bank checks with stubs, the drive-in movie theater parking layout, and a cash-registering and account-checking system designed to prevent collusion between waiters and cashiers have been found to be nonpatentable as methods of doing business.

Ideas. On first impression, the last three classes of nonpatentable subject matter—ideas, scientific principles, and mental processes—may seem to be identical. However, they are distinguishable. Each varies in degree from the preceding class in its relationship to patentable subject matter—tangible solutions for problems. Ideas are merely vague and abstract thoughts. Scientific principles are detailed and specific statements of an idea. Mental processes are intellectual applications of a scientific principle. None of these three classes involve a tangible solution to a problem. As stated, an idea is a mere vague and abstract thought. Although novel and useful, an idea is not patentable by itself. Only the means for carrying out the idea are patentable. For example, when Jules Verne, the science fiction writer of the late nineteenth century, conceived and wrote about his idea for traveling to the moon in a rocket ship, his idea was not patentable by itself. However, if Verne had devised a rocket ship for carrying out his idea, he could conceivably have obtained a patent on the rocket ship because it would be a tangible solution for applying the idea. Today an idea for traveling instantaneously from place to place by means of a teletransportation mode is not patentable by itself. However, it remains to be seen whether someone will devise a tangible—patentable—solution for the fulfillment of such an idea.

Scientific Principles. The fifth implied judicial exemption is scientific principles. As stated earlier, a scientific principle is a detailed and specific statement of an idea. Although the conception of a scientific principle or a mathematical expression may explain a long-standing phenomena or mystery of nature, it is not patentable no matter how sound or how acceptable the discovered principle is to the scientific community. Thus Newton's laws of motion and Einstein's mathematical expression of $E = mc^2$ are not patentable kinds of subject matter. Only a tangible application of such scientific principles and mathematical expressions is patentable.

When Samuel Morse discovered the principle of electromagnetism and developed the telegraph as a result, he filed patent claims not only for the specific device but also for the "use of the motive power of the electric or galvanic current . . . , however developed, for marking or printing intelligible characters, signs or letters at any distances. . . ." The Supreme Court found that the specific application of the principle of electromagnetism was patentable but that the latter claim was so broad that it was in effect a claim for the principle itself. Thus the claim was considered invalid because it embraced the whole scientific principle. As an illustration the Court said that although Robert Fulton had obtained a patent on the steamboat, he could not have claimed the "exclusive right to use the motive power of steam, however developed, for the purpose of propelling vessels." If such a patent was granted, the Court pointed out, it would embrace all later steam-powered developments (e.g., the railroad locomotive), which were clearly not contributions of Fulton.

A more recent illustration of this exemption is found in a situation where a party applied for a process patent on a computer program that worked out a mathematical equation the patent applicant had derived. After working through the mathematical equation to obtain the same answer that the computer program reached, the Supreme Court in a 1972 decision concluded that a process patent could not be issued because the claimed invention merely carried out an application of the mathematical formula.

Mental Processes.   The sixth implied judicial exemption is mental processes. A mental process is an intellectual, as opposed to a tangible, application of a scientific principle. An example of a process found nonpatentable because it was a mental process was a method of prospecting for oil. It is known by geologists that underground oil deposits emit certain gases. Concentrations of these gases are always found in the presence of oil. The applicant sought a process patent on a method for reliably and readily determining the presence and amounts of concentrations of these gases in an area. The applicant's method required the sinking of boreholes in the area being prospected. After a vacuum was created in the hole, the concentration of any gases flowing into the vacuum from the surrounding soil would indicate the presence or absence of oil deposits nearby. The court said that although the method required both physical and mental steps, novelty resided in the mental steps. There was nothing new about drilling a borehole or creating a vacuum. The novelty resided in determining, registering, counting, observing, measuring, comparing, recording, and computing the gas concentrations indicative of the presence of oil.

Express Statutory Exemption Under the Atomic Energy Act

Although the Patent Act says nothing specifically about what kinds of subject matter are not patentable, as we have seen, the courts have said that certain subject matter is impliedly exempted from patentability by a reading of 35 U.S.C §101. Furthermore Congress has enacted a statute that expressly exempts certain kinds of otherwise patentable inventions from being patented. The statute is the Atomic Energy Act of 1954. This statute says that no patent shall be granted for an invention useful "solely in the utilization of special nuclear material or atomic energy in an atomic weapon." Any person who has made such an invention is required to file with the Atomic Energy Commission (AEC) a complete description of the invention. In lieu of filing such a report, the inventor may file a patent application with the Patent Office. The commissioner of patents has the duty to refer all such applications to the AEC. Also, any invention "useful in the production or utilization of special nuclear material or atomic energy" shall become the property of the AEC if it was made pursuant to a government contract. However, the AEC may waive this right whenever it deems appropriate.

Even if the invention was not made pursuant to a government contract, the AEC may still direct the Patent Office to issue the patent to it instead of to the inventor. If the inventor protests, judicial resolution of the controversy may follow.

OTHER STATUTORY HURDLES FOR AN INVENTION TO CLEAR

As seen earlier, 35 U.S.C. §101 of the Patent Act spells out what can be the subject of a U.S. patent. However, even if certain subject matter is in the patentable category, a patent may be denied. The Patent Act spells out these specific conditions in 35 U.S.C. §§ 102 and 103.

Anticipation

No patent—if the invention was known or used by others in *this country* or patented or described in a printed publication in *this or a foreign country* before the invention thereof by the applicant [35 U.S.C. §102(a)].

This bar to patentability is called anticipation. It can be raised in three ways. First, the invention, although not patented and not published, may be "known or used by others" in the United States. Second, the invention may have already been patented in the United States or a foreign country. Third, the invention may have been described in a printed publication anywhere in the world. Thus the alleged invention is a "Chinese copy" of another device, patented or unpatented, that was known or used by others before the alleged invention was made.

If the invention was made (reduced to practice) in March, it would be a bar to patentability if it was known or used by others in this country, even though not published, prior to March of the same year. The rationale is that, objectively speaking, the person was not really an inventor. It would be no bar to patentability in this country if the invention were merely known or used in a foreign country before March, but not patented and not the subject of a prior printed publication abroad. However, there would nevertheless be a bar to obtaining a U.S. patent if the invention was described before March (the date of the invention) in a publication printed anywhere in the world, as long as it was available to the general American public.

Prior Printed Publication, Public Use, and On Sale

No patent—if the invention was patented or described in a printed publication in *this or a foreign country* or in public use or on sale in *this country*, more than one year prior to the date of the application for patent in the United States [35 U.S.C. §102(b)].

Under the unequivocal terms of this statutory requirement a disclosure in a U.S. or foreign publication or a public use or a sale of the invention in this country, more than one year before the U.S. application date, will forestall the right to a patent. Diligence in filing the patent application is mandated by this "one-year" rule.

The first part of this section relating to printed publications may seem, at first blush, repetitive in light of the previous section. However, there is a distinction. This section relates to the date of filing the patent application; the previous section, to the date of invention. The Patent Office presumes, until shown otherwise, that the date of filing the patent application is the date of invention, called the "constructive" date of "reduction to practice," unless the applicant can "carry back" the date of invention by swearing under oath to an earlier date for the actual reduction to practice of the invention. The applicant can swear back to a date of invention only up to one year before the filing date of his patent application because if a prior patent or printed document is published more than one year before this application filing date, a patent on the application will be barred. The date of invention is successfully carried back in these circumstances if the applicant's oath establishes one of two situations: first, reduction to practice before the date of the prior patent or printed publication; or second, conception of the invention before the date of the prior or printed publication coupled with the inventor's diligence from that prior patent or publication to the date of reduction to practice.

The factors bearing on whether a document is a "printed publication" within the meaning of the statute are the number of copies made, availability, accessibility, dissemination, and intent. For a document in the United States one copy has been found to be a sufficient publication as long as all the other four factors were present. Thus, the sole copy of a master's thesis on a shelf of a university library has been found to be a sufficient publication. Also, a microfilmed copy of a secret patent application captured from the German Patent Office at the end of World War II and stored in the Library of Congress in Washington, D.C., has been found to be a sufficient publication. However, a similar microfilmed copy of a captured secret German patent application was not considered to be a printed publication because the single extant copy had been misindexed. The Court found the requirement of accessibiltiy to be lacking and therefore the document did not constitute a printed publication.

For a printing outside the United States, a less rigorous rule is applied. In a case involving eighty copies of a British document, one court required the document to be generally available to the American public before it would be considered a printed publication barring a U.S. patent.

The courts have distinguished between experimental and public use in construing the one-year rule. Experimental use of the invention, even though exposed to the public, does not necessarily constitute a public-use bar. For example, in a leading Supreme Court case decided in 1878, an inventor of a new kind of pavement constructed a section of the pavement along a toll road for use by the public. After six years he decided that the new pavement was durable and sought a patent. The patent was granted and in subsequent litigation the use was found to be experimental, not a public use. The Supreme Court said that although the use of the pavement was public in one sense, the invention was not in public use in the statutory sense because the nature of a street pavement is such that it cannot be experimented upon satisfactorily except along a public road. The use of the invention by the inventor himself, and any other person under his direction, by way of experiment, and in order to bring the invention to perfection was not regarded as a public use in the statutory sense.

Thus exposure to public view is not the test of a public-use bar. Nevertheless, even though an invention may not be observable by the public, a public use may still be found. One such instance reported in an 1881 Supreme Court decision involved a new type of corset that an inventor let his girl friend wear before he applied for a patent. The Supreme Court found a public-use bar for three reasons. The Court said that, first, it is sufficient that only one of the patented devices be used publicly. Second, it is sufficient that only one member of the public use the article. Third, because some devices by their very nature are meant to be used only out of public view, the controlling factor must be whether the inventor allowed his invention to be used with or without any limitations. This rationale has maintained its vitality through all these years without disturbance. It has been applied recently to inventions far removed from anything that the Supreme Court could have imagined in 1881. For example, an airplane mechanic came up with a solution for eliminating the periodic need for replacing worn lugs connecting a floating fairing to the last stationary stator section of the JT-4 jet engine used in commercial aircraft. Two techniques were suggested. One was incorporated inside three engines; the other was incorporated inside only one engine. The engines were installed on jet aircraft used in the ordinary course of business. A patent was issued to the mechanic but, in subsequent litigation, was found invalid because the installation was considered to constitute a prior public use. The rationale of the old 1881 case was adopted.

Again, remember the public-use and on-sale bars apply only to activities in this country. Public uses and sales abroad, unlike the patent or printed publication bar, do not prevent a U.S. patent from issuing. Also, the on-sale bar has not been interpreted literally by the courts. It is not any offer to sell the invention that comes within the meaning of being "on sale." Most lower federal courts have said that only an offer made after the invention is fully completed and deliverable satisfies the requirements of this bar. The purpose of this bar is to prevent an inventor from having the advantages of a monopoly for longer than the statutory period by preventing him from exploiting the invention after it is fully developed but for more than one year prior to the patent application date.

Abandonment

No patent—if the person has abandoned the invention [35 U.S.C. §102(c)].

Abandonment is a question of the intent of the inventor. This bar requires diligence on the part of the inventor to file and prosecute the patent application. The reason behind the rule is that it is considered in the public interest for an invention to pass into the public domain as soon as possible. A person can abandon his invention either expressly or impliedly. Express abandonment occurs where the inventor takes some affirmative action openly relinquishing his invention. Such an express abandonment occurs when an inventor dedicates his discovery to the public and refuses to seek a patent. For example, a professor, after delivering a speech at a convention describing his invention, declared that his invention could be utilized by anyone who so desired and stated his intention not to seek a patent thereon.

Although the intent of a person to abandon the invention can be expressly made, it is more often inferred from the conduct of the inventor if such conduct is inconsistent with the right to a patent. Implied abandonment has been found to occur in two ways. First, the patent applicant may fail to claim all that he is entitled to claim in the Patent Office. Any subject matter disclosed in the patent application but not claimed in the subsequently issued patent is considered to pass into the public domain. However, if the patentee has failed to make claims on disclosed subject matter through error without deceptive intent, he may capture the unclaimed subject matter if he files an application for a reissue patent within two years of the date of the original patent grant. Second, the inventor may impliedly abandon his discovery by failing to apply for a patent within a reasonable period after completion of the invention. This bar arises only after the invention is completed. Also, what is a reasonable period does not depend on the mere passage of time but rather on the action or inaction of the patent applicant in each case during the period from completion of the invention to the filing of an application. An example should explain the distinction.

In one case an inventor conceived of a tobacco harvester and reduced it to a rudimentary form of practice in 1947. However, no patent application was filed. In 1949 the inventor went to work for an employer who developed a similar tobacco harvester and obtained a patent in early 1955. In the meantime the inventor had left in 1953 to work for a competitor on his original harvester design. After obtaining patents in mid-1955 and 1957, the inventor sued his former employer for patent infringement. The former employer raised the defense that the inventor's patents were invalid because the invention had been abandoned for six years since it had been originally reduced to practice in 1947. The court agreed with the former employer's position. The court said that although mere delay is insufficient to constitute abandonment, "nonclaim for a period of time of considerable duration will result in abandonment" because the purpose of the patent law was being defeated where the "public's right to a free use of the invention" was unnecessarily postponed. Thus the inventor's inaction during the period

from completion of the invention to the filing of an application constituted abandonment of the invention. Nevertheless, an inventor's inaction during the period from the filing of an application, followed by
a failure to prosecute it for any reason (e.g., lack of money or a mis-
understanding with one's patent attorney), to a refiling of the same
application does not necessarily constitute an abandonment of the
invention.

Prior Foreign Patenting

No patent—if the invention was first patented by the applicant in a
foreign country *prior* to the date of the application for patent in this
country on an application filed *more* than twelve months *before* the filing
of the application in the United States [35 U.S.C. §102(d)].

When an inventor first files a foreign-patent application on which
a patent is subsequently granted by a foreign country, he must have
filed a U.S. application within a year after the filing of the foreign
application. If the inventor does not do so, he runs the risk that this
subsection will bar the granting of a U.S. patent. The risk is avoided
only if either the U.S. patent issues first or the foreign patent does not
issue. The foreign patent may not issue because either the inventor
abandoned the foreign application or the foreign application was turned
down.

Several examples may help clarify this subsection. First, suppose a
foreign application is filed in January 1970. A corresponding U.S. application is filed in either December 1970 or February 1971. A foreign
patent issues in January 1972. If the U.S. application was filed in December 1970, a U.S. patent is not barred because the invention was first
patented in a foreign country *after* the date of the U.S. application on
a foreign application filed *less* than twelve months *before* the filing of
the U.S. application. Even if the U.S. application was filed in February
1971, a U.S. patent is still not barred because the invention was first
patented in a foreign country *after* the date of the U.S. application
even though on a foreign application filed *more* than twelve months
before the filing of the U.S. application.

Second, suppose a foreign application is filed in January 1970 and
the foreign patent issues in November 1970. A U.S. application is filed
in either December 1970 or February 1971. If the U.S. application was
filed in December 1970, a U.S. patent is not barred even though the
invention was first patented in a foreign country *prior* to the date of
the U.S. application because the foreign application was filed *less* than
twelve months *before* the filing of the U.S. application. However, if the
U.S. application was filed in February 1971, a U.S. patent would be

barred because the invention was first patented in a foreign country *prior* to the date of the U.S. application on a foreign application filed *more* than twelve months *before* the filing of the U.S. application.

One more example should suffice. Suppose a foreign application is filed in January 1970. A U.S. application is filed in either December 1970 or February 1971. A U.S. patent issues in January 1973. A foreign patent issues in January 1974. Regardless of whether the U.S. application is filed in December 1970 or in February 1971, the U.S. patent is valid because the invention was first patented in the United States, and *not* first in a foreign country.

The focal point of this subsection is always the date of the filing of the U.S. patent application. From this reference point inquiry is made as to whether a foreign application has been filed within the previous twelve months; then inquiry is made as to whether a foreign patent has issued or may issue before the U.S. patent.

Because foreign patents are not enforceable in the United States, this subsection encourages a foreign inventor to file a U.S. application within twelve months of his earliest foreign filing date if he wants to capture the U.S. market for his invention. If a foreign patent is obtained and a U.S. patent is not, the invention passes into the public domain in the United States and anyone can use it in the United States without fear of an infringement suit by the foreign inventor.

Prior Inventor

No patent—if the invention was described in a patent granted on an application by another filed in the United States before the invention thereof by the applicant [35 U.S.C. §102(e)].

This subsection first appeared in the 1952 Patent Code to codify the rule of a 1926 Supreme Court case. In that case A filed a patent application in January 1911. B filed a patent application in March 1911 on subject matter described but not claimed in A's application. A patent issued to A in February 1912; to B, in June 1912. B later sued C for infringement. C defended on the grounds that B's patent was invalid because the subject matter was not new. The Supreme Court agreed with C's defense, finding that B's patent did not satisfy the requirement of novelty because the subject matter was described, although not claimed, in a U.S. patent already granted to A.

This subsection modifies the rule of this case. It operates to prevent the issuance of a patent to B only where he cannot "swear back" to a date of invention that predates A's application date. A U.S. patent must issue to A on subject matter described but not claimed by A before this bar will come into operation. If a patent does not issue to

A, this subsection does not bar the issuance of a patent to B. If a patent issues to A on subject matter also claimed by B, a patent to B would be barred, not under this subsection, but under 35 U.S.C. §102(a) for anticipation by the prior art. If a patent issues to B first, it will be considered invalid under this subsection only if a patent subsequently issues to A.

As mentioned earlier, the date of filing the U.S. application is considered the date of invention unless the inventor can swear back to an earlier date. There does not appear to be any time limit as to how far back one can swear. However, the earlier date of invention must be proved by strong and convincing evidence. Furthermore, the rule of this subsection has been judicially extended to cover the situation where the first patent applicant can also swear back to an earlier date of invention than the date of the filing of his application. In such a case the later patent applicant must be able to swear back not only before the first applicant's filing date but also before the first applicant's earlier date of invention if he is to avoid this bar for lack of novelty.

Noninventor

No patent—if he did not himself invent the subject matter sought to be patented [35 U.S.C. §102(f)].

This rule applies a different test of inventorship than the previous section. It is used to bar a patent to a person who has appropriated the invention from another. Also, it is used when more than one person works on an invention, as is most often the case in industrial settings.

Sometimes it happens that several individuals are listed as the joint inventors. The rule cautions applicants to list only the actual inventors and not also mere co-workers or supervisors. The test goes to the substantiality of the contribution of each person to the finished development and the nature of the relationship of each such person to the project. In one case the court said that, "it must appear by clear and convincing proof that the two inventors collaborated in evolving the patented device. The two must have 'worked together for a common end, which was finally accomplished by the contributions and united efforts of both.'" Each inventor must make some contribution to both the conception and the reduction to practice. However, the "idea" person may be an inventor even if he contributes no actual work to the building of a model. Whether or not such a person is an inventor depends on how detailed is his idea. In another case a court said that it must be shown that the person "had an idea of the means to accomplish the particular result, which he communicated to the employee in such detail as to enable the latter to embody the same in some practical form." Thus the presentation of such a detailed plan for a working model is considered a sufficient contribution to the "reduction to practice" phase of the inventive effort. On the other hand, a person who simply is employed to build the invention but who has solved some conceptual problem in reducing the idea to a working model may also be considered an inventor. The suggestions from employees must amount to a new method or arrangement which makes up a complete invention. It may or may not embrace the substance of the originator's idea; however, such a suggestion will be considered sufficient to deprive the original inventor of any claim to sole inventorship.

In conjunction with these warnings as to who is or is not an inventor, it should be pointed out that in situations involving either employee inventorship or assignment by all inventors to a common party, an attack on the validity of a patent for misjoinder or nonjoinder of inventors is not favored by the courts. Any such charge is considered a technicality and is usually resolved in favor of the patent owner. In every other situation the question as to who is an inventor may be a live issue. However, clear and convincing evidence of deliberate misjoinder or nonjoinder to defeat one's rights as a joint inventor is necessary to sustain such an attack. Finally, such a charge is not avoided by assignment of the patent to another for the defense carries over against the assignee.

If a joint inventor refuses to join in making a patent application or cannot be found, the remaining joint inventors may file the patent application with a notice to the Patent Office of the nonjoined inventor. Such a notice does not adversely affect the rights of the nonjoined party if the person changes his mind or is later found. Also, if another person is not joined or is misjoined by error without deceptive intent, the application can be amended without any adverse effects on the patentability of the invention.

Priority

No patent—if before the applicant's invention the invention was made in this country by another who had not abandoned, suppressed, or concealed it. In determining priority of invention there shall be considered not only the respective dates of conception and reduction to practice of the invention but also the reasonable diligence of one who was first to conceive and last to reduce to practice from a time prior to conception by the other [35 U.S.C. §102(g)].

This subsection usually comes into play in a priority fight between two or more inventors in a Patent Office interference proceeding. Also, it may be used by parties as a defense of patent invalidity in infringement suits.

The first clause of this subsection is intended to deny a patent to later inventors of the same discovery unless the earliest inventor has made his invention but has committed acts inconsistent with the right to a patent before filing a U.S. application. Such acts as abandonment, suppression, and concealment constitute a forfeiture of the right to a patent because they are inconsistent with the policy behind the patent law of encouraging public disclosures as soon as possible. This policy is thwarted if an inventor, who has not sought a patent for a number of years, is subsequently allowed to obtain a patent and further exclude others from using his invention for seventeen years.

What constitutes abandonment was discussed earlier. One example of what constitutes suppression and concealment is maintenance and practice of an invention as a trade secret. In one case an inventor conceived and reduced to practice a new type of computer in 1957. Later, another inventor conceived and reduced to practice the same kind of computer. The later inventor filed a patent application in 1959. After learning of the later inventor's application, the first inventor filed his patent application in 1963. An interference proceeding was initiated in the Patent Office and a patent was eventually awarded to the later inventor. The earlier inventor was denied priority. The court said that the later inventor had diligently reduced to practice and sought a patent in good faith without knowledge of the activities of the earlier inventor. The later inventor was regarded as the first inventor in law, although he was not the first inventor in fact, because the earlier inventor had deliberately suppressed and concealed his invention from the public for six years by keeping it a trade secret. He sought a patent only after he was spurred into activity by awareness that the later inventor's patent claims would capture the market from his invention.

The second clause of this subsection deals with a different priority question. This second clause provides a rule to be followed where two persons, unknown to each other, have made the same invention at about the same time and subsequently filed patent applications claiming substantially the same invention. Only one of the inventors is entitled to the patent. Whenever such a question of priority arises, the issue is usually resolved on the basis of the evidence offered by the parties to substantiate the conflicting claims of priority.

In one case the inventor's action during the period from completion of the invention to the filing of the patent application was found not to be a forfeiture. In 1953 inventor A reduced to practice a device designed to speed up the operation of automatic elevators. In 1954 inventor B applied for a patent on a similar device. In the meantime inventor A was continuously at work on the installation and testing of his device, during which time several failures had occurred. He apparently wanted his device to work perfectly before applying for a patent. When he learned that a patent was about to issue to inventor B, he immediately filed a patent application and provoked an interference action in the Patent Office. In 1961 the Board of Patent Interferences found that inventor A had not forfeited his right to a patent during the time of continuous experimentation after the first reduction to practice until the filing of the patent application. The appellate court agreed.

Herein lies the importance of keeping accurate, understandable, and bound lab notebooks, preferably witnessed by others, from the time the idea for the invention is first conceived. Such notebooks are admitted as contemporaneous writings and frequently determine the outcome of the contest. It sometimes happens that the person who has last reduced to practice his invention can prevail over another claiming an earlier date for reduction to practice if he can show by records that he conceived his idea before the other and worked diligently on the invention from the time of conception until the time the idea was reduced to practice.

Obviousness

No patent—if the differences between the subject matter sought to be patented and the prior art are such that the subject matter as a whole would have been *obvious* at the time the invention was made to a person having ordinary skill in the art to which said subject matter pertains. Patentability shall not be negatived by the manner in which the invention was made [35 U.S.C. §103].

Before the 1952 Patent Code was enacted, there was a judge-made criterion for a technical development to be patentable known as "invention." Because this notion of "invention" had become confusing, a statutory standard of "nonobviousness" was incorporated into the 1952 Act—an effort by Congress to provide an objective test of patentability. For fourteen years there was uncertainty among patent scholars as to whether nonobviousness was a new concept or simply a new name for the old concept of invention. Numerous pro and con law review articles were written on the issue. Finally the U.S. Supreme Court resolved the matter in 1966 in the case of *Graham* v. *John Deere Co.* The Court ruled that nonobviousness was intended to be simply a better expression for the old requirement of invention. The Court had three inventions before it. Two were found obvious in view of the prior art in one case; the third invention was found nonobvious and therefore patentable in another case. The Court said that three basic factual inquiries were necessary to determine nonobviousness: first, the scope and content of the prior art; second, the differences between the prior art and the claims at issue; and third, the level of ordinary skill in the pertinent art. If there is still doubt as to whether or not the invention is obvious, three secondary factors should be considered: first, commercial success; second, the long felt but unsolved needs; and third, the failure of others. The three basic factors must always be evaluated first in making any determination as to obviousness.

These three basic nonobviousness factors are resolved in the first instance by a Patent Office examiner. If the examiner decides that the invention is not beyond the skill of those with ordinary skill in the pertinent prior art existing at the time the invention was made, no patent will be granted because the invention is considered obvious. The reason for considering the obviousness of an invention only at the time it was made is that it is too easy for one to find the "solution" quite simple when examined by hindsight.

The first invention considered by the Court in this 1966 trilogy was a spring clamp for vibrating plow shanks. The spring clamp absorbed the shock from the plow shanks, thus preventing damage to the plow frame itself as the shanks plowed through rocky soil. The prior art included a patent issued three years before to the same inventor. The prior patent disclosed plow shanks that were not rigidly connected to the spring clamp on the plow frame. In practical application it was found that in plowing through rocky soil, the plow shanks wobbled and sometimes caused the whole plow to fishtail behind the tractor. Also, the vibrations of the plow shanks were causing wear on the plow frame. After learning of this problem, the inventor bolted the plow shanks fast to the spring clamp so that the vibrations caused by movement through the rocky soil were absorbed by the spring clamp, thus eliminating the wear on the plow frame. The inventor then applied for another patent. The Court found that the new invention was obvious in light of the prior art—in this case, the inventor's own earlier patent. The new arrangement was considered merely what any mechanic skilled in the particular art would have done when confronted with such a problem.

The second invention found to be obvious in the same decision was a plastic, finger-operated pump sprayer with a hold-down cap. The invention was, in essence, a built-in dispenser for containerized liquids, such as common household insecticides. It was made in 1956 and patented in 1959. Before this invention, insecticide manufacturers had been unable to develop a sprayer that could be integrated into their containers. The recognition of a solution to this long-standing problem in the industry met with immediate commercial success. However, there were three prior U.S. patents issued in 1938, 1952, and 1953 on similar mechanical closure devices for containers used in other unrelated industries. Although the similar devices had nothing to do with insecticides, the Court considered the prior patents relevant because the pertinent art was said to be mechanical closure devices, not insecticides. Thus these patents were prior art, making the alleged invention obvious in the eyes of the Court. Each of the improvements were found present in one or another of the prior patents. The Court remarked that the problem could have been solved beforehand if someone had simply made a patent search of the knowledge available in the Patent Office. The fact that the solution to this longstanding problem was commercially successful was considered irrelevant because the existence of the prior patents made the solution obvious. Thus the Court invalidated the patent issued.

As mentioned, the patentability of the third invention was upheld as unobvious in a separately decided case argued the same day as the case involving the other two inventions found to be obvious. Before beginning his oral argument, the attorney for the patentee is reported to have poured ordinary drinking water into a glass on the speaker's podium. He then pulled two small metal bars from his pocket and plunked them into the glass of water. Then he connected alligator clips from the metal bars to a small light bulb. Nothing happened. The Supreme Court justices on the bench, attentive to what the patent attorney was doing, were then told that this was the invention claimed to be unobvious in the suit. Some of the justices raised their eyebrows and looked at each other or at the attorney askance. The attorney then presented his oral argument for about thirty minutes. As he was proceeding, the light bulb began to glimmer. By the time he had finished the bulb was glowing brightly.

The invention was a nonrechargeable electrical battery, consisting of a magnesium electrode, a copper chloride electrode, and an electrolyte of plain tap water. The inventor had first reduced it to practice in 1938. He applied for a patent eleven days after Pearl Harbor was attacked and a patent was issued in June 1943. In the meantime, he had shown his invention to the Army and Navy, but it was rejected as impractical. However, in late 1943, at the peak of World War II, the government changed its mind and adopted it for use in Army jeeps and later adapted it to many other uses without notifying the inventor. He did not find out about the use by the government until 1955. He then brought suit in the Court of Claims for patent infringement to recover monetary damages. His claim was granted and the government appealed to the Supreme Court.

The government claimed that the invention was anticipated under §102(a) by two prior foreign patents, one dating back to 1880, and two prior printed publications, one dating back also to 1880. In addition, the government said that the invention was obvious under §103 in view of two U.S. patents, one dating back to 1883. Taken together, the government contended these prior art references showed that the electrodes of the invention were mere substitutions for those used in the previously patented batteries. One patent used magnesium and silver chloride in an acid solution; the other used zinc and copper chloride in a different acid solution. Magnesium was said to be an equivalent electrode for zinc; silver chloride, an equivalent electrode for copper chloride. None of the prior art references used ordinary water. However, this was said to be unimportant by the government.

The prior art also taught that the batteries using water had to have another electrolyte destructive to magnesium in order to be successful. Furthermore, the batteries, which could not be shut off or heated up even in normal use, were considered impractical. This invention had all of these supposedly detrimental characteristics, yet it worked. The reason was unobvious. The use of these two particular electrodes in water balanced out all of these detrimental effects.

In addition, there were several other advantages to this new kind of battery. No dangerous fumes were generated as in conventional batteries using acids. The battery could be stored indefinitely without any fluid in its cells. It was activated within thirty minutes merely by adding water. The battery delivered electricity at a voltage that remained essentially constant, regardless of the rate at which current was withdrawn. Its capacity for generating current was exceptionally large for its size and weight. Full capacity could be obtained quite efficiently over a wide range of currents. It performed with little effect on its voltage or current at temperatures ranging from -65°F to 200°F. Considering all these factors together, it became clear to the Court that this invention was unobvious.

Another case decided bearing on "obviousness" before the present code was enacted points out how the secondary factors can be important. At the turn of the century, newspaper was made by the Fourdrinier machine, which could not produce more than 500 feet of paper a minute. This was considered the practical limit of the machine. If the machine was run much faster, the paper would ripple up and be wasted. Manufacturers had been working on the problem of how to increase the production speed of the machine for years. Then along came a newcomer who looked at the machine and realized why the rippling occurred. The reason was that the paper, while still in fluid form, moved down a slight incline to the solidifying rollers only at the speed of 500 feet per minute. The solution was simple: make the incline as high as possible so the paper fluid would move faster and therefore paper would be produced more rapidly. It worked on the first try and production speed was increased to 700 feet per minute. The inventor obtained an improvement patent and when the paper manufacturers heard about it, they all presumably kicked themselves for not seeing the forest for the trees. The industry adopted the concept within a year but refused to pay royalties on the increased production because they claimed the invention was obvious. The Supreme Court thought otherwise. Here was a good example of a longstanding but unsolved industrial problem whose solution resulted in an instant commercial success of the invention. As a result of these secondary factors the Court decided the invention was not obvious at the time it was made.

The last sentence in 35 U.S.C. §103, on first impression, appears to be unrelated to the rest of the section. It was tagged onto the tail end of this statutory criterion in order to overrule a judge-made rule that the test of obviousness required that it be shown that the invention was conceived in a "flash of creative genius." The hardship of this rule was to prevent the issuance of patents to those who made an invention by hard trial-and-error work. Thus Congress acted to reassure inventors that the patentability of their discoveries would "not be negatived by the manner in which the invention was made."

PROCEDURES FOR OBTAINING U.S. PATENTS

The Patent Office

The U.S. Patent Office is administered under the hierarchy of the Department of Commerce. Located along the Potomac River in Arlington, Virginia, the Patent Office possesses one of the most refined technical libraries in the world. The technical fund of knowledge—and the business of the Patent Office in passing on the merits of some 100,000 patent applications per year—is based on an elaborate system of classifying technical literature composed of U.S. and foreign patents and other technical literature. A corps of some 1,250 patent examiners allocated among all technical areas of patentable subject matter constitutes the personnel principally responsible for determining whether a patent application contains patentable subject matter and, if so, the scope and limitations of the claims to be allowed.

The commissioner of patents heads the Patent Office and is appointed by the president, subject to the advice and consent of the Senate. The Commissioner supervises all the work of the Patent Office and prescribes rules governing procedures in the Patent Office and registration of attorneys and agents to practice before the Patent Office. Also, the commissioner decides certain questions presented in petitions brought by patent applicants.

Selection of a Patent Attorney

Although an inventor may present his own patent application to the Patent Office, he commonly runs into considerable difficulties and the patent he may eventually obtain may not adequately protect his rights in the invention. Therefore most inventors retain a patent attorney (or occasionally a patent agent). Both must have a college degree in either engineering or science. A patent attorney is distinguished from a patent agent in that the patent attorney additionally has a law degree and is admitted to practice law in at least one state. Thus a patent agent cannot conduct litigation in a court or perform other services that would be considered the "practice of law" within any particular state.

The Patent Office keeps a public register of the names and addresses of all those individuals who are admitted to practice. To be admitted to practice before the Patent Office, a person must pass a rigorous examination as to both his patent law knowledge and his moral character. This is done to ensure inventors that they will be rendered competent technical, legal, and ethical services. Only about 2 per cent of the attorneys in the United States are registered patent attorneys, most of whom practice in large urban population or industrial centers or as "in-house" corporate patent counsel.

Registered patent attorneys and agents are prohibited from advertising for business. Some business organizations advertise their services as patent promoters. However, such organizations cannot represent inventors before the Patent Office and are not subject to Patent Office discipline for misconduct.

Selection of a patent attorney, like selection of a general lawyer, physician, or accountant is commonly based on referrals by others, by reputation in the field, and by level of experience in the general area of interest. The patent bar, small and sophisticated a group that it is, is further broken down into varying areas of technological and legal areas. There are patent attorneys who concentrate in chemical, pharmaceutical, electronic, or other areas. The choice of a patent attorney may depend in part on the sophistication of the technical subject matter. Moreover, there are patent attorneys who concentrate their practice in litigation and licensing matters, others who confine their practice to prosecution of patent applications in the Patent Office, others who perform in both areas. Indeed, when efforts are made to secure foreign patents, the U.S. patent attorney commonly refers this work to a patent attorney in the foreign country of interest, while retaining general supervisory authority over the foreign patent efforts. Most patent law firms are well staffed to deal with issues arising in all these areas.

Developing a Description of the Invention

In the earliest stages of invention development the inventor will need to develop, with drawings, sketches, and memoranda, an informal description of the invention that will enable the reader to understand precisely what the inventor believes may be the subject of a patent. Final and complete engineering drawings are not necessary; a straightforward, readily understandable description of the technical subject matter will suffice. These documents, preferably dated and witnessed by another (or others) who understands the development, will aid in documenting the earliest time of conception of the invention and may prove highly useful in the event a controversy ever develops over the date of conception. In all events these documents have two immediate purposes:

1. They enable the patent attorney to grasp quickly the subject matter with which he will be dealing.
2. They provide a basis for the patent searcher to understand the nature of the development, which is absolutely necessary for him to carry on his searching responsibilities. As the invention is refined, changed, or modified, the development of documentation will enable the patent attorney to keep abreast of the refinements in thinking on the part of the inventor and help insure that the patent application, if prepared, corresponds to the inventor's current thinking.

A patent on an application for an invention that has been reduced to drawings and specifications but for which no working model has been made is known as a "paper" patent. A good example of a commercially valuable paper patent was the pioneer patent for the submersible offshore oil-drilling rig for which no model was made until after a patent issued.

The Preliminary Search

As we have seen, it is of no consequence that an inventor subjectively believes he has developed an invention, for the test of patentability is one based on objective standards. Some objective facts can be determined at the outset, but not necessarily all. Therefore the first objective test is an evaluation of what the invention discloses in light of "prior art"—is there a prior published teaching such that the Patent Office would find the invention old or obvious? To try to answer this question, the patent attorney will arrange for a *search*, sometimes called a patentability search—in the public search room of the U.S. Patent Office, where the technical literature available to the Patent Office examiners is duplicated and similarly classified. Even an examiner's more elaborate technical literature on the subject may be canvassed.

This search is conducted by professional searchers in Washington, D.C., commonly associated with patent law firms, by some free-lancers, and sometimes by the patent attorney himself. Many large corporations maintain their own staff of searchers to process their continuous flow of technical developments. The search cannot be considered a totally reliable criterion for evaluating patentability, but is the best-known procedure to follow. Unreliability arises because technical prior art may not be physically found in the Patent Office, such as is the case where foreign publications or obscure technical publications are relevant, or because judgment calls are necessary as to where to search, or because the limitations of time and money may not permit as exhaustive a prior art search as is really necessary.

In all events an evaluation of the closest prior art uncovered by the search allows the patent attorney to formulate a fairly informed decision as to whether the invention (1) is probably patentable or not and (2) if patentable, whether the likely scope of patent protection will be broad or narrow. These factors form the basis of a decision whether to proceed further.

Application Proceedings

Having completed a preliminary search and having determined to seek a patent, the first step in the administrative process is the preparation and filing of a patent application in the U.S. Patent Office, together with the appropriate oath and filing fees.

Under previous Patent Acts a model was also always required. However, the present Patent Act makes submission of a model optional with the examiner, a requirement rarely invoked. A specimen is sometimes requested where the application covers a composition of matter such as a chemical or a food. There is one type of invention for which a model is always requested: a perpetual motion machine—for understandable "doubting Thomas" reasons.

In any event the patent application must include a *specification,* which is a description or a disclosure of the invention, an explanation:

> . . . in such full, clear, concise, and exact terms as to enable any person skilled in the art to which it pertains, or with which it is most nearly connected, to make and use the same, and shall set forth the best mode contemplated by the inventor of carrying out his invention [35 U.S.C. §112].

This requirement is the inventor's side of the contractual duty to the public; it is a requirement of full disclosure of the invention, not partial disclosure or inadequate disclosure lacking important details. The description must be complete so "as to enable any person skilled in the art" to make the invention. The inventor cannot disclose one mode and seek a patent while failing to disclose the best mode in order to practice the latter as a trade secret. For example, in one case the patentee had obtained a process patent for goldplating. A broad range of temperatures and currents were disclosed, which included the conditions for practicing the process. However, the patentee gave examples that produced poor results and did not state the precise conditions of temperature and current that achieved the best results. The court found that the patent was invalid because the best mode contemplated by the inventor for carrying out his invention was not set forth. In another case the patentee had obtained a patent on a composition of matter for a therapeutic preparation used in the treatment of iron deficiency anemia. In subsequent litigation for patent infringement, a defendant pointed out that the patentees had failed to disclose a preheating step in the manufacturing process that was suggested by a co-worker to produce a better result. The patentees countered that they believed the step to be unnecessary. The court held that the patent set forth the best mode contemplated by the inventors, although not a better mode contemplated by another, of carrying out the invention.

The preparation of the specification and claims is the forte of the skilled patent practitioner, trained in the subtle nuances of translating the technical disclosures of inventors into the multitudinous standards of disclosure reflected in the statutes, the Patent Office Rules of Practice, the examination standards of the Patent Office examiners, as well as the case law in the field. This is a technical writing at its most demanding level, requiring technical skill as well as legal and organizational ability of the highest order.

Once the patent application is filed in the Patent Office, the application is taken up by an examiner, who reviews the application for adequacy of disclosure, and, based on his own independent search of prior art, takes action on the key issue of whether any or all of the claims define an invention over the prior art. Commonly, the examiner, in the form of "official action," initially rejects claims over earlier patents or publications, saying that this prior art teaches the claimed invention. The patent attorney, on receiving the examiner's "official action," then reviews the examiner's position, evaluates the patents cited by the examiner (if the search was good, hopefully there will be no surprises here), and files an "amendment" to the application—changes to the text, revisions to the claims—aimed at more concisely defining the invention, accompanied by arguments why the prior art cited by the examiner does not operate to forestall patent protection as defined in the revised claims. This battle goes back and forth between the examiner and the inventor's attorney until an agreement or an impasse is reached. An agreement is reached when the examiner and the attorney no longer dispute whether or not a patent should issue and, if so, what the precise language of the claims will be. An impasse is reached when the attorney still disputes the examiner's refusal to allow any or all claims.

Divisions, Continuations, and CIPs

A patent application filed later for a separate invention, carved out of a pending application, is called a division. A division, sometimes called a divisional application, must be filed by the same party who filed the earlier or parent application. Also, the division must disclose and claim only that portion of the subject matter in the earlier application that relates to the invention sought to be patented. No new subject matter may be introduced. Also, the filing date of the division has the benefit of the filing date of the earlier parent application, if filed before the patenting, abandonment of, or termination of proceedings on the parent application.

A division is filed in response to a patent examiner's determination that the earlier application covers two or more independent or distinct inventions. Because each patent issues for only one invention, an applicant will be required to file such a divisional application to pursue his efforts to secure complete patent protection. If an applicant files a division when the examiner has not first decided that the earlier application covers two or more inventions and patents later issue on both the earlier and the later applications, the patent owner may find in subsequent litigation he will have to deal with the issue of double patenting—a subject to be discussed in detail in the next subsection.

A patent application filed later for the same invention sought to be patented in an earlier pending application is called a continuation. A continuation must be filed by the same party who filed the earlier application. Also, the continuation must disclose the same subject matter in the earlier application. The filing date of the continuation has the benefit of the same filing date as the earlier application. A continuation is sometimes filed in response to a patent examiner's final rejection of any or all claims in the earlier application. Thus a persistent applicant may make a new set of claims in the continuation that is covered by the same disclosure repeated from the earlier application. The continuation entitles the applicant to a further examination by the patent examiner. Thereafter the earlier application will be abandoned by the applicant in favor of the continuation.

A patent application filed later for the same invention sought to be patented in an earlier application but adding new subject matter is called a continuation-in-part, or a CIP. The CIP has its own filing date with respect to the newly disclosed subject matter. A CIP does not have to be filed by the same inventive entity that filed the earlier application if the examiner orders the earlier application to be divided because it contains more than one invention. If such an order is made, a sole applicant may file a CIP derived from an earlier application filed by joint inventors.

Double Patenting

An applicant must be careful when he files a number of applications that he claims different subject matter in each application. Otherwise, all claims duplicated in more than one application will be rejected for *double patenting*. There are two kinds of rejections for double patenting. The first type of rejection is based on 35 U.S.C. §101, which states that a person "may obtain *a* patent" for an invention. The second type of rejection was judicially created. It is based on the public policy that an inventor should be prohibited from prolonging his patent monopoly if claims in a second application are obvious in light of, and therefore not patentably distinguishable from, claims in an application already allowed.

An example should clarify this second type of rejection. In 1962 two chemists obtained a patent for a process for preparing highly polymeric linear polyesters. In 1965 they filed an application for a process of preparing linear aromatic polyesters. The Patent Office rejected this second application on the grounds of double patenting because the subject matter was obvious in light of their earlier patent. The applicants appealed to the CCPA, which upheld the rejection.

It is interesting to note that just a week earlier the CCPA allowed a patent to issue on a second application that was obvious in light of the applicants' earlier issued patent because the applicants had made a terminal disclaimer of any remaining time in the patent term of the second application after the first patent would expire. The court considered the public policy argument against double patenting of subject matter obvious in view of an applicant's earlier patent to be moot where a terminal disclaimer is filed. The court added that a terminal disclaimer is not effective to overcome the first type of rejection for double patenting because the same invention, rather than similar inventions, is involved.

It should be pointed out that rejections for double patenting are made only where the same inventive entity is involved. If different inventors made the subject matter in both the earlier patent and the later application, even though the inventions may be now commonly owned, the later application will not be rejected for double patenting but rather for obviousness under 35 U.S.C. §103 in view of the prior art—the earlier patent.

File Wrapper Estoppel

Sometimes after claims have been made by the applicant and rejected by the examiner because of prior art, the patent attorney may amend the claims and accompany the amendments with arguments as to how the amended claims are distinguished from the prior art cited by the examiner, what the amended claims do not cover, and what is really the scope of the invention. When the examiner and the attorney finally agree as to the precise language of these amended claims, the arguments made to win the examiner's acceptance of the claims will appear in the "file wrapper"—the collection of papers constituting the prosecution history of the patent in the Patent Office. These arguments may become important if any future litigation involves the scope of the invention. The patent owner will be "estopped" from asserting that the invention covers subject matter contrary to that urged in the arguments appearing in the file wrapper.

The leading case that expounded this doctrine concerned the basic patent for the pinball machine game which so engrosses the attention of many teenagers. In this 1942 case decided by the Supreme Court, an aspect of file wrapper estoppel dealing with the scope of a narrowed claim was involved. The applicant had obtained a patent in 1938 on a "contact switch for ball rolling games." It appeared that one of the original claims filed in the Patent Office covered a "conductor means carried by the table." The examiner rejected this claim because he considered it old in the pertinent art. In order to obtain the examiner's approval the attorney limited the claim by changing the language to a "conductor means embedded in the table." The patentee then brought infringement suits against the manufacturers of six other pinball machines, all of which had conductor means carried by the table but only two of which had the conductor means embedded in the table. The manufacturers argued that the patent was not infringed because the original claim had been so limited during its prosecution in the Patent Office that the patent did not embrace the six accused devices, as the patentee was now contending. The Supreme Court said that the patent owner was estopped from asserting charges of infringement against four of the six devices. Thus the doctrine of file wrapper estoppel means that the patentee cannot recapture coverage he has surrendered by amendment or argument whether or not the examiner was correct in his insistence upon the changes. If the applicant is dissatisfied with the examiner's position, he should appeal to the Board of Appeals. If he accepts a narrower claim in order to get his patent earlier, the patentee is bound by its language. Such language along with the accompanying arguments appearing in the file wrapper will be strictly construed against him in any future lawsuit.

Interference Proceedings

Sometimes two or more inventors file applications at about the same time claiming substantially the same invention. Because a patent can be granted to only one of the inventors, an interference proceeding is initiated in the Patent Office. Besides an interference between two or more applications, such a proceeding may be initiated between an application claiming the same invention and a patent that has already issued less than one year before the claim was made. About 1 per cent of the total number of applications are placed into interference proceedings. A study of interferences terminated between 1950 and 1959 showed that the applicant who was the first to file prevailed three out of four times over the party who filed later.

Such a proceeding is conducted before the Patent Office Board of Patent Interferences. The board consists of three interference examiners. The question of whom will be granted the invention is a question of the one being prior in time also being prior in right. Such a priority question depends on the dates of conception and reduction to practice for each inventor. The date for reduction to practice is, subject to countervailing facts, the date of filing the application unless the inventor can carry it back by swearing under oath to an earlier date and by presentation of evidence such as laboratory notebooks and affidavits of collaborating witnesses. If inventor A shows himself to be the first to reduce his invention to practice, he will be granted the patent unless inventor B, being the last to reduce to practice, proves that he was the first to conceive and also that he has exercised reasonable diligence in reducing the invention to practice after the date of conception of inventor A.

Judicial review of the board's ruling may be obtained by the losing party in either one of two ways. First, a civil action may be filed against the successful party in federal district court or, second, the loser may appeal directly to the Court of Customs and Patent Appeals.

Public-Use Proceedings

Sometimes a person, after learning that another party has filed a patent application, will protest to the Patent Office that a patent should not be granted. Although any member of the public may protest, the Patent Code does not provide an opposition proceeding. Protests are merely acknowledged by the Patent Office and referred to the examiner handling the patent application for his information.

Only in one instance may a protest be acted upon at the Patent Office. If the protest alleges that the invention sought to be patented has been in public use for more than one year before the application was filed, a public-use proceeding may be instituted. The protestor must file a petition with the commissioner of patents during the pendency of the challenged application. Most public-use proceedings grow out of interference proceedings in which one of the litigants charges that the other's invention has been in public use. Where such a charge is made, the interference proceeding is halted until the public-use proceeding is completed. A petition for initiation of a public-use proceeding must be supported by affidavits and must make a prima facie showing of a prior public use. Otherwise, the proceeding will not be instituted. Finally, if the Patent Office makes a decision favorable to the patent applicant on the question of public use, the petitioner will not be heard further in the prosecution of the patent application. Of course, if the ruling is favorable to the petitioner the patent application will be rejected.

Appeals and Judicial Review

In order to break the impasse over an examiner's rejection of claims a persistent inventor and his patent attorney may appeal to the Patent Office Board of Appeals. The board is composed of the commissioner of patents, three assistant commissioners, and up to fifteen examiners-in-chief. However, only three examiners-in-chief usually sit for each appeal. A brief must be filed by the applicant in support of his position. The examiner likewise files a brief supporting his position. Also, if desired, the inventor's patent attorney may have an oral hearing.

If the board rules against the applicant, judicial review may be obtained. The applicant may file a civil action against the commissioner of patents in the federal District Court for the District of Columbia or he may appeal to the Court of Customs and Patent Appeals. In the civil action the applicant will present his full case to the trial judge who will decide whether or not a patent should be issued. In the CCPA the court will confine its review to the Patent Office records to determine whether the board's ruling should be affirmed or reversed. Most applicants seek judicial review by the CCPA because the judges are generally more knowledgeable in technical matters than the D.C. district court judges and, more importantly, because the CCPA, unlike the district court, does not work under a presumption that the expertise of the administrative agency should be weighed to resolve doubts against the appealing applicant and in favor of the Patent Office. Thus during the fiscal years 1961 through 1971, the CCPA reversed the Patent Office in 25 to 46 per cent of the cases each year whereas the D.C. district court reversed the Patent Office in from 0 to only 11 per cent of the cases each year.

Ultimate review is, of course, to the Supreme Court. However, patent validity cases are infrequently taken by the Supreme Court. For example, after the Supreme Court decided the validity of three patents in 1966, it did not decide another patent validity case until it rendered an opinion on the validity of a combination patent in 1969.

Correction of Patents by Disclaimer or Reissue

After a patent issues, the owner sometimes finds to his dismay that through his own fault the patent is defective in some manner. To alleviate such a problem, the patentee may either file a disclaimer or apply for a reissue patent. The owner may disclaim one or more claims of his patent if he considers them invalid. Such a disclaimer is thereafter treated as part of the original patent. A disclaimer of all claims constitutes a dedication of the patent to the public.

Of the 325,000 inventions patented during the years 1966–1970, about 1,000 reissue patents were applied for and granted. The reissue patent replaces the original patent and is granted only for the remainder of the term of the original. No new subject matter may be added. Also, the patentee must show that the defect occurred through an error made without any deceptive intent. Furthermore, the reissue must be applied for within two years of the original patent grant.

Although a reissue may solve a problem for the patentee, it may create problems for someone else. After the original patent has been issued, a party may begin manufacturing a competing product that does not infringe the patent. However, if a reissue is subsequently granted, he may become an infringer. Whether or not the party has any intervening rights was originally a question of equity for a court, but now has been codified in the present Patent Act. Intervening rights are personal defenses. A third party may not assert someone else's intervening rights on his own behalf.

Where the claims in the reissue repeat the claims in the original patent, there is no problem of intervening rights because the question of whether or not a party infringes the original patent is unaffected by the grant of a reissue. If a party infringed the original patent, he will also be infringing the reissue. The problem of intervening rights arises where the claims in the reissue are broader than the claims in the original patent. There are two types of protection for any intervening rights of a party. The first type is absolute for the time period after the original patent was granted but before the reissue was granted; the second is discretionary with the court for the time period after the reissue is granted.

Where a party had not infringed the original claims but now infringes the reissue claims, the statute extends absolute protection against any charge of infringement for manufacture, use, or sale after the original patent was granted but before the reissue was granted. Also, where a party had not infringed the original claims but now infringes the reissue claims, the statute allows protection to be extended in the discretion of the court against any charge of infringement for manufacture, use, or sale after the reissue was granted. Such discretionary protection may be given in two ways. First, the court may permit the infringement of the reissue patent to continue unabated even after the reissue is granted. Second, the court may permit the making, using, or selling of a product or an apparatus or the practice of a process to begin where substantial preparation was made in good faith during the time period after the original patent was issued but before the reissue was granted. For example, in a 1958 case an inventor obtained a patent on a truck body designed to carry wooden cases containing soda bottles. Another party, after learning of the patent, examined it carefully and built a different truck body designed for the same purpose. The party went to considerable expense to convert its entire business into large-scale production of the truck body. Thereafter, the patentee, after realizing that he had not claimed all that he was entitled to claim, applied for and obtained a broadened reissue patent. The patentee then sued the other party for infringement. The court found that the defendant's truck body infringed the reissue although it had not infringed the original patent. Nevertheless, the court refused to award damages for the defendant's activities before the grant of the reissue. The defendant's intervening rights were considered absolute. Furthermore, the court refused in its discretion to grant an injunction against the continued manufacture, use, and sale of the truck body because the defendant's substantial investment made in the interim between the grant of the original patent and the grant of the reissue was considered sufficient to give it an intervening right against any charge of infringement of the reissue. However, the court did grant an injunction against any further expansion of the defendant's business.

"Patent Pending" and Like Marks

After a U.S. patent application has been filed, the applicant who decides to lease or sell his invention commercially may mark it with the phrase *patent pending*. There is no legal effect of these words; nevertheless, the phrase does serve to give notice to the world that one may be running the risk of infringement if he makes, uses, or sells the invention without permission of the owner after the patent issues. However, before the patent issues, anyone may make, use, or sell the invention without liability. Patent protection does not begin until the patent is granted. Use of the phrase *patent pending* where no patent application has been filed is punishable by a fine of $500 for each offense. Because such false markings are considered against the public interest, anyone may sue the violator for half of the fine. The other half goes to the federal government. A similar prohibition levies the same fine for a false marking with the word *patented* or words of similar import.

Secrecy of Patent Office Disclosures

Application for patents shall be kept in confidence by the Patent Office and no information concerning the same given without authority of the applicant or owner unless necessary to carry out the provisions of any Act of Congress or in such special circumstances as may be determined by the Commissioner [35 U.S.C. §122].

This statute guarantees a patent applicant that any disclosures made to the Patent Office during the pendency of an application will be kept secret until a patent issues. To assure inventors that this rule will be adhered to by federal employees, a criminal prohibition against disclosing any such secrets has been enacted.

The Patent Office is required to transmit any information concerning an application relating to atomic energy, outer-space activities, and the national security to the Atomic Energy Commission, the National Aeronautics and Space Administration, and the various Department of Defense military branches, respectively. Such information is passed along without authorization from the patent applicant to help carry out the provisions of various Acts of Congress under which these agencies operate.

The file of a terminated interference involving a patent, the file wrapper of an issued patent, and recorded assignments of patents are areas of public information. The courts have recognized that pending patent applications are not public documents until they develop into patents. However, both pending and abandoned applications have been the subject of a limited disclosure made under a court order where the application is relevant to matters in litigation. Otherwise, the Patent Office wraps a blanket of secrecy around all pending, abandoned, and rejected applications, except those that are abandoned but are referred to in an issued patent. Applications for which no patents were issued are preserved in the Patent Office for a period of twenty years, after which time they are destroyed, unless marked for preservation for some special reason.

Outside of the Patent Act, Congress has legislated that the public-disclosure requirements of the Freedom of Information Act do not apply to matters specifically exempted from disclosure by statute (35 U.S.C. §122 for the Patent Office) and to trade secrets obtained from a person in a privileged or confidential manner. These exemptions have been posited by the courts as a bar to access by the public of both pending and abandoned applications in the Patent Office.

FOREIGN PATENTS

The procedures for obtaining a foreign patent and the scope of protection granted vary greatly among the industrialized countries of the world. Most of the developing countries have adopted their patent system from one of the major industrial countries. Because of this diversity of procedure and protection, no generalizations can be made about foreign patents. The patent laws of each foreign country in which a party is considering filing an application must be consulted. Many foreign countries discourage filing of patent applications by foreigners by imposing a progressive tax on the patent as it ages, by requiring that the patent be "worked" in the country upon penalty of forfeiture, or by exempting large areas of subject matter from patentability, for example, pharmaceuticals. Also, the United States imposes some limitations on efforts to obtain a foreign patent on any invention made in the United States.

Nevertheless, efforts are being made to establish a uniform worldwide system for the protection of industrial property. Initial progress has been made in the patent area. The United States has entered into several treaties with different groups of foreign countries. The nine members of the European Common Market are also moving toward a uniform patent system.

Limitations on Foreign Patenting of Inventions Made in the United States

The United States imposes patentability limitations on certain kinds of inventions, the qualifying categories being all those made in the United States for a technical process, a machine, an article of manufacture, a composition of matter, an improvement of such processes and products, and an industrial design. All inventions made in a foreign country, designs created in the United States of a nonindustrial nature, and botanical plants do not come under these limitations. It should be noted that these limitations do not depend on the citizenship of the inventor but rather on the location where the invention was made.

One of the limitations imposed by Congress is that even if a U.S. application is filed first, the applicant cannot file a foreign application until six months have passed unless permission to file earlier than six months is given by the commissioner of patents. If a foreign application is filed within six months of the U.S. patent application without such a license from the commissioner, a U.S. patent will not be granted. Nevertheless, to alleviate this harsh rule, the license may be granted retroactively where the foreign patent application was inadvertently filed abroad and the application does not disclose an invention in which the federal government has a property interest and that might be detrimental to the national security.

The other limitation is that an inventor may be barred altogether from filing a foreign patent application if a secrecy order against the disclosure of the invention is imposed by the commissioner of patents at the request of the chairman of the Atomic Energy Commission or the secretary of defense because the invention is considered detrimental to the national security. The person filing a foreign application in violation of either of these limitations is subject to imprisonment for up to two years and a $10,000 fine or both. However, so far as it can be ascertained, nobody has ever been penalized under this provision.

U.S. Patent Treaties with Foreign Nations

The United States is presently a party to a number of treaties covering the protection of patents with foreign countries. Most of these treaties established reciprocal rights or priority as to an invention for both domestic and foreign inventors in all contracting countries. Such a right is important because some countries permit an invention claimed by one of its citizens to be patented even if it has already been made by another in a foreign country. Also, some of these treaties are initial steps toward establishing an international patent system.

The oldest treaty that is still in force is the Inter-American Convention on Inventions, Patents, Designs, and Industrial Models entered into by the United States in 1912. The treaty was adopted by the United States and twelve Central and South American countries. The most important provision of this treaty gives any person who has deposited a patent application in one of the contracting countries a right of priority in all the other signatory countries during a period of twelve months for a patent on an invention and of four months for a patent on a design of an industrial nature. This provision is now a part of the Patent Act. Bilateral Treaties of Friendship, Commerce, and Navigation containing similar reciprocal rights of priority were signed between 1946 and 1954 with eight other countries that were either our former enemies or were noncombatants in World War II.

The fourteen members of the North Atlantic Treaty Organization (NATO) also signed an agreement in 1960 to respect secrecy orders imposed by any member country upon all inventions relating to defense for which patent applications have been filed. Thus an inventor will not be able to avoid a U.S. secrecy order by filing a patent application in any NATO member country. However, Italy did not ratify the agreement and only eight of the fourteen members have adopted a 1967 revision of the implementing procedures of this pact.

The latest treaty entered into by the United States is the Locarno Agreement Establishing an International Classification for Industrial Designs, signed in 1968 and finally ratified in 1972. Nine other countries, including the U.S.S.R., adhere to the agreement. The pact allows a citizen of any signatory country to research the existence of rights to any industrial design in any of the other signatory countries. The agreement also establishes a uniform system of design patent protection. Each contracting country reserves the right to use the international classification as either a principal or a subsidiary system. The U.S. Patent Office has been applying the international classification to its issued design patents since January 1969 as a subsidiary system.

There is also an international organization of which the United

States is a member. The Convention of the Union of Paris for the Protection of Industrial Property was originally established in 1883 and has been revised five times, the latest revision being in 1967. The agreement in effect allows a foreigner to have in all member countries the rights that each member country grants to its own citizens. The new agreement was partially adopted by the United States in 1970. Most of the approximately eighty member countries have signed the pact. The most important article of the latest revision expands the priority rights of foreigners in the signatory Eastern European countries and makes patent protection in these Eastern European countries more readily available to citizens of the other foreign signatory countries. Another important article states that the use of an invention on a ship or an aircraft of a member country temporarily in another member country is not an infringement of any patent in that country. This provision was incorporated into the U.S. Patent Code in 1952 as a result of an earlier revision of this international organization.

European Common Market System

Each European country presently has its own patent system with different procedures and various scopes of protection. In lieu of undertaking the Herculean task of discussing each foreign patent system, only the emerging system being developed by the European Communities (EC), usually called the Common Market, will be reviewed. This combined system should be operational in 1978. Because the total number of patents granted by the nine individual members of the EC comprises most of the patents granted in Europe, this combined patent system of the Common Market countries is one of primary interest to those dealing with foreign patents.

In September 1973 representatives from twenty-one European countries met in Munich to begin the process of setting up a "European System for the Grant of Patents." One month later, the nine member countries of the EC and five other countries signed a European Patent Convention (EPC) for this system. The chief virtue of the EPC is one of practicality. It enables the patent applicant to file a single application in one language and by one examination procedure. When granted, the patent will extend to any or all of the countries that signed the Convention, as designated by the applicant.

The EPC provides for a European Patent Office (EPO) to grant "European" patents. It will be made up of administration, examination, opposition, and revocation divisions with boards of appeal above the last three divisions. The EPO will be located in Munich and will be staffed by approximately 1,700 officials when it is fully operational. Before examination by the EPO, a Receiving Section located at The Hague is to inspect the application as to form. Next, the application will be compared with a novelty search report on the state of the art obtained from the International Patent Institute at The Hague. The application will then be published to allow any interested party to present his views on the patentability of the invention. The Hague will be responsible to render such publication within eighteen months after the priority date of the application. After such publication and after the applicant has paid a fee and asked for examination, the application will move to Munich. The report on the state of the art and any comments presented by interested parties will be examined together with the application. The examiner will inform the applicant of any objections he may have and the applicant may respond to such objections within a specified time limit. On the basis of the examination, the EPO will grant or deny a patent. The grant will give protection in all the member countries for a period of twenty years from the date of application, not from the date of patent issuance. Anyone could, within nine months from the date of publication of the patent, give notice to the EPO of opposition. The EPO will inform the patent owner of the opposition and allow him to comment. After hearing from both parties, the EPO could decide either to revoke the patent, or to require an amendment of the patent, or to reject the opposition. An application for a European patent will be filed at the EPO in Munich or its branch at The Hague or at the competent authority of a member nation, which would forward it to the EPO. When the application is filed, the applicant must designate those European countries in which he wants protection, with the understanding that he must choose all or none of the individual members of the EC.

Infringement actions would be started in the courts having jurisdiction under national law. The courts will decide suits in accordance with their own national law. However, if a revocation has been initiated at the EPO, the national court would have to stay the infringement suit until the EPO terminates the revocation proceeding.

A separate convention attached to the European Patent Convention provides for a new patent called a Community patent, which will be a single unitary patent for the nine member states of the EC. The EPO will grant this Community patent and its revocation will be dealt with by the Revocation Division of the EPO. Appeals from the Revocation Division will be to a Revocation Board within the EPO and then to the Court of Justice of the EC at Luxembourg. The Court of Justice will also interpret the patentability and other provisions of this "Second Convention" on a Community patent.

Japanese System

For anyone dealing in foreign patents on an international scale, a familiarity with the law of Japan is helpful. A foreigner applying for a patent has the same rights as a Japanese citizen. However, Japanese patent law has some nuances that must be considered; for example, entire fields are exempted from patentability; a "race" statute exists for filing applications; there is an annual patent "tax," a compulsory licensing provision, and protection for utility models not reaching the high standard of patentability and industrial designs.

To be patented an invention must be the "creation of a high level technical idea utilizing natural laws." Only processes and products of an industrial nature are patentable. Furthermore, a number of specific products are exempted from patentability. These include foods, human medicines and any process for mixing two or more medicines, products made by chemical means, material made by any method of transforming atomic nuclei, and subject matter potentially detrimental to the public health, order, or morals. "Patents of Addition" may be obtained by a patentee for improvements on his previously patented inventions.

Much as in the United States, a person is not entitled to a patent if the invention was publicly known or in public use by others in Japan, or described in a printed publication in Japan or a foreign country, or identically described in an application for a patent or a utility model filed in Japan by another before the patent application is filed in Japan. Applications are filed in the Japanese Patent Office. If more than one application is filed for the same invention by different inventors at about the same time, the first applicant to file is given the patent, unless, of course, he obtained the invention by improper means. Thus a premium is placed on winning a race to the Patent Office.

The technical scope of the patent grant is defined in the specification by a description of the scope of the patent claim. The term of the patent is fifteen years from the date of the publication of the application for objection by the public, but not to exceed twenty years from the date of filing. An annual "tax" must be paid in order to maintain the patent. Failure to pay the fee will result in loss of the patent.

The Japanese government may order a license to be given to another private party under three circumstances. First, the director-general of the Patent Office may grant a compulsory license where the "patented invention has not been appropriately carried out" for more than three years in Japan. Second, the minister of international trade and industry may grant a compulsory license where the invention "is specially necessary for the public interest." Third, an owner of either a basic or an improvement patent may obtain a compulsory license of each other's patent through the director-general of the Patent Office unless the grant of such a license "amounts to unreasonably injuring the interests of the other person."

A party "works" his invention when he produces, uses, assigns, leases, displays for the purpose of assignment or lease, or imports (if made abroad) his patented product or process. Failure to work the invention in Japan creates the risk of the grant of a compulsory license to others by the government against the patentee's will. Infringement of a Japanese patent occurs where another party does any of the acts constituting a working of the invention without authorization by the patentee. A party may also infringe the patent by selling unpatented items that are capable of use only either in a patented process or in the manufacture of a patented product. Infringement may be intentional or negligent. Upon an accusation made by the patent owner to the proper authority, an intentional infringer may be liable for a criminal offense.

Rights to a "utility model" are protected not by the Patent law but rather by the Utility Models law. An invention covering a product that is not as "high level" as required by the patent law but that has practical utility of form, structure, or combination can be registered. The term of a utility model right is ten years from the date of publication but not to exceed fifteen years from the date of filing. A request for examination of a utility model must be made within four years of the filing date. Otherwise, the application will be considered withdrawn. Also, rights to an industrial design are protected not by the Patent law but rather by the Design law. Industrial designs must be new and ornamental. They must relate to the form, pattern, coloring, or a combination of these features. After registration the industrial design is published in the *Official Design Gazette*. The term of protection for a design is fifteen years from the date of registration.

THE PATENT OFFICE AS A TECHNICAL LIBRARY

Resources Available

The Patent Office has its technical resources divided into three sections: Record Room, Search Room, and the Scientific Library. All of these facilities are open to the general public. The Record Room provides access to the file wrappers (patent prosecution documents) of all of the approximately 4 million U.S. patents issued since 1836. Prior patents issued from 1790 to 1836 did not require the making of any claims and therefore are merely of historical interest. The Record Room also contains other documents open for public inspection. The most important of these are assignments of the patent by the inventor to others, such as manufacturers and employers.

The Search Room contains the approximately 4 million U.S. patents issued since 1836. Also, the patents are categorized according to a classification system of over 300 subject classes and 64,000 subclasses. Another set of all the U.S. patents are arranged in order of issuance. All these patents are duplicated and distributed to twenty-one major public libraries throughout the United States. The Search Room also contains a complete set of the Patent Office *Official Gazette,* a weekly abstract publication of newly issued patents, trademarks, and related affairs.

The Scientific Library contains bound volumes of more than 8 million foreign patents and the official gazettes of foreign patent offices. The Scientific Library also contains over 90,000 bound volumes of scientific and technical periodicals as well as over 120,000 books on scientific and technical subject matter.

Such vast resources constitute a scientific bookworm's dream come true. Besides casual use by the general public, such material has very valuable commercial and legal purposes.

"Collection of Art" Studies

The Patent Office's technical libraries often serve as a research tool for manufacturers considering new products for commercial development. Many corporations routinely obtain copies of all patents issued in certain subject classes in order to keep abreast of any new advances in the area. Many inventors are first contacted by an interested manufacturer as a result of information learned through the Patent Office.

It is a common practice for a corporation considering entry into a particular commercial field first to assemble and review a collection of the pertinent art. Such a collection aids the corporate technical personnel in getting educated in the particular technology.

Defenses in Trade Secret Suits

Where an article or the process of making it is found not patentable or where no patent protection is sought, a manufacturer may seek to practice his invention as a trade secret. When a competitor adopts comparable technology, the manufacturer may sue the competitor for appropriation of the trade secret where there is reason to believe that the alleged trade secret was obtained by improper means. In defense of the suit for appropriation of the alleged trade secret, the alleged misappropriator can defend his actions on the grounds, among others, that the plaintiff's technology is not really a trade secret but rather a technical development already in the public domain. A common source of evidence for supporting such a contention is the Patent Office's technical library.

Infringement and Validity Searches

It would obviously be unfortunate if a manufacturer went through the expense of tooling up for a new product only to find that someone else already has a patent on the technology. Therefore, before a manufacturer takes steps to put a new product on the market or otherwise undertakes the expense of using in-plant technology for commercial purposes, a search will frequently be made to determine whether there may be an infringement of a U.S. patent or patents. Such a search is commonly known as an "infringement" search.

Based on the results of that search, the manufacturer or seller may decide to "design around the claims," acquire rights under the troublesome patents, take the chances of defending an infringement suit, or abandon the project. In all events, the remote possibility remains that the infringement search may have missed a key patent or a patent may subsequently be discovered. Patent attorneys probably have nightmares about such topics as these, because based on the results of the infringement search, millions of dollars may be gambled on the new manufacturing and marketing venture.

It follows that the stakes are commonly high enough to evaluate the next question: If we are sued for infringement of this troublesome patent, can we win the suit based on invalidity of the patent rather than proving noninfringement? To answer this question, a "validity" search will be conducted to determine the strengths and weaknesses of the troublesome patent.

Not relying on the patent examiner's search and findings alone, the validity search is a thorough, in-depth investigation of the validity of the troublesome patent in light of the prior art. This search frequently goes far beyond all previous searches: the preliminary search made before the patent applications were first filed, the patent examiner's own search, and the infringement search made before the marketing decision. Based on the prior art gleaned from the validity search, an assessment can be made as to whether or not a court would find that the best-known prior art would render the patent invalid.

OWNERSHIP AND CONVEYANCING OF PATENT RIGHTS

Although the patentee may convey patent rights to the government as well as to private parties, only the relationship between the patentee and private parties will be discussed here. The relationship between a patentee and the government is so different that it merits discussion in a later section dealing with government contracting involving patents by the armed services and the federal agencies.

Short of selling a patent outright, the patentee may convey only some of his patent rights. Such partial conveyance may be by assignment or by various forms of licenses. However, before examining these types of conveyances between the patentee and others, the nature of common law "shop rights" between an inventive employee and his employer is worth exploring.

Common Law Shop Rights

The shop-right doctrine was judicially created to give to an employer an implied, irrevocable, nonassignable, nonexclusive, royalty-free license to use an employee's invention. In order to establish a shop right, the employer must show that it was made on company time with company facilities and materials. Thus, the mere existence of the employer-employee relationship does not create the shop right. Nevertheless, a shop right may attach whether or not the employee has been hired as an inventor and whether or not the employee is required by oral or written contract to assign his invention to the employer. The shop right attaches for the employer whether it is a private concern or a governmental agency. The existence of a shop right is an equitable notion of state law. The Patent Act gives no such federal right to the employer. However, neither does it disallow such a right.

Absent an agreement, the employee who obtains a patent on an invention retains all rights granted under the patent as to the rest of the world except that the employer may be entitled to a shop right in the patented invention. If a shop right exists, the employer may practice the patented invention without a duty to pay royalties to the employee. The shop right will continue during the entire term of the patent and does not terminate if the employee leaves the company before the patent expires. Sometimes the existence of a shop right is doubtful where the employee has not been hired to invent and he has done much of the work on his own time, off company facilities, and without company materials. In such a situation, a shop right may be found if the employee acquiesced in the use of the invention by the employer for company purposes.

Assignments

An assignment is a written instrument transferring all or some of an inventor's interest in a patent application or the patent. Upon assignment of an entire right, title, and interest, the assignee becomes the sole owner of the patent application or the patent. Assignment of a partial interest gives the assignee fractional ownership, e.g., a half or a quarter interest in the undivided whole with the inventor. If there is more than one owner of a patent, any of them, no matter how small his interest, may make, use, or sell the invention for his own profit; may grant licenses to others to make, use, or sell the invention; and may sell all or some of his own partial interest, without regard to the other joint owners, unless there is a contract governing their relationship as joint owners. Therefore, it is generally wise for the co-owners to enter into a contract governing the rights and duties between themselves.

An assignment should be acknowledged before a notary public and then recorded in the Patent Office within three months from its date. If it is not recorded within the three-month period, the assignee runs the risk that it will be found void by the courts against a subsequent bona fide purchaser who paid a valuable consideration without notice of the earlier assignment. Because the entire document making up the assignment is a public record, many assignees may not want the terms of the assignment to be public knowledge while the patent application is still pending. Therefore, an assignee of a patent application will often not record until a patent is about to issue.

When a patent application is found meritorious and there has been an assignment by the inventor of his entire interest before the issue fee has been paid, the Patent Office will issue the patent directly to the recorded assignee in the name of the inventor. Often the assignee is a corporate employer who has conducted the patent application proceedings at its own expense. If the recorded assignment shows only a partial interest the patent will be issued to the inventor and the assignee as joint owners. If there has been no assignment recorded, the Patent Office will issue the patent in the name of the inventor alone.

Licenses

Instead of assigning his patent outright to others, the patentee may keep the legal title in his own name and grant licenses of some or all of his rights to others. Because the patent owner has the right by statute to exclude others from making, using, or selling the patented invention, others desiring to exploit the patent must first obtain permission to do so from the patent owner or run the risk of being charged with patent infringement. The patent owner grants such permission by means of a license. There are various forms of licenses; however, all involve the substantive right to make and/or use and/or sell the patented invention.

Exclusive. An exclusive license for the remaining term of the patent is tantamount to an assignment. Such a license gives to only one party the sole right to make, use, and sell. Even the patent owner is prevented from making, using, or selling his own invention. If a third party infringes the patent, the exclusive licensee has the right to join the patent owner in an infringement action against the alleged infringer, to make the patent owner an involuntary plaintiff in such an action, to bring such an action in the patent owner's name without its consent, or to make the patent owner a defendant in such an action if the patent owner has become hostile toward the exclusive licensee.

Nonexclusive. A nonexclusive license gives to a party the right to make and/or use and/or sell; however, the patent owner retains the right to practice the invention and to grant licenses to any number of other parties. The nonexclusive license is merely an assurance that the patent owner will not charge the licensee with infringement for any conduct that would otherwise be an infringement. If the patent owner does not sue others who are infringing the patent, the nonexclusive licensee has no right to enforce the patent against such infringers without the consent of the patent owner.

Cross Licenses. A cross license is an agreement that provides for the licensing of a patent by one patent owner in return for a license under a different patent owned by another. Such a license sometimes becomes an economic necessity where neither party is willing to sell or assign its patent to the other but also neither party can make, use, or sell its patented invention to its best commercial advantage without the benefit of the other party's patent. Therefore the owners of the patents will cross-license each other for the right to use each other's patent.

Cross licenses are most often made between owners of "interfering" or "blocking" patents. Such interfering or blocking patents cover different aspects of the same invention. For example, if a basic patent is owned by one party and an improvement patent on the same invention is owned by another party, a cross license is warranted because the parties must have the benefit of both patents in order to practice the improvement to its best commercial advantage.

Also, inventor A may obtain a patent on item X. Inventor B may obtain a patent on item Y. Both A and B may realize that items X and Y in combination with a third item, Z, which may be in the public domain, constitute a new and useful combination, XYZ. Therefore, A and B may cross-license each other to make, use, and sell each other's patented invention so that they both can produce XYZ without incurring any liability for infringement of each other's patent.

Package Licenses.   Some corporations are in the business of developing and managing patents. They may employ many brilliant minds in research and development organizations churning out patentable inventions. Others may buy up many patents in a particular field. Both types of firms make a profit by licensing their patents in a "package." Sometimes a "package license" contains hundreds of patents. A manufacturer in a certain industry pays a royalty for the use of all the patents in a desired package. Such a deal keeps the manufacturer free to exploit new developments with a minimum of cost in both time and money.

"Voluntary" package licensing is an acceptable practice. This simply means that a licensee may voluntarily desire to take a whole package of patents, including some that he neither needs nor intends to use, and still pay royalties for the entire package of patents.

Pools.   Sometimes a number of patent owners, usually small competing corporations, each owning one or more important patents in their field, may "pool" all their patents together by transferring title of all patents to a trustee or other third party, with licenses back under the pooled patents. This practice gives each of the competitors access to greater technical resources so as to compete more readily. Often such a pool is the result of a settlement of a many-sided legal battle over infringement of the patents involved. The pooling arrangement usually allows each participant to take a license under some or all of the other patents in the pool.

Duration.   The duration of any patent license, unless specifically stated to be a shorter period, is the entire remaining term of the patent. The license may not extend beyond the patent term because when the patent expires the subject matter passes into the public domain and the patent is thereafter unenforceable.

Quantity Limitations.   Quantity limitations involve a license clause that either limits the quantity of items a licensee manufactures under a product patent or limits the number of times a licensee may use a patented process. Although the Supreme Court has not ruled on the legality of this practice, some lower federal courts have upheld such license provisions only where the quantity limitation is made with reference to the patented product or process itself.

A quantity limitation is similar to a limitation on the duration of a patent license. A quantity limitation relates to the number of patented items produced; a durational limitation relates to the time period over which patented items may be produced. Whenever a quantity limitation is imposed, it is usually applied by a small company that owns a key patent that is licensed to larger competitors in an effort to save part of the commercial market for itself.

Field-of-Use Limitations. If a patent owner's invention is capable of being used in two or more commercial fields, a field-of-use limitation provides that the prospective licensees in different fields will not use the invention outside of their own field. By way of illustration, a party held a reissue patent on a composition of matter that was a therapeutic preparation for the treatment of iron deficiency anemia. The drug could be used on both humans and animals. Therefore, in order to make his patent more attractive to potential commercial exploiters, the patent owner decided to license only two drug manufacturers, one in the human medicinal field and the other in the veterinary field. The manufacturer of human medicines was forbidden to use the invention in the veterinary field and the manufacturer of veterinary drugs was forbidden to use the invention in the human medicinal field. A federal court later found the field-of-use limitation perfectly legal.

Territorial Restrictions. A license may be geographic in nature. This type of license has been specifically approved by the Patent Act. Such a license gives a party the exclusive right to make, use, and sell the patented invention in a defined geographic area, e.g., a metropolitan area, a state, or a group of states. Other parties may be given exclusive rights in other geographic areas. In this way the patent owner is able to assure each manufacturing licensee that it will have no competition in the first sale of the patented invention in the defined territory. If the patent license imposes no territorial restriction, the Supreme Court has stated that the license allows exploitation throughout the United States.

Grant-back and License-back Provisions. The patent owner may require as partial consideration for the license that the licensee "grant-back" or "license-back" to the patent owner partial or all rights in any improvements that the licensee may make on the patented invention. A license-back under the patent issued on the improvement is usually nonexclusive. Occasionally, assignment of all rights to an improvement is provided for in a grant-back.

A common purpose of license-back provisions is simply to enable the patent owner to practice any patented improvements developed by the licensee. An exclusive grant-back or assignment of such improvement patent rights would foreclose the licensee who developed the improvement from practicing it because title to the improvement patent would belong to the owner of the basic patent.

Know-how and Technical Assistance. Many times a prospective patent licensee may have an interest in obtaining a license but does not have the know-how to use the technology to its best commercial advantage. Although the patent license itself is enabling, the licensee may need additional technical assistance in bringing the patented invention to efficient commercial production. In such a situation, the parties may agree that along with the patent license the owner will help the licensee to exploit the patent through know-how disclosure and technical assistance. Such technology is frequently conveyed along with the patent license in a variety of ways: technical instruction manuals, educational courses for the employees of the licensee, or technical assistance agreements whereby several of the patent owner's engineers and technicians are assigned to work for the licensee for the time it takes to tool up and get production on its way, as well as ongoing technical consulting arrangements.

Sublicenses. A provision in the license may provide that the licensee is or is not authorized to sublicense or that he may do so only with the consent of the licensor whether the license is exclusive or nonexclusive. In the absence of a sublicensing provision in a nonexclusive license, the licensee has no implied right to sublicense. However, in the case of an exclusive license that is so absolute as to amount practically to an assignment, an argument can be made that the licensee has an implied right to sublicense. In fact, no case has squarely held that an exclusive licensee does not have the implied right to sublicense within the territorial or other limits, if any, to his exclusivity. A sublicense, of course, cannot survive the term of, or be broader than, the license itself.

Compulsory Licensing Under the Clean Air Act. The Clean Air Act of 1970 is the first federal law providing for compulsory licensing of a patent by its owner if a federal court so orders. Because an owner has the right not to license his patent to anyone if he so desires, Congress passed the mandatory licensing provision to emasculate this right in order to aid in the national fight against air pollution.

Three conditions must be satisfied before the owner will be ordered by a court to license its patent. The attorney general of the United States must certify to a federal district court having jurisdiction over the patent owner to the presence of three factors: first, the patented invention enables any person required to comply with the standards governing hazardous pollutants from both stationary and moving sources to so comply; second, no reasonable alternatives are available; and third, the unavailability of the patented invention tends to create a monopoly. If the court agrees that all three of these factors exist, it may issue an order requiring the owner to license the patent under terms that the court decides are reasonable.

Shortly after its enactment, there was an attempt made to repeal this mandatory licensing provision as unnecessary on two grounds: first, there is no reason for believing that the owner of such a valuable patent would deliberately refuse to issue licenses; second, the provision takes away the freedom to contract and any resulting bargaining power of the owner to obtain the best return on its investment because the prospective licensee knows that he can always seek the attorney general's help to get a license whenever the patent owner refuses to accept whatever low offer the prospective licensee cares to make. This attempt at repeal was not successful. It remains to be seen whether more attempts will be made and whether such compulsory licensing provisions will be included in future federal legislation.

ROYALTY ARRANGEMENTS

Although a license may or may not call for the payment of royalties, most licenses require their payment. The Supreme Court said in 1964 that a "patent empowers the owner to exact royalties as high as he can negotiate with the leverage of that monopoly."

Percentage-of-Total-Sales Arrangements

The amount of royalties to be paid is most often determined by a percentage of the gross sales volume of the licensee for the patented invention. Such a system is used because it allows easy calculation and auditing of the royalty due. It is difficult to determine the amount of royalties due under a package license, especially if several hundred patents are involved. Many of the patents may be used in many different items in combination either with one or more other patents or with unpatented parts. Some of the patents in the package may never be used. In such a situation the royalty due is usually based on a percentage of the total sales made by the licensee. In negotiations over the license, the parties often agree on a percentage-of-total-sales royalty arrangement if they consider it would be too complex and too time-consuming to figure out the royalty due under any other formula. Basing the package license royalty on a percentage-of-total-sales measure has been found reasonable by the Supreme Court if done in the absence of coercion and is for the convenience of the parties.

Number of Actual Units

Less frequently, the royalty due is based on the number of patented units made, used, or sold by the license under the patent. This type of royalty arrangement is most often employed where a patent covers a manufacturing process or where there is no "selling price" for a patented product, such as would be the case in the manufacture of a patented subcomponent not sold by itself.

Minimum and Maximum Clauses

Sometimes the patent owner, in order to encourage full use of his patent by a licensee, will insert minimum and maximum royalty clauses. The license may call for royalties to be paid on the gross sales volume of patented units or a minimum royalty due each year, whichever is larger. Thus a floor is put under the amount of royalties due so that less aggressive parties are discouraged from taking a license if they believe that their sales will not justify paying the minimum royalty. Less frequently, the royalty clause may then call for a maximum royalty due each year if the gross sales volume of patented units passes a certain peak. Thus a ceiling may be put on the amount of royalties due so that parties that do take a license are encouraged to work the patent in order to reach the point after which no additional royalties are payable.

Sliding-Scale Arrangements

There are two basic types of sliding-scale royalty arrangements. The first type is based either on the gross sales volume of patented units or, less frequently, on the number of patented units produced. Usually the license initially sets forth a table of royalties that are due in decreasing percentages-of-total-sales or dollar amounts as either the gross sales volume of patented units or the number of patented units produced increases, respectively. Thus an incentive is created to maximize the use of the patent.

The other type of sliding-scale royalty arrangement is based on the number of still unexpired patents included in the license. This type of arrangement, usually covering a small group rather than a large package of patents, automatically decreases the royalty rate or amount due as each licensed patent expires. Such a system might work as follows: An owner of three patents licenses them in a package at 3 per cent of the gross sales volume of all goods incorporating the patents. The first patent expires in 1980. At that time, the royalty rate due is reduced to 2 per cent. When the second patent expires in 1984, the royalty rate is again reduced, this time to 1 per cent.

Royalty-free or Nominal Royalty

Even though most licenses require the payment of royalties, a royalty-free or nominal-royalty license is sometimes granted. Such a license may be given to a party that the patent owner believes has good grounds for defeating a patent infringement suit and, at worst, for invalidating the patent. More often, a royalty-free provision may appear in a cross license made between two parties or in a pooling arrangement made between three or more parties.

Most-Favored Licensee Clause

If a party cannot obtain a royalty-free or a nominal-royalty license, the next best provision to seek is a "most-favored licensee" clause. Such a provision allows the licensee to obtain the same more favorable royalty terms from the patent owner that any later licensee may receive.

Payment Period

Finally, it should be pointed out that any royalty arrangement must cover only activities taking place during the term of the patent. If the patent owner prefers, for tax or other purposes, to receive royalties payments over a period of time extending beyond the patent term or if the licensee, after obtaining the license, later finds that it cannot pay all the royalties when they become due, installment payments may be arranged extending beyond the patent term. Such an arrangement is legal so long as the royalties are paid only for activities occurring before the patent expires.

GOVERNMENT CONTRACTING

During the period covering the fiscal years 1963 through 1973, an average of almost 9,000 inventions resulted each year from the efforts of private contractors under federal research and development

(R&D) programs. These developments have caused the creation of various governmental policies over the rights to the inventions.

Title and License Theories

There are two opposing theories as to how these rights should be handled. Advocates of the title theory say that the government should take title to a patent for an invention created under its contract or grant. The reasoning behind this theory is that the government is entitled to own the patent on an invention if it paid for the research necessary to develop the invention. Advocates of the license theory say that the inventor should be allowed to keep the title to exploit it commercially and that the government should obtain only a royalty-free license under the patent. The reasoning behind this theory is that if the government takes more than it needs, the incentive to invent is thereby diminished. It is further argued that vesting title in the government would limit the commercial availability of the patented invention because the government does not exploit patents in the market place.

Statistics indicate that the advocates of the title theory prevail much more often than the advocates of the license theory. During the fiscal years 1963 through 1970, the rights to an average of 8,500 inventions made as a result of R&D by a private contractor were distributed yearly, with the government taking title to about four out of five inventions and taking only a license for the rest of the inventions.

Statutory Policies

There are several statutes governing the patent policies of specific agencies. Each of these statutorily created policies are different. Some of these agencies with their own statutory patent policies are the government's larger contracting agencies.

The first patent policy appeared in the legislation creating the National Science Foundation (NSF) in 1950. The policy is one of a general nature. Each contract must contain provisions over rights to any patents obtained on any resulting inventions. The provisions call for the NSF to balance the public interest with the equities of the inventor. The first detailed patent policy came in the Atomic Energy Act of 1954. This Act adopted the title theory. The titles to all inventions under contracts awarded by the Atomic Energy Commission (AEC) are taken by the government. Nevertheless, the AEC may waive this right in situations that the AEC "may deem appropriate." An even more detailed patent policy was adopted in legislation creating the National Aeronautics and Space Administration (NASA) in 1958.

Whenever any invention is made in the performance of any work under any NASA contract, the government will take title. However, NASA may waive this right where the "interests of the United States will be served thereby."

Presidential Policy

Outside of the statutorily created patent policies, the present government attitude is the result of two presidential statements on patent policy, one proclaimed in 1963 by President Kennedy and another amending the earlier statement, proclaimed in 1971 by President Nixon. The two statements, comprising the current policy, reject both the title and license theories as an overall government approach. Instead, each agency, not already governed by a specific statute, is allowed to decide for itself how the patent rights should be allocated within the presidential guidelines.

Because no specific legislation controls the patent policy of the government's largest contracting agency, the Department of Defense, it now acts under the direction of the policy set forth by the presidential statements. The patent provisions for the DOD appear in the Armed Services Procurement Regulation (ASPR). The General Services Administration (GSA), which has the duty of prescribing general procurement policies and procedures for all executive civil agencies has established patent provisions in the Federal Procurement Regulations (FPR), which as of early 1974 have been indefinitely suspended due to court litigation challenging them. All civilian agencies, not guided by a specific statute, will, when and if these GSA regulations become effective, act under this patent procurement policy although some of these agencies, such as HEW, have separate regulations governing employee inventions and the licensing of government-owned patents.

Instead of undertaking the monumental task of discussing the patent policy of each government agency, an analysis of guidelines set forth in the presidential statements will be made with occasional specific references to both the ASPR and the tentative FPR. According to the presidential statements, the initial decision as to whether the government agency will take either title to or a license under a patent obtained on an invention developed as a result of R&D under a contract or grant should be made at the time the contract is given. However, a contract sometimes provides that the decision will be deferred until a later time. Thus, both the ASPR provides (and the tentative FPR provides) three different patent clauses from which a government agency through its procuring activity can choose, depending on whether the agency wants to take the title or a license or to defer the decision.

When the Government Takes Title. The government will generally take title if the contract or grant has one of four main purposes:
first, for use by the general public; second, for use in public health,
safety, or welfare; third, for work in a technical field basically developed by the government where title in the contractor or grantee would
result in its domination of the commercial field; or fourth, for the
operation of a government facility.

If the government decides to take the title, the contractor or
grantee is usually left with a nonexclusive royalty-free license under the
patent. Nevertheless, the contractor may acquire greater rights than
a nonexclusive license at the time the contract is made if the head
of the government agency certifies that such action will best serve
the public interest. The contract may provide that after an invention
has been developed, greater rights may be acquired by the contractor
where the head of the government agency determines that the acquisition of such greater rights is consistent with the presidential statements
and one of two other factors are also present: the grant of greater rights
is either a necessary incentive to call forth private risk captial to make
the invention practical or that the government's contribution to the
invention is small compared to that of the contractor. The deferred
decision will turn on the public interest involved and the intentions
of the contractor to develop the invention for commercial use. Where
the contract provides that the government will take title and the contractor is left with a guarantee of a deferred decision as to greater rights
under the patent, the deferred decision usually goes in favor of the
private contractor. For example, during the fiscal years 1969 and 1970,
more than 99 per cent of slightly more than 3,000 requests for greater
rights were granted in some form. However, if the contractor desires
title to any patent developed, it is better to have the contract initially
state that title will be given to the contractor and the government will
take a license.

If the government obtains title to the invention and the contractor
is given a nonexclusive license, the government agency may later change
the nonexclusive license into an exclusive one if it decides that a degree
of exclusivity is necessary to encourage further development and commercialization of the patented invention. If the government does not
elect to secure a patent in a foreign country, the government agency
may permit the contractor to acquire such rights.

Under the most recent presidential statement, if the government
has title to an invention, the patent may be exclusively licensed to a
private concern. Although the exclusive licensee may be someone
other than the contractor that developed the patented invention, usually the developer is given the right of first refusal. Under authority

of the presidential statement, the GSA has developed regulations governing the licensing of government-owned patents. The authority of the government to dispose of its patents through exclusive licensing was challenged successfully in a 1974 federal district court decision. Further litigation will clarify this practice of granting exclusive licenses by the government.

When the Contractor Takes Title. At the time the contract is made, the contractor may obtain the right to take the title or an exclusive license under a patent for any resulting invention where two conditions exist: first, the purpose of the contract is to build upon either existing technology owned by the contractor for use by the government agency; and second, the contract calls for work in a field of technology in which the contractor has both acquired technical competence as demonstrated by its know-how, experience, and patent position, and has established a commercial position for itself.

Where the contract provides that the contractor obtains title to the patent, the government takes a nonexclusive royalty-free license under the patent to use the invention. However, the contractor may be required to provide written reports at reasonable intervals, when requested by the government agency on the commercial use that is either being made or intended to be made of the patented invention developed under the government contract. Both the DOD and the GSA provide for such a clause in the ASPR and in the tentative FPR, respectively.

Even though the title to a patent is given to the contractor, the government agency will normally reserve certain rights. One such right gives to the agency a nonexclusive, nonassignable, royalty-free license to make, use, and sell the patented invention throughout the world by or on behalf of the federal government. This right may be extended so that the license allows the federal agency to act also on behalf of the domestic state and municipal governments if the agency head determines that it would be in the public interest.

Other rights that the government agency will normally reserve to itself include the right to sublicense any foreign government pursuant to a treaty if the agency head determines it would be in the national interest and the right to obtain the exclusive territorial rights to the invention in any foreign country in which the contractor does not elect to secure a patent. Furthermore, the government agency may reserve a "march-in" right where certain circumstances arise. The march-in right allows the government to require the granting of either a nonexclusive or even an exclusive license to a responsible party on reasonable terms unless the contractor can show that he either has taken effective steps within three years after the patent issues to bring the invention to commercial use or has made the patented invention available for licensing on reasonable terms or can show cause why he should retain the exclusive rights for a further period of time. However, the march-in right will be exercised only to the extent that the patented invention is required for public use under government regulation, or as may be necessary to fulfill health or safety needs, or for other public purposes stipulated in the contract but not being adequately carried out by the contractor.

Background Patents.   The government policy as to so-called background patents applies whether the government or the contractor takes title to the patent on an invention developed under the contract. For instance, a contractor may hold patents A, B, and C. A government agency funds the contractor to develop D. The agency may include a contract provision whereby the contractor agrees that he will license the background patents A, B, and C to others upon their written application after the government agency asserts a march-in right to order licenses granted. Most private contractors resist such a contract provision as to their background patents because of the possibility that the license applicants will be commercial competitors of the contractor.

Authorization and Consent to Infringe

All government contracts contain a clause authorizing the contractor and giving the government's consent to infringe any patent if necessary to carry out the contract. Such clauses are included pursuant to a federal statute. Most government agencies include a broad authorization and consent provision in R&D contracts. Such agencies include DOD and NASA. A more limited clause is used in supply contracts by these same agencies. Even if authorization and consent is not specifically given in a provision of a government contract, it may still be implied. The comptroller general has ruled that, as a matter of law, a contracting official of a government agency has no authority, except in very limited situations, to withhold authorization and consent to infringe privately owned patents.

The ASPR differs from the FPR and the regulations of the few agencies acting under special statutorily created patent policies in that the ASPR specifically negates the applicability of the implied warranties of the Uniform Commercial Code against patent infringement.

Indemnification by Contractor for Infringement

Sometimes when a government agency solicits bids for a contract, there is one bidder that has a patent or patents in the relevant technology. Because it may be necessary to use the patent, the other bidders may decide to infringe the patent if the owner will not give them a license under the patent. If such a situation is foreseeable, the government agency may require the other bidders to idemnify the government against any liability that may arise if the successful bidder is not the patent owner but finds it necessary to infringe the patent. This requires competing bidders of the patent owner to include the cost of the infringement in their contract bid. If the agency did not require indemnity and the contract is let to a low bidder that intends to infringe, the government might ultimately pay more to achieve the objective of the contract (because of the resulting infringement litigation judgment) than it would have paid if it had originally let the contract to the higher-bidding patent owner. This is the philosophy behind the indemnification clauses in government contracts.

The government solicits bids for R&D and supplies either by formal advertising or by negotiation with several competitors. Indemnification by the contractor for financial liability for patent infringement is usually not required by the government in R&D contracts and grants. However, it is generally required for supply contracts, both formally advertised and negotiated, either covering subject matter that may infringe a patent owned by one of the bidders for the contract or covering subject matter that normally is or has been sold or offered for sale commercially. Under ASPR, supply contracts made by the military services for weapons systems do not normally contain a patent indemnity clause, even if the particular component in the weapon system being purchased is also sold commercially.

Where a contract contains both R&D and supply provisions, indemnity is sometimes used. Only the AEC is known always to use patent indemnity clauses for contracts calling for both R&D and supplies.

Administrative Settlement of Infringement Suits

Only in a few instances is an administrative procedure available where a patent owner may settle a claim against the government for patent infringement regarding a government procurement. However, where such procedures are available, the method of claim settlement is limited in scope.

Special statutorily created boards may grant compensation to a patent owner for infringement by the AEC or NASA. The DOD has an informal procedure for settling administrative claims for patent infringement by the military services. The GSA, although it spends billions of dollars each year on supplies, has no authority to settle any alleged patent infringement claim made prior to suit resulting from its procurements, regardless of the merits of the claim. Without an administrative settlement, the only recourse left to the patent owner is to sue the government in the Court of Claims in order to obtain compensation for the unauthorized use of his patent by a federal civil agency.

STARTING AN INFRINGEMENT SUIT

We will now explore the enforcement of patent rights. Patent infringement can be committed by either the government or a private party. The trial of a simple patent infringement case averages about five days per patent in suit, frequently preceded by monumental pretrial discovery activities. The longest suit, involving twenty-six patents, required 183 trial days. Because the courses of action and the remedies available against the government and a private party are so different, separate treatment is necessary.

Against the Government

A suit for patent infringement may be started against the federal government by filing a complaint in the United States Court of Claims for money damages. An injunction against the government cannot be obtained where the patent is being used "by or for" the government without the consent of the patent owner. Also, an injunction against a government contractor or subcontractor who is infringing the patent is not available if the patent is being infringed "with the authorization or consent" of the government.

The present statute limiting private lawsuits against the federal government to money damages is the tortuous result of several earlier statutes and court decisions. In 1910 Congress waived for the first time the sovereign immunity of the federal government for the infringement of patents. This statute was interpreted by the Supreme Court in 1911. The Supreme Court refused to grant an injunction for infringement against the U.S. Army, which was manufacturing patented guns in its arsenals. However, in 1918 the Court allowed an injunction against private government contractors for infringement. Congress acted quickly that same year to emasculate the decision by providing an exclusive remedy in the Court of Claims for money damages where a patent is infringed by the federal government or its contractors.

The basic policy behind this statute limiting a person's remedy to money damages is that government programs should not be delayed or halted by injunctions granted in patent infringement actions. Monetary compensation is considered adequate relief. The rationale behind this policy has been judicially extended to public services rendered by both state and municipal governments. Thus, the courts will not grant an injunction for patent infringement against a state or local government agency performing a public service if the court order would be against the public interest. This principle, known as the *Activated Sludge* doctrine, became established as the result of a series of seven cases brought from 1934 to 1947 against the cities of Chicago, Illinois, and Milwaukee, Wisconsin, by the owner of several patents for the purification of sewage by aeration. Although all the various courts found the patents valid and infringed by the sewage authorities of the two cities, the courts refused to halt the operation of the sewage disposal systems and limited the patent owner to recover monetary damages for the past and future unauthorized use of the patent.

Whenever the federal government is sued for an infringement committed by a contractor or subcontractor, the government can bring in the contractor as a third-party defendant only if there is an indemnification clause in the contract. If the government is found liable, the contractor will be required to indemnify the government.

Lawsuits filed in the Court of Claims are tried before a trial judge who may sit in any city. The same trial judge controls the discovery of evidence, the pretrial proceedings, and the actual trial. The trial is initially limited to the issue of liability. Most cases are settled out of court. However, if the case reaches the trial stage, the trial judge will write a report including findings of fact and an opinion. The trial judge's report is reviewed by a three-judge panel of the Court of Claims. There are seven judges on the full court. The court will either enter judgment for the patent owner or dismiss the complaint.

If an invention is the subject of a patent application but a patent has not been issued because the Patent Office has imposed a secrecy order on the grounds that the invention is detrimental to the national security, the inventor may sue the government for money damages in either the Court of Claims or the federal district court in which the inventor resides if the government is using the invention without permission or if the Atomic Energy Commission has communicated patent application data to other countries without the applicant's consent.

Against a Private Party in the United States

The federal court system has exclusive jurisdiction of all patent infringement suits. A suit for patent infringement may be started against a private party in one of three ways.

First, the patent owner may file a complaint against the accused infringer in a U.S. district court. The suit may be brought "where the defendant resides, or where the defendant has committed acts of infringement and has a regular and established place of business."

Second, after being charged with infringement, even though no lawsuit has been filed, the accused party may sue the patent owner under the Federal Declaratory Judgment Act, seeking a declaration from a federal district court that it is not infringing the accuser's patent or that the patent is invalid. Such initiative by the accused party may be desirable, for example, where the patent owner is harassing the alleged infringer's customers with charges of infringement but the accuser has failed to file a suit to back up its threats. Thus if the accused party thinks he has a good defense, he will be able to force the complaining patent owner to "put up or shut up" by bringing the declaratory judgment action. Once the alleged infringer learns that the patent owner is charging infringement against him or his customers, the accused party may want to file such a declaratory judgment action quickly beforehand in order to try the case on its home turf or in a preferred court.

A statistical study points to a difference in the judicial attitudes of the various federal circuits toward patent owners and alleged infringers. Results that have been compiled for the period immediately following the Supreme Court decision in Graham v. John Deere Co. in 1966 until early 1971 show that two federal circuit courts of appeal found more of the patents before it valid and infringed than all other circuits, whereas one circuit decided all its patent cases in a manner favorable to accused infringers. For instance, the Fifth (Deep South states) and Seventh (Great Lakes area) Circuits found 37 per cent of thirty-five patents and 34 per cent of seventy-six patents valid and infringed, whereas the Eighth (Northern Plains states) Circuit decided all of its eighteen cases in a manner favorable to accused infringers. This same study is later referred to in the discussion of the defense of patent invalidity.

If a party wants to sue the foreign owner of a U.S. patent who is not otherwise found in the United States to resolve charges of infringement or related rights under the patent, he may file suit only in the United States Federal District Court for the District of Columbia, unless the foreign patent owner has designated a U.S. agent to receive service. When a foreigner without requisite U.S. contacts obtains a U.S. patent, he is required by statute to submit himself to the jurisdiction of this court.

The third way in which a charge of patent infringement may be brought against a private party is as an outgrowth of a civil action for breach of either a contract or a license involving a patent. Such an action must be brought in a state court like any other suit for breach of a contractual obligation, unless the parties are citizens of two or more different states. Where there is a diversity of citizenship and the amount in controversy exceeds $10,000, the federal district court may take jurisdiction of the case under the federal diversity statute, not the patent statutes. Nevertheless, even if there is no diversity of citizenship between the parties, the suit may still be transferred from the state court to a federal district court under the federal removal statute. In order for such a removal to be ordered, there must be at least one of three circumstances present: first, a claim or right arising under the Constitution, treaties, or laws of the United States; second, none of the defendants a citizen of the state in which the action is brought; or third, a separate and independent claim that would be removable if sued upon alone, is joined with one or more otherwise nonremovable claims. Nevertheless, if an action is brought either to enforce or to void a contract, federal jurisdiction is not established merely because the contract relates to patents. To constitute a suit within the jurisdiction of a federal district court, it must appear that some right or interest under the patent laws will be either defeated by one construction or sustained by another construction of these laws. Thus although questions of patent infringement are entirely within federal jurisdiction, questions of patent invalidity may be decided by a state court if raised as a defense to a state civil action for breach of a contract or a license.

Against an Importer

Where a U.S. patent is being infringed by a foreign manufacturer in a foreign country, there is no recourse for the U.S. patent owner except under a foreign patent, because a U.S. patent is not enforceable against acts done outside the United States. Furthermore, the Patent Act provides no protection against an importer of foreign infringing goods until after the goods are sold in this country. Nevertheless, outside of the Patent Act, a remedy is afforded. If the foreign manufacturer attempts to import infringing goods, the owner of the U.S. patent may file a complaint with the U.S. Tariff Commission. The commission will halt importation of the accused goods until a determination as to the existence of "[u]nfair methods of competition and unfair acts in the importation of articles" is made. Although the statute makes no reference to patent infringement, this phrase has been construed by the courts to prohibit the importation of infringing goods. If a finding of infringement is made, the importer may obtain review only in the Court of Customs and Patent Appeals. If the findings of the Tariff Commission are upheld, the president will order the secretary of the treasury to refuse entry to the accused goods. The ban will continue in effect until the U.S. patent expires.

INFRINGEMENT

Infringement is a judicially created doctrine established as an outgrowth of tort law: it is an act that is in violation of the patent rights of another, regardless of whether or not the act was innocently done without knowledge of the other's patent rights. Infringement arises in connection with acts relating to the unauthorized manufacture, use, or sale of the claimed invention. Congress did not find it necessary to codify the doctrine of infringement until the present Patent Act was passed in 1952. In the present statute, Congress states that a patent has all the attributes of personal property and that a patentee has a remedy by a civil action for infringement. Additionally, the Patent Act defines three types of infringement: direct, active inducement, and contributory.

Direct

Whoever without authority makes, uses, or sells any patented invention, within the United States during the term of the patent therefor, infringes the patent [35 U.S.C. §271(a)].

Direct infringement may be proved in one of two ways: literally or under the doctrine of equivalents.

Literal Reading on the Claims.   Literal infringement is the simplest form of direct infringement. Recall that the scope of the patent right is limited by the claim language resolved between the patent applicant and the Patent Office. In one of the two leading cases on the definition of direct infringement, the Supreme Court said in 1950 in the *Graver Tank* case that "resort must be had in the first instance to the words of the claim. If accused matter falls clearly within the claim, infringement is made out and that is the end of it."

Doctrine of Equivalents.   Because courts came to recognize that to allow the imitation of a patented invention that does not copy every literal detail of the patent claim could sometimes turn a patent into an empty right, the doctrine of equivalents was created. In another leading case on the definition of direct infringement, the Supreme Court said in 1929 in the *Sanitary Refrigerator* case that "one device is an infringement of another . . . if two devices do the same work in substantially the same way, and accomplish substantially the same result, . . . even though they differ in name, form or shape." In this particular case, the invention related to a latch of the swinging-lever type, particularly adapted for use on early modern refrigerators. The inventors obtained a patent in 1921 and the patented invention became a commercial success. After examining the patent, the defendant obtained a patent on a device identical in function and similar in structure. After beginning commercial exploitation of its patent, the defendant was sued for infringement of the earlier patent. The Supreme Court found that even though the prior art comprising door latches was crowded and that the plaintiff's patent was not a pioneer patent, the patented invention was still entitled to some range of equivalents. After a recitation of the claims, the Court concluded that the slight change in the form of the accused device was merely a colorable departure from the patented invention and therefore was a direct infringement under the doctrine of equivalents. It is interesting to note that the accused device was also patented. Even though a later device may also be patented, the Supreme Court said in 1869 that it may still be an infringement of an earlier patented invention.

Transposition of Elements. Direct infringement under the doctrine of equivalents is not avoided by the transposition of elements in a patented invention. For instance, an inventor obtained a patent on a machine for automatically eviscerating Monterey sardines at a 95 per cent efficiency level. Before this time, eviscerating machines were only 50 per cent to 60 per cent effective so that manual inspection was needed thereafter for each individual fish in order to reach the 95 per cent evisceration required by the California State Board of Health. The patented invention was therefore an instant commercial success in the fish canning industry. The defendant canner studied the patented machine and changed around the arrangement of many of the parts so that the resulting machine was not similar in structure but still accomplished the same result. The inventor sued for infringement and recovered. The court said that the transposition of parts in the machine did not avert infringement where the realignment continues to perform the same function as before.

Addition of Elements. Direct infringement under the doctrine of equivalents is not avoided by the addition of elements to the patented invention, even if an improvement results. For example, an inventor obtained a patent on a buoyant, flexible, waterproof filler pad to be used in cushions, mattresses, life preservers, pillows, and the like. A national retail chain store imported a chaise lounge that embodied the patented article and the inventor sued for infringement. The retailer defended on the ground that its article contained additional parts constituting an improvement over the patented invention. The patent called for a plurality of strips that could be attached to the frame of a chair by tabs. In the retailer's article the connecting strips were heat-sealed to the caps of sheet plastic placed over the ends of the metal frame of the chair. The court said that the addition of sheet plastic, although an important improvement, did not avoid infringement under the doctrine of equivalents because the same result was accomplished.

Omission of Elements. Direct infringement under the doctrine of equivalents is always avoided by the omission of an element specifically recited in the claims of the patent. This does not mean that infringement can be avoided either by the substitution of one element for two or more elements in the patent or by the substitution of two or more elements for one element in the patent. Such changes fall under the doctrine of equivalents just as if one equivalent element was substituted for the replaced element described in the patent.

An illustration as to how the omission of an element avoids infringement would be helpful. An employee of the 3M Company obtained a reissue patent on a vinyl plastic tape designed primarily for use in electrical insulation work. The patent claim specified an adhesive insulating tape composed of a film backing mixed with a non-volatile liquid plasticizer, a soft and viscous resinous plasticizer, and an adhesive coating united to the inner surface of the film backing. Later, Sears, Roebuck & Company started selling a vinyl plastic tape identical to the patented product except that the film backing did not contain a liquid plasticizer. The patent owner sued but the court made a finding of noninfringement. The court said that there was no infringement, even though the same result is obtained, because the accused article was not covered by the claims of the patent and therefore is not an equivalent product.

Legitimate Design-Around. One may study a patent and analyze the language of the claims in order to strive to make a product that will perform the same function but not infringe the patent. Designing around a patent is wholly proper. It is a beneficial result sought by the U.S. patent system in order to inspire others to make different and better products, because adequate protection to an inventor who acquires a U.S. patent is assured by the doctrine of equivalents as the outer boundary. Thus a court has to measure infringement by a yardstick with the doctrine of equivalents on the near end of the stick and the doctrine of legitimate design-around on the far end of the stick. The length of the yardstick taken up by the doctrine of equivalents depends on the particular patented invention. A pioneer or basic patent may be entitled to a very long portion of the stick; a small improvement in a crowded art may be entitled to only a short distance on the near end of the stick. For example, an inventor obtained a patent on a new type of ear muff. The single claim of the patent stated that the ear muff comprised a head band

> terminating in enlarged portions, the enlarged portions being slitted, with the adjacent portions of the slit lapped and secured together to form such enlarged portions in approximate cone shape, the *lapped portions forming a pocket,* and a securing strip for the article with its terminals secured in said pockets.

The defendant, after examining the patent, began making a similar ear muff and was sued for infringement. The court decided that because the prior art comprising ear muffs was crowded, the patented invention was entitled to only a very narrow range of equivalents. Because the defendant's ear muffs did not have a pocket and because the terminals of the securing strip of the accused device were not secured in any pocket, the court made a finding of noninfringement. The defendant had thus "designed around" the troublesome claim and avoided infringement.

Experimental Use. Experimental use, as contrasted with commercial use of a patented invention, does not constitute actionable infringement, according to a group of nineteenth-century decisions. Thus use for the sole purpose of gratifying curiosity or a philosophical taste, or for mere amusement, was found in the late 1800's not to be an infringement. The reason given for this judicial exemption is that an unauthorized use of the patented invention must be done with an intent to profit commercially before an infringement will be found. Another apparent reason is that one of the main purposes of the U.S. patent system is to encourage experiments upon already patented subject matter in order to improve processes and products and thus advance the progress of the useful arts.

A good example of an experimental use that was found not to constitute an infringement involved a government contract. An inventor obtained patents on two compositions of matter that were metal alloys containing cobalt, nickel, and carbon plus a metal or metals capable of forming hard carbides especially adapted for use in high-speed cutting tools. The federal government awarded a contract to develop heat-resistant blades in gas turbines. The contractor used the patented metal alloys in carrying out research and development. The patent owner sued the federal government for direct infringement but the Court of Claims found that the patents were not infringed because the patented metal alloys were used only for testing and for experimental purposes.

Experimental use for commercial purposes, as in the ordinary course of business or for profit, is an infringement. For example, an inventor obtained a patent on a process for quick-freezing large catches of fish on board commercial fishing vessels. The patented process was used experimentally on two voyages of a vessel during tuna fishing operations. As a result of the experiment, the ship's engineer decided that it was not necessary to use the patented process to freeze fish adequately on board the vessel. The patent owner sued for infringement and recovered. The court concluded that the process described in the claims of the patent was used commercially, although experimentally. Nevertheless, there was infringement regardless of whether or not the patented process proved to be practicable or preferable over other methods.

Infringing Reconstruction Versus Permissible Repair. Before the Supreme Court decided two important cases in 1964, there was a doctrine of patent law that stated that one infringes a patent by reconstructing or by rebuilding a worn-out patented device but that one is permitted to repair the device without infringing the patent. This distinction was effectively abolished when the Court refocused its attention to the question as to whether or not the device being reconstructed or repaired was originally licensed or sold by the patent owner. The Court said that if the patent owner had initially licensed or sold the patented device, it did not matter whether the device was later reconstructed or repaired. There was no infringement because the license or sale effectively permitted any subsequent modifications of the patented device by the licensee or purchaser. However, if the device initially sold was not licensed or sold by the patent owner, there was a direct infringement and any subsequent reconstruction or repair continued the infringement and did not alter the effect of the original infringement.

Active Inducement

Whoever actively induces infringement of a patent shall be liable as an infringer [35 U.S.C. §271(b)].

One federal court of appeals has described active inducement of infringement as a term "as broad as the range of actions by which one in fact causes, or urges, or encourages, or aids another to infringe a patent." If a party is to be found guilty of active inducement of infringement, three facts must be proved: first, the defendant must have had knowledge that an infringement of a patent by a third party would occur; second, the defendant acted with the intent that a third party make, use, or sell the accused infringing subject matter; third, the third party infringed the patent. There are not many cases that involve active inducement of infringement. However, there is one case that provides a very thorough discussion of active inducement to infringe. Here, a railroad supervisor obtained a patent on both a machine and a process for correcting railroad track misalignments that he licensed to a manufacturer of railroad track maintenance equipment. A competitor began selling a machine with an operating and maintenance manual that explained how to practice the patented process. The patent owner and his exclusive licensee accused the defendant of active inducement of direct infringement, among other charges. The defendant was found liable by the federal district court after three findings were made: first, that the use of the accused machine by third-party customers of the defendant was a direct infringement; second, that the defendant had knowledge that its third-party customers were not entitled to practice the patent because it had been so notified in writing by the patent owner; and third, that a cursory reading of the explicit manual and other advertising literature conclusively demonstrated an intent on the part of the defendant to induce the third-party customers to practice the infringing subject matter. However, the appellate court reversed only because it disagreed with the first finding of direct infringement.

Contributory Infringement

The doctrine of contributory infringement, although existing since about 1870, was not codified by Congress until the Patent Act of 1952 was passed.

> Whoever sells a component of a patented machine, manufacture, combination or composition, or a material or apparatus for use in practicing a patented process, constituting a material part of the invention, knowing the same to be especially made or especially adapted for use in an infringement of such patent, and not a staple article or commodity of commerce suitable for substantial noninfringing use, shall be liable as a contributory infringer [35 U.S.C. §271(c)].

This paragraph of the statute, although lengthy and complex, can best be understood if it is broken down into its constituent parts. Such an explanatory breakdown was made in a commentary by one if its chief draftsmen, Mr. Pasquale Federico, soon after the present Patent Act was codified.

> Contributory infringement under this paragraph requires the presence of the following factors:

1. The thing sold must be "a component of a patented machine, manufacture, combination or composition, or a material or apparatus for use in practicing a patented process." The thing sold is presumably not itself patented since if it were patented the question of contributory infringement, as distinguished from direct infringement, would scarcely arise and the paragraph would have little or no apparent purposes.

2. The thing sold must constitute a material part of the invention, that is, of the patented invention.

3. The thing sold must be especially made or especially adapted for use in an infringement of the patent.

4. The seller must have knowledge of factor 3.

5. In addition the thing sold must not be "a staple article or commodity of commerce suitable for substantial noninfringing use."

Before examining any cases interpreting this statute, a knowledge of the stormy history of the doctrine of contributory infringement is helpful. The doctrine of contributory infringement is a judge-made rule of equity that grew out of the rules involving liability of joint tort-feasors or wrongdoers. The doctrine was effectively abolished by the Supreme Court in 1944 in a decision widely known as the *Mercoid I* case, which held that a patent owner could not sue sellers of unpatented *nonstaple* articles incorporated into a combination patent as contributory infringers. Congress resuscitated the doctrine by enacting §271 of the present Patent Act in 1952. The Supreme Court made an attempt to reconcile the *Mercoid I* case with the statute in a case decided in 1961 that effectively restated the *Mercoid* position. However, the Court finally followed the congressional intent to overrule the *Mercoid* cases in the *Aro II* case in 1964.

A good example of the application of this statute was the *Aro II* case. That case involved a combination patent on the once popular convertible tops that first appeared on 1952 model cars. The patent— one for a "Convertible Folding Top with Automatic Seal at Rear Quarter"—covered the combination, in an automobile body, of a flexible top fabric, supporting structures, and a mechanism for sealing the fabric against the side of the automobile body in order to keep out the rain. Because the fabric portion of the patented combination wore out after about three years of use, the defendant went into the business of producing fabric components designed as replacements for the worn-out fabric portions. A fabric replacement could be installed by a car owner himself. The patent owners sued the manufacturer of the fabric components for contributory infringement.

The Supreme Court found that factors 1, 2, 4, and 5 were present. The convertible top replacement fabric sold was a component of a patented combination but was not itself patented. The fabric sold constituted a material part of the patented invention. The defendant seller had knowledge that the fabric sold was especially made for use in an infringement of the patent. The fabric sold was *not* a staple article suitable for substantial noninfringing use; rather, the fabric sold was a nonstaple article suitable for substantial infringing use. However, the Supreme Court found that factor 3 was not completely satisfied. Although the fabric sold was especially made for use in a direct infringement, the Court said that there was no contributory infringement because the accused contributory infringer did not have knowledge, not only that the convertible top combination was patented, but that its replacement fabric was a direct infringement until the patent owner charged it with contributory infringement in a letter dated in early 1954. Thus the Court limited recovery to a period thereafter.

Acts Before the Patent Issues and After the Patent Expires

A patent owner may not recover for infringement if acts constituting infringement were committed before the patent issues or after the patent expires. Before the patent issues, the disclosure of the invention sought to be patented is kept secret by the Patent Office and the patent monopoly begins only on the issue date of the patent. The third party, committing acts that would be an infringement if done during the term of the patent, may have developed the accused device either independently, through legitimate channels, or by improper means. In every instance, there is no remedy for preissuance infringement under the patent laws. After the patent expires or is found invalid by a court of law, the invention passes into the public domain. There can be no infringement thereafter because the patented invention is free to be used by everyone. That is a dividend to the public of the U.S. patent system.

Acts Outside the United States

For an infringement to be actionable, the accused acts must occur within the territorial limits of the United States. It is not an infringement if a party either makes, uses, or sells the patented invention in a foreign country. A transfer of the title to goods infringing a U.S. patent executed in the Foreign Trade Zone in New York City while the goods are enroute from one foreign country to another is a sale actionable as a direct infringement. However, the making of a patented invention partially in the United States and the completing of it in a foreign country is not actionable. This is the interpretation made by the Supreme Court in 1972. In the case that made this construction, a patent owner held two combination patents for deveining shrimp, which inventions were a boon to the shrimp-processing industry. A manufacturer made the patented machinery in three sections and shipped them to foreign competitors of the patent owner with directions for assemblage. The patented combination would be completed in less than an hour. The patent owner sued for direct infringement and the manufacturer defended on the grounds that the patented invention was not made within the United States. The Court in a 5–4 decision ruled that the statutory term "makes . . . any patented invention within the United States" means *entirely* makes, not *substantially* makes where a patented combination is involved.

DEFENDING AN INFRINGEMENT SUIT

When a party is sued for patent infringement, there are a number of defenses that may be raised. The defendant must succeed on only one of the many available defenses in order to prevail in the lawsuit, whereas the patent owner must overcome all the defenses to succeed.

Congress has specifically listed the defenses available to an accused infringer in the present Patent Act.

The following shall be defenses in any action involving the . . . infringement of a patent and shall be pleaded:

(1) Noninfringement, absence of liability for infringement or unenforceability,

(2) Invalidity of the patent or any claim in suit on any ground specified . . . as a condition for patentability,

(3) Invalidity of the patent or any claim in suit for failure to comply with any requirement of sections 112 or 251 of this title,

(4) Any other fact or act made a defense by this title [35 U.S.C. §282].

Many of these defenses were mentioned earlier in this chapter but are recounted here for the sake of completeness.

Noninfringement

The burden of proving infringement is on the accuser. The accused party may present evidence to oppose the charge of infringement. The defense of noninfringement goes directly to the question of whether or not the accused subject matter falls within the claims of the patent in suit. This is done by comparing the specific language of the patent claims with the accused subject matter. If the accused subject matter is not described by the patent claims, the defense of noninfringement is successful.

The term *file wrapper estoppel* (pp. 41–42) is a shorthand name for one way of construing the body of evidence in a case most favorable to the accused infringer so as to show noninfringement. The doctrine of file wrapper estoppel acts to prevent a patent owner from asserting against a party accused of infringement that the scope of the patent claim covers subject matter inconsistent with that indicated by the arguments supporting patentability that appear in the file wrapper (prosecution record) at the Patent Office. The doctrine is, in effect, a limitation on the doctrine of equivalents (pp.75–76) used to prove direct infringement.

If charged with direct infringement (pp. 75–79, the accused party may also defend on the grounds that he has neither made nor used nor sold the patented invention within the United States during the term of the patent. If charged with active inducement of infringement pp. 79–80), the accused may deny that any of his acts induced either direct or contributory infringement or he may show that there was no direct or contributory infringement which he could actively induce. If charged with contributory infringement (pp. 80–82), he may defend on several grounds: first, he did not sell either a component of a patented invention or an article or apparatus for use in a patented process; second, if he did sell such a component, article, or apparatus, it did not constitute a material part of the patented invention or it was a staple or commodity of commerce suitable for substantial noninfringing use; third, if he did sell such a component, article, or apparatus, he did not have knowledge that it was especially made or adapted for use in an infringement of a patent; or fourth, there was no direct infringement to which his acts could be considered a contribution.

Patent Invalidity

In the early part of this chapter, conditions were discussed that, on the threshhold, determined in the Patent Office whether a patent should initially issue. These conditions become relevant again with respect to the patent's validity when an infringement suit is brought. Because the prosecution of the patent application in the Patent Office was carried out by only one party, the accused infringer has a right to contest in an adversary proceeding whether these conditions were actually met.

Because an invalid patent cannot be infringed, a court will usually be asked to rule on the validity of a patent incident to deciding the issue of infringement. Thus a patent owner can find himself in a worse position than when he started the lawsuit because he may not only lose the lawsuit for infringement but also lose his patent because of invalidity. Therefore a defense of patent invalidity appears in almost every infringement suit. The defendant usually has everything to gain and nothing to lose by raising this defense.

Technically, a legal presumption of validity attaches to every patent when it is issued by the Patent Office. Congress has enacted a statute to make this presumption clear. Nevertheless, the strength of this defense of patent invalidity should not be underestimated. An indication of its success is evident from a study undertaken of all federal appellate court decisions on patent validity in infringement suits decided after the *Graham* v. *John Deere Co.* litigation in 1966 until early 1971. The study shows that of the 294 patents contested, only eighty-nine, or about 30 per cent, were found valid. The percentage found valid varied from 0 per cent in the Eighth Circuit (Northern Plains states) to 48 per cent in the Fifth Circuit (Deep South states).

The legal presumption of validity applies only to prior art that has been considered by the Patent Office; it is only a presumption and is not binding on a court. A court will independently rule on questions of utility, novelty, and nonobviousness. There is no presumption that a patent is valid over prior art not considered by the Patent Office and presented for the first time to a judge for ruling in a contest over validity.

The significance of the presumption varies with the patent in suit. Extrinsic factors other than prior art may affect the strength or weakness of the presumption. For instance, one court said that a patent, resulting from an application involving four separate official actions, seven amendments, and at least two interviews personally attended by the applicant and his patent attorney with the examiner, "should not lightly be held invalid." Another court said that a "significant" presumption of validity attends a patent issued after the Patent Office Board of Appeals has considered the nature of the invention and decided that it is patentable. Other courts have said that the presumption was strengthened by immediate commercial success of the patented invention, by widespread imitation by numerous competitors necessitating the institution of several infringement suits, and by a prior judicial determination of validity.

On the other hand, different extrinsic factors may weaken the presumption. For example, one court said that the issuance of a patent on the basis of an innocent misrepresentation of fact made to the Patent Office "serves only to destroy" the presumption, assuming the misrepresentation had a substantial bearing on the issuance of the patent. Another court said that the presumption is "diminished" by the fact that an interference proceeding in which the patent was involved was settled by agreement rather than by a decision of the Patent Office Board of Patent Interferences. Also, a court said that the presumption "is weaker" in instances of combination patents, because a rather severe test must be applied in light of the difficulty of finding unobviousness in an assembly of old elements. Nevertheless, the burden of proof upon an accused infringer attempting to establish invalidity of the patent is heavy. Overcoming the presumption of validity, like the presumption itself, varies with the patent in suit. Some courts have taken the position that, ordinarily, a party must prove invalidity "by clear and convincing evidence." However, where the presumption of validity is weak, other courts have said the burden of proof is carried if the "evidence has more than a dubious preponderance."

Any one of the following grounds may result in a patent being declared invalid. This checklist may be handy for a party about to be embroiled in an infringement suit.

1. The patented invention may be nonstatutory subject matter. It may not be a technical process, machine, article of manufacture, composition of matter, improvement of any of the above, design, or botanical plant. See pp. 11–16. The patented invention may be mere printed matter, a naturally occurring substance, a method of doing business, a mere abstract idea, a scientific principle, or a mental process. See pp. 16–20.

2. The patented invention may be barred by the Atomic Energy Act. See p. 20.

3. The patented invention may not be novel. It may be anticipated by the prior art (pp. 20–21), described ahead in a U.S. patent granted to another (pp. 20–21), or made beforehand in the United States by another who had not abandoned, suppressed, or concealed it (pp. 28–30).

4. The inventor may have lost the right to a patent. More than one year before the patent application was filed, the invention may have been the subject of another patent or a prior printed publication, or it may have been in public use or on sale. See pp. 21–23. The inventor may have abandoned the invention (pp. 23–25), already obtained a foreign patent (pp. 25–26), or did not himself invent the patented subject matter (pp. 26–28).

5. The patented invention may have been obvious to one with ordinary skill in the art at the time the invention was made. See pp. 30–34.

6. The description of the invention in the patent may not be specific enough to enable any person skilled in the pertinent art

to make the invention or does not set forth the best mode contemplated for carrying out the invention. See p. 36.

7. The invention may be the subject of double patenting. See pp. 40–41.

8. The patent may have been barred for foreign filing without a license. See pp. 25–26.

Unenforceability—Estoppel

A patent may be unenforceable because its owner may be "estopped" for some reason from asserting a charge of infringement against the defendant.

Collateral Estoppel. Collateral estoppel is a judge-made rule that precludes a patent owner from asserting a charge of infringement if the patent has already been found invalid in earlier litigation involving its owner and a different accused infringer.

It should be noted that this doctrine does not work in reverse. An owner whose patent has been found valid in an initial suit against one infringer may not thereafter avoid relitigation of the validity of the patent in a subsequent suit against another infringer. The reason is that the later accused infringers would be effectively denied their "day in court" if all of them are forced to rely on the validity attack made by the first accused infringer, no matter how poorly done.

Equitable Estoppel. Equitable estoppel is a judge-made rule that precludes a patent owner from asserting a charge of infringement because his previous actions are inconsistent in some way with the right to assert such a charge. The purpose of the doctrine of equitable estoppel is to prevent the patent owner's inconsistent actions from resulting in injustice to the accused party who had been misled by the patent owner's earlier acts, even though the accused party is guilty of infringement. To create an equitable estoppel, a false representation or concealment of material facts must be made by a person with knowledge of the real facts to a person without such knowledge. The representation must be made with the intention that it shall be acted on by the latter person. The person must have relied on or acted on the representation so that he will suffer injury or prejudice by a later repudiation, contradiction, or inconsistent assertion by the patent owner. For example, an inventor obtained two patents relating to an apparatus for administering therapeutic treatments to patients. The patents were assigned to a corporation which publicly claimed that some of its competitors were infringers. Upon learning of the announcement to the trade, one of the competitors inquired directly to seek verification and explanation of the charges. In response, the patent owner denied that any assertion of infringement had been made against the inquirer but refused to indicate whether it considered the competitor's devices to be infringing. However, the patent owner gave its assurance that those believed to be affected would be directly advised of the situation. One of the competitor's machines was then obtained by the patent owner and subjected to testing. Almost a year later, in a deposition given in connection with other litigation, the patent attorney for the owner stated that it did not then contend and did not, to the best of his knowledge, previously contend that any device manufactured by the inquiring competitor infringed the patents. Based on these events the competitor considered this statement to be a clear confirmation that the owner did not consider the patent to be infringed. Thus the competitor continued to manufacture and sell its own devices. Shortly thereafter, the patent owner sued four of the competitor's customers for infringement. The competitor intervened and raised the defenses of invalidity and equitable estoppel. The court found the two patents to be invalid and not infringed. The court went on to decide that, in any event, the patent owner was estopped from bringing the charges of infringement because its prior conduct had led the competitor justifiably to rely and act on its earlier statements. The patent owner's present inconsistent conduct would cause unexpected economic injury to the competitor and the court would not allow any such inequity to result.

Laches and the Statute of Limitations.   *Laches* is a label attached to a particular type of equitable estoppel. It is limited to those situations where equitable estoppel applies because of the patent owner's earlier inaction. Laches is a judge-made rule of equity that prevents a patent owner from enforcing his patent against a party for infringement because he has slept on his rights while the infringer made expenditures in the belief that he was not infringing the patent or that, if infringing, he would not be sued.

Thus laches is the neglect, for an unreasonable length of time, under circumstances requiring diligence, to do what should have been done, resulting in injury or prejudice to another party. Six years of inaction with knowledge is presumptive laches. This period is imposed by the courts for the sake of consistency with the statute of limitations, which limits the bringing of charges for infringement to six years after the accused act has been committed.

By the way of illustration, an inventor obtained a patent for pump construction. In 1956 he sent a written notice of infringement to a competitor. For a year thereafter there was some correspondence about cross licensing but no agreement was reached. Eight years after the last communication, the patent owner filed an infringement suit. The accused infringer raised the defenses of invalidity, noninfringement, and laches. The court found that the patent was valid and infringed but that it was unenforceable because the patent owner was barred by laches from asserting the charge of infringement. The court said that there was an unreasonably long delay without explanation for asserting its patent rights resulting in economic injury to the defendant so that it became inequitable to allow the patent owner to recover any damages or obtain a court order preventing any future damage.

It should be noted that the mere fact of a long delay is not sufficient to establish laches. For example, in another case the inventor of the process for using frequency modulation (FM) in radio obtained two pioneer patents in 1933. In 1940, a small radio manufacturer began infringing the patent. Shortly thereafter, the patent owner approached the infringing party with an offer of a license. Negotiations began but stopped in late 1941 because of the outbreak of World War II, during which time the inventor gave a royalty-free license to everyone in support of the war effort. In 1948 the patent owner started infringement suits against the largest competitors in the radio manufacturing industry. The stress on his personal relationships caused by the numerous lawsuits drove the inventor to suicide in 1954 and within a few months, the defendants settled with his widow for $1 million. Shortly beforehand, another suit had been brought against the initially accused small radio manufacturer. The accused infringer raised the defense of laches, among others. The suit dragged on for thirteen years until the court finally found the patents enforceable. The court said that the infringement suit was not barred by laches because the delay from notice in 1940 until bringing suit in 1954 was not unreasonable. The court felt that the outbreak of World War II and the subsequent intervening lawsuits against larger competitors justified the delay. Furthermore, the earlier suits were notice to all other infringers of the patent owner's intent to sue them later.

Unenforceability: Patent Misuse

An accused infringer has the opportunity to defend an infringement suit by charging the patent owner with misuse. Patent misuse is predicated upon a finding that the patent owner has committed acts that have for their purpose the illegal expansion of the scope of the patent monopoly. This defense may be raised by any accused infringer regardless of whether the action alleged by the defendant to be a misuse was committed by the patent owner against the accused infringer or against a third party.

Patent misuse is a judge-made rule of equity that grew out of the doctrine of "unclean hands"—a person who himself has done wrong cannot come into court to seek redress against one who has done him a wrong in return. The doctrine of patent misuse arose in 1917 in the *Motion Picture Patents* case. In this landmark case, an owner held a patent on a motion picture projector. The patent owner sold the machine with a license restriction that it be used only with motion picture films that it supplied. The defendant sold films to be used in the patented machine and the patent owner sued for contributory infringement. The Supreme Court found that no contributory infringement existed. The Court said that the patent cannot be allowed to cover unpatented products that were not elements claimed in the patent. Although the term *patent misuse* was not used, the Supreme Court said in a later case that the doctrine began its development in this 1917 decision.

The high-water mark of this doctrine was reached in 1944, when the Supreme Court inferred that the mere bringing of a suit for contributory infringement was a patent misuse. This occurred in the 1944 *Mercoid I* case. Feeling that the Supreme Court had extended the doctrine of patent misuse too far in this case, Congress found it necessary for the first time in the history of the patent system to codify the doctrine of infringement and to limit the doctrine of patent misuse. This was done in 1952 in the present Patent Act. The limitation on the doctrine of patent misuse appears in 35 U.S.C. §271(d).

Statutorily Exempted Acts.   What *is* patent misuse was not codified in order to give such an equitable doctrine room to develop in the courts. However, Congress did state three types of actions that, when taken by the patent owner, were *not* misuse. These actions are listed in §271(d). Each type of action is covered in a separate clause. In order to understand subsection (d), it is helpful to examine each of the three clauses individually.

No patent owner otherwise entitled to relief for infringement or contributory infringement of a patent shall be denied relief or deemed guilty of misuse or illegal extension of the patent right by reason of his having . . . derived revenue from acts which if performed by another without his consent would constitute contributory infringement of the patent . . . [35 U.S.C. §271(d)(1)].

Clause (1) states the first type of permissible action. The meaning of this clause is that the patent owner can do acts that, if performed by another without the patent owner's consent, would constitute ordinary contributory infringement under §271(c). If the patent owner makes a profit from such acts, there is no misuse.

As an example, suppose that the patent owner sells a component of the patented invention. The thing sold is not itself patented but it constitutes a material part of the patented invention and is especially made and adapted for use in the patent. In addition, the thing sold is not a staple article or commodity of commerce suitable for any other substantial use. If another did this without the patent owner's consent, he would be guilty of contributory infringement. However, the patent owner can take this action without being guilty of misuse.

A case decided shortly after the 1952 Patent Act shows very well the meaning of clause (1). In 1956 a manufacturer held a combination patent relating to alternating current supply systems for consumption circuits having negative resistance characteristics. The manufacturer sold ballasts, i.e., resistances used to stabilize the current in the circuits, to customers with an implied license to use the patented system without charge. The ballasts were not themselves patented. A competitor made and sold a device that was similar to the patented combination. The patent owner sued for direct infringement and the competitor raised the defenses of noninfringement, invalidity, and unenforceability. The district court found the patent uninfringed and invalid for anticipation by the prior art. Nevertheless, for purposes of a possible appeal, the district court also proceeded to decide the issue of unenforceability. The defendant contended that the patent was unenforceable because the sale by the owner of unpatented articles for use in the patented combination constituted a patent misuse, citing the *Mercoid* cases. The court rejected this contention, saying that the recently enacted statute, §271(d), changed the prior case law. Because the ballasts sold constituted a material part of the patented invention and were especially made for use in the patent, they were a nonstaple article. Thus if the ballasts had been sold by another without the consent of the patent owner, such sales would constitute contributory infringement. However, because the patent owner had derived revenue from these same sales, there was no misuse under clause (1) of §271(d).

> No misuse if patent owner—licensed or authorized another to perform acts which if performed without his consent would constitute contributory infringement of the patent . . . [35 U.S.C. §271(d)(2)].

Clause (2) states the second type of permissible action. The meaning of this clause is that the patent owner can license others to do acts that if performed without the patent owner's consent would constitute contributory infringement.

Congress did not find it necessary to add that the patent owner could license others to do acts that if performed without the patent owner's consent would constitute direct infringement, because a patent owner has always been able to do this under the patent grant.

As an example, suppose that the patent owner licenses another to sell a component of the patented combination. The component sold is not itself patented but it constitutes a material part of the patented invention and is especially made and adapted for use in the patent. In addition, the component sold is not a staple article or commodity of commerce suitable for any other substantial use. If a party did this without the patent owner's consent, he would be guilty of contributory infringement. However, the patent owner can license the party and others to take this action without being guilty of misuse.

Another example of the type of conduct made permissible by this clause is best illustrated by an actual case. An inventor obtained a patent on both a process and a machine for the treatment of cotton fibers. The patented machine contained an impurity-crushing roller device that was not itself covered by a claim in the patent but it constituted a material part of the patented combination. The patent was assigned to a manufacturer who then charged a competitor with contributory infringement for selling four different constructions of a machine containing such impurity-crushing rollers. As the result of negotiations the competitor agreed to take a license under the patent and to pay royalties to the patent owner to continue use of the accused machine. After a few years the licensed competitor changed its mind, decided to stop paying royalties, and sued for a declaratory judgment that the patent was invalid and unenforceable. The unenforceability charge was based on the grounds that the patent owner's alleged attempt to obtain a monopoly on unpatented goods, namely, the impurity-crushing rollers, constituted a patent misuse. The patent owner counterclaimed for contributory infringement and the court found the patent valid, infringed, and enforceable. The court said that the impurity-crushing roller device, although unpatented, was a nonstaple especially made for use in the patent and thus the licensing arrangement was not a misuse of the patent because clause (2) of §271(d) allows a patent owner to license others, including accused infringers, to perform acts that if performed without the owner's consent would constitute contributory infringement.

No misuse if patent owner—sought to enforce his patent rights against infringement or contributory infringement [35 U.S.C. §271(d)(3)].

Clause (3) states the third type of permissible action. The meaning of this clause is that the patent owner can sue to enforce his patent against direct infringers under §271(a), active inducers of infringement under §271(b), and contributory infringers under §271(c). If the patent owner brings such suits, there is no misuse.

The congressional intent of this clause in the 1952 Patent Act became clear very quickly after its enactment. In the first case to interpret this clause, a manufacturer held three patents on rotary drilling bits. Several individuals went into the business of reconstructing the wornout drilling bits and reselling them. The patent owner sued these "retippers" for infringement in three separate concurrent suits. The accused infringers defended on several grounds, one being that the mere bringing of this type of lawsuit constituted a patent misuse, as implied by the Supreme Court's 1944 *Mercoid I* decision. In 1954 a court of appeals reviewed the three suits and said, in short order, that the new statute, clause (3) of §271(d), allowed an owner to enforce his patent against infringers without being guilty of misuse. In 1955 the Supreme Court refused to hear the case, thus letting the court of appeals decision stand.

Outside of these specifically exempted acts, the courts have applied the doctrine of patent misuse to various other activities.

Enforcement of Patent Against Sellers of Unpatented Staple Goods.
The courts will find a misuse if an owner attempts to enforce his combination patent against sellers or users of unpatented staple articles capable of being used outside the patent in suit, where such sellers are not inducing infringement and such sellers are not actually infringing the patented combination.

The Supreme Court first recognized this type of patent misuse in the *Carbice* case decided in 1931. In this leading case the patentee held a combination patent on a refrigerating transportation package for ice cream. The package used dry ice as a refrigerant. The defendant sold dry ice to be used in the patented device and the patent owner sued for contributory infringement. The Supreme Court found no contributory infringement. Although the term *patent misuse* was not specifically used, this case made the first definitive statement of the principal involved: relief for infringement will be denied to an owner whenever he has attempted to extend his patent coverage over unpatented staple products that are common articles of commerce, in this case, dry ice.

Shortly after §271(d) was enacted in 1952, there was some confusion in the lower federal courts as to the statute's effect on this type of misuse. Commentaries by the two chief draftsmen of the Patent Act indicate that this type of misuse is to continue unaffected but it is not to be extended to unpatented nonstaple products that are new articles of commerce suitable only for substantial infringing use.

Royalty Charges After Patent Expiration.
After a patent expires, its owner can no longer charge royalties for the making, using, or selling of the patented product or process. If the owner does so, he is

guilty of misuse and will not be allowed by the courts to enforce his royalty "rights" against anyone. For example, an owner held twelve patents covering both machines and processes for picking hops. The owner sold for a flat sum a machine that incorporated seven patents and charged farmers each hop-picking season for use of the patents at a minimum royalty of $500 or $10 per 600 pounds of picked hops, which-ever was greater. The farmers who purchased the machines refused to pay royalties after the last patent expired in 1957 and the patent owner sued. The Supreme Court found that the defendants did not have to pay the royalty charges for use after the patent expired.

Mandatory Package Licensing. Where a patent owner requires that any licensee desirous of receiving the right to make, use, or sell under certain patents must also take the right to make, use, or sell under other patents, there is being imposed a "mandatory" or "coercive" package license, as contrasted with a permissible "voluntary" package license. This type of condition, where the patent owner refuses to license any patents other than in a predetermined group, constitutes a patent misuse. For example, a patent owner held thirty-five patents connected with the tempering of glass. A manufacturer, attempting to enter the glass market, sought a license under only four patents. The patent owner refused to license any patents less than all of them together. The prospec-tive licensee would be required to pay a royalty on the total package, regardless of the number of patents actually used. Thereafter, the manu-facturer commenced production of glass and the patent owner sued for infringement of the four individual patents. The manufacturer defended on the grounds of invalidity, noninfringement, and unenforceability. The court found the patents valid, infringed, but unenforceable because the owner had misused the patents by imposing mandatory or coercive pack-age licenses on licensees and by refusing to license prospective licensees under any other terms. Nevertheless, it should be noted that mandatory package licensing is not a misuse where the packaged patents are interlocking. Patents interlock if none of the patented devices can be used without infringing all the patents.

By way of illustration, a patent owner sued a competitor for in-fringement of two patents covering devices for skimming and filtering the water in swimming pools and vacuuming the sides and bottom of such pools. The competitor raised the defense, among others, that the patents were unenforceable because the patent owner imposed a man-datory package license of the interlocking patents upon licensees. The court found the patents enforceable because no commercially feasible device could be manufactured under either of the patents without in-fringing the other. Thus there was no misuse because the mandatory package license was the only practical way of making the patents available for public use.

Prohibiting Manufacture of Competing Goods.   A patent will also be unenforceable if its owner requires that the licensee must not manufacture competing products upon pain of termination of the license. Although the Supreme Court has not condemned this type of license clause specifically, lower federal courts have decided that such a clause constitutes a misuse. In one case the patent owner issued licenses to various manufacturers of metal washers. Each license contained a clause to the effect that the licensee agreed, while the license was still in effect, that it would not manufacture any other form of nontangling spring washers except those covered by the patent in suit. The owner sued a competitor who defended on the grounds that the patent was invalid, not infringed, and misused. The court found the patent valid and infringed but not enforceable because its owner had misused it by imposing the manufacturing limitation on its licensees. The court said that the owner had disentitled itself to recover for infringement by using its patent monopoly to drive competing unpatented goods from the market.

Purge of Patent Misuse.   Even though a patent may be unenforceable against an infringer because its owner has committed acts constituting misuse, he may recover for later acts of infringement after he has "purged" himself of the misuse. This purging must encompass not only the elimination of the abusive acts or practices, but also the effects of the misuse. Only thereafter can the patent owner renew his fight against infringers.

Purging patent misuse is sometimes more easily said than done. For example, between 1942 and 1956 an inventor obtained four patents on various electrical devices and licensed them to a manufacturer. Shortly after the fourth patent issued, the licensee sued another manufacturer for infringement. The accused party raised the defenses of invalidity, noninfringement, and unenforceability. In January 1960 the court rendered an opinion that the last patent was valid, infringed, but unenforceable because the licensee had been misusing the patent by committing antitrust violations (to be discussed in the next section) since the date that the last patent issued. Thus the defendant, although found guilty, continued to infringe unabated.

A week after the court's opinion the losing patent licensee distributed to its employees and sales representatives a summary of the court's decision. At the end of the month it notified all of its customers, distributors, and jobbers that it was no longer practicing its prior abusive practices. Such written notices were sent to 6,600 customers and to over 1,800 distributors and jobbers. On the same date all sales personnel were instructed to refrain from any of the prior abusive practices. During the next week the board of directors, at a special meeting, adopted a new sales policy eliminating the earlier condemned acts. During the next two months the patent licensee published a statement of its new sales policy at its own expense in seven trade magazines. In the following year and a half the patent licensee repeated and emphasized its new sales policy at staff and departmental meetings and at semiannual sales meetings addressed by its attorney. In the meantime the patent licensee went back into court to sue the same defendant for infringement. This time the court allowed the recovery but limited it to infringement occurring after August 1961, over one and a half years after the court's first decision.

Duty to License.   There is no duty on a patent owner to license in the abstract and some courts have loosely said that there is even no duty to license in order to purge a misuse. However, a so-called duty to license may arise in the context of patents on processes, combinations, or new uses, as well as for violations of the antitrust laws.

It is already established law that a patent owner cannot condition the grant of a license upon the purchase from himself of unpatented staple elements incorporated into the patent and enforce the patent by suing competing sellers of the unpatented staple elements for contributory infringement. To do so constitutes a misuse. Denials by the patent owner of requests for licenses by competing staple sellers may be taken as evidence of such conditioning. However, offers of licenses negate any such implication.

If those who wish to practice the patented combination have a choice as to from whom they can purchase the unpatented elements and still be able to practice the invention, there is no misuse because there is no conditioning. The method of doing business whereby a patent owner sells an unpatented staple article with an implied license to use it in his patented invention is not in itself unlawful, and the patent owner may lawfully collect his license fee out of the proceeds of the sale of the unpatented staple article, so long as there is no intent to condition the license upon its purchase. Thus, although the patent owner may continue to earn his royalty income on his own sales, he must provide that those who wish to purchase from a competitor may do so and still be able to practice the invention.

Moreover, a number of cases have made clear that a patent owner cannot avoid misuse by offering alternative licenses that are discriminatory or that are so arranged that the potential licensee cannot tell in advance whether the license would in fact be discriminatory. Although a patent owner may thus be guilty of misuse if he affirmatively offers alternative licenses that amount to an illusory offer because they are unfair or discriminatory, he will not be held to have misused his patent for failure affirmatively to offer alternative licenses at all, unless there is a proof of intent to monopolize the market for the unpatented staple article.

Absence of Liability

The last, but not least, defense to be discussed is the mere absence of liability. Absence of liability is a simple defense whereby a party shows that the patent owner is suing the wrong party or that the manufacture, use, or sale of an accused device by the defendant is done with authority under an assignment, license, or release made by a properly authorized party.

PATENT–ANTITRUST LAW

The Interface Between Antitrust Policy and Patent Policy

Standing alongside the monopoly protection accorded patented technology are a series of federal statutes called the antitrust laws. Generally speaking, these antitrust laws prohibit unreasonable restraints of trade and various specific kinds of trade conduct that Congress has determined to be anticompetitive. Some of these trade restraints are unlawful in themselves, so-called per se violations of the antitrust laws, and some are unlawful only if they may or do give rise to certain anticompetitive effects.

The conventionally stated objective of these antitrust laws is to foster vigorous competition in the market place. The patent laws forming the basis of the American patent system have as their objective the fostering of the incentive to make public disclosure of inventions through the seventeen-year right to exclude others from making, using, or selling the patented invention. Tensions between these objectives arise principally from the manner in which patent rights are exploited through licensing and the manner in which patent rights are accumulated. These conflicts are loosely referred to as patent–antitrust law. Typically, a recurring issue in patent–antitrust disputes is whether a particular restriction in a patent license is reasonably necessary to afford the patentee the rewards of his invention or whether the restriction goes further and constitutes an unreasonable restraint of trade. We turn now to a brief summary of the various federal antitrust statutes involved.

Federal Antitrust Laws Affecting Patent Rights

The Sherman Act. In 1890 Congress enacted the Sherman Antitrust Act, the statute forming the cornerstone expression of federal policy with respect to competition. Section 1 of the Sherman Act prohibits agreements, combinations, and conspiracies amounting to unreasonable restraints of trade. Section 1 of the Sherman Act prohibits such conduct as price fixing between competitors, division of customers or markets between competitors and competitor group boycotts, these offenses being per se violations—unlawful without any showing required as to specific anticompetitive effects. It is generally of no consequence that one or more competititors happens to be utilizing patented or licensed technology. Section 2 of the Sherman Act prohibits "monopolization" and "attempts to monopolize" a relevant market either throughout the United States or any trading area of the United States. Combinations and conspiracies to monopolize or attempts to monopolize are also precluded.

The federal antitrust laws do not prohibit a company from acquiring a monopoly position, standing alone. Judge Learned Hand said in the landmark 1945 *Alcoa* case: "A single producer may be the survivor out of a group of active competitors, merely by virtue of his superior skill, foresight and industry. . . . The successful competitor, having been urged to compete, must not be turned upon when he wins." This means that a patent owner who acquired the patent rights by proper means can literally secure a monopoly position in the market for a "better mousetrap" where the patent rights are so strong and so broad as to prevent competition in the "better mousetrap" market. Of course, after the patent monopoly expires, "better mousetrap" competition is free to enter the market and erode that monopoly position through conventional economic forces of price, quality, and service competition.

The words *monopolization* and *attempt to monopolize* as used in Section 2 of the Sherman Act primarily involve market or company behavior along with market structure. Thus unlawful, predatory practices to restrict competition, and even practices that standing alone are lawful but that taken as a whole are restrictive of competition, usually constitute the genesis of an antitrust action under Section 2 of the Sherman Act. Market size and shares are factors in such proceedings. Speaking generally, monopolization has been defined as the possession of monopoly power in a relevant market, coupled with attainment of that power by unfair means or the use of that power unfairly to exclude competition. In practice, however, it has proved very difficult for a firm having monopoly power to defeat a claim of monopolization. For example, in the *Alcoa* case, the court said that monopoly power is used unfairly by merely "progressively [embracing] each new opportunity as it opened, and [facing] every newcomer with new capacity already geared into a great organization, having the advantages of experience, trade connections, and the elite of personel." Thus the existence of monopoly power, although insufficient in and of itself to establish an antitrust violation, is the critical element in analyzing a firm's exposure under the "monopolization" clause of Section 2. *Monopoly power* has been defined as the "power to fix prices or exclude competition." Evidence of this nature is rarely available, however, so normally courts look to the defendant's percentage share of the market. There is no precise demarcation between a monopoly share and a nonmonopoly share of the market, but the cases do offer some guidance. As a general rule, 85 to 90 per cent of the market would constitute monopoly power, but it is at least doubtful whether 60 per cent would be enough, and certainly 30 per cent is not. It is the definition of the market that determines the defendant's market share—the narrower the market is pegged to the defendant's business the more likely its market share will approach monopoly power. The market is usually defined, from a product standpoint, to include the products that defendant makes and sells and that it is alleged to be monopolizing, and all products that are reasonably competitive with defendant's products—price, use, and qualities considered.

In the patent–antitrust area, the monopolization and attempt-to-monopolize prohibitions will not normally affect the patent owner so long as he merely exercises his statutory right to prevent others from making, using, and selling the patented invention. On the other hand, attempts to extend the patent monopoly beyond its legitimate scope will create antitrust problems under Section 2. This is where company behavior and market definitions come into effect, as we shall see from discussions later in this chapter.

Section 3 of the Clayton Act. Section 3 was enacted by Congress in 1914 to reach specific kinds of business transactions involving a seller's exercise of economic leverage in one product to force sales of another product, called tie-in transactions, as well as requirement contracts—giving rise to adverse competitive effects. The Act provides in pertinent part:

> It shall be unlawful for any person . . . to lease or make a sale or contract for sale of goods, . . . or other commodities, whether patented or unpatented, for use, consumption, or resale within the United States . . . or fix a price charged therefor, or discount from, or rebate upon, such price on the condition, agreement, or understanding that the lessee or pur-

chaser thereof shall not use or deal in the goods, . . . or other commodities of a competitor or competitors of the lessor or seller, where the effect of such lease, sale, or contract for sale or such condition, agreement, or understanding may be to substantially lessen competition or tend to create a monopoly in any line of commerce.

IBM Corp. v. *United States,* decided by the Supreme Court in 1936, illustrates the application of Section 3 of the Clayton Act where the goods or commodities involve patented machinery. IBM held a patent on a punch-card tabulating machine. IBM leased the machines on the condition that the lease would terminate if non-IBM cards were used by the lessee in the machines, thus requiring machine lessees to fill their needs for unpatented punch cards from IBM. The Department of Justice charged that this tie-in arrangement violated Section 3 of the Clayton Act. The Supreme Court agreed, noting that the requisite adverse competitive effects were evidenced by the manufacturer's 81 per cent market share of unpatented punch cards. IBM's defense that the tie-in requirement was necessary to ensure satisfactory machine performance was rejected because it was not shown to be a necessary quality control measure; IBM could have established punch-card specifications to achieve this end so that competing punch-card suppliers would not be foreclosed from that market.

Section 5 of the Federal Trade Commission Act. In 1914, when Congress enacted the Clayton Act, it also enacted legislation that established the Federal Trade Commission and that gave the FTC power to secure cease and desist orders against corporations and others engaged in "unfair methods of competition."

It has long been recognized that the scope of Section 5 includes conduct prohibited by the Sherman and Clayton Acts and goes on "to stop in their incipiency acts and practices which, when full-blown, would violate those Acts." An example of the application of Section 5 of the FTC Act in patent-related cases is the famous tetracycline litigation. Here the Federal Trade Commission charged that Pfizer and American Cyanamid made false and misleading statements to officials of the Patent Office in an effort to secure a patent on the "wonder drug" tetracycline, and that the subsequent use, for purposes of excluding competition, of the patent so obtained, constituted a violation of Section 5. The courts ultimately upheld the commission's position, and relief in the case required compulsory licensing of the tetracycline patent as well as licensing of substantial amounts of proprietary know-how and technical information relating to the manufacture of tetracycline. In related civil litigation involving the same facts, private plaintiffs received over $100 million in settlement of claims alleging overcharges by the defendant pharmaceutical companies; in subsequent criminal and civil actions these defendants prevailed.

Section 7 of the Clayton Act. Section 7, as amended in 1950, prohibits corporations subject to FTC jurisdiction from acquiring: "assets of another corporation ... where in any line of commerce in any section of the country, the effect of such acquisition may be substantially to lessen competition, or to tend to create a monopoly." Although the mainstream enforcement efforts under Section 7 have focused on mergers and related corporate asset acquisitions involving competitors or prospective competitors (horizontal acquisitions) or involving suppliers or customers (vertical acquisitions), Section 7 can reach corporate patent asset aquisitions from other corporations that give rise to the requisite anticompetitive effects.

An example of a patent acquisition in violation of Section 7 involved competitors in the truss-plate manufacturing market. Truss plates are flat metal plates having barbs perpendicular to the plane of the plate. The plates are used to secure the wooden support elements of preassembled roof trusses. At the time of this case, Automated Building Components, Inc. (ABC), was a dominant factor in the manufacture of truss plates. Its competitor, Component Engineering Company, had earlier been forced to liquidate because of flood damage to its plant, and at the liquidation sale ABC acquired some of the capital equipment and a patent application held by Component. After a patent issued based on the acquired application, ABC sued Trueline for violation of ABC's patent rights. Trueline countered with a Section 7 claim, stating that the acquisition of the patent application was an asset acquisition the effect of which was substantially to lessen competition in the manufacture of truss plates. The court agreed with Trueline, noting that ABC had not manufactured the patented plate and further that the owner of Trueline had attempted to acquire the patent application at the liquidation sale but that it was outbid by ABC.

Federal Antitrust Enforcement

The U.S. Department of Justice. The Antitrust Division of the U.S. Department of Justice has, over the years, been the principal enforcer of the Sherman and Clayton Acts against patent owners engaged in anticompetitive practices beyond the permissive scope of the patent monopoly. The Justice Department can bring criminal and civil actions in the federal district courts for Sherman Act violations, whereas Clayton Act charges involve civil actions only. The Antitrust Division has a Patent Unit composed of a small but highly sophisticated group of patent–antitrust lawyers charged with monitoring, investigating, and litigating patent–antitrust abuses in U.S. industry.

The Federal Trade Commission. Traditionally, the FTC has concentrated its antitrust enforcement efforts under Section 5 of the FTC Act in challenging anticompetitive distribution practices that at most have swept in patents as peripheral matters. Its relative inactivity in the patent–antitrust field has been largely due to accommodation between the FTC and the Department of Justice with respect to allocation of enforcement priorities. It is worth noting, however, that because Section 5 of the FTC Act reaches conduct that may not be a full-blown violation of the Sherman Act, it materially reduces the burden of proof the government must carry in order to prevail. As previously noted, the FTC's enforcement power is generally limited to issuance of injunction-type cease and desist orders, which, if violated, subject the offender to civil penalty actions in the federal district courts.

Private Treble-Damage Suits. Particularly with the advent of class-action suits, a major deterrent to patent–antitrust misconduct is the exposure to lawsuits by injured parties for treble damages plus reasonable attorneys' fees. Such actions may be brought by injured parties for violations of the Sherman and Clayton Acts. No private cause of action exists, however, for violations of the Federal Trade Commission Act.

The Relationship of Patent Misuse to Antitrust Law

Before reviewing several of the patent-related activities condemned under the antitrust laws, it should be pointed out that most patent-related antitrust violations also would support a finding of patent misuse. However, the Supreme Court has indicated that all patent misuses are not necessarily antitrust violations. The difference is important. A patent misuse that is *not* an antitrust violation makes the patent unenforceable until the misuse is purged. However, a patent misuse that is *also* an antitrust violation not only makes the patent unenforceable but also makes the patent owner liable for treble damages to parties injured by the violation. Thus although a patent misuse that is not an antitrust violation does not necessarily help empty the patent owner's pockets, a patent misuse that is also an antitrust violation may do just that.

Specific Patent—Antitrust Problem Areas

A patentee that uses the lawfully procured patent merely to exclude others from making, using, or selling the patented invention will not incur antitrust difficulties. And when the patentee manufactures and sells the patented product or uses the patented process in his business (i.e., "in-house" use of the patent), based on these facts alone he should not run afoul of the antitrust laws, even though the patent permits him to exclude competing products and processes from the market. These statements may seem overly simplistic, but because of recent extensions of the antitrust laws to strike down various patent-related practices, it is important to point out the safe ground that remains for the patentee. On the other hand, because the patent monopoly is a limited exception to the prohibitions of the antitrust laws, use of the patent to secure a competitive advantage outside the scope of the patent grant is likely to create antitrust issues. These issues usually arise during the course of the patentee's dealings with others—sales of patented products, cooperation in patent pools, granting licenses, and the like. In order to focus on troublesome areas, let us look at some examples of patent-related transactions that have come under antitrust scrutiny.

Resale-Price Maintenance. Resale-price maintenance, or "vertical price fixing" as it is also known, involves the imposition by the patent owner over minimum or maximum resale prices upon a purchaser of patented goods. Such a practice is condemned under Section 1 of the Sherman Act as an unreasonable restraint on trade. The only permissible exception to this rule is by virtue of the Miller–Tydings Act and the McGuire Act. These Acts, amending Section 1 of the Sherman Act and Section 5 of the FTC Act, provide that if state fair trade laws permit, it shall not be unlawful to prescribe by contract minimum resale prices of trademarked products, so long as those products are in free and open competition with products of the same general class produced by others. Fair-trade laws sanctioning resale-price maintenance in varying degrees exist in approximately forty states, but because these are exceptions to a general rule against price fixing, a patentee should be careful to insure that his situation is in complete accord with the technical requirements of the fair trade laws that come into play.

It is worth noting that a manufacturing patent owner who established resale prices for a manufacturing licensee of patented goods was found, under the "rule of reason," not to have violated the Sherman Act in a 1920 Supreme Court decision. The rationale in the case was that a manufacturing patent owner has the right to protect its own market for the patented goods by imposing upon competing manufacturing licensees a resale price higher than that the manufacturing patent owner charges its own customers. Lower federal courts have limited the holding of this case to apply to the first resale only and the Antitrust Division of the Department of Justice attempted to have this decision overturned in 1948 and again in 1965. Both attacks were unsuccessful. The 1965 Supreme Court decision was a 4–4 split, which indicates that the continuing vitality of the 1926 decision is open to serious question today.

Exclusive-Dealing Requirements. Where the patent owner's license expressly forbids the licensee to use or to deal in the goods, patented or unpatented, of competitors of the patent owner, there is an arrangement known as an exclusive-dealing requirement. Such a clause will be an antitrust violation condemned by the Clayton Act Section 3 if the effect of the arrangement may be substantially to lessen competition or create a monopoly.

An illustration of this type of antitrust violation in operation is a case involving a manufacturer that held a patent on dead ends for electrical cables. This patent owner required electrical supply companies desiring to deal in the patented dead ends to buy all its electrical products from the patent owner as a condition of purchasing any products, including the patented dead end, from the patent owner. The court found the requirement that the electrical supply companies deal exclusively with the patent owner to be an antitrust violation under Section 3 of the Clayton Act. The economic significance of the tie-in was summarized as follows:

> The plaintiff is the largest manufacturer and seller in the United States of helically preformed reinforcements and attachments for use on electric cables. It is the dominant company in this specialized field, its only competitors (Fanner and Indiana Steel & Wire Co.) being its two licensees. The patent No. 4 dead ends are now widely accepted in the electrical industry, and, therefore, good business practice requires jobbers and distributors of armor rods to carry preformed dead ends in stock.

Another form of exclusive-dealing arrangement is the so-called requirements contract. Requirements contracts usually call for a purchaser to buy all or a specified portion of his requirements of a given product from the contracting supplier, thus foreclosing competitors from competition for the purchaser's business. The amount of business foreclosed to other suppliers is determinative of whether the anticompetitive effect necessary to establish a violation has been shown. In the leading case the Supreme Court held that annual requirements contracts by a major oil company tying up 16 per cent of the retail gasoline outlets and 6.7 per cent of actual gasoline sales on the western area of the United States constituted a violation of Section 3. On the other hand, in a 1960 case a twenty-year requirements contract for the sale of coal to an electrical generating company foreclosing 1 per cent of the market each year was held not to constitute a violation.

Looking at the requirements contracts in a patent context, in one case the court found a violation of Section 3 when a holder of a welding process patent offered special price incentives to its licensees to enter into full requirements contracts whereby the licensor would supply all the licensee's requirements of welding rods used in the process. The requirements contracts were not mandatory to securing a license under the patent, but the court found particularly anticompetitive the special price incentive arrangement.

Tie-In Arrangements.   Where a contract expressly requires the purchaser of certain products to purchase other, less-desired products of the supplier as a condition for buying the preferred product, there is an arrangement known as a tie-in. Tie-in contracts are usually violations of the antitrust laws and many cases illustrating this violation have involved patented products or processes.

The test for a finding of per se illegality in tying cases under Section 1 of the Sherman Act is that the supplier have sufficient economic power in the tying product appreciably to restrain competition in the tied product and a "not insubstantial" amount of interstate commerce is affected. Per se violations of Section 3 of the Clayton Act result when the supplier has a monopoly position in the tying product *or* if a substantial volume of commerce in the tied product is restrained. It is significant that the economic power required for a Section 1 violation is presumed when the tying product is patented.

In the patent field, tie-ins often involve conditioning the sale or lease of certain desired patented goods on the requirement that the dealer or user also purchase certain unpatented goods. Often the unpatented goods are not wanted for price reasons or are inferior to other similar unpatented goods available on the open market. In the leading case on this point involving patents, a patent owner licensed a patented machine for depositing salt tablets into canned products during the canning process. One license provision required licensees to purchase from the patent owner all the unpatented salt tablets used in the patented machines. The Department of Justice sued the patent owner for antitrust violations. The Supreme Court found that the license provision was an unreasonable restraint of trade under the Sherman Act and an illegal tie-in arrangement under the Clayton Act.

A violation of the antitrust laws can also result even though both the tied and tying products are patented, because the antitrust laws do not ordinarily permit a compounding of the statutorily conferred monopolies. However, there may be technological justifications for a tying arrangement that will save it from antitrust vulnerability. In one particular case a manufacturer of feed storage equipment owned a patent on a glass-lined silo and another patent on an unloading device. The patented unloader had a sweep-arm, installed inside at the bottom of the silo, which, when operated, directed the settling stored material out through a slot in the base of the silo. For seven years the patent owner, if requested, sold its unloader separately from its silo. During this period eighty unloaders were sold to thirty-six customers who did not use these patented silos. Half of these customers complained that the unloaders were incompatible with their own silos. Eventually one third of the complaining customers returned an unloader for a refund. Because of these complaints the patent owner adopted a policy of not selling unloaders unless they were installed in the manufacturer's own patented silo. Later, when the patent owner refused to sell the unloader separately from the silo, a disappointed purchaser sued for an antitrust violation under Section 3 of the Clayton Act. The court determined that this tie-in of patented goods to other patented goods was in the sound business interest of the patent owner and that a substantial hardship would result in a continuing injury to its reputation if the tie-in was not allowed. Thus, applying a "rule of technological reason," the court found the tie-in to be legal.

Bulk-Sale Restrictions. *Bulk-sale restriction* is a term used to describe the practice of selling drugs or other chemicals in bulk to a party on condition that the party agree to resell the drug only in a limited form, such as a dosage form. The leading case on this point was decided in 1969. Here, one defendant, Glaxo, owned various patents on a process for manufacturing in bulk an antibiotic drug for treating external fungus infections. The other defendant, ICI, owned patents on the dosage form of the drug. The two defendants pooled their patents and licensed three U.S. wholesalers to sell the drug. However, the right to sell the drug was restricted by the patent owners in that the licensees were limited to reselling the drug in dosage form and were prohibited from reselling the drug in bulk form. Because the source in the U.S. market for the drug consisted of only the three wholesalers, the effect of the bulk-sale restriction was to make the drug unavailable from the licensees to others in the United States in bulk form. The Department of Justice challenged the limitation as an unreasonable restraint of trade. The patent owners defended on the ground that the bulk-sale restriction was necessary in order to prevent the drug from falling into the hands of dealers who could buy large quantities and repackage it in smaller dosages in order to make a profit at the expense of the licensees' own markets. The Supreme Court agreed with the government's position that the bulk-sale restriction was an antitrust violation under Section 1 of the Sherman Act because it unreasonably restrained trade by effectively keeping the dosage-form wholesale market free of competition with the licensees. The bulk-sale restriction on the licensees foreclosed competition from purchasers who would convert the drug from bulk form into dosage form for sale to retail outlets, thus leading to price reductions for the general public.

Quantity Limitations on Unpatented Goods. Although it has been considered acceptable for a patent owner to impose on his licensees quantity limitations on the number of patented goods produced or on the number of times a patented process is used, a quantity limitation may not be imposed on the number of unpatented goods produced by the licensee. This issue usually arises when the unpatented product (to which the quantity restriction applies) is produced by a patented process or machine. Although the Supreme Court has ruled on this issue only in the context of a sweeping anticompetitive scheme, several lower federal courts have said that such a practice is a per se violation of the antitrust laws.

In the first case to condemn this practice, a patent owner had patents on a brick-setting machine licensed to six manufacturers in the city of Chicago. The license limited the number of unpatented bricks that each licensee could make. If a licensee exceeded the quota, a penalty five times the royalty rate in addition to the basic royalty rate was imposed for the amount of excess bricks produced. After one of the licensees exceeded the quota and refused to make the additional payment, the patent owner sued for royalties. The licensee defended on the grounds that the license provision was unenforceable because it violated the Sherman Act. Both the trial court and the appellate court agreed that the quantity limitation on unpatented goods was an antitrust violation voiding the license clause because it was primarily intended to control the production and prices of unpatented bricks in the Chicago metropolitan area.

Divisions of Markets. The Supreme Court has stated that horizontal territorial limitations agreed to by competitors "are naked restraints of trade with no purpose except stifling of competition." Under this rationale, a division of markets among competitors, by assigning exclusive rights to territories, customers, or products is normally a per se violation of the Sherman Act. Similarly, vertical restrictions, by which a supplier attempts to restrict the territory in which his customer resells a product, have been condemned.

In contrast with these established antitrust principles is Section 261 of the Patent Act, which specifically provides that a patent owner may grant an exclusive right under his patent to the "whole or any specified part of the United States." This statute, therefore, sanctions a patent owner's imposition of certain territorial restrictions on his licensees. This is a limited right, however, and one federal district court found that the patent owner may not additionally impose territorial restrictions on the resale of patented goods after the first sale of the goods by a licensee to its sublicensed customer. In this 1973 case an owner of a patent on a washer for threaded fasteners licensed a manufacturer to make and sell the patented product in the fourteen-state territory of the northeastern United States. The manufacturing licensee was permitted to sublicense others to make and/or sell the patented product as long as the sublicensees also agreed to be bound by the territorial restriction. After one of the nonmanufacturing sublicensees resold outside its assigned territory, the patent owner sued for breach of contract. The sublicensee counterclaimed with an antitrust violation under Section 1 of the Sherman Act. The court found that the territorial restriction on the initial sale of the patented goods imposed on the licensee was permissible under the Patent Act but that the territorial restriction on the resale of the patented goods imposed on the sublicensee was a per se antitrust violation. The court said that once the licensee sold the patented goods, the patent owner could exercise no future control over the territory in which the nonmanufacturing sublicensee might resell the patented goods because the goods had passed beyond the scope of the patent owner's right to impose territorial restrictions under the Patent Act.

Although the Patent Act allows a patent owner to divide markets territorially among its licensees, or to license certain territories while retaining exclusive rights for himself in others, the Act does not allow the patent owner to control the territory or application to which a licensee sells unpatented products made by use of a licensed process or machine. Similarly, the Patent Act may not sanction a division of territories among patent owners in competition with each other or with nonpatent owners, although there does not appear to be a case directly on this point. Division of customers among competing patent owners would also seem to be outside the scope of the limited exception of Section 261, although, again, there are no cases on the point. On the other hand, there is an abundance of authority condemning a division of territories or customers among competitors when patents are not involved, and there appears to be good reason to expect an extension of the rationale of these nonpatent cases to instances where multiple patent owners are involved. This conclusion is predicated, in part, on the fact that there has been a case involving division of product markets among competing patent licensees. In this case five corporations, competitors in the machine tool industry, were licensed under separate agreements to use three pioneer patents relating to the machine tool industry. These companies, in effect, pooled their patents, along with the rights in any improvement patents, in the name of a holding company that gave exclusive licenses to each of the members of the pool to make, use, and sell different types of tools. The Department of Justice sued to break up the pool as an unreasonable restraint on trade in violation of the Sherman Act. The court agreed with the government's position, finding that the corporations were engaged in a conspiracy, the purpose of which was to confine the manufacture of machine tools by each of them to fields of specialization that were not competitive with each other, in order to give each of them an unfair advantage in the various tool markets.

Unilateral Refusal to Deal. The Supreme Court announced in *United States* v. *Colgate & Co.*—a 1919 nonpatent case, that a businessman is free "to exercise his own independent discretion as to parties with whom he will deal. And, of course, he may announce in advance the circumstances under which he will refuse to sell." Since that time the Supreme Court has severely limited this rule in other nonpatent cases. In the patent context several lower federal courts have ruled against challenges that the patent owner's refusal to deal with or to license others is, by itself, an antitrust violation. Nevertheless, where the patent itself covers a product that constitutes an entire relevant market and the patent owner has engaged in so-called predatory acts directed at others, such as customers or potential competitors, the owner's unilateral refusal to deal, taken together with all its other anticompetitive practices, may be found to be part of an attempt to monopolize in violation of Section 2 of the Sherman Act.

Concerted Refusal to Deal. Where two or more competitors join together and refuse to deal with a certain party or class of parties, there is usually a per se antitrust violation called a concerted refusal to deal, more commonly known as a group boycott. This may happen where a patent owner gives one or more existing licensees the right to veto the grant of future licenses. Such a veto effectively creates a group boycott against the disappointed would be licensee. The patent owner and the licensees who hold the veto power are considered co-conspirators.

A group boycott may also occur in a patent pool where the participant member agrees to exclude all or some competitors from receiving a license from the pool. For example, in one case several U.S. firms through their Canadian subsidiaries formed a pool of some 5,000 Canadian radio and television patents. The pool had the exclusive right to license all the patents in one package. The license was strictly limited to manufacture in Canada and no license was available to importers. The chief purpose of the pool was to protect the member firms and licensees from competition by foreign companies seeking to import their products into Canada, and the pool's efforts to prevent importation of radio and television sets from the United States were highly organized and effective. Agents systematically policed the market, warnings were given to dealers against selling products not made under a license from the pool, and threats of infringement suits were regularly and effectively made to persuade dealers not to handle foreign-made sets. For many years a large U.S. manufacturer attempted to enter the Canadian market, but its Canadian dealers were warned off by the pool and efforts to secure a license from the pool were unsuccessful because the pool would not grant the license unless the U.S. firm would manufacture in Canada. After refusing to agree to such a condition, in 1958 the U.S. manufacturer began to import radio and television products into Canada. The pool continued its campaign against the imported goods, limiting the U.S. manufacturer to 3 per cent of the market. In late 1959 one of the U.S. members of the Canadian pool brought a suit against the manufacturer in the United States for infringement of one of its U.S. patents. The defendant counterclaimed for antitrust violations under the Sherman Act for unreasonably restraining trade in U.S. foreign commerce. In 1969 the case finally reached the Supreme Court. The Court found that the U.S. patent owner was a member of a foreign conspiracy engaging in a concerted refusal to deal. As a member of the group boycott, the U.S. patent owner was found liable in treble damages for $35 million.

Although some patent owners have engaged in group boycotts, group boycotts have also been directed against patent owners. For example, in one case an inventor obtained a 1958 patent on a new type of knitted fabric. The new fabric was lightweight and particularly suited for use in the production of winter garments such as thermal underwear. More importantly, it could be made on both weft (circular) and warp (curved) knitting machines. Before this invention, the only fabric to gain consumer acceptance could be made only on the warp knitting machines. Users of the weft knitting machines desiring to sell fabric for use in manufacturing insulated winter garments had to purchase their requirements from users of the warp knitting machines. Faced with this unexpected loss of business, twelve fabric manufacturers that used only warp knitting machines refused to negotiate with the inventor for a license. They also entered into a written agreement in which they agreed to share the costs of a lawsuit that they brought to have the patent declared invalid. However, the court determined that the patent was valid and also found that the suing manufacturers were concertedly refusing to deal in an effort unreasonably to restrain trade in violation of the Sherman Act.

Cross Licenses. Cross licensing between patent owners is a practice which is not, by itself, an antitrust violation. However, antitrust problems may be created by the inclusion in the cross license of terms that either may unreasonably restrain trade in violation of Section 1 of the Sherman Act or may constitute an attempt to monopolize under Section 2 of the Sherman Act.

In one case two competing manufacturers applied about the same time for patents on dropout electrical fuse cutouts. The Patent Office declared an interference, allowing broad claims in one patent to issue to one of the manufacturers and narrow claims in two patents to issue to the other manufacturer. Because the patents were interlocking, the competitors entered into a royalty-free cross license in which one of the parties was given the exclusive right to sublicense both patents. The sublicensing party then set resale prices for all products made under its own patent. Although both patents were necessary to make any commercially feasible device, the scheme went beyond the limited cross license necessary to solve this problem. The Supreme Court concluded that the entire arrangement embraced a price-fixing scheme for the commercial device, and therefore was an unreasonable restraint of trade under the Sherman Act.

In another case a U.S. and two European manufacturers of competing zigzag sewing machines entered into a royalty-free cross-license arrangement among themselves in settlement of an impending Patent Office interference. The U.S. firm, then having 70 per cent of the domestic market, brought a charge of patent infringement against its largest competitor, a Japanese importer that controlled 20 per cent of the U.S. domestic market. After the settlement, the Antitrust Division of the Department of Justice brought an antitrust action against the U.S. firm. The Supreme Court found that there was a conspiracy to monopolize in violation of the Sherman Act. The conspiracy, facilitated by the cross-license arrangement, arose from the course of dealing among the parties, resulting in the U.S. firm's obligation to enforce the patents against Japanese imports for the benefit of all three parties.

Pools. Pooling arrangements, by themselves, are not necessarily antitrust violations. The Supreme Court first made this determination in a 1931 case involving the gasoline-cracking industry. In this case four corporations formed a patent pool as a result of a settlement of infringement suits brought against each other. The Department of Justice attacked the pool as an unreasonable retraint on trade under Section 1 of the Sherman Act and as an attempt to monopolize under Section 2 of the Sherman Act. Applying the rule of reason, the Supreme Court found the pool to be legal because the arrangement was no more than a reasonable settlement of a legitimate conflict over the patent rights of all parties.

A pool does not have to result from the settlement of a lawsuit to be legal. However, in any other type of pool, care must be exercised to insure that operation of the pool is not exclusionary or discriminatory. The pool generally should be open to all present and prospective competitors to avoid an antitrust charge that the arrangement constitutes a concerted refusal to deal in violation of the Sherman Act.

Field-of-Use Limitations. A field-of-use limitation imposed upon a licensee by a patent owner is not, by itself, an antitrust violation because such a condition "is reasonably within the reward which the patentee by the grant of the patent is entitled to secure." This is the reasoning of the Supreme Court in the 1938 *General Talking Pictures* case. There, a manufacturer held patents relating to vacuum tube amplifiers. An exclusive license was granted to one party in the commercial field of sound recording and reproducing, which embraced talking-picture equipment for theaters. About fifty nonexclusive licenses were granted in the noncommercial field, which embraced home radio broadcast reception, amateur radio reception, and private experimentation. One of the nonexclusive licensees started selling the patented amplifiers commercially and the patent owner sued. The infringer defended on the grounds that the field-of-use limitations were illegal. The Supreme Court upheld the provision by a 6–2 vote, with the dissent arguing that such a restriction was an unreasonable extension of the patent monopoly.

Grant-back and License-back Provisions. Grant-back and license-back provisions, by themselves, have also been found by the Supreme Court not to be antitrust violations. The leading case on grant-backs is the 1947 *Transparent-Wrap Machine* case. An inventor obtained a basic patent on a machine for making transparent packages, simultaneously filling them with articles such as candy, and sealing them. An exclusive license to make and sell was given to a manufacturer. The license contained a provision by which the exclusive licensee agreed to grant back to the owner of the basic patent any improvement patents which the exclusive licensee might later obtain. Thereafter, several improvement patents were obtained but the exclusive licensee refused to sign over their ownership. When the owner of the basic patent threatened to terminate the license, the exclusive licensee sued for a declaratory judgment that the grant-back provision in the license was illegal. In a 5–4 decision the Supreme Court applied the rule of reason and found that such a provision is not, by itself, an antitrust violation. In this situation the clause was considered reasonable partial consideration for the grant of an exclusive license on the basic patent.

Although license-back provisions have not been seriously questioned, the Antitrust Division of the Department of Justice has criticized grant-back provisions. Also, it is conceivable that a grant-back provision could be attacked in a license issued by a corporate patent owner as a violation of Section 7 of the Clayton Act on the theory that it provides for an asset acquisition in the form of the improvement patents of a corporate licensee. The acquisition would be illegal only where, in the particular line of commerce to which the patents relate, the effect of such acquisition may be substantially to lessen competition or to tend to create a monopoly.

Nonuse, Accumulation, and Suppression of Patents. After an inventor obtains a patent, he may do nothing with it because the patented invention is not commercially feasible, or there are alternative products that are cheaper and of better quality, or the raw materials required for production are not available at practical cost, or the patent owner does not have sufficient risk capital and is unable to obtain adequate financial backing for commercial exploitation. There is no legal obligation that one "work" the patent in the United States as there is in some foreign countries. The Patent Act gives the owner only the "right to exclude others from making, using, or selling the invention." Thus the mere nonuse of a patent is not an antitrust violation.

It is not uncommon for corporations to attempt to purchase or to obtain a license under newly issued patents in the particular technology in which they are commercially engaged, and the mere accumulation of patents is not, by itself, an antitrust violation. On the other hand, accumulation of patents may be illegal in special circumstances, and the Antitrust Division of the Department of Justice has warned that any deliberate plan to accumulate patents, by purchase, grant-back, or otherwise, and then not to use them may constitute suppression of potential competition and thus be treated as monopolization or an attempt to monopolize under the Sherman Act.

Also, as we have seen, acquisition of patent rights by a corporation may constitute an illegal acquisition of assets under Section 7 of the Clayton Act; such accumulations may also be tested against Section 5 of the FTC Act, which prohibits "unfair methods of competition."

Discriminatory Royalty Charges. Another activity of patent owners that has received judicial scrutiny is the practice of charging different royalty rates to different licensees or classes of licensees. Although the Supreme Court has not condemned this practice standing alone, some lower federal courts have decided that such conduct, done without reasonable business justification and taken together with other anticompetitive practices, is an antitrust violation. For example, an owner of a patented shrimp-peeling machine licensed canners along the Gulf of Mexico and the Northwest Pacific Coast. The royalty rate charged to canners along the Northwest Pacific Coast was double the royalty rate charged to canners along the Gulf of Mexico. In a series of four lawsuits spread out over a period of fifteen years, the patent owner sued the manufacturer and various users of a competing shrimp-peeling machine for infringement. In three of these cases the defendants counterclaimed for antitrust violations, and a fourth antitrust claim was filed by various lessees of the patent owner charging antitrust violations. The same court, hearing two of the antitrust claims in a consolidated proceeding, sustained a jury verdict that the patent owner was guilty of monopolization under the Sherman Act by charging discriminatory royalty rates with the intent to create a competitive advantage in favor of the Gulf of Mexico canners to the detriment of the Northwest Pacific canners. Although this action by the court is open to question because of the absence of benefit to the patentee from the alleged extension of the patent monopoly, the case was settled before the appeal could be heard. Another court found that the conduct in question constituted a patent misuse making the patent unenforceable but not subjecting the patentee to any valid antitrust claim; and the court hearing the fourth antitrust claim found that the antitrust action was barred by the statute of limitations, because the suit was filed more than four years after the cause of action accrued. In the meantime the FTC had sued the patent owner under the FTC Act for engaging in an unfair method of competition and a cease and desist order issued against the patent owner's continuing refusal to treat Northwest Pacific and Gulf of Mexico shrimp canners on equal terms. The commission's finding that the lease price discrimination had "substantially and unjustifiably injured competition in the shrimp canning industry" was upheld on appeal.

Fraud on the Patent Office. Another important activity that could give rise to an antitrust violation is the fraudulent procurement of a patent from the Patent Office. Although what constitutes a fraud on the Patent Office has not been defined exactly, the courts have generally required the showing of certain factors before finding fraud. Some of the factors courts have considered include: that there was a misrepresentation about which the patentee knew (the misrepresentation could be in the form of a false statement or a withholding of pertinent information); that the patentee had intent to deceive the Patent Office into issuing the patent; that there was a misrepresentation determinative of a legal or factual issue material to the issuance of the patent; that the Patent Office, through its examiner, relied upon the misrepresentation; and that the misrepresentation caused the issuance of a patent that otherwise would not have issued. It is not necessary to prove injury because it is inferred from the mere fact that the fraudulently procured patent issues that the public is injured. Any patent obtained in such a fraudulent manner is, of course, invalid.

The enforcement of a fraudulently obtained patent may be an antitrust violation under Section 2 of the Sherman Act, as either monopolization or an attempt to monopolize, depending on the relevant market and the scope of the patent improperly acquired, or an unfair method of competition in violation of Section 5 of the FTC Act. Also, there is a federal statute that has been interpreted to make it a crime for a patent applicant, attorney, or agent to make any false or fraudulent statements or representation to the Patent Office. The statute imposes a fine of not more than $10,000 or a prison term of not more than five years, or both.

The policy behind these judicial holdings is that, as the Supreme Court stated, the "far-reaching social and economic consequences of a patent, therefore, give the public a paramount interest in seeing that patent monopolies spring from backgrounds free from fraud or other inequitable conduct and that such monopolies are kept within their legitimate scope."

Since the articulation by the Supreme Court of the underlying nature of an antitrust violation involving fraud on the Patent Office, the lower federal courts have substantially expanded the scope of conduct embraced by this rule. The lower federal courts have found numerous sources of fraud. Some only involve the patent applicant: the oath or declaration of inventorship, affidavits, omissions of data that should be included in a specification, omission of bad experimental results, or related false or misleading representations of fact. Some only involve the patent attorney. The most common source of a fraud claim probably is the nondisclosure of statutory bars such as the one-year public-use or on-sale bar to patentability. Other bases for fraud claims may include nondisclosure of known pertinent prior art, depending on the circumstances. Closely related grounds for unenforceability will arise from failure to report a settlement between parties in a Patent Office interference proceeding, as required by a 1962 amendment to the 1952 Patent Act.

The leading case establishing fraud on the Patent Office as a basis for a nonconspiracy antitrust violation was *Walker Process Equipment, Inc.* v. *FMC Corp.*, decided by the Supreme Court in 1965. The patent owner filed a suit against a competitor for infringement of a patent covering knee action swing diffusers used in aeration equipment for sewage treatment systems. The competitor raised the defenses of invalidity and noninfringement, and counterclaimed for an antitrust violation on the grounds that the patent owner had monopolized the relevant market by enforcing a fraudulently obtained patent. The competitor had discovered that during the prosecution of the application in the Patent Office the applicant had sworn under oath that he neither knew nor believed that the invention had been in public use in the United States for more than one year prior to his filing the application where actually the applicant was a party to such a prior public use before the permissible period of time. The lower court, although finding the patent invalid and not infringed, dismissed the counterclaim. The Supreme Court reversed, stating that the perpetration of an intentional fraud on the Patent Office to obtain a constitutionally permissible monopoly may be an antitrust violation under Section 2 of the Sherman Act. However, the Court added that good faith of the patent applicant would furnish a complete defense and that such good faith would embrace an honest mistake known as technical fraud. Also, to establish monopolization or an attempt to monopolize in violation of the Sherman Act, "it would then be necessary to appraise the exclusionary power of the illegal patent claim in terms of the relevant market for the product involved."

In addition to possibly constituting a Sherman Act violation, fraud on the Patent Office was part and parcel of an unfair method of competition in violation of the FTC Act in a series of earlier cases discussed previously involving the corporate owners of the patent on the wonder antibiotic drug, tetracycline.

With this analysis of patents concluded, we now turn to the other side of the coin: protection of technology and related property rights by not disclosing to the public—the lore of trade secrets.

 **Trade Secrets, Know-how, and Unsolicited Disclosures**

INTRODUCTION

The preservation of technology and commercial information as a trade secret is a judicially protected alternative to taking advantage of patent and copyright avenues of monopoly protection. If the intellectual property is maintained and preserved in secrecy, the courts will prevent its misappropriation by improper means. In this chapter we will explore what is and is not a trade secret, how rights in a trade secret are preserved, lost, and misappropriated as well as exploring the closely related topic of submitting unsolicited ideas and suggestions to business enterprises in the hopes of financial reward.

ORIGINS

Rome

It was the era of ancient Rome when legal systems began to take a view of what might be termed the unfair taking of trade secrets. Although scholars deny that legal proscriptions against unfair competition

117

existed before the Middle Ages, Roman law protected rights in trade secrets covering information such as dyeing and pottery processes. Where a slave was enticed by his master's competitor to divulge the trade secrets of his master, the master's remedies against his competitor lay in an action for corrupting a slave. By this action, a slave owner could receive double damages from the person who had induced his slave to disclose the trade secrets. The theory behind the action was that the value of the slave had been lessened.

English Common Law

Perhaps the first reported English case about trade secrets was *Newberry* v. *James,* decided in 1817. Dr. James invented certain pills for the gout and rheumatism and a powder for the cure of fevers and he sold the medicines to Newberry. To prevent the secret formulas for the medicine from being lost, Dr. James also made the secret formulas known to Newberry, who agreed not to disclose the formulas. Although most of the medical formulas were patented, one of the agreements covered Analeptic Pills, for which no patent had been obtained. For this reason the case can be considered a trade secrets case. After Dr. James went to meet his reward, his son, and later his grandson, did business with Newberry. That grandson, defendant Robert George Gordon James, received the right to the sale of the medicines as well as the ensuing profits. Newberry sued and alleged that James threatened to divulge the secret of the preparation and asked for an injunction. The court declined to grant an injunction because disclosure of the secret formula would be necessary to determine whether or not the secret had been unfairly appropriated. However, Newberry was permitted to recover damages. Three years later, however, the same court granted an injunction against an employee of a veterinarian who copied medical formulas and after leaving this employment, sold the information. Injunctive relief was justified on the ground that a confidential relationship was breached. The court thus introduced a concept that has been greatly relied upon for generations in the litigation of such disputes between employer and ex-employee.

In a well-known 1851 case, the plantiffs were Alexander and John Morison, surviving partners in the firm called Morison, Moat & Co., Hygeists. James Morison, the father of Alexander and John, had communicated the secret of how to prepare the medicinal compound he had invented to his partner, Thomas Moat, under a contract that forbade Moat to disclose the secret to anyone. James Morison and his partner Moat agreed that they would not disclose the ingredients or method of making the medicine to anyone other than a new partner. When James

Morison died, he left by his will the formula for his medicine to his sons, Alexander and John, to be used in the partnership. But after termination of the partnership, Thomas Moat's son began using the medical formula that had belonged to his father's partnership. He had acquired knowledge of the formula while he had conducted affairs of his father at his firm. To make things worse, defendant Moat represented the Morison's Universal Medicine to be a product of his own ingenuity.

The Morisons denied that Moat ever became a partner in the place of his father, or was so treated and acknowledged by the other partners. The secret was not considered by the court to be a partnership asset. However, by virtue of bonds executed by Morison and Moat when they formed their partnership, they made an agreement that gave Morison the right to stop Moat from disclosing the secrets. Morison did not tell the secrets to Moat's son, who came in as a servant after his father's death, not as a partner. Moat's son learned the secret from his father. The court found that there was an equity against Moat's son deriving from the breach of faith and of contract on Thomas Moat's part in divulging the secret, and an injunction was granted against Moat's son from further exploitation of the secret by compounding the medicine. The court summarized the development of English trade secret law:

> In some cases, it has been referred to as property, in others to contract and in others, again, it has been treated as founded upon trust or confidence meaning, as I conceive, that the court fastens the obligation on the conscience of the party, and enforces it against him in the same manner as it enforces against a party to whom a benefit is given, the obligation of performing a promise on the faith of which the benefit has been conferred; but upon whatever grounds the jurisdiction is founded, the authorities leave no doubt as to the exercise of it.

The United States

The first significant trade secret case in the United States was *Vickery* v. *Welch,* decided by the Supreme Judicial Court of Massachusetts in 1837. In that case Welch contracted to transfer to Vickery chocolate mills along with the right to Welch's exclusive secret process for making chocolate. Welch turned over the chocolate mills and the secret art to Vickery but refused to obligate himself not to disclose the trade secret to others. Vickery brought an action for damages and won. In addition, the court held that Welch was under a legal duty not to disclose the secret to outsiders, rejecting Welch's argument that such a duty amounts to an unreasonable restraint of trade.

Having thus held that a contract not to divulge a trade secret was not an unreasonable restraint of trade, the Supreme Judicial Court of

Massachusetts decided another landmark trade secret case, *Peabody* v. *Norfolk,* in 1868. Peabody, the plaintiff, had invented and adapted machinery and a process for manufacturing gunny cloth from jute butts. He made the gunny cloth in a large factory and employed defendant Norfolk as his machinist. Ancillary to the main contract of employment was an agreement between Peabody and Norfolk that Norfolk would not disclose to outsiders the knowledge he gained of Peabody's machinery and process. Norfolk left employment with Peabody and, contrary to his agreement, disclosed these secrets to persons unknown to Peabody and utilized the secrets to go into competition with his former employer in the manufacture of gunny cloth from jute butts. The court enjoined Norfolk's violation of the contract and observed:

> If he invents or discovers, and keeps secret, a process of manufacture, whether a proper subject for a patent or not, he has not indeed an exclusive right to it as against the public, or against those who in good faith acquire knowledge of it; but he has a property in it, which a court of chancery will protect against one who in violation of contract and breach of confidence undertakes to apply it to his own use, or to disclose it to third persons.

A trade secrets case first reached the U.S. Supreme Court in 1889, which was the last restraint-of-trade case decided by the Supreme Court before passage of the Sherman Act in 1890. Fowle had acquired rights to a secret medicinal compound known as Wistar's Balsam of Wild Cherry for "certain complaints and diseases." Park later legitimately acquired rights to use the same compound. Between 1849 and 1864 Fowle and Park both sold the medicine in competition with one another in an area between the Rocky Mountains and the Pacific Coast. Thereafter, Fowle and Park entered into a contract whereby Park sold to Fowle his franchise of the medicine for use in the territory west of the Rocky Mountains for an unlimited period of time. Thereafter, Park continued to sell the medicine under the same name in that area. Fowle sued for an injunction and accounting against Park. The Supreme Court held that the agreement was not so unreasonable as to justify refusal to enforce it. Fowle had relied in part on *Vickery* v. *Welch* to support his cause. Setting the trend for many cases to be decided in future years, the Court noted that "[t]he policy of the law is to encourage useful discoveries by securing their fruits to those who make them."

THE JUDICIAL APPROACH TO TRADE SECRET CASES

Trade secrets have been a significant class of intellectual property accorded judicial protection broadly based on the twofold inquiry into

(1) whether there really is a "secret" in the first place and (2) whether there exists any duty on the part of the person who learns the secret not to use or disclose it. Courts have offered various definitions as to what constitutes a trade secret, none wholly satisfactory. The definitions given have depended in part on the circumstances of each case and perhaps on the results the courts have wanted to reach. In wrestling with the question of whether there is a "secret" in the first place, courts have been influenced by the degree of unfairness that inheres in the disclosure or threatened disclosure by the person who gained knowledge of it.

A 1963 Ohio case illustrative of this unfairness notion is *B. F. Goodrich Co.* v. *Wohlgemuth,* where the court's decision seemed to gloss over the test of a real secret where the unfairness facts seemed strong. For about six years Wohlgemuth was employed by B. F. Goodrich and became a key person in that company's development of a space suit comprised of approximately 1,600 parts. Wohlgemuth had a thorough knowledge of several of the secrets and confidential facts through his own work and that of his colleagues with whom he worked.

Wohlgemuth resigned from Goodrich when he was offered a higher salary by International Latex Corporation, which competed with Goodrich in the pressure-space-equipment field, having entered the field some fourteen years after Goodrich. International Latex became responsible for developing a space suit for the NASA Apollo project. Soon after being awarded this NASA contract Wohlgemuth started work for International Latex. Goodrich tried to enjoin Wohlgemuth from disclosing to International Latex the secrets he had gained knowledge of while in its employ. The Court of Common Pleas of Summit County, Ohio, while denying the injunction, recognized that by hiring Wohlgemuth, Latex was attempting to acquire his valuable experience and that if he was assigned to work in the space suit division of the Latex Company not only could he give the Latex Company his valuable experience, but he would have the opportunity to divulge trade secret information of B. F. Goodrich.

The Court of Appeals of Summit County, Ohio, took note of Wohlgemuth's attitude at the time he left Goodrich. In reply to an objection by a Goodrich staff member to his taking a job with a competitor, Wohlgemuth replied to the effect that "loyalty and ethics had their price; insofar as he was concerned, International Latex was paying the price." The court noted Wohlgemuth's statement that "[o]nce he was a member of the Latex Team, he would expect to use all of the knowledge that he had to their benefit." The court declared that any revelation of the trade secrets of Goodrich to a "competitor is in equity a breach of faith and reprehensible to a court of equity." Although there was no evidence that Wohlgemuth had disclosed Goodrich's trade secrets to

Latex, the court determined from Wohlgemuth's attitude that a substantial threat of disclosure existed. Accordingly, the court granted an injunction against Wohlgemuth. The court recognized Wohlgemuth's right to take a job with a competitor

> and to use his knowledge (other than trade secrets) and experience, for the benefit of his new employer, but a public policy demands commercial morality, and courts of equity are empowered to enforce it by enjoining an improper disclosure of trade secrets known to Wohlgemuth by virtue of his employment. Under the American doctrine of free enterprise, Goodrich is entitled to this protection.

The court did not attempt to define what the trade secrets were or were not. The court's conclusion turned on the "irreparable injury" Goodrich might suffer by disclosure of the secrets to Latex by Wohlgemuth. It is worthy of note, however, that the Ohio court mentioned sources of various definitions of trade secrets and adopted for the purposes of this case the elements of trade secrets as they are set forth in the Restatement of the Law of Torts:

> A trade secret may consist of any formula, pattern, device or compilation of information which is used in one's business, and which gives him an opportunity to obtain an advantage over competitors who do not know or use it. It may be a formula for a chemical compound, a process of manufacturing, treating or preserving materials, a pattern for a machine or other device, or a list of customers. . . . A trade secret is a process or device for continuous use in the operation of the business. Generally it relates to the production of goods, as, for example, a machine or formula for the production of an article. . . .

It is noteworthy that the Restatement further states that "[a]n exact definition of a trade secret is not possible." In other words, that which constitutes a trade secret must be determined from the facts of each case.

A case that contrasts with *Wohlgemuth* in result is a 1958 case called *Sarkes Tarzian, Inc.* v. *Audio Devices, Inc.* Tarzian, the plaintiff, was an operator of local television and radio stations in Bloomington, Indiana, and manufactured and sold components for silicon rectifiers. The defendant, Audio, was a large manufacturer of recording tape and discs and also manufactured and sold silicon rectifiers in California.

Eight employees of Tarzian left that corporation to work at Audio's rectifier division. Tarzian sued Audio, alleging that its former employees had knowledge of its trade secrets used in manufacturing and selling silicon rectifiers and that Audio had engaged in a conspiracy with its former employees, by employing them, to deprive Tarzian of its trade secrets and its advantage over its competitors. Tarzian asked for an injunction, accounting of profits, and damages. In answer to the complaint, Audio denied any conspiracy between itself and Tarzian's former employees and claimed no trade secrets were involved. Tarzian pointed out that the techniques, materials, and products developed at Audio, by its personnel, including the former employees of Tarzian, were well known in the industry and were described in many publications circulated in the trade and available to the public.

The court quoted the Restatement of Torts definition of trade secrets but went on to state:

> What is a trade secret is difficult to define. However, on the whole, it must consist of a particular form of construction of a device, a formula, method or process that is of a character which does not occur to persons in the trade with knowledge of the state of the art or which cannot be evolved by those skilled in the art from the theoretical description of the process, or compilation or compendia of information or knowledge.

Notwithstanding the trial court's attempt to arrive at its own definition of a trade secret, the court, in deciding for Audio and the former employees of Tarzian, made little reference to its trade secret definition. After a review of the facts surrounding the departure of Tarzian's employees, the court found that Audio had not enticed them into its employ, but that the employees had left Tarzian for legitimate business reasons. The court noted that Audio had not tried to get a "free ride" by using know-how developed at Tarzian's expense and had made no attempt to copy Tarzian's products. The court observed that the equipment that Audio ordered from Tarzian's suppliers were not from secret sources of supply to which only Tarzian had access and that there was no evidence that Tarzian's former employees had taken with them any written information, blueprints, or related documents.

In reaching the conclusion that no trade secrets were violated, the court posed the following question for itself: "Has Tarzian developed a production process which is such a deviation from what was known and taught in the art that it has acquired a secret which its former employees were entitled to respect, contract or no contract, and Audio could not appropriate to itself?" The court could only answer its question by analyzing the procedure anyone must follow in order to build a silicon rectifier. Having done this, the court observed that "[w]hether a method is or is not orthodox does not determine its validity as a secret. It is whether it is unique and unknown in the trade that is important, or whether there is discovery in selecting between alternative steps" of manufacture of a silicon rectifier. The court found that these matters were common knowledge in the trade because of available literature and thus was able to conclude that Tarzian did not utilize any secrets in the trade at the time the employee-defendants left its employ. Interestingly, the court observed that the differences in the processes of manufacturing silicon rectifiers by Tarzian and Audio appeared to be the result of a conscious attempt by Tarzian's former employees "not to infringe upon whatever element of selectivity between alternate procedures there may have been in the Tarzian process." The decision was affirmed by the U.S. Court of Appeals.

Opposite results, then, were reached in the *B. F. Goodrich* and *Sarkes Tarzian* cases. In *Goodrich* the court looked at the attitude of Wohlgemuth as manifested after leaving Goodrich and somehow found that Wohlgemuth had knowledge of trade secrets belonging to Goodrich. The element of secrecy, not present in *Sarkes Tarzian,* was found in *B. F. Goodrich* because the evidence showed that trade secrets had resulted from a great deal of expense and effort, and Goodrich had taken strict security measures to maintain the secrecy of several of the processes and technical know-how used in space-suit manufacture.

The difference in the results can be explained at least in part by the presence of unfairness and secrecy in *B. F. Goodrich* and a threat of trade secret disclosure justifying injunctive relief and the apparent absence of unfairness and secrecy in *Sarkes Tarzian,* which justified the court's refusal to grant relief. Unfairness and secrecy, then, are two essential elements a court will tend to look for in any factual situation where a trade secret issue has been raised. Without unfairness courts seem not so willing to determine that there is, in fact, a true secret.

TRADE SECRET SUBJECT MATTER

Chemical Formulas

Chemical formulas are often the subject of trade secret protection. They range from such items as food compositions to industrial chemicals. A food formula, or recipe, for cheese was given trade secret status in an 1891 case. In that case, the defendant, Lena Gross, owned a cheese factory in the town of Monroe, New York, and with the help of her husband, Conrad Gross, her brother-in-law, August Gross, and her father, John Hoffman, manufactured cheeses known as Fromage de Brie, Fromage d'Isigny, and Neufchatel. The formulas for processing the cheeses were kept a guarded secret and were known only to Lena and her agents.

Lena then contracted with one Adolph Tode and Ferdinand Wolff whereby Lena sold her entire factory together with the good will and trademarks of the business. She also agreed to communicate to Tode and Wolff the secret formula once they paid her for the cheese business and that she, Conrad Gross, John Hoffman, and August Gross would not communicate the secret formula or manufacture nor sell these cheeses. After this agreement, however, Lena's husband, Conrad, while on a business trip to New York City, sold a few boxes of cheese under the name Fromage d'Isigny, which bore trademarks substantially the same as those sold by Lena to Tode and Wolff. This cheese was similar to that formerly manufactured by Lena Gross.

August Gross, Lena's brother-in-law, also kept for sale in New York City boxes of cheese marked or stamped Fromage d'Isigny. The court found that the cheese Conrad Gross sold under the name of Fromage d'Isigny as well as that kept for sale by August Gross marked Fromage d'Isigny was never sold by Tode and Wolff nor made or manufactured by them but that it was a similar product. The court held that the primary object of the contract was to maintain the secrecy of the cheese formulas. It was not necessary that Lena Gross herself breach the contract because she had agreed that her agents would not sell. The court, having found defendants breached the trade secret agreement, awarded damages to Tode and Wolff.

Cosmetic formulas may be the subject of trade secrets. For example, a lipstick formula was protected in *Michel Cosmetics, Inc.* v. *Tsirkas.* Tsirkas, while employed with Michel Cosmetics, Inc., learned the secret lipstick formulas of Michel Cosmetics. After leaving Michel Cosmetics, Tsirkas set up his own corporation and began manufacturing and selling lipsticks made from his ex-employer's formulas. The court held that Michel Cosmetics was entitled to an injunction and damages for lost profits.

In *Cowley* v. *Anderson* a formula for rat poison was recognized as a trade secret. Cowley developed a rat poison and then entered into a contract with Anderson which provided that for five years Anderson could sell the product in a certain territory including Kentucky and other states. Cowley's product was prepared under a secret formula, the constituent elements of which were a trade secret relating exclusively to Cowley's business. Anderson, with a purpose to work out his own formula for the manufacture of an identical or similar rat poison for sale to the public, analyzed Cowley's product and experimented with it without Cowley's knowledge. Although Anderson was able to identify only two of the elements of Cowley's poison, arsenic and anise oil, he was thereby able to formulate a poison called Zip. While still under contract with Cowley, Anderson sold Zip to former customers of Cowley. This was held to be a misappropriation of Cowley's trade secret. The court stated that Anderson's wrongdoing contravened the policy of the law because it amounted to a breach of his duty toward Cowley, quite apart from the financial injury to Cowley's business. Thus it might be said that Anderson was the rat and Zip his poison. The court stated, however, that had Anderson prepared Zip as a measure of protection against the day when Cowley might terminate the contract such an act would not have been such a breach of the obligation of good faith owed to Cowley.

As might be expected in this technological age, industrial formulas are often the subject of trade secrets. In *Marcann Outdoor, Inc.* v. *Johnston,*

> the defendant Johnston developed unique formulae or processes for photographic emulsion. By them, a proof of a proposed four-color advertising end-product can be made quickly and on a small scale, so as to depict exactly the final billboard print or other advertising product planned. The evidence indicates this is a valuable trade-secret property.

Johnston sold to Marcann, an advertising firm, the exclusive right to these industrial formulas as well as "future developments" of the formulas. However, Johnston hindered Marcann's use of the product, and contacted a competitor of Marcann with the apparent intention of disclosure. The court held that the issuance of an injunction against such activities was justified but that the injunction did not prevent Johnston from doing other work in the graphic arts field or from using formulas not sold by him to Marcann.

Another industrial-formula trade secret was involved in the 1939 decision of *Platinum Products Corporation* v. *Berthold.* Berthold had developed an original and secret formula for a catalytic lighter fluid for use in the Vestalite cigar lighter. He sold his secret to Platinum Products and also entered into an employment contract with that corporation to prepare the fluid for the lighter and not to work for a competitor. It was found that competitors of Platinum Products, knowing of Berthold's restrictive employment contract, induced him to leave Platinum Products and to divulge to them the trade secret developed by Berthold but belonging to Platinum Products. The Court of Appeals of New York affirmed the lower court's judgment in favor of Platinum Products enjoining the use of the trade secret and for an accounting and damages.

Industrial Processes

Processes are another type of subject matter that are frequently the subject of trade secrets. An illustrative case involving a manufactured product is *Sun Dial Corp.* v. *Rideout.* Here Williams organized the Sun Dial Corporation to manufacture precision dials and panels through a secret process. He had previously worked for Linotone Corporation, which made similar products. Some of Williams' employees left Sun Dial and established their own company to compete with Sun Dial. They had acquired their knowledge of dialmaking while working for Sun Dial, and the process they used was like the Sun Dial process in all material respects, differing only in minor details.

The former employees of Sun Dial tried to show that Sun Dial's processes were the same as those learned by Williams while he was employed at Linotone. The court found that Sun Dial's process differed substantially from Linotone's because Linotone's processes were characterized by etching the metal surface as compared with Sun Dial's surface relieving. This factor plus Sun Dial's substantial research and development and the measures Sun Dial took to keep its processes secret lead the court to conclude that Sun Dial's processes were trade secrets. Accordingly, the appropriation and use of these trade secrets by Sun Dial's former employees was enjoined.

An industrial process was also the subject of a trade secret in the very significant and interesting case of *E. I. du Pont de Nemours & Company* v. *Christopher*. It was, in the court's words, "a case of industrial espionage in which an airplane [was] the cloak and a camera the dagger." Rolfe and Gary Christopher, photographers in Beaumont, Texas, were hired by an unidentified person to photograph a duPont plant under construction which was designed to produce methanol by a process that gave duPont an advantage over its competitors. The company had taken strict security measures to maintain the secrecy of this process but because the plant was still being constructed, the process technology was visible from above and thus discoverable by aerial photography. The court held that the Christophers had improperly discovered the trade secrets of duPont, observing that to "require DuPont to put a roof over the unfinished plant to guard its secret would impose an enormous expense to prevent nothing more than a school boy's trick."

Know-how

The various cases mentioned so far involving formulas and processes may also be described as involving methods and techniques, or know-how. The term *know-how*, in fact, can be used to describe practically any technical subject of a technical trade secret so that secret know-how is almost synonymous with "trade secret" technology. On the other hand, technical know-how, not a trade secret, is a category of knowledge that any technical employee is free to take with him from one job to another.

One case that illustrates secret know-how as a trade secret in an interesting way is a 1960 California decision, *Ojala* v. *Bohlin,* one reason being that neither the term *trade secret* nor the term *secret know-how* is used. However, it can be considered a secret know-how or trade secrets case. Instead, the court stated in more general terms that the "gravamen of the action is unfair competition . . . ," which is that area of law that embraces the law of trade secrets or secret know-how.

Ojala, the plaintiff, conceptualized and designed the Hollywood Fast Draw Holster, which permitted the cocking of a single-action revolver and free turning of the cylinder while it was being withdrawn from the holster. Ojala sold and later advertised these holsters in *Guns* magazine. Just prior to the advertisement, Ojala took his holster patterns to Bohlin, the defendant, who agreed to manufacture the holsters for $20 each. Ancillary to the main contract was an agreement by Bohlin that he would not compete with Ojala by making or selling such a holster. The court stated that information on designs made available to Bohlin by Ojala were "otherwise unobtainable," thereby implying that Ojala had kept his knowledge of how to make the holsters a secret. When Bohlin raised his price for manufacturing the holsters, Ojala himself began to make the holsters again. Bohlin then advertised in *Guns* magazines the "lightning-draw" holster, which was practically the duplicate of Ojala's Hollywood Fast Draw Holster, and stated in the ad that he had "pioneered" the lightning-draw holster. The court found that Bohlin had not pioneered his holster but had unfairly appropriated the design of Ojala's holster.

Trade secret know-how not involving technology is also illustrated in the colorful opinion in *Arthur Murray Dance Studios of Cleveland* v. *Witter.* Judge Hoover of the Court of Common Pleas of Ohio commenced his opinion in the following fashion:

> When the defendant, Clifford Witter, a dance instructor, waltzed out of the employment of the plaintiff, the Arthur Murray Dance Studios of Cleveland, Inc., into the employment of the Fred Astaire Dancing Studios, the plaintiff waltzed Witter into court. . . . At the time Witter took his contentious step, Arthur Murray had a string attached to him —a certain contract prohibiting Witter, after working for Arthur Murray no more, from working for a competitor. That Arthur Murray and Fred Astaire are rivals in dispensing Terpsichorean erudition is not disputed. Now Arthur Murray wants the court to pull that string and yank Witter out of Fred Astaire's pedagogical pavilion.

The court's refusal to pull the string that would have yanked Witter out of Fred Astaire's pedagogical pavilion upon which he had willingly waltzed was based on the plain fact that the know-how imparted by Arthur Murray to Witter that he later used at Fred Astaire was never proved to be secret by Arthur Murray because "[t]he essence of his proof on this point [was] merely 'I taught Clifford Witter my method of teaching.' How does that prove secrecy? . . . Labelling it 'my method' does not make it a secret."

Ojala, duPont, and Goodrich all had been able to show the presence of that all-important element of secrecy; Arthur Murray had not. The importance of proving each element of a trade secret is pointed out in the *Arthur Murray* case: "more Ships of Justice have gone down for failure to sense the treacherous reefs of generality than for any other reason."

Pricing Information

Some trade secrets have no independent value but gain it from the extent to which possession of the secrets by businessmen enables them to operate their businesses in a superior manner and to the ultimate detriment of their competitors. This does not represent any recent trend. The Supreme Court of South Dakota, in *Simmons Hardware Co. v. Waibel,* decided in 1891 that a secret price code and the key thereto known only to Simmons Hardware and its traveling salesmen were properly the subjects of a trade secret. Waibel, a customer of Simmons Hardware, had wrongfully obtained the price code from Meeck, one of the salesmen of Simmons Hardware. The price code had been prepared by Simmons at a cost of many thousands of dollars. When Simmons learned that the price code had been taken by defendant customer Waibel, Simmons demanded return of it. Before complying with the demand, however, Waibel copied the code and threatened to divulge it to the customers of Simmons. Waibel contended that because he had copied the secret code into a Simmons catalogue he had acquired from another Simmons customer, he had not taken the property of Simmons Hardware. But the court enjoined the threatened disclosure, observing that although the original catalogue was of minimal value, that value increased greatly by the addition of the Simmons price code. Because that enhanced value was the result of the expense and efforts of Simmons, it became his property and was entitled to legal protection.

Although information as to pricing was found to constitute a trade secret in *Simmons Hardware,* many other cases hold that pricing information is not a trade secret. This does not necessarily represent a genuine division of authority but suggests that more often than not, pricing information is not really a secret in the first place. For instance, in *Taylor Freezer Sales Co. v. Sweden Freezer Eastern Corp.,* Sweden Freezer brought suit to enjoin its former employee, Auerhahn, and his new employer, Taylor Freezer, from exploiting Sweden Freezer's alleged trade secrets, some of which dealt with pricing policies. The court pointed out that in none of the allegations regarding trade secrets was there any showing that the information for which protection was sought was secret or confidential, and accordingly trade secret protection was denied.

Products

Products themselves sometimes have remained the subject of trade-secret protection despite sale and commercialization of them. One example is found in *K & G Oil Tool & Service Co.* v. *G & G Fishing Tools Service,* where the product for which trade secret protection was sought was a magnetic fishing tool. The "fish" to be caught by this tool was junk in oil wells such as broken drilling bits, drill stems, and other foreign metallic material from oil wells. Defendant G & G Fishing Tools subleased the K & G tool to drilling operators for 25 per cent of the rentals charged. G & G agreed that it would not disassemble the K & G tool and thereby acquire K & G's trade secrets of how the fishing tool was made. K & G brought an action for damages and an injunction against G & G for wrongfully copying, manufacturing, and employing a magnetic fishing tool that was very much the same as the tool developed by K & G. The jury found that G & G did not learn how to build the K & G tool or a tool similar thereto by observing it in an assembled or unbroken condition but learned of its internal makeup by taking it apart despite the agreement that it would refrain from doing so. The court found this to be a breach of confidence and contract by G & G. It was of no consequence that the method of building the fishing tool could possibly have been learned by an external examination of the product.

Computer software is a type of product that may be subject to trade secret protection and is also a timely topic for discussion. Trade secret protection was given to computer programs in *Hancock* v. *State*. Hancock, an employee of Texas Instruments, a corporation, possessed computer programs of his employer. Through another, he attempted to negotiate with Texaco, a client of Texas Instruments, the sale of fifty-nine of the programs. Hancock and his intermediary were foiled when a supposed Texaco agent turned out to be an investigator. The computer programs listed in the indictment against Hancock were the personal property of the manager of the Dallas Computer Center of Texas Instruments. Trade secret protection was not derived from the common law but from a Texas theft statute. Hancock argued that the computer programs alleged to have been stolen were not personal property and therefore were not the subject of theft. The court looked to the Texas Criminal Statute for a definition of property: "The term 'property,' as used in relation to the crime of theft, includes . . . *all writings of every description, provided such property possesses any ascertainable value.*" According to this definition of *property*, the court concluded that the computer programs were property within the meaning of the statute and went on to find that Hancock had violated the statute. The unfairness of Hancock's conduct was so blatant that the court never looked into the question of secrecy.

Computer hardware was the subject of trade secrets in *Telex Corp.* v. *IBM Corp.*, decided by an Oklahoma federal district court in 1973, where IBM charged Telex with misappropriating various trade secrets. The major portion of Telex's business was to offer for sale interchangeable replacements for products manufactured by IBM. Telex desired to compete with IBM by selling its products at lower prices than those of IBM. To achieve this Telex hired IBM employees who had the necessary know-how and in some cases knowledge of IBM's trade secrets in order to copy IBM's products, sometimes before they were announced to the public.

Telex hired one James, an IBM employee, who possessed substantial confidential information concerning plans for IBM's future products. Among other things, James conveyed to Telex confidential information concerning tape, disc, memory, and printer products developed by IBM. As a result, Telex was able to manufacture very similar products and thereby diminish the advantage IBM would otherwise gain over its competitors by conducting independent research and development efforts. The court found that James had wrongfully taken IBM's trade secrets and that Telex was aware that the information James conveyed to it was confidential.

After hiring James, Telex hired several other IBM employees to learn IBM's trade secrets. Among these were Grover, whom it hired to learn confidential information regarding IBM's unannounced advance tape subsystem known as Aspen, and Clemens, whom it hired to learn confidential information concerning IBM's advanced disc subsystem known as Merlin. The court found these and other products to be the proper subjects of trade secrets and spoke of the resulting unfairness to IBM in terms of the unjust enrichment of Telex.

Customer Lists and Information

Customer lists represent a frequently litigated area of trade secret law. Whether or not protection will be extended may depend on whether or not a restrictive covenant not to compete is present and on what jurisdiction you happen to be in. Roger Milgrim, a leading authority in the field, observes: "Whereas a clear majority rule cannot be stated as to the status of customer lists in the absence of restrictive covenants, it is almost universal that a customer list which has some basis for a claim of secrecy can be protected by a restrictive covenant." Customer list cases involving such restrictive covenants not to compete are usually dominated by discussion of contract law principles rather than trade secret law principles and require that restrictions imposed on former employees be reasonable as to time and geographical area and no more than necessary to protect the interests of the ex-employer.

In *Town and Country House & Homes Serv., Inc.* v. *Evans* trade secret protection was given to a retail list of customers for house-cleaning services although the employee in question had refused to sign a covenant not to compete with his former employer. While Evans worked for Town and Country, he solicited plaintiff's customers, telling them he was going to start his own house-cleaning business. He did so and took along a substantial number of his former employer's customers with him when he quit. The court held that this conduct was unlawful under the general principles of agency law for "[i]n the absence of clear consent or waiver by the principal, an agent, during the term of the agency, is subject to a duty not to compete with the principal concerning the subject matter of the agency." Evans had to account for profits made from the customers he had solicited while he was employed with plaintiff and was enjoined from doing business with these customers in the future. The court found error in the lower court's finding that the customer list did not constitute a trade secret. In the event that a trade secret was found, Evans would be enjoined from servicing not only the customers he had solicited while employed with plaintiff, but all customers on plaintiff's customer list.

A California court gave trade secret protection to a wholesale customer list where a restrictive covenant was absent in *Peerless Oakland Laundry Company* v. *Hickman*. Hickman was a former employee of Peerless, which had supplied linens to customers in Oakland since 1930. Hickman had been employed as a route supervisor and sales manager and had sufficient opportunity to learn the customer lists of Peerless. The lower court found that the information he acquired was a trade secret and confidential to Peerless. Hickman left employment with Peerless and a couple of years later started his own linen supply business. He solicited business from former Peerless customers, some of whom had been customers of Peerless for over twenty years, thereby diverting business from Peerless to himself. The court stated the rule that "in the absence of an enforceable contract containing covenants to the contrary, equity will not enjoin a former employee from soliciting business from his former employers provided *such competition is fairly and legally conducted."* Whether or not Hickman was guilty of unfair competition depended on whether or not the information he exploited was secret and confidential. The court pointed out that "[w]hile the mere identity of the customers may not be considered confidential, it may become such if it contains additional and confidential information about the customers." Under this test, the court found that Hickman had such additional information as to make such use unfair competition against Peerless.

Business information other than customer lists but that nevertheless pertains to customers can also be the subject of a trade secret. A case in point is *Robinson Electronic Supervisory Co.* v. *Johnson,* decided by the Supreme Court of Pennsylvania. Johnson, Sr., and Johnson, Jr., had been employed by Robinson and had necessarily become familiar with the special customer needs and problems for which their employer serviced with special security protection from fire, burglary, and so on, by central alarm service. The Johnsons attempted to utilize this knowledge by setting up a competing business with a financier-businessman in the same city. The court said that this customer information was the subject of a trade secret and that use of this information to the detriment of Robinson was an act of unfair competition and properly enjoined.

Sources of Supply

Another category of information that is subject to trade secret protection involves sources of supply. In *Storey* v. *Excelsior Shook & Lumber Co.* the subjects of the trade secrets were sources of supply, customer lists, and other data. Plaintiff Storey employed defendants Vossnack and Schaffel in the W. M. Storey Lumber Company prior to which time neither man knew of the lumber producers or customers engaged in the trade. But while employed by Storey, Vossnack and Schaffel at all times had complete access to the names and addresses of the customers and lumber products, and other trade information. After Vossnack and Schaffel were made directors of W. M. Storey Lumber Co., Inc., they conspired to take away Storey's business. They resigned from their positions with Storey and set up the Excelsior Shook & Lumber Company through which they made use of information learned from Storey and solicited the business of Storey's customers and lumber producers. The court awarded damages to Storey for his loss of business and enjoined Vossnack and Schaffel from further exploiting the confidential information they had learned from their former employer.

Although customer lists and sources of supply are not know-how, the unfair taking of such trade secrets has a similar impact as unfair taking of secret know-how. Quite often a case involving sources of supply will involve other types of information that are the equivalent to know-how so that the character of sources of supply as nonsecret know-how dims in importance. In *Water Services, Inc.* v. *Tesco Chemicals, Inc.,* Glad, the former employee of Farris Chemical Company, a subsidiary of the plaintiff, Water Services, Inc., was found to have unfairly disclosed to Tesco Chemicals, Inc., the design and composition of a fully automatic system to purify water and sources of supply for parts that Farris, Glad's former employer, had used to manufacture the Treat-A-Matic system. The Fifth Circuit did not make Glad very happy with its pronouncement that "Glad will not be allowed to bite the hand that fed him his expertise." The court found that Farris had protected the composition of the Treat-A-Matic system by keeping secret the identity of the components and their suppliers. Glad, while employed by Farris, had learned this information and was hired by Tesco Chemicals so as to exploit Glad's knowledge to enable Tesco to manufacture a water-purifying system that could compete with Treat-A-Matic. Tesco developed the Tescomatic system, which was strikingly similar to the Treat-A-Matic system. Competitors had been unable to duplicate Treat-A-Matic before. The court found that Glad had violated a covenant not to compete that was valid and enforceable and that the Treat-A-Matic supply sources were protectable as a trade secret.

Merchandising Methods and Business Information

Although many types of information can be the subject of a trade secret, a couple of types of information are generally found to be inappropriate for trade secret protection. Merchandising methods represent a class of information the courts appear to have uniformly held not to qualify as trade secrets. The reason the courts have so held is that merchandising methods are necessarily of a commonplace and public nature and are thereby precluded from being kept secret. One case that illustrates this is *Furr's, Inc.* v. *United Specialty Advertising Company.*

Mr. Goulding, sales representative of Furr's, paid a call to the United Specialty Advertising Company to try to sell to United Specialty its Cash Surprise Bonus Card, which it had developed to be furnished with banners and bag stuffers. Customers who got their cards punched out by making several purchases received $1 bonuses and further opportunity for a surprise bonus. Eventually United Specialty purchased $12,200 worth of the cards but was informed by Furr's that United could not use the cards in one of its areas because Furr's had sold cards to one of United's competitors, Food Mart, in that area. In response to this, United Specialty retained an advertising agency to develop a promotion it could use to meet Food Mart's competition. The agency came up with the Cash Circle Card, which was very similar to the Cash Surprise Bonus Card. Furr's sued United Specialty for damages and injunction.

In deciding that the Furr's bonus cards were not trade secrets, the Texas court observed that the use of such cards was not new and the idea behind the cards was disclosed by the cards themselves, which had been advertised very extensively in the newspapers. Moreover, the court pointed out that United Specialty did not receive information about Furr's cards through a confidential relationship and that one does not violate the law by merely using someone else's idea.

The second kind of subject matter that courts hold to be unworthy of trade secret status is general business information. It can be readily perceived that the reason for this is, once again, the lack of secrecy surrounding such information.

A case illustrating how general business information cannot be the subject of a trade secret is *Bimba Manufacturing Company* v. *Starz Cylinder Co.* Here Charles Bimba, the plaintiff, conceived and produced an air cylinder. He hired defendant Harold Carlstead to be his accountant and upon Carlstead's recommendation incorporated his cylinder business. Carlstead turned over to defendant Americo Amadio one of Bimba's uncopyrighted catalogs that had been distributed widely throughout the United States. The catalog showed pictures of Bimba's unpatented cylinders as well as drawings that showed dimensions and size, internal and external, of the cylinders. Subsequently, Amadio and defendant Nicholas Fushi began to get ideas about going into the cylinder-manufacturing business. Fushi knew defendant Frank Starzyk, who had an economic and industrial background. After being shown one of Bimba's catalogs, Starzyk thought he could make a cylinder like the one in Bimba's catalog. Starzyk said upon deposition that he used Bimba's catalog as well as a Bimba cylinder as a guide in constructing a competing air cylinder but did not use any additional information from Carlstead.

Although the cylinders the Starz Cylinder Company produced were the same size as Bimba Manufacturing Company's most popular model, there were several differences between the two brands. For example, the Starz piston was not threaded whereas Bimba's was, and the air vents of the two brands of cylinders were of different sizes.

When Bimba learned of his new competition, he told Carlstead that Carlstead was no longer his accountant. A few years later, Bimba sued the Starz Cylinder Company and others alleging that Carlstead had disclosed to Starz Cylinder its trade secrets so as to enable Starz to copy and use the designs shown in Bimba's catalogs.

The lower court having decided that Carlstead disclosed to Amadio,

Fushi, and Starzyk and to the Starz Cylinder Company trade secrets concerning Bimba Manufacturing Company's business, its suppliers, its methods of manufacturing cylinders, and its customer lists and having enjoined and found damages for such alleged activities, the Appellate Court of Illinois considered, as one of the critical issues, whether Bimba really possessed trade secrets that the defendants conspired to steal. Said the court:

> In order for business information to be a trade secret, it must have value to the business; it must take a form different from ordinarily acquired general information. For an owner's customer information to be a trade secret, it must have a particularity that gives it a business value derived from the information itself. It must be in a form susceptible to appropriation.

Even though such ordinarily acquired information is distilled, perhaps thereby achieving a modicum of enhanced value, it still does not attain trade secret value.

Very aptly, the court stated that "[o]ne cannot market his goods, disclose how it is made, and yet call its method of production a secret," and further stated that "[w]idespread publication and advertising will destroy any right of action to preserve as a secret that which is disclosed." Not only had Bimba failed to treat his design of the air cylinder as a secret but, in addition, there was no showing that the techniques Bimba used to manufacture his cylinder had ever been communicated to Carlstead. The court therefore concluded that Bimba Manufacturing Company had no trade secrets and that the defendants did not wrongfully appropriate anything.

SOURCE OF THE TRADE SECRET

"The source of the alleged trade secret is necessary to show both ownership and the state of secrecy of the [information] from the trade in general." So stated the Supreme Court of Pennsylvania in a footnote to the well-known trade secrets case *Wexler* v. *Greenberg*, as it summed up the principle of the opinion it rendered. It was the application of this principle that enabled the court to decide in whose favor the equities of the case ran.

From 1949 to 1957 Greenberg, a highly skilled chemist in the sanitation and maintenance field, was employed with the Buckingham Wax Company as its chief chemist. There he spent half his time developing new formulas for his employer by analyzing and duplicating the products of Buckingham's competitors. He was therefore familiar with the formulas of Buckingham. From 1952 to 1957 Brite Products Co., Inc., purchased the manufactured products of Buckingham and then sold them as its own products. In 1957 Greenberg sought employment with Brite and became treasurer, a director, and chief chemist of Brite. He also acquired a substantial financial interest in Brite.

Before Greenberg's employment with Brite, that company's business had consisted exclusively of distributing a line of sanitation and maintenance chemicals. Under Greenberg's supervision, however, Brite went into the business of manufacturing the chemicals it had previously purchased from Buckingham. The evidence showed that Brite's chemicals were manufactured by the use of formulas "substantially identical" to those of Buckingham. These formulas of Buckingham had been developed while Greenberg was chief chemist and were undoubtedly known to him. It had been noted by the court that while Greenberg was employed with Buckingham there did not exist between them a written or oral contract of employment or any restrictive agreement. The court was thus confronted with the problem of deciding to what extent Buckingham, without the aid of any express contract, could restrict Greenberg in the areas to which he could apply his knowledge of formulas he himself had developed while employed with Buckingham. This is a particularly important problem in light of the omnipresent interchange of employment among skilled employees who develop technology. Recognizing the gravity of its decision, the court stated:

> We must therefore be particularly mindful of any effect our decision in this case might have in disrupting this pattern of employee mobility, both in view of possible restraints upon an individual in the pursuit of his livelihood and the harm to the public in general in forestalling, to any extent widespread technological advances.

The court stated that Buckingham, the employer, had to show a legal basis upon which to predicate relief. In the absence of a covenant restricting Greenberg's use of the formulas he developed, the legal basis for relief could rest upon a confidential relationship between Greenberg and Buckingham. The issue, therefore, was whether or not a confidential relationship existed.

The court addressed itself to the fact that a confidential relationship in these cases and its ensuing pledge of secrecy usually arise upon the disclosure by the employer to the employee of a pre-existing trade secret. Obviously, such a confidence did not arise between Greenberg and his former employer because Greenberg had made the disclosures to Buckingham. The court was also unwilling to find that the relationship of employment itself created a duty of nondisclosure. The court declined to find such a relationship here because the formulas Greenberg developed for Buckingham were not the result of corporate experimentation or research but were the product of Greenberg's own talent and experience. Greenberg merely modified formulas learned from competitors, and received virtually no guidance from Buckingham in doing so.

Accordingly, the court decided that Greenberg was a rightful user of the formulas in question because he himself had been the source of the formulas.

The source of the information also played a pivotal role in *GTI Corporation* v. *Calhoon*. GTI Corporation hired defendants Calhoon, Davis, and King, who had formerly worked for Sylvania Electric Products, for the purpose of bringing knowledge they had learned at Sylvania in the manufacture of welded stud leads to one of GTI's plants. The employment contracts Calhoon, Davis, and King signed obligated them to disclose to GTI any ideas, improvements, discoveries, or inventions they made during their employment. While they were employed with GTI, Calhoon, Davis, and King manufactured welding machines, which were similar to those used by Sylvania, to match the Sylvania capability, and in the course thereof continued to learn about the design and use of stud lead welding machines.

Calhoon, Davis, and King terminated their employment with GTI after a few years and incorporated themselves as Metpar Manufacturing, Inc., to manufacture welded stud leads similar in specification and identical in purpose to the leads manufactured by GTI, Sylvania, and others. GTI sought to enjoin Calhoon, Davis, and King from using its alleged trade secrets and to direct the assignment to GTI by Calhoon, Davis, and King of any ideas or improvements that one or more of them may have made relating to GTI's business.

The court reasoned that there was nothing different about the machines that Calhoon, Davis, and King had developed for GTI and that GTI had not reposed in its former employees any secret or confidential information regarding its machines. GTI failed to show that its former employees conceived and developed any features during their employment that were trade secrets. GTI also failed to prove that the machines subsequently designed by Calhoon, Davis, and King utilized trade secrets. Any improvements that may have been made were merely supplements to machines well known in the trade. The court stressed the fact that Calhoon, Davis, and King had really learned their trade with Sylvania and elsewhere and that at Metpar Manufacturing Co., Inc., they utilized their general skills, knowledge, and experience rather than any trade secrets belonging to GTI. Thus, just as in *Wexler* v. *Greenberg*, the court based its decision to deny relief on the fact that the party seeking the relief had not been the true source of the technology.

SECRECY

Means of Appropriation as an Aspect of Secrecy

A case that illustrates means of appropriation as an aspect of secrecy is *Knudsen Corporation* v. *Ever-Fresh Foods, Inc.* The Knudsen Corporation owned by subsidiary, Dairy Fresh, Inc. (DFI). Defendant Rosenfeld had been employed by Knudsen as vice-president of DFI and had been in charge of salesmen, warehousing activities, and contact with customers. Rosenfeld left DFI and set up a competing company with defendant George Rabinoff, named Ever-Fresh Foods, Inc. Knudsen sued and claimed that Rosenfeld had trade secret knowledge regarding Knudsen's handling of DFI pricing, marketing, and sales strategy. Knudsen also complained that Rosenfeld knew DFI customer lists and how it dealt with its customers and used this information in the development of Ever-Fresh Foods, Inc. The defendants, however, were able to show that the marketing and pricing strategies were the subjects of common knowledge in the delicatessen trade. Quoting from the Restatement of Torts §757, Comment *a,* the California district court stated that, "the significant difference of fact between trade secrets and [those] which are not secret is that knowledge of the latter is available to the [user] without use of improper means to procure it, while knowledge of the former is usually available to him only by such means." The court found that Rosenfeld's considerable experience in the delicatessen business and his role in forming the Delicatessen Council of Southern California gave him access to the information alleged to be subject matter of the trade secrets. There was no trade secret because the requisite secrecy was not achieved: Rosenfeld was able to gain the information through proper means. What is meant by proper and improper means will be explored more fully later.

A case that recites the same general principle regarding secrecy but that contrasts in result is *Clark* v. *Bunker,* decided by the Ninth Circuit Court of Appeals in 1972. There the alleged trade secret consisted of a detailed plan for creation, promotion, financing, and sale of contracts for "prepaid" funeral services. Defendant Bunker, having lost the decision in the court below, argued on appeal that because plaintiff Clark had authorized seven other corporations to use the plan, had discussed it with the managing director of a national association of morticians, and had described the plan in a special bulletin, the plan was not secret. However, the court found that although the preceding disclosures were made by Clark, these others held the plan a secret and the special bulletin described the plan in only a general way. Moreover, the bulletin was not published until after Bunker had gotten the information through a breach of confidence and exploited it.

The court stated that secrecy was not nullified because Bunker through a special effort might have garnered the same information from public sources. Considerable effort would be required to assemble the detailed elements of the plan from these public sources. Accordingly, the court found that trade secret protection was justified. The difference in results between *Knudsen Corporation* v. *Ever-Fresh Foods, Inc.* and *Clark* v. *Bunker* was that in the former case defendant Rosenfeld had within easy grasp without using any improper means the information for which trade secret protection was sought. Quite logically, the information was no secret to Rosenfeld. On the other hand, Bunker did not have such access to the information as Rosenfeld had enjoyed; although the information could conceivably have been acquired through public sources, secrecy existed because "except by the use of improper means, there would be difficulty in acquiring the information."

Originality

Another aspect or element of secrecy is that "[a]lthough a trade secret need not be so unique or novel as to be patentable, it must possess at least that modicum of originality which will separate it from everyday knowledge." So declared the Fifth Circuit Court of Appeals in *Cataphote Corporation* v. *Hudson.* The court explained that:

> patent laws are designed to encourage invention and the arts while trade secret law is designed to protect against a breach of faith and reprehensible means of learning another's secrets. For this latter, limited protection, novelty *in the patent law sense of a substantial advance over prior art* is an improper standard.

Cataphote Corporation, a manufacturer of spherical microscopic glass beads, brought a suit to enjoin its former employee, Cecile Hudson, and his new corporation, Hudson Industries, Inc., from using what it alleged to be its trade secrets involving six techniques used in manufacturing the glass beads. Important to the court's decision was its finding that the six processes alleged to be trade secrets involved principles of general scientific knowledge in the glass bead industry or principles of even more basic and widespread common knowledge. One of the techniques sought to be protected involved "principles so common that in form they are utilized on every household gas cook stove." Another of the processes was found to bear greater similarity to a patented process that had become part of the public domain than to Cataphote's alleged trade secret.

But courts do not neatly isolate such issues as originality. Hudson had an ancillary point in his favor. The court found that Hudson's native talent was the key to his success rather than any secret information he acquired from his employment with Cataphote of seven years before. Thus the court's decision partially turned on that same inquiry into the source of the trade secret as *Wexler* v. *Greenberg*. But, chiefly, the court predicated its decision on the quality of "everyday knowledge" about the alleged trade secret subject matters that prevented them from achieving the requisite element of secrecy. As the Fifth Circuit had stated in a prior opinion in the same litigation, "[t]he subject matter of a trade secret must be secret. An item or process of public or general knowledge in an industry cannot be appropriated by one as his own secret." Accordingly, Cataphote was unsuccessful in enjoining Hudson from the use of these techniques in his competing corporation.

Although the major elements of a process may be known to a trade as they were in *Cataphote,* it is still possible for the secrecy requisite to be achieved if the combination of these elements is nevertheless secret. This point is brought out in *Ferroline Corp.* v. *General Aniline & Film Corp.,* where the trade secret subject matter was the process for manufacture of iron pentacarbonyl. The defendant, General Aniline & Film Corp., claimed that this process was disclosed by patents it held as well as by other prior art teachings. Although it was true that each of the basic elements of Ferroline's process was generally known, they were not generally known *as a combination* in a complicated process. In this way, that modicum of originality was achieved.

In a similar case, Servo Corporation had disclosed to General Electric in an inspection its complicated process for developing a hot-box detector that had utility in the railroad industry for detecting an unusual amount of heat escaping from freight car boxes. Servo Corporation claimed that prior to the inspection by General Electric, it had kept the combination of all the elements of the hot-box detector a secret. General Electric, on the other hand, attempted to show that each and every element of the detector had been disseminated to the industry in trade journals and industrial fairs before the inspection and that General Electric had been able to put together its own detector from such sources of information. However, the Fourth Circuit Court of Appeals was of the opinion that because the combination had not been publicly disclosed before the inspection, General Electric had acquired its knowledge of the combination by the inspection of its subsequent use of this information amounted to a breach of confidence it could not avoid by piecing together bits of data in retrospect.

Relative Versus Absolute Secrecy

Although a few cases suggest that the secrecy in a trade secrets case must be absolute, i.e., the secret must be known only to the owner, these cases are in the minority in relation to the number of cases that state that secrecy need only be relative or qualified. A leading case that states this view is *Vulcan Detinning Co.* v. *American Can Co.* decided by a New Jersey court in 1907. The Vulcan Detinning Company had been formed in the United States on the basis of the acquisition by the organizers of a secret detinning process from a concern called Tinfabriek in Vlissingen, Holland. Although Tinfabriek had unfairly appropriated the process from a German manufacturer, that unfair appropriation was not what caused the lawsuit. One Assmann, to whom was entrusted the secrecy of the detinning process in the form of a formula by Vulcan Detinning, left Vulcan and enticed three others from Vulcan to join with him in installing, for the American Can Company, two plants using Vulcan's detinning process. That the court did not require an absolute secrecy to Vulcan's trade secret, which was obviously lacking because it was utilized by two concerns in Europe, was evidenced in the court's opinion:

> In the application of these general principles the secrecy with which a court of equity deals is not necessarily that absolute secrecy that inheres in discovery, but that qualified secrecy that arises from mutual understanding, and that is required alike by good faith and by good morals.

Accordingly, Assmann and the American Can Company were enjoined from using Vulcan's detinning process. A more recent case expressing the view of *Vulcan Detinning* is *Space Aero Products Co.* v. *R. E. Darling Co.*, decided in the Maryland courts in 1965. Darling, the plaintiff, had developed a process for making oxygen silicone flexible breathing hoses that were sold to the Douglas Aircraft Company and to the Navy. Four of the defendants had worked for Darling before leaving its employ to go into competition with Darling. Norris Manufacturing, a former supplier of silicone products to Darling, financially aided these four former employees in incorporating Space Aero. Although no one else had been able to duplicate Darling's breathing hose previously, the Space Aero Company was able to do so within twenty days after its corporate charter was granted. In affirming the lower court's finding that Darling had a protectable trade secret, the Maryland court stated:

> Absolute secrecy is not essential but a substantial element of secrecy must exist so that there would be difficulty in others properly acquiring the information. . . . A trade secret owner, however, does not abandon his secret by a limited public publication for a restricted purpose.

Loss of Secrecy

Laxity and Lack of Notice.   It would seem obvious to anyone, layman and lawyer alike, that secrecy is the sine qua non of a trade secret.

It is therefore not surprising that the courts so often find that trade secret protection was not justified due to lack of real secrecy. This is usually due to laxity on the part of the would-be possessor of the trade secret in keeping the subject matter truly secret rather than to some other element of the case such as the type of information for which trade secret protection is sought. A relatively recent case that well illustrates this situation that so frequently arises is *J. T. Healy & Son, Inc.* v. *James A. Murphy & Son, Inc.*, decided by the Supreme Judicial Court of Massachusetts in 1970. The defendants, James A. Murphy and others, former officers, directors, and employees of Healy, were charged with wrongful appropriation of secret information to set up a rival business. James A. Murphy had worked for the Healy corporation since 1936 and in 1958 he became a secretary, director, and vice president of Healy. The Murphy Company was incorporated in 1963 and had its principal place of business in Attleboro, Massachusetts, where the Healy Corporation also had its principal place of business. Both companies were engaged in the jewelry findings business. Jewelry findings are pieces of metal, such as brass, silver, or gold, that are created through the use of dies. The jewelry findings are then sold to jewelry manufacturers, who finish the pieces. The master in the lower court proceeding had found that two of the processes used to make the jewelry findings, called the pattern application and twisted-corrugated methods, were trade secrets, but the court was of the opinion that his conclusions were too indefinite as to what features he regarded to be trade secrets. These processes were utilized as part of the rest of the operation and there were no partitions to shield them from disclosure. "There was no written notice to employees nor admonishment against discussing the processes when they should be outside the plant. No employee was required to sign a non-disclosure agreement. This was company policy based on the theory that the best way to guard the secret was not to excite undue interest." The court construed this

> to be a consciously adopted plan to do nothing affirmative to admit that anything was secret. It not only is suggestive that the whole idea is an afterthought but is completely at variance with the rule that individuals must be constantly admonished that a process is secret and must be kept so. We regard non-action pursuant to the so called policy as an insuperable reason why these processes cannot be trade secrets. . . . [I]f the person entitled to a trade secret wishes to have its exclusive use in his own business, he must not fail to take all proper and reasonable steps to keep it secret. He cannot lie back and do nothing to preserve its essential secret quality, particularly when the subject matter of the process becomes known to a number of individuals involved in its use or is observed in the course of manufacture within

plain view of others. . . . [O]ne who claims that he has a trade secret must exercise eternal vigilance. This calls for constant warnings to all persons to whom the trade secret has become known and obtaining from each an agreement, preferably in writing, acknowledging its secrecy and promising to respect it. To exclude the public from the manufacturing area is not enough.

The plaintiff bears the burden of proving secrecy; he must show that secret status has been achieved and he has no presumptions in his favor. The court found that the plaintiff had failed to sustain its burden and thus plaintiff lost the case.

In a more recent decision, *Jet Spray Cooler, Inc.* v. *Crampton,* the Supreme Judicial Court of Massachusetts stated that "[t]he language in the *Healy* case makes it clear that one seeking to prevent the disclosure or use of trade secrets or information must demonstrate that he pursued an active course of conduct designed to inform his employees that such secrets and information were to remain confidential."

Jet Spray Cooler was a manufacturer and seller of "visual display beverage dispensers" in Waltham, Massachusetts. Crampton and other defendants were formerly employed by Jet Spray Cooler and another plaintiff corporation that operated as a unit out of the same offices and at the same plant. They subsequently became the officers, directors, employees, and stockholders of Cathco, Inc., a competitor in the manufacture and sale of beverage dispensers. One Jacobs, the president and treasurer of the plaintiffs, originated the first magnetically pumped visual display beverage dispenser. While employed with Jet Spray Cooler, defendant Crampton had access to the customer lists. Other defendants had access to financial and sales records and sources of supply. Another, as chief engineer, had responsibility for improving and redesigning the beverage dispensers. These defendants had been found to be "trusted employees" and, accordingly, critical information was made available to them to enable them to make improvements in the business.

The court recited the principle that although an employee has the right to take his knowledge and skill with him to other employment, he may not use or disclose confidential or secret information which he gained with his former employer. Therefore, the major issue confronting the court was whether or not Jet Spray Cooler had kept this information a secret. The court stressed the point that in order for a confidential relationship to be created, the one wishing to create such a relationship must express his intention to the other party. The court found that only with respect to one report were sufficient precautions taken to preserve secrecy. The fact that Jet Spray Cooler, Inc., had procured only one copy of the report for its use and had personally given it to one of the defendants, Armstrong, constituted enough notice or precautions to preserve secrecy so that in this situation there was no need to give to Armstrong periodic warnings and constant admonitions of secrecy.

Another case that followed this principle was *Lowndes Products, Inc.* v. *Brower,* decided by the Supreme Court of South Carolina in 1972. Plaintiff Lowndes Products, Inc., was a manufacturer of nonwoven textile fabric. Some of the defendants who were "key employees" of Lowndes, left that company in 1969 and with the help of other of the defendants formed B.L.S. Corporation, which competed with Lowndes in the manufacture of nonwoven textile fabric. Lowndes sued B.L.S. Corporation to enjoin it from using what it considered to be trade secrets belonging to it. Although the court found that Lowndes had trade secrets, injunctive relief was denied because Lowndes had failed to take the necessary steps to preserve their secrecy. The court made the following observations with regard to the laxity of the plaintiff in protecting its secrets:

> Lowndes' employees were not required to sign employment contracts containing secrecy agreements. Nor were they required to execute noncompetition agreements. Employees were rarely, if ever, admonished concerning the "secrecy" of Lowndes processes or equipment, not even upon an employee's termination.
>
> Plant security at Lowndes was, at best, minimal. There was no "sign-in" system or badge system. Doors customarily remained unlocked. A hurricane fence surrounded the plant, but it appears to have been maintained as a deterrent to vandalism rather than as a deterrent to competition. No signs were posted in the plant to remind employees of the alleged secrecy of Lowndes' operations. Upon occasion specifications of equipment or processes appear to have been posted on the walls.
>
> Access to the Lowndes plant appears to have been less than fully restricted. Employees were generally free to "roam" throughout the plant. Supply and maintenance personnel visited frequently and freely. There were instances where actual or potential competitors were given tours of Lowndes' facilities.

The court summed up its opinion by observing that the evidence revealed that an atmosphere of congeniality and accommodation was encouraged by Lowndes' management toward its employees and visitors. The court later stated that it refused to grant the injunction solely because a "court of equity will not grant injunctive relief in a case where the owner of the trade secrets did not endeavor to protect itself."

In *Gallowhur Chemical Corporation* v. *Schwerdle,* where one of the plaintiffs, a Dr. Sowa, divulged one of the alleged trade secrets in a lecture, the court observed that "one may not venture on liberties with his own secret, may not lightly or voluntarily hazard its leakage or escape, and at the same time hold others to be completely obligated to observe it."

In *Republic Systems and Programming, Inc.* v. *Computer Assistance, Inc.* the trade secret subject matter alleged was customer lists for computer software. In finding that the customer lists did not qualify as trade secrets the court noted that: "Many of the clients were openly listed in plaintiff's advertising brochures as 'representative clients' . . . . Furthermore, efforts to keep the names . . . secret were meager at best."

In *Wheelabrator Corporation* v. *Fogle,* Wheelabrator Corporation attempted to stop its former employee, Fogle, from using what it alleged to be its trade secrets for the process of making steel shot to be used as an abrasive. Wheelabrator argued that it had preserved the secrecy of its processes by having Fogle sign a contract as he began work for Wheelabrator that stated that Fogle would respect the trade secrets of his employer. The court noted, however, that Fogle was in a poor bargaining position when he signed the contract and more importantly that Wheelabrator had not taken further precautions to guard its alleged trade secrets. Although Wheelabrator showed that it had fenced in the manufacturing facilities and had guard houses at the entrances, the court did not accept these as adequate precautions, noting that:

> No distinction . . . was made between the shot plant and other manufacturing facilities within the fenced area. The shotting plant was afforded no greater security than the admittedly non-secret facilities. The location of the guard houses also indicates only a general security management. They were located at the general entrances providing no greater security for the shotting plant than other facilities. Moreover, there was uncontroverted testimony that often these guard houses were unmanned. These precautions indicate a security arrangement "only to the extent that many manufacturers are accustomed to exclude the general public from an inspection of their methods."

Although Wheelabrator had issued two notices that purported to admit only authorized personnel to the shot plant, it was not feasible to carry this announced policy out so that admission was not really restricted. The court further noted:

> . . . the apparent routineness that customers, potential customers, independent contractors, and repairmen were allowed admission to the plant. . . . [M]any of the people that were allowed to tour the plant were engineers and professionals some of whom [Fogle] personally conducted in descriptive tours. Almost all, if not all, of the alleged secret processes were visible, and only a few interior modifications to machinery were not observable. Significantly there was no evidence of contractual relationships between those touring the plant and Wheel-

abrator. Nor was there evidence of admonitions or notice to the independent contractors and repairmen as to the allegedly confidential nature of the operations.

The court also noted that Wheelabrator, in an annual report, published a photograph of the heat treating equipment it had alleged to be secret. This the court held to be a public disclosure. In light of this disclosure and the lax security arrangements, the court found "that the alleged trade secrets lack the first essential element for trade secrecy—namely secrecy itself." For these reasons, Wheelabrator had failed to sustain its burden to show the presence of the elements of a trade secret and accordingly it was denied the relief it sought. It is worth noting that although Wheelabrator may have had the intent to keep its processes secret as evidenced by the contract Fogle signed with it, "that intent will be disregarded where absence of evidence of proper precautions against disclosure is found. . . . To limit a man in the exercise of his knowledge there must be a strong showing that the knowledge was gained in confidence."

It would be a misinterpretation of *Wheelabrator Corporation* v. *Fogle* to conclude that a written agreement between the employer and the employee is not advisable. It is probably the best way of initially putting the employee on notice that he will be under an obligation not to disclose the employer's trade secrets. It is advisable that the contract describe what the trade secrets topically cover; the contract should also contain a clause stating that improper use of the trade secret information would amount to a breach of confidence and would subject the employee to liability. Even before the signing of such a contract, the employer can take a precautionary step. He can investigate the record of job applicants with respect to their handling of trade secrets for former employers.

As is easily apparent from the preceding cases, it is important that access to the secret information be limited to those who need to know. Further, those employees who do need to know should be put on notice that they are in this special category so that they will not divulge the information to those who do not need to know. Not only should access to the information be restricted, but access to trade secrets areas should be restricted to those who must go there. In addition, written trade secret material should be stamped "Confidential" and pertinent wastepaper should be burned or otherwise disposed of on the premises.

It is as important that affirmative precautions to preserve secrecy be taken when employment is terminated as when it is begun. The employee should be placed on notice of his continuing obligation of nondisclosure. The employee should also be required to return any secret or confidential papers relating to the employer's business, including those papers written by the employee himself. A further precaution to be taken when feasible is to inform the subsequent employer of the topical areas of trade secret information that the ex-employee knows.

Independent Efforts of Others. The preceding cases have emphasized the importance of guarding secrecy to maintain trade secret status. Without minimizing this crucial factor in trade secret law, it should be pointed out that even the most thorough sysem of secrecy maintenance does not insure the continued existence of one's trade secret. Such is the import of *Drew Chemical Corporation* v. *Star Chemical Company*. The Drew Chemical Corporation claimed as one of its trade secrets the secret know-how or process for producing their beaded combination stabilizer-emulsifier product for ice cream. The individual defendants had formerly worked for Drew and as key employees they had been familiar with Drew's secret process. Drew's ordinary employees, the industry, and the public at large did not receive the information concerning this process and Drew was the only manufacturer who sold such a product to the dairy industry. The defendants, after leaving Drew, formed the Star Chemical Company. Star, for awhile, produced a beaded combination stabilizer and emulsifier by a process similar to that employed by Drew. The Star Company abandoned its efforts, however, because its experimental process, although similar to Drew's, did not appear to be promising. The court found that Drew's know-how at one time qualified as a trade secret. However, between the time of the filing of the suit and trial as many as ten companies entered into manufacturing a product similar to the one formerly manufactured by only Drew and Star. As a result, the court found that "Star, as well as the rest of the world, is entitled to make use of this process and manufacture the combination product." Thus, no matter how well a secret is preserved by a company, legitimate discovery by others can cause the original trade secret to evaporate. This would only occur, however, where because of the subsequent discovery, the matter formerly a secret became public knowledge. The cases are clear on the principle that one cannot claim as his trade secret that which has become a part of the public domain. In *Drew Chemical*, for example, had only one other corporation subsequently discovered the secret process and used it, the process might have remained a trade secret, if it was available to others only by improper means or through a confidential relationship.

Issuance of a Patent. Another important way in which trade secrecy can be lost is through its publication via issuance of a patent grant. One case that illustrates this proposition is *Bickley* v. *Frutchey Bean Company*. For thirteen years defendant Lloyd DuBois worked for Bickley, one of the first and evidently best manufacturers of bean-sorting machinery in the country, and then went to work for defendant Frutchey Bean Company. DuBois helped the Frutchey Bean Company develop its own bean sorter. Bickley claimed that the Frutchey bean sorter had been built by utilizing trade secrets DuBois had learned from it. The Frutchey Bean Company claimed that Bickley had disclosed its trade secrets by the issuance of patents that had expired. The court documented the principle that issuance of a patent destroys the secrecy necessary for a trade secret:

> If a discovery is one which constitutes invention and for which a patent is issued, the right of further secrecy is, of course, lost, for a legal disclosure and public dedication have then been made, with a right of limited and temporary monopoly granted as the reward.

The court found that nine of the twelve trade secrets Bickley claimed were disclosed by patents, most of them belonging to Bickley. The other information not covered by patents was found to be in the public domain. For these reasons, Bickley had no rights against the Frutchey Bean Company.

For effect on trade secrecy, there is an important distinction between issuance of a patent and a patent application; the issuance of a patent is a publication whereas a patent application is not because the U.S. Patent Office is required to keep patent applications in secrecy. An interesting problem could arise if the patent application was rejected because the subject matter was found by the Patent Office to be "obvious." The question is whether that subject matter could still be considered a trade secret if it is obvious "to a person having ordinary skill in the art."

Sale of the Product and Reverse Engineering. Although it is theoretically possible for a product to remain the subject of a trade secret despite its sale and commercialization, sale of the product often spells the end of secrecy when it is possible to discover the technology through product analysis or reverse engineering. A case that well illustrates this principle of trade secrets law is *Carver* v. *Harr.* Plaintiff Carver had invented a ventilating blackout screen made especially for ship portholes. Carver had applied for a patent but prior to its issuance claimed that his invention was protectable as a trade secret and sought to enjoin Harr from making and selling the blackout screens or divulging information regarding it to others, having alleged but not proved that Harr had learned about the invention in confidence from Carver. The stumbling block to Carver's suit was that the novelty of the invention lay only in the way the parts of the screen were arranged. Thus, anyone with skill in such matters could obtain full knowledge of the invention by simply examining and analyzing one of the screens.

Despite this kind of disclosure, which could be expected, there were no requests or promises to keep the information secret. The court assumed that the invention was disclosed to the purchasers and observed that "[t]rade secrets are not given protection against all the world, but only against one who has learned the secret by improper means or by virtue of a confidential relation." The court concluded that although Harr may have been under an implied duty not to use Carver's invention for his own purposes, such a duty ceased when Carver, in soliciting business or by making deliveries, disclosed the design of the screen to a great number of people. The consequence of such disclosure is competition and Harr was free to enter into the scramble for the business.

Publication. There are various forms of publications through which secrecy may be lost. Issuance of a patent, already discussed, is one such form of publication. In *Tom Lockerbrie, Inc.* v. *Fruhling*, decided by a Wisconsin federal district court in 1962, the subject matter of the alleged trade secret was an apparatus for cooling water to be circulated through a tank to an external heat exchanger, also known as an air-agitated ice builder, commonly used in the dairy industry. The court found that because Lockerbrie had widely circulated trade literature that fully disclosed the design of the apparatus, he had thereby failed to maintain the requisite element of secrecy, and trade secret protection was denied.

Advertising is a form of publication through which secrecy may be lost. A good example of such a publication is found in *Mycalex Corp. of Am.* v. *Pemco Corp.* Mycalex Corporation, a producer of Mycalex, a combination of mica and glass used as an insulator, contracted with defendant Pemco to supply it with a substance known as frit for use in the manufacture of Mycalex. In order to enable Pemco to improve the quality of the frit for Mycalex's Corporation's use, Mycalex Corporation acquainted officials of Pemco with the way in which frit was used in the production of Mycalex. Later Pemco and another corporate defendant began manufacturing a product that was competitive with Mycalex. Mycalex Corporation filed suit against Pemco and the other corporation to enjoin such manufacture, claiming that Pemco was illegally using trade secret information it had gained from Mycalex Corporation as its supplier. Although Pemco alleged that it had learned how to manufacture the glass-bonded mica material from General Electric without using improper means, the court was willing to base its conclusion on the grounds that the know-how was not the subject matter of a trade secret because in Mycalex Corporation's catalog there appeared, as an advertisement, a clear and elaborate description of "how Mycalex is made." The court observed that the law requires more than merely calling a particular process a secret. Information for which trade secret protection is sought must bear the "indicia of secrecy," and the Mycalex Corporation's advertisement negated any such indicia. Accordingly, trade secret protection was denied.

Advertising as well as sale of the product were the means by which secrecy was lost in *Wissman* v. *Boucher*. The subject matter of the alleged trade secret was a collapsible metal fishing rod. The court reasoned that this unpatented fishing pole could not receive trade secret protection because any reasonably experienced machinist, upon seeing it advertised or purchasing it on the open market, could easily imitate the product.

IMPROPER MEANS

Whether or not liability arises in connection with use of another's trade secret depends on the means used to acquire the trade secret. We have already seen that whether or not the acquisition of a trade secret is proper may turn on the precautions taken to keep the information secret and whether the information was really secret in the first place.

Employer–Employee Relationship

Trade secret litigation frequently arises from the employer–employee relationship, as can be seen by many of the examples already discussed. The most important aspect of this employment relationship for trade secret purposes is that it is a fiduciary relationship. It is because of this element of an employee's duty of loyalty to his employer that the employee is bound not to divulge or use the trade secrets of his employer while he is still an employee, with obligations continuing after the employment relationship has terminated.

Misuse While Still an Employee. A case illustrating how an employee might use a trade secret by improper means while still an employee is the 1963 New York case of *Harry R. Defler Corp.* v. *Kleeman.* The most valuable asset of the Defler Corporation was the business records that revealed the particular requirements of the firm's clients and provided analyses of the materials available from the various industrial producers supplying the firm. One Kleeman, the general manager and vice president, necessarily had access to these records and was made aware of their confidentiality. About a year after he was hired, Kleeman hired Schneider to work as a salesman. Kleeman and Schneider, even though working for the Defler Corporation and in breach of their obligation of loyalty to its interest, set upon a course of action with a plan to divert to themselves the very business they had been employed to secure for the Defler Corporation. They and their wives set up Carchem Products Corporation, which dealt almost exclusively with customers and suppliers of the Defler Corporation. Kleeman and Schneider continued to reap the benefits of their employment with the Defler Corporation and took unfair advantage of the customer information contained in the Defler Corporation's business records in order to solicit customers for Carchem. They used the name of the Defler Corporation to secure credit for Carchem and charged Defler for telephone and travel expenses of Carchem. They even went so far as to pay the legal fees incurred with regard to the incorporation of Carchem out of the funds of the Defler Corporation.

After Schneider left the employ of the Defler Corporation, Kleeman not only acquiesced in Schneider's subsequent piracy of Defler Corporation's customers but withheld his knowledge of such piracy from the other corporate officials. The court set forth the well-established principle:

> that an employee, who has had entrusted to him confidential information pertaining to the conduct and clientele of his employer's business which he would not have obtained were it not for his status as a trusted employee and which affords him an advantage over other competitors to whom the information is not available, may not subsequently use that information to further his own ends.

The court was applying this principle to two defendant employees, only one of whom had departed from the employ of the plaintiff corporation. It is interesting to note here that the court considered as part of the damages owing to the Defler Corporation the salary that the corporation paid the two employees after they had set up the rival Carchem Products Corporation.

A contrast to the *Defler* case is found in a 1912 Massachusetts case, *American Stay Co.* v. *Delaney*. Delaney, an employee of the American Stay Company, by no improper means, developed inventions which amounted to new and competing machinery to that of the American Stay Company while he was in the employ of that company although it was not his responsibility to orginate inventions. The court reasoned that although the law would not permit Delaney to unfairly appropriate American Stay's trade secrets, he was under no obligation to deny himself the benefits of his inventive talents, even though they were stimulated by the performance of his duties of employment. Under these conditions, Delaney had a legal right to invent and develop these new and better machines. Unlike *Defler,* the American Stay Company could not recover the wages paid to Delaney as the Defler Corporation had recovered the wages paid to Kleeman and Schneider. The reason for the different results is that in *Defler* the defendant employees had used the trade secret information by improper means, whereas in *American Stay* there was nothing improper about the acquisition or use of Delaney's inventions because Delaney was the source of the information.

The case of *Southern California Disinfecting Co.* v. *Lomkin* presents an interesting example of improper means. Lomkin, the defendant employee, while still an employee of plaintiff Southern California Disinfecting Co., entered into a conspiracy with Calar Chemical Company to represent himself as being associated with Calar to plaintiff's customers with the purpose of diverting the business from plaintiff to Calar. In carrying out this conspiracy, Lomkin utilized the confidential customer information belonging to plaintiff Southern California Disinfecting. After a substantial amount of such piracy had occurred, Lomkin left the employ of Southern California Disinfecting and took with him valuable and confidential customer information to use for the benefit of Calar. In finding liability on the part of Lomkin and Calar, the court noted that this was "not the usual commercial hitchhiking of a former employee but rather it is trade secret larceny."

Misuse After Termination of Employment

An illustration of the proposition that an employee's obligation not to take the trade secrets of his employer by improper means survives and continues long beyond the period of employment is found in the case of *Pasadena Ice Co.* v. *Reeder.* All of the defendants were former employees of the Pasadena Ice Co., and they formed Purity Ice Co. As employees for the Purity Ice Co. they used the trade secret customer information they had gained as employees of Pasadena. Several of the defendant employees had been out of the employ of Pasadena for over a year. The defendants argued that because they had ceased employment with Pasadena for a time before being employed by Purity they had breached no duty. The court rejected this argument, observing that the courts have held that injury to the employer results from the improper use by the employee of the trade secrets of the employer. Because such improper use may occur after as well as before the employer has hired replacements for his former employees, the employer may sustain substantial injury at such a time and accordingly the employer merits legal protection in cases of that character.

A case in which improper means was not employed by a group of former employees but that nevertheless recognized the survival of this nondisclosure obligation is *Metal Lubricants Company* v. *Engineered Lubricants Company*. Metal Lubricants dealt mostly in lubricating oils that it made for certain kinds of machine metal work. The main office and manufacturing plant were in Chicago. One of the sales and warehousing offices was located in St. Louis. One Donald Wachter, the Division Manager of the St. Louis office, together with the vast majority of the sales and administrative staff of that office resigned from Metal Lubricants because of dissatisfaction with the policies of its operation. Under the leadership of Wachter, they formed a competing concern, Engineered Lubricants Company. Metal Lubricants brought an action against these former employees, alleging, among other things, that their former employees, through Engineered Lubricants, had taken by improper means the trade secrets belonging to it that related to customer lists, customer information, product specifications, and formulas.

The court noted that Wachter's replacement, the new division manager, had supervised and approved of everything that the former employee defendants had taken with them when they left Metal Lubricants. These included salesmen's copies of invoices showing the customer's name and address, the type of oil purchased, and the price. It was apparent to the court that customer information and the prices charged by Metal Lubricants could easily be retained by memory or could be quickly compiled by checking with old customers.

As to the formulas and product specifications, the kind of ingredients to the lubricants was generally known, but the exact ingredients and their proportions were often kept secret. Testimony showed that Engineered Lubricants subjected lubricants of Metal Lubricants to independent product analysis to determine what the exact molecular components of the products were. Accordingly, Metal Lubricants was denied relief because it could not prove that the defendants had taken the information by improper means.

W. R. Grace & Company v. *Hargadine* is an interesting 1968 decision in which the Sixth Circuit Court of Appeals found former employees to have taken trade secrets by improper means. After W. R. Grace & Company had merged with and then purchased all of the assets of another company, DuBois Chemicals, Inc., the minority of officers and employees of DuBois who had opposed the merger and sale formed an operating company, Intercontinental Chemical Corporation, to compete generally in the same industrial chemical fields in which DuBois had previously operated and was continuing to operate as a division of W. R. Grace.

Grace sued Universal, Intercontinental, and Clyde C. Hargadine, the former executive vice president and general manager of DuBois, for improperly taking trade secrets previously the property of DuBois. The court noted that Hargadine had had access to the trade secret information of DuBois and knew from whom he could obtain the product formulas and customer information if he did not already possess this information himself. In order to induce DuBois employees to become a part of the new venture, Hargadine told them repeatedly that "we have the DuBois formulas."

The court noted that the former employees who had left DuBois, in contrast to those in the *Metal Lubricants Company* case, had, without authorization, kept customer lists and other customer service information when they went with Hargadine. In addition, Universal was found to have improperly appropriated trade secret chemical formulas belonging to Grace. The court accordingly restrained the former employees from using the trade secrets they had obtained by improper means and were assessed damages as well.

A factor in deciding whether or not improper means were used by a former employee in obtaining or taking a trade secret involves "appropriation by memory." In *Jet Spray Cooler, Inc.*, v. *Crampton* the Supreme Judicial Court of Massachusetts stated that the "fact that no list or paper was taken does not prevent the former employee from being enjoined if the information which he gained through his employment and retained in his memory is confidential in nature." Thus the court stated the majority view of the courts today regarding trade secrets in general. Another case representing this view is *Sperry Rand Corporation* v. *Rothlein*. Rothlein and the other defendants had been employed with the Sperry Semiconductor Division of Sperry Rand Corporation in the development and manufacture of silicon alloy junction transistors. The record of the case showed that strict security precautions were taken and the defendants signed agreements that they would not divulge secret information either during or after their respective periods of employment.

Rothlein and other defendants became dissatisfied with Sperry Rand and set up a competing company, the National Semiconductor Corporation, for the manufacture of silicon alloy fusion transistors and other devices. The defendants claimed that the drawings used by their new company were constructed not by copying from Sperry Rand drawings, but from memory. The court replied: "It may be and if so, it was a remarkable display of memory, for numerous measurements were in thousandths of an inch. But it does not matter whether a copy of a Sperry drawing came out in a defendant's hand or in his head. His duty of fidelity to his employer remains the same."

This same principle was followed in another case involving a technological trade secret, *A. H. Emery Company* v. *Marcan Products Company*. The Emery Company charged that a former employee, Mills, had, by improper means, taken trade secrets to manufacture and sell a hydraulic load cell used in weighing machines that competed with a cell manufactured and sold by Emery. While Mills was employed by Emery as an engineer he became thoroughly familiar with the design, construction, and manufacturing methods for the cell. Later Mills became a salesman for Emery, but because he was not considered to be sufficiently productive he was discharged. Mills, in collaboration with defendant Marcan Products Corporation, enlisted the aid of another former employee of Emery Company, Northrop, to supply drawings that he made from memory and that he had learned from Emery. The trial court ruled that "it is as much a breach of confidence for an employee to reproduce his employer's drawings from memory as to copy them directly" and concluded "that Northrop violated his obligation to keep confidential the engineering data disclosed by the parts drawings when he reproduced those drawings from memory" and that Mills was in no more defensible a position than if he had taken copies of the drawings from the Emery files. The Second Circuit Court of Appeals, in affirming the trial court, held that the information contained the Emery parts drawings, which Northrop had reproduced from memory for use by the defendants, was entitled to trade secret protection.

The cases are less uniform with regard to customer lists, but the majority view is still that appropriation by memory is just as improper as appropriation by written list. A representative "appropriation by memory" case involving customer lists is *American Republic Insurance Company* v. *Union Fidelity Life Insurance Company*. Lindgren and Anderson had worked for plaintiff American Republic Insurance Company as insurance agents and obtained their customer leads from responses to national advertising campaigns conducted by American. The lists of customers accumulated in this manner were not available to American's competitors. Lindgren and Anderson left American to work for defendant Union Fidelity Life Insurance Company and used the American customer lists there. It was argued on behalf of the defendants that their solicitation of customers was not improper, because the lists were committed to memory and not written. But the Oregon federal district court found that whether the lists were memorized or not would not lead to a different result. The modern trend clearly is to reject any distinction between written and memorized information.

Breach of Fiduciary Duty as Contrasted with Trade Secret Law. At this point it is appropriate to digress slightly from the law of trade secrets in order to pay recognition to another legal principle that bears great similarity to the trade secret principles regarding the employer–employee relationship. To put it succinctly, an employee owes to his former employer not only a duty not to use trade secrets belonging to that former employer improperly, but also a duty not to use other confidential information improperly that may not technically qualify as trade secrets. This may be termed as a fiduciary obligation or duty of loyalty to his ex-employer.

A leading case that illustrates this principle of law is *Duane Jones Co. v. Burke,* decided by the Court of Appeals of New York in 1954. The plaintiff, Duane Jones Company, an advertising agency organized by Duane Jones in 1942, brought an action against ten of its former employees, the Manhattan Soap Co., Inc., and Scheideler, Beck & Werner, Inc. The Manhattan Soap Co., a soap manufacturer of which Burke had been a director and the treasurer, was, until August, 1951, the principal client of the Duane Jones Company. Scheideler, Beck & Werner, Inc., was an advertising agency comprised of the former employees of Duane Jones.

It was these defendants that the Duane Jones Company alleged had entered into a conspiracy to deprive it of its customers as well as its key employees. We shall concern ourselves here mainly with the allegation concerning deprivation of customers, because that is the aspect of the case that bears similarity to trade secrets law, that is, customer lists and customer information.

On June 28, 1951, several of the Duane Jones employees met to discuss plans either to start a new advertising agency or to buy out the interest of Duane Jones, because they were unhappy with his role as president of the company. Defendant Scheideler told those assembled that several of the Duane Jones customers that he serviced approved of such possible moves and suggested that other employees of Duane Jones discuss these possibilities with the customers they serviced. One of the then employees of Duane Jones, Hayes, informed Duane Jones that the employees wanted to buy him out and that "if he did not agree to a sale they would resign en masse within forty-eight hours." According to Jones he said to Hayes: "In other words, you are standing there with a Colt 45, holding it at my forehead, and there is not much I can do except give up?" . . . Hayes replied: "Well, you can call it anything you want, but that is what we are going to do."

Hayes had informed Jones that the customers were "already presold" on the alternative plan. As a result, Jones retired from the agency but the sale was never consummated. Gradually, as the employee defendants resigned or were discharged for cause, the defendants Scheideler, Werner, and Beck set up Scheideler, Beck & Werner, Inc., a competing advertising agency to the Duane Jones Co., which opened for business on Park Avenue on September 10, 1951. Soon after opening, the new advertising agency employed over one half of those formerly employed by Duane Jones. One of its clients was the Manhattan Soap Co., which had been solicited away from Duane Jones by defendant Scheideler before Scheideler had completely terminated his services with Duane Jones. In addition to Manhattan Soap, the former principal client of Duane Jones, upon or shortly after its opening Scheideler, Beck & Werner, Inc., had as advertising clients G. F. Heublein, International Salt, Wesson Oil, C. F. Mueller Company, The Borden Company, Marlin Fire Arms, McIlhenny Corp., Haskins Bros., and Continental Briar Pipe, all of which had been clients of Duane Jones before the formation of Scheideler, Beck & Werner. With the possible exception of the Wesson Oil account, all of these companies had been actively solicited by employees of Duane Jones, both before and after their termination with Duane Jones. According to defendant Scheideler, the Wesson account "walked in off the street" without solicitation. However, Scheideler had serviced Wesson for four years for Duane Jones and had discussed with Wesson executives the possibility of buying out Duane Jones before the June 28th meeting. Scheideler wrote a letter to Duane Jones dated August 24, 1951, one day after the incorporation of Scheideler, Beck & Werner, Inc., informing Jones that they had asked Duane Jones customers and personnel to join a new agency.

The court was of the opinion that these former employees had breached the fiduciary duty that they had owed to Duane Jones, Inc. stating that their conduct fell beneath the standard imposed by the law of agency, which required that these former employees at all times act in a manner consistent with their trust and bound them to act in the utmost good faith and loyalty in the exercise of their duties. The court also cited the principle that such a duty can extend beyond the period of actual employment. The basis for the application of the principle in this case was that the conspiracy began while the employment relationship was still intact. Accordingly, the individual defendants were held liable for benefits secured by them after termination of their employment, because these benefits were derived from opportunities resulting from their relationship of employment with Duane Jones. The case contained no allegations that any trade secret rights had been violated, but, as has been seen, focused on the breach of fiduciary duty that the employees owed to the Duane Jones Co.

Other cases that recite this principle of law are also worthy of mention. One such case is *Tlapek* v. *Chevron Oil Company*, decided by the Eighth Circuit Court of Appeals in 1969. Defendant Tlapek had been employed by Chevron Oil as a geologist. Through the use of confidential information made available to him by Chevron Oil, Tlapek developed a "unique theory" that a large quantity of oil could be found in Columbia County, Arkansas. While still employed with Chevron Oil, Tlapek proposed that his employer embark on his proposed venture. Chevron Oil was interested in Tlapek's theory but decided not to act immediately. Tlapek was disappointed and after informing Chevron Oil that he intended to resign to get further education he was promptly terminated. Tlapek then began to raise the money necessary to take out leases on the land that he thought had oil and subsequently executed and recorded the leases. Chevron Oil brought suit against Tlapek, claiming ownership of the leases that were acquired through Tlapek's use of confidential information in violation of a fiduciary duty to Chevron Oil. Although the court was of the opinion that the information Tlapek had used to arrive at his "unique theory" was trade secret in nature, it answered Tlapek's claim that the information did not contain trade secrets by stating that the information was disclosed in confidence and was therefore protectable. In doing so, the court quoted the Restatement of Torts, Section 757, Comment (b) as follows:

> *Information not a trade secret.* Although given information is not a trade secret, one who receives it in a confidential relation or discovers it by improper means may be under some duty not to disclose or use that information.

Another such case is *Nucor Corporation* v. *Tennessee Forging Steel Service, Inc.*, decided by the Eighth Circuit Court of Appeals four years later in 1973. Plaintiff Nucor Corporation was a manufacturer of steel joists and had several joist-manufacturing plants, one of which was in Grapeland, Texas. Munn, president of Tennessee Forging, a competitor of Nucor, asked White, an employee of Nucor, to draw plans for construction of a steel joist plant to be operated in Hope, Arkansas, and agreed to pay White for his services. White got the construction plans for the Grapeland plant and asked a Nucor engineer to devise plans for a joist plant, using the Grapeland plans as a guide. Two days after the engineer delivered the plans to White, White left employment with Nucor and started his own consulting firm. Tennessee Forging agreed to pay White $2,700 for preparing the plans and to retain White as a consultant at an annual salary of $25,000. The trial court had held that White had not breached an obligation not to disclose the plans because they were not really trade secrets. The appellate court, however, found authority to state that "employees have a high duty not to disclose confidential information received by them as employees to competitors regardless of the fact that the information disclosed might not technically be considered a trade secret."

In a footnote to its opinion the court quoted with approval the following portion of the Restatement (Second) of Agency:

§395. Using or Disclosing Confidential Information.

Unless otherwise agreed, an agent is subject to a duty to the principal not to use or to communicate information confidentially given him by the principal or acquired by him during the course of or on account of his agency or in violation of his duties as agent, in competition with or to the injury of the principal, on his own account or on behalf of another, although such information does not relate to the transaction in which he is then employed, unless the information is a matter of general knowledge.

§396. Using Confidential Information After Termination of Agency.

Unless otherwise agreed, after the termination of the agency, the agent . . . (b) has a duty to the principal not to use or to disclose to third persons, on his own account or on account of others, in competition with the principal or to his injury, trade secrets, written lists of names, or other similar confidential matters given to him only for the principal's use or acquired by the agent in violation of duty. . . .

The court found specifically that Nucor considered the Grapeland plans to be confidential information, because it took measures to preserve their secrecy by not permitting outsiders and competitors to view them. Accordingly, the court found that White had breached his fiduciary duty not to divulge Nucor's architectural plans to Tennessee Forging.

One final area of breach of fiduciary duty is worthy of mention here. This involves the situation where an unfaithful employee engages in an effort to convert surreptitiously his predeparture "eleventh-hour" negotiations with a prospective customer to his own benefit or that of a new employer. Courts hold that such information is confidential although not technically a trade secret in nature. Even absent a covenant not to compete, courts hold that it is a breach of a common law fiduciary duty for an employee who is in the process of negotiating for his employer to exploit his status in the negotiations by secretly transferring business opportunities engendered by these negotiations to a new employer or to his own benefit as an individual.

Right to Earn a Living. Whether or not an ex-employee has taken a trade secret of his employer by improper means will sometimes depend upon how the ex-employee's general right to earn a living is reconciled with the former employer's right to restrain his former employee from utilizing or divulging the former employer's technology. Earlier in this chapter this same issue was discussed within the area "Source of the Trade Secret." One of the cases discussed there, *Wexler* v. *Greenberg,* is a leading case on the principle of the ex-employee's right to earn a living. Greenberg, it will be recalled, left his employer, Buckingham, where he had been chief chemist, to work in a similar capacity with Brite Products Co., Inc., where, the Pennsylvania Supreme Court found, Greenberg was able to use the "trade secrets" that he had developed from analysis of products of competitors of Buckingham. The court observed that in the absence of a restrictive covenant entered into between employer and employee and where no trade secret is involved, an employee's skills, abilities, and subjective knowledge that he acquires through the experience of employment remain the property of the employee after termination of the employment relationship and he has a perfect right to take further advantage of these powers.

While recognizing the need for some postemployment restraints on the employee to protect the "valuable developments or improvements" that the former employer has invested in as well as the need for the modern businessman to divulge to certain appropriate personnel confidential information relating to his business, the court also paid particular heed to the fact that

> any form of post-employment restraint reduces the economic mobility of employees and limits their personal freedom to pursue a preferred course of livelihood. The employee's bargaining position is weakened because he is potentially shackled by the acquisition of alleged trade secrets; and thus, paradoxically, he is restrained, because of his increased expertise, from advancing further in the industry in which he is most productive.

The Pennsylvania Supreme Court went on to state its conviction that in the balancing of each of these two factors the weight of authority of both English and American decisions tends to favor the interest of the employee's right to earn a living.

A case that offers an interesting comparison to *Wexler v. Greenberg* is *E. I. duPont de Nemours & Co.* v. *American Potash & Chemical Corporation*, decided by a Delaware court in 1964. Plaintiff duPont Company brought the suit against American Potash and Chemical Corporation and Hirsch, a former employee of duPont who had left to work for Potash, to prohibit Hirsch from disclosing its alleged trade secrets and confidential information to Potash and further to preclude Hirsch from working for Potash in connection with the operation and development of a chloride process or in connection with the manufacture of TiO_2 (titanium dioxide) pigments by a chloride process. As in *Wexler*, no covenant not to compete was present, although when Hirsch went with duPont he entered into a contract with his employer that he would not "use or disclose any of [duPont's] trade secrets without its prior written consent."

When Hirsch joined duPont, it was in the process of learning how to manufacture TiO_2 pigments by a chloride process. This was a long, involved, and expensive effort on the part of duPont. From 1950 to 1955 and from 1960 to 1961 Hirsch played an important role in duPont's research and development of this process. Hirsch became unhappy with his work at duPont; and, Potash, interested in developing the chloride process for the manufacture of TiO_2, hired Hirsch for a management position one day after he had resigned from duPont. Prior to hiring Hirsch, Potash had attempted to purchase a license from duPont to grant it patent and know-how rights regarding the manufacture of TiO_2, but when duPont refused to license any of its secret know-how, Potash discontinued licensing negotiations with no agreement consummated.

Hirsch signed an agreement with Potash that he would not divulge "any information that he knows to be proprietary or confidential information, data, development or trade secret of a third party without the prior written consent of said third party." But, nevertheless, duPont argued that if Hirsch were to be placed in a job with Potash that related to Potash's efforts to develop the chloride process for manufacturing TiO_2, he would disclose duPont's trade secrets.

duPont was successful in securing a restraining order to prevent Hirsch from disclosing its trade secrets relating to the manufacture of TiO_2 by its chloride process. The question came to the court on Hirsch and Potash's motion for summary judgment, meaning that the court had to decide whether there was any issue of fact to be decided; if so, the decision would have to await a trial.

Just as the Brite Products Co. had no expertise in manufacturing chemicals prior to hiring Greenberg, Potash lacked the prior know-how for manufacturing TiO_2 by a chloride process. duPont, in fact, was the only successful commercial manufacturer of TiO_2 by a chloride process. This presents a factual contrast with the *Wexler* case in that other competitors of the Buckingham Wax Company had the same products and in fact it was through the analysis of their products that Greenberg was able to arrive at the chemical formulas used to make Buckingham's products. By comparison, it would seem that duPont had more to lose by disclosure of its trade secret know-how to Potash than Buckingham Wax had to lose by disclosure of its chemical formulas to Brite Products, because Buckingham already had competitors. The position of duPont with regard to its know-how in the manufacture of TiO_2 by its chloride process was comparable to the leadership that B. F. Goodrich enjoyed in the space suit industry in *B. F. Goodrich Co.* v. *Wohlgemuth*.

In *Wohlgemuth* the former employee was restrained permanently and in *duPont*, a preliminary injunction was granted to restrain the former employee and Potash's motion for summary judgment was denied, which meant that the court's final decision would have to await trial. In addressing itself to the principle of the right to earn a living, the court in *duPont* stated that:

> Among the substantial and conflicting policies at play in this situation are the protection of employers' rights in their trade secrets on the one hand, versus the right of the individual to . . . pursue his calling without undue hindrance from a prior employer on the other. . . . Reasonable legal protection tends to encourage, as here, substantial expenditures to find or improve ways and means of accomplishing commercial and industrial goals. . . . However it is hard to ask a man to work in a trade secret area and thereby circumscribe his possible future liberty of action and the use of the knowledge and skills which are inextricably interwoven with his knowledge of the trade secrets.

The way in which a court is swayed by these competing principles will often influence the finding by a court as to whether or not improper means are used in the disclosure or use of a trade secret, or whether there is a secret in the first place.

Credit Investigations

At least one case, *Copley* v. *Northwestern Mutual Life Company,* decided by a U.S. federal district court in 1968, involves a credit investigation that is interesting to note because of the absence of any pre-existing fiduciary relationship between the parties. The defendant Retail Credit Company made the investigation on behalf of defendant Northwestern Mutual of plaintiff C&B Blueprint Company of which plaintiff Copley was a partner. Before disclosing any information to Retail Credit, Copley exacted from Retail Credit its assurance that the "information would not be released to any persons other than the insurance company." Copley alleged that shortly after disclosing the information, Retail Credit informed plaintiffs' competitors of the information in the face of its agreement not to do so. The parties devoted "considerable space" in their briefs as to whether or not a confidential relationship existed between Copley and the Retail Credit Company at the time the disclosures occurred. The court found that

> This is beside the point, for to be actionable, it is only necessary that the disclosure constitute a breach of the confidence reposed in the one to whom the secret was originally transmitted. Thus, the important factor is a *communication in confidence* rather than a *confidential relationship* such as between agent and principal or attorney and client.

With this principle of law in mind, the court was able to hold that Copley stated a claim for which relief could be granted.

Manufacturer–Supplier

Because supplier relationships are sometimes afforded trade secret protection, whether they involve a manufacturer and his independent contractor or supplier, it will be useful to examine cases in the area to determine in what instances improper means are found to have been employed in the appropriation of trade secrets.

Where an independent contractor is hired by a manufacturer, it is generally held that disclosures of trade secret information by the manufacturer to the independent contractor are confidential in nature. This principle of law is well illustrated in *Kamin* v. *Kuhnau,* decided by the Supreme Court of Oregon in 1962. Plaintiff Kamin had developed a garbage truck that compressed the garbage inside through the use of a hydraulically operated plow. Kamin hired defendant Kuhnau to build these trucks for him. After Kuhnau had built about ten trucks for Kamin, they had a disagreement over the amount Kuhnau was to receive from Kamin for building the trucks; as a result, their relationship was terminated, although Kamin alleged that the relationship was terminated because Kuhnau wanted to enter into competition with Kamin. The first question to be decided by the court was "whether the disclosure to . . . Kuhnau of plaintiff's design for a garbage packer unit was made under such circumstances as to raise an implication of a promise by Kuhnau not to appropriate the design to his own use." The court stated that no such promise could be implied if the compressor garbage truck was in common use in the local market but "[i]t was established that garbage truck bodies of the type made by plaintiff had not been on the local market." The court found that Kamin's design gave him a commercial advantage over his competitors and stated that "[t]his advantage constitutes value, and the disclosure of the information which creates the advantage may be sufficient to raise the implied agreement not to appropriate it."

As to Kuhnau's argument that Kamin's truck design was disclosed by advertising or could otherwise be ascertained by reverse engineering, the court explained that the "real question is not whether the disclosee could have obtained the disclosed information elsewhere, but rather whether in fact he *did* so obtain it."

The court found that there was an implied agreement between Kamin and his independent contractor, Kuhnau, that Kuhnau would not appropriate Kamin's design. The court took note of the fact that Kamin paid Kuhnau for help in developing Kamin's idea. The parties could not have contemplated that Kuhnau would be free to exploit what had been perfected "through painstaking and expensive experimentation." Accordingly, the court held "that defendant Kuhnau violated his duty to plaintiff by appropriating the information derived through their business relationship."

One should not automatically assume that trade secret protection will always be granted where the independent contractor relationship is present, for it is still necessary that all the requirements of a trade secret be met. Such is the import of *Boucher* v. *Wissman,* decided by the Court of Civil Appeals of Texas in 1947. Plaintiff Wissman had, after some experimentation, developed a fishing pole that was "novel in its conception and utility, so that it can be used as a fly rod, casting rod or fishing pole, and, when dissembled, serves as a container, and, with rubber tips placed on each end, converts the assemblage into a walking stick."

Wissman employed defendant Boucher and another doing business as the Southwest Tool & Die Company to manufacture the fishing pole after other firms had made earlier models of the pole. However, as Wissman was not satisfied with the way in which Southwest Tool & Die constructed the pole that company was advised that its services would no longer be needed. Wissman brought suit against Boucher and others to stop them from making the fishing pole in competition with him. The court noted that the defendants had not agreed to keep secret any matters relating to the pole and had not agreed not to manufacture it in competition with Wissman. More importantly, the court considered the pole to be a "mere mechanical difference in the use of a product" and observed that

> [t]he assemblage of the various parts composing the fishing pole . . . is susceptible to be copied and manufactured by any one possessing mechanical ability of the most simple nature. . . . Matters which are completely disclosed by the inventor and by the articles themselves, as here, are not secrets after the articles have been put on the market to be reviewed by all people.

The court was simply stating that secrecy was not shown and consequently Boucher did not employ improper means in the acquisition of what had been alleged to be a trade secret embodied in the fishing pole device.

With regard to the relationship between supplier and purchaser, it must be remembered that the supplier risks disclosure and loss of a trade secret embodied in a product when he markets that product. A case in point is *Northrup* v. *Reish,* decided by the Seventh Circuit Court of Appeals in 1953. In 1945 plaintiff Northrup began to develop an idea, an oven liner, to take care of boil-overs in cooking ovens and to catch food drippings in broilers of cooking stoves. In 1946 he took his idea to the Consumer Products Corporation for assistance in further developing the idea and for possible financing and manufacturing. At Consumer Products Northrup was interviewed by defendant Reish, who, according to Northrup, gave assurances that Northrup's idea would not be improperly disclosed. Northrup left with Reish some samples of the oven liner that were embossed in a pebbled form so as to stiffen the liner. Both parties agreed, however, that the oven liner was not yet in marketable form. Soon thereafter, Reish became ill and had no further contact with Northrup until 1947. Meanwhile, Northrup began marketing his oven liner, which carried a rectangular type of embossing, under the trademark "Oven Maid." Shortly after Reish resigned as president of the Consumer Products Corporation that company purchased foil from Northrup to market as oven liners.

When Reish next came in contact with Northrup, Reish, having formed Reish Products, Inc., purchased forty-eight dozen of Northrup's oven liners. Later, Reish approached Northrup with a request for Northrup to supply Reish with oven liners, which Reish would then market under his own trade name and trademark. After Northrup refused Reish's request, Reish contracted with the Nu Products Company to make oven liners for Reish Products, Inc. Reish furnished Nu Products with a sample of Northrup's oven liner, which he had purchased from Northrup, whereupon Nu Products built a machine for Reish to make oven liners, which Reish then sold under his trademark "Ovnap" in a distinctive package that was not confusingly similar to the package in which Northrup sold his "Oven Maid" oven liner. In finding that Northrup did not have any trade secret rights in the oven liner that he could assert against Reish, the court gave the following explanation of why Northrup lost any trade secret he might have had when he began selling the "Oven Maid":

> Packages of the oven liners, as marketed by [Northrup], described their purpose and illustrated the manner of their use by both pictures and words. The containers in which [Northrup's] oven liners were sold told the public everything that [Northrup] had told Reish about the oven liners. After the liners had been so marketed [Northrup] no longer had any secret about their composition, their style of embossment, their size, their shape, the method of their use, nor their disposal after they were too soiled for further use.

The court emphasized that it was only after Northrup had marketed his oven liner, and after asking Northrup to supply him with his oven liners, that Reish entered into competition with Northrup. The court took this as evidence that Reish's prior dealings with Northrup were not a "part of a malicious scheme to steal [Northrup's] idea."

A supplier's trade secrets were found to have been used by improper means in *Forest Laboratories, Inc.* v. *Pillsbury Company,* decided by the Seventh Circuit Court of Appeals in 1971. Forest Laboratories brought the action against Pillsbury for misuse of trade secrets belonging to it that related to the packaging of effervescent sweetener tablets which lengthened their shelf life. The evidence showed that Forest Laboratories communicated to the Tidy House Corporation its secret method of packaging the tablets that it then supplied to Tidy House. Later, Pillsbury purchased the assets of the Tidy House Corporation, which then became known as the Tidy House division of Pillsbury. Forest Laboratories continued to supply the tablets to Pillsbury until Pillsbury commenced doing business with Formulation, Inc., as its new supplier. It was after this event that Forest Laboratories brought the action for misappropriation of its trade secret packaging know-how by Pillsbury.

Dealing first with the requirement that there be an actual trade secret, although some of the packaging steps were found to be generally known in the trade, four of the steps were found to be trade secrets. Of these four, one step belonged to Forest Laboratories. It was described as follows: "Before packaging, the tablets are to be tempered in a room having 40% or less relative humidity for a period of between 24 to 48 hours."

The improper use by Pillsbury had occurred one year prior to the issuance of a patent covering this process. The court ruled that after issuance of the patent, Pillsbury could not be held liable because the key "element of secrecy evaporated with the issuance of the patent."

On the question of whether or not there was a confidential relationship between Forest Laboratories and Pillsbury, Pillsbury contended that no such confidential relationship existed, because the information for which trade secret protection was sought was communicated to the Tidy House Corporation prior to its acquisition by Pillsbury. The Seventh Circuit did not uphold the trial court's conclusion that Pillsbury implicitly assumed the liabilities of Tidy House; nevertheless, it found that a confidential relationship existed, because Pillsbury was given actual notice of the confidentiality of the trade secret information that Forest had given to Tidy House. Because the evidence did not show that Pillsbury had paid anything specifically for the trade secret belonging to Forest, Pillsbury was found to be liable for damages to Forest. In finding such liability, the court quoted with approval, §758(b) of the Restatement of Torts as follows:

> One who learns another's trade secret from a third person without notice that it is secret and that the third person's disclosure is a breach of his duty to the other, or who learns the secret through a mistake without notice of the secrecy and the mistake. . . .
>
> (b) is liable to the other for a disclosure or use of the secret after the receipt of such notice unless prior thereto he has in good faith paid value for the secret or has so changed his position that to subject him to liability would be inequitable.

Industrial Espionage

What is industrial espionage? It may be briefly defined as the practice of spying on a company by deception or other improper means in order to gain knowledge of that company's secrets. It is not a term of special legal significance but a popularized expression of trade secret misappropriation by outsiders. It may be set off from the kind of improper means of taking trade secrets already seen in this chapter in that it involves more premeditated conduct and is therefore perhaps more pernicious.

That industrial espionage may involve theft as well as spying is illustrated by an industrial espionage plot against the IBM Corporation that was first reported in 1973. The case allegedly involved the unlawful smuggling of plans for two of IBM's major information storage devices. Reportedly, the smugglers then sold the plans to IBM's competitors. The damages to IBM through loss of sales for these two systems were estimated by one source to be as high as $460 million.

It isn't at all difficult to perceive that smuggling away plans is "improper means." However, a much more expansive concept of what may constitute improper means in an industrial espionage setting was rendered by the Fifth Circuit Court of Appeals in 1970 in the highly celebrated and fascinating case of *E. I. duPont de Nemours & Company* v. *Christopher,* which was discussed earlier in this chapter (p. 127). The Christophers, it will be recalled, were photographers who were hired by an unknown person to take aerial photographs of an unfinished duPont plant in order to learn duPont's secret process for producing methanol. The Christophers argued "that they committed no 'actionable wrong' . . . because they conducted all of their activities in public airspace, violated no government aviation standard, did not breach any confidential relation, and did not engage in any fraudulent or illegal conduct." As reasonable and cogent as the Christopher's argument appeared to be, the Fifth Circuit emphatically disagreed. In applying Texas substantive law, the court found particularly applicable §757 of the Restatement of Torts, which it quoted as follows:

> One who discloses or uses another's trade secret, without a privilege to do so, is liable to the other if
>
> (a) he discovered the secret by improper means, or
>
> (b) his disclosure or use constitutes a breach of confidence reposed in him by the other in disclosing the secret to him. . . .

The court was somehow able to find that duPont had a cause of action against the Christophers by reading very broadly the rule of subsection (a) of the Restatement. The court specifically found that a breach of confidence was not a necessary ingredient to a cause of action for obtaining another's trade secret by improper means. The court stated that "[t]o obtain knowledge of a process without spending the time and money to discover it independently is *improper* unless the holder voluntarily discloses it or fails to take reasonable precautions to ensure its secrecy."

The court held that duPont had not failed to take such reasonable precautions. Aspects of the secret process were visible from the air because the roof to the plant had not yet been completed. The court stated that "we need not require the discoverer of a trade secret to guard against the unanticipated, the undetectable, or the unpreventable methods of espionage now available." The court was clear to point out, however, that it recognized the need for a competitor to "shop his competition for pricing and examine his products for quality, components, and methods of manufacture." Similarly, the court qualified its decision by stating that it did "not mean to imply . . . that everything not in plain view is within the protected vale, nor that all information obtained through every extra optical extension is forbidden."

The *Christopher* case represents a judicial expansion against industrial espionage. Electronic eavesdropping could be more easily proscribed under the rule in *Christopher,* because many forms of electronic surveillance such as wiretapping are already illegal. Notwithstanding this, corporate rooms in which trade secret information is discussed are sometimes periodically "debugged"; telephones are sometimes frequently checked for wiretapping; corporate executives are cautioned against phone conversations discussing trade secret information.

State statutes have provided little protection against highly sophisticated forms of industrial espionage, because they usually concern only tangible property. Legislative expansion that provides more liberal protection against industrial espionage has occurred in some states. For example, a New Jersey statute provides for protection against the copying or theft of a commercial *intangible.* It reads in part that:

> Any person who, with intent to deprive or withhold from the owner thereof the control of a trade secret, or with an intent to appropriate a trade secret to his own use or to the use of another,
>
> (a) steals or embezzles an article representing a trade secret, or,
>
> (b) without authority makes or causes to be made a copy of an article representing a trade secret,
>
> Is guilty of a misdemeanor, if the value of the article stolen, embezzled or copied, including the value of the trade secret represented thereby, is less than $200.00, and of a high misdemeanor if such value is $200.00 or more.

It is interesting to note that some loopholes exist even in the modern New Jersey statute. It would not be a violation of the statute to make an unauthorized reading of a secret written report, whereas photographing that same report would be a violation. Although a recording of an unauthorized reading of a secret document would come within the statute, a recording of a discussion containing the same secrets would fall outside the statute. The reason is that a discussion or conversation is not an "article" under the statute.

Industrial espionage does not necessarily involve theft or sophisticated forms of surveillance. Simple misrepresentation may be the means by which a competitor seeks to learn the secrets of a businessman. In *Franke* v. *Wiltschek,* decided by the Second Circuit Court of Appeals in 1953, defendant Wiltschek and his partner, defendant Blatt, represented to plaintiffs that they wanted to market their product, a compressed perfumed face cloth that opened up to its natural size when immersed in water. At first, plaintiffs were not interested but Wiltschek persevered and finally gained the interest of plaintiffs. In order to represent themselves as a competent sales agency, Wiltschek and Blatt told plaintiffs they had a sales force of thirteen men, when in truth they had none. As negotiations were about to be consummated, at the request of Wiltschek and Blatt, they were shown the process by which the face cloths were made. The parties then reached an agreement whereby the plaintiffs supplied defendants with sample products, signs, and displays so that Wiltschek and Blatt could embark on a trial sales period. Soon thereafter, Wiltschek and Blatt terminated their agreement under the pretext that the face cloth was not saleable. The court was of the opinion that Wiltschek and Blatt had probably never intended to sell the product for plaintiffs. Instead, it was likely that the defendants had made such a representation in order to learn the trade secrets of the plaintiffs. This is evidenced by the fact that a few months after the agreement was terminated a corporation of which Wiltschek and Blatt were directors and vice presidents began putting out a face cloth similar to that of plaintiffs and at a lower price.

The court found that defendants Wiltschek and Blatt had violated trade secrets rights of plaintiff by breaching the confidential relationship that they had created with plaintiff when they misrepresented themselves as potential salesmen. That the defendants could have learned the secrets from an expired patent or by analysis of the product was no defense. When the defendants gained their knowledge by way of the confidential relationship that they had created, they "incurred a duty not to use it to plaintiffs' detriment. This duty they . . . breached."

A similar case of industrial espionage, *Air Waukies, Inc.* v. *Pincus,* was decided by a New York court in 1950. Plaintiff Air Waukies, Inc., was the successor in interest to Mary Frances Lee, who had originated and developed a combined arch and sole footpad. Defendants Oxman and Pincus represented to Mrs. Lee that they were interested in becoming a distributor for her arch and sole footpad. During the negotiations, Oxman and Pincus gained knowledge of Air Waukies, Inc.'s sources of supply and also obtained a sample of the product, which they used as models "for imitative purposes." The court was convinced that Oxman and Pincus had "ulterior motives" in entering into the negotiations. This was evidenced when

> the defendant complained about the contract solely as an expedient to make possible the breakdown of negotiations and thus enable the defendant to go forward on its own in the manufacture of these footpads and on the basis of the knowledge and information and samples of footpads illegally obtained from the plaintiff.

As in *Franke* v. *Wiltschek,* the court found that Oxman and Pincus had acquired Air Waukies, Inc.'s trade secrets by improper means because their actions amounted to a breach of trust.

Dress design has been the subject of espionage by competitors. Before looking at some cases on this point, however, it should be noted that copyright protection is not available for dress design, although it is possible to obtain a design patent for protection of a dress design. In *Montegut* v. *Hickson, Inc.,* decided by a New York court in 1917, where plaintiff Montegut had made it a practice to sell her dresses only to bona fide customers for their personal use, defendant Hickson, Inc., hired a person to impersonate "herself as a private customer, buying the gowns to wear herself, and thus misled and deceived the plaintiffs into turning over their models to" Hickson, Inc. Although Hickson, Inc., had a "legal right to copy and to sell as its own creations the exclusive models designed by the plaintiffs," it could do so only if fair and proper means were used. The court held Hickson's means of obtaining the dress designs of Montegut to be fraudulent and deceptive.

Another case of dress design espionage is *Dior* v. *Milton,* decided by the New York courts in 1956. Christian Dior exhibited his new dress designs in private showings in Paris, France, all of those attending having promised not to disclose or copy any of the designs and styles. However, some of those attending the showing concealed the fact that they were working for defendant Milton, furtively copied the designs and models of Dior, and conveyed them to Milton and "co-conspirators unauthorized to receive and use them in the United States and elsewhere." The court found that Milton had violated the law of unfair competition but did not base this finding of liability on trade secrets law. Instead, the court rested its decision on the ground that the law of unfair competition provided the dress designers with a remedy for "commercial immorality."

In *Eastern Extracting Co.* v. *Greater New York Extracting Co.*, decided by a New York court in 1908, defendant Biderman, who had organized defendant Greater New York Extracting Co., misrepresented himself as a laborer to plaintiff Eastern Extracting Co. in order to gain employment there. His purpose in doing so was to observe Eastern Extracting Co.'s secret process for extracting alcohol from barrels. Biderman accomplished his mission in two days and never bothered to return for his wages. The court found that Biderman had taken the Eastern Extracting Co.'s trade secret by improper means, noting particularly the element of dishonesty involved. As the court put it: "Fair competition is always encouraged; but a man cannot, through deceit and by means of an appeal for employment as a laborer and assistance to earn his bread, enter the household of his benefactor and steal his belongings."

Similar espionage was involved in *Attorney General* v. *National Cash Register Co.*, decided by the Supreme Court of Michigan in 1914. Although the action was brought under the Michigan antitrust laws rather than trade secret law, the court found defendant National Cash Register's activities of placing its own employees in the offices of competitors to learn their secrets as well as hiring spies for the same purpose to be among those activities that justified the imposition of a fine against National Cash Register.

Sophisticated executives and negotiators are aware of the ingenuity of competitors, potential suppliers, licensees, and customers (but surely not all of them!) to gain confidential information, be it in the form of technology, cost data, or bargaining information. The foreign adversary in heavy negotiations who "doesn't speak English"; the "taxi driver" with a Ph.D. in some obscure technology discussed by the passengers moments before in the corporate headquarters. The list is long; the list of precautions is equally long. The full extent of industrial espionage and related activities is probably much greater than reflected by the number of cases brought to adjudication.

NEGOTIATIONS AND UNSOLICITED IDEA DISCLOSURES

Every day of every year individuals with "bright ideas" write to a General Motors Corporation or to an Ace Storm Door Company, with the hopes of selling the "bright idea" at a price sufficient to ensure comfortable retirement on the southern coast of France. Broadly speaking, what usually happens is a disappointment to the untutored individual, for the corporations routinely send back form letters and standard contracts that are not very attractive to pursue. Why is this? Certainly some percentage of these ideas, however small, has at least some merit and feasibility. Why are corporations so cautious? This seeming anomaly has its roots in the development of a body of law broadly characterized as unsolicited ideas.

Both corporations and idea submitters are concerned with protecting themselves from losses flowing from any such disclosures. Corporations wish carefully to avoid antagonizing the public by discouraging the submission of new and creative ideas. However, from a practical standpoint, only a very small percentage of the ideas that a corporation typically receives for evaluation are ever found to be of any significant value. But the occasional useful idea appears to justify the great expense incurred in maintaining elaborate systems of controls to avoid liability resulting from unsolicited disclosures.

The context in which disputes arise in this area usually involves a claim by an idea submitter for compensation or damages due him as a result of the alleged use of his idea by the corporation. These claims frequently involve the law of contracts, equity, and trade secrets. The types of ideas submitted and the manner of their disclosure are as varied as are the personalities of the submitters. Motion picture companies, radio and television networks, and diverse publishing companies are by their very nature particularly prone to become parties to this type of litigation, because they are constantly involved in the traffic of unsolicited ideas. Accordingly, their actions serve as the basis for a considerable amount of the case law on the subject of liability for the unsolicited disclosure of ideas.

Rights in Ideas

The scope of legal protection afforded to an idea is dependent upon the nature of the idea and its value both to its author and to the corporation to which it is submitted. It also depends on the circumstances surrounding the disclosure. In determining whether improper means have been used by the idea recipient, the courts are influenced by the existence or degree of unfairness that inheres in the situation.

The patent and copyright laws provide for an absolute right to exclude others in the area of inventions and copying writings that qualify under the provisions of those respective statutes. As we have seen in the preceding chapter, an idea in and of itself is not patentable, however new and useful or even revolutionary and beneficial to humanity it may be. Moreover, any right to exclusive use of an idea is lost by its unrestricted disclosure. To quote Mr. Justice Brandeis, the "general rule of law is, that the noblest of human productions—knowledge, truths ascertained, conceptions and ideas—become after voluntary communication to others, free as the air to common use."

Copyright law does not afford any greater protection to unembodied ideas than do the patent laws. Only the written expression of those ideas can be protected from copying under the copyright law. The protection does not prohibit the mere use of the expressed ideas. Thus the copyright law is a highly limited area for protection of ideas. Alternatively stated, because there is a strong public policy against monopolies on ideas, only the form, manner, and sequence of the expression of ideas are secured to the author. Once copyright attaches, an action for infringement will lie to protect against substantial copying of the copyrighted work or writing.

Ideas may not be protected by statutory copyright, and similarly there is authority for the proposition that the common law protects only the author's or inventor's rights in the written expression of his ideas as soon as they are committed to paper or some other concrete form. Once reduced to tangible form, he may treat his ideas as any other property that he owns. He may preclude others from first using the written expression of his ideas and his ability to so restrict use ends only upon his own first publication, dedication, and voluntary disclosure of his work to the public. To the extent that the author does not publish or otherwise dedicate his ideas to the public the written expression of these ideas will be protected by common law copyright.

Two California cases in which the ultimate basis for recovery was contract rather than copyright take the position that, in accordance with state statute, only the written expression of ideas rather than ideas alone are protectable. The Supreme Court of California, in the case of *Weitzenkorn* v. *Lesser*, an action for the misappropriation by a motion picture company of plaintiff's literary composition entitled "Tarzan in the Land of Eternal Youth," allowed recovery for defendant's copying of the submitted script. The court implied that if plaintiff had merely submitted an idea for a motion picture sequence, her submission would not have been protected. The later California case of *Desny* v. *Wilder*, involved the submission of an idea and synopsis for a motion picture based on the life story of Floyd Collins, a local figure who had died following a two-week entrapment in an underground cave. Paramount Pictures, defendant's employer, produced and released a motion picture the theme of which bore a striking similarity to plaintiff's submitted idea and synopsis. The court cited the *Weitzenkorn* case for the proposition that the plaintiff must show that his story or synopsis is a literary composition rather than the mere restatement of an idea. However, the protection of ideas based on a property theory has been allowed in the areas of advertising slogans and formats for radio and television shows.

It is imperative that some measure of protection be afforded to the creative innovator in order to encourage and perpetuate a free flow of creative business and literary and scientific ideas. In the absence of patent or copyright protection, a number of alternate theories of recovery are available to the idea submitter in his effort to prevent the wrongful appropriation of his ideas by a recipient. Each of these theories will be considered in a factual context assuming the submission of an idea, be it artistic or technical, to a corporation or other form of business organization and a subsequent claim by the submitter for damages arising out of the allegedly unlawful use of the idea. As a prelude to the examination of the individual basis of recovery, there are two elements that generally must be shown in varying degrees depending upon the recovery theory, in order to succeed. They are concreteness and novelty.

Concreteness

In order for an idea to be protected it must be "concrete." Each of the theories to be discussed requires a showing of some degree of concreteness. The case law avoids precisely defining the term. It is clear, however, that no recovery may be had for the appropriation of an abstract idea not reduced to a concrete form. One case has held that an idea is concrete only when it can be immediately used without any further embellishment. In *Plus Promotions, Inc.* v. *RCA Manufacturing Company,* the court refused to grant relief to plaintiff for his disclosure of an idea that would increase the sale of musical records manufactured by defendant. Plus Promotions, Inc., orally suggested to RCA that it induce famous artists to make recordings and that it pay them for the "reasonable value of their services" rather than on a royalty basis. The records would be sold under the names of the artists at a low price that could be afforded by persons of modest means. Newspapers rather than dealers would be responsible for the sale and distribution of the records. The court intimated that because defendant would be required to reduce the whole idea to a detailed marketing plan, plaintiff's idea did not possess the requisite concreteness necessary in order to permit recovery.

The more pragmatic approach recognizes ideas as being concrete when they have been developed to the point that, with the aid of the originator, they are capable of being implemented within a short period of time. *Jones* v. *Ulrich,* an action for an injunction and an accounting for the alleged misappropriation by defendant Ulrich of plaintiff Jones' invention, held that an idea is sufficiently concrete when it has been developed to the point where, under Jones' direction and with Ulrich's aid, the idea could be reduced to usable form within twenty-four hours. Another court said that writing was essential to a showing of concreteness. Still other courts have decided that an idea may be sufficiently concrete even though not embodied in written form. Writing may be some evidence of concreteness but it is certainly not conclusive.

The heart of the concept of concreteness lies in the requirement that an idea be developed to such a degree as to afford its author some form of property right. The test of concreteness is at best vague and uncertain. Some courts require that elaborate detail be proved before concreteness will be found. In *Booth* v. *Stutz Motor Car Co.*, decided by the Seventh Circuit Court of Appeals in 1932, the submission of a design for a new automobile was accompanied by blueprints, drawings, sketches, and diagrams. The court found the idea sufficiently concrete to allow recovery for its appropriation.

Despite the difficulty in arriving at precisely what is meant by the term *concrete*, it is clear that there is an inverse relationship between the amount of concreteness and novelty necessary to sustain an action. Where an idea is clothed with a high degree of novelty, it generally will be afforded protection in its more abstract form. Conversely, where an idea is not very ingenious, a higher degree of concreteness is usually required before it will be protected.

Novelty

The next prerequisite to a recovery for the appropriation of an idea by another is a showing of novelty. Take, for example, the situation in *Masline* v. *New York, N.H. & H.R.R.*, where plaintiff Masline offered to sell the defendant railroad company valuable information that allegedly would provide a handsome increase in its annual profits. An agreement was reached and plaintiff disclosed his plan that defendant should sell advertising space in its railway stations, depots, rights of way, on its fences, and in its cars. Defendant did sell such space and refused to compensate Masline as provided in their agreement. The court refused to honor Masline's claim on the grounds that the idea was neither original nor novel. The court took "judicial notice that the idea of selling advertising space is in the common knowledge and use of the people. . . . [W]all space, natural or artificial, has been used for advertising purposes at least from before the destruction of Pompeii to the present time."

Another New York case, *Soule* v. *Bon Ami Co.*, involved the disclosure of an idea to a corporation for the purpose of increasing its profits. The idea was that the company should raise its prices and thereby increase its profit margin. It is obvious that the implementation of this idea would and did increase profits; it is also obvious to businessmen that profits will increase if prices are raised. This idea was neither novel nor original and, therefore, no recovery was allowed.

The degree of novelty required to sustain a cause of action will vary depending upon the theory of recovery. For example, in an action based on an express contract, the courts might very well require a minimal showing of novelty because it is reasonable to assume that the parties might intentionally contract for the disclosure of a nonnovel idea. When, however, recovery is sought on an "implied contract theory," to be discussed shortly, the traditional view is that novelty must be shown. In opposition, California decisions have held that novelty should not be required in actions for recovery in implied contract. In *Donahue* v. *Ziv Television Programs, Inc.*, plaintiff Donahue submitted the written format for a television series, together with twelve story outlines, one screenplay, and a proposed budget to defendant television company. Ziv Television produced a television program entitled "Sea Hunt" which allegedly used Donahue's story outlines without compensating him for their use. The court held that an idea need not be novel to be the subject matter of a contract because it may be valuable to the person to whom it is disclosed simply because the disclosure takes place at a certain time. Accordingly, Donahue won. In the area of confidential relationship disclosures, the courts have been less insistent on a showing of novelty. As with the case of express contracts, this tolerance grows out of a respect for the agreements, whether express or by virtue of a special relationship, by which both parties have chosen to be bound.

Bases for Recovery

Having concluded that the idea is at least nominally both concrete and novel, the submitter will proceed to disclose or try to disclose his idea to a corporation with the expectation of compensation for its use. Should the corporation make use of the idea and then refuse to compensate its author, it may be held liable on one of a number of grounds: express contract, implied contract, quasi contract, or confidential relationship.

Express Contract. The disclosure of an idea to a corporation may be protected by an express contract between the parties, the terms of which normally call for the compensation of the submitter at an agreed amount should the corporation ultimately make use of the idea. The act of contracting, with its attendant meeting of the minds, is thought to eliminate the need for such protective requirements as novelty. For example, in a 1946 New York case, plaintiff High and defendant Trade Union Courier Publishing Co. orally agreed that if High would disclose information that would enable defendant to secure an exemption from paying telephone excise taxes and acquire a refund of taxes already paid, Trade Union Courier would pay him 35 per cent of all refunds and future savings. High then disclosed the existence of an Internal Revenue Code provision exempting the operation of a newspaper or public press from payment of taxes upon telephone service. Trade Union Courier refused to pay the agreed-upon compensation and an action was brought against it, one count of which was for breach of contract. The corporation claimed that because the matter disclosed was a public statute, it was not novel and no compensation to High would result. The court held that "an idea, if valuable, may be the subject of contract. While the idea disclosed may be common or even open to public knowledge, yet such disclosure if protected by contract, is sufficient consideration for the promise to pay." Hence the requirement of novelty was discarded here in favor of the terms of an agreed-upon contract.

An express contract may fail for lack of consideration should it be found that the idea is so common that it is universally known. This type of idea differs markedly from the one described in the preceding case, because an Internal Revenue provision was considered somewhat obscure and much less than common knowledge. Courts have refused to find contracts where the ideas submitted were not new and valuable on the theory of lack of consideration. In *Soule* v. *Bon Ami Co.*, the court refused to find consideration to support a contract where plaintiff had represented himself as possessing "valuable information" when, in fact, his information (to raise prices and thereby increase profits) turned out to be old and of little value. In *Masline* v. *New York, N.H. & H.R.R.*, the court stated that "[w]hen information is proferred as the consideration for a contract, it is necessarily implied, is indeed the essence of the proffer, that the information shall be new to the one to whom it is proferred." Both of these cases indicate that although courts are prepared to recognize the subject matter of contracts in this area, those contracts must be supported by valuable consideration.

Implied Contract.   The behavior of reasonable men and that which has come to be accepted as normal in society have given rise to the theory of implied contract. Express contract by definition involves an express manifestation of intent to be bound by words, whereas an implied contract arises from consent expressed by conduct. In the absence of an express contract, the law may infer a promise to compensate for services rendered. As applied to the law of ideas, the theory of implied contract requires the subject matter of the contract to be both concrete and novel. Once these requirements are met, any person who discloses a valuable idea to a producer who commercially solicits the submission or who voluntarily accepts it knowing that it is tendered for a price will be entitled to recover. Voluntary receipt by the corporation is a critical element in finding liability. The California Supreme Court in *Desny* v.

Wilder stated that, "[t]he idea man who blurts out his ideas without having first made his bargain has no one but himself to blame for the loss of his bargaining power." Courts do not imply promises to pay for an idea even if the idea is valuable and is put to profitable use by the recipient if the originator placed his idea in the public domain by publishing it. Because the recipient in this type of case has no advance notice of the impending submission, his conduct in receiving the idea will not give rise to an implied promise. However, if the submitted idea is embodied in some form (book, screenplay, scenario, or drawing) subject to property rights, a promise to pay may be implied from the use of the property itself.

There are exceptions to the preceding rules. The most important one exists in those businesses that, by their very nature, impliedly solicit ideas from the public. The entertainment industry relies on unsolicited ideas for television, radio, and movie shows, and they have established a custom of paying for any ideas that are ultimately used. In cases where this type of situation exists, courts will imply a contract for a reasonable compensation. Note, however, that the corporation always has the power publicly to revoke any implied standing offer that it might have made. Once the revocation becomes effective, no promise to compensate for the use of unsolicited or involuntarily received ideas will be implied.

Liability in implied contract will attach more readily in those cases where an unsolicited idea is voluntarily received by a corporation. Voluntariness in this context requires some advance notice to the corporation that an idea is about to be submitted and the existence of an opportunity for it to stop any disclosure of that idea. If, however, the corporation chooses to sit back and permit the disclosure to be made, then it may be subjecting itself to liability for the use of that idea. Even though the disclosure is unsolicited, it is considered made with the implied consent of the recipient, and some courts consider the recipient's inaction and failure to reject as a negative form of solicitation. The courts have placed an affirmative duty on the corporation to act or else be bound by its inaction.

Where advance notice of an idea submission is given and the recipient permits that submission to be made, an implied contract to compensate for its use is established. The most common factual circumstance in which this obligation arises involves the submission to the corporation of a letter stating the existence of an idea and a statement that it will soon be submitted for consideration. This letter is followed by a second letter (let's assume after a reasonable interval) containing the actual disclosure. Inaction between the first and second letter may imply the agreement just described. Unless otherwise agreed upon, the amount of compensation for the use of an idea will be determined by the courts based on the standard of reasonableness. It is not always dependent upon profitable use. In *Downey* v. *General Foods Corporation*, decided in 1971, a New York court held that the plaintiff may be entitled to a recovery notwithstanding the fact that defendant's use of the idea resulted in a monetary loss. Although the showing of a profit from the use of an idea is not critical, it provides a more adequate basis upon which recovery can be assessed.

An implied contract only becomes binding on a corporation when the unauthorized use of an idea occurs. Absent this use, there can be no recovery. It should be kept in mind that the contract itself is established upon submission of the idea to the corporation and its acceptance whereas the duty to compensate arises only when the corporation makes use of that idea. In *Thompson* v. *California Brewing Company*, decided by a California court in 1961, a test of Thompson's marketing idea was held to be use, because such test disclosed the idea to a substantial segment of the public and further marketability of the idea was thereby destroyed.

Quasi Contract. Quasi contract, sometimes labeled contract implied in law, is often confused with contract implied in fact. In *Weitzenkorn* v. *Lesser*, a California court stated that "[q]uasi-contracts, unlike true contracts, are not based upon the apparent intention of the parties to undertake the performances in question, nor are they promises. They are obligations created by law for reasons of justice. . . . Quasi-contractual recovery is based upon benefit accepted or derived for which the law implies an obligation." Critically absent from the quasi contract is the mutual manifestation of an intent to be bound, whether it be by words or actions. Essentially, recovery on this theory is based upon a legal fiction created by the courts in order to afford substantial justice to parties to an otherwise remediless situation. Many courts in idea cases have attempted to condition recovery under a quasi contract theory upon the existence of a number of attributes that traditionally apply to express or implied-in-fact contract cases. One federal district court established the requirement of confidential relationship as the prerequisite to recover on this theory. *De Filippis* v. *Chrysler Corp.*, involved an action by De Filippis for an accounting and an injunction based on Chrysler's alleged use of De Filippis' invention relating to a transmission mechanism for automobiles, without plaintiff's authority or consent, and to recover under quasi contract for this alleged use. The case was dismissed on the grounds that De Filippis failed to show (1) that the idea was disclosed in confidence, (2) that the idea disclosed was novel, or (3) that the idea was subsequently appropriated by defendant for its own use. Earlier, the same court in *Davis* v. *General*

Foods took the position that, absent a showing of express or implied-in-fact contract, any trust in the fairness of another is misplaced and no misreliance can arise thereon.

Confidential Relationship. Where plaintiff discloses his idea to defendant in the context of a confidential relationship, disclosure by defendant to third parties in violation of that relationship will give rise to an action for breach of fiduciary obligation or for a violation of trade secret rights. *Jones* v. *Ulrich* provides an example of a fiduciary relationship that will impose liability for unauthorized disclosure. In that case, Jones submitted an idea to Ulrich in order that Ulrich might embody the idea in a working model. A model was constructed, manufacture of the product was begun, and defendant refused to render an accounting of profits from its sale of said product. The court, allowing recovery by plaintiff, stated: "To hold that such a person may accept such disclosures and in turn put them to his own use without responsibility to the inventors would be to deny to the inventors the mechanical skill they so vitally need to first make the pilot model and demonstrator of their invention, and later manufacture the same, and would as a result materially impede the industrial progress of the nation."

Some courts have held that a confidential relationship must arise out of an express or implied agreement whereby the defendant consents to such a relationship. Unauthorized disclosure to third parties is thus treated as a breach of contract. Another approach permits recovery in equity irrespective of the existence of a formal contract. This approach grants relief on the basis of quasi contract. The difference between these two approaches is important because remedies and defenses will vary depending upon whether the action is legal or equitable in nature. If plaintiff can establish a contractual relationship coupled with a confidential disclosure, then he will be granted contractual relief and any limitation stated above under the section on express or implied contract will generally not apply. Where, however, a quasi contractual and confidential relationship exists, the somewhat broader equitable remedies will attach.

Where the basis of recovery is that of a confidential relationship, the possibility of finding relief under the law of trade secrets looms on the horizon. It will be useful to take a look at some cases involving negotiations and unsolicited idea disclosures in which trade secret rights were asserted and to observe how these cases often turn on the presence or absence of a confidential relationship.

An agreement was involved in *Hisel* v. *Chrysler Corp.*, decided by a federal district court in 1951. The idea that Hisel wanted to sell Chrysler was that of using an "Inserted license-place holder. The front plate is inserted in front fender in glass-covered, insulated, metal box; the rear plate in trunk compartment in a like box."

In accordance with the conditions under which Chrysler would accept ideas from persons outside the corporation, when Hisel submitted his idea he signed an agreement which stated in part, "I do hereby, in consideration of its examining my suggestion, release it from any liability in connection with my suggestion or liability because of use of any portion thereof, except such liability as may accrue under valid patents now or hereafter issued." Chrysler responded to Hisel by telling him that his idea "had been discussed with its engineers, and stated 'that the idea is not new to them since others have submitted similar plans in the past.'" As to the agreement that Hisel signed, the court found that "[t]he clear intent, manifest in the . . . agreement, is repugnant to any implication of confidential relationship existing between [Hisel] and Chrysler Corporation. . . ." Because of the absence of a relationship of trust and confidence between Hisel and Chrysler and because of the fact that Hisel's idea was well known to the auto industry, the court dismissed Hisel's complaint against Chrysler, finding that Chrysler had not taken Hisel's idea by any improper means.

In *Smith* v. *Dravo Corp.*, decided by the Seventh Circuit Court of Appeals in 1953, trade secret protection was granted for information gained in negotiations for purchase of a shipping container business. There was an absence of any agreement between the parties as to the confidentiality of the information given to the Dravo Corporation or as to the rights of either party to the information. However, the court found that information concerning the structural design of the containers and prospective customer lists had been disclosed in confidence to Dravo. The court stated:

> Here plaintiffs disclosed their design for one purpose, to enable defendant to appraise it with a view in mind of purchasing the business. There can be no question that defendant knew and understood this limited purpose. Trust was reposed in it by plaintiffs that the information thus transmitted would be accepted subject to that limitation.

Consequently, the use of this information by Dravo was found to be a breach of confidence and improper. The fact that Dravo could have learned the structural design of the containers by close inspection and analysis was no defense. As the court put it, the "mere fact that such lawful acquisition is available does not mean that he may, through a breach of confidence, gain the information in usable form and escape the efforts of inspection and analysis."

The unsolicited disclosure in *Irizzary* v. *Harvard College* involved Irizarry's plan and idea to publish a foreign tax service. Irizarry and

Harvard exchanged correspondence about such a project until Erwin Griswold, then Dean of the Harvard Law School, informed Irizarry that he did not "care to pursue the matter further." Subsequently, the Harvard Law School, in cooperation with the United Nations, began to prepare for the publication of a "World Tax Series" and as a result Irizarry brought suit against Harvard. The court commented on this situation as follows:

> In the present case it is perfectly clear that no . . . implied contractual or fiduciary relationship arose. For the plaintiff's initial letter to Griswold, which was wholly unsolicited, disclosed and described the plaintiff's entire idea. . . . Such a gratuitous unsolicited disclosure as the plaintiff made to Griswold could not impose upon the defendants a contractual or fiduciary relationship.

The negotiations involved in *Food Processes, Inc.* v. *Swift & Company* involved the licensing of a patent from plaintiff Food Processes, Inc. to defendant Swift & Company. Although the negotiations were broken off, Food Processes claimed, in addition to patent infringement, that Swift & Company had misappropriated various trade secrets that it had disclosed during the course of negotiations. For example, one of the allegedly misappropriated trade secrets was specified as the "cost of constructing an installation to practice the process." The court found that the cost disclosed to Swift differed from the cost of constructing an installation that used the process for sterilizing canned food. Moreover, the court stated that it was "unable to ascertain how the cost of a plant might be considered a confidential trade secret, in any sense." Although the court stated that it was "cognizant of the law regarding implied notice of trade secrets and that a confidential relationship is implicit in license negotiations," it nevertheless required some overt showing on the part of Food Processes, Inc., that these alleged trade secrets were being disclosed in confidence to Swift. Instead the court found that

> all disclosures regarding the . . . process made to Swift and others, in the course of negotiations with them as prospective licensees of the patent in suit, were revealed openly, freely, and with no restrictions, express or implied.

Accordingly, trade secret protection was denied because the "essential element of confidential relationship [was] lacking. . . ." The principle to be seen in this case is that where the essential element of secrecy or confidence is not met, the defendant will generally not be found to have taken the alleged trade secret by improper means.

However, in *J & M Building Specialties, Inc.* v. *Marwais Steel Company,* where Marwais sought out trade secrets belonging to J & M

Building Specialties in negotiations that broke off, the court did not explicitly find a confidential relationship, although it did state that there must be "either a covenant or a confidential relationship upon which to predicate relief." Yet the court found that Marwais had taken the trade secrets by improper means. That the court did not find it necessary to a specific finding of either a covenant or a confidential relationship can probably be explained by the degree of unfairness that would have resulted had not relief been granted. J & M Building Specialties had a unique design for metal door frames and disclosed these to Marwais Steel, who had never designed, fabricated, or sold metal door frames but was interested in doing so. After negotiations broke off without a contract, Marwais began manufacturing a metal door frame that incorporated plaintiff's unique design concepts.

The Second Circuit Court of Appeals has simplified matters somewhat by recognizing that as to license negotiations, there is a confidential relationship between the parties. The case that recognized this principle was *Speedry Chemical Products, Inc.* v. *Carter's Ink Company,* decided in 1962. Carter's entered into licensing negotiations with Speedry with the purpose of obtaining a satisfactory licensing agreement to market the "Magic Marker" developed by Speedry under Carter's label. These negotiations broke off without any agreement and some eighteen months later, Carter's came out with its own product "Marks-A-Lot" to compete with Speedry's "Magic Marker." Speedry claimed that Carter's had taken by improper means trade secrets that had been disclosed to it during the license negotiations. The court found, however, that Speedry had not disclosed any trade secrets to Carter's during the negotiations and that Carter's had developed its own product through its own research and experimentation. The Second Circuit, however, agreed with Speedry's contention "that it is not necessary to show an express agreement to hold in confidence and not to use trade secrets obtained as the result of a . . . confidential relationship. . . . During the negotiations for the license agreement such a confidential relationship existed."

Another case that recognized the principle of confidence during license negotiations was *Allis-Chalmers Mfg. Co.* v. *Continental Aviation & Eng. Corp.,* decided by a U.S. district court in Michigan in 1966. At issue in that case was whether a former employee of Allis-Chalmers, Wolff, could go to work for Continental in an area where Wolff might be disposed to disclose trade secrets belonging to Allis-Chalmers. The court held that the trade secret information of which Wolff had knowledge had retained its character as a trade secret, although it had been the subject of license negotiations between Allis-Chalmers and Continental. Said the court: "Any disclosures which may have been made to Continental were made under circumstances which give rise to a relationship of trust and confidence between Allis-Chalmers and Continental, so that this information retains its nature and value as a trade secret."

The court did not mention any agreement between the parties to show the existence of a confidential relationship, but it did note the adequate degree of notice that Allis-Chalmers gave as to the confidentiality of its industrial processes.

> The plant is fenced and guarded and visitors are restricted. Passes must be issued to authorized personnel and all visitors must have passes and be accompanied by an Allis-Chalmers employee while in the . . . plant. Before entering the fuel systems laboratory, which is within the engineering department, a special pass is required that can only be issued by one of four people. Files containing drawings and copies of patent applications are locked and all engineering drawings are labeled "Confidential—Property of Allis-Chalmers." . . .

It is quite possible that the court was influenced by this notice in finding that the confidentiality of the industrial know-how of Allis-Chalmers extended to the license negotiations. At any rate, notice can be seen as an important element to the propriety of means of appropriation.

Methods of Protecting Submitted Ideas

Recognizing that the unqualified disclosure of an idea normally results in the loss of rights to compensation for its use, it becomes necessary to consider those protective devices that may be employed to minimize such risks. The patent and copyright laws provide the optimum protection for ideas embodied in inventions or literary compositions that fall within their purview. Absent statutory protection, there are certain steps that an idea submitter might take to insure protection from unauthorized use by a corporate submittee. The most important devices relate to the timing and method of disclosure.

An idea should never be disclosed without first giving the recipient an opportunity to resist disclosure. To submit an idea blindly is to invite use for which no recovery may be allowed. The submitter should first inform the intended recipient of the existence of an idea that he believes should be of value to the recipient. The initial communication should explicitly state that the idea is being disclosed for the purpose of sale and that compensation for its use is expected. The submitter should seek a satisfactory contractual relationship prior to any disclosure. This contract should give the corporation every opportunity to reject the idea if it is found to be valueless and the duty to compensate would arise if the corporation (1) learns of the idea from the submitter and (2) puts it to use. Some minimal compensation might be paid to the submitter for the mere act of disclosure, should the parties so agree, but it is doubtful that a corporation would be willing to pay value for the act of disclosure without some indication of the nature and subject matter of the soon-to-be-revealed idea. An agreement concerning compensation should be made as part of a predisclosure contract. For example, in *High* v. *Trade Union Courier Publishing Co.*, plaintiff High and defendant Trade Union Courier entered an agreement that provided that High would receive 35 per cent of all savings to Trade Union Courier resulting from the disclosure. Only after this agreement was reached did High disclose his idea that would result in a proposed tax saving to Trade Union Courier.

Still other issues should be considered before disclosure. As seen, whether or not a court might find that a trade secret was acquired by improper means through contract or related negotiations could likely depend on whether or not the communication of the alleged trade secret information was made in confidence. In recognition of this significant factor, the party owning what he considers to be trade secrets might strive to make as part of the predisclosure agreement a stipulation that the disclosure of information that he would like to sell or license is made in confidence and that the recipient will make no use of nonpublic information received without prior written consent of the discloser. The recipient corporation would want to have as part of the predisclosure agreement a stipulation that it is free to use information in the public domain or information that the recipient already has. Both parties may be willing to acknowledge that the secrecy restrictions will last only for a specified period of time. In those cases where such a formal agreement does not appear feasible, the idea may be disclosed in a setting conducive to recovery on the grounds of implied contract, quasi contract, or confidential relationship—all of which the sophisticated corporation will strive to avoid.

Defenses to Idea Submission Claims

A number of defenses by a corporation to idea submission claims have already been discussed. Defenses now to be discussed are lack of consideration, agent's lack of authority to bind the corporation, lack of concreteness or novelty, independent conception, and abandonment.

Lack of Consideration. Where an express contract has been alleged as part of the claim for compensation for use by a corporation of a disclosed idea, consideration must be shown in order to support such a theory. Consideration is the inducement to a contract that is offered by one party to an agreement and accepted by the other as an inducement to that other's act or promise. Two things are essential to a showing of legally sufficient consideration: (1) something must be given that the law regards as of value, and (2) that something must be treated by the parties to the agreement as the agreed price or exchange for that purpose.

If the corporation can show lack of consideration, then the claim will fail. Two cases discussed earlier, *Soule* v. *Bon Ami Co.* and *Masline* v. *New York, N.H. and H.R.R.*, illustrate this point. Where an idea is submitted as consideration for a contract, the subsequent showing that the idea was actually worthless will destroy the alleged contract. The rationale employed in these cases is that the contract contemplated that something of value would be disclosed and the disclosure of an idea that is common and universally known is essentially valueless as consideration.

Agent's Lack of Authority. While the corporation does have an independent legal status, it can only operate through its employees and agents. The ability of any of these individuals to bind the corporation depends upon an application of the principles of the law of agency. If an agent has the actual or apparent authority to deal with and negotiate concerning the idea submissions, then any such activity by him will bind the corporation he represents. Absent ratification by the corporation or the application of the estoppel doctrine, the lack of express or implied authority by an agent will necessitate a finding of no liability to the corporation for the individual's unauthorized acts. Therefore, through the defense of lack of authority, a corporation is in the position of being able to disclaim liability for the acts of its unauthorized agent. Hence the value and limitations of this defense are readily apparent: although this principle may be of little or no practical value to a recipient corporation acting through its executive employees in the normal course of business, midnight deals with a corporate pal in a dimly lit bar may prompt efforts to invoke the defense.

Lack of Concreteness and Novelty. A corporation may successfully defend an action for the unauthorized use of an idea by showing that the idea was neither concrete nor novel. Two cases, *Lueddecke* v. *Chevrolet Motor Co.* and *Booth* v. *Stutz Motor Co.*, illustrate the problems involved in sustaining a defense based on lack of concreteness. In the *Lueddecke* case defendant corporation succeeded in defending an action for unauthorized appropriation by showing that plaintiff's idea was useless without further experimentation and investigation. Accordingly, the court held that the lack of concreteness was fatal to the success of plaintiff's action. The *Booth* case provides an example of the degree of concreteness that will all but insure success by a plaintiff in a misappropriation case. In that case, blueprints, drawings, sketches, and diagrams were submitted that embodied plaintiff's idea in every detail. The court had no reasonable choice but to find the requisite concreteness.

The defense of lack of concreteness is available, depending upon which theory of recovery plaintiff pursues. The defense is available in actions on quasi contract, implied contract, and confidential relationship. In actions based on an express contract, the defense is normally unavailable because most courts favor the proposition that concreteness is not an essential element in plaintiff's case based on that theory.

The defense of lack of novelty succeeds upon a showing that plaintiff's idea was either a copy of another's work or that the subject matter of the idea previously existed in some other form. Such showings would not succeed, however, in jurisdictions where the only degree of novelty required is such that the disclosure need only be novel to the defendant. Inasmuch as the parties might contract for the disclosure of a nonnovel idea, the defense of lack of novelty is limited in those actions based on express contract. Traditionally, however, the defense is available in actions on quasi contracts and implied contracts.

Independent Conception.   An absolute defense to a charge of idea appropriation results upon proof that the idea alleged to have been appropriated previously was independently developed and conceived by the defendant corporation. This, of course, is an aspect of lack of novelty. This independent development is most likely to occur within the corporate research and development area that has as its main function to provide a constant flow of new and useful ideas for future use by the corporation. In this posture these corporate departments often develop plans and ideas that are also by coincidence the subject matter of later submissions to the corporation by outsiders. Problems arise because the discoveries and inventions of the research department are not necessarily made public. They may be publicized only through use, and, in fact, a corporation uses only a small percentage of all the ideas formulated by its research and development staff. Therefore it is often the case that an unsolicited idea disclosure that appears to its author to be original and novel is identical to suggestions made months or years earlier by the research department. This is a matter of simple coincidence and the result is that the independent submitter sues for damages and the corporation defends on the ground of independent conception. This defense of independent conception is affirmative in nature; consequently, the defendant must trace the line of development and show that no connection exists between the independent conception and the unsolicited disclosure.

Abandonment. The voluntary and unprotected public disclosure of an idea constitutes an abandonment of rights in that idea. The law of abandonment was stated in *William A. Meier Glass Co., Inc.* v. *Anchor Hocking Glass Corp.,* as follows:

> It is well established that a common law property right may be abandoned by conduct from which such intent may be inferred. A publication is defined as the act of making public or known, as by offering for sale or disposition the subject matter in question. A general publication consists of such a disclosure, communication, circulation, exhibition, or disposition of such matter tendered or given to one or more members of the general public as it implies abandonment of the property right or its dedication to the public.

Once a corporation can prove that an abandonment has occurred, it has a complete defense to any charge of unlawful appropriation.

Corporate Protection from Unsolicited Disclosure

Although the corporation is possessed of a number of defenses to claims for compensation arising from the use of unsolicited ideas, it will much prefer to practice "preventative liability" by defining and limiting the circumstances under which it will accept and consider such disclosures. A number of alternate courses of action are available to the corporation. The first requires the execution of a release by the submitter before the corporation will even consider his idea. This release empowers the corporation to determine, in its sole discretion, the originality of the material and the amount of compensation, if any, that is to be paid for its use. Note, however, that a release of this type is only of value when it has been voluntarily executed. Often the submitter will decline to execute the release for fear that he will lose all of his rights in the idea. In such a situation, the corporation might simply refuse to give the unsolicited ideas any further consideration unless the release is executed.

A fairly common approach used by corporations who might be the recipients of idea submissions is to require an agreement on the part of the submitter that there is no confidential relationship express or implied between the parties. Such an agreement might also contain a provision to the effect that the sole recourse for the submitter shall be such rights as he has secured under the patent and copyright laws.

An alternate approach involves the execution of a contract whereby the parties agree that a determinable compensation will be paid for the use of the idea. This compensation may be a lump-sum payment or a fixed percentage of the ultimate value to the user, perhaps measured by gross sales. This type of agreement requires as a condition precedent to compensation that the idea be used by the corporation. In the absence of any such use, no right to compensation will accrue to the submitter. A number of corporations require in these contracts that any submitted material susceptible to patent protection be the subject matter of an application for such protection at the time the disclosure takes place. Otherwise the submissions will not be considered.

The circumstances of submission may not afford the corporation an opportunity to refuse receipt. Often the idea is disclosed without any previous warning. A number of protective practices can and should be established for the proper handling of these submissions to establish good-faith effort to avoid actual knowledge of the idea among knowledgeable corporate personnel. Thus the first critical step is to insure that the personnel in a position to use or communicate the idea on an informed basis be insulated from these unsolicited disclosures. This can be accomplished, for example, by setting up an incoming-correspondence-filtering system whereby secretarial or clerical level personnel screen all material ultimately destined for the operational areas of the corporation. This system must be the product of education programs that instruct these employees to return the disclosures with accompanying contract forms to be filled out and included upon resubmission.

A corporate consideration always to be remembered when dealing with idea submission problems is that the buying public includes most if not all of the idea submitters. Therefore, public relations should temper the otherwise legalistic approach to this problem.

BASES OF TRADE SECRET PROTECTION

The courts have never developed a central theme for the legal basis of protection of trade secrets. In the 1851 English case of *Morison* v. *Moat* already discussed on pp. 118–119, the court, in summarizing the development of English law, adverted to property, contract, and trust or confidence as various bases upon which trade secret protection can rest. In addition to the bases mentioned in *Morison* v. *Moat,* to be discussed here is the basis of unjust enrichment or quasi contract.

It will be recalled that these theories of trade secret protection, with the exception of property, have already been discussed to some extent on pp. 177–185. What is to follow here is a discussion of these theories as applied to trade secrets law in general.

Property

The view that trade secrets are a kind of property is accepted by most jurisdictions. As the Seventh Circuit Court of Appeals put it in *Ferroline Corp.* v. *General Aniline and Film Corp.*, decided in 1953, "[w]e are dealing with a type of intellectual property—in effect, a property right in discovered knowledge." In one 1939 case, *Godefroy Mfg. Co.* v. *Lady Lennox Co.*, a Missouri court went so far as to say that "it is universally held that secret formulas and processes are property rights. . . ." In light of the many cases already seen in this chapter that have spoken of the confidential relationship as a basis for the protection of trade secrets, one might wonder at this statement. This seeming contradiction can be at least partially explained by the fact that many cases join these two concepts so that both theories are considered as proper bases of protection by the same courts. For example, the Missouri court in *Godefroy Mfg. Co.*, having asserted the universality of the property concept, went on to state that trade secret protection will be rendered "against those who, through a breach of trust or violation of confidence, attempt to apply the secret to their own use or to impart it to others." Similarly, in *Brown* v. *Fowler*, decided by the Court of Civil Appeals of Texas in 1958, it was stated that the rule "seems to be that one who has a secret formula or process has a property right therein, which . . . will be protected as against those who, through breach of trust or violated confidence, attempt to apply the secret to their own use."

The U.S. Supreme Court, in *E. I. duPont de Nemours Powder Co.* v. *Masland,* decided in 1917, went one step further than the courts Masland to prevent him from using or disclosing certain secret processes that simply join the two concepts. duPont had brought suit against that he had learned while he was in the employ of duPont. At issue was whether Masland should be permitted to disclose the alleged trade secret to his expert witnesses. Mr. Justice Holmes, who delivered the opinion of the Court, noted that the case had been considered as presenting a conflict between a property right and a right to make a thorough defense. In *dictum* that was to become famous and quoted by many courts, Mr. Justice Holmes stated:

> We approach the question somewhat differently. The word "property" as applied to trademarks and trade secrets is an unanalyzed expression of certain secondary consequences of the primary fact that the law

makes some rudimentary requirements of good faith. Whether the plaintiffs have any valuable secret or not the defendant knows the facts, whatever they are, through a special confidence that he accepted. The property may be denied, but the confidence cannot be. Therefore, the starting point for the present matter is not property or due process of law, but that the defendant stood in confidential relations with the plaintiffs. . . .

The Court ruled that it would be within the discretion of the trial judge to decide whether, to whom, and under what conditions the disclosure should be made.

It might appear that the acceptance of this language in *Masland* would tend to erode the concept that there is a property right in trade secrets. However, among those cases that join the concepts of property and confidence are cases that state that there is a property right in trade secrets but that also cite *Masland*.

Although trade secrets may generally be considered as property, they are such in only a limited sense. This limitation was well stated in a New York decision, *Eastman Co.* v. *Reichenbach,* in 1892 as follows:

the word "property," as applied to trade secrets and inventions, has its limitations; for it is undoubtedly true that when an article manufactured by some secret process, which is not the subject of a patent, is thrown upon the market, the whole world is at liberty to discover, if it can by any fair means, what that process is, and, when discovery is thus made, to employ it in the manufacture of similar articles. In such a case, the inventor's or manufacturer's property in his process is gone. . . .

Although the concept of property in trade secrets is thus limited and also perhaps somewhat diluted by the concept of the confidential relationship as well, the property view has significant implications. For example, in *Homer* v. *Crown Cork & Seal Co.,* decided by the Court of Appeals of Maryland in 1928, the court ruled that so long as the trade secrets in question had not lost their value as property through disclosure, they were to be considered as part of the assets of Crown Cork & Seal and were therefore of unimpaired value in determining the worth of its shares of stock. Similarly, in *Radium Remedies Co.* v. *Weiss,* decided by the Supreme Court of Minnesota in 1928, the trade secret formulas of the Radium Remedies Company for the medicinal remedy "Py Radium" were considered by the court to be the principal items of the corporate assets and of value as such.

Another aspect of trade secrets as property is that they may be assigned, that is, the right to them may be transferred from one party to another. The assignment of trade secret rights in *Grand Rapids Wood Finishing Co.* v. *Hatt,* decided by the Supreme Court of Michigan in 1908, amounted to a sale of secret formulas for furniture polishes. Prior to the making of the contract effecting the assignment, Hatt was the owner of these formulas for the manufacture of furniture polishes and was involved in the business of manufacturing and selling the polishes to retailers. Grand Rapid Woods Finishing Co. was also a manufacturer of furniture polishes and sold them at wholesale. The contract between Hatt and Grand Rapids stated that the secret formulas were sold and assigned over to Grand Rapids in consideration of which Hatt would receive commissions from the profits that Grand Rapids realized from the sale of the polishes made from these formulas. Hatt, as part of the contract, agreed that he would not sell or divulge the formulas to anyone during the life of the contract, which was to extend for twenty years. About six months after this contract was executed, Hatt sold his rights under the contract to the secretary and bookkeeper of Grand Rapids. Hatt then began to manufacture and sell the polishes made under formulas covered by the contract under his own name and also attempted to sell one of these formulas. The Grand Rapids Wood Finishing Co. brought suit against Hatt to prevent him from manufacturing polishes under formulas assigned to Grand Rapids and from divulging any of said formulas. Hatt's main defense was that the contract was void as an unreasonable restraint of trade. The court rejected this defense, stating that in many cases, the principal worth of a manufacturing business lies in the secret process through which its products are made and is "as much a lawful subject of disposal as property as the articles themselves manufactured. A contract to sell such process is therefore valid and binding."

The New York case of *In re Brandreth's Estate* supports the view that trade secrets are taxable as property. One of the issues in that case was how to value shares of stock in the Porous Plaster Company for purposes of applying a transfer tax. The individuals to whom the shares of stock were transferred, and would therefore be taxed, the four daughters of Brandreth, argued that the three secret formulas under which the Porous Plaster Company compounded and manufactured pills and plaster did "not belong to the corporation" and were "of no value to it." The court reasoned, however, that because the earning capacity of the company was derived in large part from these trade secrets, they should be considered as part of the value of the shares of stock to be taxed. In this sense, then, trade secrets can be considered as taxable property.

Confidential Relationship

Although it has been seen that most jurisdictions adhere to a property concept in trade secrets and that some cases join the concepts of property and confidence as bases of protection, there are also many decisions that rely on confidence without mentioning property as a basis of protection. It is interesting to note that the jurisdictions in which these cases were decided are, in several instances, the same jurisdictions in which there have been decisions based on the property concept. This indicates, along with the cases that join the property and confidence concepts, that the courts do not find any substantial conflict between the two concepts.

It is undoubtedly true that the most common incidence of confidential relationship seen in trade secrets cases is the relationship between employer and employee. The frequency with which this exhibits itself in litigation is due to the fact that it is impossible for a corporation to operate its business without confiding to its key employees the secrets that gave it a commercial advantage over its competitors. This confidential relationship between employer and employee need not depend on an express covenant in a contract of employment for its existence. In *Extrin Foods Inc.* v. *Leighton,* decided by a New York court in 1952, where defendant former employees of plaintiff Extrin Foods were found to have unfairly appropriated secret food formulas and processes belonging to Extrin Foods, the court stated that:

> [e]ven though the contract of hiring contained no express covenant, the individual defendants by an implied agreement bound themselves not to disclose, reveal or appropriate secret processes or formulae. . . . Liability under these circumstances is predicated on the breach of this duty rather than on a specific property right of plaintiff.

Similarly, in an earlier New York case, *Rubner* v. *Gursky,* decided in 1940, where Gursky was found to have improperly taken the trade secrets of his former employers and to have thereby breached the confidential relationship existing between him and his employer the court observed that a fiduciary duty existed between employer and employee and that duty need not depend on an express contract, because it is an implied term in all contracts of employment.

Another case that is instructive on the confidential relationship between employer and employee and that invokes the property concept as well is *By-Buk Co.* v. *Printed Cellophane Tape Co.,* decided by a California court in 1958. At a time when the By-Buk Company, a manufacturer and seller of industrial adhesive tape, was developing new machinery, it took into its employ one Black and trained him in the assembly and later the operation of this machinery. By-Buk put Black on notice of the secrecy of the processes embodied in the machinery and took steps to prevent others from learning of these processes. After only a few months of employment with By-Buk, Black terminated his employment and went to work for the Printed Cellophane Tape Company. Black divulged to his new employer the secret processes he had learned while employed at By-Buk and, subsequently, two machines were constructed that were identical to By-Buk's machines and embodied the secret processes. With the use of these machines, the Printed Cellophane Tape Company went into competition with By-Buk by producing the same articles, which were known as die-cut masks and overlapping discs. In finding that By-Buk was entitled to relief, the court stated that it didn't matter whether or not Black had made an express agreement with By-Buk not to divulge By-Buk's trade secrets. The court simply took the position that an employee is under the implied obligation not to divulge or use confidential information that he acquires by reason of his employment. Such information is the property of the employer and the employee holds that property in trust for the employer and cannot use it in violation of his trust.

The preceding cases show that the element of confidence is something that arises out of the employment relationship, even though there is not necessarily a clause in the contract of employment that states that the relationship of the parties to the contracts is one of confidence. There are also cases that find that the relationship of confidence between employer and employee arises by operation of law rather than out of contract. One case that illustrates this proposition is *Monsanto Chemical Co. v. Miller,* decided by a federal district court in 1958. Miller had been employed with Monsanto Chemical Company on two different occasions. In his first period of employment with Monsanto, Miller was party to a contract that expressly obligated him not to divulge Monsanto's trade secrets relating to the design, construction, and operation of electric furnaces for the production of elemental phosphorus. Upon Miller's second period of employment with Monsanto, he entered into no such contract. After leaving Monsanto the second time, Miller became employed by a firm that was making an effort to get into the business of constructing electric furnaces for the production of elemental phosphorous. Miller disclosed to his new employer and other defendants the trade secret information he had learned from Monsanto. The absence of a contract during Miller's second period of employment presented no obstacle to the court as it found Miller to have breached a confidence owed to Monsanto.

It was unnecessary for the court to find that Miller's written contract from the first period of employment served as a basis for finding an obligation of confidence upon termination of Miller's second period of employment with Monsanto. The court found no difference between Miller's earlier contractual obligation and the obligation imposed upon him by the common law.

Whether the relationship of confidence between employer and

employee is found to have been imposed by law or contract, the courts have little difficulty in finding that the confidence exists. Other cases arise, however, that do not involve the employment relationship or other relationships where the court can easily find confidence. In such cases, the circumstances that gave rise to the relationship must be examined as well as the question of what the parties understood the nature of their relationship to be. If something of value has been communicated in confidence an understanding that the recipient of the information is not at liberty to use it to his own advantage may reasonably be implied. Also, if the disclosure is made for limited purposes, the implication that arises is that any other use of the information would violate the intent of the parties.

Although it has been stated that where a party to a confidential relationship improperly discloses trade secrets belonging to the other party to that relationship, the party making the improper disclosure is liable to the other party, it may be necessary in a given situation to carry this proposition one step further. The third party to whom the improper disclosure is made is equally liable where the third party has knowledge of the breach of confidence and nevertheless uses the trade secrets to its own advantage.

The application of this principle of law is seen in *Minnesota Mining & Mfg. Co.* v. *Technical Tape Corp.*, decided by a New York court in 1959. The Technical Tape Corporation was a competitor of the Minnesota Mining and Manufacturing Company ("3M") in the manufacture of masking tape and cellophane tape. However, the Technical Tape Corporation was unable to match the quality of 3M's tape. The techniques by which 3M was able to make its high quality tape were the subjects of trade secrets that 3M took strict security measures to protect. In order to gain knowledge of 3M's trade secrets, Technical Tape induced one of 3M's chemists to enter into its employ by offering him a substantially higher salary. Technical Tape was thereby able to learn and make use of 3M's trade secrets in improving the quality of its tapes. In finding that Technical Tape was liable to 3M, the court specifically noted that Technical Tape had full knowledge of 3M's former employee's obligation to keep in confidence the trade secret information that had been reposed in him by 3M.

Unjust Enrichment

As discussed previously, the concept of unjust enrichment is also known as quasi contract, because the essential element in recovery under the quasi contract theory is that of unjust enrichment. Trade secrets cases that rely on unjust enrichment as the basis for protection are not nearly so numerous as the cases that rely on the other bases of protec-tion discussed here. One of the few trade secrets cases that appear to rely exclusively on unjust enrichment as a basis of protection is *Matarese* v. *Moore-McCormack Lines,* decided by the Second Circuit Court of Appeals in 1946. Matarese was a man of little education who, having worked around the docks most of his life, became employed with Moore-McCormack Lines as a stevedore. Matarese informed one Furey, an agent of Moore-McCormack Lines, that he had devised a method that would greatly facilitate the loading and unloading of cargo and thereby save costs to Moore-McCormack as well as prevent many stevedore accidents. Furey made a trip to the home of Matarese, where he was shown working models employing Matarese's idea. According to Matarese, Furey was satisfied with the models and promised Matarese one third of what his employer would save through the use of the device. After testing Matarese's device, Moore-McCormack put several of them to use. When Matarese asked for compensation, he was assured that he would be paid in the future. Sometime later, however, Matarese was discharged without having been compensated. Consequently, Matarese brought an action against Moore-McCormack. Because Matarese was unable to prove that there had been a contract between himself and Moore-McCormack, he based his claim upon the theory that his former employer had been unjustly enriched when it used the loading and unloading devices, which Matarese had originated, without compensating Matarese. The main legal issue before the court was the validity of Matarese's claim of unjust enrichment. In defining what was meant by unjust enrichment, the court stated that:

> The doctrine of unjust enrichment or recovery in quasi-contract . . . applies to situations where as a matter of fact there is no legal contract, but where the person sought to be charged is in possession of money or property which in good conscience and justice he should not retain, but should deliver to another.

The court settled the issue of unjust enrichment in favor of Matarese, having found that Moore-McCormack had made substantial savings by utilizing Matarese's device. It should be noted that although the court spoke only of unjust enrichment as the basis of protection, the relationship between Matarese and Moore-McCormack, being that of employer and employee, was one of confidence. Most cases that mention unjust enrichment as a basis of protection also expressly depend on the existence of a confidential relationship as an element of this protection.

In *E. W. Bliss Company* v. *Struthers-Dunn, Inc.,* decided by the Eighth Circuit Court of Appeals in 1969, the trade secrets issue revolved around allegations that former employees of the E. W. Bliss Company had improperly used trade secrets belonging to their former employer in connection with their subsequent employer, Struthers-Dunn, Inc. The case was on appeal from the entry of a preliminary injunction against the defendants in a federal district court. The court took this opportunity to state its view of the bases for protection of trade secrets. Although the court recognized the confidential relationship as one of the essential elements of a cause of action for the unlawful taking of a trade secret, the court stated that the "essence of the wrong is the obtaining of unjust enrichment and unfair competitive advantage through inequitable conduct." One of the cases that the court cited as support for this last statement was *Atlantic Wool Combing Co.* v. *Norfolk Mills, Inc.*, where the First Circuit Court of Appeals in 1966 had made the same statement but made an additional clarification by adding that the inequitable conduct that led to unjust enrichment and unfair competitive advantage was "usually a breach of confidence." An analysis of the facts of Atlantic Wool Combing Co. provides a particularly good illumination as to why the court invoked the doctrine of unjust enrichment.

The Atlantic Wool Combing Company and Norfolk Mills, Inc., were competitors in the dehairing of raw cashmere. Norfolk Mills, however, was a newcomer in the field, having established its plant some eleven years after Atlantic Wool began conducting its business. There were only six to ten American companies engaged in dehairing cashmere, and each company designed and built its own machinery, traditionally maintaining the secrecy of its process. Atlantic Wool had devised a particularly efficient process and contracted with one Lawton, the proprietor of a machine shop, to build the dehairing machinery in accordance with designs, drawings, and instructions supplied by Atlantic Wool. Lawton had agreed with Atlantic Wool "not to make the parts for anyone else."

An Atlantic Wool employee, one Letoile, was a mechanic involved in the maintenance of the dehairing machinery and was on notice of the secrecy of the process embodied in the machinery. Letoile left the employ of Atlantic Wool and went to work for Norfolk Mills, which was aware that Atlantic Wool had made some improvements in its machinery that it regarded as confidential. Letoile gave Norfolk Mills specific information as to the nature of these improvements and further informed his new employer that Lawton had made the parts. Norfolk Mills then asked Lawton to build for it new machinery that incorporated the improvements devised by Atlantic Wool and provided no exact specifications of its needs. When Lawton duly complied with the request of Norfolk Mills, it was found that he still had the designs and blueprints that belonged to Atlantic Wool. Further, the machinery Lawton built for Norfolk Mills was identical to the machinery he had built for Atlantic Wool.

From these facts the rationale of the doctrine of unjust enrichment presents itself rather clearly. Why should the law permit a party such as Norfolk Mills to take through a breach of confidence the trade secrets developed through the industrious efforts of another when the effect of such taking is to put the party who developed the secret process at an economic disadvantage? The answer to this question lies in the unfairness that would result in permitting this kind of conduct.

Contract

Contract as a basis for the protection of trade secrets has already been touched upon insofar as contract is a basis for recovery in the area of unsolicited idea disclosures. It has also already been seen that trade secrets as property may be the subject of contract and that the relationship of confidence can arise out of contract. The distinction between express and implied contracts will not be belabored here as this has been amply discussed on pp. 177–180. It will be sufficient to say here in summary that an express contract is created by words and an implied contract by conduct.

Because trade secrets can be protected under the theories of property, confidential relationships and unjust enrichment, one might question the need for contract for such protection. Nevertheless, the vast majority of corporations have as part of their employment agreements express contractual provisions that protect trade secrets and rights. One can infer from this that certain advantages must lie in the use of such contracts. It has already been seen in *J. T. Healy & Son, Inc.* v. *James A. Murphy & Son, Inc.*, discussed on pp. 143–144, that a court will take these contracts into consideration as evidence that the owner of the trade secret took the necessary steps to preserve secrecy. Another way of stating this is that a contract helps serve to put the obligee on notice as to the confidentiality of certain information. *Empire Steam Laundry* v. *Lozier*, decided by the Supreme Court of California in 1913, stated this principle from a slightly different perspective. The trade secret involved in the case was a customer list and the owner of that trade secret was the Empire Steam Laundry. Lozier, as an employee of Empire Steam Laundry, made a contract with his employer to the effect that he would supply Empire Steam Laundry with the names and addresses of the customers he serviced and that upon termination of his employment he would not solicit the business of these customers. When Lozier unexpectedly quit the employ of Empire Steam Laundry and went to work for a rival, he continued to solicit laundry work from the customers he had serviced while with Empire Steam Laundry. As a result, Empire Steam Laundry brought suit against Lozier to prevent him from wrongfully exploiting this trade secret information. Although the court found that the contract was not a necessary prerequisite to Empire Steam Laundry's cause of action, it was advantageous to Empire Steam Laundry because "its consideration plainly evince[d] the intent of the parties, the one to protect itself against the doing, the other to abstain from doing the very things which the court finds that [Lozier] upon the termination of his employment immediately proceeded to do."

By the same token, outside of the employer–employee context, where a confidential relationship is generally held to exist, the omission of a provision regarding the protection of any trade secrets in a contract presuming to cover the rights and liabilities of the parties may lead a court to decline to find that trade secret protection exists.

This is exemplified in *Manos* v. *Melton,* decided by the Michigan Supreme Court in 1960. Manos and Melton had formed a corporation, Perfection Industries, Inc., to do work in the plating business, in which each owned or controlled equal portions of the stock. A few years later, Melton made known his desire to disengage from his work with Perfection Industries. As a result, Manos and Melton drew up a contract providing for the sale of Melton's interest in Perfection to Manos. Soon after this sale was consummated, Melton went to work for the Precision Hard Chrome Company, a competitor of Perfection Industries. Melton showed Precision certain techniques for "reverse etching" drive shafts, the result of which was that a substantial amount of business was diverted from Perfection to Precision. In finding that Manos did not deserve trade secret protection for these techniques, the court took special note of the fact that there was "no mention of secret process in the written agreement. Nor [was] there any testimony from which it could reasonably be implied that the agreement constituted a prohibition on defendant to refrain from demonstrating what he knew about the 'reverse etching' process." Accordingly, the court could find no breach of the contract and the implication of confidence was negated by this omission.

A case of similar import is *Laughlin Filter Corp.* v. *Bird Machine Co.,* decided by the Massachusetts Supreme Judicial Court in 1946. The Laughlin Filter Corporation had licensed to the Bird Machine Company the right to make and sell two types of centrifugal machines to separate solids from liquids. The license was to continue until expiration of patents covering the techniques by which the machines were built. After the Laughlin Filter Corporation revoked the license under a reserve power it had in the contract, the Bird Machine Company continued to make and sell similar machines. Laughlin Filter brought suit to prevent Bird Machine from so doing but apparently because there was some dispute as to whether any of the patents were actually embodied in the machines made under the license, Laughlin Filter chose not to rely on the patents but instead alleged that the know-how that had been licensed was in the nature of trade secrets. However, because the license contract contained no language that described any of the know-how information as being confidential, the court found that Laughlin Filter had no basis for maintaining its suit under trade secret law.

Although the omission of a provision regarding trade secrets in a contract of employment would not be nearly so fatal as were such omissions in the last two cases discussed, the inclusion of provisions regarding the protection of trade secrets in contracts of employment is advisable. This view is supported by a New York court's opinion in *L. M. Rabinowitz & Co., Inc.* v. *Dasher,* decided in 1948. L. M. Rabinowitz & Co. was a manufacturer of hook and eye tape to which was attached metal hooks and eyes capable of being joined together so as to fasten garments to which the tape was attached. L. M. Rabinowitz & Co. had acquired an unpatented invention for a machine that automatically sewed the hooks and eyes to the tape. Dasher, while employed with L. M. Rabinowitz & Co., was in charge of the maintenance and operation of these machines. Subsequently, Dasher left the employ of L. M. Rabinowitz & Co. and with other defendants built hook and eye tape machines that were very similar to those Dasher had become familiar with at L. M. Rabinowitz & Co. As a result, L. M. Rabinowitz & Co. brought suit to prevent Dasher and others from manufacturing and using these machines.

The complaint of L. M. Rabinowitz & Co. stated two causes of action. The first was based on the confidential relationship that existed between Dasher and L. M. Rabinowitz & Co. by reason of which the latter claimed to be entitled to protection against Dasher's divulging or using secrets concerning the plaintiff's machines that were confidentially disclosed to Dasher. The second cause of action was based on a written contract between Dasher and L. M. Rabinowitz & Company in which Dasher had agreed not to disclose any of the secrets of L. M. Rabinowitz & Company during the course of his employment or for ten years thereafter. Dasher had also agreed not to enter into competition with L. M. Rabinowitz & Company for a period of ten years after he terminated his employment with it.

Although the court stated that Dasher's obligation not to disclose confidential information he had learned from his employer was implied in his contract of employment, it stated further that "[t]he fact that such an express contract had been made . . . fortifies the plaintiff's position that the parties understood the value which the plaintiff attached to secrecy and it emphasizes the trust which the defendant assumed in entering into this confidential relationship." The court found that L. M. Rabinowitz & Co. was entitled to an injunction that prevented Dasher and others from constructing and using the machines.

A case espousing the same view is *Todd Protectograph Co.* v. *Hirschberg,* decided by a New York court in 1917. Hirschberg had been employed with the Todd Protectograph Company and during the course of his employment he became familiar with a list of Todd Protectograph's customers as well as other confidential information concerning its trade methods. Hirschberg had entered into a contract with Todd Protectograph to the effect that he would not divulge any confidential information obtained by him during his employment and that he would not become employed with a competitor within one year after the termination of the contract. According to the court, Hirschberg breached this contract after termination with Todd Protectograph. This resulted in a suit against Hirschberg by Todd Protectograph. Although the court found that the law implied an obligation upon Hirschberg not to reveal trade secret information, the court stated that "[t]he right to such relief is strengthened where a contract between the parties exists relating to the subject." Accordingly, Todd Protectograph was held to be entitled to a decree that prohibited Hirschberg from revealing the trade secrets of his former employer or from working for a competitor for a period of one year.

Covenants Not to Compete: An Alternative Approach. Particularly in an area where a corporation lacks certainty that it can prevent trade secret misappropriation because, for example, it is not sure how secret its alleged trade secrets will turn out to be under the hostile climate of a court contest, the corporation should give serious consideration to the alternative approach of relying on covenants not to compete to keep former employees away from its competition for a reasonable period of time. Such use of covenants not to compete has the advantage of being a relatively simply way to safeguard marginally protectable, short-term trade secrets in that the corporation may thereby avoid the highly difficult burden of proof it would otherwise have to sustain in trade secret litigation.

The reasonableness of covenants not to compete is governed by state law but the principles by which reasonableness is judged are nevertheless fairly uniform. Of key importance is the balancing of the former employee's right to earn a living with the former employer's right to preserve the confidentiality of information he has developed at his own expense to give him a commercial advantage over his competitors but that he necessarily confided to his former employee during the course of employment. The use of covenants not to compete provides a greater measure of certainty of success. Of equal significance are the cost benefits from a management standpoint that flow from their use. It is much less expensive to have covenants tailored to be lawful than to sue in tort in such difficult causes of action as trade secrets cases can become.

Although the *Dasher* and *Hirschberg* cases are similar in that they each found trade secret protection to be justified by the common law and that the position of the parties seeking protection of their trade secrets was further strengthened by existence of provisions in the contracts of employment that bound Dasher and Hirschberg not to reveal confidential information, these two cases differed in their treatments of the covenants not to compete contained in each of the two contracts. In *Dasher* the court held that it would be unreasonable to prohibit Dasher from working for a competitor of L. M. Rabinowitz & Co. in the hook and eye tape business for the eight years remaining after two years had expired since Dasher's termination of employment with L. M. Rabinowitz & Co. as the contract had provided. The court took note of Dasher's long experience in the hook and eye tape business that had preceded his employment with L. M. Rabinowitz & Co. and the fact that this was the only field for which he was particularly suited. The court stated that "equity does not look with favor upon covenants restricting a man from earning his livelihood for a long period of time" and found that to impose this contractual provision on Dasher would be "unjust and oppressive."

Conversely, the court in *Hirschberg* found that Hirschberg's covenant not to compete with Todd Protectograph for a period of one year following termination of his employment there was reasonable and hence enforceable. From the fact that a ten-year covenant not to compete was held to be unreasonable and unenforceable in one case and a one-year covenant not to compete was held to be reasonable and enforceable in another case, it can be correctly inferred that the duration of a covenant not to compete is one factor a court will consider in judging the reasonableness of the covenant. The other factor is the reasonableness of the geographic scope of the covenant not to compete. However, when the object of a covenant not to compete is to protect trade secrets, the territorial restrictions involved may not be the subject of inquiry, because disclosure of confidential information wherever made can deliver the subject matter of the trade secrets into the public domain, thereby precluding further protection to the information under trade secret law. Where, however, the subject matter of the trade secret is customer lists or customer information, the territorial restriction of the covenant not to compete must be reasonably related to the location and nature of the employer's customers. In other words, whether the court is looking at the duration or the geographical territory that the restriction covers, the restriction must be no more than is reasonably necessary to protect the one for whose benefit the promise is made.

Hazards of General Contract Language.   One final word of caution regarding the use of contract to protect trade secrets is in order. It is advisable, when drawing up such a contract, to alert the person who is not to divulge trade secrets just what information is to be protected by the contract. The wisdom of such advice is illustrated by *Motorola, Inc.* v. *Fairchild Camera and Instrument Corp.*, decided by a federal district court in 1973. The controversy in this case arose when eight executives left Motorola for employment with Fairchild Camera. One of the charges made by Motorola against these ex-employees and Fairchild Camera was the misappropriation of its trade secrets. Each of these ex-employees had signed a contract with Motorola stating that he would maintain strictly confidential during his employment and for two years after the termination thereof information "of a confidential or secret nature such as product, machine, and process developments, whether patentable or not patentable manufacturing 'know-how' and specifications, cost and pricing practices, customers' lists, records of customers' requirements and usage, personnel records, company financial records, and the like." Although this contract language might be considered to be a vague general description of the kinds of information that would be considered to be trade secrets, the court was of the opinion that the language advised the employees neither generally nor specifically what things Motorola "considered proprietary." In short, this was insufficient notice. The court noted that in other similar companies in the same industry, employees were given lists of information that the companies considered to be trade secrets and upon termination these companies required a "signed document acknowledging specifically identified and claimed trade secrets." The absence of such specific identification on the part of Motorola was one factor which led the court to dismiss Motorola's complaint against Fairchild Camera. Thus the lesson of this case is clear to those wishing to give adequate trade secret notice by contract.

ACQUISITION AND CONVEYANCING OF TRADE SECRETS

Internal Development

Ownership.   We have seen in numerous instances that where an employer is the owner of a trade secret, employees and others to whom such a trade secret has been confided by the employer are under a legal obligation not to use it improperly or disclose it to others. It has also been seen, however, from a discussion of *Wexler* v. *Greenberg* and related cases on pp. 136–138, pp. 160–163, that the employer, although the owner of the trade secret, may not be able to enjoin his former employee from using a trade secret because, as in *Wexler*, for example, the employee was the source of the trade secret and the court was swayed by the right of the employee to continue to earn a living following the termination of the employment wherein the trade secret was developed. However, the fact that the former employee was the source of the trade secret and wishes to use this trade secret in subsequent employment to earn a living will not necessarily persuade a court that the former employer under whose aegis the trade secret was developed is not entitled to prevent the former employee from using his trade secret.

A federal district court in Connecticut was not so persuaded in *Sperry Rand Corporation* v. *Rothlein*, decided in 1964 and already discussed in the area "Misuse after Termination of Employment." There, it will be recalled, Rothlein and other employee defendants left Sperry Rand to set up a competing company, the National Semiconductor Corporation, for the manufacture of the silicon alloy fusion transistor and other devices, and in so doing utilized trade secrets they had learned at Sperry Rand. The court expressly recognized that Rothlein and the other defendants had themselves developed the trade secrets that they attempted later to use in competition with Sperry Rand. That the court refused to find that Rothlein and the other defendants were therefore privileged to use these trade secrets can be explained by a couple of facts that were not present in the *Wexler* case. Wexler alone had conceived the trade secrets that his employer later unsuccessfully tried to prevent Wexler from using, whereas the trade secrets in Sperry Rand had been developed by many employees who worked together on Sperry Rand's research and development staff. Wexler had not made any agreement that trade secrets that he developed would become the property of his employer. On the other hand, Rothlein and the other defendants in *Sperry Rand* expressly agreed that they would not, either during or subsequent to their terms of employment with Sperry, divulge to unauthorized persons any secret information, whether acquired or developed by them in the course of employment or obtained from other employees.

Wexler can be further distinguished from *Sperry Rand*. In *Wexler*, the trade secret formulas were developed by Greenberg through a relatively simple process of reverse engineering the products of competitors. Under these circumstances it was not necessary for Greenberg's employer to provide him with technical assistance and supervision. In *Sperry Rand*, however, the trade secret information was the result of corporate research and development that called for a more supportive role on the part of the employer, Sperry Rand.

On the question of ownership, the differences in the results of *Wexler* and *Sperry Rand* merit further clarification. In *Sperry Rand* the former employer was held to be the owner of the trade secrets and the former employees were denied the use of these trade secrets. In *Wexler,* the trade secrets remained the property of the former employer, but in addition, Greenberg was given the privilege of using these same trade secrets in subsequent employment. Thus, on the question of ownership, these two cases both hold that the former employers remain the owners of trade secrets, although they were developed by former employees who wished to use these secrets in competition with their former employers.

Several other trade secrets cases hold that where the former employee develops the trade secret by himself or with the help of his co-workers, ownership of these trade secrets vests in the employer. Among these cases is *Head Ski Company* v. *Kam Ski Company,* decided by the federal district court in Maryland in 1958. When Howard Head embarked on a course of developing a plastic and metal ski that utilized aircraft construction techniques, he hired defendants Meyer and Kaminski, both of whom he had worked with in previous employment. Head formed the Head Ski Company and was eventually very successful in producing the ski he had envisioned. Meyer and Kaminski left Head and went into business by themselves to produce skis, eventually forming the Kam Ski Company. The ski that Meyer and Kaminsky produced embodied many of the materials and processes that they themselves had helped to develop while employed by Head. The Head Ski Company brought suit against Meyer, Kaminski, and their Kam Ski Company for having taken by improper means trade secrets belonging to the Head Ski Company. The court found that the processes and materials used by Kam Ski that Kaminsky and Meyer had helped to develop while employed by Head qualified as trade secrets. The court held, by implication, that these trade secrets belonged to the Head Ski Company and enjoined the Kam Ski Company from continuing to use them. The result in this case is identical to the result in *Sperry Rand.* In both cases the former employees had signed written agreements with their former employers that they would not divulge trade secrets, and in both cases the trade secrets were developed as part of a team effort.

It is not safe to assume from the foregoing cases, however, that the employment relationship itself gives the employer ownership of inventions made by the employee during the course of his employment. A case that sheds some light on the established rule of law in this area is *Wireless Specialty Apparatus Co.* v. *Mica Condenser Co.*, decided by the Supreme Judicial Court of Massachusetts in 1921. The Wireless Specialty Apparatus Company, in order to engage itself in the business of producing magneto condensers, directed its employees in experimentation that led to certain inventions relating to such production. Some of the employees who were responsible for these inventions left Wireless Specialty and attempted to use these inventions elsewhere. As a result, Wireless Specialty brought suit against these former employees, the Mica Condenser Co., and other corporations to enjoin such use, claiming that use of these inventions was a misappropriation of its trade secrets.

The court addressed itself to the question of who owned the inventions, observing what it considered to be a well-established principle that where an employee develops an invention during the course of his employment, and although at the employer's expense, that invention remains the property of the employee unless by the terms of his employment or otherwise he agreed to transfer the ownership, as distinguished from its use, of the invention. The court also recognized, however, that where an employee is hired to accomplish a particular result, he cannot, upon the accomplishment of that result, claim ownership. In reconciling these two principles in application to the facts before it, the Massachusetts court reasoned that because the defendant former employees had been hired by Wireless Specialty solely to develop the inventions in question, they understood or ought to have understood that Wireless Specialty intended to maintain the secrecy of these inventions. The relationship of trust and confidence that thereby developed between employer and employees prevented the former employees from successfully claiming ownership in the inventions. The fact that there was no express agreement that ownership would vest in the employer was not fatal to Wireless Specialty's cause of action because such an agreement was implied by the just described circumstances. Accordingly, Wireless Specialty won the case.

Another case in which the question of ownership of trade secrets arose is *Daniel Orifice Fitting Co.* v. *Whalen*, decided by a California court in 1962. Whalen had been employed by the Daniel Orifice Fitting Company to conceive and design improvements to piston-controlled check valves that were produced by the company. For a number of years Whalen dutifully performed these functions for the benefit of his employer. In 1956, however, although Whalen continued to devise these improvements, he declined to contribute the fruits of his labor to Daniel Orifice but instead shelved them away for his own use at a later time. That time came in 1959, when Whalen resigned from Daniel Orifice to set up a corporation, Whalen, Inc., to compete with Daniel

Orifice in the manufacture and sale of a line of valves and other related products. Daniel Orifice sued Whalen and his corporation to prevent them from using or disclosing to others the valve improvements in the form of drawings and patterns that Whalen had devised while employed with Daniel Orifice. What made the question of ownership interesting in this case was that Whalen had worked on the new improvements and designs in question away from the plant of Daniel Orifice and on his own time. Notwithstanding these facts, the court ruled that the product of such work rightfully belonged to Daniel Orifice. Moreover, the fact that Whalen had turned over to Daniel Orifice the plans and improvements he had devised before he began diverting them for his own benefit meant to the court that Whalen considered himself bound to do so under his contract of employment.

Shop Rights. Closely related to the question of ownership of trade secrets is the common law doctrine of shop rights, because although an employer may be denied ownership of his employee's invention, he may nevertheless be entitled to a royalty-free right to use it through this doctrine. It has already been seen in the preceding chapter that the shop-right doctrine is applicable where the invention is protected under the patent laws. Because the reason for the application of the shop-right doctrine is the fact that the employer has contributed to the completion of an invention by virtue of the use of company time, facilities, and materials, the employer can obtain the shop right whether the invention is protected by the patent laws or trade secret law. In the case of trade secrets, however, where the employee never discloses his secret to his employer, the shop-right doctrine would naturally never come into play.

One case in which the shop-right rule arose in a trade secret context is *Kinkade* v. *New York Shipbuilding Corp.,* decided by the New Jersey Supreme Court in 1956. Kinkade was employed with the New York Shipbuilding Corporation as a tinsmith in a crew whose work involved the installation of sleeping bunks in ships. The extreme complexity of the installation method led Kinkade to conceive a more simple method while he was at home one night. Kinkade disclosed his idea to his supervisor, who thought it was a "good idea" and said it would be used on the next ship. From that point on New York Shipbuilding's facilities, time, and materials were used toward the implementation of the new bunk installation method, which eventually proved to be a success. When New York Shipbuilding failed to compensate Kinkade, he brought suit against his employer. The court ruled that although there had not been sufficient publication of Kinkade's design to destroy the secrecy necessary for trade secret protection, the case was controlled by the shop-right rule rather than trade secret principles. The court explained that in order for the employer to be the owner of an invention developed by its employee, in the absence of an express contract, the employer must demonstrate that the inventor was hired specifically to use his inventive powers for the benefit of his employer. Failing this, the employer can gain an irrevocable but nonexclusive royalty-free shop right to the invention by establishing that the invention was conceived and developed during company time with the help of coworkers and with the employer's materials and facilities. The court found that New York Shipbuilding had succeeded in meeting this test. Kinkade had on his own time only conceived the abstract idea, which he had reduced to a crude design on a scrap of paper. The rest of the development of the design was solely at the time and expense of the company. Because Kinkade failed to show an express or implied promise on the part of New York Shipbuilding to compensate him for the use of his design and invention, the situation was controlled by the shop-right rule.

Licenses

Licenses as Methods of Transfer. We have already seen in this chapter, pp. 192–193, that trade secrets may be transferred by way of assignment. The distinction between an assignment and a license is that the licensor keeps legal title, whereas the assignor relinquishes such title. Because the one transferring trade secrets will usually want to retain legal title so that he still has control over the use of the trade secrets by others, licensing is a more common method of transfer than assignment, apart from corporate acquisition and unsolicited disclosure transactions. Trade secrets are sometimes licensed as part of the same contract that licenses patent rights. An agreement must be reached between the licensor and the licensee as to the economic value of the trade secret to be licensed. Factors to be considered in deciding upon value include savings of time and expense compared to independent development, short-term and long-term economic advantages to be reaped by use of the secret by the licensee, and the lead time advantages arising from degree of difficulty others would encounter in acquring the secret or other competitive technology by independent discovery or development.

Although trade secret violations are generally governed by tort law, in the trade secret licensing situation contract law provides the means for seeking legal redress. A case that well illustrates this proposition is *Aktiebolaget Bofors* v. *United States,* decided by the District of Columbia Court of Appeals in 1951. Aktiebolaget Bofors was a Swedish corporation that manufactured and sold munitions and was the owner of a secret process that enabled it to produce a superior 40-mm. antiaircraft gun. Wishing to acquire this secret process, the U.S. Navy Department entered into a contract whereby Bofors granted to the Navy Department, for $600,000 an "Exclusive and irrevocable license to make, use and have made in the United States for the United States use" the Bofors 40-mm. guns for army and navy use and ammunition therefor. After Bofors disclosed its trade secret, the United States government not only began using it to manufacture the guns and ammunition but also transferred the guns and ammunition to other nations.

Bofors claimed that these transfers were in violation of the license restrictions and argued informally that a royalty arrangement be worked out for the unauthorized use of the trade secret or, in the alternative, that the dispute be submitted to arbitration. When these efforts were of no avail, it brought an action against the government under the Federal Tort Claims Act for damages in the amount of $2 million. The court necessarily addressed itself to the question of whether the cause of action was properly presented as arising in tort. The court explained that when one takes the trade secret of another by improper means, he "violates his property right and commits a tort." The tort lies in the unlawful appropriation. But in the licensing situation the trade secret is acquired by lawful means and the one so acquiring the trade secret by license is free to use it in any way he wishes unless the license contains a restriction as to its use. If the licensee contravenes that restriction, he commits no tort but is liable for a breach of contract because the duty he breaks was created by the license contract. Thus in order to prevail in a cause of action for violation of a trade secrect license, a contract must be pleaded and proved. Because the Federal Tort Claims Act does not permit recovery where the basis of recovery is contract, the Court of Appeals affirmed the trial court's dismissal of Bofors' complaint.

The way in which contractual provisions or the absence of them can govern the outcome of trade secret license litigation is illustrated in *Venn* v. *Goedert*, decided by the Eighth Circuit Court of Appeals in 1963. Defendant Goedert had obtained a license in the form of a franchise for making and selling cookies from plaintiff Venn. Upon termination of Goedert's franchise, Goedert continued to make and sell a line of cookies similar to that covered by the franchise. The court ruled that because the parties had not agreed as part of the license that Goedert would refrain from making and selling a similar line of cookies upon termination of the license, Venn could not prevent Goedert from so doing.

Duration of the License. Although the licensee may be permitted to use a process similar to that covered by a license after the license has terminated, the licensee is generally prohibited from using the very same secret subject matter covered by the license once the license is terminated. The very opposite situation presents itself where the licensee ceases to use the trade secret subject matter of the license prior to the agreed-upon termination date of the license. The question is whether the licensee is obligated to continue to pay royalties after he has stopped using the secret but before the agreed-upon expiration date of the license has passed. One case that provides an answer to this question is *Montgomery* v. *Kalak Water Company of New York, Inc.,* decided by a New York federal district court in 1961. The subject matter of the trade secret license was a formula for a medicated water called Kalak Water. The license for use of the formula was entered into in 1915 and was to last for ninety-nine years. The licensees were to pay royalties based on sales of "quart bottles" of the medicated water. The license contained no provisions to cover the event of substantial change or abandonment of the formula by the licensee. In 1960 the licensee abandoned use of licensor's formula and began producing a medicated water under a different formula. The court accepted the licensee's argument that it was therefore not obligated to continue to pay royalties under the license after 1960.

The present state of the law does not provide a clear answer as to whether trade secret royalties can be exacted from a licensee after the subject matter of the trade secret covered by the license has become public knowledge. One answer to this question is provided by *Warner-Lambert Pharmaceutical Co.* v. *John J. Reynolds, Inc.* In 1881 J. W. Lambert, the predecessor in interest to plaintiff Warner-Lambert, entered into a license with Dr. J. J. Lawrence, the predecessor in interest to defendant John J. Reynolds, Inc., whereby Lambert acquired from Lawrence the use of the secret formula for Listerine mouthwash in consideration for which Lambert agreed to make periodic payments to Lawrence and his successors based on the amount of Listerine mouthwash manufactured or sold. According to the court, the agreement was to remain in effect as long as Lambert and his successors manufactured or sold Listerine mouthwash. However, Warner-Lambert sought a judgment declaring that it was no longer under a duty to pay royalties for use of the formula because the secrecy of the formula evaporated when it was published in various medical publications through no fault of Warner-Lambert or its predecessors. None of the agreements between the predecessors of Warner-Lambert and John J. Reynolds contained any language as to what would happen if the formula for Listerine became public knowledge. Warner-Lambert argued that its obligation to pay under the license was coextensive only with secrecy of the formula rather than its use and that it was a forbidden "perpetuity" that the law would not enforce. But enforce it the court did, as it could find no support for

Warner-Lambert's argument. The court ruled that the agreement could terminate only when Warner-Lambert ceased manufacturing or selling Listerine mouthwash. The court took note of the fact that for twenty-five years after public disclosure of the formula, Warner-Lambert's predecessor continued to pay royalties before asserting its right to stop paying these royalties because of the disclosure. This the court found to be "strong evidence that the obligation to pay still continues in force and effect, if any such evidence were needed." Certainly one lesson of the *Listerine* case is that a prospective licensee of a trade secret should insist on a provision in the license that would terminate the obligation to pay royalties upon public disclosure of the trade secret. The licensor might reasonably insist, however, that the licensee obligate himself to pay royalties for some time after possible public disclosure of the trade secret in view of the head start the licensee gains over his competitors by virtue of the initial confidential disclosure under the license.

The validity of the holding in the *Listerine* case is now somewhat questionable under a U.S. Supreme Court case, *Lear, Inc.* v. *Adkins,* decided in 1969. Lear hired Adkins, an inventor and engineer, in 1952 to aid in solving problems it was having in developing gyroscopes. Lear and Adkins agreed that "new ideas, discoveries, inventions, etc. related to . . . vertical gyros become the property of" Adkins and that Adkins would grant a license to Lear on all ideas he might develop "on a mutually satisfactory royalty basis." Soon after this agreement was reached, Adkins developed a method of building the gyroscope that improved its accuracy at low cost; Lear immediately incorporated it into its production process. In 1954 Adkins filed a patent application to cover these improvements. At about the same time, Lear and Adkins entered into license negotiations that eventually concluded in 1955 with an agreement that provided that if the "Patent Office refuses to issue a patent . . . or if such a patent so issued is subsequently held invalid . . . Lear at its option shall have the right forthwith to terminate the specific license so affected or to terminate this entire Agreement. . . ." Lear finally obtained his patent in 1960. Meanwhile, however, in 1957, Lear searched the files of the Patent Office and found a patent that it contended had fully anticipated Adkins' discovery and for this reason stated that it would no longer pay royalties on gyroscopes produced at its Michigan plant, although it did continue payments on a smaller number of gyroscopes produced at Lear's California plant until 1959.

When Adkins obtained his patent in 1960 he initiated a lawsuit in the California courts and when the case reached the U.S. Supreme Court, he maintained his argument "that since Lear obtained special benefits before 1960, it should also pay royalties during the entire patent period (1960–1977), without regard to the validity of the Patent Office's grant." In rejecting this argument, the Supreme Court cast considerable doubt on whether a licensee of a trade secret is obligated to continue to pay royalties when the trade secret, subject of a licensed patent application, becomes publicly disclosed by issuance of the patent that is held invalid, because the Court ruled in *Lear* that Lear would not have to pay royalties under the license if it proved that Adkins' patent was invalid. However, it should be noted that the Court relied at least in part in making this ruling on the terms of the 1955 agreement, which stated that royalties would be paid until the "patent . . . is held invalid." Of course, that was not the situation in the *Listerine* case, because that trade secret had not been the subject of a patent application which matured into a patent that thereafter either was held invalid or expired. However, an argument can be made that the Supreme Court intended its holding to reach situations like those in the *Listerine* case by its reference to the "strong federal policy favoring the full and free use of ideas in the public domain."

In 1972 a California court in *Choisser Research Corp.* v. *Electronic Vision Corp.,* although without referring to the preceding language in *Lear,* expressly held that the *Listerine* case is no longer law under *Lear.* In this case a license agreement was entered into between Waddell Dynamics, Inc., and Choisser Research Corp. ("CRC") in 1966 in which Waddell agreed to pay CRC royalties for " 'know-how,' designs, and unpatented inventions." In the event no patent or patents issued, the term of the agreement was to be the greater of the useful life of the unpatentable inventions, designs, and design rights covered under the agreement or ten years. In 1968 CRC consented to the assignment of the license agreement to the Electronic Vision Corporation ("EVC"). As part of the agreement, Waddell agreed that it would not divulge any information regarding the subject matter of the license for a period of three years, or until July 31, 1971. In a suit for back royalties by CRC against EVC, the court ruled that EVC must pay royalties up to and including July 31, 1971, but not after that date, because the subject matter of the license was at least theoretically no longer a secret.

To add further to the uncertainty of the answer to this question, a leading trade secret licensing case, *Painton & Company* v. *Bourns, Inc.,* decided by the Second Circuit Court of Appeals in 1971, would appear to favor the result in *Listerine* to the result in *Choisser* with Judge Friendly's statement that "[i]n thousands of contracts businessmen have divulged such secrets to competitors, dealing at arms' length and well able to protect themselves, on the faith that mutually acceptable provisions for payment . . . will be enforced by the courts."

Trade Secret–Antitrust Problems. The antitrust point of reference for agreements concerning trade secret rights is usually Sections 1 and 2 of the Sherman Act, which as we have seen in Chapter 2, pp. 98–99, prohibit contracts in unreasonable restraint of trade, monopolization, and attempts to monopolize where either the interstate or the foreign commerce of the United States is involved. The problems that the Sherman Act raises initially arise from the fact that rights in trade secrets permit the owner to exclude or control others in the use of the property. In the sense that appropriation by improper means can be stopped somewhat akin to copyright infringement principles, each trade secret owner is the possessor of a legal, albeit limited, monopoly. However, when the permissive boundaries for commercially exploiting this limited monopoly are overstepped, antitrust liability can follow. When the trade secret owner simply uses this internally developed property in his own business—for example, by using a trade secret process to manufacture a commercial product—he is not likely to run into antitrust problems solely on this basis.

Contrasted with the situation where the trade secret owner uses his rights "in-house," some difficulty may be encountered once he decides to license to others the authority to exploit his trade secret rights. The uninitiated owner of a trade secret might react to this suggestion with the rejoinder that because he has the exclusive right to use his secret barring independent discovery by others, and by licensing others to use it he is promoting competition, he should be able to attach any conditions to the license he may choose. This is not the law, however. In light of the policy of free and open competition embodied in the Sherman Act, the courts will find that once the trade secret owner decides to exploit the trade secret by licensing, he must satisfy the same antitrust standards as are applicable to other commercial transactions and agreements.

TERRITORIAL RESTRICTIONS. An aspect of trade secret licensing that is most likely to become the focal point of antitrust scrutiny is territorial restrictions contained in the license. Territorial restrictions in a license of trade secrets are generally more vulnerable from the antitrust point of view than those in a patent license because trade secrets are not protected as are patents through any statutory schemes of national scope. However, the rule of reason is usually applicable with respect to territorial restrictions in the trade secret context. The application of a rule of reason means that a court will make an inquiry into the purpose and effect of an arrangement in order to see whether it is reasonable and therefore legal.

It will be recalled that a territorial restriction in a trade secret license was held to be reasonable and therefore enforceable in the 1889 pre-Sherman Act case of *Fowle* v. *Park,* decided by the U.S. Supreme Court and discussed earlier in this chapter, p. 120. However, the courts have not spoken authoritatively on the question of when a license of valuable and secret unpatented technology can validly include, as an "ancillary restraint," a territorial limitation. In some cases, the courts have failed to reach the question, concluding that the know-how involved did not amount to a valuable trade secret or else that the territorial restrictions went too far to be reasonably related to the license itself.

In the famous *duPont Cellophane* case, a French firm, eminent in the cellophane field, granted to duPont, which was in the early stages of developing its cellophane business, the exclusive right to manufacture cellophane in North and Central America under the French secret process. The French company agreed not to compete in duPont's territory. On a challenge by the government under the Sherman Act, the district court rejected the former's argument that a "territorially limited license under a secret process is *per se* illegal." The district court held the territorial limitation in question to be a reasonable ancillary restraint to the license agreement "since the participants were not in fact competitors" and the beneficial result of the agreement was the "creation of the American cellophane industry." The U.S. Supreme Court affirmed the judgment of the district court but did not expressly pass on this particular feature of the licensing arrangement.

Although such a territorial limitation in a license between two sizable industrial concerns who are competitors in the same business will not receive the same lenient treatment under the present state of antitrust development, the recourse to the rule of reason would appear still valid at least in limited circumstances.

FIELDS OF USE. Field-of-use restrictions by which licensee and licensor agree not to compete with one another in the use of the licensed trade secret are similar in nature to territorial restrictions and are also governed by resort to a rule of reason, as with patent licenses, p. 112. In *A. & E. Plastik Pak Co.* v. *Monsanto*, decided by the Ninth Circuit Court of Appeals in 1968, A & E challenged a trade secret license between itself and Monsanto, the licensor, as a violation of the Sherman Act because of a contested provision in the license in which A & E promised not to compete with Monsanto in the public sale of a durable type of plastic sheet but would use it for internal purposes only. The court reasoned that the latter provision did not appear to be an agreement between competitors not to compete, for in the absence of the licensed secret know-how, A & E would not have any opportunity to compete with Monsanto in the sale of the plastic. Although the court did not ultimately decide this antitrust issue in the case, it stated that in order to decide this issue, an inquiry would need to be made into "whether the restriction may fairly be said to be ancillary to a commercially supportable licensing arrangement, or whether the licensing scheme is a sham set up for the purpose of controlling competition while avoiding the consequences of the antitrust laws."

GOVERNMENT CONTRACT ASPECTS OF TRADE SECRETS

When the federal government enters into a contract with a private party, there often arises a need on the part of the government to know certain information covered by the contract. The government's need for such information, which often involves trade secrets, may arise from its desire to stimulate competition for orders and thereby reduce the costs of future procurement. The government may also want this information to enable it to make available to the public new processes and products. The primary need, however, is for use and repair of items ordered under a contract. The rights of the parties to this information are often referred to as "data rights"; problems arise where rights are asserted by the government to data that might disclose trade secrets. The threat of such disclosure can be a cause of greater concern to private contractors than the loss of patent rights. Although competitors can infringe patents in the performance of government contracts as a matter of law, if trade secrets are protected, they can make it difficult for competitors to take government business.

The type of government contracting relationship to be discussed here is the government–contractor relationship. The problems arise when the government wishes to order items under the contract that may require disclosure of trade secrets. The government–contractor relationship also may involve the situation where trade secrets are developed under a research and development contract or where background trade secrets are intertwined with research or development work under the contract. The contractor's need to protect his trade secrets does nothing to lessen the government's need for information that contains these secrets.

Agency Data Policies

Because there is a dearth of legislation pertaining to government contracting aspects of trade secrets, the government agencies have taken a variety of positions as to any protection to be afforded trade secrets of government contractors. The Armed Services Procurement Regulation (ASPR) for the Department of Defense (DOD) states that as a general policy, the government wishes to acquire only those technical data rights which are necessary for it to meet its needs. ASPR states that DOD takes unlimited rights in the following six types of data:

(1) technical data resulting directly from performance of experimental, developmental, or research work which was specified as an element of performance in a Government contract or subcontract;

(2) technical data necessary to enable others to manufacture end-items, components and modifications, or to enable them to perform processes, when the end-items, components, modifications or processes have been, or are being, developed under Government contracts or subcontracts in which experimental, developmental or research work was specified as an element of contract performance, except technical data pertaining to items, components or processes developed at private expense;

(3) technical data prepared or required to be delivered under any Government contract or subcontract and constituting corrections or changes to Government-furnished data;

(4) technical data pertaining to end-items, components or processes, prepared or required to be delivered under any Government contract or subcontract, for the purpose of identifying sources, size, configuration, mating and attachment characteristics, functional characteristics and performance requirements ("form, fit and function" data, e.g., specification control drawings, catalog sheets, envelope drawings, etc.);

(5) manuals or instructional materials prepared or required to be delivered under a Government contract or subcontract for installation, operation, maintenance, or training purposes; and

(6) technical data which is in the public domain or has been or is normally furnished without restriction by the contractor or subcontractor.

Except as provided in the preceding cases technical data pertaining to items, components, or processes developed at private expense will be acquired with limited rights. This means that the government can use the data internally for purposes of use and repair but cannot disclose it or use it for manufacture.

When DOD needs trade secrets with unlimited rights but to which the contractor intends to give only limited rights, having a right to do so under the criteria just set forth, such data should be identified before the award of the contract is made, if possible, and an agreement with respect to this should be made a part of the contract. This is known as "predetermination of rights in technical data." This procedure is not supposed to be used to require the contractor to furnish with unlimited rights that which he is entitled to furnish with limited rights. If the government's need for unlimited rights is strong enough, ASPR provides for specific acquisition by DOD of unlimited rights in technical data to which DOD would normally take only limited rights.

When the contractor submits data to which DOD is to have only limited rights, in accordance with ASPR each piece of data should be marked with a restrictive legend. The contractor should indicate which parts of the data the legend pertains to by circling, underscoring, or otherwise noting the specific parts of the data to which limited rights apply. Further, the contractor should explain the indication used to identify the limited-rights data.

DOD has the right to require the contractor to provide clear and convincing evidence that restrictive markings were properly used. Technical data received without restrictive markings are taken by DOD with unlimited rights unless within six months the contractor is permitted to place restrictive markings on such data by satisfying certain requirements set forth in ASPR. Notwithstanding what the ASPR says, if the trade secret owner has a strong enough bargaining position, he can refuse to sell to the government unless there is an ASPR deviation changing data requirements to his satisfaction.

Pursuant to NASA research and development contracts, the contractor is allowed to refrain from disclosing trade secrets that pertain to standard commercial items or trade secrets relating to items developed outside the contract and offered for sale to the general public as long as sufficient identification of the item is made to NASA. Because the NASA contractor is given the option of refraining from disclosing proprietary information, he is not permitted to put restrictive markings on the information he supplies to NASA.

The Atomic Energy Commission (AEC) employs a standard short provision that gives the government unlimited rights in all information concerning the work under the contract. But under an AEC regulation, this provision does not embrace "background secret processes, technical information, and know-how." However, the regulations provide sample alternate provisions, if the government wishes to acquire such information.

The Department of Transportation (DOT) uses a standard provision in its contracts that gives the government unlimited rights in information to be supplied under the contract. Contrasted with this, however, is a DOT regulation that provides that in certain instances where a contractor argues that particular information is confidential, the contracting official may change the clause so that the government would not have such unlimited rights.

The Office of Saline Water of the Department of the Interior uses a standard provision similar to that of NASA when a standard commercial item is to be included in the final product being ordered under the contract. The provision permits contractors to refrain from disclosing trade secrets, provided an adequate identification of the withheld trade secret is provided. This requirement for identification negates the regulation somewhat because the identifying information must enable others to manufacture and employ the final product being developed under the contract. Moreover, there is another requirement that the contractor must be willing to license others to utilize, for purposes of water desalination, any proprietary data concerning the product being developed under the contract. However, this licensing requirement does not extend to information related to items developed outside the contract.

Authority to Acquire Data

The acquisition of trade secrets by government agencies is expressly authorized by Congress for only a few government agencies. They include the Department of the Interior, the Environmental Protection Agency, and the Department of Defense. Although Congress has not expressly delegated this authority to most other agencies, such authority results by implication.

Disclosure of Data

The Solid Waste Disposal Act contains a provision that states, in effect, that where information containing trade secrets is developed under a government contract, the contract shall contain a provision that provides that this information will be made easily available to industries using methods of solid-waste disposal and industries that provide "devices, facilities, equipment, and supplies to be used in connection with solid-waste disposal."

A number of statutes require that information developed under contracts with specific agencies be made available to the public. Because such information includes trade secrets, many potential contractors are reluctant to deal with these agencies. However, most of these agencies have not implemented the authority granted under those statutes as to trade secrets, especially in view of the specific exemption against the public dissemination of trade secrets under the Freedom of Information Act.

Remedies for Disclosure of Data

Congress has not seen fit to provide many administrative remedies for trade secret violations and, generally speaking, executive agencies lack authority to settle claims. One remedy exists in the Foreign Assistance Act. This provides, in effect, that where the government uses or discloses trade secrets and in violation of restrictions imposed by the owner, the exclusive remedy of the owner is to sue the United States government for damages in a federal district court or the Court of Claims. However, the head of the government agency involved derives authority from this Act to settle by payment before suit. The claimant must accept the tender with "full satisfaction" in order for the claim to be paid.

Although there is generally no judicial remedy for the improper disclosure or use of a trade secret by the government, it may be possible to obtain jurisdiction in a federal district court or the Court of Claims in cases where the action against the government has a contractual basis or where an action under the Federal Tort Claims Act is appropriate.

One case in which a judicial remedy in the form of a preliminary injunction was granted against the government is *International Engineering Co.* v. *Richardson,* decided by the federal district court for the District of Columiba in 1973. The International Engineering Co. (IEC) had entered into a contract with the Air Force to develop a missile guidance subsystem. Concomitant with the development of this missile guidance subsystem, IEC developed an advanced navigation system that was included within the scope of the original contract by subsequent modification. In order to evaluate the latter system, the Air Force project engineer asked IEC to furnish three technical reports that contained a "detailed description of the internal operations . . . of IEC's precontract components. . . ." IEC complied with this request but affixed restrictive markings to each of the reports with the understanding that the government would take only limited rights in the data. However, the Air Force contracting officer objected to these restrictive markings and after the last payment on the contract advised IEC without explanation that the three reports would not be considered restricted and that the government would take unlimited rights in the data. To prevent public release of the reports, IEC sought an injunction, having already unsuccessfully protested to the government that the data contained trade secrets that should not be made public.

Because the court was of the opinion that IEC would eventually be successful, it granted a preliminary injunction to prevent public release of the reports pending a final determination on the merits. The court ruled that the procedure by which the contracting officer had made his decision to remove the restrictive markings on the three IEC reports was contrary to the requirements of the Armed Services Procurement Regulations, which required "that contracting officials make a meaningful inquiry and good faith effort in the exercise of their discretion." The contracting officer had acted only on the untested advice of the project engineer and thus having failed to make an independent determination, his arbitrary decision did not comply with the minimal due process requirements of the procurement regulations.

Only the government employee divulging such secrets may be held criminally liable. The federal statute providing for this sanction imposes a maximum fine of $1,000 or imprisonment not exceeding one year, or both, and provides that the individual committing this violation "shall be removed from office or employment."

Subcontractor Data

The subcontracting relationship involves the same trade secret issues that we have seen in the prime contracting relationship. In some instances the problems are even greater, because a subcontractor may be extremely reluctant to disclose to a prime who may be his competitor in other work, even when such disclosure is on a limited basis.

REMEDIES

We have seen that one very important aspect of trade secrets is that they give to their owners a commercial advantage over their competitors. It is this fact that has generated a law of trade secrets, because competitors wishing to eliminate that advantage sometimes are tempted to do so by improper means. When this happens, the law seeks to make the trade secret owner who has been wronged whole again through the use of the remedy of damages and to stop or prevent the improper use or disclosure of trade secrets by injunction where the need for such relief is established.

Injunction

In order for the need for injunctive relief to be established, the one seeking the injunction must show that he will suffer irreparable injury in the absence of such relief. Hence where damages at law are adequate relief, an injunction will not issue. The fact is, however, that damages are rarely an adequate form of relief for trade secret disclosure. For this reason injunction is the form of relief that is most commonly sought.

One very interesting question for which the courts have not provided us with a uniform answer is whether the wrongdoer, having destroyed a trade secret by his improper disclosure to the public, is free to use the matter formerly the subject of trade secret protection on the grounds that others are so permitted, because of evaporation of the trade secret. This is something like a situation where a wife murders her husband and then pleads for mercy at sentencing time on the ground she is a widow.

The *Shellmar* rule, developed by the Seventh Circuit Court of Appeals in 1937 in *Shellmar Products Co.* v. *Allen-Qualley Co.*, concludes that the one who wrongfully destroyed the trade secret is not entitled to use it (forever?) even though secrecy has ended. The theory behind this position is that the wrongdoer should not be permitted to profit by his own wrong. On the other side of the fence is the *Conmar* rule, developed in 1949 by the Second Circuit Court of Appeals in *Conmar Products Corp.* v. *Universal Slide Fastener Co., Inc.* Under this rule the one who wrongfully discloses a trade secret and thereby ends the trade secret protection that the owner had formerly enjoyed is permitted to use the former trade secret information, under the theory that because others can use the information, the wrongdoer can no longer cause irreparable injury to the former trade secret owner.

Some courts, instead of following strictly the application of either rule, find a middle ground by issuing an injunction against the wrongdoer for only a limited period of time. For example, in *Schulenburg* v. *Signatrol, Inc.*, decided in 1965, the Illinois Supreme Court was troubled by the fact that the duration of the injunction that had been imposed by the trial and appellate courts was unlimited. The court decided to limit the period of the injunction to the length of time it would have taken the defendants to develop the information they had unlawfully appropriated.

It is not only the initial wrongdoer (usually the ex-employee) who may be enjoined. The party to whom the trade secret is improperly disclosed may also be enjoined. An example of this is found in a 1956 Missouri federal district court decision, *Jerrold-Stephens Co.* v. *Gustaveson, Inc.* There, Gustaveson, Inc., had induced one Walters to leave the employ of Jerrold-Stephens Co. and to come into its employ in order to take advantage of trade secret information that Jerrold-Stephens had confided to Walters as its employee. The court applied a well-settled rule that where an employee leaves his employer knowing his ex-employer's trade secret information and then discloses it to a competitor to the detriment of his former employer, the subsequent employer will be enjoined from using such trade secret information.

Where the injunctive relief is based upon contract and such relief is sought after the duration of the restrictive covenant has expired, it would not seem logical to allow injunctive relief. This logic was recognized by the Supreme Court of Vermont in *Abalene Pest Control Service, Inc.* v. *Hall*, decided in 1966. Defendant Hall was employed by plaintiff Abalene Pest Control and predecessors in interest from 1947 to 1962. Hall's contract of employment stated that for two years after termination of employment, Hall would not compete with his employer either on his own or as an agent for another. Hall also agreed that for five years following termination of employment he would not disclose to anyone but his employer names and addresses of customers and customer information, nor would he solicit customers in the territory to which he had been assigned. After Hall left Abalene Pest Control in 1962 and before two years had expired since that date, he formed the L & N Pest Control Service, which competed with Abalene Pest Control. Although Abalene Pest Control was successful in winning a temporary injunction preventing Hall from competing with it and from soliciting its customers, the temporary injunction was dissolved by the final judgment of the Chancery Court. By the time the case was appealed to the Supreme Court of Vermont, the period of the two-year covenant not to compete had expired and was therefore moot. However, the court was able to enforce the five-year provisions of the contract, because that period of time had not elapsed.

Once a secret has been disclosed, the damage has been done and injunctive relief would often seem futile. Therefore if a showing is made by a plaintiff that the threat of disclosure is substantial and imminent, a preliminary injunction may issue before a disclosure has been made. We saw just this situation in *B. F. Goodrich Co.* v. *Wohlgemuth,* discussed earlier in this chapter, pp. 121–122. There, it will be recalled, Wohlgemuth left B. F. Goodrich to work for International Latex to compete with Goodrich in the pressure space-equipment field. Although there was no evidence before the court that Wohlgemuth had disclosed Goodrich's trade secrets to Latex, Goodrich was able to show to the court's satisfaction on the basis of Wohlgemuth's attitude that a substantial threat of disclosure existed and an injunction against Wohlgemuth should therefore issue. Had Goodrich waited until Wohlgemuth disclosed its trade secrets to International Latex, injunctive relief might have been futile. This illustrates the importance of moving fast for injunctive relief.

The battleground for a trade secret war between the trade secret owner and the feared misappropriator is customarily fought in the trenches of a preliminary injunction proceeding where relief is commonly sought days, or at most, weeks, after the trade secret owner suspects disclosure problems. In order to secure a preliminary injunction the party seeking this form of relief must show to the court's satisfaction that it is likely that he will ultimately prevail in a trial on the merits and that without the preliminary injunction he is likely to suffer irreparable harm. Many crucial rights are decided in a preliminary injunction proceeding because in the long course of litigation events leading to a trial, absent such a preliminary injunction, the value or availability of injunctive relief may dim considerably many months or even years later.

Damages

Although an injunction is usually a more significant form of remedy than damages, damages can still be important to the party who has been wronged by improper use or disclosure. They may be awarded as a supplement to injunctive relief or as the only form of relief.

Perhaps the most intriguing question with regard to damages is how they are measured. The fact that the means by which they are measured is based on probability is no reason for not granting such relief. This is so because the evidence in a case may show a cause of action that justifies damages and yet the damages may be difficult to determine. Nevertheless, damages should not be based on speculation or conjecture. One might logically conclude that either the damages to the injured plaintiff or the actual gain of the wrongdoer could serve as a basis for estimating the amount of damages to be awarded to the plaintiff. Rudolf Callman, a leading authority in the field, suggests that "[t]he plaintiff's probable loss may sometimes be the more significant measuring rod than the defendant's actual gain." The famous jurist Judge Learned Hand, of the Second Circuit Court of Appeals, observed in the 1929 case of *Harley & Lund Corporation* v. *Murray Rubber Co.* that the proper measure of damages is the "difference between the plaintiff's position after the defendants learned its secrets and before." This seems logical, for the purpose of damages is to put the plaintiff in the monetary position he would have been in had the improper use or disclosure of trade secrets not occurred. However, in a case where business is diverted directly from one party to another because the latter improperly appropriated the trade secrets of the former, the profits thereby accruing to the wrongdoer would appear to be a measure of the loss to the injured plaintiff.

In *Servo Corporation of America* v. *General Electric Co.*, decided by the Fourth Circuit Court of Appeals in 1965, where General Electric had unlawfully appropriated information belonging to the Servo Corporation, the court measured damages by what would have been the cost to General Electric in acquiring the same information by lawful means. This illustrates what has become known as the "head start" rule and has been employed by other courts as well.

Trademarks and Franchising

INTRODUCTION

This chapter deals with words and symbols used in association with suppliers' products and services to distinguish or differentiate these goods and services in the market place. Trademarks (for goods) and service marks (for services) are shorthand designations of origin and source that form a vocabularly basis for consumer choice. Basic considerations in this marketing field involve the ways in which enforceable rights are obtained, preserved, and lost. The general objective of avoiding market place confusion forms the thread of continuity in this field of law.

DEFINITIONS

It will be helpful to begin with a clarification of the terms *trademark, service mark, collective mark,* and *certification mark.* These terms identify the precise words used as shorthand designations of origin with which we will be concerned. However, it should be kept in mind that a mark may be variously classified, depending on how or by whom it is used. An example is the *L* for *Lions Club* that is used both by persons to indicate membership in the organization and by the Lions Club to designate the many community services it renders. Although the particular or peculiar nature, character, or function of marks will be considered later in greater detail, for our immediate purposes, it will be sufficient to turn to the definitions incorporated in the Lanham Trademark Act of 1946, the basic federal legislation in the field.

Trademark

The Lanham Act defines a trademark as "any word, name, symbol, or device or any combination thereof adopted and used by a manufacturer or merchant to identify his goods and distinguish them from those manufactured or sold by others." Note a distinction between a trademark and a trade name. A trade name is commonly a company name or a corporate name used to identify a business, vocation, or occupation. *General Motors* is the world-known trade name of a corporation, General Motors Corporation, which manufactures and sells products with varying trademarks like *Chevrolet, Frigidaire, GMC,* and the like. This does not mean that General Motors Corp. theoretically would have to stand idly by while a competitor came into the market place with a "General Motors" automobile; but the technical distinction in definitions shape the kind of legal action involved. On the other hand, a trade name may also be a trademark, as is the case with Chrysler Corp. selling *Chrysler* trademarked automobiles or Coca Cola Company selling *Coca-Cola* trademarked soft-drink products.

Service Mark

The definition of a service mark under the Lanham Act is

A mark used in the sale or advertising of services to identify the services of one person and distinguish them from the services of others. Titles, character names and other distinctive features of radio or television programs may be registered as service marks notwithstanding that they, or the programs, may advertise the goods of the sponsor.

A service mark is generally no different than a trademark other than the fact that it is associated with services rather than goods. Such service marks as *Hertz, Avis, Holiday Inn, McDonald's, TWA, PanAm, Greyhound,* and *Amtrack* illustrate the extent to which service marks are in the mainstream of the world of commerce.

Services such as fast-food restaurant services particularly lend themselves to a mode of distribution called franchising, whereby the owner of the service mark licenses others, called franchisees, to utilize the service mark under strict quality controls that the franchisor-licensor desires to be associated with the use of his service mark. *Howard Johnson's* is such a mark. However, *Howard Johnson's*, as with a great many marks, may be distinguished both as a service mark and a trademark, depending on the usage to which reference is made. Where the name is used to identify products associated with the business, it is a trademark, and the trademarked goods may be sold in conjunction with the services that the mark also designates (*Howard Johnson's* ice cream sold in *Howard Johnson's* restaurants) or apart from such services (*Howard Johnson's* frozen fried clams sold in supermarkets).

Certification Mark

A certification mark is defined by the Lanham Act as

a mark used upon or in connection with the products or services of one or more persons other than the owner of the mark to certify regional or other origin, material, mode of manufacture, quality, accuracy or other characteristics of such goods or services or that the work or labor on the goods or services was performed by members of a union or other organization.

An essential characteristic of a certification mark is the fact it is used by someone other than the owner of the mark. However, it is important to distinguish between the function of a certification mark (for goods or services) and a trademark or service mark that is used by licensees or franchisees (the *Howard Johnson's* example). A certification mark does not identify goods or services and distinguish them from those manufactured or sold by others, nor does it identify a single business as the source of such goods or services. It indicates only that the goods or services with which the mark is used meet standards or requirements that have been established by the owner of the mark, who does the certifying.

As already noted, in some instances the same mark may be used to identify both goods and services associated with a single business or owner. However that is not the case with a certification mark. In order to maintain the character and function of a certification mark, the owner may not use it in connection with his own goods or services, even goods or services that are different from those to which the certification mark is applied. Unlike marks generally, a certification mark may include a geographically descriptive term to indicate regional origin of the product on which the mark is used. Thus, *Grown in Idaho* is a familiar marking on potatoes, as is *Roquefort* on cheese made from sheep's milk and cured in the natural caves of Roquefort, France. An example of a mark that certifies characteristics of the products or services with which it is used is the Underwriters' stamp or seal of approval. This mark appears on a variety of goods—including safety matches, photographic film, fire fighting equipment, automotive equipment, and appliances—to indicate that "representative samplings of the product conform to the safety standards established by (Underwriters' Laboratories, Inc.)." *AP* (meaning "approved product") is a mark used on modeling clay, poster paint, crayons, water colors, and related art products that have been certified by the Crayon Water Color and Craft Institute as "nontoxic."

The standard or standards to which a certification mark applies need not be indicated by the mark itself. *Approved product,* as in the last-mentioned mark, or *Bonderized* for metal castings and forgings, say a great deal about the product on which the marks appear; however, certification marks are often more specific as to the standards certified, as, for example, *Certified Washable* (American Institute of Laundering) and *Certified Cleanable* (National Institute of Rug Cleaning).

Collective Mark

Under the Lanham Act the term *collective mark* means a "trademark or service mark used by the members of a cooperative, an association or other collective group or organization and includes marks used to indicate membership in a union, an association or other organization." The term *collective mark* encompasses marks used by members of a collective group or organization on goods that they produce (collective trademarks) or in connection with services that they render (collective service marks) to identify such goods or services and to distinguish them from those of nonmembers. To the extent that ownership and use of the mark are separated, a collective mark resembles a certification mark and with respect to a given fact situation it may be difficult to differentiate between these two classes of marks. Functionally, however, the marks are completely different. Although there will be a certain uniformity or similarity among goods or services bearing a trade or service mark owned by a collective group and used by its members, such goods or services will not have been certified as complying with quality standards. Identification of the "collective" source, not certification, is the particular province of the collective mark. In addition, a collective mark may indicate membership in the owner group or membership association. The identifying names and insignia of the Greek letter fraternities and sororities and other fraternal groups are well-known collective membership marks. The marks of such organizations appear, for example, on jewelry or lapel buttons; but collective membership marks may also take the form of metal plates (AAA) or patches (National Ski Patrol).

KINDS OF MARKS

Following the definition of marks used in the Lanham Act, a mark "includes any word, name, symbol, or device or any combination thereof." This description is not all-inclusive and marks have been recognized in subject matter that cannot be classified as a word, name, symbol, or device. These and related topical categories will be reviewed against the Lanham Act standards for federal trademark registration, it being understood that the word *trademark* is being used in a broad sense to embrace trademarks and service marks.

Words and Phrases

Contrary to popular belief, a word or combination of words need not be invented or coined to be a good trademark and, in fact, most marks are not. However, such words must differentiate the goods or services with which they are used from similar goods and services. Words that the whole world is free to use to designate a product or service or to describe its character or quality, or its intended use, are not distinctive and the phonetic or foreign equivalent will not necessarily convert them into a trademark. On this basis, federal registrations have been denied to *Kwixtart* for electric storage batteries and to *Flor-Tile* for tile flooring. *Yo-Yo* is an example of an improper trademark use of a foreign word inasmuch as it is the Filipino word for the popular toy. Similarly, registration has been denied to *La Posada* (Spanish word meaning "inn") for lodging and restaurant services and to *Ha-lush-ka* (phonetic equivalent of Hungarian word for "noodle") for egg noodle products.

With respect to marks that comprise a plurality of words, some of which are federally registrable and some of which are not because they are "free," the owner will not have an exclusive right to the nondistinctive portion and, in applying for registration, may be required to disclaim that portion. An example is the use of a geographical term or name as part of a mark ("of New York" or "from California"), because any manufacture or merchant may accurately describe the geographical origin of his goods or services. The problem that arises lies in determining whether the remaining or nondisclaimed portion of a mark consisting of several words (or words and symbols) is, in and of itself, a good trade or service mark. It may be that the nondistinctive portion is so essential to the mark as a whole that the disclaimer will not render the composite mark registrable. This is particularly significant in determining whether a slogan is a trademark. While registrations exist for marks in which every word was disclaimed apart from the particular combination for which registration was sought, generally, where no portion of the mark is salvageable as distinctive, registration will be denied. A *Product of Kimberly-Clark Research* was rejected as a trademark for the reasons that *Kimberly* and *Clark* were merely surnames and the remaining words were simply descriptive.

Colors

In most instances colors perform a decorative and ornamental function and, because of the limited number, a color in and of itself cannot be appropriated to the exclusive use of any individual or corporation as a mark. However, a color may serve as an integral part of a valid trademark and when used in connection with a distinctive shape or design may be granted trademark protection. Thus, trademarks have been found in a red dot on rubber heels for shoes and a red crown painted on the necks of bowling pins. Where, however, the colored design appears to be decoration only, evidence that the purchasing public recognizes the design as a trademark must be shown before protection will be granted. Such evidence was forthcoming with respect to a blue band on a drum container for paint driers. However, decorative bands of red and blue on the tops of men's ribbed socks were held not to be a trademark in the absence of proof that the colored bands also served to identify their origin.

Pictures and Symbols

Trademark protection is sometimes sought for pictures that are used either alone or in conjunction with words or other symbols. Whether or not such protection will be granted again depends upon the relationship between the picture and the goods or services with which it is used. If it is primarily descriptive in nature, it will be denied trademark protection. If the picture is otherwise distinctive and serves as an indicant of origin, its chances of success are improved considerably. The girl in a red swimming suit, applied to Jantzen swimming apparel, is a well-known pictorial mark, as is the running greyhound used in connection with bus transportation services. But where a picture is so commonly associated with a particular product as to become a generic designation for that product, it cannot be used exclusively by one manufacturer or merchant. For example, a picture of a hog is generic in connection with ham or bacon, as is a picture of a cow on butter, cheese, and other dairy products.

The use of certain pictures or symbols is regulated by statute. The Lanham Act specifically excludes the flag, coat of arms, or other insignia of the United States as subject matter for trademarks. Other statutes grant certain organizations, like the American National Red Cross and the Boy Scouts, the exclusive right to use their marks and symbols. The character and name of *Smokey Bear* are similarly restricted to the use of the Department of Agriculture. That is not to say that a picture of a bear or a cross or a campfire will never be considered a mark for commercial purposes. The image of a bear in conjunction with the word *Cub* has been registered for small aircraft. However, to the extent that such pictures and symbols, as actually used, infer an association with the well-known organization, they will be denied protection, as a matter of public policy, and denied registration as "deceptive" subject matter under the Lanham Act.

Numerals and Letters

Numerals and letters, individually or in groups that do not make up a word, can be very successful marks. Often used in a distinctive form or design and frequently derived from the business or corporate name of the owner, such marks are easily remembered. Although, like colors, the number of letters and numerals are limited, there appears to be no limit to the public's acceptance and differentiation among marks consisting of these elements alone: *MG, GE, RCA, AAA, CBS, IH, F-5, 707, 7-Eleven, 007, 4711, 2'N'1, 3-in-One.* Moreover, the same combination of letters may be used and registered by two separate and unrelated businesses. *ABC* is an example. The mark is well known in connection with broadcasting services. However, it has also been registered for seminar and educational services to the construction industry. In such cases the seeming conflict may be avoided, or resolved in the Patent Office or between the owners of the same mark, on the basis of clearly distinguishable commercial uses and the design format of the particular letters or numerals.

Label and Package Designs

Today more than ever, the purchasing public is conscious of package design and almost every element of a product's "dress" or its package (color, size, shape) may be an important factor in a customer's decision to buy. However, only those features that function as an identification of origin may be appropriated under a claim of trademark significance.

Distinctive symbols or devices constituting but a part of the design of a package or label—the "Flying Red Horse" or the well-known "mule team"—are more easily associated with source and are recognized as trademarks. Generally, overall label and package designs function only as background decoration for other words. However, if a background has been promoted as a separate mark and is inherently distinctive (or through use, becomes distinctive of the product with which it is used), it is or can become a good trademark. Frequently a description of the design will be picked up in advertising—"Pick the Polka-Dot Package." "Look for the Checked Blue Gingham Wrapper." Promotion of this type will be helpful in demonstrating that a package or label design was adopted for and serves the purpose of source identification.

Because color alone will not qualify as a trademark, the use of color will not convert a basic, conventional label or package shape into a design mark unless the arrangement and proportions are inherently distinctive. On the other hand, a label or package design, including the color, may be protected on the ground of unfair competition, irrespective of the technical question of trademark. Although the basis of such relief is the likelihood that consumers will be confused when faced with products that are "dressed" similarly, recent cases indicate that if the buying public can read the label and the manufacturer is identified, a general impression of similarity between packages for the same goods will not be enjoined unless the overall design has acquired a significance as an indicant of origin in addition to primarily serving as an element of ornamentation.

Configuration of Containers and Goods

Normally configuration of containers and goods are not trademarks, and if the configuration is primarily or essentially functional, it cannot become a trademark. However, configuration of containers for goods, like other package designs, may function as a trademark. If the product it holds is identified with a particular source by the distinctive shape, the container will be protected and registered. The overall design of a building may be similarly protected as a mark for the services rendered there. However, unless the design has acquired public recognition without a sign that identifies the business, registration will be denied.

Notwithstanding that concepts of unfair competition had been employed to protect distinctive package dress, including containers, and that the Lanham Act made the "protection of the new right coextensive with the law of unfair competition as it was in 1946," it was not until 1958 that the first container was federally registered as a trademark. However, that registration, for the Haig & Haig "Pinch Bottle," was issued essentially because the distinctive appearance was the only way of identifying or asking for the particular whiskey. Since that time, a number of containers, including the "Coke" bottle, have been registered upon a showing that distinctiveness or secondary meaning had been acquired. However, the total number is small and most such configurations are registered under another provision of the statute, which permits the registration of "any . . . package (or) configuration of goods" if it is *"capable* of distinguishing the applicant's goods or services." The test has been described as requiring a determination that the particular shape *"might* be a [registrable] . . . trademark, upon proof of *established* secondary meaning." The configuration will qualify for registration if it is nonfunctional and was adopted with the intention that it should be associated with the manufacturer, and not to make the product easier to make or to use or to pack, whether or not the purchaser is likely to deduce origin from its shape. As will be discussed in another section, marks registered on this basis are less significant in terms of protection than marks that are or have become distinctive of the goods or services with which they are used. However, such registrations, like all registrations, do tend to ward off potential infringers and should be sought where a package design or configuration (or label, symbol, name, and so on) is not otherwise registrable. Registrations have issued for the shape of charcoal briquettes, cookies, and medical tablets.

Slogans

Slogans or phrases adopted to advertise a product are not defined in the Trademark Act of 1946. However, they may function as trademarks and will be judged on the same basis as any word, name, symbol, or device for which registration is sought. Although frequently descriptive (that is, inherently nondistinctive of the product or service with which it is used), a slogan nevertheless may be registered on the Principal Register if it has acquired distinctiveness through use or on the Supplemental Register if it is capable of distinguishing such product or service. The Patent Office will consider the extent to which the slogan has been used, where it has been used, how much it has been advertised, whether advertising and sale of the product have created a commercial impression of one mark, and what it means to purchasers. Thus trademark recognition has been found in the following slogans: *Every Body Needs Milk* for promotional services in the dairy industry, *Pay Less-Get More* for retail liquor store services, *The Test Is in the Touch* for a textile fabric and garments made of such fabrics and *I dreamed I . . .* [starred on television, etc.] *in my Maidenform bra.* On the other hand, a slogan that has a double meaning is not primarily descriptive and is entitled to protection, because it is distinctive, without regard to the question of its actual or potential impact on purchasers. *Moving Air Is Our Business* was registered for electric fans on this basis.

Sounds

Sounds are also not defined in the 1946 Trademark Act, and only in recent years have such "devices" been considered for registration, in contrast to other subject matter not specifically denominated by the statute. A sound is or is not registrable for the same reasons as any other mark. Some sounds that have been registered are the NBC call sign in the form of chimes, the sound of a coin spinning on a hard surface, which is used in the advertising of banking services, and the five electronically produced notes used by ABC. Radio programs are identified by sound marks and these include the full sweep of harp strings, the tintinnabulation of the Liberty Bell, and the sound of a creaking door.

Prohibited Marks

The Lanham Act specifically proscribes federal registration of marks consisting of the flags and other insignia of governmental entities and the name, portrait, or signature of a living person or a deceased president of the United States (during the lifetime of his widow), without written consent. What is not registrable appears rather straightforward. It may include such things as actual copies of flags or seals or close simulation of the currency of the United States. However, as noted earlier, the statute does not indicate that any and all "flags," or symbols commonly associated with government bodies or public organizations, will be unregistrable. The question of registrability may devolve to another category of forbidden marks requiring a determination as to whether the subject matter "falsely suggest(s) a connection with persons, living or dead, institutions, beliefs or national symbols." Under this provision the names or insignia of a commercial organization will be considered where known by or brought to the attention of the Patent Office. A business is not an "institution" within the meaning of this provision, but it is a "person" and a commercial trademark or name will be protected against registration of a word or symbol that, when applied to the applicant's goods or services, is likely to suggest an association or connection that it does not have. Although necessarily a subjective determination, the standard has been described as requiring, at the very least, the same likelihood of confusion as must be found to deny registration of a mark that "resembles a mark registered in the Patent Office or a mark or trade

name previously used in the United States by another and not abandoned, as to be likely, . . . to cause confusion . . . mistake, or to deceive."
The concept of confusing similarity encompasses all facts surrounding
the use of the opposing marks, or marks and trade names, including the
appearance, sound, and meaning of the words and the relationship of
the goods and/or services. It may be raised by the Patent Office to deny
registration to an individual applicant or to resolve a conflict between
marks that has been brought to its attention in an opposition or cancellation proceeding.

Other matter that is prohibited from becoming a good mark is that
which is "immoral, deceptive or scandalous." In one case, the Court of
Customs and Patent Appeals adopted the following dictionary definitions of *scandalous:*

> 1. Causing or tending to cause scandal; . . . shocking to the sense
> of truth, decency, or propriety; disgraceful; offensive; disreputable. . . .
> 2. Giving offense to the conscience or moral feelings; exciting rep-
> robation; calling out condemnation. . . .

This seems to be all-inclusive, but it is actually necessary to consider the
article to which the mark has reference before determining whether a
mark is scandalous. Thus, in this case, the word *Madonna* and representation of the Virgin Mary as a trademark upon wine was held to be
scandalous. *Messias* was also denied registration as a trademark for wine
and brandy inasmuch as it was considered to be the phonetic equivalent
of the word *Messiah,* which in Judaism, means the "promised, expected
deliverer of the Jews," and in Christianity, "Jesus," "the deliverer," or
"Christ." The applicant argued that the term *Messiah* does not carry with
it a definite meaning as applied to the Old Testament and is now commonly used in a broader sense to describe any redeemer, expected deliverer, or liberator of an oppressed people or country. However, the
Patent Office still felt that the term would be offensive to the American
public when applied to alcoholic beverages and refused to register this
term.

The Patent Office also considers a mark scandalous if the name
of any religious order or sect is applied to a product whose use is forbidden to followers of such sect or order; it considers such a mark
disrespectful to such persons and feels that it tends to disparage their
beliefs. On this basis *Senussi* was rejected as a trademark for cigarettes
because *Senussi* is the name of a Moslem sect whose followers are
forbidden to use cigarettes. However, the word *Amish,* in association
with the representation of a man in Amish clothing smoking a cigar,
has been registered for cigars where it was shown that nothing in the
religious principles or teachings of the Amish sect forbids the raising

of or use of tobacco, cigars, or chewing tobacco, and that at least 75 per cent of the Amish males smoke cigars and/or chew tobacco.

Subject matter that, when applied to specific products, is found to be vulgar or obscene will be denied registration. Applications in the Patent Office have been rejected for *Bubby Trap* for brassiers and for *Balls* on deodorant. On the other hand, *Libido* was not considered to be immoral in connection with cologne. *Acapulco Gold* was similarly deemed to be registrable for suntan lotion on the rationale that to the average purchaser of such goods the words suggested the "resort city of Alcapulco noted for its sunshine and other climatic attributes," and not marijuana.

LIMITATIONS ON ACCEPTABLE MARKS: TO USE, IDENTIFY, AND DISTINGUISH

Up to this point we have been discussing the various kinds of words, names, symbols, or devices that may be trademarks. Not all such subject matter, of course, will be recognized as such. First of all, going back to the definition of *trademark*, the word, name, symbol, or device must be *used* so as to *identify* the goods or services with which it is used and *distinguish* them from other goods and services. Each of these elements must be found in the particular subject matter for which protection or registration is sought. In addition, however, the Lanham Act, tracking closely the common law of trademarks, sets forth specific limitations on what otherwise would be registrable words.

Distinctiveness

The primary function of a trade or service mark is to indicate source or origin by distinguishing the goods or services with which it is used from other goods and services of the same general characteristics. If it serves this purpose, or is capable of doing so, it is "distinctive." A mark may be distinctive at the time it is adopted or, through use and advertising, it may acquire distinctiveness. It may be distinctive when used in connection with one product (*Red Rose* on tea) and nondistinctive when used with another (*Red Rose* on a rose bush). It may also lose all of its distinctiveness, as when a mark becomes the common or generic name for the goods or services (*Escalator* for moving stairs), or it may become less distinctive by virtue of the common usage in other marks of one or more of its features (*Lux* as a suffix in trademarks on paints).

The extent to which a mark will be protected relates directly to the degree of distinctiveness it possesses and additional factors to be considered are whether the mark, when applied to the particular goods or services with which it is used, is descriptive or deceptively misdescriptive or is a surname or a geographical name (except certification marks that may indicate regional origin). These factors will render a word or symbol unregistrable under the Lanham Act on the Principal Register, except· where it can be proved that it has become distinctive through the acquisition of a secondary significance or meaning. Otherwise, such nondistinctive marks may be registered on the Supplemental Register, providing they are "capable of distinguishing applicant's goods and services."

Secondary Meaning

Arbitrary and fanciful marks are granted the maximum protection under the law; but as the measure of novelty and originality declines, so does the owner's power to limit imitation of his mark. Marks that are nondistinctive may, nevertheless, become valuable trademarks through the acquisition of secondary meaning. Once a term ceases to be descriptive, for example, and commences to indicate the origin of a product, it has acquired a secondary meaning. Secondary meaning confers title and results in the attachment of the common law right to prevent infringing imitation of the mark in its trademark meaning. The owner, however, cannot act to prevent the use of the term in its primary (e.g., descriptive) and unprotectable meaning.

The touchstone of secondary meaning is prolonged, exclusive use of a mark in such a manner that it serves to indicate the origin of the goods upon which it appears rather than simply referring to the article itself. Some terms are so inherently descriptive that they will never acquire a secondary meaning no matter how long the term of use. An example is *Raisin Bran,* which, despite its lengthy existence, has never served to indicate anything other than the product itself. Other examples include *Ready to Eat* as applied to snack products and *Grapey* for grape-flavored gum. Also, words or pictorial representations that are generic with respect to the product or service and designs or configurations that are essentially functional or ornamental will never become good marks.

The burden of showing secondary meaning is on the owner of the mark. The problem is that there is no simple test for determining whether a mark is functioning as an indicant of origin. However, factors that will be considered are length of use, volume of sales resulting from that use, and the manner, extent, and target of any advertising campaigns. *Dollar-a-Day* has been registered for car rental services notwithstanding that the phrase described the terms by which the services were rendered. Significant to the finding that the mark had acquired secondary meaning or distinctiveness was a $200,000 national advertising campaign covering sixty-three locations that served 400,000 customers and the fact that the phrase had not been used by competitors.

Descriptiveness

Because there are only a limited number of words available in the English language to describe a product or service, or its characteristics, neither protection by the courts nor registration under the federal statute will be granted to descriptive terms or pictures unless they have acquired distinctiveness or secondary meaning. A descriptive term has been defined as "any one that would normally and naturally be employed by a manufacturer in describing the particular goods upon which the mark is used." However, there is a legal distinction between marks that are "merely descriptive" and those that are "merely suggestive," the latter being inherently good marks. "The difficulty is that such marks shade gradually, almost imperceptively, from one type into the other."

Notwithstanding some questionable decisions, it is fairly well established that a word or phrase is merely descriptive, with reference to the goods or services with which it is used, if it (1) describes the manner in which the product or service is packaged or marketed (*Matchbox* for miniature toys packaged in simulated matchboxes); (2) describes the position of the product with respect to the goods on which it is used (*Kat-E-Korner* for a zipper that is placed across the corner of a garment bag); (3) describes the function of the product (*Asphalt-Pak* for shipping containers for asphalt); (4) describes the essential ingredient of the product (*Rich n' Chips* for chocolate chip cookies); (5) describes a desirable characteristic of the product (*Easy Peel* for labels and tags with adhesive backing and *Chunky Cheese* for cheese-flavored salad dressing); (6) describes a functional feature of the product (*Blue Dot* for flash bulbs featuring a blue dot that indicates atmospheric air has been exhausted); or (7) indicates a method of use of the product (*Noclamp* on glue). On the other hand, if the mark merely suggests a possible end result to be derived from the use of the product (*Show Car* for metal polish and cleaner used on automobiles) or suggests one but not all purposes for which the product may be used (*Brown-in-Bag* on plastic cooking bags), or suggests the nature of the product (*Wig-Lac* for hair spray), or is incongruous in its entirety (*Polytissue* for combination paper and plastic table covers), or is merely laudatory (*Super Wale* for a fabric), the mark is registrable without having to show secondary meaning. Moreover, coined words will be protected "with a higher moat or a higher fence than is required to be built around publicly owned descriptive words or phrases," even if "highly suggestive" (*Skinvisible* for transparent medical and surgical tape), if there are other ways to describe and advertise the product.

A distinction has been drawn for purposes of protection and registration between descriptive marks that have acquired distinctiveness and those that have not. However, certain words are totally incapable of distinguishing the goods or services with which they are used and are unregistrable notwithstanding long use. One example is the common or generic name for a product. Words in this category have been defined as the "ultimate in descriptiveness" and will not be protected to the use of any one manufacturer or merchant of the products they describe (*Rubber Rope* for rope made of rubber). Similarly, ordinary or commonplace words or expressions of no distinctiveness or uniqueness are not registrable ("a truly fine pale beer," "the cigar supreme," and "America's most luxurious mattress"). Aside from other considerations, such a phrase must have "at least some degree of ingenuity in its phraseology or in its application to the goods; it ought to say something at least a little different from what might be expected to be said about a product, or say an expected thing in a somewhat unexpected way." This standard of registrability has been described as "a low order of distinctiveness"; however, expressions that the Patent Office considers capable of serving as a trademark (*We Smile More*) will not necessarily pass muster for protection against infringement where, in the court's opinion, they are common and ordinary and "do not apply to any particular person or organization."

Deceptive and Deceptively Misdescriptive Terms

Terms that, when applied to specific goods or services, are deceptive or deceptively misdescriptive are not usually proper marks. However, it is important to note that a mark is not invalid simply because it is misdescriptive. There are many such well-known marks that have become distinctive. For example, *Glasswax* for a metal polish suggests ingredients that do not exist and *English Leather* toiletries are not made in England. The Lanham Act only denies registration to those misdescriptive terms that would really deceive the public if used as trademarks. If it is likely that a majority of potential purchasers might be deceived as to a material fact about the product with which the mark is used, it will be declared nonregistrable. Note that this is a "balancing" test and, consequently, the possible deception of a few individuals at the time the mark is questioned will not render a mark invalid.

There have been relatively few cases concerning deceptively misdescriptive marks as compared with the mass of cases on merely descriptive terms. One such case involved the mark *American Beauty* for sewing machines and attachments that, with the exception of the driving motor and the cabinet, were manufactured in Japan. As applied to these machines, the mark was deemed to be geographically misdescriptive, as it led purchasers to believe that the product was of American origin, when it in fact was not. In denying registration, the court stated that "[i]t gives the false indication of geographical origin to that segment of the purchasing public which may be interested in the country of origin and in purchasing American-made goods and it is likely to deceive them."

Similarly, *Vynahyde* and *Dura-Hyde* have been denied registration as deceptively misdescriptive terms for a plastic material. Inasmuch as *hyde* is the phonetic equivalent of *hide,* which is accepted by the public as referring to the skin of an animal, the court held that the use of the terms on nonleather goods had the capacity to deceive the public as to the nature or characteristics of the product with which they were used. On the other hand, deception is not likely where the mark for which registration is sought is "so incongruous and ludicrous" as to be arbitrary. This was the rationale for resolving the question of registrability in favor of the user of *Ice Cream* on chewing gum.

Geographically Descriptive Terms

Geographical terms, like other descriptive words, may not be appropriated to the exclusive use of any one manufacturer or merchant unless they become distinctive. When used in the geographically descriptive sense, such terms include *American, Dixie, Antartica,* and *Nationwide. Continental* has been similarly construed as a "word in common use, more or less descriptive of extent, region and character, and, like the words 'Columbia,' 'International,' 'East Indian,' and some other geographical adjectives, it cannot be exclusively appropriated as a trademark or trade name" unless secondary meaning has developed, such as *Hershey* for chocolates; *Waltham* for watches; *American, Allegheny,* and the like for commercial airline services.

Terms that may be protected as a trademark or part of a trademark because they are not "primarily" geographical in nature include *Northern, Southern, Eastern,* and *Western; Metropolitan;* and *Globe.* The use of the term *primarily* in the Lanham Act eliminates any possibility that terms having only remote geographical connotations will be denied registration (absent secondary meaning) when used in this sense.

Surnames

Unless and until it has become distinctive or is otherwise capable of distinguishing the goods or services with which it is used, a mark that is "primarily merely a surname" will not qualify for registration. This attitude restricting trademark use of surnames reflects the public policy that every individual has the right to use his own name in connection with his business. Judicial protection of names in the absence of registration or without regard to whether the name is a trade or service mark is based on the same policy consideration. However, there the right to use one's name will be resolved with regard to the likelihood of confusion with another use of the same name. Confusing similarity will also operate to preclude registration of a name where a conflict is known or brought to the attention of the Patent Office; but registrability under this section of the statute will depend initially on the primary significance of the name to the purchasing public.

The fact that another meaning exists for a word does not necessarily indicate that it will not be considered primarily as a surname, particularly if the other meaning (in a foreign language or as a geographical name, for example) is remote. On the other hand, the fact that there is no other meaning will not affect registrability if, considering the product with which it is used, the word is not likely to be recognized as a surname. For purposes of registration, it is unimportant that the mark consists of an uncommon name or has been derived from the name of the applicant, if the ordinary meaning is that of a surname. Such surname significance, however, will be diminished by the inclusion in the mark of the first name of a person or other words, like geographical terms ("of Vermont"), and by the use of two surnames. Conversely, the addition of initials or the abbreviation of the word *company* will not change a mark as a whole from being primarily merely a surname.

There is no simple test for determining the meaning conveyed to the purchasing public by a word that is also a surname. Essentially subjective, interpretations of the statutory standard may be, occasionally, irreconcilable. However, where a mark has not been used sufficiently long to have become distinctive of the goods or services with which it is used, the owner should consider a survey to determine primary significance to the purchasing public. Such evidence was ultimately persuasive in the registration of *Calaway* for a diet bread inasmuch as it demonstrated that both purchasers who do and do not normally use such bread viewed the word as suggesting a low-calorie bread rather than a surname.

ACQUIRING RIGHTS IN A MARK
THROUGH USE AND REGISTRATION

The rights created by the adoption and use of a word, name, symbol, or device to identify goods or services and distinguish them from the goods and services of others, and to exclude others from the use of the same or similar word or symbol, have their origins in the common law. Although the medieval guilds provided the impetus for greater use of marks on goods as indicia of origin and quality, regulation was by no means uniform. The common law sought to standardize the principles by which trademarks would be protected. Directed at a society whose commercial activities were, by and large, limited geographically, the common law recognized prior use of a trademark, within any given area, as the yardstick by which protection would be measured in an action against subsequent users. The consequence, of course, was that it was possible for two users to acquire rights in the same mark in different regions of the country. Modern-day provisions for registration of marks mitigate this result to some extent. However, the basic tenet that common law rights in unregistered marks are coextensive with the facts of actual use of the mark is substantially as true today as it was a century ago. Such rights exist independent of federal and state statutes and do not depend upon them for their creation.

Adoption and Use as a Mark

Rights in a trademark or service mark—to own, to protect, to license—are acquired by adopting and using the mark on goods or in connection with services for the purpose of indicating the source of such goods and services. Actual use of the mark, not plans or hopes to use, is paramount in this country to the acquisition of rights in a mark. This is not the case in some foreign countries, where it is possible to obtain the right to use, and to exclude others from using, a mark simply by virtue of registration without having made any use of the mark. These so-called defensive registrations are, in effect, a license to steal a well-known mark in the sense that they operate to exclude, in the country where such registrations are obtained, the use of marks that have become established and well known through use elsewhere. In the United States, however, the extent of an owner's rights is determined by the facts of actual use. The "use" that gives rise to rights in a mark normally involves the application of the mark to the product or, as in the case of a service mark, to literature, brochures, ads, and signs used in the promotion and sale of services. The trademark may be placed on a box or on the shipping container, on a tag or label or, where physical attachment is impossible, on the dispenser from which the product (for example, gasoline) is sold. Such affixation will satisfy the requirement that a word or symbol be used as a trademark. In addition, the Lanham Act provides that a mark may be placed on "displays associated" with the product. This language has been construed by the Patent Office as requiring a "close physical association of these devices with the goods." Recently, however, the Court of Customs and Patent Appeals specifically rejected this view and ruled that the use of a mark for sandwiches on a restaurant menu constituted a use on displays associated with the goods inasmuch as the phrase was relative and, depending on the actual circumstances of use, could mean "actual contact, or proximity, or contiguity." On the other hand, use of a mark on a building sign or in a catalog or in advertising will not be sufficient use as a mark for goods or products, although such uses may be sufficient for a service mark use.

Attachment of the mark to goods need not be permanent or placed on the goods at the production stage. The primary purpose of a trademark to identify the source of the goods is fulfilled at the time of purchase and, so long as the mark is applied prior to sale to the ultimate consumer, it is immaterial what happens after a purchase has taken place.

To be federally registered, however, a mark not only must be used as a trade or service mark, it must be used as a mark *in commerce* that may be lawfully regulated by Congress. Sales of goods or services within the boundaries of a single state (intrastate commerce) nail down that use of a mark that will create ownership in the mark and give the owner the right to stop another use of the same mark within the actual trading area of use. In order to satisfy the federal registration requirements, however, such transactions must have occurred in commerce between two or more states, in foreign commerce, or in intrastate commerce that affects interstate commerce, this latter category having particular significance with service mark usage.

Normally a single shipment or sale in commerce will be sufficient to establish rights in a mark used in connection with goods or services and to support a federal registration, even where subsequent sales or shipments are delayed for many months, providing the circumstances indicate a continuous course of action to get the product on the market, as, for example, with marketing tests or adjustments to the product to correct an imperfection. However, a "sweetheart" shipment, although interstate, is not a shipment *in commerce* where "it was not dispatched as part of an established business in the product." Bona fide use is similarly not established where a trademarked product is limited to friends of the owner or the interstate shipments are made only within the applicant's own business enterprise.

Importance of "First Use" in Time and Geographic Area

Although adoption and use of a mark in association with goods or services are essential to establishing rights in a trade or service mark, these rights, which flow to the first user in time, extend under common law principles only to the specific trading areas of use where there are conflicting claims to the same mark. Although there may exist some qualification to this principle in the context of areas of prospective business expansion, and although ownership may be limited or totally abrogated by other factors previously mentioned respecting bona fide and lawful use as a mark or distinctiveness, whether inherent or acquired, the common law rule, still applicable in the absence of a registration, recognizes concurrent ownership and use of the "same mark upon goods of the same class, but in separate markets wholly remote the one from the other." And even though a federal registration is notice to the world of the registrant's claim of ownership of the registered mark, another unregistered use of the same mark for the same goods or services commenced prior to the date of federal registration may continue as a lawful use and operate to restrict the rights of the prior user and registrant. Under such circumstances, the "rights which the (registrant) might otherwise have are not available to it . . . and the case resolves itself into a question under the law of unfair competition and the respective rights of the parties without regard to the registration under the Lanham Act."

The question of registrability itself may devolve to the single issue of priority. Under the statute, the date of first use, which may be used in the first instance to resolve conflicts between marks for which registration is pending, must be specified in the application. In the more usual case, however, the question of prior use will be brought to the attention of the Patent Office and, if established, may preclude registration of the same mark on the same or related class of goods or services, even when the earlier use of the mark was in intrastate commerce.

As can be expected, sometimes difficult problems arise in situations where a small company adopts and uses a trademark in interstate commerce, let us say, in the Middle Atlantic region of the United States, and then files an appliction for federal registration that is thereafter granted. Meanwhile, in our hypothetical situation, another regional company innocently has adopted and is using the very same mark for the very same goods or services in Arizona. Our Arizona company never used the mark in interstate commerce and for that matter may have never heard of the Patent Office and all this business about federal registrations. In all events, time passes, our Mid-Atlantic trademark owner has expanded nationally and when he moves into the Arizona market, finds to his surprise the pre-existing Arizona trademark use. The Arizona trademark owner has vested "first use" rights in his trading area that are not taken away by the other's federal registration. Particularly with the advent of franchising as a burgeoning mode for geographic expansion of mark usage, this trading-area-by-trading-area vesting of trademark rights has generated sometimes significant marketing obstacles. However, different rules apply in situations when (1) a first user in a limited part of the United States secures a federal registration for his trademark, (2) the subsequent user of the same mark for the same goods (or the same service mark for the same services) adopts and uses that mark after the other's federal registration issued, and (3) the federal registration owner thereafter moves into the subsequent user's trading area. In this situation the subsequent user may be stopped from using the mark.

Federal, State, and Foreign Registrations

Federal registration of a qualifying mark can provide the trademark owner with various benefits under the Lanham Act. We shall see that a federal registration gives rise to a cause of action in federal district courts for trademark infringement. With respect to a mark registered on the Principal Register of the Patent Office, procedures are opened up to stop infringing imports; the registration gives the world constructive notice of the owner's claim for the goods or services involved; and after the registration has been in effect for five years it becomes subject to cancellation only on limited grounds, generally involving fraudulent procurement, illegal marks, abandonment, improper control over certification marks, or the mark becoming a common descriptive name.

There exist state trademark registration programs in most states based on a model state trademark bill developed by the U.S. Trademark Association. These state statutes provide machinery for securing a state registration of a trademark adopted and used within that state. Filing procedures are simple; examination is basically as to form and does not embrace the more elaborate examination procedures provided by the Patent Office in administering the program of federal trademark registrations under the Lanham Act. Thus marks that would not pass muster with the Patent Office may well be granted a state registration. Recalling that rights in a mark flow from its adoption and use, state registration laws provide little or no substantive rights to the owner of a mark not already available under common law principles of unfair competition. The time and expense of securing state registrations is usually not justified, especially where federal registration has been obtained.

Foreign trademark registrations are based on the law of each foreign country of interest. The principal area of concern to American companies expanding to new markets abroad lies in the laws of some countries that permit registration of a mark without adoption and use in that country. The net effect of this situation is that an enterprising citizen of that country will register his "ownership" in a mark that the American company has spent millions of dollars to promote as a household word, and when export plans or foreign direct investments contemplate use of the mark in such a country, the American company finds some chap to be the "owner" who is quite willing to negotiate an assignment of his ownership at a fee commensurate with his questionable motives. As we shall see, the Patent Office does maintain a Supplemental Register for marks that, although not qualifying for registration on the Principal Register, must nevertheless first be registered in the United States in connection with a particular foreign country's registration requirements.

CONVEYANCING OF TRADEMARKS

Licensing and the Quality Control Requirement

The Lanham Act provides that "where a registered mark . . . is . . . used legitimately by related companies, . . . such use shall not affect the validity of such mark or its registration, provided such mark is not used in such manner as to deceive the public." A related company is defined as one "controlled by the registrant or applicant for registration in respect to the *nature and quality* of the goods or services in connection with which the mark is used." The upshot of these somewhat complicated sections of the Act is that the owner of a mark may license others to use the mark so long as the licensor controls the "nature and quality" of the goods or services offered by the licensee. If he does not control the licensee's use of the mark, the mark will become unenforceable. The antithesis of controlled use is what is commonly referred to as a "naked license." Let us look for a moment at the distinction between the two concepts, the reasons why quality controls are necessary, and the types of quality controls that should be employed to protect a licensed mark.

The business value of the trademark has rested historically on its ability to identify for consumers the source or origin of the goods or services with which the mark is used. Trademarks and service marks gave the businessman a vehicle by which he could distinguish his products or services from those of his competitors and establish a market position as the sole and continuing beneficiary of the reputation for quality, price, or service that became associated with the goods or services. In the last quarter century, this historic function of trademarks has been eclipsed to some degree by the use of marks as an essential tool in mass advertising of consumer goods and services. Justice Frankfurter caught the essence of this use in his opinion in *Mishawaka Rubber & Woolen Mfg. Co. v. S. S. Kresge Co:*

> The protection of trade-marks is the law's recognition of the psychological function of symbols. If it is true that we live by symbols, it is no less true that we purchase goods by them. A trade-mark is a merchandising short-cut which induces a purchaser to select what he wants, or what he has been led to believe he wants. . . . Whatever the means employed, the aim is the same—to convey through the mark, in the minds of potential customers, the desirability of the commodity upon which it appears.

Thus as consumers are induced to purchase goods or services by "brand name" through mass advertising, there is a need for the law to insure that the purchaser will receive products or services of consistent quality under the same "brand name." This does not mean that the products or services have to be "high-quality" products under any objective standard. Rather, consistency is the aim, and when someone other than the owner of the mark, because of a license, offers the same goods or services as the owner, the purchaser, who buys because of the name used on the label, or in advertising, should not face the risk of getting a baldly different-quality product or service each time he makes a purchase. Moreover, if the owner of the mark is not concerned with the quality of the licensee's goods, and if the mark cannot be viewed as some assurance of consistency, there is no incentive in legal theory to allow the owner to enjoin use of the mark by anyone who so chooses. In effect, use without control causes the mark to lose its distinctiveness, and it is no longer serving as a trademark. This is what happens when the owner grants a naked license; thereafter, others are free to use the mark without legal sanction.

What, then, is meant by the requirement that the licensor control the nature and quality of the licensee's use of the mark? The "consistency" objective is usually achieved by issuing detailed specifications under which the licensee must make the product or implement the service. For example, one of the prominent fast-food franchising companies has a license-franchise agreement covering its service mark (and its related systems of doing business under the mark) that extends for seven legal-sized pages of fine print. The licensing agreement literally covers everything the franchisee does from the time his doors open until they are closed, and it even sets the time that those openings and closings take place. The control cannot stop with specifications either—regular policing or checking must be made by the licensor to insure that the specifications are being followed, and noncompliance must be corrected. Often the trademark-licensed product will be made using "secret" ingredients that the licensor supplies and that help to insure consistent quality of the goods of the licensee. This is the case, for example, in the soft drink industry, where trademark licensors of such soft drink syrup as Coca-Cola, Pepsi, 7-Up, and many others have built worldwide businesses combining a secret syrup formulation with a widespread licensing program whereby licensee bottlers actually "make" the end-product soft drink that is bottled or canned and sold to the public.

In terms of economic impact it is probable that service mark licensing programs in such fields at fast-food selling emerge as the most significant area of licensing in the United States. According to congressional testimony presented by the Federal Trade Commission, in 1973 there were more than 85,000 franchisors and more than 385,000 franchisees in the United States.

Sale and Assignment; The Importance of Goodwill

A mark may be sold and assigned along with the goodwill of the business in which the mark is used or with that part of the goodwill of the business connected with the use of and symbolized by the mark. This principle is expressly set forth in Section 10 of the Lanham Act to the extent of marks federally registered or the subject of pending applications for registration, but the principle applies equally to marks not embraced by the Lanham Act. However, with respect to Lanham Act marks, an assignment recording procedure is specified as follows:

> Assignments shall be by instruments in writing duly executed. Acknowledgment shall be prima facie evidence of the execution of an assignment and when recorded in the Patent Office the record shall be prima facie evidence of execution. An assignment shall be void as against any subsequent purchaser for a valuable consideration without notice, unless it is recorded in the Patent Office within 3 months after the date thereof or prior to such subsequent purchase. A separate record of assignments submitted for recording hereunder shall be maintained in the Patent Office.

A 1970 federal district court decision, *Syntex Laboratories, Inc.* v. *The Norwich Pharmacal Company*, illustrates the practical importance of proper assignments in the context of enforcing trademark rights through infringement proceedings. In April 1969, Syntex Labs acquired by assignment from another company, Reid-Provident Laboratories, rights in the trademark *Vagitrol,* a prescription drug. *Vagitrol* was the subject of a federal registration issued in 1964 to the Reid-Provident corporate interests. The assignment provided among other things that Syntex was to receive the entire right, title, and interest in the *Vagitrol* mark with the goodwill and business associated with the mark. Although no patents or trade secrets were involved, Syntex was to receive all related technical information and know-how; Reid promised not to make or sell any product like *Vagitrol* for two years hence and a royalty form of payment to Reid was contemplated.

Syntex started marketing *Vagitrol* in late September of 1969. Three weeks earlier, Norwich came into the market with a similar product, called *Vagestrol.* Syntex sued for trademark infringement. Norwich defended on the grounds there was no likelihood of confusion and that, in all events, Norwich really was "first user" as between the parties because the assignment to Syntex was defective and thereby did not allow it the benefit of the prior dates of use by Reid-Provident. The court, in a preliminary injunction proceeding, rejected all efforts of Norwich to claim priority of use based on a defective assignment to Syntex. With respect to the key question of whether goodwill was transferred along with title to the mark, the court found it sufficient that nothing relevant to consumer confusion or to Syntex's complete takeover of the production and marketing of *Vagitrol* was withheld by Reid-Provident, the assignor. The court found that Syntex had complied with all necessary requirements to protect the consumer against confusion arising from the assignment.

An illustration of the effect of failing to assign a mark with goodwill—an assignment in gross—is found in the 1969 Ninth Circuit decision, *Mister Donut of America, Inc.* v. *Mr. Donut, Inc.* Here, Mister Donut of America (plaintiff) commenced a retail doughnut store operation in 1955 and expanded from Massachusetts to a coast-to-coast operation of some 200 shops. Plaintiff opened a shop in California in 1966. At that time defendant, Mr. Donut, Inc., was operating in Orange County, California, using the same name on a much smaller scale: its first shop opened in 1957 and by the time of trial defendant had seven franchised operations.

Plaintiff sued the California-based operation for infringing its *Mister Donut* federal trademark registration. This federal registration, however, was its downfall, because it was assigned to it in gross without any goodwill. The plaintiff had filed an application in the Patent Office to register *Mister Donut* shortly after its 1955 adoption and use in interstate commerce. The Patent Office rejected the application because of a 1947 registration issued to one Mr. Ragsdale in Washington state for *Mr. Donut.* Plaintiff found out that Mr. Ragsdale was deceased, so it purchased an assignment of the Ragsdale *Mr. Donut* rights from the estate and recorded the assignment in the Patent Office in 1956, one year before defendant innocently started up *Mr. Donut* operations in California. But no goodwill was associated with the assignment; Ragsdale had quit the doughnut business in 1951 and did not use the mark thereafter. There was no pretense that the Ragsdale estate transferred any merchandise, equipment, recipes, customer lists, or the like. The assignor had no goodwill, thus assigned none, and plaintiff received no rights. Under such circumstances, the plaintiff could not forestall the defendant in the area of its use in Orange County, California.

CONFLICTS BETWEEN MARKS, INFRINGEMENT, AND UNFAIR COMPETITION

The Concept of Infringement

As we have seen, the function performed by trademarks, whether or not federally registered under the Lanham Act, is to identify the source of origin of the goods or services. There are two major purposes to be performed by such identification, namely, the protection of the manufacturer from unfair competition through the infringement of his mark and resulting trading by another upon his goodwill, and the protection of consumers who might be deceived into purchasing the goods of one manufacturer mistakenly believing them to be the goods of another. Accordingly, where two marks are either so similar standing alone, or are sufficiently similar so that when attached to certain goods they cause confusion as to the source of origin of those goods, use of the conflicting mark may have to be discontinued to prevent the likelihood of such confusion.

Because trademarks serve to identify the source of origin of a manufacturer's goods, protection of a manufacturer's trademark rights in such goods extends only to the improper marketing of another's goods in such a way as to constitute infringement. A mark is infringed whenever another person markets goods bearing a mark that is so similar to a protected trademark that there results a likelihood of confusion as to the source of the goods. Section 32 (1) of the Lanham Act provides for a civil right of action against anyone who, in commerce, without the consent of the trademark registrant, either uses any reproduction or colorable imitation of any trademark in connection with the sale or advertising of goods or services, where such use is likely to cause confusion or mistake, or to deceive purchasers as to the source of origin of such goods or services, or who applies any such reproduction of a mark to labels, packages, or advertisements for the sale of such goods or services. In addition to this Lanham Act remedy for infringement of federal registrations, the owner of a trademark that was never federally registered may still prevent infringement of his mark in an action for common law trademark infringement. Moreover, although the Lanham Act was intended to pre-empt state interference with uniform federal standards for protection of trademarks, a trademark owner may also prevent infringement of his mark under applicable state laws that are not inconsistent with federal law. Further common law relief may be available in an action for unfair competition or for dilution of the mark. Although federal courts are vested with exclusive jurisdiction in actions involving federal trademarks, these state claims may be joined with an action for trademark infringement under the Lanham Act, and brought within the pendent jurisdiction of the federal court.

The Effect of Federal Registration

In addition to establishing the likelihood of confusion resulting from the use of an identical or similar mark by another in connection with his products or services, the plaintiff in an action for trademark infringement must also establish the exclusive right to use his mark in connection with his goods and services in a trading area, his prior and continuous use of it, and its validity as a protectable trademark. These issues are established in a common law infringement proceeding in much the way that they are established before the commissioner of patents in an application for registration, as will be discussed. Registration on the Principal Register does not create any additional rights in a trademark than exist at common law. Because, however, a mark must qualify for registration under the Lanham Act by meeting the common law requirements for a valid and protectable trademark, registration under the Act carries with it the procedural advantages of facilitating proof with respect to these issues in an action for trademark infringement. Specifically, the Act provides that registration is admissible as prima facie evidence of the registrant's exclusive right to use the registered mark in commerce on the goods and services specified in the registration, subject to any stated conditions or limitations. Once the right to use the mark has become incontestable under the Act, after five consecutive years of use after registration, the registration is conclusive evidence of such exclusive right, subject to a few equitable defenses.

Additionally, the Act provides that such registration constitutes nationwide constructive notice of the registrant's claim of ownership of the mark, thus eliminating the need to establish actual notice to the defendant of the use of the mark in a different geographical area. Thus, a second user's good faith use of such mark in such area after it has been federally registered by a prior user will not operate to insulate him from liability, as was the case at common law. Aided by these evidentiary provisions, the plaintiff in an action for trademark infringement can concentrate on establishing the likelihood of confusion resulting from the use of the challenged mark.

The Concept of "Palming Off"

Related to the offense of trademark infringement is the common law tort of "palming off," often referred to as "passing off." This tort is committed when one manufacturer or seller attempts deceivingly to market or "palm off" his goods as those of another. It traditionally has been required that the copying be accompanied by an intent to pass one's goods off as those of another. Moreover, for the tort to be completed, there must result actual confusion as to the source of the goods.

The offense of palming off is commonly perpetrated by the concurrent use by the offender of a mark, package, or design so similar to that of another that consumers mistakenly believe the offender's goods originate with the person whose property has been affected. Similarly, the offense is also committed when a dealer or other third party makes an unauthorized substitution of the goods of one manufacturer when the goods of another are requested by the customer. Thus, it is palming off to serve a glass of another brand of cola to a restaurant customer who specifically requests Coca-Cola, without verbally advising the customer that the product served is manufactured by someone other than that of the product ordered, and without providing him with an opportunity to accept or reject the substituted product. Interestingly, the defendant in one case had posted signs stating he served his own brand of cola in his establishment instead of the well-known brand, and had directed his waitresses to so advise any patrons ordering that brand of cola. The court declared that customers were entitled to receive actual, oral notice of the fact that the defendant did not serve the requested brand and could not be required to watch for signs nor to rely on receiving information from waitresses who did not always observe the directed instructions. Although the defendant may have acted in good faith in taking the steps enumerated to avoid confusion as to the source of origin of the goods, he was held responsible for the failure of his employees to comply with his instructions, which failure, in light of their knowledge of the source of the product, could not be deemed innocent.

The Likelihood of Confusion Standard

The offense of trademark infringement is not as difficult to prove as the tort of palming off. Hence it is not necessary in such actions to establish that the defendant is guilty of palming off, that he has deliberately infringed the plaintiff's mark, or that instances of actual confusion have occurred. Rather, the standard required for a finding of trademark infringement under the Lanham Act is merely the likelihood of confusion, mistake or deception as to the origin of the goods. This is the same standard that precludes registration of a mark on the Principal Register if, when applied to the goods of the applicant, it so resembles a mark that has already been registered, or that is in current use, as to be likely to cause confusion, or to cause mistake, or to deceive the public as to the source of the goods. This same standard also applies in actions at common law for infringement of an unregistered trademark. An infringer may not avoid liability for infringing a mark registered under the Lanham Act merely by confining his infringing mark within intrastate commerce. The Act's commerce requirement refers only to the impact that use of the infringing mark has upon interstate commerce; hence any impact that affects the registrant's use of his mark in interstate commerce is sufficient to bring the Act into play.

Although the standard of likelihood of confusion is a legal one, resolution of trademark infringement actions must be decided upon a balancing of several factual considerations presented in each case. It is not surprising, therefore, that courts are fond of stating that prior precedents weigh little in this balancing process. A finding by a trial court, based on a factual analysis that confusion is likely to occur in a particular case, is entitled to affirmance by an appellate court where the facts are in dispute unless the finding is "clearly erroneous." Where, however, there is no factual dispute, but the issue of confusing similarity is based solely upon a comparison of the trademarks themselves, appellate courts often claim they are in as good a position as the trial courts to decide such issue.

As may be reasonably expected from the foregoing considerations, the likelihood of confusion standard for trademark infringement often may lead to what appear to be inconsistent, or even conflicting, decisions. However, the similarity of the competing marks is only the first step in the decisional process. Other factors that are typically assessed in an infringement proceeding include the similarity of appearance of the packaging or trade dress of the products, the strength of the plaintiff's mark, the extent to which the goods are competitive or related, the geographic area of concurrent sale, the likelihood that the first user will bridge either a product or geographic "gap," the channels or methods of distribution of the goods, the sophistication of the purchasers, the intention of the defendant in selecting his mark, and the existence of actual confusion. In addition, several defenses may be advanced to defeat a claim for trademark infringement notwithstanding the apparent satisfaction of the likelihood of confusion standard. What has been described as a determination based upon the visceral reactions of the trial judge as to the likelihood of confusion in actuality often consists of a sensitive balancing of several factors in the context of market conditions. Our discussion will now proceed to a review of the various factors analyzed by the courts in such proceedings, as well as an examination of the types of evidence considered in assessing the likelihood of confusion.

Similarity of the Marks. Because trademarks are used to identify the source of products with which they are associated, often the first inquiry in an infringement action is the confusion likely to be directly attributable to the similarity in appearance, sound, and meaning of the marks. Obviously, the greater such similarity, the greater the likelihood of confusion when such marks or names are applied to identical or closely related products. The test for confusing similarity of marks is not, however, a side-by-side comparison, but rather is an over-all view in light of the manner in which consumers actually purchase the products. Where marks are phonetically similar, it may often be clear that confusion is likely to result from their use on goods in a common line of commerce. Thus the mark *Kiki* when applied to ladies' headbands, tights, and hosiery is understandably likely to cause confusion with the same mark when applied to a lady's panty garment, and the mark *Comcet* when applied to computer services has been held likely to cause confusion with the mark *Comsat* when applied to a communications service, the similarities existing with respect to both appearance and sound. Likewise, the mark *Chester Laurie* when applied to men's clothing was held to infringe the mark *Chester Barrie* when applied to the same class of products; the words *Your Maternity Shop* infringed the mark *Maternally Yours* when each was used in connection with the sale and advertising of maternity apparel; and the mark *Valcream* infringed the mark *Brylcream* when each was applied to an identical cream-style hair dressing for men.

One may not lawfully use a close facsimile of another's mark by merely misspelling it or using a foreign derivative, or otherwise altering it. The proprietor of the mark *Dyanshine* for shoe polish was accordingly able to enjoin the use of *Dye and Shine* on a similar product, and the Polaroid Corporation was able to enjoin the use of *Polaraid* for refrigeration and heating systems because of the phonetic similarity of the marks. On the other hand, as will be seen, a high degree of similarity in sound, appearance, or meaning of the marks may not result in a likelihood of confusion when the effect of other factors, especially that concerning the different nature of the products, is considered in conjunction with the marks.

Where the marks have a nearly identical meaning, however, but are dissimilar in sound or appearance, the likelihood of confusion is more difficult to establish. Thus, the mark *Dawn Donuts* was held not to be confusingly similar to the mark *Daylight Donuts* when used on identical products in concurrent areas, notwithstanding the claim that the words *dawn* and *daylight* conveyed the same concept of early morning baking and freshness. Likewise, although no confusion was likely between the marks *Sunfish* and *Barracuda,* confusion was held likely to result between the marks *Sunfish* and *Goldfish* when such names are applied to small sailboats.

In addition to the similarities of appearance, sound, and meaning, a mark may contain some salient feature that, when made a part of another mark, may cause confusion. The term *Dutch* was found to be of such significance when applied to cigars that the mark *Little Dutchman* was held likely to cause confusion with the mark *Dutch Masters,* and the mark *World Carpets* was held infringed by the mark *Dick Littrell's New World Carpets* despite the fact that each sold carpets at different levels of competition. Likewise, the term *fish* was considered a salient part of a trademark so as to establish a "family of marks" containing that term when applied to sailboats. One court considered the location of the primary portion of a mark to be determinative of the likelihood of confusion issue. Although use of the marks *Miss U.S.A.-World* and *Miss U.S.A.-World Beauty Pageant* were enjoined with respect to the mark *Miss U.S.A.,* use of the term *Miss World-U.S.A.* was not enjoined for use in connection with the promotion of beauty contests. It was reasoned that the interjection of the term "World" would alter the principal emphasis and thereby avoid confusion with the well-known *Miss U.S.A.* mark.

Similarly, prefixes and suffixes may be relevant to a determination that confusion is likely between marks that are otherwise quite dissimilar. The sameness of a prefix will be of particular interest since the customer is more likely to remember the first letters or syllable of a word. However, where a suffix is an essential feature of a well-known mark it cannot be adopted for the same product even if the first part of the mark is different. On this basis *Q-Tips* prevailed over *Cotton Tips* for cotton-tipped swabs. On the other hand, the suffix *Lite* was deemed too common and not worthy of protection as part of the mark *Carolite* for plastic lighting panels in an action charging that defendant's use of the mark *K-Lite* on the same product constituted an infringement. Similarly, the term *Tavern* was rejected as constituting the salient part of the *Ye Olde Tavern* mark and was not infringed by *Planters Tavern Nuts*. The court emphasized the manner in which the products were actually purchased, and found, among other things, that no evidence had been introduced that would show that this was the part of the mark to which customers referred when making purchases.

Trade Dress, Symbols, and Slogans. Closely related to the similarity of appearance, sound, and meaning of the trademarks themselves is the Gestalt-like impression that is evoked by the packaging, labeling, and total appearance of the product, often referred to as its trade dress. The use of conflictingly similar symbols, colors, designs or other designations may cause a likelihood of confusion, as may the use of slogans that emphasize certain features associated with a competing product. In one case, the defendant's use of the famous Beefeater guard symbol for plaintiff's gin—in identical form and color employing the same descriptive language in defining the historic role of the figure in using the mark as a trade name in connection with its restaurants —was compelling evidence as to the likelihood of confusion. The significance of design marks is further demonstrated by the fact that the Planters Peanut Company, owner of the registered design mark

was successful in opposing the registration of a design

for a "peanut-king figure," containing the inscription "Fit for a King," in connection with the advertisement of its products. The court reasoned that the dissimilarities between this mark and the opposer's well-known humanized peanut design, bearing the inscription "Mr. Peanut," did not resolve the likelihood of confusion issue. Rather, it held that the right to "humanize" the product by means of a design mark did not constitute mere descriptive illustration of the product, and was worthy of protection from another's attempt to trade on the goodwill established through use of the design despite the differences between the illustrations. Where, however, alphanumeric symbols such as *K-4* and *C-4* are used in a trade as generic terms to designate pattern configurations or quality grades and the like rather than the origin of the products, the question is not likelihood of confusion between trademarks and the use of one will not be enjoined as against the other.

A good analysis of the importance of trade dress as a factor to be considered in a claim for trademark infringement appears in *Ye Olde Tavern Cheese Products, Inc.* v. *Planters Peanuts Division, Standard Brands, Inc.* Among the features discussed was the kind of script used in printing the names, the backgrounds upon which they were superimposed, the emphasis given to the words, the order of placement of certain words in the name, the use of symbols on packaging, and the type size, and color of packaging. Taken as a whole, the court concluded that the differences in the appearance of the products precluded finding a likelihood of confusion. Conversely, the similarity in appearance of the products; identity as to the size and shape of their containers and cartons; similarity of price, color, advertising, and other features of their respective trade dress were significant in establishing infringement as between the *Brylcream* mark and the *Valcream* mark when applied to men's hairdressings.

Where some feature of a popular slogan is utilized in connection with a competing manufacturer's products, the necessary association of that feature to an identification of source of the product is often difficult to establish. For example, although the slogans *Use Arrid . . . To Be Sure* and *To Be Sure* had been used in connection with a personal deodorant, it was held to be descriptive of, rather than a trademark for, the product and not entitled to protection against the trademark *SURE* for a similar product. Similarly, a manufacturer of bath oil preparations was permitted to continue using the legend *Joy of Bathing* on its labels despite the claim by the maker of *Joy* perfume and toilet water that such use constituted an infringement of its registered mark. On the other hand, use of the mark *Tornado* as a name for a detergent was held to be likely to cause confusion with the Ajax slogan *White Tornado* and *Cleans Like a White Tornado*. A distinction was drawn between this case and that involving the deodorant products partly on the ground that *Tornado* was more fanciful when applied to a cleaner than was *Sure* when applied to a deodorant.

Distinguishable are cases in which the slogans themselves are so similar as to be likely to cause confusion as to the source of the products that are totally different. On this basis, *Where there's life . . . there's Bud* for beer was found to be infringed by the slogan *Where there's life . . . there's Bugs* for a combination insecticide and floor wax.

Strong Versus Weak Marks. The scope of protection afforded a trademark is directly related to the strength of the mark: the stronger the mark, the greater is the protection generally afforded. A mark is considered strong when it is fanciful, is distinctive, and has enjoyed a sufficiently continuous use in connection with a manufacturer's products that it has come to be understood as designating the source of such products. Such marks are often coined and no impoverishment of the language results from the granting of their extensive use by a single manufacturer. Thus, such marks as *Kodak, Acrilan,* or *Exxon,* enjoy greater protection than marks that involve words in common usage.

A word need not be entirely arbitrary to be deemed strong, however. Relatively strong marks may be derived from common words, for example, *Comsat* taken from the words "communications" and "satellite," or *Ekco* from the name "Edward Katzinger Company." Moreover, the use of dictionary words and common symbols when applied in a fanciful way may produce a strong mark. Hence *Greyhound* with the picture of a running dog is a strong mark when applied to passenger bus transportation services, although not strong when applied to dog racing.

A related consideration is the defendant's choice of his own name with which to identify his goods. A second user's good faith adoption and use of his own name as a trademark, absent intent to trade on the goodwill of another, may generally not be enjoined, because one is traditionally entitled to utilize his own name as a means of identifying his goods or services. Where a second user adopts a personal name confusingly similar to one already being used as a trademark or trade name, however, as was the case in *Chester Barrie, Ltd.* v. *Chester Laurie, Ltd.*, such use will be properly enjoined.

If the effect of the second user's good faith use of his own name in connection with his business is to cause confusion as to the source of his goods, the courts will require some differentiation or modification so as to obviate any mistaken association on the part of the buying public. For example, although John L. Stetson was permitted to use his name in connection with his hats, he was required to distinguish affirmatively that the source of his products was not identical to and that he was in no way connected with, the famous Stetson hat company. In other situations there may be no way to differentiate one's name sufficiently to avoid competing unfairly as demonstrated by an interesting case arising in New York. The Findlay brothers, David and Wally, had been involved in the family's well-known art business, Findlay Galleries, Inc., which had branch offices in several cities. Each specialized in art of the same period and nationality. The brothers separated, David in New York and Wally in Chicago. Wally later opened his *Wally Findlay Galleries* in New York practically next door to his brother's gallery known as *Findlay's on 57th Street*. Although the court assumed that Wally's use of his name was in good faith, it ruled that such use nevertheless constituted unfair competition and a bare majority of the court refused to permit him to use the Findlay name in connection with an art gallery on the same street. It reasoned that Wally could find another location, or be restricted to the use of some other name, not including *Findlay*, such as *W.C.F. Galleries*, at his present location.

Where the second user's own name is used in connection with, or as part of, an allegedly appropriated mark, courts generally distinguish between cases in which the alleged infringer's name is unknown and where it is well known as denoting a particular brand or source; in the latter case there is generally not likely to be confusion as to source. Thus, the use of the prominent name *Planters* in conjunction with the term *Tavern Nuts* was considered as abrogating any likelihood of confusion with *Ye Olde Tavern* mark for nuts.

A significant factor in assessing the relative strength of a mark is the extent to which the mark or portions of it have been used by others in addition to the person seeking to prevent its infringement. Although one court considered it significant that the *Greyhound* mark and symbol had not been used to designate any trade or product other than the plaintiff's, another court's finding that the mark *Mustang,* in conjunction with the symbol of a running horse, had been used in connection with a variety of products and had been registered a number of times alone and in combination with the representation of a horse, was evidence that it was a weak mark and not entitled to broad protection in the vehicle field. If marks in use in a particular line of commerce so resemble each other as to have become common to that class of goods or services, protection may be limited to the precise mark and even to the specific goods in connection with which it has been registered.

Courts also may base their determination of the relative strength of a mark on the descriptive nature of the word or name as, for example, *Allstate, Nationwide,* or *National.* In addition, the amount of advertising and promotional efforts expended in building up a mark and the extent of its public recognition are also considered.

Related Goods. Because a trademark functions as an indicant of origin of the product or service with which it is used, the owner of a valid mark has historically been able to prevent its infringement arising from subsequent use of a similar mark on identical or competing products. However, protection of a valid mark may extend beyond the specific goods of the trademark owner to products or services that are so closely related that use of the same or similar mark with other goods and services would be likely to lead purchasers into believing that the goods originated from a common source. For example, the *Greyhound* mark has been proscribed for use on taxicabs where it already had become associated with passenger bus services. Where the products or services are of a substantially different type, a closer balancing of the relevant factors is generally required, with more emphasis given to the degree of similarity between, and the strength of, the respective marks. Thus the mark *Ekco* when used in connection with kitchen utensils was considered confusingly similar to the mark *Wekco* when used in connection with mops and related products. Similarly, the mark *Comsat* when applied to a satellite communications service was found to be infringed by use of the mark *Comcet* when used to identify communications computers.

The extent of protection under the related goods theory can be considerably broad. One court, emphasizing the similarity of the marks and the piracy of the gin distiller's symbol and descriptive lore, held that the mark *Beefeater* for gin was infringed by use of the marks *Beef/Eater* and *Beefeaters* for restaurant services. The court reasoned that because a common denominator existed with respect to the products involved—both were consumables—there existed a likelihood that the public would be confused into believing that the defendant's restaurants were in some manner connected with the plaintiff's gin distillery.

Protection of exceedingly strong marks may extend beyond related goods to non-related goods. An example is the *Kodak* mark for cameras and accessories which has been protected against registration of the *Kodak* mark for cigar and cigarette lighters. Although the products were not deemed related, it was reasoned that no harm would be inflicted upon anyone by refusing the concurrent registration of such a classic example of an invented trademark. In another leading case, the Rolls-Royce Company, maker of famous automobiles, was able to enjoin the use of its mark by the manufacturer of radio tubes largely because of the strength of its mark.

Similarly, because its trademark *Black Label* had achieved a secondary meaning with respect to source identification, the Carling Brewing Company was able to enjoin the use of that mark as a brand name for cigarettes, and use of the name *Miss Seventeen* was barred as a mark for girdles in an action by the publisher of *Seventeen* magazine. In this latter case the theory of relief was based upon the conclusion not that confusion as to the source of the products would exist, but that the public would be likely to associate the magazine with sponsorship of such product, thus injuring its reputation and goodwill. On the other hand, the scope of the related-goods doctrine may be dramatically reduced where the conflicting marks are considered weak. Thus Sears' *Allstate* mark for, among other things, automobile insurance and safety-driver training programs was found not to be infringed by the identical term when used in connection with an auto driving school. In addition to finding that Sears had a weak mark, the court reasoned that although the respective products and services were sold to common purchasers, they were marketed through different distribution channels. Further, even though there existed a relationship between the services rendered by the insurance company and the driving school to the extent they shared a common purpose, namely, the instruction of prospective drivers, the difference in the motivation behind each party in achieving the result was sufficient to differentiate the respective uses of the same mark.

In like fashion, *Ship Shape* for men's hair spray was allowed against an earlier use of the same mark for a comb and brush cleaner on the basis of the different purposes served by the product. Although the court recognized that both products were related to hair grooming, an analysis of the products in their entire context, or "Gestalt perception," convinced the court that the likelihood of confusion standard had not been met. In this case, as well as that involving the *Allstate* mark, consideration was given to the lack of direct competition between the products and to the fact that the first user had no plans to extend the mark to the product that the opposing party was marketing. Conversely, where such product expansion reasonably may be expected, this fact will strengthen the conclusion that the products are sufficiently related so as to warrant the relief sought in order to prevent confusion as to source.

On the other hand, the fact that there already exists an overlap in the products produced by the parties, although the conflict relates to products that are different, will not necessarily give the first user an edge and he may have to be content with sharing the mark.

In the *Mustang* case, the mark accompanied by the picture of a running horse, for campers and travel trailers, was held not to be infringed by the use of the same mark and symbol on Ford Motor Company's *Mustang* model automobiles, notwithstanding that Ford advertised and sold certain of its other vehicles as "campers," "camper specials," and "recreational vehicles," and some of its franchised dealers sold other brands of campers and travel trailers in addition to its Ford products. Because Ford as the source of the *Mustang* automobile was always indicated and the mark was otherwise in common usage, the protection was restricted to the specific products on which the first user had used the mark. It may thus be seen that although the related-goods doctrine may act in some situations to expand trademark protection, the scope of such protection may be narrowed considerably where the mark is a weak one and where an analysis of other relevant factors tips the balance against finding that the public is likely to be confused as to the source of origin of the products.

Geographic Areas of Sales. Under the common law, the concurrent use of similar marks on similar or related products was permitted in different geographic areas without knowledge of the other's use, on the theory that such goods did not compete with each other and that the public was not likely to be confused as to their source. The right to use a mark in a certain geographic area was derived from the priority of its actual use there, and the trademark owner entered a new trading area subject to the existing rights of another user in that area, except where the second user intentionally sought to infringe the other's mark. The original user was also permitted a buffer zone of sorts and could protect his mark in an area of "legitimate trade expansion." Thus, in a common law action for "innocent" trademark infringement, the plaintiff must establish the priority of use of his mark in the area in question, in addition to the other elements of the action.

Registration under the Lanham Act serves as constructive notice of the claim of ownership and use of the mark in interstate commerce. Thus by eliminating the defense of good faith lack of knowledge, the Act affords nationwide protection to registered marks, regardless of the areas in which the registrant actually uses the mark. Such far-reaching protection may be limited, however, by the innocent use of a registered mark by another in a separate geographic area. Under Section 33 (b) (5) of the Act, such use will be established by the adoption and continuous use of the mark in such geographic area without knowledge of the registrant's prior use, from a date prior to the registration or publication of the mark. Where this criteria is not satisfied, however, the courts nevertheless may examine in an infringement proceeding the likelihood that the registrant will expand his activity into the area of second use.

Litigation in this area has largely involved chain stores or franchised businesses, which often have a history of geographical expansion. In a leading case in the area, *Dawn Donut Co. v. Hart's Food Stores, Inc.*, Dawn, a wholesale doughnut distributor, had registered its *Dawn* mark prior to the second user's first use and had licensed that mark in connection with retail doughnut shops in various places within the State of New York. The defendant used the same mark in connection with the retail sale of doughnuts and baked goods entirely within a six-county area surrounding Rochester, New York. The plaintiff had not licensed its mark in the defendant's area for more than thirty years, and its closest licensed retail establishment was more than 60 miles from defendant's trading area.

Although the court recognized that the plantiff's registration had occurred prior to the defendant's first use, it refused to issue an injunction against the defendant's continued use of the mark, accepting the trial court's finding that it was a matter of "common knowledge" that customer purchases of such products were usually confined to an area of no more than 25 miles from their homes. Determinative of the central issue as to the likelihood of confusion resulting from the second use of the mark was the conclusion that because the plaintiff was found not likely to expand the retail use of its mark into the defendant's area, customer confusion was not likely to result so long as the respective retail sales of the parties were confined to their separate areas. Upon a showing of such intent to expand, however, the plaintiff would be entitled to enjoin the defendant's further use of the mark. The case is significant for two reasons. In the first place, it well illustrates that the effect of registration of a mark under the Lanham Act alters the common law rule and provides constructive notice to a second user of such mark as to the first user's claim of ownership of it. Accordingly, prior use in a particular trading area that commences subsequent to registration by another will not give a second user the right to its continued use if the registrant at some future time decides to enter that market. The case further demonstrates that ownership of a registered mark does not necessarily carry with it the right to its exclusive use, nor to enjoin its subsequent use, even in connection with the sale of identical commodities. Rather, such rights continue to be related to the geographic area in which the mark is used. The implication for a company that has not registered its mark is obvious. If use of the mark is contemplated in a geographic area distinct from the area of its present use, such right may be determined by a veritable race to establish such use before the mark is used there or is registered by another company.

In two other cases second users of a mark were successful in establishing their innocent use, in a separate geographic area, of a registered mark prior to its registration, a defense to an action for infringement under the Lanham Act, and were accordingly entitled to preserve their uses of the nationally known marks *Burger King* and *Mr. Donut* to narrowly confined trading islands surrounded by expanding chains bearing the same marks. Despite the mobile nature of modern society, some courts continue unrealistically to focus on the fact that marketing of such franchised food products is largely restricted to small geographic areas, concluding that public confusion is not likely to occur despite the reality of widespread travel from one market area to another.

Channels and Methods of Distribution.   Closely related to the factors of product and geographic competition is a consideration of the channels and methods of distribution of the respective products in question. To the extent that these channels coincide, the likelihood that confusion can be established is strengthened. For example, the facts that beer and cigarettes are often sold together, and consumed together, were factors weighing in favor of a finding that confusion would be likely where the mark *Black Label* was used as a brand name for each. Likewise, this consideration was relevant where such items as film and cigarette lighters were sold at a common counter in drugstores.

On the other hand, it was emphasized in one case that products related to men's hair grooming that bore highly similar names were distributed differently, with plaintiff's comb and brush cleaner being marketed primarily through barber shops, beauty parlors, and drugstores and defendant's hair spray generally being sold through drug, variety and grocery stores. It was noted that these marketing channels were for the most part distinct, and that where they were similar, such outlets were known for selling a wide variety of articles, thus reducing the likelihood of confusion. Likewise, in the *Allstate* case, the facts that the plaintiff's auto and other insurance was not marketed in the same manner, nor sold through the same establishments as the defendant's driver instruction course contributed to the conclusion that plaintiff's mark was not infringed by defendant's use of the same one. In another case this factor was related to the different media in which the respective products were advertised, namely, newspapers and magazines having general circulation and on television, as opposed to technical and scientific magazines journals having a more restricted circulation.

It should be noted, however, that relatively minor weight is generally given to this factor in the decisional process. Where other factors tend to tip the scale in favor of granting relief, the lack of similarity of distribution will not militate against such relief. Thus, although a carpet manufacturer marketed its products only at the wholesale level of distribution, it was able to enjoin the use of the name *World* in conjunction with an illustration of a hemisphere of a globe by a carpet retailer when its mark contained similar features.

Customer Identity and Sophistication. As we have repeatedly seen, the standard for trademark infringement is the likelihood of confusion among members of the general public. The concept is akin to the "reasonable man" standard in the law of torts. As defined by one court, the plaintiff must demonstrate the "likelihood that an appreciable number of ordinarily prudent purchasers will be confused." This is not to suggest, however, that the care or sophistication with which customers make their choices is not to be considered. Where products are complicated and expensive, and where a significant selection process is likely to be used, the presence of such factors will often militate against a finding that confusion is likely to result. Such care is expected to be taken in the purchase of substantial items such as automobiles, campers, and trailers; auto insurance and auto driving instruction; cameras and studio television; and microwave and military electronic equipment. However, even sophistication of purchasers does not always ensure the absence of confusion, for even buyers of specialized equipment such as computers may assume that related corporations having confusingly similar names are the source of noncompeting goods. For the same reason, the fact that one product may cost substantially more than a similar product is not sufficient to negate the finding of a likelihood of confusion, because the trademark owner should not be prohibited from changing the price of its merchandise. Moreover, purchasers may well believe that a company producing a premium product has undertaken to market a more economical line where the names and other characteristics of the products are confusingly similar. The fact that the respective products are likely to be sold to the same types of purchasers may also influence a court that confusion is likely to occur.

On the other hand, it seems clear that where products are relatively inexpensive and are in common usage, less care in selection is likely to be exercised. Accordingly, confusion is more apt to result from the use of similar marks on sundry items such as hairspray and hair dressing, or on other products that are subject to impulse buying. Moreover, although the standard is one of the ordinary purchaser utilizing normal care, evidence of carelessness or inattentiveness by customers is not to be disregarded.

Defendant's Intent in Selecting His Mark. Although the intent of the defendant in using the plaintiff's mark is a central issue in an unfair competition action for palming off, the intent to infringe another's trademark is not a prerequisite to establishing liability under either a common law or Lanham Act proceeding. Because the essence of an infringement action is merely to demonstrate the likelihood of confusion as to the source of the products, even the innocent infringement of another's mark may be enjoined. Most courts, however, view evidence of copying or imitation of another's mark, or the marketing of a product in such a manner as to trade on the reputation of another, as an important factor in establishing the likelihood of confusion. Accordingly, the court in *Maternally Yours, Inc.* v. *Your Maternity Shop, Inc.* considered significant the fact that the second user, with knowledge of the prior owner's mark, adopted a confusingly similar name, located its store within two blocks of plaintiff's store, imitated plaintiff's format and slanted script in its advertising, used similar packing boxes, and adopted confusing telephone listings. Similarly, although the court in *Harold F. Ritchie, Inc.* v. *Chesebrough-Pond's, Inc.* gave considerable weight to so-called objective evidence of intent demonstrated by the copying of the physical identity and color of a men's hair dressing, imitation of both plaintiff's trade dress and advertising, and selection of an identical retail price, it regarded as even more significant evidence of "subjective" intent on the part of the defendant to cause confusion. Such evidence related to the manner in which the defendant had selected the name and dress for its product, which included side-by-side comparison with the tube and carton in which plaintiff's product was packaged, topped off by a series of "blind product [marketing] tests" in order to determine the degree of customer preference between the products. Likewise, evidence of wrongful intent, as demonstrated by the change of defendant's name to one similar to plaintiff's, continued use of such name after rejection of its application for registration, the parallel change of its corporate name following that of plaintiff, and adoption of an English marketing theme similar to plaintiff's, where its goods had no actual connection with that country although plaintiff's were British made, were considered overwhelming evidence of the likelihood of confusion.

Although evidence of intent to create confusion may be dispositive of the issue of likelihood of confusion, the absence of such intent may also be taken as evidence that confusion is not likely. On the other hand, some courts refuse to go that far, usually for the reason that good faith is no defense to an action for trademark infringement, or that the sine qua non of such action is customer confusion.

Actual Confusion. Instances of actual consumer confusion need not be demonstrated in order to establish liability for either common law or Lanham Act trademark infringement; however, where such instances have occurred, they are generally regarded as highly probative of the likelihood of confusion standard. It is often exclaimed that such evidence is in fact the best proof that confusion is likely, and the reason for its high evidentiary value is obvious. In addition, instances of confusion by persons other than consumers may often be relevant to the likelihood that consumers will be confused. Where evidence disclosed that on two occasions the plaintiff's clothing salesmen were asked by members of the trade about the availability from the plaintiff of the defendant's clothing, and where a national sports magazine had misdirected its request for a photograph depicting the defendant's merchandise for an advertisement to the plaintiff, the court reasoned that such instances formed the basis of a reasonable inference that consumer confusion was likely. Similarly, testimony by sales persons concerning the mental condition of purchasers may have probative value, as may instances of confusion within the trade, the media, or a commercial directory. Even the likelihood of confusion among investors has been found to be an adequate predicate for relief. In one case the court, recognizing an agency's expertise in matters subject to its regulation, found relevant the fact that the Securities and Exchange Commission had required the defendant to state in its prospectus that it was not related to the plaintiff company, and the defendant's subsequent acquiescence, where it had adopted a name similar to the plaintiff's. Likewise, evidence of the refusal of an application for registration under the Lanham or other statute is entitled to consideration.

It should be borne in mind, however, that the existence of actual confusion is only one of several factors examined by the courts and the impact of this factor may be slight where the court determines that the quantity of such evidence is insufficient to be probative of general consumer confusion, or where the nature of the evidence proffered is such that it is qualitatively unpersuasive in the eyes of the court. For example, where evidence was introduced to show instances of approximately 100 letters and statements that had been misdirected over a period of years, such evidence was deemed to be insignificant in light of the fact that each party's daily volume approximated 1,000 and 600 pieces of mail, respectively. Moreover, the court dismissed the evidence as "clearly due to palpable carelessness on the part of clerks or other subordinate employees." Where evidence of consumer confusion is introduced, it is essential that it be probative of the issue of confusion as to source.

The inability to demonstrate adequately the connection with one manufacturer resulting from use of a mark or slogan by another may justify disregarding responses to consumer surveys. More often, such survey evidence is regarded as inconclusive because the design or sequence of the survey questions may be biased in suggesting certain responses, the persons interviewed may not be prospective purchasers of the relevant products, the interviewers are not sufficiently trained or skilled, or the survey responses are not rendered in the context of the market place and hence fail to consider those factors that are relevant to an actual purchasing decision. The use of survey evidence is not objectionable on "hearsay" grounds, because it is not admitted to prove the truth of the responses, but only to show that some responses have been made that evidence consumer confusion. It is generally required, however, that the persons who conducted the interviews testify as to what they were told and the manner in which they characterized and recorded the responses. Thus, due to the inability to determine which factors were responsible for the survey responses, the inability to test or check the validity of the selected sample and the making or recording of the responses, and the improbability that actual purchasing decisions can be effectively analyzed by use of questions chosen by one party, survey results are generally deemed to have little evidentiary value. Although carefully designed and administered surveys could no doubt be prepared, such an approach must avoid minimizing the importance of more subjective factors, such as the similarities of product appearance, design, trade dress, methods of distribution, and customer sophistication, as well as those other factors that enter into actual purchasing decisions. Moreover, it should be recalled that it is a balancing of all the relevant factors that determines the likelihood of confusion when the impact of the use of the allegedly infringing mark is viewed in the context of the market place.

Judicial Remedies for Trademark Infringement

Upon a finding of trademark infringement, and the absence of any equitable defenses that would preclude such relief, the trademark owner is entitled to an injunction against the defendant's use of his mark in a manner that would be likely to cause confusion. This remedy exists under the common law of trademarks and is codified in the Lanham Act. Injunctive relief is limited, however, by equitable considerations and is available only to the extent necessary to avoid confusion. The court may order the total cessation of the use of the infringing mark in connection with the advertising or sale of the products involved in the action, or in connection with related products, upon a showing that such relief is necessary to avoid confusion. Courts are generally careful in fashioning relief that will protect not only the trademark owner from infringement but that will still permit a second user his legitimate rights to use a similar mark, provided sufficient care is taken to distinguish his product from that of the trademark owner and to disclaim any association with that firm. Thus, although the owner of the *THERMOS* mark for vacuum bottles was entitled to enjoin the use of that word in a trademark sense, concurrent use of the mark in its generic sense as descriptive of vacuum bottles having thermal retention properties was permitted under certain conditions. Among these were the conditions that the word appear entirely in lower case letters and be preceded by the defendant's possessive name.

Limitations as to the scope of injunctive relief may also necessitate a modification of the mark, such as interspersing a nonconfusing element, so that prominent emphasis is placed upon a distinguishable element of the mark. An example involved the several beauty-pageant marks utilizing the words *Miss U.S.A.* Similarly, injunctions may prohibit the use of a common element of a name or mark without reference to the defendant's full name or other distinguishing information, or it may restrict use of the infringing mark to a particular geographic area.

The Lanham Act further provides that relief against an innocent infringer engaged solely in the business of printing the mark for others is limited to an injunction against further printing. Likewise, when the infringement innocently appears in an advertisement in a newspaper, magazine, or other similar periodical, injunctive relief against the publisher is available only with respect to future issues, provided that preventing publication does not delay delivery of the issue beyond its regular time.

In addition to prohibitory provisions with respect to use of a mark, courts may fashion certain mandatory provisions under the Act. A court may require that the defendant affirmatively disclose, either orally or in writing, in response to customer requests for, or inquiries concerning, the product of another manufacturer that he does not sell such product but will substitute his own. The court may also order the offender to deliver to the trademark owner all labels, advertising, or other materials in its possession containing the offending mark, that it use its best efforts on a continuing basis to attempt to withdraw from its customers or others such offending material and offer it to the trademark owner for destruction, and that it provide to the court and the trademark owner a written report under oath setting forth the manner in which it has complied with the injunction. Application may be made for modification of any order upon a showing, in light of changed circumstances or experience, that the decree is no longer necessary or has failed to achieve fully the object toward which it was directed. In addition, the court has power under the Act over the registration of marks, and may determine the right to registration, order cancellation or restoration of registrations, or otherwise correct the register with respect to any party to the action.

In addition to injunctive relief, a successful party in an action for trademark infringement may recover monetary damages where injury, in addition to confusion, can be established. Although monetary recovery under the common law was reserved for instances of intentional infringement or diversion of trade, as in palming off, the Lanham Act provides that monetary recovery can be had for damages suffered by the infringing use of any reproduction or imitation of a registered mark in connection with the advertising or sale of goods in commerce, provided the registrant has given notice of the registration of his mark by employment of the sign ® or by use of the term *Reg. U.S. Pat. Off.* or its equivalent. Monetary recovery, where allowable, is intended as compensation for the loss of business, injury to reputation, or other injury suffered as a proximate result of the infringing use. The court is required to assess damages "according to the circumstances of the case" to a maximum of treble the amount actually found. Where infringement of a registered mark is based on copying or imitation of the mark coupled with application of the registered mark to labels, signs, advertisements, and the like intended to be used in connection with the sale or advertising of goods in commerce, the registrant will not be entitled to damages unless it is shown that the defendant knew that such printing was "intended to be used to cause confusion, or to cause mistake, or to deceive."

In addition to compensatory damages, the court may award to the plaintiff the profits derived by the defendant from sales of products or services utilizing the infringing mark. It has traditionally been held that such a measure of damages provides the trademark owner with appropriate protection only where the defendant's goods directly compete with those of the plaintiff. It has more recently been recognized, however, that an accounting for profits serves the additional purposes of deterring willful appropriation of another's mark and preventing public confusion as to the source of the defendant's goods. Accordingly, an accounting for profits may be an appropriate measure of recovery even where the respective parties do not directly compete with each other for trade.

Defenses to an Action for Trademark Infringement

Notwithstanding the establishment of a likelihood of confusion as to the source of a particular product or service, several defenses may be interposed to defeat an action for trademark infringement. As with any legal claim, monetary relief is barred if sought after the passage of too great a period of time from the date of the actionable wrong. There is no statute of limitations provision contained in the Lanham Act, so that the legal right to the recovery of monetary damages based upon a past infringement is, under our dual system of federal and state law, based upon the applicable statute of limitations in the state in which the action is brought. However, because infringement may be regarded as a continuous tort, each misuse constitutes a new right of action.

Because the desired form of relief will certainly include an injunction against any continued use of the infringing mark—an equitable, rather than a legal, remedy—somewhat different considerations apply with respect to defending against such relief. Essentially, injunctive relief will be denied to a trademark owner only where it is no longer equitable to enforce his rights in such mark. It is therefore necessary that the trademark owner establish a record of having scrupulously "policed" his mark, to learn of any infringements of which he could be reasonably expected to be aware, to so warn the suspected infringer, and request that he discontinue use of the suspected infringing mark. In one case where the plaintiff was aware for a period of approximately eleven years of the defendant's use of a similar trademark but took no action to assert its rights under its mark, it was denied an injunction against the defendant's continued use of the mark under the equitable doctrine of "estoppel by laches." The court noted that the defendant had applied for registration of its mark to which the plaintiff unsuccessfully had filed an opposition, and that the plaintiff had delayed for more than another year before finally bringing an action. Because the defendant had expended considerable sums during this period in advertising its mark and enlarging its business, the court concluded that it would be inequitable to require it then to cease using the mark. The court observed that in balancing the relative hardships of the parties in such cases, the fact that the defendant's early sales were small and its mark not well known required the plaintiff to assert its rights within a reasonable time so as to minimize the disadvantage to the defendant by requiring him to choose another mark before substantially expanding upon it. The court also drew a distinction between situations in which the second use of the mark is made in connection with different, as opposed to similar products, and determined that in the latter case, fairness required the plaintiff to assert its rights earlier than would be necessary in the latter case. This view was based upon the reasoning that where the products are different, the initial trademark user has a less valid reason for preventing the other's use and its rights are accordingly more easily lost if not asserted at an early time.

On the other hand, it has been held that the mere passage of time is generally insufficient to invoke the doctrine of laches; there must be a reliance by the second user, to his eventual detriment, that in failing to protect its mark the trademark owner does not consider such use an infringement. Of course, courts in assessing the rights of the parties examine more than the mere passage of time and weigh all of the circumstances attendant to the situation. Thus it may be found in some cases that laches will bar the granting of monetary damages or an accounting for profits, but will not preclude injunctive relief against further use of the mark by the second user, especially where the apparent acquiescence to the second user is merely delay in enforcing his rights.

We have seen, however, that the defendant's good faith in the use of its infringing mark is not a defense to an action for trademark infringement. Moreover, lack of knowledge as to the existence of a confusingly similar mark in a separate geographic area has been eliminated as a defense by the Lanham Act provision that provides that registration is constructive notice of the claim of its validity. These defenses are inapplicable, even under the common law, since the essence of trademark infringement is the likelihood of consumer confusion, not the intentional passing off of one's goods as those of another. There are, however, several other defenses that may be asserted against an action for trademark infringement that are specifically enumerated in the Lanham Act, even where the trademark registrant's exclusive right to use his mark has become incontestable under the Act. In the first place, it may be demonstrated that the registration or incontestable right to use the mark was obtained fraudulently. This provision is related to another portion of the Act that provides that any person may, at any time he believes he will be damaged by the registration of a mark on the Principal Register, apply to cancel such mark if its registration was fraudulently obtained, and thus presents a statutory vehicle by which to invalidate the mark. To establish such defenses, not only must it be demonstrated that materially false or fraudulent statements were knowingly made by the registrant, but the Act's statutory presumption in favor of the validity of a registered mark must also be overcome.

Another defense available under the Act is that the mark has been abandoned by the registrant. Abandonment requires either demonstration of an intent to discontinue use of the mark in connection with the goods or services with which trademark rights were acquired, or a course of conduct by which the mark loses its significance as an indication of the origin of the products or services with which it is connected. Nonuse for two consecutive years is presumptive evidence of intent to abandon a mark.

A third available defense under the Act is that the mark is being used by the registrant or one connected with him to misrepresent the source of the goods or services in connection with which the mark is used. This defense is akin to the equitable defense of "unclean hands"— the courts will not enforce a right for one who himself is guilty of similar misdeeds. Moreover, no likelihood of consumer confusion will follow from a second user's infringement where the registered mark itself does not accurately identify the true source of the goods. Additionally, the Act provides a defense upon a showing that the allegedly infringing mark is the infringer's own name or is used as descriptive of his goods or their geographic place of origin.

Two other defenses available under the Act are derived from the defendant's use of his mark prior to the registration or publication under the Act of the plaintiff's mark. The first relates to the defendant's continuous use in a geographic area, without knowledge of the registrant's original use of his mark, prior to the date of registration or publication of such mark. The second protects a party who has registered and used his mark under a preceding statute without abandonment prior to the registration or publication under the Lanham Act by the trademark allegedly infringed. These defenses are limited to the geographic area in which the defendant's mark is proved to have been innocently and continuously used, or in which it was used prior to the defendant's registration or publication, respectively.

A final defense enumerated under the Act is that the registered mark has been or is being used to violate the antitrust laws of the United States. It is not sufficient, however, to show merely that the trademark owner is violating the antitrust laws, or that his trademarked products are somehow involved in such violations. Rather, it must be demonstrated that the trademark itself was being used as the basic and fundamental vehicle by which to violate the antitrust laws. In such a situation, the Lanham Act provides that federal registration is conclusive of registrant's exclusive right to use the mark after five years following registration, with a few exceptions, including use of the mark to violate the antitrust laws. Unlike the field of patent misuse discussed in Chapter 2 the extent of this defense has not been fully clarified in the courts.

Unfair Competition and Dilution as Related Theories of Protection

It is generally recognized that the law of trademarks is but a branch of the more generalized law of unfair competition and is governed by essentially the same considerations. The owner of a trademark may often include an action for unfair competition in connection with its claim for trademark infringement, the basis of which is that through use of the contested mark, the alleged offender is somehow trading on the plaintiff's goodwill or otherwise unfairly competing with him in some other manner. Because the basis for each of the claims centers around the manner in which the defendant has chosen to compete with the plaintiff, the unfair competition claim involves substantially the same legal and factual issues as that for trademark infringement. Although it is based upon state law, it can nevertheless be entertained by federal courts as "substantial and related" to a federal claim under the Lanham Act.

In order to establish a successful claim for unfair competition arising from the use of a conflicting mark, the party must establish essentially that which is required for proving trademark infringement. As with a claim for trademark infringement, the activity need not approach an intentional palming off, and the courts tend to weigh the same factors as discussed in relation to trademark infringement. Although there may be slight variations in the common or statutory laws of each state, the standard in such actions continues to be the establishment of the likelihood of confusion as to the source of origin of the defendant's goods.

Historically it has been important that the parties be in actual competition to assert a claim for unfair competition. However, the tort has become closely harmonized with that of trademark infringement and such a requirement no longer obtains. Thus, in the leading case of *Triangle Publications, Inc.* v. *Rohrlich,* the publishers of *Seventeen* magazine were able to enjoin the use of the mark *Miss Seventeen* for young ladies' girdles on the theory that the public would be likely to view the magazine as approving or sponsoring such articles. Although the trial court denied relief upon a theory of trademark infringement because the products were not sufficiently related, it nevertheless found that unfair competition had occurred by means of the use of the similar mark to trade upon the established goodwill of the magazine. Similarly, in *Polaroid Corp.* v. *Polaraid, Inc.,* relief was granted under the theory of unfair competition where a manufacturer of refrigeration and heating systems adopted the mark *Polaraid* in what the court deemed to be an intentional attempt to trade upon the well-known *Polaroid* mark, which was used in connection with cameras and optical equipment. It is not clear that relief under a theory of trademark infringement would not be available in such types of cases today under the expanded related-goods theory; but the benefits of including a claim for unfair competition are apparent and should be sought especially where the owner's mark is not sufficiently strong to provide protection against its use on unrelated products.

Another theory upon which relief may be predicated is that of trademark dilution. This state remedy is designed to prevent injury to business reputation and to protect a strong mark from gradual deterioration through its continued use by persons other than the trademark owner, and would appear most helpful where relief cannot be predicated upon trademark infringement or unfair competition. It is sparingly used, however, and courts generally require that the mark be distinctive and that there be established some fraud or intentional passing off before an injunction will be granted. The language of many state antidilution statutes specifically provides that there need not be competition between the parties nor confusion as to the source of the goods. Although some courts have seemed to require a showing of the likelihood of confusion as to source, at least where intentional trading upon the reputation of a prior user was not apparent, others appear increasingly willing to grant relief, even absent such confusion, where the mark is sufficiently strong and its successive use threatens to weaken its distinctiveness. Thus, in the *Polaraid* case, another basis upon which relief was granted was that of trademark dilution, the court declaring that if such relief were not available in the absence of confusion, the dilution concept would add nothing to the established law of unfair competition. In all events, although dilution remains a sparingly applied concept, it would appear to be worthy of greater judicial recognition as a means of preventing tarnishing or overexposure of a distinctive business name.

Trading upon the reputation of another may itself form the basis of commercial activity in the form of social commentary. In such an instance, traditional notions of infringement, unfair competition, and dilution may not be available to prevent such activity. An interesting example of the limitations placed upon the use of these doctrines is found in *Girl Scouts of the United States of America* v. *Personality Posters Mfg. Co.* Personality Posters published posters consisting of a smiling girl, obviously pregnant, dressed in the well-known green uniform of the Junior Girl Scouts. The poster also bore the well-known slogan of the Girl Scouts: "Be Prepared." The Girl Scouts sought to enjoin distribution on several grounds, including that of trademark infringement, unfair competition, dilution of its trademark, as well as defamation. The court denied preliminary relief on all claims and, with respect to those of infringement and unfair competition, on the ground that no evidence had been presented that would tend to demonstrate a likelihood of confusion that the poster had been prepared by the Girl Scouts themselves. The court noted that evidence of indignation expressed to the Girl Scout organization by some members of the public tended to establish an awareness of the nature of the satirical commentary being made, and further, that the defendant's name did appear in small type on the poster. Also rejected was the theory of trademark dilution, on the ground that such use of this doctrine as had been made extended only to situations involving likelihood of confusion as to source. Additionally, the court noted that although it was not necessary to deny relief upon the ground that the First Amendment protected the right of satirical expression, posters have been found to be a form of expression that may be constitutionally protected.

Private Actions for Deception as to Origin or Description Under Section 43(a) of the Lanham Act

In addition to trademark infringement remedies available under the Lanham Act there exists a separate, self-contained provision granting a private cause of action against sellers of goods or services in interstate commerce who falsely designate origin or falsely describe the goods or services. This is Section 43(a) of the Lanham Act, which provides that:

> Any person who shall affix, apply, or annex, or use in connection with any goods or services, or any container or containers for goods, a false designation of origin, or any false description or representation, including words or other symbols tending falsely to describe or represent the same, and shall cause such goods or services to enter into commerce, and any person who shall with knowledge of the falsity of such designation of origin or description or representation cause or procure the same to be transported or used in commerce or deliver the same to any carrier to be transported or used, shall be liable to a civil action by any person doing business in the locality falsely indicated as that of origin or in the region in which said locality is situated, or by any person who believes that he is or is likely to be damaged by the use of any such false description or representation.

The primary importance of the enactment of this statute in 1946 is that it created a new federal statutory remedy for false representation of goods in interstate commerce and thereby broadly expanded the classes of injured competitors with standing to bring civil suits for this sort of unethical business conduct. Early cases decided under this new statute clearly established that it went much farther than the common law principles of unfair competition and in fact created a new federal remedy for injured manufacturers. For example, the following sorts of activity have been held to violate this act: (1) fraudulent use of an illustration of plaintiff's product to advertise defendant's inferior copy, (2) misrepresentation of artificial fur as mink, and (3) the sale of engine bearings and connecting rods in packages and containers closely imitating the trade dress used by plaintiff. Moreover, as a practical matter, Section 43(a) does not require the plaintiff to show either that his product or its trade dress has acquired secondary meaning or to show actual palming off of the competitor's imitation on customers as the basis for the granting of injunctive relief. All that is required of a plaintiff in order to obtain equitable relief is the showing of some likelihood of competitive injury arising from a false representation made by the defendant in marketing its product.

Section 43(a) has also been held to justify a cause of action against parties whose misrepresentations are harming a plaintiff but who are not in direct competition with him. For example, in *Eastman Kodak Co.* v. *Royal Pioneer Paper Box Manufacturing Co.,* an injunction was granted against the further sale by a box manufacturer to plaintiff's competitors of boxes deceptively similar to the boxes in which plaintiff returned film after development. The court noted specifically:

> Even though defendant is not in competition with plaintiff, the latter is entitled to an injunction since defendant enables plaintiff's competitors "to palm off" their services of developing films as those of plaintiff by furnishing them with packages in plaintiff's distinctive trade dress and plaintiff has been damaged by improper developing services of its competitors who have used this trade dress.

The court held that such action constituted a violation of Section 43(a) of the Lanham Act.

Similarly, in *Geisel* v. *Poynter Products, Inc.,* the defendants marketed small toys or dolls derived from creatures depicted in plaintiff's cartoons, falsely representing that Dr. Seuss (as plaintiff was known professionally) was the creator and manufacturer of these dolls. The court held specifically that a false representation that a product is authorized or approved by a particular person constitutes a violation of Section 43(a), and that plaintiff is entitled to injunctive relief upon a showing of the likelihood of customer confusion as to the source or originator of the goods. The court's language and the fact that the record contained no evidence that Dr. Seuss had ever approved or authorized the sale of any doll under his trade name indicates that Section 43(a) has some potential application to cases in which a company adopts the trade name and trade dress of a well-known manufacturer for use in the imitator's sale of a related but noncompeting product. Such an approach would give the established company a private right of action on the same facts as were formerly enforceable only through the intervention of the Federal Trade Commission—for example, in the 1937 case of *FTC* v. *Real Products Corp.,* in which the commission successfully attacked the use by a new company of the trade designation *Champion Spark Set* to merchandise its spark plug cable sets, without the consent of the Champion Spark Plug Company.

Establishing the right to money damages under Section 43(a) is quite another matter. The cases indicate that both a showing of actual deception and proof of the amount of the loss of sales or profits must be shown before money damages will be awarded. Although a blatant and continued misrepresentation by one company of its products as being those of another company gave rise to $20,000 in actual damages, in that case a son had left the family paper business, set up a rival company under a deceptively similar name, and actively solicited the business of the family firm's customers.

The Federal Trade Commission as a Policeman
Against Infringement

Any organization injured by trademark infringement or related deceptive practices of a competitor is free to complain to the Federal Trade Commission, urging the FTC to start legal proceedings to stop unfair methods of competition or deceptive acts or practices. At the outset, the reader should be cautioned against reaching the conclusion that this procedure is a panacea for private injuries of the type described. There are a number of reasons.

First of all, the FTC and the FTC alone will make the decision whether or not to start such legal proceedings. This decision is grounded on whether such an expenditure of government funds and resources is in the public interest. In situations where Company A is simply infringing Company B's trademark, the prospect for FTC intervention is remote, because budget limitations and enforcement priorities will more likely than not leave Company B to start its own lawsuit against Company A—the "public interest" is not sufficiently compelling. However, exceptions may exist, particularly where the alternative of private litigation is not feasible or is unreliable and widespread consumer harm is shown in a very concrete way. For instance, a nonprofit association that is subjected to palming off and related deception by a commercial enterprise bilking its members through, in effect, collective mark infringement, conceivably could mashal a much better public interest case than our Company A–Company B example. In years past, the FTC was more willing to enter this arena than contemporary enforcement policies suggest, and the FTC has issued a multitude of cease and desist orders against companies who have engaged in what is in effect trademark infringement giving rise to a private remedy.

Second, and equally significant, the FTC offers limited prospects for swift enforcement aimed at stopping an unlawful practice such as deception through trademark infringement: there is the job of convincing the FTC staff of the factual, legal, and public interest merits of the complaining party's position; the FTC staff may then need to conduct its own investigation; the FTC itself must then decide whether to start a legal action. While the FTC was granted preliminary injunction powers by Congress in 1973, this is a largely untested enforcement procedure for this agency. Confronted with these obstacles, the company with the desire to do something right now is most likely to start its own infringement lawsuit, where time and results are more within its own control.

Bureau of Customs Remedies Against Infringing Imports

The Bureau of Customs has regulations governing importation of products bearing infringing trademarks and trade names (and products which infringe upon United States copyright registrations as described more fully in Chapter 5). These regulations have for many years offered to American companies a convenient method of preventing foreign-based manufacturers from importing goods that bear trademarks or trade names similar to trademarks or trade names of United States companies and for preventing the importation of pirated versions of copyrighted materials. These regulations offer an alternative to, and in many cases advantages over, an infringement suit against a foreign-based competitor. However, apparently because of a lack of familiarity with the regulations, American companies generally have failed to realize the full advantages they offer.

In summary, the regulations provide that registered trademarks and copyrights, and trade names that have been in use for six months or longer, may be recorded with the Bureau of Customs by complying with several prescribed steps. After recording, customs officers will "detain" for thirty days any imported article that bears a mark or name copying or simulating the recorded trademark or trade name. Thereafter, unless the importer is able to prove to the Commissioner of Customs that his trademark or trade name is not a copy or simulation of the recorded mark or name, the articles will be seized and forfeiture proceedings instituted. Similar sanctions are imposed against the importation of articles bearing a false notice of copyright as well as pirated copies of recorded copyrighted works.

As compared to infringement suits, compliance with these regulations can be advantageous in at least two significant respects. First, the Bureau of Customs will assist in discovering unauthorized users of a recorded trademark, trade name, or copyrighted work. More importantly, if a customs official decides that an imported article infringes upon the recorded rights of a party, he can prevent the articles from entering the flow of U.S. commerce. Such action can be very important, particularly in instances where the importer may be judgment-proof or insulated from service of process. In this latter situation, unless the articles are seized before distribution, the company whose rights have been infringed, in order to protect those rights, would face the onerous task of suing a large number of outlets who may have purchased the articles for resale. The second noteworthy point regarding these regulations is that they shift the burden of proof on the question of whether or not the trademark or trade name used on the imported goods is "similar" to the recorded mark. Thus once a customs official decides that the mark on the imported goods is similar to the recorded mark, one of the few ways in which the importing company can avoid seizure and forfeiture of the goods is to prove that the marks are not similar. Conversely, if the company owning the recorded mark resorted to an infringement suit to enforce its rights, it would have the burden of proving that the marks were in fact "similar."

Customs Recording Procedure. The procedures for recording trademarks and trade names follow.

TRADEMARKS. The only trademarks eligible for recording with the Bureau of Customs under these regulations are trademarks that have been registered in the United States Patent Office under the Trademark Act of March 3, 1881, the Trademark Act of February 20, 1905, and any marks registered on the Principal Register under the Lanham Act of 1946. The mark is recorded by filing an application with the Commissioner of Customs, Washington, D.C., and the application must identify the trademark owner, including its principal business address, and (where applicable) the jurisdiction of incorporation, the place of manufacture of goods bearing the recorded trademark, the name and address of licensed users of the trademark, and a statement outlining the use authorized and the identity of any parent or subsidiary company or other foreign company under common ownership or control that uses the trademark abroad.

The application must be accompanied by a status copy of the certificate of trademark registration, bearing Patent Office certification that the applicant for recordation is the owner of title to the mark, 700 copies of the certificate of trademark registration, and a fee of $100 for each trademark and each additional class of goods (where recording is for more than one class) for which the mark is to be recorded.

After the application and documents are on file with the Bureau of Customs, the applicant will be notified of the approval or denial of the application; if the application is approved, protection under the provisions of the regulations becomes effective on the date of approval. The term of recording is concurrent with the term of registration of the mark with the Patent Office. When a trademark registration is renewed with the Patent Office, the recording with the Bureau of Customs may also be renewed by filing an application within three months of the date of the expiration of the existing registration. The application for renewal must include a status copy of the Certificate of Registration, again certified by the Patent Office to show that applicant is the owner of title to the trademark registration, a statement describing any changes in ownership with respect to the mark or changes in the address of owners or places of manufacture, and a fee of $40. The $40 fee covers all recording renewals submitted with the fee, so renewal is considerably less expensive than recording in the first instance. The rules also provide for notifying the Bureau of Customs prior to the time for renewal of any changes in ownership of the recorded mark or changes in the name of owners of recorded marks. To record these changes, notice in writing must be given to the Bureau of Customs, along with a status copy of the Certificate of Registration, again certified to show proper ownership of the registration, and a fee of $40 to cover the changes with respect to all recorded marks referred to in the notice.

TRADE NAMES. The regulations provide that any name or trade style used for at least six months to identify a manufacturer or trader may be recorded with the Bureau of Customs. Recording of trade names is permitted only for the complete business name. The application to record a trade name must be filed with the Commissioner of Customs, and it must include the name and address of the applicant, the name or trade style to be recorded, the name and principal business address of each foreign person licensed to use the mark and a statement as to the use authorized, the identity of any foreign company under common ownership or control that uses the trade name abroad, and a description of the merchandise associated with the trade name. The application must also be accompanied by statements by the owner of the mark and by at least two other persons not associated or related to the applicant—each stating that to the best of his knowledge and belief, applicant has used the mark in connection with the merchandise described in the application for at least six months, that the trade name is not identical or confusingly similar to any other trade name or registered trademark used in connection with similar goods, and that the applicant has the sole and exclusive right to use the trade name in connection with his business. The application must also be accompanied by a fee of $100 for each trade name to be recorded.

If an application to register a trade name appears in order, the Bureau of Customs will publish a notice of tentative recording of the trade name in the Federal Register and the Customs Bulletin. Interested parties may then oppose recording of the trade name. If there is no opposition, or if an opposition fails, notice of final approval for recording of the name will then be published in the Federal Register and Customs

Bulletin. The term of recording of a given trade name is indefinite and for so long as the applicant continues to use the name.

Protection Received Through Recording. The customs regulations provide that articles of foreign or domestic manufacture bearing a mark or name copying or simulating a recorded trademark or trade name shall be denied entry and are subject to forfeiture as prohibited importations. The regulations define a "copying or simulating" mark or name as an "actual counterfeit of the recorded mark or name or . . . one which so resembles it as to be likely to cause the public to associate the copying or simulating mark with the recorded mark or name." This definition is quite similar to the test that courts use to determine whether or not trademark infringement exists. Thus the effect of these regulations is that by recording a trademark or trade name with the Bureau of Customs, the owner of the mark or name will have enlisted the services of the Bureau of Customs in policing, and enforcing his rights in, trademarks and trade names against importing infringers.

When a customs official determines that a mark or name on imported goods copies or simulates a recorded mark or name, he may detain the articles bearing the mark or name for a period of thirty days. During that time the importer may obtain a release of the goods by showing that the mark or name of both the U.S. and foreign company is owned by the same person, that the company owning the recording and the importing company are parent subsidiary companies or otherwise subject to common ownership or control, that the mark or name is applied under authorization of the U.S. owner, that the objectionable mark has been removed, or that the recording party has given written consent to the importation of the article. If the importer fails to obtain release of the goods, he will be notified that the merchandise has been seized and forfeiture proceedings instituted. Once this has been done, the importer can avoid forfeiture only by showing that his mark or name is not a copy or simulation of the recorded mark or name. For any company that is confronted with significant competition from importers, and where questions of trademark infringement have arisen in the past, this portion of the regulations could be used to shift the burden of proof to the importer, as well as, in effect, to have the government bring the infringement suit at its expense.

LOSS OF RIGHTS

The most common ways in which a trademark owner may totally lose his rights in a mark are (1) by abandoning the mark, (2) by allowing the mark to become a generic word, (3) by expiration of the patent or copyright of which the mark is itself the subject, (4) by improper licensing, and (5) by assigning the mark in gross without transferring the good will.

Abandonment

The Lanham Act provides that a mark "shall be deemed to be 'abandoned' . . . . (w)hen any course of conduct of the registrant, including acts of omission as well as commission, causes the mark to lose its significance as an indication of origin." The definition embraces several of the methods by which rights in a trademark may be lost. However, in this section, the term *abandonment* will be limited to the "intentional reversion of the property rights in a mark to the public domain." Nonuse of a mark is not, in and of itself, sufficient to establish that the mark has been abandoned. There must also be an intent to abandon the mark, which may be inferred from the fact of nonuse for a substantial period of time. What will be sufficient to establish such intent depends on the facts of each case. However, when the question of abandonment is raised with respect to federally registered marks, or marks for which registration is pending in the Patent Office, reference will be made to Section 45 of the Lanham Act which makes nonuse of a mark for two consecutive years prima facie evidence of abandonment—that is to say, abandonment will be presumed unless the owner of the mark can demonstrate that there was no intent to abandon.

Though the situation occurs infrequently, the owner of a trademark may expressly abandon the mark, as, for example, by agreement with another who wants to use, or is already innocently using, the same or confusingly similar mark. Generally, however, such clear-cut facts are lacking and the requisite intent to abandon must be gleaned from other circumstances. A few cases will demonstrate the type of activities that have been held to be inconsistent with an intent to resume use of the mark where nonuse is established.

In *American Home Products Corp.* v. *Viviano*, American Home filed a petition to cancel the registration of *Zoo-Mac* for macaroni products that were manufactured in the shape of miniature animals. American Home had begun in May of 1966 to use the word *Zooghetti* as a trademark for a canned macaroni preparation and it believed that the two marks so resembled each other as to be likely to cause confusion. The petition asserted abandonment of the *Zoo-Mac* mark on the basis of nonuse for at least two consecutive years. Viviano claimed that although his company was not manufacturing a macaroni product under its mark, he had sent samples of the *Zoo-Mac* product to a number of companies, his company maintained the dies used in producing the macaroni animal shapes, and he was attempting to find some place to manufacture the product. However, the court found that these claims were not supported by the evidence. Moreover, the actual period of nonuse was shown to have included Viviano's predecessor who had not sold macaroni products under the mark since March of 1951, when the application for registration of the mark was filed. Under these circumstances there was nothing to overcome a presumption of abandonment.

In *Conwood Corp.* v. *Loew's Theaters, Inc.,* Conwood filed a petition to cancel Loew's Theaters' registration for the trademark *Stag* used for cigarette tobacco, charging that it had been abandoned as of 1970. Fifteen years earlier Loew's predecessor, P. Lorillard Company, discontinued manufacture, sale, and promotion of the cigarette tobacco, and although the company had made several shipments in small quantities of filter-tipped cigarettes using the mark *Stag* in 1968, the court found that this was not a bona fide cigarette business and the shipments were made solely in an attempt to preserve its rights to the mark. With no resumption in the manufacture and sale of *Stag* cigarette tobacco by the time testimony was taken, the court held that Loew's had not demonstrated an intent to resume use of the mark.

Courts have held that use of the mark in advertising is sufficient to show that the owner does not intend to abandon his rights even though the mark is not applied directly to the product with which it is associated. Similarly, use of the mark in correspondence with prospective customers, though the goods remained unsold, will be sufficient evidence to overcome a presumption of abandonment based on nonuse for the statutory period. Moreover, ceasing to manufacture a product will not show abandonment of the associated trademark if there are sales of the trademarked product, an inventory exists to meet current orders, and dealers use the trademark. This is generally the way an automobile manufacturer avoids loss of trademark rights on models it no longer manufactures. An illustration of this principle is shown in *American Motor Corp.* v. *Action Age, Inc.* Action Age sought to register the name *Scrambler* as a trademark for off-highway recreational vehicles. The registration was opposed by American Motors, which alleged prior and continuous use of the registered trademark *Rambler*. Action Age contended that the trademark *Rambler* had been abandoned. The court held, however, that although American Motors had discontinued use of *Rambler* on automobiles manufactured by it, there was no abandonment because of sales of Rambler parts, trademark use by dealers in used-car sales, and a large number of Rambler automobiles on the road.

The case of *Izod, Ltd.* v. *Liberty Hosiery Mills, Inc.,* illustrates the proposition that if the trademarked products are not manufactured because o* pending litigation over the trademark rights, the mark is not abandoned. Here, Izod petitioned for cancellation of a trademark registration owned by Liberty Hosiery for *Doozies* for hosiery. The evidence revealed that Liberty had made only one sale in interstate commerce of hosiery under the *Doozies* mark and had made no subsequent use of the mark. Accepting Liberty's explanation that it had not intended to abandon the mark, but that further sales had been curtailed pending the outcome of litigation concerning its rights in the mark, the court held the mark had not been abandoned. Thus, if the trademark is in use at the time the infringement action is commenced and if the owner diligently asserts rights to continue using it, and has an intent to resume use of the mark when the action is successfully terminated, then nonuse during that period is not abandonment.

If the owner of a trademark discontinues manufacture of the trademarked item, but continues to use the mark on other items in the same class, no intention to abandon is shown. A case in point involved Big Bear Stores that tried to register *Supershield* for exterior primer and exterior house paint and barn paint, asserting first use since June 1965. In February 1966 duPont filed an application to register *Supershield* for exterior clear finish, asserting first use since June 1964 when it commenced to test-market the product in two cities in New York State and several cities on the West Coast. When the initial test marketing and a subsequent test in 1966 at a lower price did not generate any significant distribution of the product, duPont proposed to use the mark *Supershield* on other products considered nearest in quality but lower in price than the original *Supershield* finish. Big Bear contended that duPont's use of the trademark was purely experimental, and that once experimentation ceased in November 1966, duPont's mark was abandoned. The court held that although duPont failed in the marketing of the original product, which was admittedly experimental and small in volume, it had nevertheless shown continuous use from June 1964 to November 1966, and the mere "change of the use of mark from one product to another variety thereof cannot constitute abandonment of the mark."

In general, if one uses a mark in business and then goes out of business, the mark is abandoned. Trademark rights are not discarded, however, by temporary suspension of business that is beyond the control of the owner of the trademark. Examples of involuntary nonuse of a mark not amounting to abandonment include court orders temporarily curtailing use, strikes, reorganization of business, scarcity of raw materials, war, and statutory prohibitions against a particular line of business involving the mark—for example, the Prohibition era effect on the liquor industry.

A trademark may be lost if there is a dissolution of the business in bankruptcy, if there is no goodwill any longer associated with the mark; however, if a receiver runs the business and the goodwill continues, the trademark will not have been lost.

If a mark is modified or changed, it is not necessarily abandoned as long as it retains its impact and symbolizes a "single and continuing commercial impression." In *Hess's of Allentown, Inc.* v. *National Bellas Hess, Inc.*, Hess's petitioned to cancel the registration of *Bellas Hess Superstore*. In tracing the alleged ownership of Hess's rights in its trademark *Hess*, the court held that *Hess's* and *Hess* are one and the same designation, and the change does not constitute a substantial change or modification in the mark so as to give rise to abandonment.

Mark Becomes a Generic Word

A generic term is the common dictionary-type designation by which a product is known. When a mark becomes generic, usually as the result of widespread public use of the word to identify the product or service with which the mark has been associated rather than one particular brand or source, the word is free to the whole world to use as such. The owner of a mark thus must walk a tight rope between, on the one hand, encouraging recognition of his mark and, on the other hand, taking steps to prevent a situation where the mark becomes so well known that it is converted into a reference term for a class of products, thereby losing its distinctiveness as an indicator of origin. This has happened to *aspirin, thermos, shredded wheat, escalator, cellophane,* and many others, but not without considerable litigation as to the status of the words. The cost of developing and preserving the exclusivity of a mark comes high. However, there are several positive steps that can be taken to police a mark to ensure that it remains a trademark.

1. *Descriptive synonym.* Trademark owners are wise to develop some way to refer to their product in addition to the trademark itself. For example, the makers of *Vaseline* have also called it petroleum jelly. This is especially advisable where the product is manufactured exclusively under a patent.

2. *Publications.* Owners should object to generic use of trademarks in publications of any sort, including trade publications and dictionaries (though mere appearance as a generic word in a trade publication or dictionary is not necessarily enough to cause loss of rights). Even patents and patent applications should not use trademarks as common nouns in the text.

3. *Extended mark usage.* If a mark is in danger of becoming generic its use can be extended to a line or family of products or services. This

will break the connection between a mark and a particular product or service, and refocus attention on the origin of the goods.

4. *Owner's use.* Of course, the trademark owner should never use a trademark as a generic term. The owner should use the word *Trademark* or *Registered Trademark,* or ® in close conjunction with the mark. The trademark should always be capitalized, because it is a proper adjective. The word *brand,* e.g., "Vaseline Brand Petroleum Jelly," will

Xerox vs. xerox.

Our Xerox trademark is among our most valuable assets.

So it's important to us that you know how it should be used. And how it should not.

If you spell Xerox with a small x, you're making a big mistake.

Since a trademark is by definition a proper adjective, it should always be capitalized.

At the same time, using a capital X doesn't give you the right to use it in a way that's wrong.

Even with a big X, you can't make a Xerox, you can't go to the Xerox and you can't Xerox anything. Ever.

As long as you use a big X, however, you can make copies on the Xerox copier, you can go to the Xerox computer and you can read a Xerox publication.

So remember, whenever you're writing our name, use a capital letter.

After all, isn't that the way you write your name?

XEROX

serve as a further indicium of trademark identity. Trademark owners concerned over a mark becoming generic should consider advertising to ensure proper use of their marks. A good example of this practice appears in the Xerox ads reproduced here.

Please don't use our name in vain.

The name Xerox is one of the most famous in America. We're very flattered.

But we'd like to remind you that just as there are ways you can use our name, there are ways you shouldn't.

Despite what you may say, there is no such thing as a xerox.

In other words, you can't make a xerox. You can't go to the xerox. And you can't xerox anything. Ever.

On the other hand, you can make copies on the Xerox copier.

You can go to the Xerox copier or the Xerox computer.

And you can read a Xerox textbook.

We're happy to have you use our name.

All we ask is that you use it the way the good law intended.

XEROX

Special problems arise when patentees break new marketing ground and introduce to the public goods or services not formerly known and therefore without a common descriptive name. Here it is particularly important to create, introduce, and insist upon use of a descriptive term · with the trademark; otherwise the trademark will become the only means by which the product may be identified. *Singer*, for example, was held to be a generic word in 1896 in reference to sewing machines, which developed in the market place under ·the aegis of patent protection. There was only one sewing machine on the market of the patented type —the *Singer*. In 1952, however, *Singer* was held to be a valid trademark, demonstrating that a trademark that has become a generic word may later be reclaimed as a trademark. And if the mark that was used on the patented product or service is in fact not generic to the product or service, the trademark rights will be unaffected by the expiration of the patent.

Once the mark, or features of it, becomes generic, others may use it to describe their products. This windfall right has limitations, however. For example, in the case that decided the status of the *Thermos* trademark, although the court upheld the validity of the trademark THERMOS, it also held that the word had become generic to vacuum insulated bottles and required the would-be infringer to confine its use of the word to lower-case type preceded by the company name and not to use the words *original* or *genuine* to describe its product.

Expiration of Patent or Copyright

Suppose a distinctive package or shape of a product is the subject of a design patent and is also protected as a trademark. Because design patents and trademarks are in essence governmentally sanctioned monopolies, is the owner of a patent–trademark allowed to protect his distinctive design from use by competitors after the patent expires by reference to trademark rights that continue to exist, generally speaking, as long as the mark is used? The courts have answered a rather unequivocal "no," but nonetheless will not allow competitors to mislead the public about the origin of the item. In one case Honeywell sought to register the configuration of its thermostat as a trademark, alleging that the configuration had been used as a mark since 1952. The mark was described in the trademark application as consisting of the arbitrary and unique combination of an outer cover ring and a disc positioned concentrically within the ring, which comprised a portion of the configuration of a thermostat. The court held that apart from considerations of whether the configuration is functional, the registration should be refused because it would extend the monopoly that the applicant had enjoyed for fourteen years from the issuance of the design patent, and the issuance of a trademark registration for the same subject matter would be "inconsistent with the right of others under the terms of the patent grant to make fair use of the ornamental design for control instruments including thermostats after the expiration of the patent and that it would serve, in effect, to extend the protection accorded the patented design contrary to the purpose and intent of the patent law." Another case involved the famous *Zippo* lighter for which the patent had expired. In upholding an imitator's right to use the Zippo design with appropriate indentification of the source and place of manufacture, the court said, "Purchasers who desire a Zippo-looking lighter at a lower price may have one. Competitors who desire to satisfy this demand may do so."

Improper Licensing

If a trademark is licensed without reference to the particular product with which the mark is associated (a "bare" or "naked" license) or for use on other products, or if the licensor is unable to exert control over product quality, then the license will entail loss of rights in the mark.

Under the Lanham Act and at common law a licensor must exercise control over the nature and quality of the product or service for which the mark is licensed or lose its rights in the mark. However, because the very *raison d'être* of a trademark is to distinguish a particular brand from among competing brands of the same product or service, it is essential that this function continues whether the product or service is produced by the trademark owner or its licensee. Normally a trademark license will give the licensor the power to monitor the methods of production and evaluate the resultant product or process in order to insure that his mark continues to represent a product or service of a certain quality. But even if the agreement does not explicitly grant licensor the right to control the quality and nature of the trademark goods, it may be read into the agreement by a court if, for example, in fact there has been reasonable inspection of trademark product quality, and where it has not been shown that the goods were below the licensor's standard of quality.

Assignments Without Goodwill

Similar to the legal technicalities that attach to an authorization to use a trademark as by license from the owner, the law requires that any agreement to transfer ownership of a mark be accompanied by a transfer of the goodwill associated with the mark. Legally, *goodwill* refers to the business or that part of the business that is represented by the mark; that is to say, every advantage the owner of the mark has acquired in connection with the use of the mark. An assignment of the mark without goodwill operates as an abandonment of the rights the assignor had in the mark and the assignee takes only the right to use the mark, and to perfect the rights based on that use, from that point forward. However, there is a presumption that rights in a mark pass with the sale and transfer of the business with which the mark was used, unless there is evidence to the contrary. If the entire assets of a business have been transferred, it is proper to assume that the trademarks used in that business have also been transferred and written trademark assignment does not have to be established, although it is obviously desirable.

CHOICE OF A MARK AND THE SEARCH
TO DETERMINE AVAILABILITY

Choosing a new mark is such a subjective decision that only the most general observations may be made. More often than not somebody "just likes it," such as the marketing vice president or maybe the president's wife. In large consumer goods industries, choice of a mark may be based on extensive consumer market research surveys and attention to contemplated advertising programs, as well as to the marks and advertising approaches of competitors. For example, the time and expense involved in selecting *Exxon* to replace *Esso* involved the highest level of marketing talent within the management circles of Standard Oil, including three years of intensive research and the rejection of one of the company's existing trademarks *Enco*—because in Japanese the word means "stalled car." In all events, we will assume that some preliminary decisions involving choice of a mark have been made, taking into account the host of factors already discussed, such as the advantages of coined names and phrases, the benefits of a corporate family of marks, related-goods considerations, strong versus weak mark considerations, and the like.

Prior to adopting and using the new trademark under consideration it is highly desirable, even customary, to arrange with trademark attorneys for a Patent Office search and evaluation to be conducted with a view to uncovering existing federal registrations of marks that may create "likelihood of confusion" problems. This is the case whether or not federal registration is contemplated, for there is a basic interest in determining whether or not the mark, if used, is an invitation to become defendant in a lawsuit for infringement, on the one hand, or susceptible of strong judicial protection against prospective infringers, on the other hand. Moreover, an exhaustive search should go beyond Patent Office records of federal registrations (and pending applications): all available sources should be checked for infringement possibilities—telephone directories, trade association directories and publications, the Thomas Register, for example. Trade names are of equal interest in the context of unfair competition problems. If foreign use is contemplated, sources within the country of interest should be checked for potential difficulties.

FEDERAL REGISTRATION OF MARKS

Introduction

The registration of trademarks was unknown at common law, where we have seen that the adoption and use of a mark resulted in the availability of protection against infringement by a subsequent user in the geographic area of the first user. It was not until the latter half of the 1800's that the major trading countries of the world undertook legislative action on the subject of trademarks. England, Germany, and the United States enacted laws that dealt primarily with the public registration of marks. These initial legislative efforts were procedural in nature and did not affect substantive common law trademark rights. Today most industrial countries of the world have registration programs of one form or another.

The Lanham Act of 1946, the culmination of earlier federal legislation in the field, not only serves to codify common law principles but also provides a dual registration system that has national and international consequences. Although it is beyond the scope of this section to develop the more intricate procedural niceties attendant to Patent Office rules and regulations involving federal registration, a general survey will be provided, along with a discussion of the opportunities available for contesting prospective or issued federal registrations through the Patent Office procedures.

When to Seek Federal Registration

An application for federal registration may be filed with the U.S. Patent Office any time after the statutory prerequisite of adoption and use in interstate commerce is satisfied. We have seen that nominal sales or use in interstate commerce will suffice, so long as bona fide third-party transactions take place. This first adoption and use in interstate commerce can be followed weeks, months, or years later by the filing with the Patent Office.

The Role of the U.S. Patent Office

The machinery for administering Lanham Act registration of marks has been assigned by Congress to the U.S. Patent Office. We have reviewed in Chapter 2 (pp. 34–35, 53–55) the range of Patent Office responsibilities and activities in the issuance of patents; comparable procedures and organization exist with respect to trademarks. Under an assistant commissioner for trademarks there is a corps of trademark examiners whose role is to pass on the merits of the thousands of trademark, service mark, collective mark, and certification mark applications filed each year. These examiners have assigned responsibilities in specified fields of commerce and are generally quite knowledgeable about the use of marks in broad lines of commerce. They, as well as the public, have access to an elaborately classified library of marks that enables comparison of an applicant's mark with existing registrations and pending applications to make assessments of likelihood of confusion.

The Principal Register

The Lanham Act provides for a "register" of marks that are entitled to the full benefits of federal registration. This is called the Principal Register. A trade or service mark adopted and used in interstate commerce is eligible for registration on the Principal Register except where the mark has the following features, described in Section 2 of the Lanham Act:

(a) consists of or comprises immoral, deceptive, or scandalous matter; or matter which may disparage or falsely suggest a connection with persons, living or dead, institutions, beliefs, or national symbols, or bring them into contempt, or disrepute;

(b) consist of or comprises the flag or coat of arms or other insignia of the United States, or of any State or municipality, or of any foreign nation, or any simulation thereof;

(c) consists of or comprises a name, portrait, or signature identifying a particular living individual except by his written consent, or the name, signature, or portrait of a deceased President of the United States during the life of his widow, if any, except by the written consent of the widow;

These provisions form the statutory basis for rejection of prohibited marks generally described on pp. 234–236. Section 2 of the Lanham Act goes on to exclude from the Principal Register any mark that

(d) consists of or comprises a mark which so resembles a mark registered in the Patent Office or a mark or trade name previously used in the United States by another and not abandoned, as to be likely, when applied to the goods of the applicant, to cause confusion, or to cause mistake, or to deceive. . . .

This Section 2(d) brings into play the standards of trademark infringement discussed on pp. 253–266; if the applicant's mark will give rise to a likelihood of confusion with a prior effective registration, the Patent Office will refuse to grant federal registration. As can be expected, this sort of judgment is susceptible of disagreement between the applicant and the Patent Office and we shall see what machinery exists for resolving such disputes.

Section 2(d) goes on to deal with situations where confusion, mistake, or deception is not likely to result from the continued use by more than one person of the same or similar mark under conditions or limitations involving the mode or place of use of the mark or the goods or services with which the mark is used, by providing for issuance of a concurrent federal registration when the applicant has become entitled to use the mark as a result of concurrent, lawful use in interstate commerce before (1) the earliest filing date of any applications involved or (2) July 5, 1947 if the concurrent user has, or has applied for, a registration under earlier federal trademark legislation. Provision is made for concurrent registrations when a court has determined that more than one person is entitled to use the same or similar mark in interstate commerce. To avoid the confusion that would likely result from concurrent use in the same geographical area, concurrent registrations may limit the place of use of the marks.

Under Section 2 another class of marks will be denied registration, unless secondary meaning can be shown, if the mark

(e) . . . (1) when applied to the goods of the applicant is merely descriptive or deceptively misdescriptive of them, or (2) when applied to the goods of the applicant is primarily geographically descriptive or deceptively misdescriptive of them, . . . (3) is primarily merely a surname;

(f) except as expressly excluded in paragraph (a), (b), (c), and (d) of this section, nothing herein shall prevent the registration of a mark used by the applicant which has become distinctive of the applicant's goods in commerce. The Commissioner may accept as prima facie evidence that the mark has become distinctive, as applied to the applicant's goods in commerce, proof of substantially exclusive and continuous for the 5 years next preceding the date of the filing of the application for its registration.

We have seen on pp. 237–238 how marks that start off as falling within the Lanham Act Section 2(d) may nevertheless acquire secondary meaning and thereby function as a proper mark. Although Section 2(e) will prohibit registration of the enumerated kinds of marks unless secondary meaning is shown, Section 2(f) in effect states that if the trademark owner can execute an affidavit that he is using and has used the mark in interstate commerce for five years on a substantially exclusive and continuous basis, the Patent Office will accept the existence of secondary meaning.

The Principal Register also includes collective and certification marks, in accordance with Section 4 of the Lanham Act.

The Supplemental Register

Marks that do not qualify for registration on the Principal Register may nevertheless be registered on what is called the Supplemental Register under a much more relaxed standard of being "capable of distinguishing applicant's goods or services," if previously used as such for at least one year. Exceptions apply to marks unregistrable under Sections 2(a)–(d) of the Lanham Act, quoted in the preceding section on the Principal Register. The one-year rule is waived if domestic registration is required as a basis for foreign registration. Suffice it to state that registration on the Supplemental Register does not accord the registrant the range of benefits accorded a mark registered on the Principal Register. It may not be used to stop imports through the Bureau of Customs; it is not prima facie evidence of validity of the registration, ownership, exclusive right to use, or incontestability benefits.

An example of a mark involving the distinction between Principal Register and Supplemental Register definitions is one that consisted of horizontally spaced pairs of vertical rows of stitches applied to the outer vertical face of a mattress. Registration was denied on the Supplemental Register by the Patent Office because the record failed to show that the average purchaser recognized such stitching as a trademark or that he would be in any way moved, by the stitching, to buy the applicant's mattress. The Court of Customs and Patent Appeals rejected that position and held that the test set forth in the statute only required that the mark, at the time registration is sought, be capable of becoming recognized by the average purchaser as distinctive of the applicant's goods in commerce. The court found the stitching design to be unique among stitching on mattresses and, hence, not incapable of distinguishing the goods upon which it appeared from those of the other manufacturers.

The concept of "capability of distinguishing" is related to the Section 2(f) concept of secondary meaning. Once a Section 2(e) mark has acquired a secondary meaning, it may become registrable on the Principal Register. However, even if the 2(e) mark does not possess the requisite distinctiveness necessary under 2(f), it may still be capable of distinguishing the applicant's goods and, hence, registration on the Supplemental Register would be permitted. An example of a mark that has been granted supplemental registration is *Oregon's Finest* for use on canned and frozen vegetables. Registration was denied on the ground that applicant's trademark was confusingly similar to *Oregon Fruit Products* that had been registered previously for canned fruits, preserves, and jams. The examiner-in-chief had considered the words "fruit products" to be broadly descriptive and, therefore, the word "Oregon" to be the dominant part of the registered mark. The Court of Customs and Patent Appeals reversed the examiner's decision and held the mark registrable on the ground that "[t]he only obligation resting upon the applicant in the instant case was to identify its product lest it cause confusion in trade and be mistaken for the product of the owner of the cited mark. The applicant has accomplished that result." The mark met the capable-of-distingushing text and was entitled to supplemental registration.

In another case the Clairol Company made application to register the mark *Innocent Beige* for hair coloring products. The examiner denied principal registration on the ground that the "wording sought to be registered is believed to be a color designation used by applicants to distinguish this shade of hair coloring from others it manufactures. As such, the wording serves only to indicate color and does not function as a badge of origin in commerce indicating that the product emanates from the applicant." However, the application was converted to one for supplemental registration, which was accepted, becaûse *Innocent Beige* was *capable* of indicating origin and distinguishing Clairol's products.

Registration on the Principal Register is much preferred to supplemental registration. However, in the event that qualification for registration on the Principal Register is impossible, registration on the Supplemental Register is preferred to none at all. It establishes a published date of record for first use, which becomes important when the owner of a mark attempts to transfer it from the Supplemental to the Principal Register. Pursuant to Section 27 of the Act, "[r]egistration of a mark on the supplemental register . . . shall not preclude registration by the registrant on the principal register established by this [Act.]"

The Form of the Application for Federal Registration

The application for federal registration is itself a simple document to prepare; indeed, unlike the preparation of a patent application, it is an activity that requires no particular expertise. The Trademark Rules of Practice of the Patent Office include sample forms for completion of the application. Of significantly more importance is the information supplied with the application, which, if not handled properly at the outset, can give rise to legal difficulties as the application is considered by the Patent Office, and unhappily, in any adversary proceeding that may develop.

The trademark applicant, usually a corporate official, must execute an oath that states that:

> he believes said corporation to be the owner of the mark sought to be registered; to the best of his knowledge and belief no other person, firm, corporation or association has the right to use said mark in commerce, either in the identical form or in such near resemblance thereto as to be likely, when applied to the goods of such other person, to cause confusion, or to cause mistake, or to deceive; and the facts set forth in this application are true.

If the available facts do not justify execution of the oath, pretty clearly a question of fraud can be raised with any willful misrepresentation to the Patent Office.

Careless attention to the dates of first use and dates of first use in interstate commerce should be avoided; only the earliest bona fide dates should be alleged by the applicant. However, care should be taken to extend back as far in time as is permitted by the facts, because the initial bona fide user will have priority of rights in the mark. Prudent conduct dictates that the sales receipts, invoices, and related documents upon which "use" dates are based be preserved, in the event of a contest over priority of rights.

Perhaps the commonest problem arising in "do-it-yourself" trademark applications arises from failure to file specimen labels, package samples, facsimiles of signs (for service marks), or the like, which show use of the mark as a *trademark* (not a company trade name) or as a *service mark* (not mere general advertising). Trademark practitioners will point to this lack of proof of mark usage as the most prevalent obstacle to prompt processing of an application for federal registration. And it is not easily corrected later, for, under the statutory standard for registration of "use" of the mark, the Patent Office requires specimens that have in fact been used prior to the application filing date. In doubtful situations, the would-be applicant should have the proper labels or signs printed and used before the application is prepared and filed. In all events, once the application is properly prepared and executed, it is filed with the U.S. Patent Office with the required filing fee.

Patent Office Examination Proceedings

Following receipt of the trademark application, the application "takes its turn" among the thousands of other applications pending with the Patent Office, in awaiting examination by the trademark examiner. The examiner reviews the application as to form, for compliance with the statutory requirements for registration on the Principal or Supplemental Register as applicable. The examiner, many months after the application is filed, will issue an "official action" detailing any grounds for rejecting the application. An opportunity to respond to the examiner is provided and this continues until all grounds for rejection are overcome and the application is allowed, or an impasse is reached and an appeal is the only course of action.

If the mark is allowed, it is then published in the official publication of the Patent Office, called the *Official Gazette,* giving the public notice that the Patent Office will issue the registration. Persons believing they will be injured by issuance of the registration have thirty days to file a Notice of Opposition. Assuming no such difficulty, the federal registration is routinely issued by the Patent Office. The duration of such uncontested Patent Office proceedings may be in the range of a year or two, because of a backlog of applications pending at all times in the Patent Office.

In the event an impasse is reached with the examiner, there is a multiple level for appeals from an adverse decision. The applicant first has the opportunity to appeal to the Trademark Trial and Appeal Board, the highest trademark tribunal in the Patent Office. If unsuccessful there, the applicant has the option of a further appeal to the U.S. Court of Customs and Patent Appeals, or to the federal judiciary via a U.S. federal district court.

Patent Office Adverse Party Proceedings

Opposition.   Any party who feels that he will be injured by the registration of the applicant's mark that has been allowed and published in the *Official Gazette,* may start an opposition proceeding in the Patent Office, where the applicant takes the position of defendant. The plaintiff, known as the opposer, is usually the prior user of a mark or trade name that more or less resembles that of the applicant.

While the opposer need not have exclusive rights in a mark in order to oppose its registration to another, it is "necessary that the opposer establish that he would probably be damaged by the registration of an applicant's mark," most commonly on the basis of a likelihood of confusion with the opposer's mark or trade name.

The rights alleged to be damaged by the grant of registration to the applicant must be those of the opposer, and not some third party. Stated differently, the opposer has no standing to assert damage to himself because of third-party rights. Furthermore, where the mark sought to be registered is descriptive of goods, damage to the opposer is presumed where he has an interest in using the descriptive term in connection with his business. For example, in *De Walt, Inc.* v. *Magna Power Tool Corp.*, applicant (De Walt) sought registration of the mark *Power Shop* for woodworking saws. Opposition was filed by Magna Power Tool Corporation, manufacturer of an all-purpose power tool known as Shopsmith. Magna claimed the words *Power Shop* were descriptive of a shop or workshop in which the tools are power rather than hand tools. It had used the terms in its advertisements of the *Shopsmith* tool. The Trademark Trial and Appeal Board sustained the opposition based on the fact of Magna's prior use of the term. The Court of Customs and Patent Appeals affirmed this holding denying registration, but the decision was based on other factors. It found that Magna's use of *Power Shop* was descriptive in nature. As such, Magna was not claiming trademark rights in the terms, merely the freedom to continue its descriptive use of those terms. The court found that the goods of both parties were essentially identical and a term descriptive of opposer's goods would necessarily be descriptive of applicant's goods. To grant registration of the term to De Walt would damage rights of the opposer to use a term that is in the public domain.

Some final observations concerning opposition proceedings should be made. First, the validity of a registered mark cannot be challenged in an opposition proceeding. That type of challenge is undertaken in an action for cancellation. Accordingly, if the opposer is the owner of a trademark registration, that registration is presumed valid in an opposition proceeding.

As regards application for supplemental registration, there are no provisions for opposition proceedings, and the determination by the Patent Office examiner that a mark satisfies the requirements for such registration will result in an issuance of registration. The fact that a registration has been issued is published in the *Official Gazette*. The only way that a third party can challenge that grant of supplemental registration is through a cancellation proceeding, the details of which are discussed in the next section.

Cancellation and Incontestability. The fact that a mark has been granted registration after the opposition period has passed does not imply that it is thereafter immune from attack in the Patent Office. The Lanham Act provides for another adverse-party proceeding in the Patent Office, called a cancellation proceeding, whereby a petitioner may seek to cancel an issued federal registration. The grounds available in an action for cancellation depend upon the type of registration involved (Principal or Supplemental) and the age of that registration. Within five years after a Principal Register mark has been issued a petition to cancel may be filed by any person who believes that he is or will be damaged by the registration of a mark. These broad grounds for a cancellation petition are sharply narrowed after five years have passed; after five years the petition to cancel is confined to situations where the registered mark (1) has become the common descriptive name of an article or substance; or (2) has been abandoned; or (3) was registered fraudulently; or (4) is a prohibited mark under Sections 2(a)–(c) of the Lanham Act; or (5) is being used by, or with the permission of, the registrant so as to misrepresent the source of the goods or services in connection with which the mark is used; or (6) the registrant of a certification mark (a) does not control, or is not able legitimately to exercise control over, the use of such mark, or (b) engages in the production or marketing of any goods or services to which the certification mark is applied, or (c) permits the use of the certification mark for purposes other than to certify, or (d) discriminatorily refuses to certify or to continue to certify the goods or services of any person who maintains the standards or conditions which such mark certifies. In addition, The Federal Trade Commission may apply at any time to cancel a registration on the preceding grounds going to issues of deception. This course of conduct, surprisingly, has rarely, if ever, been pursued by the FTC.

With respect to the cancellation of marks registered on the Supplemental Register, the Lanham Act provides:

> Whenever any person believes he is or will be damaged by the registration of a mark on this [Supplemental] register he may at any time, . . . apply to the Commission to cancel such registration. The Commissioner shall refer such application to the Trademark Trial and Appeal Board, which shall give notice thereof to the registrant. If it is found after a hearing before the Board that the registrant was not entitled to register the mark at the time of his application for registration thereof, or that the mark is not used by the registrant or had been abandoned, the registration shall be cancelled by the Commissioner.

In order to succeed in an action for cancellation, the petitioner must allege a valid ground for cancellation and show that he will be damaged by the continued existence of the defendant's registration. A party challenging a registration on the Principal Register that has been in existence for less than five years may avail himself of any of the grounds described under the previously discussed section on opposition proceedings.

Once five years have elapsed since the date of principal registration, the grounds for cancellation narrow sharply, giving rise to incontestability benefits to the owner of the Principal Register mark. With respect to marks registered on the Supplemental Register, no distinction is made based upon the age of the registration. The standards for showing damage in actions for cancellation are the same as those for opposition proceedings. This damage need only be probable and not actual.

Interference. While an application for federal registration is pending in the Patent Office, the examiner may declare an interference proceeding, somewhat analogous to patent interference proceedings discussed in Chapter 2 (pp. 42–43). Generally speaking, a trademark interference arises where an applicant is considered to have a mark raising a likelihood of confusion with another applicant, or registrant on the Principal Register whose application was copending with the other pending application, and where the first to file in the Patent Office does not also claim the first date of use. Marks on the Principal Register will not be "called back" into an interference proceeding after five years following issuance, nor will Supplemental Register marks at any time. The interference serves to sort out priority of claims based on conflicting dates of use. Although it is beyond the scope of this book to discuss the technicalities of such proceedings, it can be appreciated how concurrent use registrations may emerge from such proceedings where regional users are involved, not in geographic competition with each other.

Preserving an Issued Federal Registration

The Lanham Act provides a procedure for "cleaning out" federal registrations by the very simple procedure of requiring the owners of federal registrations to file an affidavit within six years following the date of registration, showing that the mark is still in use or that any nonuse is due to special circumstances and not to any intention to abandon this mark. Failure to file this six-year affidavit results in cancellation of the registration. This is of little consequence to the owner who has abandoned his mark, but will necessitate refiling the application for federal registration where failure to file the six-year affidavit arises from oversight. Provision is also made for filing an affidavit of incontestability, called a Section 15 affidavit. The life of a federal registration, whether on the Principal Register or the Supplemental Register, is for twenty years, unless previously canceled or surrendered. The registration may thereafter be renewed for twenty-year periods. Renewal applications generally require evidence of continued use of the registered mark in interstate commerce or an explanation for nonuse resulting from special circumstances and not from any intention to abandon the mark.

TRADEMARK–ANTITRUST

Introduction

Many of the restraint-of-trade considerations reviewed in the areas of patent–antitrust (Chapter 2, pp. 97–116) and trade secret–antitrust (Chapter 3, pp. 213–216) find their counterparts and analogies in the use of trademarks in the market place. A federal district court said in *United States* v. *Timken Roller Bearing Co.*:

> The trademark may become a detrimental weapon if it is used to serve a harmful or injurious purpose. If it becomes a tool to circumvent free enterprise and unbridled competition, public policy dictates that the rights enjoyed by the ownership be kept within their proper bounds. If a trademark may be the legal basis for allocating world markets, fixing prices, restricting competition, the unfailing device has been found to destroy every vestige of inhibition set up by the Sherman Act.

In affirming the lower court, the Supreme Court found that American Timken had combined with its two foreign subsidiaries to create an international cartel for the purpose of dividing world markets, fixing prices, and restricting imports for Timken antifriction bearings along with other products to, and exports from, the United States. The Court rejected all attempts by American Timken to justify such restraints under the aegis of a trademark licensing program, branding the aggregate of trade restraints illegal standing alone. The Court did not directly decide whether such specific restrictions could be reconciled with the antitrust laws under trademark licensing principles, because it accepted the lower court in the finding that the "trademark provisions [in the agreement] were subsidiary and secondary to the central purpose of allocating trade territories."

We turn now to typical antitrust problems raised in the management and exploitation of trademarks—problems peculiar to the nature of trademarks as opposed to marketing practices that only incidentally may involve products or services associated with trademarks or service marks.

Competitor-Level Licensing Restraints

Any analysis of competitive conduct by a trademark owner, for example, in the field of licensing, proceeds from the premise that agreements and tacit understandings between competitors aimed at a division of markets, price fixing, allocation of customers, group boycotts, and related trade restraints are, standing alone, an unlawful restraint of trade in violation of Section 1 of the Sherman Act.

United States v. *Sealy, Inc.* illustrates the application of some of these general principles in the context of a trademark licensing program involving the manufacture and sale of Sealy bedding products. Mattresses lend themselves to manufacture and sale under a trademark licensing program, probably because of the high freight charges that would be involved in the centralized manufacture and the intensity of competition in the industry from small, local manufacturers. A trademark licensing program was developed for the *Sealy* line of mattresses whereby a corporation, Sealy, Inc., was the trademark owner and licensor. The thirty *Sealy* licensees were stockholder directors in the licensing corporation and the directors in fact made the licensing business decisions of the licensor corporation. Sealy, Inc., "was a joint venture of, by, and for its stockholder-licensees." The *Sealy* licensing program involved exclusive territorial allocations that operated to prohibit *Sealy* manufacturer licensees from selling *Sealy* products outside the licensed territory. Retail price fixing, also, existed among the licensees.

The Supreme Court, viewing the program as an "aggregation of trade restraints," declared unlawful the trademark license agreement operating to restrict the licensees to manufacture and sell in assigned territories as being a horizontal arrangement among competing manufacturers of bedding products, and not a situation involving vertical distribution restraints on territories. The Court regarded the totality of the restrictions as unlawful "without the necessity for an inquiry . . . as to their business or economic justification, their impact in the marketplace or their reasonableness."

Similarly, in *United States* v. *Topco Associates, Inc.*, decided in 1973, the Supreme Court struck down territorial and customer restrictions imposed by a group of small grocery chains in the Chicago area organized into a private-brand trademark purchasing cooperative. The various selling restrictions were confined to the trademarks owned by the purchasing association, Topco Associates, Inc. The private-brand organization of small grocers was designed to enhance their ability to compete with private brands against larger integrated chain grocery stores like A & P, Safeway, and Kroger, which chains marketed private-brand trademark food products for a great many years. The presence or absence of price-fixing was not considered by the Supreme Court to be important to its decision; it was sufficient that the restrictions were horizontal agreements among retail competitors. *Sealy* and *Topco* illustrate the proposition that a trademark licensing program involving competitors is no umbrella by which competitors can avoid the stringent standards prohibiting agreements between competitors to restrain trade.

Similarly, a 1973 New Jersey federal district court decision points up the dangers inherent in efforts by a franchisor to eliminate competition between its franchisees and between the franchisees and company-owned outlets. In *American Motor Inns, Inc.* v. *Holiday Inns, Inc.,* Holiday Inns over a period beginning in 1953 added provisions to its franchise agreements for the ostensible purpose of protecting its nationwide motel system and the *Holidex* computer reservations system from abuse or misuse by its licensees.

From 1953 to 1958 Holiday granted exclusive licensees for a designated geographic area, subject to both a "best-efforts" clause and a clause prohibiting the licensee from owning or operating a non-Holiday Inn within his territory. In 1957 or 1958, this clause was broadened to read as follows: "Licensee will not, directly or indirectly, own any interest in, operate, or be in any manner connected with or associated with, any inn, hotel or motel, during the period of this license, except Holiday Inns." This broadening occurred after one franchisee who had five or six Holiday Inns refused to take Holiday Inns' license refusals for several other areas as a definitive answer. This franchisee opened up motels in these areas under his own name instead and in direct competition with Holiday Inns. The franchisor's response was to buy out this franchisee's licenses and change its agreements with the remaining franchisees by deleting a "within the licensed territory" limitation on non-Holiday Inns.

Later, the franchisor instituted a policy of declining to issue licenses for cities in which the company owned a Holiday Inn or in which the company planned to open a motel. In addition, Holiday Inns instituted a "radius letter" policy under which at least three existing franchisees closest to a proposed franchise were solicited for their comments. If any one of the three objected, an additional review step was included in the decision on the franchise application with referral from the Franchise Committee to the Executive Committee for final action. In 1972 the Executive Committee rejected 57 per cent of the applications to which objections had been registered.

Although it is clear that both the franchisor and the existing franchisees derived certain benefits from these restrictive provisions, the non-Holiday Inn clause was put squarely into issue when Holiday Inns both refused a franchise and refused to waive the noncompetition clause for a motel site at Newark Airport owned by American Motor Inns (AMI). As the largest licensee of Holiday Inns, with some forty-eight motels in operation, AMI had purchased the Newark site from the city of Elizabeth, N.J., under sealed bid and subject to a covenant requiring the successful purchaser to erect a motel on the site within a specified time period.

The reviewing court held that the non-Holiday Inns clause, standing alone, violated Section 1 of the Sherman Act, and that the totality of the restrictions—radius letter policy, company town policy, and non-Holiday Inns clause—constituted a per se unlawful horizontal combination and conspiracy to allocate territories. The court noted that, taken as a whole, these restrictions restrain both intrabrand competition and interbrand competition on the part of the largest United States motel franchisor and its licensees, who operate some 1,099 franchised motels.

Tie-In Practices and the Quality Control Licensing Problem

Issues relating to tie-in practices are of great importance in the trademark licensing context. The Lanham Act permits trademark licensing where the licensee is controlled "in respect to the nature and quality of the goods or services in connection with which the mark is used." In *Dawn Donut Co.* v. *Hart's Food Stores,* the Second Circuit interpreted this provision as placing an "affirmative duty upon a licensor of a registered trademark to take reasonable measures to detect and prevent misleading uses of his mark by his licensees or suffer cancellation of his federal registration." Because a trademark owner will customarily discharge this affirmative duty through quality control provisions in the trademark license, a collision with antitrust doctrine may not be far around the corner. Indeed, courts have extended the law relating to tie-ins to embrace arrangements whereby franchisors control the nature and quality of franchised products or services by, among other things, requiring franchisees to purchase supplies solely from the franchisor or its designated supplier.

In *Susser* v. *Carvel Corporation,* a majority of the Second Circuit Court of Appeals held that contracts obligating franchisees to purchase from Carvel or Carvel-designated sources all ingredients of the ice cream sold to customers were reasonable, because the tying trademark lacked the prominence necessary to establish market dominance and the tied products were both necessary to protect goodwill and not susceptible of advance objective specification without imposing an "impractical and unreasonable burden" on the franchisor. Seven years later, however, the Ninth Circuit, in *Siegel* v. *Chicken Delight,* built on the language of *Carvel* to affirm a contrary result on a similar set of facts. This change of outcome was partly explained by the intervening decision of the Supreme Court in *Fortner Enterprises* v. *United States Steel Corp.,* holding that market dominance was not the test to be applied in determining the economic power of the tying product, but rather "whether the seller has the power to . . . impose other burdensome terms such as tie-ins." Such power could be presumed from the uniqueness of the product combined with the existence of legal barriers preventing other sellers from offering a similarly distinctive article.

On the strength of *Fortner,* the *Chicken Delight* court held that contracts requiring its fast-food franchises to purchase "essential cooking equipment, dry-mix food items and trade-mark bearing packaging exclusively from defendant," in order to obtain defendant's trademark license, constituted per se violations of the Sherman Act. The tying product in this arrangement was the license to use the *Chicken Delight* mark, and method of preparation, an item separate and distinct from the tied mixes, packaging, and equipment. The court reasoned that the *Chicken Delight* mark was distinctive and had public acceptance, and that it conferred economic power sufficient to bring about a tie-in situation, because the registered trademark presented a legal barrier against competition, preventing competitors from offering the distinctive product themselves. Chicken Delight sought to justify the tie-in, among others, on the ground of its affirmative duty to guarantee the uniformity and quality of its product. The court concurred in recognizing an affirmative duty that devolved on the trademark licensor "to assure that in the hands of his licensee the trademark continues to represent that which it purports to represent." Nevertheless, it rejected the defense, holding that "to recognize that such a duty exists is not to say that every means of meeting it is justified. Restraint of trade can be justified only in the absence of less restrictive alternatives." Here, the court found, the device of providing specifications for the type and quality of the product to be used was an available alternative. Although Chicken Delight had contended that the needed dip, spice mixes, and cooking machinery were not susceptible to specification, the court affirmed a jury finding against Chicken Delight on this factual issue. The court did suggest parenthetically, however, that in cases where product specification would require divulging a trade secret, a tie-in might be acceptable.

The trade secret sequel to *Chicken Delight* came with the Federal Trade Commission's 1973 decision involving the franchise program of Chock-Full-of-Nuts Corporation, a New York City area restaurant chain with some thirty-six franchised outlets then operating in the area. The *Chock* decision held unlawful under Section 5 of the FTC Act a range of price-fixing and tie-in practices imposed on *Chock-Full-O-Nuts* restaurant francisees. The FTC found itself faced directly with the question left open by *Chicken Delight* as to whether trade secret formulations would justify tying in the sale of commodities with the franchise license. The FTC said no, on the ground that even a program of trade secret licensing could be used to provide alternate third-party sources of supply to the franchisees.

Chock also argued that not all the restaurant food products made by Chock lent themselves to specifications whereby the franchise could purchase food products for retail sale in the Chock-Full-O-Nuts restaurants from any desired source. Its coffee, for example, its particularly "runny pies" that it made and sold to its franchisees, were not susceptible of quality specifications to permit third-party manufacture. The FTC acknowledged the principle that with respect to such coffee and baked goods, the tie-in prohibition would not apply, leaving Chock free to require its franchisees to buy these distinctive products from Chock.

Franchisor-Imposed Exclusivity, Location, and Assignment of Territories and Customers

In order to achieve desired levels of product availability, service, and convenience of outlet locations, franchisors have frequently turned to use of specific franchisee location provisions in their franchise contract agreements. A typical location provision is the granting of a license that specifies the location at which the franchisee is to conduct his business. This sort of restriction, which has been upheld by the courts, nevertheless has several key drawbacks. From the franchisor's point of view, this provision means only that his franchise will in fact have a place of business at that location and that presumably the place of business will conform to any other requirements expressed in the franchise agreement. On the other hand, if the commodity or service being purveyed through the franchise is not one that is susceptible to over-the-counter sales from a fixed location—not for example, a fast-foods outlet or an auto dealership—this provision gives no assurance that the area surrounding the assigned location will be adequately serviced. From the standpoint of the franchisee, a simple location clause has two disadvantages: standing alone such a clause does not bar appointment of another franchisee "right next door or down the street," nor does this provision bar the franchisor itself from establishing a company-owned outlet in the immediate proximity. Either of these occurrences can deprive the franchisee of the full benefits of the goodwill he may have been responsible for developing in his locality under the franchise program.

One method for meeting these franchisee objections has been to couple the location clause with the promise of exclusivity; that is, a promise by the franchisor not to appoint another franchisee or to open up its own competing outlet within a defined territory surrounding the franchised location. The validity of such exclusive appointments has been upheld, provided that such provisions are not a part of a scheme to monopolize and provided further that effective competition exists at both the seller and buyer levels. It must be noted very clearly here that we are talking now about territorial provisions imposed by the franchisor in a *vertical* setting, where the franchisor and franchisee operate at different levels of distribution and do not compete directly with each other as we just saw in *Sealy, Topco,* and the *Holiday Inns* cases.

Another variation on the location clause, which appears to be more attractive to franchise companies that are just beginning, is the assignment of a geographic region to a franchisee on an exclusive basis. Such an arrangement gives the franchisee the sole right to develop the distribution system within that region for the franchise company. For example, franchises might be given an exclusive right to a whole state, with the ultimate decisions as to where in that state each franchise outlet is to be located left to the franchisee, and with no right for the franchisor to appoint any other franchisee at any location within that state, or, in fact, to open up an outlet of its own in the state. Provided that such an exclusive geographic provision does not absolutely bar sales by the franchisee into other areas and does not bar sales into the assigned state by outsiders, if the requisite levels of competition from other products and other sellers exist within the exclusive territory, these provisions are not necessarily objectionable. On the other hand, where the grant of an exclusive territory is coupled with a prohibition against making sales outside of that assigned area, the use of such provisions has been subject to increasing challenge by the antitrust enforcement agencies.

Deferring, for a moment, an analysis of the legality of vertically imposed territorial restrictions upon resale of products by franchisees, it is worth noting that there is a demonstrated propensity of the Antitrust Division of the Justice Department and the Federal Trade Commission to challenge such restrictions whenever they discover them. In the aftermath of the Supreme Court's 1967 *Schwinn* case and the burgeoning number of its progeny and the diversity of their holdings, virtually the only thing that is clear is the "hard-line" policy of the enforcement agencies.

It is frequently important for a franchisor to insure requisite levels of local marketing effort and market penetration for his licensed product or service in order to compete effectively against his large, vertically integrated competitors, and there is a mechanism available in many franchise programs: proper use of area-of-primary-responsibility provisions. The basic reason for the effectiveness of area-of-primary-responsibility provisions is that such provisions permit the franchisor to define with some precision the targeted market for his franchisee and at the same time provide a substantial measure of assurance for the franchisee that his capital investments and efforts to enhance the goodwill of the franchised product or service in his local area will inure to his own economic benefit. Moreover, it is appropriate for the area-of-primary-responsibility clause to contain a requirement that the franchisee use his best efforts to service that area, with failure to apply such efforts grounds for termination. Although this arrangement does not prohibit sales to customers outside the assigned area, it does emphasize that diversion of efforts away from coverage of the assigned area *first* will imperil the franchise.

Frequently, area-of-primary-responsibility clauses and programs specify sales quotas or minimum percentages of sales to be derived from the assigned area. Even under the rigorous statutory standards established by the Automobile Dealer's Franchise Act (the "Dealer's-Day-in-Court" Act), the courts have upheld termination of auto dealers for failure to achieve specified sales quotas. Where such quotas are subject to amendment on a year-to-year basis, however, it is imperative that any new quota assigned has reasonable basis in the realities of the local market. Also, great care should be taken that quotas not be used to force franchisees to drop sales of competing manufacturer's products, or to force a partial-line distributor to carry the franchisor's full line (full-line forcing).

Only in relatively recent times, beginning in the late 1940's, has the government claimed that vertically imposed territorial restrictions are illegal per se. As a result of this effort, which began about 1949, a number of consent decrees were entered into between the government and companies utilizing vertical restrictions that chose not to fight the issue. Virtually all of these cases involved considerations other than mere vertical territorial agreements, as, for example, price fixing. Moreover, a review of the major cases that have come before the courts reveals that most were brought on the basis of a conglomeration of allegedly illegal practices—price-fixing agreements, tie-in sales, horizontal territorial restrictions, and exclusive-dealing arrangements.

Unfortunately, the antitrust enforcement agencies have, over the years, paid diminishing attention to the importance and preservation of small business entities and to the significance of interbrand competition, purportedly in the interest of judicial and prosecutorial expediency. In so doing, they have overlooked Judge Hand's seminal assessment in the *Alcoa* case that: "Throughout the history of these statutes it has been constantly assumed that one of their purposes was to perpetuate and preserve, for its own sake and in spite of possible cost, an organization of industry in small units which can effectively compete with each other."

Prior to the *Schwinn* case in 1967, the Supreme Court had only one earlier occasion to consider the legality of vertically imposed territorial restrictions. It specifically ruled in that case that there was insufficient evidence available to the Court upon which it could reach a determination as to whether such restrictions should be considered under a rule of reason or accorded treatment as per se unlawful restraints of trade under the antitrust laws. This was the 1963 case of *White Motor Company* v. *United States*. There a truck manufacturer was charged with imposing both territorial and customer restrictions upon its dealers and distributors in violation of Section 1 of the Sherman Act. The district court applied a per se rule of illegality. The Supreme Court, however, reversed, rejecting the application of the per se rule to vertical restrictions, saying, through Justice Douglas, that it knew "too little of the actual impact" on competition or the "economic and business stuff out of which these arrangements emerge" to determine whether vertical restraints should be categorized as per se restrictions. Given the fact that the *White* case was a case of first impression as to the legality of vertically imposed restrictions, the argument of the Department of Justice in its brief seeking affirmance of the lower court's decision in *White* is informative. The Justice Department said, "A full inquiry into the long-term effects of territorial restrictions such as White's would be incredibly prolonged and complicated and would, in all probability, be fruitless." The approach taken by the Justice Department in the *White* case parallels the attack made in the *Schwinn* case.

Subsequently, on a full review of the facts involved, the Sixth and Seventh Circuits upheld vertical territorial restrictions in two suits brought under Section 5 of the Federal Trade Commission Act. These cases rebutted anew the government's efforts to have such restrictions declared illegal per se. Nevertheless, the solicitor general declined to seek Supreme Court review in either case. Evidently, the facts developed in the full evidentiary hearings in these cases did not make them "suitable vehicles" to convince the Court to establish a rule of per se illegality. Thus the cases before *Schwinn* established without exception that vertical territorial restrictions were not to be judged per se unlawful.

In 1967 the Supreme Court introduced an element of confusion into the approach to be taken under the antitrust laws in passing on the legality of vertical territorial restrictions by virtue of its decision in *United States* v. *Arnold, Schwinn & Co*. There the Court held that Schwinn's vertically imposed restrictions limiting the customers to whom its distributors and retailers could resell bicycles purchased from Schwinn violated the Sherman Act, but that under the Sherman

Act Schwinn could limit distribution by its agents and consignees, where Schwinn had retained all indicia of ownership (including title, dominion, and risk of loss) with respect to its bicycles. At the outset, Mr. Justice Fortas noted that:

> In this Court, the United States has abandoned its contention that the distribution limitations are illegal *per se*. Instead we are asked to consider these limitations in light of the "rule of reason," and, on the basis of the voluminous record below, to conclude that the limitations are the product of "agreement" between Schwinn and its wholesale and retail distributors and that they constitute an unreasonable restraint of trade.

Later, Mr. Justice Fortas again noted that "[t]he government does not contend that a *per se* violation of the Sherman Act is presented by the practices which are involved in this appeal" and that "[a]ccordingly, we are remitted to an appraisal of the market impact of these practices." Subsequently, Mr. Justice Fortas emphasized that the Court "must look to the specifics of the challenged practices and their impact upon the marketplace in order to make a judgment as to whether the restraint is or is not 'reasonable' in the special sense in which Section 1 of the Sherman Act must be read for purposes of this type of inquiry" and that "[o]ur inquiry is whether . . . the effect upon competition in the marketplace is substantially adverse," citing in the two latter instances Mr. Justice Brandeis' classic formulation of the rule-of-reason approach to assessing restraints of trade.

Subsequently, various justices of the Supreme Court have interpreted *Schwinn* as not establishing a broad rule of per se illegality for all vertical territorial restrictions. Concurring in the 1968 Supreme Court decision in *Albrecht* v. *Herald Co.*, Mr. Justice Douglas, who also concurred in *Schwinn*, noted that *Schwinn* was decided on the basis of the "economics of the bicycle business" in the context of a record that "elaborately sets forth information as to the total market interaction and interbrand competition, as well as the distribution program and practices" there challenged. Mr. Justice Douglas, adhering to his *White Motor* approach, went on to note that the legality of exclusive territorial franchises in the newspaper distribution business would have to be tried as a factual issue and would depend on their impact on competition. Moreover, Mr. Justice Marshall, speaking for the Court in *United States* v. *Topco Associates, Inc.*, was careful to distinguish between vertical and horizontal territorial restrictions, only the latter of which were held to be per se violations of Section 1 of the Sherman Act. Finally, Chief Justice Burger, dissenting in *Topco*, pointed out that in *Schwinn*, the "Court made it clear that it was proceeding under the 'rule of reason' and not by *per se* rule."

Other courts have also interpreted *Schwinn* as not creating a broad per se rule prohibiting all vertical territorial restraints. A case in point is *Tripoli Co.* v. *Wella Corp.*, which involved a prohibition against the resale by a wholesale distributor to nonprofessional retail users of a hair-care product intended for professional application in beauty parlors. There, a United States Court of Appeals rejected the contention by the plaintiff that *Schwinn* imposed a per se rule with respect to every postsale restraint. The court said, "This restraint must be tested, not by a *per se* rule, but by the standard of reasonableness." The court went on to point out that *Schwinn* involved postsale restraints on finished goods, bicycles, a "product so simple in use that most ultimate consumers are children." Similarly, in *Carter-Wallace, Inc.* v. *United States*, the United States Court of Claims also refused to accept the premise that *Schwinn* declared every postsale restraint to be illegal per se. A 1972 decision in the Ninth Circuit in *Anderson* v. *American Automobile Association* held that under *White* and *Schwinn* vertically imposed territorial restrictions are not per se unlawful. The Federal Trade Commission staff points to some post-*Schwinn* cases as standing for the proposition that *Schwinn* established a general per se rule with regard to territorial restrictions. For the most part, those cases either involved clear per se restraints, such as price fixing, or did not deal directly with the issue. If *Schwinn* does stand for the proposition that it established a per se rule against all territorial restrictions, then its theory is that, in the interest of efficient administration of justice, no comprehensive analysis can be undertaken by the courts of the total economic effect of vertically imposed restrictions. The results of such a theory would be the destruction of far more small business enterprises than would be helped and the awarding of a distinct competitive advantage to the large manufacturer or licensor who can afford to integrate forward into the market place.

Certification Marks, Standards, and Foreclosure from the Market

It will be recalled that the Lanham Act expressly provides for certification marks—marks that reflect conformity of a product to the standards of the certification mark owner. This is a form of "seal of approval," which may greatly influence the ability of a company to sell its product. Certification mark programs that meet standards of reasonableness, that are not an umbrella for restricting competition, and that do not unreasonably foreclose new entrants from the industry are not likely to run afoul of the antitrust laws.

In a series of advisory opinions, the Federal Trade Commission has enumerated criteria that should apply to any standardization or certification program: the program should be voluntary (unless state or federal law is otherwise), nondiscriminatory in its application to members or nonmembers of, say, any trade association; involve procedural public notice of proposed standards with an opportunity to be heard; and should provide for reasonable fees and for procedural safeguards with respect to any form of remedial action for failure to comply. Standards for certification should be kept current and should be adequately upgraded to allow for industry and scientific advances and innovation.

In the 1961 Supreme Court decision, *Radiant Burners, Inc.* v. *Peoples Gas Light and Coke Co.*, Radiant was a manufacturer of a ceramic gas burner used in heating houses and other buildings, called a Radiant Burner. It sought from the American Gas Association (AGA) their "seal of approval," or certification. The AGA was composed of competitor burner manufacturers and gas utility company suppliers. Radiant claimed that approval was withheld even though its burner was safer and more efficient than, and just as durable as, gas burners that AGA approved. Radiant charged that this arbitrary refusal to approve or to certify its burner excluded it from the market, it brought a treble-damage action, charging violation of Section 1 of the Sherman Act. The Supreme Court agreed with Radiant that such charges, if proved, would constitute a violation of Section 1 of the Sherman Act.

Fair Trade Laws Permitting Vertical Price Fixing of Trademark Products

Conventional antitrust standards have been applied in a host of cases to declare unlawful vertical price-fixing agreements. This practice most frequently involves manufacturer-imposed resale price restrictions on its wholesale or retail customers "to keep the retail price up." During the Depression Era, however, Congress carved out of the Sherman Act's vertical price-fixing prohibition some limited opportunities for states to legislate exceptions. This category of federal–state legislation is popularly called fair trade law.

In 1937 Congress enacted what is known as the Miller–Tydings amendment to Section 1 of the Sherman Act. This enabling legislation declared that it is not unlawful under the Sherman Act to enter into a vertical distribution agreement

> prescribing minimum prices for the resale of a commodity which bears, or the label or container of which bears, the trademark, brand, or name of the producer or distributor of such commodity and which is in free and open competition with commodities of the same general class produced and distributed by others, when . . . agreements are lawful

. . . under any . . . law . . . in any state . . . in which such resale is to be made, as to which the commodity is to be transported for such resale. [Such agreements are not to be violative of the Federal Trade Commission Act]

Following enactment of the Miller–Tydings Act, almost all states ended up legislating fair trade laws patterned after the enabling federal legislation. Problems developed, however, with state fair trade laws: Although the federal statute spoke of minimum prices, what about stipulated or fixed prices? What about customers of the commodities who did not agree to the minimum resale prices—the nonsigners? In 1951 the Supreme Court took a restrictive line on construing the non-signer problem and said that the Miller–Tydings Act did not authorize states to bind nonsigners who had notice of supplier's fair trade agreements.

In 1951 Congress passed the McGuire Act, which amended, in effect, the Miller–Tydings Act by restating its basic fair trade principles but also overriding the Supreme Court by sweeping in nonsigners, if state law so provided. It also stated that "stipulated" as well as "mini-mum" resale price controls could be legislated by the states, and it clarified the right of the supplier's customer (say a wholesaler) to enter into like fair trade contracts with its customer (say a retailer).

A host of state-law litigation has been generated over the years dealing with a range of technical problems involved in the efforts of manufacturers to police their state fair trade programs against price cutters, commonly retail discount stores. Although these issues extend beyond the scope of this book, it is sufficient for our immediate purposes to note that qualifying commodities must be trademarked or comparably branded as to origin and in competition with goods of the same general class. In *Eastman Kodak Co.* v. *Federal Trade Commission,* decided by the Second Circuit in 1946, the court ruled that *Kodachrome* photographic color film and black and white film were not in free and open competition with each other.

The free-and-open-competition standard is thus narrower than the related-goods standard sometimes involved in trademark infringement proceedings, where, to use the *Kodak* analogy, the courts would have no difficulty in finding that black and white film and color film are related goods.

TOPICS TO CONSIDER IN NEGOTIATING A FRANCHISE

Like spouses, cars, politicians, and morticians, franchises "ain't all bad"; rather, it is the measure of care exercised in the selection process that is often so important. Much has been written in the news media about spectacular successes and spectacular failures in the franchising field, so much, in fact, that persons interested in participating in a franchise venture are generally more aware of the issues and problems than in years past. We will not deal with the nuances of franchise business activity; presumably, the person interested in opportunities in this field has some threshold knowledge about the nature of the business involved, the commitment of time, money, and energy required. We will pick up the adventure before any papers have been signed, before any money has changed hands. This is the time to plan. This is the time to engage a lawyer in the community with some measure of sophistication in the field, who will guide the prospective franchisee each step of the way.

Perhaps as well as anyone and better than most, the Federal Trade Commission has generated what is, in effect, a checkoff list of issues to be considered prior to entering into a franchise arrangement. This is in the form of a proposed trade regulation rule that franchisors would be required to comply with in soliciting franchises. By knowing what the FTC would like franchisors to do and to disclose, the reader has a good idea of what to find out. This proposed trade regulation rule would require franchisors to provide the following information to prospective franchisees "in a clear, permanent and straightforward form, at the time when contact is first established between such prospective franchisee and the franchisor or its representative":

(1) The trade name (s) or trademark (s) under which the franchisor and the prospective franchisee will be doing business; the official name(s) and address(es) and principal place(s) of business of the franchisor, the parent firm or holding company of the franchisor, if any, all affiliated companies that will engage in business with the franchisees, and all companies which employ the franchise salesmen (if they are not employed by the franchisor itself).

(2) A factual description of the franchise offered or to be sold.

(3) The business experience stated individually, of each of the franchisor's directors, stockholders owning more than 10 percent of the stock, and the chief executive officers for the past ten years; and biographical data concerning all such persons.

(4) The business experience of the franchisor, including the length of time the franchisor [a] has conducted a business of the type to be operated by the franchisee; [b] has granted franchises for such business; and [c] has granted franchises in other lines of business.

(5) Where such is the case, a statement that the franchisor or any of its directors, stockholders owning more than 10 percent of the stock, or chief executive officers:

(i) Has been held liable in a civil action, convicted of a felony, or pleaded nolo contendere to a felony charge, in any case involving fraud, embezzlement, fraudulent conversion, or misappropriation of property; or

(ii) Is subject to any currently effective injunctive or restrictive order or ruling relating to business activity as a result of action by any public agency or department; or

(iii) Has filed bankruptcy or been associated with management of any company that has been involved in bankruptcy or renegotiation proceedings; or

(iv) Is or has been a party to any cause of action brought by franchisees against the franchisor.

(v) [We would add legal claims or pending governmental investigations of the nature described even if a suit has not been started; SEC and accounting standards require such disclosures in all events in specific situations.]

Such statement shall set forth the identity and location of the court [or government agency], date of conviction or judgment, any penalty imposed or damages assessed, and the date, nature, and issuer of each such [claim, investigation,] order or ruling.

(6) The financial history of the franchisor, including balance sheets and profit and loss statements for the most recent 5-year period; and a statement of any material changes in the financial condition of the franchisor since the date of such financial statements.

(7) A description of the franchise fee; and a statement indicating whether all or part of the franchise fee may be returned to the franchisee and the conditions under which the fee will be refunded.

(8) The formula by which the amount of such franchise fee is determined if the fee is not the same in all cases.

(9) A statement of the number of franchises presently operating and the number proposed to be sold, indicating which existing franchises, if any, are company owned and their addresses.

(10) A statement of the number of franchises, if any, that operated at a loss during the previous year.

(11) A statement that the prospective franchisee may inspect the profit and loss statements of all existing franchisees. (The names and addresses of the franchisees may be deleted from these profit and loss statements, which must be provided to any prospective franchisee requesting to inspect them.)

(12) A statement whether, by the terms of the franchise agreement, or by other device or practice, the franchisee is required to purchase or lease from the franchisor or affiliated persons or their designee services, supplies, products, signs, fixtures, or equipment relating to the establishment or operation of the franchise business.

(13) A statement describing any payments or fees other than franchise fees that the franchisee is required to pay to the franchisor or affiliated persons, including royalties and payments, fees, or mark-ups on land, buildings, leases, signs, equipment, or supplies, and the average total amount of all such fees paid by all franchisees in operation during the preceding year, expressed both as a dollar amount and as a percentage of gross sales of such average franchisee. If no franchisee has been in operation for the past year, this fact must be stated, and an estimate must be disclosed, computed in accordance with accepted accounting principles, of the maximum anticipated percentage figure.

(14) A statement of the amount and basis for any revenue received by the franchisor from suppliers to its franchisees during the past 12 months.

(15) A statement of the conditions under which the franchise agreement may be terminated or renewal refused, or repurchased at the option of the franchisor, and a statement of the number of franchisees that fell into each of these categories during the past 12 months.

(16) A statement of the conditions and terms under which the franchisor allows the franchisee to sell, lease, assign, or otherwise transfer his franchise, or any interest therein.

(17) A statement whether, by the terms of the franchise agreement or other device or practice, the franchisee is limited in the goods or services he may offer for sale.

(18) A statement whether the franchisor requires the franchisee to participate personally in the direct operation of the franchise.

(19) A statement of the terms and conditions of any financing arrangements offered directly or indirectly by the franchisor or affiliated persons, and a description of any payments received by the franchisor from any person for the placement of financing with such person.

(20) A list of at least 10 representative operating franchisees with addresses and telephone numbers, similarly situated to the franchise offered and located in the same geographic area, if possible.

(21) A statement of the territorial protection granted by the franchisor, in which the franchisor will not establish another franchisee who is permitted to use the same trade name or trademark; in which the franchisor will not establish a company-owned outlet using the same trade name or trademark; and in which the franchisor or its parent will not establish other franchises or company-owned outlets selling or leasing similar products or services under a different trade name or trademark.

(22) If the franchisor uses the name of a "public figure," a statement of the promotional assistance the "public figure" is committed to provide to the franchisor for the next year and the promotional assistance that the "public figure" will provide specifically to the new franchisee,

and a description of any fees or conditions attendant upon such assistance.

(23) A statement of the number of persons who have signed franchise agreements for whom a site has not yet been agreed upon by both franchisor and franchisee.

(24) A statement of the average length of time between the signing of a franchise agreement and the opening of the franchisee's outlet.

(25) A statement of the average length of service of personnel who are responsible for assisting the franchisee at his location, and the average number of hours such personnel spent during the past year with each franchisee that was in business for less than 1 year.

(26) If the franchisor informs the prospective franchisee that it intends to provide him with training, the franchisor must state the number of hours of instruction and furnish the prospective franchisee with a brief biography of the instructors who will conduct the training.

(27) A statement explaining clearly the terms and effects of any covenant not to compete which a franchisee may be required to enter into.

All of the foregoing information (1) to (27) is to be contained in a single disclosure statement, which shall not contain any promotional claims or other information not required by this section or required by State law. . . .

Not all of this information may be relevant or produced voluntarily, or practical to produce, but this FTC "checkoff list" forms a systematic basis for determining whether sufficient information has been disclosed upon which informed decisions may be made.

The proposed rule adds that it is unlawful for the franchisor

To make an oral or written representation of a prospective franchisee's potential income or gross or net profits not based upon the actual average figures for all franchisees not owned or operated by the franchisor or an affiliate thereof in operation during the entire preceding 12-month period, and not disclosing clearly and conspicuously immediately adjacent to any such representation that "Representations are based on the average earnings or profits of all independent franchisees in operation during the past year." These figures should not be considered as accurate representations of potential earnings or profits of any specific franchisee. Or, where no independently owned and operated franchisees have been in operation during the entire preceding 12-month period to make any representation of potential income or gross or net profits without a clear and conspicuous disclosure immediately adjacent to any such representation that 'All Representations of Potential Earnings or Profits Are Merely Estimates; No Franchisee Has Been In Operation Long Enough To Indicate What, If Any, Actual

Earnings Or Profits May Result,' or in any case, to make any such representation not based upon sound accounting practices.

. . . To make any claim in any advertising, promotional material, or disclosure statement, or in any oral sales presentation, solicitation, or discussion between a franchisor's representatives and prospective franchisees, for which the franchisor does not have substantiation shall be made available to prospective franchisees or the Commission or its staff upon demand. This provision applies, but is not limited, to statements concerning the experience or qualifications, or lack of experience or qualifications, needed for success as a franchisee.

. . . To make any claim in any advertising or promotional material, or in any oral sales presentation, solicitation, or discussion between a franchisor's representatives and prospective franchisees, which (directly or by implication) contradicts or exceeds any of the statements required to be disclosed [above].

The proposed FTC rule requires the contractual opportunity of the franchisee to have a ten-day cooling-off period after signing the franchise contract to cancel without liability. It also adds safeguards with respect to any promissory notes signed by the franchisee that prevent the franchisor from selling them to third parties in a way whereby the third party can sue the franchisee-signer of the note without the signer having the right to base a legal defense against payment or failure of the franchisor to perform under the contract or related defenses not generally available against the "holder in due course" of a promissory note.

All of these contract or informational safeguards are worth pursuing directly with the franchisor during the course of negotiations. Moreover, inquiries to the Securities and Exchange Commission and state consumer protection agencies relative to reports required to be filed by corporate franchisors constitute an independent source of data relative to the prospective franchisor. In short, rely on hard information, good accounting, and sound legal advice in deciding whether to become a franchisee.

5

Copyrights

OVERVIEW OF THE U.S. COPYRIGHT SYSTEM— THE CONCEPT OF PUBLICATION

In common with the U.S. patent system, federal copyright law owes its existence to Article 1, Section 8, Clause 8 of the Constitution. This clause permits Congress to secure to inventors for limited times the exclusive right to their discoveries, and to "authors" the exclusive right to their "writings." As will be seen in ensuing sections, the Constitutional term *writings* goes far beyond the common conception of words placed on paper, and covers all manner of creative expression of ideas in tangible form. Although we leave it to later sections of this chapter to explore in detail the scope and extent of federal copyright protection, it is important to explain here a central concept of copyright law, the concept of "publication." Publication of a "writing" is the event that, accompanied by proper formalities, invests the author with federal copyright protection. Publication, however, is also the event that divests the author of another form of protection, known as common law copyright. Thus to understand the significance of publication, it is important to be acquainted with the common law copyright an author has before he publishes.

Stated simply, common law copyright is the right of an author to the first publication of his work. If John Doe writes a book and maintains the book in secret or shows it only to his friends, no one but him may first publish the book. The common law copyright, or right of first publication, that he has is not a creature of the Constitution or of federal coypright law. Rather it is a right protected by the laws of the individual states. In this sense it is similar to the trade secret right, as opposed to federal patent or copyright law.

Common law copyright exists in all the unpublished forms of expression of an "author." Not only John Doe's book, but an artist's unpublished painting, a playwright's unpublished play, a sculptor's unpublished statue, and a composer's unpublished cantata are all protected by common law copyright against publication by anyone other than the author.

Virtually everyone is the owner of a vast body of works in which he has a common law copyright, though many never know it and few ever have cause to rely upon their rights. A good example of a subject of common law copyright is the ordinary letter. When we write a letter, and send it to our friend, relative, lover, or business associate, we have placed our creative stamp upon paper in a tangible form. Though the recipient may own the letter itself, we, the authors, own a common law copyright in the form of expression that makes up the sense and meaning of the letter. Although the recipient may sell the letter should he wish to do so, neither he nor anyone else may publish it without our permission. This is because only the author of an unpublished work may first publish it. Although the writer's common law copyright in the letters he sends may seem of dubious value, we are all familiar with books that consist solely of the collected or selected letters of famous people. Who is to say that the words we set down on paper in letters to our friends will not someday be the subject of great interest to the public at large? And if that day should come, it is we the authors, as owners of the common law right of first publication in our writings, who stand to benefit from their publication.

The boundaries of common law copyright protection are hazy. The letters, sketches, and even finger paintings we make carry with them the right of first publication, but what about other, more ephemeral things, such as the words that we utter? Over a period of years, Ernest Hemingway had numerous conversations with A. E. Hotchner, a friend and fellow author. Hotchner made notes of these conversations and after Hemingway's death, published a book, *Papa Hemingway*, in which he quoted at length from them. In a lawsuit by Hemingway's widow and estate, Hotchner was charged with infringing Hemingway's common law copyright in his conversations. The court in this case ducked the issue of whether conversations might ever be subject to common law copyright, holding that Hemingway had acquiesced in their publication by failing to indicate affirmatively that he wished to exercise control over them.

At least, however, where the nature of the conversation manifests an intent to exercise control over its publication, it would appear that the speaker maintains a common law right of first publication. In another case, for example, a writer had a conference with a newspaper editor in which she detailed the contents of some articles she proposed to write. Later, when she decided not to write them, the newspaper published an "interview" with her, in which much of her conversation with the editor was quoted. The court held that she had a common law right of first publication in her words, and that the publication by the newspaper had infringed that right. Of course, the freedom of speech and press vouchsafed by the First Amendment will serve to limit the common law protection of utterances. Thus, where the words themselves, as well as the ideas expressed are important or newsworthy, it is unlikely that the speaker can prevent their publication.

We have seen that the author of all manner of unpublished works has the right to their publication. Once he has exercised that right, his common law copyright expires and the work is in the public domain, available to others to copy freely. Only if he secures federal copyright protection at the time of publication does the work fail to pass into the public domain. And because publication is one of the elements normally necessary to securing a federal copyright, the precise definition of publication is vitally important, because on it depends both the divesting of common law and the investing of "statutory" copyright.

An eminent authority on copyrights, Professor Melville Nimmer, has defined publication as occurring "when by consent of the copyright owner, the original or tangible copies of a work are sold, leased, loaned, given away, or otherwise made available to the general public, or when an authorized offer is made to dispose of the work in any such manner even if a sale or other such disposition does not in fact occur." As can be seen from this definition, a great many actions taken by the copyright owner may constitute publication; the key is that the work be made available to the general public. Thus our author, John Doe, who has written a book and kept it secret, will publish it if he then makes it available to the general public. If the book was, for example, a doctoral thesis, and it was placed in a major university library where it was freely available to borrowers, it would quite probably be "published."

Although the preceding definition is clear and readily applicable with respect to books and other writings, there are some instances in which the fact of publication cannot be so easily ascertained. In many of these cases the existence or lack of publication arises from historical reasons rather than from common sense. As examples we will discuss the performance of written works, the sale of mechanical recordings of music, the display of works of art, and the effect of publication of a derivative work on the unpublished work on which it is based.

It has long been the rule, handed down from England during American colonial days, that the public performance or oral rendition of a written work does not constitute a publication so as to divest common law copyright. Assume for a moment that Shakespeare's plays had never been made public and distributed as folios. If the only way in which these works had become known to the public was by their performance, they would never have been published. Accordingly, Shakespeare's heirs, even to this day, would be the proprietors of a common law copyright in his works, and only they would have the right to publish them. In a more modern context, the public exhibition of a motion picture is not a publication of either the film itself or of the underlying screenplay. Of course, the public distribution of the film, entailing leasing or selling copies to distributors, would under the preceding definition of publication, constitute a publication. But the mere exhibition, no matter how large the audience, would not divest the common law copyright in the work.

An interesting example of the fact that a wide public audience does not create publication is found in a case involving the late Dr. Martin Luther King's famous "I Have a Dream" speech of 1963. When Dr. King gave his speech, he was heard by a live audience of several hundred thousand people, and on television by countless others. Dr. King subsequently registered the speech with the U.S. Copyright Office, publishing it in written form. He brought suit against a number of defendants, including several recording companies that were selling phonograph records of the speech. The defendants argued that the oral delivery of the speech to the vast audience was a publication that barred both common law and statutory copyright, because the speech was made without the formalities necessary to create statutory copyright protection. The court held that mere oral delivery, no matter the size of the audience, did not constitute a publication.

Although the public rendition of a written work does not amount to a publication, the law is much less clear as to the public sale of a sound recording of a musical composition. Before the enactment in 1909 of the present Copyright Act, the Supreme Court had held that the reproduction of copyrighted music on piano rolls did not constitute an infringing copying of the composition. From this rule that a mechanical recording was not a copy, some courts concluded that a recording did not constitute a publication. Under this rule, a composer would retain a common law copyright in his music even though recordings of the music were widely disseminated, as long as the music itself was not published in sheet form. Other cases, however, have held that the public distribution of a recording of an unpublished musical composition does in fact amount to a publication, divesting any common law right in the music. This question has yet to be resolved authoritatively.

A somewhat different view has been taken with respect to publication of works by placing them on public display. Long ago the Supreme Court held that the public exhibition of a painting at an art gallery was not a publication, when it was understood by the viewing public that copies were not to be made and when steps were taken to prevent copying.

In a recent case it was found that adequate safeguards against copying were not taken, and therefore the court found a publication eliminating copyright rights. In this case, a small model of a Picasso sculpture was publicly displayed without any apparent restrictions on copying or photographing it. When a giant final version of the sculpture was displayed with a copyright notice, the copyright was held invalid on the ground that the earlier display of the model constituted a publication that placed the statue in the public domain.

Derivative works are works that are substantially based on or derived from other works. Examples are translations of books into other languages and reproductions of paintings. By their very nature, derivative works embody most if not all of the copyrightable nature of the work they are based on. Thus a publication of a derivative work affects a publication of the underlying work. Accordingly, if an author writes a novel and then adapts the novel into a play, publication of the play without copyright notice will cause the divestment of common law copyright in the novel.

One area in which this type of divestive publication may cause a problem involves architectural plans. A number of courts have held that the authorized construction of a building based on architectural plans is a publication of the plans, divesting common law copyright in them. This holding is based on the theory that the building was made public, and thus constituted a publication of the plans for it. Other cases have held to the contrary, concluding that even public exhibition of a building does not amount to a publication, either of the building itself or of the underlying plans. Several recent cases, however, have suggested that the degree of publication is based on how accessible the building is made to the public. Thus in one case the court found that the public sale of numerous houses in a development constituted a divesting publication of the underlying plan. In another recent case a court held that construction of a building constituted a divestive publication of only those features of the plan that were discernible by a person inspecting the building. Thus the floor plan was considered published, whereas other features not observable from inspection were not.

From the preceding discussion it can be seen that the fact of publication is a crucial legal concept upon which important rights hinge. If a work is published, it loses its common law copyright protection, and if the statutory formalities of notice are not observed, there will be no federal copyright protection. This sometimes harsh result has led to the creation of a doctrine known as "limited publication." Essentially, this doctrine states that if a work is distributed to a selected group for a limited purpose without the right to distribute it further, the publication is a "limited" one. In the case involving Dr. King the distribution of press copies prior to the speech was regarded as a limited publication. It should be noted that this doctrine operates essentially to prevent the inadvertent divestiture of the common law copyright by means of distribution of a manuscript to a selected group. If the distribution is accompanied by requisite statutory notice, it will almost certainly be effective to invest statutory copyright rights.

This overview, although somewhat detailed in relation to the matters of common law copyright and publication, should give the reader an idea of the dual nature of the American copyright system. Publication is the central concept, for it demarcates between the common law right of first publication, on the one hand, and the statutory copyright, on the other. In the following sections we will treat the types of works protectable by copyright, and the rights accompanying such protection. With the distinctions between common law and statutory copyright firmly in mind, the reader should be able to understand how the various rights relate to each.

STANDARDS OF COPYRIGHTABILITY

Originality

The basic requirement to the copyrightability of a work is that it be original. The word *original* as used here means not that the work is novel or unique, but that it originates with the author. In fact, the requirement of originality is inherent in the constitutional language that copyrights may be secured to "authors," because *to author* means "to originate or create." Moreover, the requirement of originality is similarly applicable to both common law and statutory copyright. Only those works actually created by the author, and not slavishly copied, satisfy this basic criterion.

The test of originality, however, as pointed out, is not that the work be novel or unique. Even a work based upon something already in the public domain may well be original. For example, in one case, the copyrightability of mezzotint engravings based on paintings in the public domain was questioned. The court held that the engravings were sufficiently original to be entitled to copyright, stating that all that is required "is that the 'author' contributed something more than a 'merely trivial' variation, something recognizably 'his own.' Originality in this context 'means little more than a prohibition of actual copying.'" Furthermore, even a work exactly identical with another already existing work could be original with the author, if the author had created it independently of the earlier work. As stated by a well-known federal judge, Learned Hand, "if by some magic a man who had never known it were to compose anew Keats' Ode on a Grecian Urn, he would be an 'author.' . . ." From this striking example, it can readily be seen that the requirement of originality has nothing to do with the patent law's requirement of novelty. Rather, it means simply that the author's work must be his own.

Creativity

Creativity as a standard of copyrightability is to a great degree simply a measure of originality. Thus, although a work that merely copies exactly a prior work may be held not to be original, if the copy entails the independent creative judgment of the author in its production, that creativity will render the work original. For example, in the mezzotint engraving case referred to, though the resulting work was intended to be a faithful reproduction of the original painting, its production entailed the labors of a skilled engraver and the judgment of an artist in selecting colors to create the desired result. Moreover, the engraving process inevitably introduced variations from the original painting. It was these creative efforts that distinguished the reproductions from the original paintings and made them original in the copyright sense.

Another example of the types of considerations that go into evaluating the creativity of a work may be found in a case concerning the Zapruder film taken of President Kennedy's assassination. As stated by the court in a copyright case involving these films, Abraham Zapruder "was by sheer happenstance at the scene [of the assassination] taking home movies with his camera." The copyrightability of the films was attacked on the ground that Zapruder had done no more than record the actual happening of real events, and had added nothing creative to this film record. The court disagreed, noting that among the elements of creativity introduced by Zapruder were the "kind of camera (movies, not snapshots), the kind of film (color), the kind of lens (telephoto), the area in which the pictures were to be taken, the time they were to be taken, and (after testing several sites) the spot on which the camera would be operated." Creativity, then, is the introduction by the author of his own judgment and skill into the production of a work. If the work is derivative, that is, if it is based on another work, it will be the elements of creativity that serve to determine whether the work is original. If the work is itself clearly original, but of modest accomplishment, the element of creativity may sometimes of itself be the determinative factor of copyrightability. For example, the Regulations of the Copyright Office indicate that certain works are not subject to copyright. Among these are "[w]ords and short phrases such as names, titles, and slogans; familiar symbols or designs; mere variations of typographic ornamentation, lettering or coloring; mere listing of ingredients or contents." At least some of these items would appear to be excluded because they lack even minimal creativity. For example, short advertising slogans, even set to simple music, have been denied copyright protection because they lacked creativity, even though they were original in that they were not copied from other works. In one case the slogan *Tic Toc, Tic Toc, Time for Muehlebach,* set to a two-note scale to imitate the sound of a clock, was held to be uncopyrightable when both of the phrases *Tic Toc* and *Time for Muehlebach* were already in the public domain. In another case the phrase *This is Nature's most relaxing pause,* used in advertising a reclining chair, was held to lack sufficient creativity to merit copyright protection. Thus creativity is a necessary element of copyrightability, even if the work is original with the author. It is important to remember the caveat of Mr. Justice Holmes, however, that "it would be a dangerous undertaking for persons trained only to the law to constitute themselves final judges of the worth of pictorial illustrations, outside of the narrowest and most obvious limits." This caveat should extend to works other than pictorial ones, because the creative merit of works in general is a difficult thing to judge. Thus the law should be chary to impose its standards of literary or artistic merit on the creation of others. Although the preceding slogans, for example, may lack the requisite creativity to merit copyright protection, what of Ogden Nash's two-line poem concerning babies:

> A bit of talcum
> Is always walcum

Obviously, such judgments are fraught with the danger of imposing one's own standards on others, and Justice Holmes' words should be heeded "outside of the narrowest and most obvious limits."

COPYRIGHTABLE SUBJECT MATTER

We have seen that certain minimum criteria of originality and creativity must be met in order for a work to be considered copyrightable. These criteria should apply regardless of whether we are talking about statutory or common law copyright. Another question, quite apart from the preceding prerequisites, is whether the work is of a type that is susceptible of being copyrighted. With regard to common law copyright, we have already seen in the overview some indication of the breadth of coverage. Thus not only are tangible writings or works of art subject to the author's right of first publication, but even his spoken words may under some circumstances be protectable. It is probably fair to say that any original, unpublished work is protected by common law copyright as long as it is set out tangibly or in such a way as to delineate it as a characteristic form of expression, rather than merely as an abstract idea. Statutory copyright, on the other hand, covers neither so nebulous nor so broad an area. This is because the Constitution limits copyright to the "writings" of an author, and therefore only tangible writings may be protected by statutory copyright. Discussion of the types of subject matter that may be protected under the Copyright Act follows.

Statutory Categories

First, Section 4 of the Copyright Act states that, "[t]he works for which copyright may be secured under this title shall include all the writings of an author." The next section of the Act lists a number of categories in which works may be registered, but ends by saying that the list of categories "shall not be held to limit the subject matter of copyright as defined in section 4. . . ." One might conclude, therefore, that the works registrable under the Act are all "writings" of an author as set out in the Constitution. Judicial decisions, however, very definitely conclude that "writings of an author" in Section 4 is not as broad as in the term in the Constitution. This point has very recently been affirmed by the Supreme Court in *Goldstein* v. *California*, in which it was stated that "in light of [the] consistent interpretation by the courts [that "writings" as used in Sections 4 and 5 does not encompass the entire scope of Constitutionally protectable writings], . . . we cannot agree that §§ 4 and 5 have the broad scope [claimed]."

It is conceivable that there might exist works that cannot be conveniently categorized in one of the enumerated groups under Section 5, and yet might still arguably be copyrightable. As a practical matter, however, the Copyright Office Regulations limit registration to works falling within one of the listed categories. For the present we will discuss those categories, and subsequently we will look briefly at some types of works that may not fit into any category.

The categories of works specifically made registrable are set out in Section 5 as follows:

(a) Books, including composite and cyclopedic works, directories, gazetteers, and other compilations.

(b) Periodicals, including newspapers.

(c) Lectures, sermons, addresses (prepared for oral delivery).

(d) Dramatic or dramatico-musical compositions.

(e) Musical compositions.

(f) Maps.

(g) Works of art; models or designs for works of art.

(h) Reproductions of a work of art.

(i) Drawings or plastic works of a scientific or technical character.

(j) Photographs.

(k) Prints and pictorial illustrations including prints or labels used for articles of merchandise.

(l) Motion-picture photoplays.

(m) Motion-pictures other than photoplays.

(n) Sound recordings.

Section 5 ends with a proviso that the listed categories do not limit the subject matter of copyright as defined in Section 4 to include all the writings of an author. But, as noted previously, judicial construction and Copyright Office procedure effectively confine the protectable works to the listed classes. Section 5 also states that error in classification of a work shall not invalidate or impair copyright protection. Although this provision would operate, for example, to maintain the validity of a copyright in a musical comedy registered as a musical composition instead of as a dramatico-musical composition, it should not be taken to imply that the registration class is unimportant. On the contrary, significant differences in the degree of protection afforded by copyright hinge on the nature of the copyrighted work. Moreover, in some cases the nature of the work will place greater or lesser duties on the copyright owner to secure protection. Some of these distinctions will be discussed in the section concerning rights protected by copyright; others will be dealt with when *ad interim* copyrights and the manufacturing clause are discussed.

We can thus see that the nature of the work may well be of significance in establishing the rights and duties of the copyright proprietor.

Beyond these, however, the courts have tended to differentiate among certain classes of works and have traditionally established different standards of copyrightability with respect to them. One major area in which a special standard may be applied is that of "derivative works." These will be discussed separately in this section. Even among the individual classes, however, certain differences in the standards of copyrightability may be discerned.

Books.   Books constitute something of a catch-all category, which covers practically any written thing not specifically covered by another class. The category is directed to the physical form, rather than the substance of the work, and includes fiction and nonfiction, poetry, compilations, directories, catalogs, annual publications, pamphlets, and even such things as playing cards and single pages. Books may be copyrighted only upon publication.

Periodicals.   Like books, the category of periodicals is principally concerned with the physical form of the work. It includes newspapers, magazines, bulletins, and serial publications published at intervals of less than one year. Thus the dividing line between serial books and periodicals is whether the interval of publication is less or more than one year. Like books, periodicals may be copyrighted only upon publication.

Lectures, Sermons, and Addresses.   The class of lectures, sermons, and addresses is quite distinct from books or periodicals and includes all types of scripts of unpublished nondramatic works prepared in the first instance for oral delivery. Only unpublished works may be registered under this class. When published, they may be registered as books.

Dramatic or Dramatico-musical Compositions.   Dramatic or dramatico-musical compositions include plays for production in any medium, opera, musical comedy, and pantomime. Choreography may be registered under this class if the work is of a dramatic character, expressing a story or conveying a dramatic concept or idea. Works registered under this class may be either published or unpublished.

Musical Compositions.   All musical compositions in the form of visible notation, other than dramatico-musical works, are registered in this class. Sound recordings are not registrable as musical compositions. Songs, with or without lyrics, are registrable here, but lyrics alone must be registered as books. Musical compositions may be registered as published or unpublished works.

In the area of musical compositions, courts have developed peculiar standards of originality. Original lyrics can make a derivative song copyrightable, so long as appropriate permission is obtained if the basic music is copyrighted. On the other hand, originality of music itself is generally determined from its melody. Harmony, for example, is essentially a mechanical application of chords to a melody line, and generally will not make an unoriginal melody copyrightable. Similarly, musical rhythm is rarely original with a single composer, as in one case Irving Berlin was held not entitled to a property interest in iambic pentameter. Thus melody alone is normally the criterion for measuring musical originality.

Maps. The class of maps is self-descriptive and includes three-dimensional works such as globes as well as two-dimensional maps and charts. Maps may be copyrighted only upon publication. Maps also have been held to require a somewhat greater standard of originality to merit copyright protection than do other types of works. Thus the selecting of various local highlights and tourist attractions, and placing them on a general outline map of the island of Hawaii, were held not to entail sufficient originality to justify copyright. Apparently the court concluded in this case that the selection of places identified was copied from other maps, or in some cases, even if not copied, so obvious as to gainsay any originality. It might be observed that such a standard is essentially one of creativity, insisting as it does on some ingenuity beyond the obvious designation of geographic or topographic features.

Some courts have gone even beyond this creativity standard and have held that copyrightability of maps depends upon direct observation of the geographic features by the maker. Thus in one case it was held that a map in which all the features were taken from other maps or from records (such as street names) in the public domain was not copyrightable. Professor Nimmer has suggested that this "direct observation" rule imposes standards of copyrightability far beyond what is warranted by the Copyright Act.

Works of Art. This class includes all types of works of artistic craftsmanship, whether fine arts, such as paintings and sculpture, or applied art, such as jewelry, glassware, and tapestry. Works of art may be registered as either published or unpublished works. Works of applied art are clearly copyrightable even though they have utilitarian aspects. Thus in a landmark case, *Mazer v. Stein,* the Supreme Court upheld a copyright in a statuette that was employed as a lamp base. The Copyright Office Regulations comment rather cryptically on when a utilitarian work is copyrightable:

If the sole intrinsic function of an article is its utility, the fact that the article is unique and attractively shaped will not qualify it as a work of art. However, if the shape of a utilitarian article incorporates features, such as artistic sculpture, carving, or pictorial representation, which can be identified separately and are capable of existing independently as a work of art, such features will be eligible for registration.

Where the work incorporates features traditionally considered to be art, such as the statuette in *Mazer* v. *Stein,* it seems clear that it may be copyrighted. In other instances the question may be close, and Professor Nimmer has suggested that the answer may depend on "whether the shape or form of the object (as distinguished from its intended use) is dictated primarily by aesthetic or utilitarian considerations."

It is in the field of works of art that the requirement of creativity is most evident. Although a book or a play, if not copied, must have some creative element of necessity, it is creativity that distinguishes a "thing" from a work of art. Thus a stone may be split rudely with a hammer to make an original, unique shape, but that shape will not necessarily be the product of creative effort justifying copyright. On the other hand, if hewn to a shape that has an esthetic appeal, the stone may become a sculpture. Harkening back to Justice Holmes' caveat about art, the law should be reluctant to deny the status of art to things merely because they do not appeal to the masses or to the judge. We are all familiar with sculpture welded from junk automobile parts, and such sculpture is accepted as art by at least a significant segment of the public. In the end it is probably this practical test of the ordinary perception of art by the people, or by any group of the people, that determines whether a particular work is a work of art.

Reproductions of Works of Art. For reproductions of existing works of art, whether in the same or a different medium, such as etchings or drawings of paintings or sculpture, to be registrable, the reproduction must be published. Also, like any derivative work, in order for the reproduction to be copyrightable, it must be produced with the consent of the original copyright owner.

In order for a reproduction to be registered, it must have elements of originality over the work from which it is derived. The reader will remember the case discussed previously involving mezzotint engravings reproducing public domain paintings. In that case the requisite originality was found in the differences introduced into the reproduction by the engraver, which differences were characteristic of him rather than of the original painter. In another case a valid copyright was found in a fabric design based on a Byzantine motif in the public domain. The court found sufficient originality in the combined design as printed on fabric.

Drawings and Plastic Works of a Scientific or Technical Character.
Included in this class are two-dimensional drawings and three-dimensional works that "have been designed for a scientific or technical use and which contain copyrightable graphic, pictorial or sculptured copyrightable material." The term *plastic* does not refer to the modern meaning of certain synthetic resins, but means a "three-dimensional work giving the effect of that which is molded or sculptured." Examples are mechanical drawings, architect's blueprints, and anatomical models. These works may be copyrighted either as published or unpublished works.

The Copyright Office has taken the position that works that are designed for recording information and that do not in themselves convey information, may not be registered. Examples are time cards, account books, score cards, and bank checks. Some courts, however, have disagreed with this position, and have held such things as bank checks and personal data forms to be copyrightable if their format or content is original.

Photographs. The class of photographs includes photographic prints and filmstrips, slide films, and individual slides. Photographs may be registered either as unpublished works or upon publication. As the reader may remember from the discussion of the Zapruder films of the Kennedy assassination, originality and creativity in photographs (or motion pictures) may be based upon such things as the selection by the photographer of type of camera, film, lens, and so forth. The classic statement of originality in photographs is found in a very old Supreme Court decision. In *Burrow-Giles Lithographic Co.* v. *Sarony*, at issue was the copyrightability of a photographic portrait of Oscar Wilde. The Court found that by posing the subject, selecting and arranging the costume, draperies, and various other accessories, arranging and disposing light and shade, and suggesting and evolving the desired expression, the photographer had created a copyrightable work of art.

As can be seen from the factors considered by the court in the Zapruder film case, the standard of originality in photographs requires substantially less creative effort than was found in *Sarony*. In fact, probably any photograph may be copyrighted that is not solely a slavish copy of the subject. In the category of such slavish copies might be photoreproductions produced by Xerography. In such a case, the copy would not have distinguishable variations from the original work upon which a finding of originality or creativity could be based.

Prints and Labels. Two distinct types of works are registered in the class of prints and labels. One, denominated "prints or pictorial illustrations," includes greeting cards, picture postcards, and prints produced by such mechanical means as lithography or photoengraving. The second group consists of commercial prints and labels, and includes prints and labels "containing copyrightable pictorial matter, text, or both, published in connection with the sale or advertisement of an article or articles of merchandise." The textual material of labels, however, may not be registered if it consists merely of words or short phrases such as names, titles, or slogans, or a mere listing of ingredients or contents.

In a leading case in the area of the copyrightability of commercial labels, it was held that an illustration of a chocolate cake had sufficient originality to support a copyright. In a witty opinion, the court observed that "it might be said that a piece of chocolate frosted chocolate cake looks about the same throughout the generations." Still, the court found that in depicting an idealized cake, resembling "all well-baked cakes of similar type including those baked by fondly remembered grandmothers," the label evidenced enough creative effect to justify a copyright. This case, however, was a copyright infringement suit, and it might be said that the fact that the label had evidently been directly copied by the defendant influenced the court in upholding the copyright.

Although pictorial aspects of commercial labels seem to be held to essentially the same standard as other art work, courts have differed in their treatment of printed matter on labels. In one case a court upheld a copyright in a label for furniture polish, including text that was generally laudatory of the product. The court implied that the language was not solely descriptive of the polish, and held it to be copyrightable. In another case, however, a court held that the phrase *the most personal sort of deodorant* was too short and too descriptive of feminine deodorant spray to support a copyright.

Motion Picture Photoplays.   Included in the class of motion picture photoplays are motion pictures that are dramatic in character, such as "feature films, filmed television plays, short subjects and animated cartoons having a plot." Motion picture photoplays may be copyrighted as unpublished works or upon publication.

Motion Pictures Other Than Photoplays.   Motion pictures other than photoplays include published or unpublished nondramatic films, such as newsreels, documentaries, promotional films, and filmed television programs having no plot. An example of a work registered under this class was the Zapruder film of the Kennedy assassination.

Sound Recordings.   Sound recordings constitute the newest class of copyrightable subject matter defined in the Copyright Act, having been added on October 15, 1971. Unlike other statutory classes, sound recordings are specifically defined in the Act as "works that result from the fixation of a series of musical, spoken, or other sounds, but not including the sounds accompanying a motion picture." Only those sound recordings first fixed and published after February 15, 1972, are eligible for copyright. Although the copyrightability of sound recordings ends on January 1, 1975, the legislative history of the amendment establishing copyright in sound recordings indicates that permanent legislation will be part of a general copyright law revision, pending in Congress. If such a general revision is not forthcoming, it is likely that Congress will extend the provision for the copyrightability of sound recordings.

The Copyright Office Regulations define sound recordings as including "discs, tapes, cartridges, cassettes, player piano rolls, or similar material objects from which the sound can be produced either directly or with the aid of a machine or device." The statutory definition excludes motion picture soundtracks, which are probably covered by the copyright in the motion picture itself.

Sound recordings first published prior to February 15, 1972, are not protected by federal copyright. The Supreme Court, however, in *Goldstein* v. *California*, has recently upheld the power of states to forbid the direct reproduction, or "piracy," of sound recordings. This protection, however, depends on an applicable state law, and absent such a law, the producers of sound recordings must rely on relief from such theories as unfair competition.

An interesting issue respecting sound recordings is the requirement of originality, and the question of who contributes originality to the recording. It seems clear that the performance of a musical composition by a skilled musician embodies sufficient originality to satisfy the standard for copyrightability. The Congress has suggested that in some cases, originality might be inserted by the record producer, in supervising, editing, and engineering the sound recording. One court has specifically held that sufficient originality may be found in the efforts of a recording firm that organizes the talents of arrangers, performers, and technicians. Still, in some cases, such as simple recordings of inanimate sounds such as breaking surf, there may be no originality on the part of either the "performer" or the producer, and hence no copyright.

Special Problems of Copyrightability

Fictional Characters. An interesting and recurring question in copyright law deals with what protection may be afforded to an author in the characters he develops. This question may arise in two ways. First, assuming the author's work is copyrighted, is he protected against the use by others of characters based on those he developed if the allegedly infringing work does not copy anything of the copyrighted work other than the characters themselves? Second, if the author's work as a whole is not copyrighted, can he obtain either statutory or common law copyright in the characters themselves? (Or, for that matter, if the author's sole achievement is the development of a character, may the character be copyrighted?)

The first question was discussed by Judge Learned Hand in the 1930 case, *Nichols* v. *Universal Pictures Corp.* In that case Judge Hand made the following comment:

> If Twelfth Night were copyrighted, it is quite possible that a second comer might so closely imitate Sir Toby Belch or Malvolio as to infringe, but it would not be enough that for one of his characters he cast a riotous knight who kept wassail to the discomfort of the household, or a vain and foppish steward who became amorous of his mistress. These would be no more than Shakespeare's "ideas" in the play, as little capable of monopoly as Einstein's Doctrine of Relativity, or Darwin's Theory of the Origin of Species. It follows that the less developed the characters, the less they can be copyrighted; that is the penalty an author must bear for marking them too indistinctly.

Under Judge Hand's test, fictional characters may be copyrighted, but the line must be drawn between mere ideas sketching the nature of the character, and clearly limned and developed characterizations. Although a "second comer" might infringe a copyright by drawing his characters indistinguishably from those of the copyright owner, he will not be held to infringe if his characters merely share common traits. To paraphrase Judge Hand, the more developed the characters, the more susceptible they are to copyright.

The U.S. Court of Appeals for the Ninth Circuit took a more restrictive view of copyrightability of characters in a 1954 case involving the fictional detective, Sam Spade. In this case the court held that in assigning the motion picture, radio, and television rights to the book *The Maltese Falcon*, the author had not conveyed a copyright in the character Sam Spade, because the character was not copyrightable.

The Ninth Circuit's holding goes far beyond Judge Hand's statement, and would deny copyright protection even against direct copying of a unique and fully developed character, unless the character "really constitutes the story being told." Even under this test, however, the copying of certain Walt Disney cartoon characters has been enjoined on the ground that the principal appeal of cartoons lies not in their plots but in the characters themselves, and thus the characters constitute the story being told. Recently, too, a number of courts have questioned the holding of the Ninth Circuit as too strict, and Judge Hand's formulation may well have retained its vitality.

The second question mentioned was discussed obliquely in a unique and interesting case involving the television series "Have Gun Will Travel." In this case, Victor DeCosta sued the Columbia Broadcasting System for misappropriating the character Paladin, which he claimed to have developed. The facts established by DeCosta were that over a period of years he had evolved the character, affecting black shirt, black pants, the name Paladin, a medalion affixed to his black flat crowned hat, a black mustache, and a business card labeled "Have Gun Will Travel, Wire Paladin, N. Court St., Cranston, R.I.," and carrying a hidden derringer. DeCosta portrayed this character in rodeos, auctions, and horse shows. The court agreed with DeCosta that CBS had copied his character.

CBS, however, argued that because DeCosta had not copyrighted the character, he could not be protected against its use because of the pre-emption doctrine of the *Sears* and *Compco* cases, discussed in Chapter 1. To rebut this argument, DeCosta asserted that characters could not be copyrighted, citing the "Sam Spade" case, and that therefore there could be no pre-emption. The court, however, held that the Ninth Circuit's decision in the "Sam Spade" case was not good law to the extent that it held that characters were not copyrightable. Therefore, because the court had concluded that the character in order to be protected required some sort of copyright coverage, DeCosta's theory of misappropriation turned essentially into an action for common law copyright infringement. DeCosta argued that he retained a common law right of first publication in the character of Paladin, because his performances in rodeos and so forth did not constitute a divesting publication. To this the court remarked as follows:

> Here, plaintiff's "performance" consisted of two components: appearing in public and passing out cards and photographs [of himself in costume]. . . . So far as his costume and menacing appearance were concerned, it was fully conveyed on the cards bearing his photograph— which also contained the chess piece, the slogan, and the name "Paladin." The cards were passed out in great quantities over the years to all who would have them.

These actions the court found indeed to constitute a full publication of all significant features of the character; accordingly, any common law right had effectively been divested by publication.

The significance of this case is that the court rejected the Ninth Cirouit's holding that fictional characters cannot be copyrighted, barring DeCosta recovery not because there was no protectable right but because the right had been lost by publication without obtaining statutory copyright. The court held that the constitutional copyright clause extends to "any concrete, describable manifestation of intellectual creation." Although a creation that may be ineffable might not be copyrightable, the character Paladin clearly was describable, and indeed it was the publication of the character that prevented protection. As it happens, the First Circuit decision has turned out not be the denouement of the Paladin story. Recently, a federal magistrate granted summary judgment in favor of DeCosta on grounds of common law service mark infringement and unfair competition.

Choreography. As noted previously, dramatic choreographic works (such as ballet) may be registered as dramatic works. Nondramatic choreography, however, such as ballroom dancing, may not be registered in this class. Presumably, a notational form of the dance may be copyrighted as a book, but the protection afforded a book may not cover performances of the dance. This difference in protection will be discussed in the section on rights protected by copyright. For the moment, it need only be pointed out that choreography, though clearly an art form that should be protectable by copyright, is not specifically provided for in the statute and may be protected only by fitting it into a category that does not explicitly cover it.

Derivative Works. Derivative works are works that are substantially derived from another work. Obvious examples are reproductions of paintings, translations of books into other languages, dramatizations of novels, and rendering of plays into operas. As can be seen from the preceding examples, derivative works may be in the same or a different medium from the original. Because the principal criterion for copyright is originality with the author, it is obvious that a derivative work may be copyrighted only if it contains original material that distinguishes it from the work on which it is based. As seen in the case involving the mezzotint engravings, however, the amount of originality need not be great and any reasonably distinguishable variation may be sufficient.

In addition to the standard criteria for copyright, however, the Copyright Act imposes another condition on certain derivative works. Section 7 of the Act states in part as follows:

> Compilations or abridgements, adaptations, arrangements, dramatizations, translations, or other versions of works in the public domain or of copyrighted works when produced with the consent of the proprietor of the copyright in such works, or works republished with new matter, shall be regarded as new works subject to copyright under the provisions of this title. . . .

As can be seen from this section, derivative works based upon copyrighted works may themselves be copyrighted *only if produced with the consent of copyright owner.* Derivative works are distinct not only in the additional statutory requirement to copyrightability, but in certain aspects of the law of publication, and in the scope of protection. The publication of derivative works has been discussed previously, and the scope of protection will be discussed in a subsequent section.

NONCOPYRIGHTABLE SUBJECT MATTER

Ideas

As was expressed in the overview to this chapter, it is the form of expression of an idea, rather than the idea itself, that is copyrightable. This concept is especially clear when one considers an idea that is factual, such as Albert Einstein's famous mass—energy equation $E = mc^2$. An author writing a book explaining this concept of relativity would be entitled to a copyright in the book itself, that is, in the form of expression of the idea. Even Einstein, however, the originator of the idea, could not obtain a copyright on it.

In the area of fiction, the distinction between the idea and the form of expression may be more difficult to draw. To take an example, consider the book *Love Story* by Erich Segal. There is no question that as a whole this novel is copyrightable. Yet the bare bones of the plot are certainly not novel, and some critics might say the plot is hackneyed. Thus the essentials of the plot are that rich boy meets poor girl, they fall in love, his father disowns him, they are married, they struggle together in poverty, they prosper, she dies, he is reconciled with his father. Countless variations exist on this theme, and certainly the idea it expresses may not be monopolized by one author, even if he originates it. On the other hand, a similar novel, slightly changing characterizations and locale, might well be found to infringe the book's copyright. The fine line that exists in this area will be dealt with in the section on infringement of copyright. For now it is sufficient to note that it exists, and that only that which goes beyond the mere idea is entitled to copyright protection.

Titles

Long-standing judicial construction has made clear that titles of works, even if the works are copyrighted, are not themselves copyrightable. This rule applies whether statutory or common law rights are concerned. To the extent that titles are protectable, it is under the law of trademarks or unfair competition. Thus a title (for example, to a series of books) may by use become associated in the mind of the public with a particular author or publisher. In such a case the established secondary meaning of the title may generate trademark protection.

Slogans, Trademarks, Words, and Phrases

As discussed previously, Copyright Office Regulations deny copyright to words, slogans, and short phrases. Generally these expressions will lack the requisite originality to justify a copyright. In the rare instance where sufficient originality is found, as in the Ogden Nash poem referred to earlier, the brevity of the work should not bar copyright.

Many of the items in this class may validly constitute trademarks, and as such may obtain protection under the trademark law. Words, slogans, or phrases that are already trademarks are not denied copyright protection merely because they are trademarks, but because they lack originality. Thus a trademark may in some cases also be copyrighted, and nothing in the copyright law bars this situation. The most common example is in the area of commercial prints and labels. As stated in the Copyright Office Regulations, a trademark cannot be registered for copyright if it lacks copyrightable subject matter, but a print or label that meets the criteria for copyright will be registered even though it is also a trademark. For example, an illustrated label for wine might well be both copyrightable and a trademark, if it met the requirements of originality for copyright and the various requirements for trademarks as well.

Works of Utility

As we have seen, the mere fact that a work of art also has utility will not prevent it from being copyrighted. This was the holding of *Mazer* v. *Stein*. On the other hand, a work that is purely functional and whose features exist for functional rather than esthetic reasons, may not be copyrighted. For example, a piston rod, no matter how attractively formed, is solely functional and could not be copyrighted as a work of art.

The issue, already discussed, is really whether the work in question is a "writing" under the statute. If its original features are solely functional, it is not a writing. Another question of copyrightability arises with respect to certain categories of work that are clearly writings. The origin of this question is the famous 1880 Supreme Court decision in *Baker* v. *Selden*. At issue in this case was a copyrighted book by Selden that explained a new method of bookkeeping Selden had developed. The book included sample forms to be used in the Selden system. The defendant Baker was charged with copyright infringement because he sold forms functionally similar but somewhat different in appearance, for use in the same bookkeeping system. The Court assumed that the only way in which the bookkeeping system could be practiced was by using the forms copyrighted by Selden, and posited the question whether Selden's copyright gave him a monopoly over the use of the system he had developed. Thus the Court asked whether Selden could monopolize his bookkeeping system by preventing others from copying his copyrighted forms. The answer given by the Court was no. In effect, it concluded that when a copyrighted work explains an "art" or method of doing something, and copying the work is necessary in order to use the art, then copying for the purpose of such use does not constitute an infringement.

This doctrine of copying for use versus copying for explanation is critically important in the area of infringement, and will be discussed in greater detail there. But the doctrine of *Baker* v. *Selden* has been expanded by some courts and by the Copyright Office so that it now may bar altogether the copyrightability of some works of utility. The Copyright Office Regulations bar copyright for works designed for recording information which do not in themselves convey information such as "time cards, graph paper, account books, diaries, bank checks, score cards, address books, report forms, order forms and the like." Thus these works of utility would be denied copyright protection not only against copying for their intended use (which of course would be the principal purpose for copying them), but also for copying solely for explanatory purposes. For example, under the doctrine of *Baker* v. *Selden,* a blank order form could be copied for the purpose of filling it in, whereas under the Copyright Office Regulations, it could be copied even for inclusion in a book about order forms.

It would seem that the regulation goes far beyond the holding of *Baker* v. *Selden,* and indeed, as noted in a previous section, some courts have in fact upheld copyrights in bank checks and record forms. But the doctrine as expanded still has considerable vitality. In one case a copyright had been obtained in a set of rules for a contest. The copyright owner sued Procter & Gamble Co., which had apparently copied the rules almost verbatim in connection with a contest, for infringement. The U.S. Court of Appeals for the First Circuit found that the contest rules were so simple that there were a mere handful of means by which they could be expressed. Thus finding that the rules were a work of utility that would unavoidably be copied in operating the contest, the court held not merely that there was no infringement, but that the rules were not of copyrightable subject matter.

Patented Publications

As the reader may remember, ornamental designs for works of utility are capable of protection by design patents if they are novel and original. Clearly, under the doctrine of *Mazer* v. *Stein*, such a work may also be copyrighted (as a work of art) if it meets the copyright standards of originality and creativity. Similarly, many mechanical and electrical patents include drawings that would be copyrightable as technical drawings. Though both copyright and patent protection are thus possibilities for these types of works, the Copyright Office has taken the position that under some circumstances a copyright cannot be obtained. Thus, with respect to works of art, Copyright Office Regulations state as follows: "The potential availability of protection under the design patent law will not affect the registrability of a work of art, but a copyright claim in a patented design or in the drawings or photographs in a patent application will not be registered after the patent has been issued." With regard to technical drawings, the regulations state: "A claim to copyright in a scientific or technical drawing . . . will not be refused registration solely by reason of the fact that it is known to form a part of a pending patent application. Where a patent has been issued, however, the claim to copyright in the drawing will be denied copyright registration." Both of these regulations bar copyright registration once a patent has been issued. Of course, issuance of the patent would be a publication of the work, obviating copyright unless accompanied by proper notice. It is not apparent, however, why a copyright could not subsist in the work if proper notice were provided. Nonetheless, the office's refusal to register such works will act as a strong practical bar to obtaining a copyright in them.

RIGHTS PROTECTED BY COPYRIGHT

As provided in the Constitution, the rights secured to authors by copyright are "exclusive rights." That is, the author may exclude others from infringing his copyright. As in patent law, the right to exclude others does not necessarily entail the right to practice or use on the part of the patent or copyright owner. In patent law this distinction is often of significance, as where an inventor patents an improvement on an already patented invention. Without the permission of the prior patentee, the improvement patent owner cannot practice his own invention; he can merely prevent others from practicing it.

In the copyright area this type of situation arises much less frequently. A work based on the copyrighted work of another cannot itself be copyrighted unless the derivation is done with the original proprietor's permission. This permission will normally give the derivative work's author the right to use the work himself. But this right is not necessarily unlimited. For example, in one case the author of the copyrighted book *Madame Butterfly* had granted a license permitting an opera to be based thereon. A dispute arose years later as to whether the owner of the copyright in the opera could make a movie of it. The court found that the license granted by the book copyright owner had conveyed only the right to make the opera, and to perform and publish it in that medium. Therefore the opera copyright owner was unable to make a film version of its own copyrighted opera, because the motion picture rights in the book were still retained by the proprietor of the book copyright.

It can thus be seen that the rights afforded by copyright are solely to exclude others, and do not necessarily afford any affirmative rights to the copyright owner. This section will deal principally with the various exclusive rights established by statutory copyright. It is worth looking first, however, at the exclusive rights provided by common law copyright. For the most part, these rights are the same as those under statutory copyright, and include the rights to copy, publish, sell, arrange, dramatize, and so forth. Certain statutory rights, however, as will be seen, are limited in some respect. For example, the statutory copyright in a dramatic work includes the exclusive right to perform in public, whereas the public performance or reading of a nondramatic work is protected only if it is for profit. This distinction, that the public performance must be for profit, apparently does not apply in the case of common law copyright, so that a not-for-profit performance of an unpublished nondramatic work would still be an infringement. Other examples of this distinction apply in the area of musical compositions, and will be apparent in the ensuing discussion of statutory rights.

THE GENERAL EXCLUSIVE RIGHTS

All statutory copyrights, without regard to the work they cover, give the proprietor the exclusive rights "[t]o print, reprint, publish, copy, and vend the copyrighted work." Of these rights by far the most significant conceptually is the right to copy. In the final analysis it is only copying in the broad sense that copyright really protects. Thus, going back to Learned Hand, if our mythical poet should compose anew "Ode on a Grecian Urn," he may freely print, publish, sell, or perform it, even if the original "Ode" were copyrighted, because the new work was not copied. With only two exceptions, both of which are dealt with in this subsection, all of the exclusive rights provided for presuppose copying or direct rendering (as by performance) of the copyrighted work.

Copying, as used in Section 1(a) of the Copyright Act, refers to any substantial derivation from or duplication of the work, in any tangible form. Thus copying by hand the musical notes of a copyrighted work is an infringement. So, too, is duplication by such means as Xerography. Moreover, it makes no difference whether the copy is in the same medium as or one different from the original; it is still a copy.

The rights to print and reprint naturally encompass copying. Thus one who copies a copyrighted book by setting it in print and printing it has violated the proprietor's rights both to copy and to print. Still, the right to print has some significance beyond merely being a form of copying because it focuses on a particularly important aspect of literary enterprise. Moreover, this right emphasizes that the printer of an infringing copy of a copyrighted work will be liable himself to the copyright owner.

The rights to publish and to sell are the rights alluded to earlier, which do not necessarily entail copying. Thus the publication of a copyrighted work can be an infringement, even if the actual work published was an authorized copy. Publication in this sense is not confined to general publication but may include even a limited publication of the type that might not be sufficient to divest common law copyright. For example, a choir director might obtain only one authorized copy of a copyrighted musical composition, and then run off many copies for use by the choir members. This copying itself would be an infringement of the copyright owner's exclusive right to copy. The distribution to the choir members is a publication that for the purposes of common law copyright divestment would undoubtedly be considered limited. Under the Copyright Act, however, such a distribution would probably be held to be an infringing publication.

The preceding example is of publication of an unauthorized copy. Both publication and vending, however, may constitute infringement even if the copies distributed are authorized. For example, a thief may steal authorized copies of a work from the copyright proprietor. If he distributes these copies, by sale or otherwise, he is guilty of violating the copyright owner's exclusive right to vend and publish. This result, that publication or sale of even authorized copies is an infringement, is significantly limited by the so-called first-sale doctrine, which is set out in the Act in Section 27. This provision states that "nothing in this title shall be deemed to forbid, prevent, or restrict the transfer of any copy of a copyrighted work the possession of which has been lawfully obtained." Read literally, this section would mean that anyone lawfully in possession of an authorized copy of a copyrighted book could transfer it without running afoul of the copyright owner's exclusive right to publish and vend. This reading would be of no avail to a thief, but might permit others lawfully in possession of a work to sell it with impunity. For example, consider the case of a printer who is asked to print and bind a copyrighted book. Having completed his task, his possession of the book would be lawful, but could he sell it without infringing the copyright? Although a literal reading of Section 27 would suggest that the answer is yes, probably the better view is that he cannot.

The historical purpose of the first-sale doctrine is to prevent restraints on alienation. That is, once the copyright owner has parted with dominion over the work by first selling it, he may not restrain further sales. Taking the book printer mentioned as an example, the first-sale doctrine would not seem to apply, because there has not yet been an authorized first sale. The meaning of Section 27 in this type of situation was considered by one court in *Platt & Munk Co.* v. *Republic Graphics, Inc.* In this case, Platt & Munk, the owner of copyrights in certain educational toys and books, had hired Republic Graphics to manufacture them. Upon delivery, Platt & Munk claimed that the goods were defective and refused to accept them. Thereupon Republic attempted to sell the goods, relying on the general right of a seller to sell off goods that a buyer refuses to accept. Platt & Munk sought an injunction against such sale on the ground that it would infringe their exclusive right to vend the copyrighted works. Republic, on the other hand, argued that because it was lawfully in possession of the goods, under Section 27 of the Copyright Act it could sell them without infringing. The court held that in effect, Platt & Munk's refusal to accept delivery of the goods, if unjustified, was tantamount to authorizing the sale by Republic. But, the court concluded, Republic could not sell without infringing until it had shown that Platt & Munk's refusal was unjustified. Thus, the court construed Section 27 not to permit unauthorized sale by one in lawful possession of the goods, if such sale was the first sale.

The right to vend essentially entails disposition by sale. A completed sale is necessary to infringe this right, and simply offering for sale is not an infringement. Virtually all forms of transfer of possession other than by sale would be publication. The exception, a private gift of such a limited nature as not to amount to publication, is not covered by any of the exclusive rights of a copyright owner.

The Right to Make Other Versions

Section 1(b) of the Copyright Act provides a number of specific rights to make other versions of a copyrighted work. This subsection gives the exclusive right "[t]o translate the copyrighted work into other languages or dialects, or make any other version thereof, if it be a literary work; to dramatize it if it be a nondramatic work; to convert it into a novel or other nondramatic work if it be a drama; to arrange or adapt it if it be a musical work. . . ." These rights are relatively self-explanatory. The only point that need be made concerning them is that all necessarily entail copying. Thus an infringement of the right to make other versions will inherently infringe the right to copy. Accordingly, the right to make other versions is not limited to the specific forms of work set out in Section 1(b), but is effectively protected for all types of work by the right to copy in Section 1(a).

The Right to Complete Works of Art

The right to complete works of art is also set out in Section 1(b), which provides the right "to complete, execute, and finish [the work] if it be a model or design for a work of art." This right may be of some significance beyond the right to copy. As the reader will remember from our discussion of works of utility, the doctrine of *Baker* v. *Selden* permits copying when done for the purpose of use, rather than explanation. This doctrine finds application with respect to such things as architects' plans. The building of a structure based on these plans, even though copying, is not an infringement because the copying is done for the purpose of use. Thus, in one case, copyrighted architectural plans for a bridge were held not to protect against the actual construction of the bridge. In some cases where the architectural work would qualify as a work of art, the right actually to build the work may be protected by registering a model rather than a plan for it. In this case the exclusive right to "complete, execute and finish" the model would apparently protect the copyright owner against unauthorized construction of the work, notwithstanding the *Baker* v. *Selden* limitation on the right to copy. Of course, the difficulty with this approach is that the structure must first qualify as a work of art. Although the Lincoln Memorial might well qualify, it is unlikely that an ordinary house or office building would.

Rights in the Delivery, Performance, and Recording of Nondramatic Literary Works

Section 1(c) of the Act provides certain specified rights with respect to nondramatic literary works. This section grants the exclusive rights:

> [t]o deliver, authorize the delivery of, read, or present the copyrighted work in public for profit if it be a lecture, sermon, address or similar production, or other nondramatic literary work; to make or procure the making of any transcription or record thereof by or from which, in whole or in part, it may in any manner or by any method be exhibited, delivered, presented, produced or reproduced; and to play or perform it in public for profit, and to exhibit, represent, produce, or reproduce it in any manner or by any method whatsoever.

It can be seen that a number of rights are granted by this section. All refer to nondramatic literary works, and thus exclude drama, dramatico-musical works, and nondramatic musical compositions. The rights provided may be broken down into three main groups: (1) to deliver, read, or present the work; (2) to transcribe or record the work in a form by or from which it can be exhibited, presented, or produced; and (3) to perform or exhibit the work. These rights further have important limitations in connection with them.

Delivery or reading of a nondramatic work obviously includes such things as poetry reading, reading from novels, and delivery of addresses and sermons. The exclusive right provided here, however, is limited to such delivery in public for profit. These are important conditions upon the exclusive right, because if the delivery is not *both* in public and for profit, it does not infringe the right. A poetry reading to one's family is clearly not in public. Similarly, a reading at a private club that only members may attend is not in public. The delivery of a sermon at a church, however, which may be attended by anyone who wishes, is clearly public, notwithstanding the relatively small size of the congregation. The test for whether the delivery is in public is both the size of the audience and the restrictions on who may attend. If the audience is large enough, it will be public even if it is restricted to a group smaller than the public at large. For example, a delivery before only members of a fraternal group at a large national meeting would probably be public, even though non-members are excluded. On the other hand, if the group is small, lack of formal restrictions will not necessarily make it public, as in a reading to one's family at home. Even though there is no formal restriction upon others' attending, the circumstances of the reading and size of the audience will make the reading a private one.

Even if the delivery is in public, however, it will not infringe unless it is also for profit. This "for profit" requirement has been construed very broadly by the courts, especially in connection with a similar requirement respecting performances of musical compositions. Obviously, the charging of admission to hear a poetry reading would render the reading for profit. But it is not necessary that a direct admission charge be made in order for the reading to be for profit. Virtually any situation in which the delivery of the work serves to attract people who will pay money in some way involves a for-profit delivery. For example, it is relatively common for certain coffee houses to provide "beat" poetry reading, often to the accompaniment of bongos. If the poetry is copyrighted, the reading infringes the right to deliver it in public for profit, because the reading is used as an inducement to bring in customers who will spend their money at the coffee house. Arguably, the delivery of a sermon at a church could be considered for profit in that collections are made from those in attendance. This, however, seems to be too broad a view of the profit-making motive.

The right to record or transcribe insofar as it refers to nondramatic literary works is reasonably straightforward. It does not include either the limitation that the recording be public or for profit. Obviously included are the taping or recording of poetry or readings of novels.

The right to perform, like the right to deliver, is limited to public and for-profit performances insofar as nondramatic literary works are concerned. There are a number of circumstances under which a nondramatic literary work can be performed. If, for example, a nondramatic motion picture fits in this category, as it appears to, the exhibition of it would constitute a performance. Another example of a performance might arise in the case of a dramatic derivative work. Suppose that a playwright is given the right to make a play based on a copyrighted novel but is specifically denied any performance rights in the play. A public performance for profit of the play would then infringe the copyright owner's right to perform the novel. Obviously the same result would arise if the play was written without permission. Another possible instance deals with choreography. As noted previously, nondramatic choreography can be registered in its notational form as a book. Apparently, the copyright in the book would prevent others from publicly performing for profit the dance taught in the book.

Performance and Recording Rights in Dramatic Works

The rights in dramatic works are set out in Section 1(d) of the Act, which establishes the rights:

> [t]o perform or represent the copyrighted work publicly if it be a drama or, if it be dramatic work and not reproduced in copies for sale, to vend any manuscript or any record whatsoever thereof; to make or to procure the making of any transcription or record thereof by or from which, in whole or in part, it may in any manner or by any method be exhibited, performed, represented, produced, or reproduced; and to exhibit, perform, represent, produce, or reproduce it in any manner or by any method whatsoever. . . .

Like Section 1(c), Section 1(d) sets out a number of specific rights. The right to perform with respect to dramatic works is logically the most important right. Unlike nondramatic works, there is no requirement that the performance be for profit; all public performances are protected. Also, dramatic works may be copyrighted either as published or unpublished works, and Section 1(d) grants as to unpublished works the exclusive right to vend any manuscript or any record whatsoever. It is not apparent that this right extends beyond the right to vend under Section

1(a), because the first-sale doctrine and Section 27 would still be applicable.

Section 1(d) also provides the exclusive right to record drama or to place it in a form from which it may be by any method exhibited. This would obviously include sound recordings of a dramatic work, and presumably also motion pictures of the work. *Drama* as used in this section includes dramatico-musical compositions. This issue was dealt with in a case involving the rock opera "Jesus Christ Superstar." In this case, a license had been obtained permitting the public performances for profit of the music of the opera. When the licensee attempted to produce the opera, it was enjoined on the ground that the separate right to perform the work, a dramatic composition, had not been conveyed in the license of the musical performing rights.

The rights enumerated in the last clause of Section 1(d) are unclear, because they seem to protect all exhibition, performance, production, or representation of the drama by any means. It is arguable that the "public" requirement is thereby eliminated, but all of the case law seems to indicate that only public performances are protected.

Performance and Recording Rights in Musical Compositions

Section 1(e) of the Act establishes rights available to the owner of a copyright in a musical composition. To the extent that a dramatico-musical composition consists of music alone, the rights in the music are governed by this section. The performance rights in the work as a drama, or even in the recording of the music in its dramatic sequence, are governed by Section 1(d). The rights provided by Section 1(e) are

> [t]o perform the copyrighted work publicly for profit if it be a musical composition; and for the purpose of public performance for profit, and for the purposes set forth in subsection (a) hereof, to make any arrangement or setting of it or of the melody of it in any system of notation or any form of record in which the thought of an author may be recorded and from which it may be read or reproduced. . . .

Thus this section provides for several specific rights: (1) to perform publicly for profit; (2) to make any arrangement or setting of the work in any notational system; and (3) to record the work. The public-performance-for-profit provision is like that for nondramatic literary works. A great deal of case law has been developed in this area as to what is a public performance for profit. The following activities have been held to be public and for profit: (1) live playing of music by an orchestra at a restaurant, (2) transmitting of radio music into hotel rooms by loudspeaker, (3) playing a copyrighted music roll during exhibition of a motion picture, for which admission was charged, and (4) broadcasting of music by radio or television where revenues are obtained from advertising.

Modern technology has caused a reassessment of certain of these conclusions, particularly with respect to the so-called multiple-performance doctrine. In the 1931 Supreme Court decision *Buck v. Jewell-LaSalle Realty Co.*, a hotel received radio signals off the air on its master receiver and transmitted the music received to its rooms for the enjoyment of its guests. Because the guests paid for their rooms and because the hotel was a public accommodation, there was relatively little question whether the hotel's action was public and for profit. The critical question was whether a performance had occurred. The Supreme Court held that indeed a performance had occurred, not only when the radio station broadcast the music, but when the hotel piped it into its rooms. Thus all the criteria were found to be met for an infringement of the copyright. It is from the fact that performances were found both by the radio broadcaster and the hotel that the term *multiple performance* derives.

One can readily think of other instances in which the multiple-performance doctrine comes into play. A common commercial example involves piped-in music services that draw their programming from radio broadcasts. In drawing radio performances off the air and transmitting them to places of business, a second performance occurs that is both public and for profit. Another common example, which is essentially an extension of the *Jewell-LaSalle* case, is that of the tavern that provides television for the enjoyment of its patrons. Every time a copyrighted program appears, be it musical or otherwise, a public performance for profit occurs, and thus technically an infringement.

As a practical matter, the multiple-performance doctrine has not been used to reach such technical infringing performances as the TV in the tavern, in part because of the obvious difficulty in enforcing against them, and partially, no doubt, because courts might well be reluctant to extend the doctrine to cover such situations. Today the multiple-performance doctrine is in a state of uncertainty because of two recent Supreme Court decisions involving community antenna television (CATV). CATV is essentially multiple performance on a grand scale. A giant community antenna receives a television signal off the air and either feeds it directly to home viewers' sets or retransmits it by microwave or cable to more distant sets. Such transmission is done for a fee and serves a public area. Nonetheless, the Supreme Court held that it was not a performance, and held *Jewell–LaSalle* inapplicable. In so holding, the Court cast serious doubt on the continuing vitality of the multiple-performance doctrine. Indeed, it is a dispute over the applicability of this doctrine to CATV that has in large part held up a general copyright revision that has been pending in Congress for years.

The Copyright Act includes two exceptions to the public-performance-for-profit right. The first of these, known as the "Juke Box Exception," provides that the "reproduction or rendition of a musical composition by or upon coin-operated machines shall not be deemed a public performance for profit unless a fee is charged for admission to the place where such reproduction or rendition occurs." Obviously this provision construes *for profit* much more narrowly than in general, because in other instances no admission fee need be charged as long as the performance aids in the making of a profit. The other exemption deals with charitable performances of religious or secular works. This provision states

> [t]hat nothing in this title shall be so construed as to prevent the performance of religious or secular works such as oratorios, cantatas, masses, or octavo choruses by public schools, church choirs, or vocal societies, rented, borrowed or obtained from some public library, public school, church choir, school choir or vocal society, provided the performance is given for charitable or educational purposes and not for profit.

Here, *not for profit* does not necessarily mean that an admission fee or other charge cannot be made, as long as the money raised is for charity or to defray costs of a nonprofit group covered by the exemption.

The second right secured for musical compositions under Section 1(e) is the right to arrange. At first blush, it appears that this right adds nothing to the right to make arrangements under Section 1(b). However, the right under Section 1(b) is limited to arrangements that are copies of the copyrighted work, whereas the right to arrange set out under 1(e) is "for the purposes of public performance for profit." It is well established that a phonograph record is not a copy, so a recording of a new arrangement would not infringe the right to arrange under Section 1(b). However, if made for the purpose of a public performance for profit (such as radio broadcasts), the recording would apparently infringe the right to arrange under Section 1(e).

The third right under Section 1(e) is the right to record. Unlike the right to record with respect to nondramatic literary works under 1(c), or dramatic works under 1(d), the right secured by Section 1(e) is limited by the inclusion of a compulsory licensing provision. Once the copyright owner makes or permits a recording to be made of his musical composition, he may no longer exclude others from making recordings of it. Anyone wishing to make a recording may do so upon paying a statutory royalty to the copyright owner of 2 cents per recording. There are, however, a number of procedural steps that must be taken, both on the part of the copyright owner and on the part of statutory licensees.

First it should be emphasized that until the first authorized recording, the copyright owner of a musical composition retains the exclusive right to record it. Upon making the first authorized recording, the copyright owner is then obligated to file a "notice of use" with the Copyright Office, stating that a recording has been made. This may be filed at any time, but until filed the copyright owner will not be able to recover against those who record the copyrighted composition. After this notice of use is filed, any person wishing to make a recording of the composition must send by registered mail to the copyright owner a notice of intent to use with a copy to the Copyright Office. Failure to send the notice of intent to use will avoid the creation of a compulsory license and will render the would-be licensee liable as an infringer. Upon creation of the compulsory license, the copyright owner may require the licensee to report to him, under oath, on the 20th day of each month, the number of recordings made for the previous month under the license. The statutory royalty is due for each month on the 20th of the succeeding month. Failure to pay the statutory royalty within thirty days of written demand will make the licensee liable for the statutory royalties plus up to three times the amount of royalties (or 6 cents, for a total of 8 cents per recording), as well as costs and reasonable attorneys fees.

The compulsory license procedure is somewhat cumbersome and contains pitfalls that may easily trap either the copyright owner or the licensee. Moreover, it is important to note what is and what is not protected by the right to record, especially in view of the protection afforded sound recordings under the 1971 amendment to the Copyright Act. The owner of a copyright in a musical composition is entitled, upon first authorizing recording of the composition, to the statutory 2-cent royalty for each recording manufactured by a statutory licensee. This royalty, however, is paid only on the underlying composition, and has no bearing on the actual performances in the recording. For example, if Burt Bachrach composes the music to the song "Promises, Promises" and authorizes the recording of it, any one wishing to make another recording may do so, assuming the notice formalities are met, upon paying the statutory royalties. The performers and producers who made the original authorized recording are entitled to no royalty, however. This may be of significance in the area of "record piracy." By paying the requisite statutory royalties, a pirate may be able to avoid liability to the copyright owner (Bachrach), even if he simply duplicates the authorized version by making a tape recording of it, although, we shall see shortly that several courts of appeals have recently held that payment of the statutory royalty does not authorize exact duplication of recordings. Prior to the 1971 Amendment, the performers and producers of the original record could obtain relief from such piracy only under state law under theories such as unfair competition. As will be seen in the following subsection, sound recordings copyrighted as such are entitled to protection apart from the copyright in the underlying music, and in such instances, the copyright owner may be able to obtain relief against piracy directly in an action for copyright infringement.

Sound Recordings—Limited Exclusive Rights

As we have mentioned previously, prior to the Sound Recording Amendment of 1971, recordings themselves were not subject to copyright. Although the underlying work, be it a musical, dramatic, or nondramatic literary work, was protected by the right to record, recordings themselves were not protected. With copyrighted dramatic and nondramatic literary works the lack of protection for recordings was not crucial, because duplication of existing recordings or making new recordings of the work would infringe the right to record. For musical compositions, however, the right to record is limited by the compulsory license provisions, and by paying the statutory royalty to the owner of the copyright in the underlying musical work, anyone could make recordings of it once an authorized recording had been made by the copyright owner.

It was in the area of so-called record piracy that the lack of protection for sound recordings created considerable difficulty. Pirates simply duplicated the original authorized recording, selling either tapes or, less frequently, record discs. If there was no copyright in the underlying work, the pirate was free from any copyright liability. If the underlying work was copyrighted, the pirate was obliged to pay the statutory 2 cents royalty to avoid infringing the underlying musical composition. In two suits for copyright infringement, it has been held by the U.S. Court of Appeals for the Ninth and Tenth Circuits that the compulsory license provision of Section 1(e) does not authorize exact duplication of sound recordings, but only recordings of new performances of the underlying work. This conclusion is based on the proposition that the compulsory license provisions apply only to the production of "similar" versions of the copyrighted work, and do not extend to exact duplication of recordings. Some commentators and several district courts have disagreed, concluding that upon payment of the statutory royalty, even exact duplication of the authorized recording does not fringe the copyright in the underlying work. Their argument is that if exact duplication is prohibited, the owner of the copyright in the underlying work would have a copyright monopoly in an uncopyrighted recording—a result inconsistent with the compulsory license provisions of Section 1(e) and incompatible with the absence of copyrightability for sound recordings prior to the Sound Recording Amendment of 1971. The two circuit court decisions, however, are the highest court rulings on this question to date, and unless other circuit courts disagree in the future, their holding must be considered authoritative. Even where the view of the Ninth and Tenth Circuits has not been adopted, unauthorized copying may be prevented under state law of unfair competition, or where applicable, state criminal laws of the type sustained in *Goldstein* v. *California*.

The Sound Recording Amendment of 1971 adds Section 1(f) to the Copyright Act, giving the owner of a copyright in a sound recording the exclusive right:

> To reproduce and distribute to the public by sale or other transfer of ownership, or by rental, lease, or lending, reproductions of the copyrighted work if it be a sound recording: *Provided*, That the exclusive right of the owner of a copyright in a sound recording to reproduce it is limited to the right to duplicate the sound recording in a tangible form that directly or indirectly recaptures the actual sounds fixed in the recording: *Provided further*, That this right does not extend to the making or duplication of another sound recording that is an independent fixation of other sounds, even though such sounds imitate or simulate those in the copyrighted sound recording; or to reproductions made by transmitting organizations exclusively for their own use.

Although this provision is new and has not been the subject of significant judicial construction, a number of points may be made about it. First, Section 1(f) clearly provides only limited rights, and appears to be self-contained. That is, the general rights set out in Sections 1(a) and (b) do not appear to be applicable to sound recordings. Thus the rights to publish and vend, normally set out in Section 1(a), are repeated in Section 1(f) as the rights to transfer ownership, rent, lease, and lend reproductions of the copyrighted work. More importantly, the premier right of Section 1(a), the right to copy, is significantly limited in Section 1(f). Only the duplication of the actual sounds on the copyrighted recording is prohibited by Section 1(f), and the first proviso clause explicitly excepts the imitation or simulation of the sounds by an independent fixation of other sounds. Clearly, then, what would be a copy for purposes of Section 1(a) may well not be an infringing duplication under 1(f). For example, if the copyrighted recording is of a particular singer accompanied by a specific band singing a popular song, another recording of the same song by the same singer with the same accompaniment would not infringe the record copyright. Only if the copyrighted record were duplicated so that the same sounds originally fixed on the record were transferred to the new recording (as by magnetic tape), would there be an infringing copy.

In addition to the preceding, there is a further limitation on the rights in sound recordings set out in the second proviso. Thus "reproductions made by transmitting organizations exclusively for their own use" are not infringements of the copyright in the sound recording. The legislative history of the amendment makes relatively clear that this means that a broadcaster may duplicate the copyrighted recording and transmit it over the air without infringing the copyright in the recording. Another apparent limitation, not specifically set forth in the amendment but mentioned in the report of the House Committee on the Amendment, is an exemption for home recording. Thus the committee stated that "it is not the intention of the Committee to restrain the home recording, from broadcasts or from tapes or records, of recorded performances, where the home recording is for private use and with no purpose of reproducing or otherwise capitalizing commercially on it." This home recording exemption might be looked upon as a specie of fair use, discussed in the section of this chapter dealing with defenses to infringement.

Moral Rights—The Author's Image

Strictly speaking, so-called moral rights are not rights incident to copyright. Indeed, the existence of moral rights is not expressly recognized in the United States and is sometimes explicitly denied. Nonetheless, there are certain rights that an author has in his work, whether or not it is copyrighted, that courts will generally uphold on some traditional theory such as unfair competition, libel, or invasion of privacy.

The moral rights of an author most commonly recognized are the right to prevent the distortion or truncation of his work, the right to prevent false attribution of his name to works not written by him, and the right to prevent others from using his work or name so as to injure or reflect on his professional reputation or standing. Another right sometimes asserted is the right of an author to be known as the author of his work. The following examples typify the means by which courts will enforce moral rights. In one case, the right to prevent distortion was upheld under a theory of unfair competition so as to prevent a television network from inserting commercials into a motion picture for TV exhibition in such a way as to "alter, adversely affect or emasculate the artistic or pictorial quality" of the film. The right to prevent false attribution is often upheld under a theory of libel, because the use of an author's name with a work he did not create may demean his reputation, especially if the work is inferior to his own writings. Even the truthful attribution of an author's name to a work can sometimes be an invasion of privacy or constitute a libel. This is especially so when the work is unpublished. Thus in one case a college professor was able to enjoin the publication of notes taken from his lectures both on common law copyright grounds and on the ground that the use of his name with the notes implied his approval of the commercial note publication service, which service he in fact deplored. On the other hand, the truthful attribution of an author's name to a work in the public domain is normally not actionable, even if the author dislikes the context in which his work is used.

The right of an author to have his name associated with his work is sometimes stated as a right recognized in this country, but most cases state that the right is solely contractual. The author has this right only if he expressly reserves it, and otherwise there is no obligation to identify him as the author. Chapter 6 elaborates on closely related rights.

WHO CAN OBTAIN COPYRIGHT?

Introduction

The Copyright Act in Section 9 states that copyright may be obtained by "[t]he author or proprietor" or "his executors, administrators, or assigns." Obviously, all those other than the author can obtain a copyright only by virtue of their succession to the author's right. The right to obtain a statutory copyright presupposes the existence of an unpublished copyrightable work. The author will have a common law copyright in his unpublished work, and it is by succession to the author's common law copyright that those other than the author may claim copyright. Thus if an author of an unpublished work dies, his executor or the administrator of his estate succeeds to the common law copyright and may obtain a statutory copyright on behalf of the author's legatees or heirs. So, too, if the author assigns his common law right to another, his assignee may then seek a statutory copyright. The designation of the proprietor of a copyrightable work as one who may seek statutory copyright seems to add little if anything to the statutory designation of *assigns*. However, as will be seen in the section on copyright ownership, the term *proprietor* is broader than the term *assigns* or *assignee*, and thus anyone who may be called a proprietor may seek copyright.

An interesting question arises as to who is an author under the Copyright Act. The Act itself gives little guidance. As we have seen in the case of sound recordings, the author may be the performers or the producer who orchestrates the efforts of the performers, engineers, and technicians. Similarly, in the case of motion pictures, authorship can reside in the actors, the director, the cameraman, or the producer who arranges the confluence of their efforts. As a matter of practice, the law has tended to leave these questions to the contractual understandings of the parties, and in the case of sophisticated artistic or literary endeavors, the contractual arrangements are normally sufficient to eliminate any difficulties concerning authorship. In many cases, moreover, the question of authorship where multiple efforts are involved may be settled by the law relating to works done for hire.

Works for Hire

Section 26 of the Copyright Act defines the word *author* as including "an employer in the case of works made for hire." When operative, this provision makes the employer the author of a work and permits him to obtain copyright in his own name. The crucial questions that must be asked are whether an employer–employee relationship exists, and whether contractual undertakings will affect the language of the statute.

An employment relationship will exist only if the employer is entitled to direct and supervise the employee in the performance of his work. It should be noted, however, that actual supervision and direction may not be necessary, as long as the employer has the right to supervise. This is especially so when one is hired specifically to create a particular work, in which event the absence of actual supervision can hardly gainsay the employment relationship. Nonetheless, merely because one is an employee does not mean that authorship of all his works is in his employer. Thus copyright in works that are not created as part of his employment duties will be vested in the employee. This is not to say, however, that in such a case the employer may not have a "shop right" in the work as we have seen in the analogous area of patentable inventions, p. 56. If the subject matter of the work arises out of the employee's activities for his employer, or if he works on company time, it may be argued that the employer obtains a shop right, or nonexclusive, nonassignable, royalty-free license in the work extending for the duration of the copyright term.

Obviously, if the requisite right to control and supervise is not present, an employment relationship does not exist. This is typical in the case of an independent contractor, where a work is commissioned and the contractor creates the work on his own or with minimal supervision; this sort of case sometimes involves a ghost writer. In this situation it is arguable that the work belongs either to the party commissioning the work or to the contractor, but most cases hold that it belongs to the commissioning party. Nonetheless, a strong argument can be made that the commissioning party is entitled to the copyright not as the "author" of a work done for hire, but rather as the proprietor of a work authored by another. That is, by virtue of the contractual understanding between the parties, the one who commissions the work becomes the proprietor of it. This distinction is significant, because, as we shall see, the renewal rights in works done for hire vest in the proprietor, whereas in other cases they belong to the author. Thus in the case of a work done for hire, the employer is entitled to claim copyright renewal; but in the case of a commissioned work, the renewal right will belong to the author.

Notwithstanding the provisions of the Act, the parties to an employment relationship may modify their respective copyright rights by contract; an employment contract may validly reserve copyright to the employee, subject only to an exclusive license in the employer for certain rights. And, on the other hand, even work done by the employee outside the scope of his employment can belong to the employer if the contract of employment clearly shows such an intent. Here, too, however, it appears that the employer would be considered to be the owner of the copyright by virtue of contractual proprietorship rather than "authorship."

Composite Works

Section 3 of the Copyright Act provides in part that "[t]he copyright upon composite works or periodicals shall give the proprietor thereof all the rights in respect thereto which he would have if each part were individually copyrighted under this title." As a result of this provision, a single copyright notice on a composite work, such as a magazine containing short stories, cartoons, and photographs, will be effective to protect each component part. Although there is some question whether this is always true because of the application of the so-called doctrine of indivisibility, we will see later in this chapter that a novel first published as a serial in the *Saturday Evening Post* was held protected by the magazine's copyright.

An interesting question arises, however, as to who is the owner of a copyright in a component of a composite work. Obviously, if the component part carries a separate copyright notice in the name of the author, copyright will subsist in the author. But most often this is not the case, and the work bears only a single notice. In such a case it has been held that the copyright in the component part belongs to the proprietor of the composite work, but that he holds that copyright *in trust* for the author. In this way the author is protected in that publication does not cause his work to pass into the public domain, and at the same time he becomes the beneficial owner of the copyright in his work.

Governmental Works

Section 8 of the Copyright Act provides that "[n]o copyright shall subsist . . . in any publication of the United States Government, or any reprint, in whole or in part, thereof. . . ." The term *publication* has been held to refer only to printed publications, so that a copyrightable work, such as a sculpture, could be registered notwithstanding the fact that it was produced by the government. In order to be considered a "government publication," a work must have been prepared by a government employee or officer in the scope of his employment. Thus a work prepared by a government employee, not within the scope of his duties, has been held not to be a government publication even though the subject matter of the work dealt with his employment and the author utilized special knowledge gained during the scope of his employment.

Although it is not entirely clear, it would appear that a work specially commissioned by the government will be considered a government publication, even if the author acted as an independent contractor. On the other hand, a work created by a government contractor that was not commissioned, but that was developed by the contractor during the course of his duties, would not be a governmental publication. The contractor of such a work would be the author. Proprietorship, and therefore entitlement to claim copyright, would be determined by the contractual relationship between the parties. Thus the government can claim copyright as the proprietor of nongovernmental publications, and moreover, it can become a copyright proprietor by assignment of a work already copyrighted.

PROCEDURES FOR OBTAINING COPYRIGHT

The Copyright Office

The Copyright Office is a branch of the Library of Congress. The office itself is located in Arlington, Virginia, in the same general building complex as is the Patent Office, but the Library of Congress is in Washington, D.C., about a block from the Capitol. The chief officer of the Copyright Office is the register of copyrights. The register oversees all the functions of the Copyright Office, under the direction and supervision of the librarian. The Copyright Office maintains a corps of examiners who review registration applications as they are filed, making sure that they comply with the various requirements of the Copyright Act and the regulations issued by the office. For the most part these duties are ministerial, and the office will not make judgments as to the artistic or literary merits of works. Occasionally, however, registration will be refused on the ground that a statutory formality is not complied with. And, as we have seen, the Copyright Office has taken the position that some types of works are not copyrightable. In these cases, too, registration will be refused.

If the Copyright Office refuses to register a copyright, the applicant's only recourse is to bring an action against the register to compel registration. This type of action is known as mandamus, and its purpose is to force the performance of the register's duty. Mandamus actions must be brought in federal district court. Needless to say, such suits are time-consuming and expensive, and also they rarely succeed, because the court gives great deference to the register's decision and to the practice of the Copyright Office. In addition to the registration of copyrights, the Copyright Office performs important functions in supplying books for the collection of the Library of Congress. As we shall see, each registration application must be accompanied by a deposit of one or two copies of the work. From these deposited copies the Library of Congress may select those books it wishes to have transferred to its permanent collections, or to other governmental libraries in the District of Columbia. Deposited copies that are not used by the Library of Congress may be destroyed by the Copyright Office after a suitable time. However, provisions are made so that the copyright proprietor, author, or other claimant may have an opportunity to claim and remove any copy before its destruction. In the case of manuscripts deposited for copyright as unpublished works, no destruction can occur until the copyright proprietor has been given actual notice and an opportunity to claim the manuscript.

The Copyright Office is an extremely helpful government agency. It publishes many pamphlets that explain how copyrights can be obtained and registered; it also assists authors in obtaining registration. All such pamphlets and information as well as registration application forms and renewal application forms may be obtained free of charge by writing to the following: Register of Copyrights, Library of Congress, Washington, D.C. 20540. In addition, the office will perform certain searching services for a fee of $5 per hour. Thus the office will search its records, indexes, and deposits to determine, for example, whether a particular copyright has been renewed or whether copies of a work have been duly deposited. All of the duties of the Copyright Office, however, depend on the author's taking the first steps to secure copyright. In the following pages we shall see what these steps are.

Publication

As discussed in the overview to this chapter, publication is the central concept upon which American copyright law hinges. A work that is published loses common law protection, and if publication is not accompanied by certain formalities, especially proper copyright notice, the work does not gain statutory copyright protection and thus is thrust into the public domain. Although publication without appropriate notice will inject the work published into the public domain, it is not always a necessary step in obtaining federal copyright protection. Section 12 of the Copyright Act provides that certain works, copies of which are not reproduced for sale, may be copyrighted as unpublished works. The categories of works included under this section are lectures and similar productions; dramatic, musical, and dramatico-musical compositions; motion pictures, whether photoplays or not; photographs; works of art; and plastic works or drawings. Those types of registrable works that are not enumerated in Section 12 may be copyrighted only as published works. These are books, periodicals, maps, reproductions of works of art, prints and labels, and sound recordings.

The works enumerated in Section 12 may be registered by depositing with the Copyright Office a copy of the work, together with a claim of copyright. The details of deposit will be dealt with shortly, but it suffices to note here that only one copy need be deposited under Section 12, whereas registration of published works requires the deposit of two copies. Furthermore, unpublished works registered under Section 12 require only a claim of copyright, which is essentially the registration form. In contrast, published works must be accompanied by copyright notice in order to obtain statutory copyright.

The reader may have noted previously that lectures and similar works prepared for oral delivery are registered as unpublished works only. Such registration is made under Section 12. When published, these works are generally registered as books. We have seen that oral delivery of a speech is not a publication; so long as such a work is not published, as by printing and distributing it, it may be registered under Section 12. It is important to note that works registered under Section 12 are protected only so long as they remain unpublished. Upon publication, an additional registration is necessary with all the formalities required for published works. It is important, too, to note that the provision for registration of unpublished works is optional. Because only publication will divest the common law rights of the author, he may rely on these rights rather than registering his work under Section 12. If the author does in fact register his unpublished works, however, he may be held to have forfeited any common law rights and be forced to rely on statutory protection.

Notice

Publication with notice is the most important formality necessary to secure copyright protection in published works. Section 10 of the Act provides that "[a]ny person entitled thereto by this title may secure copyright for his work by publication thereof with the notice of copyright required by this title; and such notice shall be affixed to each copy thereof published or offered for sale in the United States by authority of the copyright proprietor. . . ." The reader should note the language of this section carefully. It states that copyright may be *secured* by publication with notice. These acts establish a copyright in the author. They do not, however, give the author a registered copyright, because the additional step of registration is necessary. And, as will be seen later, registration is a condition precedent to enforcing rights under the copyright. Nonetheless, publication with notice is all that is necessary *to secure* copyright in published works. Thus publication with notice operates to create copyright, whereas publication without notice bars copyright. The additional steps of registration and deposit of copies are necessary to perfect the author's right to sue, but the single most important requirement is that publication be accompanied by notice. (Of course, as we have seen, some works may be registered under Section 12 before publication, and thus do not require notice. Upon publication of these works, however, appropriate notice becomes necessary.)

What kind of notice is necessary in order to secure a copyright under Section 10? The form of notice is set out in Section 19 of the Act. This section provides that for printed literary, musical, or dramatic works, copyright notice shall consist of the word *Copyright*, the abbreviation *Copr.*, or the symbol ©, accompanied by the name of the copyright proprietor and the year in which the copyright was secured by publication. In the case of maps, works of art, reproductions of works of art, drawings or plastic work, photographs, and prints and labels, such notice need not include the year of publication, and the "initials, monogram, mark, or symbol" of the copyright owner may be substituted for his name. However, if the proprietor's name is not used with this short form of copyright notice, it must appear "on some accessible portion of [the work] or of the margin, back, permanent base, or pedestal, or of the substance on which [the work] shall be mounted."

In the case of sound recordings notice consists of the symbol ℗, the year of first publication, and the name of the owner of the copyright, or an abbreviation by which the name can be recognized or a generally known designation of the owner. If, however, the producer of the sound recording is named on the label or container of the sound recording and if no other name appears in conjunction with the notice, his name shall be considered a part of the notice.

For some types of works, the Copyright Act specifies where the notice must be placed. Thus for books or other printed publications, notice must appear on the title page or the page immediately following.

For periodicals, notice must appear either on the title page or on the first page of text for each separate number or under the title heading. For musical works, notice should be applied either on the title page or on the first page of music. Further, the statute provides that for newspapers and periodicals, one notice in each volume or in each number shall suffice.

As the reader can readily appreciate, these notice requirements are complex and sometimes ambiguous. Accordingly, a great body of judicial interpretation has been built up over the years construing the notice requirements. Moreover, although the Copyright Act provides in some instances for alternative forms of notice, there may be good reasons why one particular form of notice should be used. For example, under the Act, the forms *Copyright, Copr.*, and © may be used interchangeably. However, the only form of notice designated under the Universal Copyright Convention (UCC) is ©. As will be seen later, some authors depend on the UCC for obtaining copyright in the United States, and for them only the © form of notice would suffice unless all other U.S. formalities are met. Similarly, only printed literary, dramatic, and musical works and sound recordings require the year of publication to accompany notice under the Copyright Act, whereas under the UCC the year of publication is always required. For these practical reasons it may be advisable, and in some cases essential, to follow the UCC form of notice.

Apart from the preceding somewhat esoteric considerations, there are very real and practical problems associated with copyright notice. One problem is what year should accompany notice when the inclusion of the year is necessary. For sound recordings there is no difficulty, because the statute refers to the year of first publication. For printed literary, musical, or dramatic works, however, the answer is less clear. Here the statute states that notice shall include the "year in which the copyright was secured by publication." For a work copyrighted upon publication, of course, the year of first publication would apply. For a work—for example, a musical composition—first copyrighted as an unpublished work under Section 12 if this work is subsequently published, judicial authority seems to indicate that the year in which the work was first registered for copyright under Section 12 should be the year to accompany the copyright notice. Other questions involving the year of publication arise with respect to derivative works and works covered by renewal copyrights. For example, if a play based on a copyrighted novel is published, judicial construction indicates that it is the date of publication of the play which should appear on the notice.

Another question of notice involves the appearance of the proprietor's name with the copyright notice. It is clear from judicial decisions that the proprietor need not use his full name with copyright notice, and may use a trade or fictitious name or his initials if that is how he is known to the public. As provided by the Copyright Act, for some types of works the name may be omitted from the notice and the copyright proprietor's "initials, monogram, mark or symbol" may be used instead, but only if his name appears elsewhere on or with the work. However, if the proprietor's initials sufficiently identify him to the public, he need not include his full name elsewhere on the work in the case of those works for which the short form of notice is satisfactory. Thus in one case involving copyrighted jewelry, the manufacturer of the jewelry used only its initials with the copyright notice. The court found that the proprietor was well known in the trade by its initials, and indeed used the initials as its trade name. The jewelry was copyrighted as a work of art, entitling it to the short form of notice. Because the court found the manufacturer's initials tantamount to its name, it held there was no need for the manufacturer's name to appear elsewhere in association with the jewelry, and thus upheld the notice as valid.

Probably the most difficult problems associated with copyright notice involve the location of notice on the work. It should be borne in mind that the principal purpose of notice is to advise the public of the copyright proprietor's claim and to prevent innocent infringement of the copyright. Thus, common sense dictates that notice should be placed where it can readily be observed. We have already noted that the Copyright Act has specific requirements for the location of notice in books, periodicals, and printed music. For books and other printed publications the notice must appear on the title page or the page immediately following. The title page is generally the first page of the book specifically setting forth the title. In case of a book having no title page, the cover may be considered the title page if it bears the title, and if the work is untitled, the first page is probably the title page for purposes of copyright notice. The page immediately following the title page is normally considered to be the overleaf side of the title page, rather than the next leaf.

For periodicals the notice may appear on the title page or on the front page of text of each separate number or under the title heading. Although the Act provides that "[o]ne notice of copyright in each volume or in each number of a newspaper or periodical published shall suffice," the trade practice assumes that each separately published issue of a newspaper or periodical requires its own notice. For musical works notice shall appear on the title page or on the first page of music. Because published music rarely contains a title page as a book does, the title page for notice purposes has been held to be the cover. The preceding discussion details some of the problems associated with the location of notice on works for which the Copyright Act designates a specific location. For works not so designated, the location of copyright notice is largely a matter of judicial construction. The Copyright Office Regulations, however, give some guidance as to various forms of defective notice. Thus the Regulations list the following types of defective notice:

... (2) The elements of the notice are ... dispersed ...

(4) The notice is in a foreign language ...

(7) A notice is permanently covered so that it cannot be seen without tearing the work apart;

(8) A notice is illegible or so small that it cannot be read without the aid of a magnifying glass: *Provided, however,* That where the work itself requires magnification for its ordinary use (e.g., a microfilm, microcard or motion picture) a notice which will be readable when so magnified, will not constitute a reason for rejection of the claim;

(9) A notice is on a detachable tag and will eventually be detached and discarded when the work is put in use;

(10) A notice is on the wrapper or container which is not a part of the work and which will eventually be removed and discarded when the work is put to use. . . .

For the most part these regulations are self-explanatory. Item (2), referring to dispersal of the elements of the notice, applies where the elements (e.g., name, symbol ©, and date) are so spread out on the work that they cannot reasonably be perceived as part of a unitary copyright notice.

Apart from the preceding rules, notice will be effective if it is placed in such a way that anyone seeking to copy the work can reasonably be forewarned that a copyright is claimed. Thus valid notice has been upheld appearing on the back of a work, and even on the underside. However, a copyright notice appearing on a giant statue of a marine in full battle dress, mounted on a pedestal so that observers were some 22 feet from the site of the notice was held to be inadequate. In part this result was reached because the notice could have been placed in a more accessible spot, and in part because there was evidence that it was deliberately concealed. A final topic of interest concerning the adequacy of copyright notice relates to graphic designs, especially to fabric designs. These designs often consist of a repetition of one basic pattern upon paper or fabric. Common examples are wrapping paper, textiles, and wallpaper. In a famous decision in 1914, *DeJonge* v. *Breuker & Kessler Co.,* the Supreme Court was concerned with the adequacy of notice on a wrapping paper that carried a checkerboard pattern of clusters of holly and mistletoe. Each sheet of paper bore only a single copyright notice. The Court, through Justice Holmes, held that each cluster was individually the work of art subject to copyright, and therefore that the notice was ineffective because each cluster should have been accompanied by a separate notice.

This harsh result has been avoided by some courts by resorting to fictions as to the nature of the work copyrighted. Thus in one case the U.S. Court of Appeals for the Second Circuit was confronted with an almost identical situation. In this instance a textile fabric was imprinted with a checkerboard pattern made up of clusters of roses. The court distinguished the *DeJonge* case on the ground that the work copyrighted was not the single rose square from which the design was created, but "rather the composite design itself, which depends for its aesthetic effect upon both the rose figure and the manner in which the reproductions of that figure are arranged in relation to each other upon the fabric." Finding the copyright to subsist in the entire pattern rather than simply in the individual design making up the composite, the court concluded that one copyright notice per 16 inches of fabric satisfied the notice requirements because 16-inch units were the smallest size in which the fabric was normally commercially sold.

Perhaps the most startling case involving copyright notice on textile fabrics is the famous decision by Judge Learned Hand in *Peter Pan Fabrics, Inc.* v. *Martin Weiner Corp.* This case dealt with a common practice in the textile fabrics industry. When printing a design on fabric, the practice was to print the copyright notice on the selvage or margin of the fabric, rather than incorporate it in the design itself. When the fabric was purchased in bolts, the notice was present and was considered adequate. However, when cut and sewn to make apparel, the selvage was either cut away entirely or else sewn into the seams so that the notice was not visible unless the seams were pulled apart or the garment turned inside out. This practice was attacked on the ground that it did not satisfy the requirements of Section 10 of the Copyright Act, namely, that notice be affixed to each copy of the work offered for sale. It was argued that the sale of dresses made from the fabric was not done with adequate notice and that the copyright proprietor knew that dresses made from the fabric would not bear the proper notice. The court rejected this argument, noting that the defendants had copied the fabric knowing of the copyright notice. It held, moreover, that the incorporation of the notice into the design itself might well have impaired the design's aesthetic appeal. Therefore, the court concluded, one who knowingly copies a copyrighted design in which notice is not incorporated bears the burden of showing that notice could have been embodied in the design without impairing its market value, in order to establish the defense of improper notice.

The holding of the *Peter Pan Fabrics* case, which serves to minimize the obligation of notice where notice would impair the commercial value of the work, has been accepted in a number of other cases involving fabric designs, and seems to be becoming the rule of law in this field. Some cases, however, following the facts of *Peter Pan* rather than Judge Hand's broad language, require that there have been adequate notice when the fabric left the proprietor's hands.

Registration and Deposit

We have seen that there is a difference in obtaining copyright for published works under Section 10 of the Copyright Act, and for certain unpublished works under Section 12. For the former, publication with notice secures the copyright; registration and deposit of copies are necessary only to perfect the right to sue. For the latter, registration of a claim of copyright along with the deposit of a copy of the work is necessary to secure the copyright in the first instance. In both cases, registration entails simply filing with the Copyright Office a properly executed registration form, together with the applicable statutory registration fee. These forms, together with explanatory materials, are available without charge from the Copyright Office. Simply write to Register of Copyrights, Library of Congress, Washington, D.C. 20540.

The deposit requirements differ for works copyrighted pursuant to Section 12 or Section 10. Under Section 12, only one copy need be filed, and this section specifically provides what kind of copy needs to be filed to satisfy the deposit requirement. For lectures and similar productions, dramatic, musical, and dramatico-musical works, a complete copy must be filed. For motion picture photoplays, the title and a description along with one print taken from each scene or act will suffice. For photographs, a print will suffice. For motion pictures other than photoplays, the title and a description, along with at least two prints taken from different sections, may be filed. For works of art and plastic works or drawings, a photograph or other reproduction will suffice.

For works copyrighted by publication with notice, the deposit of copies is governed by Section 13. In most instances the deposit required is of two complete copies of the "best edition" of the work then published. The term *best edition* simply requires that the edition deposited be the best published at the time of deposit. In the case of sound recordings, the Copyright Office has stated that discs are preferred over tapes, and stereophonic recordings over monophonic ones. As between tapes, open reel is preferred over cartridge, and cartridge is preferred over cassette. In the case of a work by an author who is a citizen of another country, which work is first published abroad, only one complete copy of the best edition need be filed. However, the copy filed must have been in accordance with the manufacturing clause discussed in the following section. If the work is a contribution to a periodical, and if registration is sought specifically for the contribution, one copy of each issue of the periodical containing the contribution must be deposited.

For works of art, reproductions of works of art, drawings or plastic works, and prints and labels, the Act provides that the Register of Copyrights may waive the requirement for deposit of two complete copies if it is impracticable because of the "size, weight, fragility, or monetary value" of the work. In this case photographs or other reproductions may be deposited. Copyright Office regulations set out in detail the requirements for the deposit of photographs or reproductions in lieu of copies. These regulations provide as follows:

1. The number of sets of photographs shall be the same as the number of copies that Section 13 would normally require. Thus two sets will be necessary except for works of alien authors first published outside the United States. Each set shall consist of as many photographs as are necessary to identify the work.

2. All photographs shall be of equal size, not less than 5×7 inches nor more than 9×12 inches, but preferably 8×10 inches. The image shall be lifesize or larger, or if less than lifesize, at least 4 inches at its greatest dimension. The exact measurement of at least one dimension should be indicated on at least one photograph.

3. At least one photograph should show the copyright notice. If this is infeasible, a drawing may be included of the same size as the photographs, showing the exact appearance of the notice, its dimensions, and its position on the work.

4. The title of the work shall appear on the front or back of each photograph.

Although the criteria for depositing photographs instead of copies are established by statute, the Copyright Office reserves the right to require actual copies in any specific case. Moreover, copies will be required in the case of fine prints and two-dimensional art reproductions.

Section 13 requires that copies shall be deposited "promptly" after publication of the work with copyright notice. It further provides that no action for copyright infringement may be maintained until such copies have been filed. This requirement of prompt deposit was considered by the Supreme Court in *Washingtonian Publishing Co.* v. *Pearson.* The Court in this case held that the term *promptly* put no particular time limit on the deposit of copies. Until such copies were deposited, no infringement action could be maintained, but a delay of more than a year in depositing the copies was held not to bar suing for infringement.

Although delay in depositing copies will not, under the rule of the *Washingtonian* case, invalidate a copyright, the Act, in Section 14, does permit the register of copyrights to demand deposit. Section 14 provides that at any time after publication, upon actual notice, the register may require the copyright proprietor to deposit copies, and if the proprietor does not comply, the copyright is void and the proprietor is subject to a $100 fine and to pay the librarian of Congress twice the amount of the retail price of the best edition of the work. For proprietors in the United States the period for compliance is three months. For proprietors in foreign countries and in outlying territorial possessions of the United States the time period is six months.

We have noted that works copyrighted under Section 12 as unpublished works have different deposit requirements from those established for published works. The last sentence of Section 12 states that the "privilege of registration of copyright secured hereunder shall not exempt the copyright proprietor from the deposit of copies, under sections 13 and 14 of this title, where the work is later reproduced in copies for sale." This provision means that upon publication of a work first copyrighted under Section 12, the deposit provisions of Section 13, entailing the deposit of additional copies, must be complied with.

The Manufacturing Clause

Section 16 of the Copyright Act, commonly known as the manufacturing clause, is a parochial restriction placed in the Act to benefit the domestic printing and bookbinding industries. It has little if anything to do with the common concerns of copyright, namely the promotion of art and literary endeavor and the reward of artists and authors. Still, because this complex and archaic provision is part of the Copyright Act and because it has considerable bearing on the validity of copyrights in books and periodicals, it must be discussed. In general, the manufacturing clause provides that in order to receive copyright protection, the text of any printed book or periodical, except non-English language books or periodicals of foreign origin, must be printed from type set within the United States, or from plates made within the United States from type set therein, or, if produced by a lithographic or photoengraving process, such process must be wholly performed within the United States. With regard to books, but apparently not periodicals, the clause requires that the actual printing and binding must also be performed within the United States. The clause extends to illustrations as well as text when the book consists of both and is produced by lithography or photoengraving, and also applies to separate lithographs or photoengravings except where the subjects represented are located in a foreign country and illustrate a scientific work or reproduce a work of art.

The manufacturing clause contains certain explicit exceptions. First, works of foreign origin in a language other than English are excluded. Second, works printed in raised characters for use by the blind are excluded. Third, works produced by any means other than those specified in the clause are not included within its requirements. Obviously, too, only books and lithographs and engravings (with the noted scientific and art-reproduction exceptions), and to a lesser extent periodicals, are included. Thus, in one case a dramatic composition printed in book form was held not to be covered by the manufacturing clause. Finally, within certain limits, works with *ad interim* copyrights, discussed later in this chapter, are excluded from the requirements of the manufacturing clause. The effect of the manufacturing clause is that in order to be entitled to American copyright protection, a work of domestic origin or a foreign origin work in English must be published in an edition manufactured in the United States. There are, as noted, certain exceptions to this requirement, and the *ad interim* copyright provisions give some relief for foreign authors of English language books. Today, as will be discussed later, the burden of the manufacturing requirement has been removed altogether for qualified foreign authors by the UCC and the enabling provisions of Section 9(c) of the Copyright Act.

An interesting case involving the effect of the manufacturing clause on American authors arose in connection with the book *Candy*. This book, written by two American authors, was first published in France without compliance with the manufacturing requirements. Indeed, this famous "dirty" book was no doubt published abroad because the authors feared for its safety under U.S. obscenity laws. In any event, some six years later an American edition, complying with the manufacturing clause, was published. The book did not fall within any of the exemptions provided by the manufacturing clause, and therefore the Copyright Office refused to register a copyright in it on the ground that initial publication in violation of the clause's requirements barred copyright. This refusal to register was upheld in a 1968 decision of the U.S. Court of Appeals for the District of Columbia.

The *Candy* case implicitly holds that failure to comply with the manufacturing clause bars copyright altogether. Some older cases had suggested that failure to comply simply rendered the noncomplying copies unprotected and did not invalidate the claim of copyright, but in view of the *Candy* decision and at least one other recent case, this holding is dubious. Therefore the cautious view must be that failure to observe the strictures of the manufacturing clause will result in total loss of copyright protection in the work itself. In any event, books deposited for registration under Section 13 must of course comply with the manufacturing requirements of Section 16. Section 17 requires that an affidavit of such compliance must be filed along with the deposit, and

Section 18 provides that the knowingly false making of such an affidavit will result in a fine of up to $1,000 on a misdemeanor conviction and in *forfeiture of the copyright*. Therefore if the manufacturing clause is knowingly violated, the deposit of copies necessary as a condition precedent to bringing an infringement action will likely bar ever enforcing the copyright.

Copyright Duration and Renewals

Copyright Duration. From the definition of common law copyright, namely, that it is the author's right of first publication, it is apparent that the right exists until the first authorized publication. In other words, the common law copyright is potentially perpetual in duration, and may be claimed until such time as the proprietor chooses to exercise his right to publish. At that time the right is extinguished, and the work passes into the public domain unless statutory copyright is obtained. Statutory copyright, on the other hand, is distinctly limited in time. Indeed, were it not, statutory copyright would be unconstitutional, because under the copyright clause of the Constitution, Congress may secure to authors exclusive rights in their writings only for "limited times." Under the Copyright Act, statutory copyright endures for a term of twenty-eight years and is renewable for a similar term. Thus the maximum total time of copyright duration in a particular work is fifty-six years, after which the world is free to copy without concern over infringement. There indeed exist enterprising publishers who regularly seek out commercially worthwhile publications whose copyrights have expired. In recent years, for example, bookstores in urban markets have carried reprints of turn-of-the-century Sears Roebuck & Co. mail order catalogs whose copyrights have expired. This store of "Americana" has found a receptive Christmas season market.

One issue that arises with respect to the duration of copyright protection is the date on which the term starts to run. Section 24 of the Act provides that the twenty-eight-year term starts to run from the date of first publication. For works copyrighted upon publication with notice pursuant to Section 10, there is no difficulty in determining when the term runs. What about works copyrighted under Section 12 as unpublished works? If the twenty-eight-year term did not begin to run until the work was published, an author of a work qualifying for copyright under Section 12 could effectively obtain a perpetual statutory copyright by not publishing his works. This result would clearly be unconstitutional, and the U.S. Court of Appeals for the Ninth Circuit has held that for works copyrighted under Section 12, the term of protection runs from the date of registration.

There is one situation in which the copyright term may effectively be shortened. If the copyright notice erroneously identifies the year in which copyright was first secured as earlier than the actual year, the copyright owner will be bound by that earlier date. Thus, although the measuring term will still be twenty-eight years, the effective term will be less because the erroneous starting date will be used. For example, if the copyright notice states "© John Doe 1956" when the correct date should have been 1965, John Doe will lose nine years of his copyright term.

As this book is written, Congress is still considering major revisions in the copyright laws. Since 1962, therefore, Congress has passed a series of concurrent resolutions extending the term of copyrights. Under these resolutions, the term of all renewal copyrights that would have expired after September 19, 1962, has been extended. The effect of such extensions apply only to the renewal term of copyrights. Thus copyrights whose first term expires during the extension period must be properly renewed to continue; only those copyrights already in their renewal term are extended.

Copyright Renewal. The second twenty-eight-year term may be secured by filing with the Copyright Office an appropriate application for renewal at any time during the twenty-eighth year of the original term. Failure to so file and register the renewal will result in termination of the copyright at the end of the twenty-eighth year. Although the procedure for obtaining copyright renewal, as outlined in the preceding paragraph, appears straightforward and simple, as is so often the case under the Copyright Act, in practice it is exceedingly complex and vexacious. The reason for this complexity arises from the question of who is entitled to renewal. Section 24 sets forth who is entitled to renewal in two proviso clauses, both of which are remarkable for their opacity. The first proviso states:

> That in the case of any posthumous work or of any periodical, cyclopedic, or other composite work upon which the copyright was originally secured by the proprietor thereof, or of any work copyrighted by a corporate body (otherwise than as assignee or licensee of the individual author) or by an employer for whom such work is made for hire, the proprietor of such copyright shall be entitled to a renewal. . . .

This proviso, then, establishes that for certain classes of ownership, the copyright shall be renewed by the *proprietor*. As we shall see, this is an exception to the general rule, set out in the second proviso to Section 24, that renewals must be made by the author or his successors. What are the classes of ownership set forth in the first proviso for which renewal must be obtained by the copyright proprietor? They are (1) posthumous works, (2) composite works in which the original copyright was secured by the proprietor, (3) works copyrighted by corporations except as assignees or licensees, and (4) works done for hire.

What is a posthumous work? Suppose a play is performed often during the playwright's life but is never published by dissemination of copies until after his death. If the playwright had assigned his common law copyright in the play to another, that person would be the copyright proprietor. Upon publication, who is entitled to the renewal rights in the play, the proprietor or the playwright's heirs? In this situation the right to claim renewal should be in the author's heirs. Barbara Ringer, a noted authority in copyright law and now register of copyrights, suggests that only those posthumous works that were not disseminated in any way during the author's life should be regarded as posthumous for purposes of vesting the renewal right in the copyright proprietor.

The second category of works for which renewal rights are vested in the copyright owner is composite works in which the proprietor originally secured the copyright. The difficulty with this provision is that the second proviso of Section 24, which establishes renewal rights in authors and their successors, states that such renewal rights apply to contributions to periodicals, cyclopedic, or other composite works. Here we have apparently contradictory provisions within the same section of the Copyright Act. Several constructions are possible, but Professor Nimmer suggests that in all cases in which the proprietor first secured the copyright in the composite work, only he can claim renewal. Only when the author's contribution was separately copyrighted in his own name may the author claim renewal rights. However, as we shall see shortly, even if the proprietor must claim the renewal right, in some cases the author may still be the beneficial owner of the renewal copyright.

The next class, works copyrighted by a corporation except as assignee or licensee of the author, is so vague that no case has ever found it applicable. Obviously a corporation cannot act by itself, but only through its agents. If its agents assign or license the copyright to it, the exception operates to obviate the clause. If the work is done for the corporation by an employee hired to create it, then the works made-for-hire class applies. Apparently, then, the provision is virtually meaningless.

The final class of works in which the proprietor may claim renewal rights is that of works made for hire. The significance of the phrase *works made for hire* has already been discussed in connection with questions of authorship. The same tests apply for renewal rights. Thus if a work was created by an independent contractor, the renewal rights would be in the author. On the other hand, if the work were created by an employee hired to create it, the renewal rights would reside in the employer.

The second proviso of Section 24 states as follows:

> That in the case of any other copyrighted work, including a contribution by an individual author to a periodical or to a cyclopedic or other composite work, the author of such work, if still living, or the widow, widower, or children of the author, if the author be not living, or if such author, widow, widower, or children be not living, then the author's executors, or in the absence of a will, his next of kin shall be entitled to a renewal. . . .

This proviso, then, sets out who shall be entitled to renewal rights for works other than those covered by the first proviso. As has been already discussed, the reference to composite works in the second proviso may refer only to those contributions that the author separately copyrighted.

The various classes of those entitled to renew if the author is not alive require some amplification. First it should be remembered that the renewal can be claimed only in the twenty-eighth year of the first copyright term. Thus if the author is alive during that entire year, only he may claim renewal. If the author should be alive during part of that year but should die without claiming renewal, the renewal could then be claimed by his appropriate successor.

The first class of succession is that of the widow, widower, or children of the author. In the case of *De Sylva* v. *Ballentine,* the Supreme Court held that despite the use of the word *or,* this class is indeed a *class* of succession, so that if both widow and children are alive, they are all entitled to the renewal. The Court did not determine, however, whether the class members would share equally or whether their shares would be determined by the state laws of intestacy. This issue therefore has not been authoritatively resolved. The terms *widow* and *children* too, are subject to some dispute. It has been held that a surviving spouse should qualify as a widow even if she has remarried subsequent to the author's death. It has also been held, however, that if the author was divorced prior to his death, his surviving former wife is not his widow.

In the *De Sylva* case the Supreme Court was in part concerned with the meaning of the word *children.* In that case the author's illegitimate child was claiming renewal rights under Section 24 of the Act. The Court held that whether an illegitimate child was a "child" within the meaning of Section 24 was to be determined by looking to the applicable state law of inheritance. If the child could inherit from its parent under state law, it would be considered a child for purposes of Section 24; if not, then it would not qualify under the section. In *De Sylva* the Court found that under California law the child could claim under Section 24. In a recent decision, however, in which an illegitimate child was found not entitled under state law to inherit from its parent, a court applied *De Sylva* to deny the child's renewal claim. This latter case must be questioned, however, not because the court misapplied *De Sylva*, but because in recent years the Supreme Court has struck down as unconstitutional a number of state laws discriminating against illegitimate children.

The final two classes of succession set forth in the second proviso of Section 24 are (1) the author's executor, if he has left a will, and (2) if he has left no will, his next of kin. Although problems may arise under these provisions, they are of an exceedingly technical nature and deal largely with state laws of decedents' estates, rather than strictly with copyright law. A few salient points, however, should be made. The first of these is that the executor is personally vested with the renewal right. Thus, although as a fiduciary he must claim the right on behalf of the author's legatees, the right is immune from claims of the author's creditors, unlike portions of the estate proper. The next of kin, on the other hand, must claim in their own right, and the entitlement of the next of kin to claim is determined by state laws of succession. Beyond these few points, it must be said that questions involving entitlement to renewal right in the last levels of succession under Section 24 are beyond the scope of this book. Specific questions in this area must be referred to an attorney skilled in the field of copyright law and decedent's estates. Certain other issues involving the transfer of renewal rights are more appropriately left to the section on conveyancing.

AD INTERIM COPYRIGHTS AND RULES PERTAINING TO CITIZENS OF FOREIGN STATES

Ad Interim Copyrights for English Language Writings First Published Abroad

We noted earlier, in our discussion of the *Candy* case, that an American citizen who writes a book in English and has it printed, bound, and distributed abroad runs the risk of losing all U.S. copyright protection because of his failure to comply with the manufacturing clause. Thus, as occurred in the *Candy* decision, a subsequent edition manufactured and published in the United States may have no protection. Whether such a subsequent edition will be copyrightable depends on whether the author has complied with Section 22 of the Copyright Act, which provides for *ad interim* copyrights. Under this section, the author of a "book or periodical first published abroad in the English language" may acquire an *ad interim* copyright in his work, if he deposits a copy of his work with the Copyright Office and files a proper request for such protection within six months of the first foreign publication. The request for *ad interim* copyright status must be accompanied by a statement containing the date of publication and the name and nationality of the author and the copyright proprietor.

Upon securing an *ad interim* copyright, the copyright proprietor becomes the beneficiary of a special exemption from the manufacturing clause; he may import up to 1,500 copies of his work in order to test the market for future sales. Further, for a period of five years from the date of first publication abroad, he becomes endowed with the full panoply of statutory rights in the copyrighted material and thus may bring suit for infringement. Moreover, he may secure full-fledged statutory copyright in the work, if at any time within the five-year period he introduces in the United States a copy of his work that comports with the manufacturing clause. However, as occurred in the *Candy* case discussed earlier, there are instances in which an author who has published abroad in English, and has neglected to obtain an *ad interim* copyright, subsequently desires to publish his work in the United States. May he proceed under Section 10 of the Act and obtain a statutory copyright in a U.S. edition of his work by publication in the United States with proper notice? The court in *Candy* considered Copyright Office regulations that stated that a book or periodical written in English and first published abroad cannot be copyrighted in the United States unless an *ad interim* copyright is obtained first. The court, in an opinion notable for its lack of persuasive analysis, held that this regulation "accurately reflects the intention of Congress"; and hence, in effect, the court accepted the regulation as a valid statement of the law. As a result of this decision, works of American citizens first published abroad in English may not be copyrighted in the United States unless *ad interim* protection is first obtained and unless the U.S. edition is published within the five-year period of *ad interim* protection. Whether or not the *Candy* court's interpretation of Congress' intentions was correct is still open to challenge in other circuit courts. And although contrary decisions in other forums seem problematic at best, Professor Nimmer and several other commentators have severely criticized the *Candy* decision. Interestingly, foreign language works by foreign authors and works in English by foreign nationals whose homelands adhere to the UCC may obtain protection under the Copyright Act at any time, no matter how long their work has been in publication abroad, and they need not first obtain an *ad interim* copyright. In contrast, under *Candy*, an American who initially publishes abroad in English must obtain an *ad interim* copyright within six months or lose future United States copyright protection. Accordingly, one commentator has accused the *Candy* court and the Copyright Office of "xenophilia," because its interpretation of the law affords Americans less copyright protection than aliens. On this point, it should be noted that if copies of a work are manufactured in the United States and so comply with the manufacturing clause, they may be originally published abroad and the copyright proprietor may subsequently obtain U.S. statutory protection without complying with the *ad interim* requirements of Section 22. Accordingly, it has been suggested that the only effect of the *ad interim* provisions and the manufacturing clause is to create business for American printers and impose a burden on American authors who desire to publish first overseas.

As we have seen, under Section 16 of the Act, the *ad interim* copyright proprietor may import up to 1,500 foreign-made copies of his work. One confusing and unresolved question is whether these *ad interim* copies must bear copyright notice. Section 16 provides that the manufacturing clause will not apply to the first 1,500 *ad interim* copies "if said copies shall contain notice of copyright in accordance with Sections 10, 19, and 20." In contrast, Section 10 provides that "Any person . . . may secure copyright for his work by publication thereof with notice . . . and such notice shall be affixed to each copy . . . *except in the case of books seeking ad interim protection under Section 22 of this title*" (emphasis added). These provisions are evidently contradictory, but it is a general rule of statutory construction that when faced with two independently valid yet seemingly contradictory laws, one should search for an interpretation that harmonizes them, preserving the meaning of both. One possible harmonizing interpretation is that Section 10, as it refers to books *seeking ad interim* protection, applies solely to foreign copies of books first published abroad and does not apply once an *ad interim* copyright has been perfected and the books have been imported into the United States. Under this construction once an *ad interim* copyright is created, Section 16 would be applicable and copyright notice would have to be affixed to each copy at some time before its importation into the United States. This interpretation, however, is unsatisfactory in that the notice exemption of Section 10 is an exception to the notice that must ordinarily be affixed to copies "offered for sale *in the United States*." Thus a construction of the Section 10 notice exemption that confines its effect to foreign publications arguably does violence to the statutory wording. Nevertheless, the Copyright Office has recently promulgated regulations that appear to adopt this interpretation of the *ad interim* copyright notice requirements. As yet these regulations have not been tested in actual litigation.

To recapitualte this view adopted by the Copyright Office, proper copyright notice need not be affixed to books in English manufactured and first published abroad until such time as they are to be imported into the United States. Upon such importation, the provisions of Section 16 of the Act would require appropriate notice in order to qualify for the manufacturing exemption.

Special Rules Pertaining to Foreign Citizens

Citizens of foreign states may obtain U.S. copyright protection only if they fall within one of four categories: (1) aliens domiciled within the United States at the time the work is first published, (2) citizens and subjects of foreign states that have been named in a presidential proclamation issued pursuant to Section (9)(b) of the Act, (3) citizens and subjects of foreign states that are signatories of the Universal Copyright Convention, and (4) citizens and subjects of foreign states that have signed special reciprocal copyright protection treaties with the United States.

Foreign Citizens Domiciled in the United States.   Under Section 9(a) of the Act, a foreign citizen who is domiciled in the United States "at the time of the first publication of his work" may obtain U.S. copyright protection by complying with the provisions of the Act just as if he were a U.S. citizen. Not surprisingly, it has been argued that the privilege to obtain copyright afforded aliens domiciled in the United States under Section 9(a) does not include the right under Section 12 to register and copyright *unpublished* works, for at the time of such registration it is not certain that the author will still be domiciled in the United States at the time of publication. Recent judicial gloss on the statute, however, has not accepted this argument, and it appears that a foreign domiciliary may secure copyright protection of both published and unpublished works. However, if the copyrighted work is a musical composition, then under Section 1(e), the exclusive right to reproduce the music mechanically shall not accrue to the copyright proprietor "unless the foreign state or nation of which such author or composer is a citizen or subject, grants . . . citizens of the United States similar rights."

Citizens of Countries Named in Presidential Proclamations.   Section 9(b) of the Act authorizes the President to issue a proclamation entitling citizens or subjects of a foreign state to claim U.S. copyright when a foreign country (1) grants U.S. citizens the "benefit of copyright on substantially the same basis as its own citizens," or (2) extends to U.S. authors substantially the same rights that the U.S. copyright law extends to foreign nationals, or (3) becomes a party to an international agreement "which provides for reciprocity in the granting of copyright" and which, by its terms, permits the United States to become a party thereto.

The President's discretion under this section, as the reader might surmise, is not open to question. Thus the fact that a foreign state falls within one of the three categories described does not make its citizens eligible to assert copyright in the United States; a Presidential proclamation is necessary, and the President may refrain from issuing one if he desires. Further, the courts have indicated that when the President does issue a proclamation, his judgment may not be rescinded; for example, in one case a court refused to consider evidence that the law of a foreign country had changed and no longer qualified it for a 9(b) proclamation.

At present no court has considered whether a Presidential proclamation may be ruled invalid when it is shown that the country in question did not qualify under Section 9(b) at the time the proclamation was issued. It is likely, however, that Section 9(b) would be construed as vesting the President with absolute, unrestrained discretion to determine when proclamations should issue, and under this construction a court would be powerless to challenge Presidential action.

A foreign national claiming U.S. copyright protection in a musical composition solely by reason of a proclamation under Section 9(b) is not vested with the exclusive right to record. As we have seen, Section 1(e) provides that the right to record accrues to a foreign copyright proprietor only when by treaty, law, or convention, U.S. citizens are afforded similar rights in the foreign country. This requirement is not necessarily satisfied when a 9(b) proclamation is issued. Accordingly, it has been held that the 1(e) right to record may not be claimed by a foreigner asserting a U.S. copyright under Section 9(b) unless a separate special proclamation is issued expressly endowing citizens of his nation with eligibility for 1(e) protection. Further, though cases have not yet arisen on this point, it seems clear that claimants under Section 9(b) are *not* exempt from the strictures of the manufacturing clause, and thus cannot import foreign-made books and periodicals.

Copyright Under the Universal Copyright Convention.   Under the Articles of the Universal Copyright Convention (UCC) member countries extend copyright protection to works first published in a member country or authored by a citizen of a member nation. The United States became a member nation in 1955, and at present there are approximately fifty member nations. The Articles provide that authors properly claiming under the UCC are entitled to copyright protection if the symbol © accompanied by the name of the copyright owner and the year of initial publication appears on each published copy. Compliance with each individual nation's formalities, which is ordinarily a condition to copyright protection, is eliminated. Section 9(c) of the Act expressly incorporates this provision of the UCC. Interestingly, if an author omits UCC notice, he is not precluded from obtaining UCC protection; the UCC notice requirement merely serves to eliminate the need to comply with individual nation's statutory formalities. Where the foreign author's work does comply with another UCC country's copyright formalities, UCC notice is superfluous. For example, if a U.S. citizen omits UCC notice and uses *Copyright* or *Copr.* instead, he may still claim UCC copyright in those countries that do not include notice as one of the conditions of obtaining a copyright.

NOTICE. As we have seen, affixation of proper notice under the UCC creates an exemption from all other conditions to copyright. Thus a copyright proprietor under the UCC need not comply with the provisions in Sections 19 and 20 of the Act relating to placement and form of notice. In a sense, the UCC standards are more restrictive than Sections 19 and 20, however, in that the symbol © and notice of the year of publication are mandatory on all works.

DEPOSIT. Persons claiming U.S. copyright protection under the UCC are exempt from the provisions of Section 13 requiring deposit of two copies of the copyrighted work, although as we have seen, the requirement of prompt filing is not rigidly enforced in any case. However, the second sentence of Section 13 provides the "[n]o action or proceeding shall be maintained for infringement of copyright in any work," until the deposit provisions of the section have been followed. As this sentence relates not to the creation of copyright rights, but rather to the procedure by which one may obtain redress for violation of these rights, compliance with this section is not a condition to copyright creation but is instead a condition to a judicial remedy, and on the basis of this distinction it has been opined that UCC copyright proprietors are not exempt.

RECIPROCAL RIGHTS PROVISION OF SECTION 1(e). Under Section 9(c)(1) UCC copyright proprietors are vested with the right to record under Section 1(e) regardless of whether their own nation extends reciprocal rights to United States citizens. As the reciprocal treatment clause of Section 1(e) is in effect a condition to copyright, persons asserting copyright under the UCC are exempt from its strictures.

AD INTERIM PROVISIONS AND THE MANUFACTURING CLAUSE. Although technically the manufacturing clause is arguably not a condition of copyright, copyright proprietors claiming under the UCC are expressly exempted from its requirements by virtue of Sections 9(c)(3) and (4); indeed the wording of the UCC Articles makes it clear that the member countries intended such a result. As the *ad interim* provisions of the Copyright Act are meaningful only in conjunction with the manu-facturing clause, these provisions are irrelevant as far as works protected by the UCC are concerned.

Special Treaties. Foreign authors who cannot qualify for U.S. copyright by any of the methods discussed so far, may still be granted U.S. copyright status if their homeland and the United States have signed a special copyright treaty. A major treaty now current is the Buenos Aires Convention, under which citizens of some seventeen South American and Latin American countries may claim U.S. copy-right. Although it is not clear, it would seem that if the foreign author has complied with the copyright formalities of his native country and if his work bears notice that all rights in it are reserved, U.S. copyright is automatic, and that the conditions to copyright required by the Act do not apply.

OWNERSHIP AND CONVEYANCING OF COPYRIGHTS

Copyright Ownership

Throughout this chapter we have used the term *copyright pro-prietor*. Of course, in the first instance upon creation of a work, it is normally the author who is the copyright proprietor. Certainly this is so for the common law copyright, which comes into existence simul-taneously with the author's act of creation. However, the author of a work is not necessarily the copyright proprietor, and of course the author can convey his copyright to another, investing him with pro-prietorship.

Only the author or one who has in some way succeeded to the author's rights may be a copyright proprietor. As we shall see in the following portions of this section, such succession may result from conveyance of the copyright by the author, for example, by assignment. Beyond direct conveyances, however, there are a number of instances in which by operation of law someone other than the true author may become the copyright proprietor. One example of such ownership by operation of law involves works done for hire. As we have noted pre-viously in this chapter, Section 26 of the Copyright Act defines the term *author* as including an employer in the case of works done for hire. Thus when an employee hired for that purpose creates a work, by law his employer is deemed to be the author and is entitled to seek statutory copyright. In this case the author in fact is not the author in law, and it is the author in law who is the copyright proprietor.

Other examples of succession to the author's rights by operation of law involve takers by testate or intestate succession. As we have seen, a common law copyright is potentially perpetual in duration, and passes down to the author's heirs or legatees until an authorized publication occurs. Under Section 9 of the Copyright Act, the author or proprietor of a work, or his executors, administrators, or assigns are entitled to a copyright in the work. Suppose an author dies holding a common law copyright. If he dies intestate, the copyright will pass to his heirs by operation of the law of intestate succession. During the term of administration, however, the administrator may seek a statutory copyright. If he does so, title to the statutory copyright will vest in the heirs upon termination of the administration. During the administration, however, the administrator will be the proprietor, though for the beneficial use of the author's heirs. Similarly, if the author dies testate, his executor may seek a statutory copyright on behalf of the author's legatees. Thus either an administrator or executor can be a copyright proprietor, though his proprietorship will be in trust for the author's heirs or legatees.

Suppose that during the administration of the author's estate, the executor or administrator does not obtain a statutory copyright. Then, upon termination of the administration, the common law copyright will pass to the author's heirs or legatees. In the case of intestate succession, title in the common law copyright will have vested in their heirs by operation of law. In the case of a will, of course, the passing of title to the legatees is essentially a form of conveyance. Although it is not crystal clear from the Copyright Act, it would appear that the heirs or legatees of an author, in whom proprietorship in the author's common law copyright has vested, could then obtain a statutory copyright themselves as the author's "assigns."

Multiple Ownership

As the reader may well have observed in the preceding discussion, it is possible for more than one person to own a single copyright. Suppose that the proprietor of a statutory copyright dies intestate, leaving two children as his only heirs. Under state laws of succession, the children would be *joint* owners of the copyright; that is, each would own a one-half interest in the undivided whole. Joint ownership of a copyright can arise in a number of additional ways. Of course, in addition to intestate succession to more than one heir, the proprietor could by will leave his copyright to more than one legatee. Also, by any other form of conveyance, such as an assignment, the proprietor could transfer the copyright to more than one person. Additionally, the copyright renewal right could vest in a class of persons, making them joint owners of the renewal copyright. For example, suppose that an author has assigned his copyright to another and then dies intestate, leaving two children as his only heirs. Under the second proviso of Section 24 as construed by the Supreme Court in the *De Sylva* case, the renewal right would exist not in the proprietor, but in the children as a class. Upon renewal, the renewal copyright would be jointly owned by the children.

The final situation in which joint ownership can be created arises out of joint authorship of the work. Clearly, if two authors collaborate to write a book that is a composite of their joint efforts, they are joint authors, and the copyright in the book would be owned by them jointly, much like the situation involving joint inventorship of a patented invention. This concept of joint authorship, however, has been greatly expanded, especially by several decisions of the U.S. Court of Appeals for the Second Circuit. These decisions have virtually eliminated any requirement of intentional collaboration in order to create joint authorship. In the first case a lyricist wrote words to a song, and his publisher then engaged a composer to write music to fit the lyrics. The lyricist and composer did not work together or even under a preconceived plan to collaborate. Still, the lyricist intended his words to be set to music and the composer knew he was writing music for those lyrics. This, the court held, was sufficient to make them joint authors. The second case went a giant step further, eliminating the question of intent on the part of one of the authors. In this case a composer had written a composition with no intention that it have lyrics. The composer's assignee, however, engaged a lyricist to write words for the composition. The combination of words and music was registered as one work, and the court found that indeed it was a joint work. Thus joint authorship was found to exist when one of the authors never intended or contemplated any sort of composite work.

Joint ownership of copyrights can create a number of difficulties, irrespective of how such ownership comes about. Because each owner has an equal interest in the individual copyright, each is usually free to convey that interest, by assignment or license. However, certain responsibilities, such as a duty to account for royalties, may devolve upon joint owners with respect to their fellow owners when they convey their rights under the copyright.

Copyright Conveyancing

Common Law Copyright. Copyright is a form of intangible personal property, and common law copyright is no exception. Indeed, be cause common law copyright is unencumbered by the statutory provisions relating to transfers of statutory copyright, the rules concerning the conveyance of common law copyright are for the most part the same as for any other form of intangible personalty.

A common law copyright can be wholly assigned by the author, in which case the author has no further rights whatever in the work. Thus if an author of an unpublished play assigns his common law copyright to another, it would be an infringement for the playwright to stage a performance of the play. Moreover, the complete assignment of the common law right would entitle the assignee, as the copyright proprietor, to secure a statutory copyright upon publication of the work.

Moreover, under some circumstances a complete assignment of the author's common law copyright may be assumed from his relinquishment of control over the physical work per se. We have discussed previously in this chapter that the owner of a common law copyright may part with the work itself and still retain his right of first publication. This is especially so in the case of letters, mentioned in the overview to this chapter. Where, however, the author irrevocably sells the work he has created and does not expressly reserve to himself the common law copyright, he may be held to have assigned to the purchaser his common law rights. On the other hand, in New York this rule has been changed by statute insofar as works of fine art are concerned. Under New York law, an artist who sells or otherwise transfers a work of fine art is deemed to have reserved his right of reproduction unless he specifically conveys that right.

Apart from the author's right to assign the entire interest in his common law copyright, he may license any part thereof within the limits of the right. For example, a playwright may license the performance rights in his play, while specifically forbidding any public dissemination or written copies. As we have seen, public performance is not a publication of a work, and therefore the playwright would still retain his full rights under the common law, save for the performance rights he transferred. To the contrary, if an author of an unpublished manuscript licenses the right of first publication of his work, he reserves essentially no common law rights for himself, for upon publication the common law copyright expires.

And, of course, an author may assign a partial interest in his common law copyright, in which case he creates a situation of joint ownership between himself and his assignee. In addition to assignment of interests and licensing of rights, the owner of a common law copyright may transfer it by bequest in his will. And, of course, if he dies intestate, his interest will pass to his legal heirs. Furthermore, in virtually every state in the country, by virtue of their adoption of the Uniform Commercial Code, a common law copyright can be used as a security for a chattel mortgage. Thus upon default, the mortgaged common law copyright can be transferred by foreclosure.

There are no particular formalities to be observed in the conveyance of common law copyrights, except as may exist under state law. Of course, to create a valid transfer by will, the testamentary formalities of the Statute of Wills must be observed; and similarly, chattel mortgages involving common law copyrights may require specific formalities. But there is nothing inherent in the common law copyright itself that requires any formalities at all. Thus, an assignment can be either oral or in writing. However, under the Uniform Commercial Code it is possible that an oral conveyance of a common law copyright may not be enforceable beyond $5,000 unless there is some sufficient writing evidencing the contract. This provision, in any case, would not affect the validity of the assignment, only its enforceability. In some cases a contract of assignment has been implied merely from the conduct of the parties. This would have been the case in New York with respect to works of fine art before the passage of the statute described. Thus mere sale of the work of art would have been deemed an assignment of the common law copyright, absent a specific reservation by the seller.

Statutory Copyright.   License versus Assignment: The Doctrine of Indivisibility.   As we have seen, copyright entails a large number of exclusive rights that the proprietor is entitled to enforce. It is this bundle of rights that makes up the commercial value of copyright. And, as might be expected, the relative value of particular rights varies greatly, depending on the nature of the copyrighted work. For example, in today's market, the most valuable exclusive right in a musical composition is probably the right to perform it publicly for profit. Thus composers may derive significant revenue from such performances, especially by radio and television broadcasts. The right to print and publish the music is today relatively unimportant. Yet when the Copyright Act was enacted, radio and television were unknown and the composer's greatest revenue came from sale of printed sheet music.

Because the bundle of exclusive rights contains separable component rights of varying commercial value, a copyright owner may wish to convey some or all of these rights. An author, for example, may wish to convey all rights in his work except the motion picture rights. These he may wish to reserve for himself so that he can sell them separately, perhaps at a later time after his book has become a success. It is the distinction between conveying all and less than all of the copyright's bundle of rights that defines the difference between an assignment and a license. But although the difference between an assignment and a license is relatively simple, a sometimes applied rule of law known as the *doctrine of indivisibility* may operate to complicate the distinction.

The doctrine of indivisibility holds that the bundle of rights conferred upon a copyright proprietor is indivisible—that is, it is incapable of being assigned piecemeal. This is not to say that a copyright owner cannot convey only part of his exclusive rights. Of course he can, and such a conveyance is a license. What the doctrine means, then, is that copyright proprietorship cannot be split up by dividing the various exclusive rights. For example, if a copyright owner were to license each of his exclusive rights to a different individual and retain nothing for himself, the doctrine of indivisibility would hold that he remained the proprietor. Only by the assignment of the entire bundle to one person can the proprietorship itself be transferred.

One purpose of the doctrine of indivisibility is to preclude licensees of various rights under a single copyright from bringing a multitude of lawsuits against a defendant. Suppose, for example, that the owner of a copyright in a novel granted dramatization rights to A and motion picture rights to B. Suppose, further, that C made an unauthorized motion picture based on A's drama. Clearly C's movie would infringe the copyright in the novel, and moreover it would impinge on the rights of the licensees A and B. Because only a copyright proprietor may sue for infringement, under the doctrine of indivisibility C would be protected from separate suits by A and B.

The rationale of avoiding multiple suits against an infringer has been largely obviated by modern federal civil procedure. Today an exclusive licensee of a copyright is able to force the copyright proprietor to join him in suing an infringer. If the proprietor is unwilling to join voluntarily, the licensee can make him a defendant or in some situations an involuntary plaintiff. Because the *raison d'être* of the doctrine of indivisibility has thus been significantly undermined, it might be thought that it is no longer consequential. In one area, however, the doctrine has operated to pose an ominous threat to copyright validity, and even today it is not clear that this threat is entirely dissipated.

The case that best exemplifies this threat is the case that may well have ended it, and thus spelled the demise of any significance to the doctrine of indivisibility. In *Goodis* v. *United Artist Television, Inc.*, at issue were the television rights in the novel *Dark Passage*. United Artists was the producer of the television series "The Fugitive," which was based on Goodis' novel. Although United claimed a contractual right to produce the series, Goodis disputed this and as a result sued for copyright infringement. It developed that Goodis, after he had written the novel, had entered into a number of license agreements. Thus he had sold the motion picture rights in the novel to Warner Brothers, and the serialization rights to Curtis Publishing Co. In accordance with its agreement with Goodis, Curtis published the novel in serial form in the *Saturday Evening Post* before the entire novel was published by Goodis' publisher. As published by Curtis, the serialization bore no copyright notice in Goodis' name. Rather, it was covered solely by the single copyright notice that Curtis affixed to each copy of the magazine.

Under Section 3 of the Copyright Act, a single copyright notice on a periodical protects all parts of the periodical that are copyrightable. However, as we have seen, it is not certain how far this coverage extends. Because Curtis was a mere licensee, having only one of the many exclusive rights included in the copyright bundle, United Artists argued that under the indivisibility doctrine Curtis could not be a proprietor and therefore could not obtain a valid copyright in the novel. Thus it was argued that publication by Curtis had been without proper notice and had thrown the work into the public domain.

The court rejected United's arguments. It held that whatever the merits of the doctrine of indivisibility as affecting the standing to sue, it should not be applied to throw a work into the public domain on such technical grounds. The court stated: "We are loath to bring about the unnecessarily harsh result of thrusting the author's product into the public domain when, as here, everyone interested in 'Dark Passage' could see Curtis' copyright notice and could not have believed that there was any intention by Goodis to surrender the fruits of his labor." If the *Goodis* case is followed by other courts, the doctrine of indivisibility will lose any major significance and will no doubt pass into oblivion as an important aspect of copyright law. Until that time, however, it does pose the threat of causing works unwittingly to be thrust into the public domain.

ASSIGNMENTS. An assignment is the conveyance of an interest in the entire bundle of rights that make up copyright. As we have seen, a copyright proprietor can assign only a partial interest in his copyright, thereby creating joint ownership. Nonetheless, the assignee in such a situation is a proprietor, for he owns an undivided partial interest in the copyright. If the conveyance transfers less than the entire bundle of rights, it is a license rather than an assignment.

Under the Copyright Act, the assignment of statutory copyrights must be in writing. In the case of assignments executed abroad, the instrument of assignment must be acknowledged under oath by the assignor before a consular or other officer of the United States who shall affix on the instrument the appropriate seal. Section 30 of the Copyright Act provides that assignments shall be recorded in the Copyright Office within three months after execution (or six months in the case of assignments executed abroad). Failure to record an assignment will not affect the validity of the copyright, but it will cause the assignment to be void as against any subsequent purchaser or mortgagee for consideration without notice whose assignment is recorded. Thus the fact that an assignment is not recorded will not matter insofar as disputes between the assignor and assignee, or between the assignee and a subsequent assignee who took with notice of the first assignment, are concerned. However, if the first assignment is not recorded and the second assignee pays valuable consideration, takes without notice of the first assignment, and records the second assignment, he will be the proprietor of the copyright notwithstanding the former assignment.

A few additional points should be made about recordation of assignments. First, as we have noted, Section 30 only concerns the effect of recordation on subsequent assignees. Therefore failure to record an assignment will not prevent an assignee from recovering from an infringer. Also, a second assignee who takes without notice and records his assignment will prevail over a nonrecording first assignee only if he has paid "valuable consideration." Merely nominal consideration will not meet the test. Thus in one case a second assignment for which the consideration paid was $1 plus an obligation to pay royalties, should any accrue, was held not to be for "valuable consideration." Finally, Section 32 of the Copyright Act provides that upon recordation an assignee may substitute his name for that of the assignor in the copyright notice. This provision has one significant consequence. As we have seen, copyright notice must be in the name of the author or proprietor. Suppose that an assignee of a copyright does not record the assignment, but nevertheless publishes the work with notice in his name. It has been universally held that such notice is not statutorily adequate, and that the work is thus thrust into the public domain.

LICENSES. A license is a transfer of less than the entire bundle of copyright rights. Examples of licenses are grants of motion picture rights, public performance rights, and dramatization rights. With the likely demise of the doctrine of indivisibility as an important aspect of copyright law, the distinction between licenses and assignments has become less important. As we have seen, this is especially so where a license is exclusive, so that the licensee is the only person entitled to exercise the particular rights he has been granted. Thus an exclusive licensee can effectively sue infringers on his own behalf by joining the copyright proprietor as a party to the suit.

There are, however, some significant differences between assignments and licenses. Unlike assignments, licenses may be in the form of oral contracts. Also, although an assignment gives the assignee the right to reassign, a licensee may not grant sublicenses unless he is explicitly authorized to do so by the license. Furthermore, although an assignment requires no consideration to be valid, as long as it is in writing, a license is like any other contract and must be supported by consideration to be enforceable. Also, it should be clear that there is no requirement that licenses be recorded. However, if an exclusive license is recorded in the Copyright Office, it may be held to give constructive notice so as to defeat subsequent assignees as to the rights licensed.

MORTGAGES. Section 28 of the Copyright Act also provides for the mortgaging of statutory copyrights. Mortgage instruments must be in writing. Although it is not absolutely certain, it appears that under Section 30, a mortgage should be recorded in the Copyright Office to preserve the mortgagee's rights against a subsequent mortgagee or assignee. The reader should note that the Uniform Commercial Code requires filing of financing statements in order to perfect security interests in intangible personal property. However, the Code establishes an exception in the case of property "subject to a statute . . . of the United States which provides for a national registration or filing of all security interests in such property. . . ." Because it is not entirely certain that Section 30 of the Copyright Act requires or "provides for" recordation of mortgages, the cautious course would be for a mortgagee of a statutory copyright to comply with both Section 30 and the Uniform Commercial Code.

DEATH TRANSFERS. Section 28 of Copyright Act provides specifically that copyrights may be bequeathed by will. It is clear that copyrights may also be transferred in accordance with the laws of intestate succession. In either case, state law will govern the transfer. The requisite formalities for testamentary transfer, therefore, are determined by state decedents' estates law.

ASSIGNMENT OF RENEWAL RIGHTS. As we have seen, statutory copyrights are renewable for a second twenty-eight-year term, and with certain exceptions, the renewal right is in the author or his statutory successors. Renewal, however, cannot be effected until the beginning of the twenty-eighth year of the original copyright term. Because until that time it is impossible to tell who will be entitled to claim renewal, the copyright renewal right is considered to be an "expectancy" rather than a vested right until the beginning of the final year of the original term. Thus the author of a copyrighted work has an expectancy in the renewal right; if he is alive in the twenty-eighth year, his expectancy will mature into a vested right. At the same time, however, the author's wife as well has an expectancy in the renewal right. If her husband dies before the final year of the original copyright term and she survives, her expectancy will vest.

Indeed, many expectancies are created when a copyright is obtained. The author, his wife, his children, his legatees, and his next of kin all have some chance of having the renewal right vest in them. Obviously, the more contingent the expectancy is, the more remote the likelihood of its vesting. For example, if an author is twenty-five years old when he obtains his copyright, and he has a wife and two children, it is quite unlikely that the renewal right will ultimately vest in the author's brother. Thus the brother's expectancy is rather remote.

The renewal right, or more properly the expectancy of a renewal right, may be assigned by its owner. In the leading case in this area, *Fred Fisher Music Co. v. M. Witmark & Sons*, the Supreme Court considered an assignment of the renewal right by the authors of "When Irish Eyes Are Smiling." The original copyright had been obtained by the coauthors in 1912, and in 1917 they assigned their renewal rights to Witmark. By 1939 only one of the coauthors was still living. In that year Witmark, relying on the 1917 assignment of renewal rights, registered the renewal. The remaining living author, however, also filed a renewal registration, and then assigned his purported renewal copyright to Fred Fisher Music Co. The question that the Supreme Court had to decide was whether the 1917 assignment was effective—that is, whether an author can assign his renewal right when it is merely an expectancy. The Court concluded that indeed he could, and if the expectancy then vested because the author survived until the twenty-eighth year of the original copyright term, the renewal right would belong to the assignee. Therefore the Court held the 1917 assignment valid, and because the assignor had lived to the twenty-eighth year, the renewal copyright belonged to Witmark.

Although an assignment of the renewal expectancy is thus valid, it must be remembered that it remains only an expectancy until it vests. Therefore if the assignor is not alive in the twenty-eighth year, his expectancy never vests and the assignee gets nothing. In one case a coauthor of the song "Moonlight and Roses" assigned his renewal rights to Miller Music Corp. Prior to the beginning of the twenty-eighth year, he died, leaving no wife or child, but three brothers. During the twenty-eighth year, one of the brothers registered a renewal as next of kin, and assigned the renewal copyright to Charles N. Daniels, Inc. The Court held that Daniels was the owner of the renewal copyright, because Miller's assignment was only of an expectancy, and when the assignor died, so did the expectancy.

The reader can easily see the pitfalls involved in obtaining assignments of renewal expectancies. The assignment is valid, but whether it is worth anything depends on circumstances entirely beyond the control of the assignee—whether in the twenty-eighth year the expectancy will vest in the assignor, which in the case of assignments by authors, means whether the author will be alive. As we have seen, any expectancy may be assigned, be it the author's, his children's, or his next of kin's. This fact gives the assignee of an author's expectancy some chance to protect himself. If he can collect assignments from all those likely to be entitled to renew if the author dies, he may be relatively certain that at least one of the expectancies he has been assigned will vest, and then he will be entitled to claim the renewal right.

Unfortunately, this tack has certain pitfalls that can upset the assignee's plans. Suppose that the assignee of the author's renewal right obtains assignments of the expectancies of the author's wife, their children, and the author's brothers. He may feel that he will be protected in the event that the author dies before the twenty-eighth year. However, unbeknownst to our poor assignee, the author has an illegitimate child. And to compound the assignee's woes, the author dies before the twenty-eighth year while living in a state in which illegitimate children may inherit. Therefore under *De Sylva* the illegitimate child is entitled to renewal. Accordingly, the assignee finds that he must share his renewal copyright. Or to make matters even worse, suppose that when the twenty-eighth year rolls around, not only is the author dead, but so are his widow and their legitimate children. In that case the only remaining link the assignee has to the expectancy is through the author's brothers. But because children take before next of kin, the illegitimate child would own the renewal outright, and the assignee would have nothing.

Consider another example of the pitfalls of taking expectancy assignments. Suppose in the former example that there was no illegitimate child, but that the author died leaving a will, and bequeathed his renewal right to his best friend. This bequest would fail if the widow or children were alive in the twenty-eighth year because of the statutory order of succession. However, if the the widow and children were dead, the author's executor would be able to claim the renewal right on behalf of the legatee. Again the assignee's efforts would have yielded him nothing.

An assignment of a renewal expectancy must be for good consideration. Moreover, courts will not imply an assignment of the renewal right unless such an intent is clear. Thus in one case an author transferred "right, title and interest by way of copyrights or otherwise . . . in and to all my musical compositions. . . ." There was no explicit mention of renewal rights, and several years later the author separately assigned his renewal expectancy to another. The court held that the second transfer was valid, declaring "that a copyright renewal creates a separate interest distinct from the original copyright and that a general transfer by an author of the original copyright without mention of renewal rights conveys no interest in the renewal rights without proof of a contrary intention." It is not an invariable rule, however, that an assignment that does not mention renewal rights will not transfer those rights. In one case a song writer conveyed all his rights, title and interest in the song "forever." The court held that this language evidenced an intent to convey even the renewal right.

As mentioned, assignments of renewal rights are enforceable only if for good consideration. This is essentially an unconscionability standard, however, and courts will not strike down an assignment of renewal rights merely because in retrospect the rights seem worth more than they appeared to be worth at the time of the assignment. Thus in the absence of some fraud on the part of the assignee, or a grossly unconscionable consideration, such as $1, such assignments will be upheld.

Finally it might be mentioned that an effective assignment of renewal rights gives the assignee the unqualified right to renew, even if the author later refuses to cooperate with him. Thus assignment of the renewal right is deemed to imply the grant of an irrevocable power of attorney to the assignee to apply for renewal in the name of the author.

Performance Rights Societies

We have previously discussed the various exclusive rights that copyright gives the proprietor. And we have pointed out that the most valuable right in musical copyrights is the right of public performance for profit. It is this right that protects the proprietor from unauthorized performances on radio and television and in movie theaters, as well as in dance halls, restaurants, hotels, and so forth. The reader may well have wondered how this right can be enforced. An individual performance of a song, after all, is an ephemeral thing. Unlike a copy of a book, it is not tangible. Moreover, it occurs daily and in many places all over the country. Thus it can be distinguished, for example, from a public performance of a play. A dramatic performance of a work is not likely to be occurring simultaneously and frequently all over the country, and a playwright might reasonably be expected to be able to discover infringing performances of his work. A composer, on the other hand, could discover only a tiny fraction of the infringing performances of his music.

It was these very problems—the fleeting nature of infringing performances and their widespread and frequent occurrence—that led in 1914 to the founding of the American Society of Composers, Authors, and Publishers, commonly called ASCAP. ASCAP is composed of thousands of members—composers, lyricists, and music publishers. Each member grants to ASCAP what is designated as an assignment of the exclusive right to perform publicly for profit. The right granted is only the nondramatic performance right, and in works such as opera, the right of dramatic performance is reserved to the copyright proprietor. Although called an assignment, the grant is of less than all the rights, and therefore might more properly be called a license. In any event, the distinction is no longer terribly important, and when ASCAP seeks to enforce the performance right by infringement suit, the individual copyright proprietor is joined as a party.

ASCAP licenses (or perhaps more properly, sublicenses) the performing rights in the compositions of its members. Any person wishing to make a public performance for profit of a musical composition may obtain a license from ASCAP. ASCAP grants essentially two types of licenses. The first of these is called a blanket license and covers all the musical compositions in ASCAP's repertory. A flat annual fee is charged, which varies with the nature of the licensee. Thus a licensee upon obtaining a blanket license is entitled to perform any or all of the music in the ASCAP repertory, as often as he wishes. The fee will bear no relationship to the number of ASCAP compositions performed. The second type of license offered by ASCAP is called a "per program" license. This license is also a bulk license, in that it covers the entire ASCAP repertory, but it entitles the licensee to perform ASCAP compositions only for a single specified performance. Here a fee is charged for each such performance.

ASCAP seeks vigorously to enforce the performance rights of its members, and frequently sues for infringement when it learns of unlicensed performances. Because ASCAP's musical repertory includes the majority of works not in the public domain, it is exceedingly difficult for an entire concert, for example, to avoid using any ASCAP music. The sums collected by ASCAP as license fees are divided among members according to a complex formula. In this way members are able to receive significant remuneration for their otherwise practically unenforceable performance rights.

In addition to ASCAP is another major performance rights society, Broadcast Music, Inc., commonly called B.M.I. B.M.I. operates on essentially the same basis as ASCAP. The history of the formation of B.M.I. is a fascinating tale of a power struggle between ASCAP and the broadcast industry. Although the details are beyond the scope of this chapter, it might be noted that B.M.I. was created by the national radio networks as a rival to ASCAP when ASCAP attempted to raise its license fees to broadcasters. A boycott of ASCAP music ensued, and for a time only such public domain works as "Jeannie with the

Light Brown Hair" were played on radio. Today B.M.I. is a significant factor in the performance rights industry.

Much of the history of ASCAP and most of the details of its present operations are intertwined with antitrust problems. As the reader may well appreciate, the great volume of music rights controlled by ASCAP and its "bulk-only" licensing practices have raised serious antitrust questions. These will be dealt with briefly in the section of this chapter dealing with copyright–antitrust problems.

GOVERNMENT CONTRACTING

There are variations in the law that differentiate copyright problems from patent problems so that a simple analogy with the patent policy of government contracting discussed, in the chapter on patents, is not realistic. Any anticompetitive effects that may flow from allowing contractors to obtain copyrights are much less significant than those from allowing contractors to obtain patents. The copyright prevents only the copying of the work and does not control the use of the ideas expressed in the work. Unlike a patent that protects the concept of an invention, a copyright merely protects the form in which an idea is expressed. Furthermore, it is possible that a key patent will give a party a clear commercial advantage in an entire industry. The same is not true for a copyright.

Sometimes the preparation of a specific work by a government contractor or grantee may be the primary object of a contract or grant. Other times a work may be prepared as a by-product of a research and development contract or grant. Furthermore, different subject matter requires different copyright policies as to public dissemination. Obviously, educational materials involve different considerations than technical materials.

During the 1950's most government agencies began to allow contractors and grantees copyrights in works produced as a by-product of the contract or grant. However, such permission was not given where the work was the primary object of the contract or grant. More recently, some agencies have developed policies allowing private parties under some circumstances to obtain a copyright on works produced as a primary object of a contract or grant. These agencies are the Department of Defense, the Office of Education, and the National Science Foundation. Some agencies still refuse to allow private parties to obtain a copyright on works produced under their sponsorship. In these cases unless appropriate in-house efforts to secure copyright are undertaken, such material will fall in the public domain.

Despite the variety of approaches now taken by the numerous agencies as to copyrights, no effort has been made to bring about uniformity. Nothing comparable to the two Presidential Memoranda and Statements of Government Patent Policy exists in the copyright area. The numerous agencies have either developed or failed to develop copyright policies without any standard guidelines. Furthermore, as in the case of patents, there is no single statute governing the question as to who is entitled to obtain copyrights in works produced under government contracts or grants. Nevertheless, many of the same statutes covered in the discussion of patents also affect copyright policy. Thus some statutes might be interpreted as barring certain government agencies in some cases from allowing contractors and grantees to claim a copyright in material created under a contract or grant.

If copyrighted works are used by the government or a government contractor in such a way as to infringe the copyright, provision is made for recovery by the copyright owner in the U.S. Court of Claims. Furthermore, the agency officials are authorized to settle, prior to suit, claims that might be brought against the agency for copyright infringement. Only a few agencies have been given express authority to acquire interests in copyrights independent of the settlement of a claim.

COPYRIGHT INFRINGEMENT

Introduction

As we noted earlier, both the Copyright Act and the common law endow the copyright proprietor with exclusive rights in the copyrighted material. The holder of a common law copyright may prevent others from publicly duplicating the protected work; the proprietor of a statutory copyright, too, has numerous exclusive rights in the copyrighted material. For both types of copyright, the right publicly to copy is not limited to the initial medium or form of the copyrighted work, but extends to adaptation, translation, arrangements, abridgements, and so forth. When someone else usurps these extensive rights to copy, an *infringement* is said to have occurred, and the copyright proprietor is entitled to demand legal sanctions that, as we shall see, are quite severe.

Although copyrights are said to confer on the copyright proprietor certain exclusive rights to duplicate the copyrighted material, our everyday experience abounds with proof that not every borrowing from a copyrighted work can constitute an infringement. For example, this book could not have been written without reference to the scholar-ship of others; moreover, the recent best seller *Jonathan Livingston Seagull* has been termed a restatement of *The Little Engine That Could.* Television networks boldly imitate successes of their competitors —"Bewitched," a series featuring a blond housewife-sorceress who involves her husband in ridiculous situations with witchcraft created by wrinkling her nose, is followed by "I Dream of Jeannie," a comedy featuring a blond genie who involves her husbandlike housemate in magical mischief created by blinking her eyes. Archie Bunker, who dislikes minorities, enjoys bigots and has a loud, coarse vocabulary, is the prototype for Maude, who likes minorities, dislikes bigots, and has a loud, coarse vocabulary. In popular music, there is a never-ending battle to make each new song sound like the previous month's million seller. In short, in every medium some borrowing from the intellectual property of others is permissible. As is evident from this book's use of instructive quotations from the works of others, even a certain amount of verbatim copying is allowed. How the courts have arrived at a definition of infringement that reconciles these instances of permissible borrowing with the extensive *exclusive* property rights afforded both statutory and nonstatutory copyright law is the subject of this chapter. It is not a simple topic, and one of the dangers lawyers face in advising their clients in matters pertaining to copyright is that a court may misconstrue the law and reach an unexpected and un-fortunate result. Indeed, a skillful attorney is a necessity in copyright litigation, for more than one judge has echoed the sentiments of the court in *Shapiro, Bernstein & Co.* v. *H. L. Greene Co.*:

> This action for copyright infringement presents us with a picture all too familiar in copyright litigation: a legal problem vexing in its diffi-culty, a dearth of squarely applicable precedents, a business setting so common that the dearth of precedents seems inexplicable and almost complete absence of guidance from the terms of the Copyright Act.

The Elements of Infringement

The tort of copyright infringement consists of two basic elements: (1) entitlement to copyright protection [copyright entitlement] and (2) an appropriation of that entitlement by some form of copying [copying].

Copyright Entitlement. What a plaintiff must prove in order to demonstrate copyright entitlement varies according to whether he asserts a common law or statutory copyright. Entitlement to a common law copyright is generally shown by introducing the work in question and demonstrating that it is novel, concrete, and unpublished. If the plaintiff is asserting a statutory copyright, he must prove originality, copyrightability, proper registration, and authorship by a person whose citizenship made him eligible for copyright protection. In addition, the plaintiff must show valid title if he is not the original author. However, the copyright registration certificate constitutes prima facie evidence that plaintiff possesses these incidents of ownership and upon its admission into evidence the burden shifts to the defendant to disprove entitlement to statutory copyright protection. There is some question as to whether the registration certificate is also presumptive evidence that all publications of the work have carried proper copyright notice, and courts differ as to whether the plaintiff or the defendant must carry the burden of truth on this matter.

Copying. VERBATIM COPYING. Once either common law or statuory copyright entitlement is established, the plaintiff must prove copying. When copying is verbatim the matter is settled. Defendant has infringed unless he can show that his copying constitutes a "fair use" of plaintiff's work. The concept of fair use is perhaps the most difficult area of copyright law and is discussed at length in the section dealing with defenses. The great majority of infringement actions, however, involve copying on a far more sophisticated level than do the few cases involving word-for-word transcription.

NONLITERAL COPYING. It is clear that a law prohibiting only verbatim copying would afford little protection indeed. Yet once literal appropriation ceases to be the test, a court is faced with two difficult problems. First, it must determine how much resemblance between works is too much. To this end, it is ruled that there must be *substantial similarity* between the two works under consideration. Secondly, it is necessary to determine whether the substantial similarity results from copying or from independent creation, for unlike the law of patents, no infringement of a copyright occurs if a second person independently creates a work identical to another work previously copyrighted. To insure the substantial similarity is not coincidental, the plaintiff must show that the defendant had *access* to the copyrighted material.

Access. Whereas substantial similarity is the first and foremost issue in the mind of a plaintiff, the courts, in deference to the policy of encouraging independent creation, focus initially on access. Not surprisingly, defendants rarely admit access, and hence access is generally shown through circumstantial evidence. For example, evidence that plaintiff's work has been widely circulated or that defendant's work was composed with inexplicable speed has been held to raise an inference of access. Moreover, even if plaintiff can adduce no evidence of access at all, which is sometimes the case, access will be inferred where the similarities between two works are so striking that independent creation seems highly unlikely. The presence of common errors in two works generally will raise a presumption of access. Indeed, compilers of directories, maps, and other similar works often intentionally insert errors to facilitate the detection and proof of copying. But no matter how striking the similarities, no liability for copying will result if the defendant can persuade the court that the similarities are coincidental and that his work is solely his own independent creation. Defendant's burden of proof on this issue is heavy; that he has plagiarized subconsciously is no defense; he must show total independence. As we might expect, when two works are highly similar, courts are skeptical of claims that the resemblance is purely coincidental. For example, in one case, the defendant, in attempting to explain why his work was virtually identical to the plaintiff's, stated that he and the plaintiff had both been influenced by the popular tune "Humoresque" and consequently had independently produced extraordinarily similar works. The court, in rejecting this implausible assertion, noted: "Buchanan tells us that Kekule's 'idea of the carbon-ring came out of the lurid imagery of the morning after a party'; many a chemist had had a like experience without such a fruitful result."

Substantial Similarity. Once access is proved, the inquiry turns to the issue of substantial similarity. To prove substantial similarity the plaintiff must show that the defendant's work is so similar to his own that we may reasonably infer copying. It is not enough merely to prove access convincingly and then argue that any similarity has probably resulted from plagiarism. Although proof of a striking degree of similarity will suffice to establish access, a striking showing of access will not diminish the degree of similarity that must exist in order to establish copying. It would be contrary to the policy of the copyright laws for the courts to view access with suspicion and thus perhaps discourage the dissemination of copyrighted materials and impede research. Actual unauthorized use of the plaintiff's property is a prerequisite to a finding of infringement; and only when the similarity between two works is great can a court be certain that this prerequisite is satisfied. Intent and opportunity to infringe are not enough. Accordingly, in one case, where the defendant admitted that, "it undertook to make a slavish copy of plaintiff's copyrighted dolls," it was held that an infringement action would not lie if by reason of "crude workmanship" defendant failed to produce a substantially similar doll.

Thus in every infringement case in which nonliteral copying is alleged, the key issue is substantial similarity. Yet it is clear that the term *substantial similarity,* when used in copyright infringement cases, carries considerably different connotations than it does when used in everyday conversation; for example, we have already noted that many similar works do not evoke infringement problems. We may explain these different connotations by saying that for infringement purposes we consider only the copyrightable portions of the copyrighted work; if the similarity extends solely over noncopyrightable material, there is no infringement.

Dictionaries perhaps represent the most instructive and elementary model. Suppose someone were to copyright a dictionary purporting to contain all the new words added to the English language from 1970 to the present. Could he enjoin someone else from publishing another dictionary also purporting to define new English words of the same period? Our common sense tells us that the answer is no, and indeed, the law reaches the same result. Were the author of our hypothetical dictionary able to impound all others, he would in effect possesses a monopoly in his idea, and as we have seen, it is a rudimentary principle of both patent and copyright law that no one can monopolize ideas. Indeed, monopolization of ideas is prohibited by the First Amendment, for the "arena of public debate would be quiet indeed, if a politician could copyright his speeches . . . and thus obtain a monopoly on the ideas contained."

In our earlier discussion of the uncopyrightability of ideas, we observed that anyone can publish on Einstein's theory of relativity or produce a play concerning two lovers whose families are mutually hostile. Despite these observations, it is well established that there is a property right in a particular combination of ideas, or in the particular form in which ideas are embodied. Obviously, the line that exists between nonprotected "abstract ideas" and protected "particular combinations of ideas" or "expression" is fuzzy, if identifiable at all. Justice Story once opined that drawing a distinction between an idea and the form in which it is expressed might well be more a matter of metaphysics than jurisprudence. Not surprisingly, then, courts have often found difficulty in drawing this distinction, and insight into why this line seems so elusive is best obtained by examining how the courts have dealt with this problem in actual cases.

The area that contains most of the decisions relating to the line between ideas and expression is the field of narrative and dramatic works. Of course, where merely the dialogue or the wording of a narrative or dramatic work is allegedly infringed, it will be held that the copyrighted expression has been appropriated when the second author's paraphrasing comes too close to the original. But clearly, there is more to the expression of a narrative work than its arrangement and choice of words, as there is more to a play than merely its dialogue. To be meaningful, copyright protection of such works must extend to the very heart of the author's expression. With respect to narrative and dramatic works, one often quoted commentaor has said that copyright protection should cover the *pattern* of a work as embodied in its "sequence of events, and the development and interplay of [its] characters."

However, it is one thing to describe those portions of a work that merit protection, but it is another to decide when these have been appropriated in an actual case. In practice, it has proved exceedingly difficult to determine when one work has misappropriated the protectable "pattern" of another. To this end, a court must undertake a detailed comparison of the works in question. The procedure by which courts undertake and evaluate this comparison was first set forth by Judge Learned Hand in the famous case of *Nichols* v. *Universal Pictures Co.* Judge Hand explained:

> [W]hen the plagiarist does not take out a block in situ, but an abstract of the whole, decision is . . . troublesome. Upon any work, and especially upon a play, a great number of patterns of increasing generality will fit equally well, as more and more of the incident is left out. The last may perhaps be no more than the most general statement of what the play is about . . . but there is a point in this series of abstractions where they are no longer protected, since otherwise the playwright could prevent the use of his "ideas," to which, apart from their expression, his property is never extended [citations omitted].

Application of this formulation calls for a two-step evaluation that has since become known as the "pattern test." First, one must identify the "most detailed pattern" common to both works, and secondly, he must decide whether this pattern is protectable or is in the public domain. This two-step procedure becomes much easier to comprehend when viewed in operation. *Nichols* v. *Universal Pictures Co.* provides a convenient example.

In *Nichols,* the plaintiff was the author of "Abie's Irish Rose," an extraordinarily popular Broadway comedy that concerns two young lovers, one Catholic and one Jewish, whose parents are mutually hostile. Defendant was the creator of "The Cohens and the Kellys," a motion picture with a plot similar to "Abie's Irish Rose." In applying the first part of the pattern test, the court undertook a point-by-point comparison of the two works in question. When "Abie's Irish Rose" opens, the young couple has secretly married, and the young boy is concerned with preparing his prosperous orthodox Jewish parents for the shock of his mixed marriage. To this end, he convinces his bride to pose as a Jewess, and he introduces her to his parents, letting it appear that he is interested in her, but concealing the marriage. The father, who has always been "obsessed with a passion that his daughter-in-law shall be an orthodox Jewess," approves of the girl, and soon summons a Rabbi to perform the nuptual rites. The girl's father is then called to the scene. He believes that his daughter is to wed an Irish Catholic. Accompanied by a priest, he arrives during the Jewish wedding ceremony, but too late to interrupt it. At its conclusion, he and the father of the boy engage in a grotesque argument, and while they are arguing, the priest marries the couple a third time. Eventually, in the final act, we see the young couple living in their own abode one year later, having been banished by each father. The couple has twins, a boy and a girl, but the fathers believe that only one child has been born. The fathers embark separately to visit the young family and meet, one bearing gifts for a girl, the other for a boy. They argue about the sex of the grandchild, only to reconcile, embrace, and live happily ever after when they learn that there are twins, and that a child will be named for each father.

In the "Cohens and the Kellys," the families are impoverished, mutually belligerent neighbors. The girl is a Jewess, the boy an Irish Catholic. The couple marries secretly not long after the movie begins. The Jewish father discovers from an attorney that he has inherited a large fortune, and accordingly, he moves into an ostentatious mansion. Each time the Irish youth calls, the girl's father drives him off. The Jewish father subsequently becomes ill from arguing with the father of the boy, and is compelled to go to Florida to recuperate. When he returns, he is distressed to learn that his daughter has married the Irish youth and has borne his son. Soon thereafter, the Irish boy's family comes to visit the grandchild, and a violent scene ensues, during which the Jew disowns his daughter. With her husband, she departs to her father-in-law's home. Soon thereafter, the attorney informs the girl's father that his fortune truly belongs to the Irishman. The Jew refuses to accept the attorney's offer to conceal this knowledge, and he proceeds to the Irishman's house and repeats what the attorney has told him. There upon a "reconciliation ensues," and the two fathers decide to share the money.

Upon completing its comparison, the court noted the paucity of common points in the development of the two works, both with respect to events and the interplay of characters. It found that the main theme of "Abie's Irish Rose," a religious antagonism, was not at all reflected in "The Cohens and the Kellys." The court pointed out that in "The Cohens and the Kellys," the mixed marriage apparently did not offend the Irish family at all and it apparently angered the Jew only because he was rich and the Irish family poor when the marriage was first brought to his knowledge. Further, it was emphasized that although the grandfathers are reconciled in both works the reconciliation stems from a different cause in each. In "Abie's Irish Rose," it arises out of the grandfathers' mutual love of the grandchildren; in "The Cohens and the Kellys," it comes about through the Jew's honesty and the Irishman's generosity; the "grandchild has nothing whatever to do with it." Thus, the court completed the first step of the pattern test—finding the most detailed common pattern. It concluded: "The only matter common to the two is a quarrel between a Jewish and an Irish father, the marriage of their children, the birth of their grandchildren and a reconciliation." The second step is to determine whether this common pattern is in the public domain, and consequently may freely be copied. In *Nichols*, the common pattern was found to be hackneyed, well known, and not protectable. Accordingly, it was held that the defendant copied merely the plaintiff's ideas, and did not appropriate her expression.

As we can see from the *Nichols* case, both steps of the pattern test create at least as many problems as they solve. Consider the first step—finding the common pattern. This pattern is composed of the cluster of similarities between two works, each similarity being a point in the pattern. The decision as to which sequences or character relationships are similar enough to be included in the "common" pattern is necessarily arbitrary. For example, in *Nichols*, the court found that the marriage of the children was a common point in each work, but it did not mention the fact that in each the marriage was secret, nor did it include in the pattern the fact that the central quarrel in each work was precipitated by disclosure of the marriage. The second step of the pattern test is to determine whether the common pattern constitutes merely an idea (and thus is in the public domain) or whether it embodies the author's expression and thus is protectable. In this step we see that the pattern test, which purports to guide us in drawing the line between an idea and its expression, ultimately gives us no guidance at all; the problem is still: which sequences of events and interrelationships of characters constitute ideas and which constitute expression?

The cases in which the pattern test has been expressly or implicitly applied illustrate the shortcomings of the test. For example, in one case the two works under consideration involved a sickly husband whose wife secretly prostitutes herself to pay his hospital bills. His illness compels him temporarily to leave home in order to convalesce in a milder climate. Upon his return, he discovers his wife with another man, and though he learns the truth behind the illicit union, he spurns his wife's explanations, renounces her love, and abandons her. Although both works shared this pattern, the court held that the expression of the first was not copied by the second. Indeed, when such a detailed similarity between the sequence of events and the interplay of the characters of two works is held to signify merely that both authors have utilized the same "idea," it is clear that only when the "patterns" of two works are almost exactly identical down to the minutest incident will it be held that the expression rather than the idea has been duplicated. For instance, in another case, the plaintiff composed a screenplay depicting the life of Clara Barton. The plaintiff embellished the famous nurse's life considerably; for example, she created a fictional lover named Tom Maxwell, who dies, and in a letter, bequeaths Clara a legacy in gold dust. Other fictional touches were added, as well, including an imagined controversy between Clara and the New Jersey school board. The defendant's biography of Clara Barton "reproduced in substantially similar form" all of the fictional events created by the plaintiff, even the names of plaintiff's fictional characters were appropriated. Although the court went through the motions of pattern test analysis, we hardly need the pattern test to aid us in finding infringement in such a case. Indeed, in the final analysis, the pattern test, and other alternative tests that have been proposed, are ineffecive guides. In the end, we must admit that Learned Hand was correct when he said, thirty years after he had conceived the pattern test in *Nichols:* "Obviously, no principle can be stated as to when an imitator has gone beyond copying the 'idea' and has borrowed its 'expression.' Decisions must therefore inevitably be *ad hoc.*"

Whereas the pattern test, even with all its inadequacies, seems aptly suited to infringement cases involving narrative and dramatic works, it is an ineffective guide in many other situations. For example, where one manufacturer's statue is alleged to be an unauthorized reproduction of another's work of art, where do we look for a pattern common to both works? Indeed, in one case, involving, ironically enough, an alleged infringement of an artistic pattern, it was suggested that the pattern test is frequently ineffective. Even in those areas in which one would imagine that pattern analysis would be fruitful, it has not been productive. For example, superficially it would seem that in the field of musical compositions, pattern analysis would aid greatly. Because all such works are segmented into intervals and can contain a limited number of notes, conceivably two musical compositions could be superimposed, their common pattern becoming visible to the eye. Yet such an approach overlooks the elementary but crucial fact that music appeals to the ear, not the eye, and what appears under a bar-by-bar comparison to be a similarity, when translated into the inscrutably abstract language of musical sound, may be something altogether different.

Indeed, of all the different areas of copyrightable works, the one that bears the most similarity to fictional and dramatic works, and in which analysis of the sort required by the pattern test ought most readily to be useful, is the area of derivative works, for in these works the line between the protected and unprotected portions seems relatively clear. This is particularly true of maps, compilations, and directories that contain only public domain material. In such works, the protectable pattern is to be found in the sequential arrangement of data, printing, indexing, coloring, and other features of arrangement. Biography, histories, and other similar works containing public domain materials raise more complex problems, however, for they are composed of descriptions of fact and call for the author to exercise discretion in both his choice of words and his choice of events. Though presented in a new directory, a phone number will convey only one bit of information, and no directory, no matter how arranged, would be complete without all of the numbers. In contrast, histories of the same period may describe different events and in two works the narrative descriptions of such events will vary. Thus such works lend themselves more readily both to originality of composition and subtlety of appropriation than do compilations and directories. Consequently, it is sometimes said that the former are entitled to more protection than the latter.

But when derivative works contain new material, as well as material in the public domain, the resulting problem of separating the ideas of the original material from their expression is essentially no different from the same problem in cases involving works of fiction. For example, there are numerous cases involving compilations of court decisions wherein the compiler appended to the public domain case reports his own analytical summary of their contents. The courts have held that in such situations two possible categories of wrongful copying may occur: (1) copying of the schematic organization and pagination of the cases and (2) copying of the analytic headnotes. As to the first, the form of arrangement is clearly divisible from the public domain content of the cases, but as to the second, if copying is not verbatim, a more elaborate inquiry must be made as to whether only the ideas in the headnotes or the expression itself has been copied. There seems to be no reason why this inquiry, in the case of headnotes of a derivative work, should not be governed by the rules and analysis that are determinative when the preface to a novel is at issue. Indeed, generally, this is the case.

However, there are a special group of cases concerning nonliteral copying of derivative works that have turned on a unique and questionable rule. To understand the special factors that have been determinative in these cases, and to comprehend why they arguably should not be dispositive at all, it is necessary briefly to reconsider some of the key concepts relating to copyright protection of derivative works.

As we noted earlier, derivative works are treated as entirely new works; that is, the copyright protection afforded to a derivative work depends solely on the originality of the derivative work and not the work from which it is derived. Thus to be granted copyright protection the derivative work must meaningfully embellish or extend the material from which it is derived; for example, alteration of the page numbers of a public domain law book is insufficient to render the altered book copyrightable. It is axiomatic that material in the public domain, whether facts or ideas, or even a pattern of facts and ideas, does not become the property of the author of a derivative work composed therefrom. If the material contained in a derivative work is in the public domain, the derivative work is afforded copyright protection solely with respect to its particular arrangement of the public domain materials. Logically, then, although an author may arrange public domain material with originality, as by the judicious selection of incidents to include in a biography, and although he may restrain other authors from copying his work verbatim, he may not prevent others from appropriating the public domain material in his work and restating it in a similar biography via a different form of expression. In other words, it follows from the principles governing copyrightability of derivative works that a later author may use a derivative work as a source book for facts and ideas, and thus, take advantage of the research of his predecessors.

Indeed, insofar as maps are concerned, this is the rule. In those jurisdictions in which direct observation on the part of the cartographer is not a prerequisite for copyrightability of a map, a map maker may borrow from sources in the public domain and create a new map. In so doing he may utilize any information contained in a copyrighted map, as long as the particular form of expressing that information is not appropriated. Thus, where one person has used particular signs and keys to designate objects on maps of New York City so that fire insurers could tell at a glance the characteristics of certain buildings, infringement does not result when another person prepares a similar map of Philadelphia using the identical signs and keys. This case demonstrates that a map maker may borrow the ideas of a previous work. Yet facts and data may also be borrowed if they are in the public domain. Accordingly, in making a map of the High Sierras, a cartographer may copy the names of creeks, lakes, and trails from the copyrighted map of the explorer who first charted the area and who invented the names. The general rule is that latter-day map makers "are entitled to use, not only all that has gone before, but even the plaintiff's contribution itself, if they draw from it only the more general pattern, that is, if they keep clear of its expression." Although this statement is entirely consistent with the rules governing originality of derivative works, most courts would restrict its application to cases involving maps.

In cases concerning derivative works other than maps, the courts have tacitly recognized a distinction between ideas and facts. Ideas are always held to be in the public domain and may always be borrowed. But where facts or the fruits of research are concerned, courts are reluctant to allow a newcomer to borrow from the work of another. Accordingly, where compilation or rearrangement of public domain materials is laborious or necessitates great expense or research, courts generally have protected the author's labor as well as his expression, and not only have they forbade others from copying the particular arrangement of material, but they have prohibited others from using the work as a source book. An interesting and typical case is *Toksvig* v. *Bruce Publishing Co.* The plaintiff published a biography of Hans Christian Andersen. The book was developed over a period of three years and was based on profound research in Danish sources, Andersen's original letters, and conversations with persons who knew of Andersen's life. The defendant's book was created in eleven months and was derived from the material in plaintiff's book. The court, in holding for the plaintiff, felt it necessary to repudiate defendant's contention that as the biography contained only facts within the public domain, it was a proper source book for later biographers: "The question is not whether Hubbard could have obtained the same information by going to the same sources, but rather did she go to the same sources and do her own independent research?"

Similar language has appeared in many cases, especially those involving directories, and it has become the general rule that a subsequent author cannot borrow abstract public domain material from a previously copyrighted work in order to save labor and expense, although a late comer may use a prior work for purposes of verifying his independent research. The most influential of these decisions has been *Leon* v. *Pacific Telephone and Telegraph Co.* In *Leon,* the defendant took plaintiff's alphabetically ordered copyrighted telephone directory and rearranged the listings, ordering them by number. A more clearcut case of copying the idea and not the expression cannot be imagined; nonetheless, the court held that defendant had infringed.

The cases in accord with *Toksvig* and *Leon* have been justly criticized as inconsistent with the concept of originality in copyright law. Although these cases emphasize the speed with which a later author could compose a competing work were the first compiler's labors not protected, another court has observed that "it is just such wasted effort that the proscription against the copyright of ideas and facts . . . [is] designed to prevent." Though it is indeed desirable to protect scholars from having their labors appropriated, such protection is best afforded by the law of unfair competition, which protects commercial intangibles, rather than the law of copyrights, which protects original writings, not original research.

The Ordinary Observer Test for Substantial Similarity.   We have seen that some of the material in a copyrighted work may be unprotected by the copyright. Such material may be freely copied. Yet those portions of the work that are protected may not be copied at all. It is on these protected portions of plaintiff's work that the issue of substantial similarity focuses. Initially, it is up to the court to determine which portions of plaintiff's work are entitled to copyright protection. The question of whether the similarity between two works relates to protected or nonprotected portions is solely a matter of law and is decided by the court. In contrast, once the court has determined that the protectable expression of two works is similar, it is up to the jury to decide whether similarity is sufficiently substantial to show copying. Obviously, the issue then becomes: how much similarity is substantial? The courts' answer to this question has been peculiarly unsatisfactory. It is said that two works are substantially similar when an ordinary observer, upon exposure to both works, would spontaneously detect copying. For example, in the leading case, in which the defendant's movie "The Freshman" was alleged to infringe the plaintiff's story "The Emancipation of Rodney," the court concluded: "[W]e think it is fairly clear that, given an interval of two or three weeks between a casual reading of the story and a similar uncritical view of 'The Freshman,' it would not occur to such a spectator, in the absence of a suggestion to that effect, that he was seeing in motion picture form the story or any part of the 'Emancipation of Rodney.'" This quotation highlights the problems inherent in the ordinary observer test. Substantial similarity exists when copying is apparent to the casual, uncritical eye. On the simplest level, this standard is awkward because neither the judge nor the jury can easily identify with an uncritical observer. In litigation, plaintiff's "suggestion" of copying permeates the courtroom, and the trier of fact by definition will always be in the position of a critical analyst, not a casual observer. He will necessarily have to guess at the reaction of an average audience.

In recognition of the difficulty a juror faces in assessing the reaction of a casual observer, some courts have held that expert testimony is inadmissible on the issue of substantial similarity. Such courts reason that if it takes expert testimony to point out similarities, then they are trivial and are not relevant to the ordinary observer test. It is undeniable, however, that although two works may seem similar to a layman, the apparent similarity very likely may stem more from the layman's lack of sophistication than from the second author's piracy. And, in complicated works, copying that is obvious to an expert may be invisible to the average observer. By excluding expert testimony in such cases, a court may insure an unjust result. This is particularly true in cases involving musical compositions. The uneducated ear simply cannot detect highly skilled copying of musical compositions. Indeed, few ordinary men can tell whether a song is sung in four-four or three-four time, and even fewer can identify a melody's key. It is inescapable, then, that a jury composed of such men is unable, without expert aid, to decide fairly whether one waltz infringes another. Yet a court cannot admit expert testimony and still obtain a result consistent with the ordinary observer standard. Clearly, the standard itself is inequitable. Professor Nimmer has summarized the issue accurately:

> Certainly there can be no dispute that the "spontaneous and immediate" reactions of the ordinary observer are relevant evidence. . . . There is, however, reason to dispute the doctrine insofar as it makes the visceral reactions of the trier the ultimate test of copying (assuming access). The Copyright Act is intended to protect writers from the theft of the fruits of their labor, not to protect against the general public's spontaneous and immediate *impression* that the fruits have been stolen.

Unfortunately, despite persuasive criticism, judicial acceptance of the ordinary observer test is almost universal, and there is no evidence that it is diminishing. The Second Circuit, however, has developed a rule intended to attenuate the prohibition against expert testimony. In that forum, under the holding in *Arnstein* v. *Porter*, it is said that the determination of substantial similarity is bifurcated into two separate inquiries. First, the trier of fact must decide whether the similarity between the two works is the result of copying. On this inquiry, expert testimony is admissible. Secondly, it must be determined whether the copying is "illicit," that is, "whether defendant took from plaintiff's works so much of what is pleasing to the ears of lay listeners . . . that defendant wrongfully appropriated something which belongs to the plaintiff." On this score the impression of the ordinary hearer is the touchstone, and expert testimony is inadmissible.

Although the *Arnstein* formulation is perhaps an improvement in that it allows expert testimony where it is often useful, as the reader has no doubt noted, the formulation is internally inconsistent. For example, suppose a jury is convinced by expert testimony that the defendant has copied. As we have seen, substantial similarity is merely a signpost of copying. Thus if copying has been established, this should end the discussion of substantial similarity, and the second half of the *Arnstein* formulation—whether or not the copying is insignificant and may be disregarded—should be an altogether separate consideration. As Judge Clark pointed out in *Arnstein* in his dissenting opinion:

> I find nowhere any suggestion of two steps in adjudication of this issue, one of finding copying which may be approached with musical intelligence and assistance of experts, and another that of illicit copying which must be approached with complete ignorance; nor do I see how rationally there can be any such difference. . . . If there is actual copying, it is actionable, and there are no degrees; what we are dealing with is the claim of similarities sufficient to justify the inference of copying.

Copying, in any amount, is a technical infringement. The determination of substantial similarity consists merely in the search for "similarities sufficient to justify the inference of copying." Once "illicit copying" becomes a factor, we are beyond the question of substantial similarity and are engaged in a consideration of substantial *copying*. This distinction was disregarded by the Second Circuit in *Arnstein*, probably because although it desired to admit expert testimony on the question of whether copying should be inferred, the court did not wish expressly to repudiate the traditional ordinary observer test. However, it is preferable, and conceptually more precise, to keep the concepts of substantial similarity and substantial copying entirely separate. Of course, courts are understandably reluctant to impose liability on a defendant who has copied only a very small amount of plaintiff's work. For example, one court questioned whether a defendant could be held liable were he to copy only one line of plaintiff's work. It was opined that the answer would depend on the qualitative substantiality of the copied line. For example, appropriation of the lines "Quoth the Raven, Nevermore" or "O Captain! My Captain! Our fearful trip is done!" might be held to create liability, whereas, a famous but less crucial line, such as, "Call me Ishmael," might be copied without detracting from the original. Some courts have said that when the defendant's work copies an insignificant amount of plaintiff's work, there is insufficient *similarity* between the two works to support a judgment of infringement. Such statements are conceptually inaccurate. When copying is demonstrated, substantial similarity exists by definition. Thus it is conceptually more exact to say that copying, though an infringement technically, will not give rise to a legal remedy where the amount copied is qualitatively *de minimis*. Copying is *de minimis* and insubstantial, when, in the judgment of the trier of fact it does not sensibly diminish the value of the original, and does not measurably appropriate the original author's effect. Therefore it may be said that in proving the elements of a claim of copyright infringement, (1) copyright entitlement and (2) copying, the plaintiff, in order to prevail on his proof of his second element must show that the copying is not *de minimis*.

Remedies

In a preceding section we have traced the boundaries of the copyright proprietor's rights in copyrighted material. As we have seen, these boundaries are often easy to describe in general but difficult to locate in a particular case. As a result, copyright infringement is not uncommon. Because of the frequency of infringement and because infringement amounts to a complete taking and use of plaintiff's intellectual property, the copyright proprietor's ability to protect his property and recover when it is appropriated is an important element of his property right under the copyright laws.

Jurisdiction and the Problem of State Sovereign Immunity. By statute, actions to obtain relief for infringement of a statutory copyright must be brought in federal district courts. In contrast, actions for infringement of common law copyrights, as they are based on state law, ordinarily must be brought in state courts except where, because of diversity of citizenship standards, the federal court system is available.

Additionally, it should be noted that when a statutory copyright infringement action is brought against the United States or one of its agents, the district courts are not the proper forum for the litigation, and instead jurisdiction is vested in the United States Court of Claims. But when a copyright is infringed by an agent of a state government, there may be no court in which remedy is available. Under the doctrine of sovereign immunity, a government may not be sued without its consent. The federal government has been held to have waived its immunity with respect to infringement of copyright, but in many states it is still the general rule that the sovereign and its agents are immune from suit. Although very few cases have considered this problem, it is likely that in such states the principle of sovereign immunity will operate to bar suits against the state or its agents for infringement of a common law copyright. Yet when a state agent infringes a statutory copyright, the issue is more complicated. It would seem that both the Supremacy Clause of the Constitution, under which state laws are invalid to the extent that they conflict with properly enacted federal statutes, and the underlying rationale of the sovereign immunity doctrine, that "there can be no legal right as against the authority which makes the law on which the right depends," compel the conclusion that a state may not interpose sovereign immunity as a bar to statutory copyright actions against its agents. Nevertheless, one court in a harshly criticized decision held that a state school district could not be sued for infringement of statutory copyright. This court did not consider the Supremacy Clause at all, but rather rested its holding on the Eleventh Amendment, forbidding suits in federal court by a citizen of one state against another state. Apparently no court has considered the problem subsequently, and it is uncertain whether this case will be followed. In patent infringement cases in which the identical issue has been decided, the courts have split, and no guiding principle has emerged.

Persons Liable as Infringers. Before we turn to a consideration of the specific remedies that may be requested by a plaintiff in a copyright infringement action, it is important to identify those persons who may be held liable for infringement and from whom the plaintiff may exact his remedy. As we have seen, the copyright proprietor's rights, both under the copyright act and common law, grant him exclusive privileges; for example, no one else is permitted to copy the copyrighted work. Innocence, as we shall see, is no defense. Does this mean that when a plagiarist feigns originality, and submits a book for publication, the publisher is liable for infringement? The answer is positively yes. Indeed, both the publisher and the printer of a plagiarized book are liable for infringement, and if a substantially similar movie is made from the plagiarized work, the creator of the screenplay, the producer of the movie, and the owners of each theater in which the picture is shown will all be liable and may be joined as codefendants. Each of these parties will be engaged in conduct prohibited by the copyright laws; the plagiarist will have copied, the screen writer will have dramatized without consent, and the theater exhibitor will have offered an unauthorized performance for profit.

A more difficult problem is presented when the plaintiff attempts to impose vicarious liability on a defendant. In such a situation it is argued that although the defendant himself has not engaged in infringing conduct, by reason of his relationship with a third person he should be held liable when that person commits an infringing act. In the law of tangible personal property, vicarious liability arises most commonly when a master–servant, parent–child, or partnership relationship is involved. However, in cases involving infringement of copyright, vicarious liability is imposed more liberally, and one may be held liable for the infringing acts of another even when none of these relationships exists. The rule, as stated in a leading case, is that liability will be imposed whenever the "right and ability to supervise coalesce with an obvious and direct financial interest in the exploitation of copyrighted materials." Consequently, it has been held that the owner of a ballroom is liable for the infringing performances of his orchestra, even when selection of the music to be performed is expressly reserved to the musicians. And in *Shapiro, Bernstein & Co.* v. *H. L. Green Co.*, a department store that granted an independent company a license to run its record department on a commission basis was held liable when its licensee manufactured and sold pirated recordings, notwithstanding the fact that the department store had no knowledge of the infringing sales. However, it has been ruled that such cases are not controlling when a mere landlord–tenant relationship exists, and absent some direct pecuniary interest in the infringing conduct a landlord is not liable for the infringing acts of his tenant, even when they are committed on the leased premises. Ordinarily, a landlord's power to supervise his tenant's conduct is far more limited than the department store's supervisory authority in the *Shapiro* case. Further, in *Shapiro* the department store owner's remuneration, a percentage commission, stemmed directly from the infringing sales, whereas in a typical landlord–tenant relationship, the tenant is legally bound to pay a fixed amount, and it is nearly impossible to determine whether any of the amount paid constitutes profits derived from an infringement.

Although an employer is often held liable for the infringing acts of his employee, it has been said that the employee himself will not be held liable where he has committed an infringing act pursuant to his employer's command without knowledge that he was infringing, and where he has no authority to exercise his own judgment in the matter.

The remedies available to a plaintiff in a copyright infringement action vary, depending on whether the action is for infringement of a common law or a statutory copyright.

Remedies for Infringement of Common Law Copyrights. When a common law copyright is infringed, the plaintiff may obtain monetary compensation by one of two alternative remedies. First, and most directly compensatory, he may demand recoupment for the decline in the market value of his copyrighted work resulting from the infringement. However, because the amount of such a depreciation is not easily proved, this remedy is often illusory. Consequently, an alternative means of recovery has evolved whereby instead of recouping damages a plaintiff may claim all the profits the defendant has made by reason of his infringement. In special cases, as when the defendant has infringed deliberately, or in reckless disregard of the plaintiff's rights, a court may, in its discretion, allow the jury to award punitive damages. Punitive damages are often called exemplary damages, for their purpose is to deter future infringers by making an example of the defendant in the instant case.

If the plaintiff learns that another is planning to infringe his common law copyright, he may bring suit to enjoin the threatened infringement. Similarly, upon obtaining judgment for one act of infringement, he may demand a permanent injunction. Whether an injunction is proper in cases involving common law copyright is a matter of individual state law, and some states grant equitable relief more readily than others. Accordingly, a skillful attorney will bring suit in a state that favors the type of relief he desires.

Remedies for Infringement of Statutory Copyrights.   Just as remedies for infringement of a common law copyright are controlled solely by state law, the Copyright Act alone governs remedies for infringement of copyrights created under the Act. The Act provides for several categories of monetary recovery, injunctive relief, and, in appropriate circumstances, impoundment and destruction of the infringing work. The provisions on monetary recovery are by far the most significant.

MONEY DAMAGES.   *Damages and Profits.*   Under the Act's monetary remedies section, "any person" who infringes a statutory copyright incurs liability for "such damages as the copyright proprietor may have suffered due to the infringement, as well as all the profits which the infringer shall have made from such infringement." Further, the statute provides that "in proving profits the plaintiff shall be required to prove sales only, and the defendant shall be required to prove every element of cost which he claims."

If *as well as* is construed to mean "in addition to," then the Act provides a drastically greater measure of recovery than does the common law, which as we have seen requires plaintiffs to choose between damages and profits. Indeed, Congress, in enacting the copyright statute, intended that plaintiffs would recover either damages *or* the infringer's profits, whichever proved to be greater. The Supreme Court, however, in *F. W. Woolworth Co. v. Contemporary Arts, Inc.* tacitly approved recovery of both damages and profits and the majority of modern courts have held that cumulative recovery is correct under the Act. It is clear that under the rule of cumulative recovery, there is a significant possibility that a plaintiff may obtain a windfall. For example, suppose plaintiff's copyrighted novel is infringed by a screenplay written by defendant A, the screenplay is produced by defendant B, and the resulting motion picture is exhibited by defendant C. As we have seen, A, B, and C would be liable as infringers; each would be separately responsible for the damages he had caused. Hence A could sue all three simultaneously and recover his damages fully. Further, each defendant would be liable for the profits he derived from his infringing acts. If the plaintiff had himself sold the film rights to his novel, he would probably have received a lump sum equaling the value of the screen rights. This sum would represent the amount that plaintiff could recover from infringers A, B, and C as actual damages. There would still be a need for a screen writer, a producer, and an exhibitor, all of whom presumably would make a profit. Yet under the Copyright Statute, plaintiff receives the profits belonging to A, B, and C. Thus the plaintiff, as a result of the infringement, would receive a bonus. Moreover, the plaintiff's damages are often measured by tabulating the number of sales that the plaintiff lost by reason of the infringement. Thus where the defendant sells to persons who would have bought from the plaintiff, the receipts from each sale by the defendant will be doubly counted, once as part of the defendant's profits and once as part of the plaintiff's lost sales.

Several commentators, citing the unfairness of a double recovery, have suggested that the statute be construed so as to include payment of damages as an element of defendant's cost of calculating his profits. By this unnatural statutory construction, both damages and profits could be awarded by virtue of the wording of the Act, yet the net result would be that only the larger of the two amounts could be recovered. The courts, however, have not accepted this suggestion. Indeed, the Supreme Court has implied, in a case not directly concerning this question, that such a strained interpretation of the statutory damages provisions would be incorrect.

Both in common law and statutory infringement actions, actual damages are often speculative, and proving them is usually difficult. On the other hand, in both cases proof of profits is relatively easy; the plaintiff need merely establish the total income that the defendant realized from his infringing acts. The defendant then has the burden of proving each cost and expense that should be deducted from his gross income. Taxes paid on the income derived from the infringing acts, general production expenses, overhead, costs of labor and materials, and similar types of expenses have been held to be fairly deductible in computing the defendant's profits.

In patent infringement cases, by contrast, when an infringing defendant has added noninfringing, valuable improvements to the plaintiff's patented product, the profits the infringer derives from the machine or device will be apportioned, and only those profits directly attributable to the infringement will be awarded. In two early cases, the Supreme Court held that it was impossible to demonstrate what proportion of the profits of defendant's plagiarized books had accrued by reason of the appropriated material. As the Court did not suggest any cases in which separation of profits would be appropriate, for years it was rigidly held that if the defendant could not clearly demonstrate exactly which profits resulted from his noninfringing improvements, he should be held accountable for the full amount, whether or not this result seemed fair. As the defendant had caused the uncertainty by confusing his noninfringing contributions with material appropriated from the plaintiff, it was felt that the defendant should not be heard to complain, and because of the Court's reluctance to speculate wrongly, it awarded all of the profits to the plaintiff.

In 1940, however, the Supreme Court, in *Sheldon* v. *Metro-Goldwyn Pictures Corp.*, distinguished its two earlier decisions and articulated a more flexible standard for determining when the defendant's profits should be apportioned. Under *Sheldon,* when it is clear that the appropriated material has created only a part of the defendant's profits, the Court, in recognition of the impossibility of "mathematical exactness" should undertake a "reasonable approximation" of the proper degree of apportionment. In *Sheldon,* defendant's motion picture infringed defendant's play. The Court recognized that the drawing power of a motion picture is largely a function of the talents of its stars and its director; its story is often secondary.

Frequently, it is obvious that the defendant's noninfringing contributions have created a great percentage of a work's profits. In such cases, courts have liberally applied the rule of apportionment. Thus in one case, although defendant presented no expert testimony or other evidence demonstrating that the noninfringing portions of his legal treatise attracted purchasers, apportionment was ordered by reason of the fact that only one section of defendant's book (which constituted one third of his treatise) contained infringing material. In ruling that the defendant's failure to introduce expert testimony on the issue did not preclude apportionment, the court stated: "where an infringer's profits are not entirely due to the infringement, and the evidence suggests some division which may rationally be used as a springboard it is the duty of the court to make some apportionment." Where the effect of the defendant's contribution is less obvious, courts tend to require the defendant to present expert testimony or other evidence showing that apportionment is proper.

Statutory "in Lieu" Damages. The Copyright Act provides that "in lieu of actual damages and profits," a court may award within statutorily prescribed limits "such damages as . . . appear just." When the infringement arises from a newspaper reproduction of a photograph, the damages that may be assessed under this section shall not exceed $200 or be less than $50; when a non-dramatic work is infringed by a motion picture and the infringer acted in good faith, the maximum assessment is $100; in all other instances statutory in lieu damages may be assessed from a minimum of $250 to a maximum of $5,000. It should be noted, however, that if the defendant continues his infringing conduct after he has been served with written notice of plaintiff's claim and has had time to act upon it, then these maximum limitations do not apply.

The Act contains several guidelines that courts in their discretion may use in computing an "in lieu" damages award. When the copyrighted work is a painting, statue, or sculpture, the optional assessment is $10 "for every infringing copy made or sold by or found in the possession of the infringer or his agents"; for all other types of works, $1 per copy is suggested. Another guideline concerns dramatic, dramatico-musical, choral, or orchestral compositions; the optional measure is "$100 for the first and $50 for every subsequent infringing performance."

The statutory guidelines are by no means compulsory, and courts may and often do ignore them completely. Further, it should be emphasized that these guidelines are subordinate to the statutory $5,000 maximum and $250 minimum limits and cannot be used to justify astronomical or inconsequential awards. However, as we have seen, when the defendant continues his infringing acts after receiving notice of plaintiff's claim, the $5,000 "in lieu" damages ceiling does not apply; in such a case, if the court desires, damages may be assessed under the optional guidelines for each infringing performance or copy without limit.

Early decisions on the meaning of the in-lieu-damages provision held that the statutory wording was to be construed strictly; thus it was held that statutory damages could be awarded only when neither the plaintiff's actual damages nor the infringer's profits could be ascertained. However, the Supreme Court, in *F. W. Woolworth Co.* v. *Contemporary Arts*, held that such a rule was incorrect. In *Woolworth*, the defendant department store without consent copied plaintiff's statuette "Cocker Spaniel in Show Position." Defendants realized a gross profit of $899.16, and plaintiff suffered damages that were not ascertainable. The court stated:

> [A] rule of liability which merely takes away the profits from an infringement would offer little discouragement to infringers. . . . The statutory rule, formulated after long experience, not merely compels

restitution of profit and reparation for injury but also is designed to discourage wrongful conduct.

Accordingly, it was held that "lack of adequate proof" of the amount of damages *or* the amount of profits "would warrant resort to the statute in the discretion of the court." Indeed, at present, it is the general rule that even when *both* damages and profits are ascertained, the court, in its discretion, may assess statutory damages in lieu of actual damages and profits, although the plaintiff has no right to demand in-lieu damages in such a case.

Although ordinarily statutory damages are applied at the discretion of the court, there is one situation in which the court has no discretion and in which statutory damages, at least the minimum amount, must be assessed. This situation arises when the plaintiff can prove that he has suffered damages by reason of the infringement, but cannot prove either the extent of the damages or the amount of profits derived therefrom by the defendant. Indeed, in one case the Supreme Court indicated that the minimum award of statutory damages is obligatory even when the plaintiff can prove only the fact of defendant's infringement and cannot demonstrate that he has been damaged or that the defendant has profited. Subsequent cases appear to have tempered this decision somewhat, and presently, at least some courts would hold that the assessment of statutory damages where no injury has been proved lies within the court's discretion.

Although the minimum statutory damages awards may seem unfair in particular cases, without them many copyright proprietors would be unable effectively to enforce their rights. As one commentator has said: "The guaranteed award serves to deter potential infringers and at the same time, ease the burden of enforcement for copyright owners." This statement is particularly true with reference to such associations as ASCAP and B.M.I., which enforce their members' rights in copyrighted music and recordings. Clearly, the damages and profits resulting from one playing of a record are generally insubstantial, and without the $250 minimum award, many users of records and sheet music would refuse to pay a license fee and would instead risk a possible suit for infringement.

Multiple Infringements. The remedies we have discussed are available for each infringement. The number of infringements contained in a concatenation of infringing activity is not crucial when actual damages and profits are sought, because these amounts remain the same whether defendant's conduct is held to constitute one continuous infringement or a number of successive independent appropriations. When statutory damages are requested, however, because there is a possible $5,000 recovery for each separate violation, the number of infringements at issue is of paramount importance.

The leading case in the area of multiple infringements is the 1919 Supreme Court decision in *L. A. Westermann Co.* v. *Dispatch Printing Co.* In *Westermann,* the defendant, in two separate editions of its newspaper, published advertisements containing plaintiff's copyrighted illustration. The court first made it clear that multiple reproduction of a single copyrighted work constitutes only a single infringement for purposes of applying statutory damages. Thus although many copies were printed of each edition of the newspaper, each edition could give rise to one statutory damages award. The same principle applies to simultaneous multiple copies of any work, including books, records, or photographs.

The facts in *Westermann* presented a slightly different situation, however. Each edition of a newspaper is a distinct, original publication. Moreover, the two infringing advertisements were sponsored by different companies. In view of these facts, the Court held that "independent infringements" had occurred, and two awards of statutory damages were approved. The Court declined to state a general rule to govern all situations in which the same work is reproduced in successive publications. As a result, individual courts have focused on various portions of the *Westermann* opinion, and there is little accord as to when multiple infringements occur. Several courts have opined that the key factor in *Westermann* was that different advertisers sponsored the two ads. Accordingly, these courts have held that where subsequent publications are "merely a continuation or a repetition of the first," statutory damages may be assessed only once. At least one court has ruled that each daily individual publication in a newspaper, even if part of a series, constitutes a separate infringement. Other courts have suggested that the defendant's technical printing arrangements may be dispositive, with multiple infringements being the correct holding where the printer has to reset copy for each publication. Still another suggestion is that analysis should focus on what we might call the steps involved in defendant's conduct. If successive publications stem from the same set of preparatory steps—that is, contractual arrangements, type setting, sales agreements, and so on—and if the time intervals separating them are brief, then under the "step" analysis only one assessment of statutory damages will be permitted. Some courts have recognized a special rule with respect to performances by an individual musician or singer, and accordingly, it has been held that for separate performances of the same work, multiple statutory damages awards may not be assessed. At present, the question of whether successive publications of an infringing work justify multiple statutory damages awards is usually answered on a case-by-case basis, with the court making its own interpretation of the *Westermann* case. To complicate matters further, it has been ruled that *Westermann,* in which a single illustration was copied twice, should be distinguished from the situation in which two different portions of a single work are copied, with one portion appearing in one edition of a paper, the other in the next. In such a case, each publication constitutes a separate distinct infringement for which statutory damages may be assessed.

It should be noted that the Copyright Act provides for one exception to the normal rules governing multiple publications of an infringing work. When a motion picture infringes a "dramatic or dramatico-musical work," if the "maker" of the motion picture infringed innocently and without negligence, only one statutory damages award may be recovered from the maker "and his agencies for distribution."

Although the *Westermann* case clearly concerned a situation in which two or more publications copy one copyrighted work, the Court took pains to differentiate the situation in which two or more copyrighted works are copied in one publication. The Court explained:

> The statute says that the liability thus defined is imposed for infringing "the copyright in any 'copyrighted' work." The words are in the singular, not the plural. Each copyright is treated as a distinct entity, and the infringement of it as a distinct wrong, to be redressed through the enforcement of this liability.

Thus a defendant whose work contains portions appropriated from several separate copyrighted works may be assessed maximum statutory damages for each appropriation. Although this rule is conceptually rudimentary, in actual practice it is often extremely difficult to apply, for it is most often invoked when defendant's work allegedly infringes several separately copyrighted versions of the plaintiff's work. Usually, each successive version is very similar to its predecessors; therefore if the defendant's work infringes one it ordinarily infringes the others. In view of the inequity of holding the defendant liable for multiple infringements under such circumstances, two courts have held that only one statutory damages award may be assessed. However, one influential case has held the contrary. As is so often the case in copyright law, the issue is unresolved.

Recovery for Infringement of the Right to Record. As we have seen, Section 1(e) of the Copyright Act provides for compulsory licensing of recording rights in copyrighted music. If the copyright owner has not given any authorization to record his work, he may recover damages and profits or statutory in-lieu damages if his composition is recorded, just as he might for any other form of infringement. Yet once a copyright proprietor permits another to record his copyrighted musical composition, anyone else can make subsequent recordings. If the person who makes the recording complies with the statute and files notice of an intent to use the copyrighted composition, he may manufacture as many records as he desires; under the licensing provisions the copyright proprietor is entitled to a royalty of 2 cents per recording. If a person who has filed notice of intent to use refuses to pay this royalty, the copyright owner may recover his royalty and in the court's discretion "by way of damages and not as a penalty" he may be awarded an additional sum, not to exceed 6 cents per recording. But when the defendant has not filed a notice of intent to use, as required by Section 101(e), no license to record comes into existence. In such event, the copyright owner's remedies are not limited by Section 101(e), and under Section 101(b) he may recover his damages and the infringer's profits or may resort to the statutory provisions for in-lieu damages.

INJUNCTIONS. The Copyright Act empowers a court in its discretion to enjoin violations "of any right secured" by the Act. Whether or not an injunction will be granted depends upon whether a preliminary or a permanent injunction is requested, and on the balance of equities in a particular case. Although the law relating to preliminary injunctions is often recondite, particularly where, as is frequently the case in copyright cases, First Amendment considerations are involved, a few general guidelines are recognized. Generally, the plaintiff must demonstrate that if the injunction is not granted he will suffer severe harm that cannot be remedied by money damages. The extent of the plaintiff's prospective injury is balanced against the harm the defendant will suffer if the injunction is imposed. Further, the plaintiff must convince the court that an injunction is not against the public interest and that ultimately, at trial, he is likely to prevail. Courts in different districts apply their own formulations of these principles. A permanent injunction will be imposed against the defendant in addition to damages, when there is the strong possibility of future infringements.

IMPOUNDMENT AND DESTRUCTION. Although a detailed discussion of the correct procedures and the applicable rules is beyond the scope of this book, it should be noted that under Section 101(c) of the Act, a court may order "all articles alleged to infringe a copyright" impounded. After finding that the articles indeed do infringe the plaintiff's copyright grant, the court is empowered to destroy "all the infringing copies" as well as "all plates, molds, matrices, or other means for making such infringing copies as the court may order." In addition, Sections 107 and 108 of the Act provide that foreign-made, unauthorized copies of copyrighted *books* (or even authorized copies that are violative of the manufacturing clause), "shall be seized and forfeited by like proceedings as those provided by law for the seizure and condemnation of property imported into the United States in violation of the customs revenue laws. As these provisions protect against pirated *books* only, without further protection the copyright proprietor would be vulnerable to importation of other foreign-made infringing works, as seizure at the moment of entry or at any time prior to the commission of an infringing act would be prohibited. Thus a foreign copyright buccaneer could send in infringing works, sell them, have the receipts wired abroad and stashed away, and would be generally safe from actions in U.S. courts and perhaps even actions in foreign tribunals. In recognition of such a possibility, the Bureau of Customs has promulgated regulations designed to protect all copyright proprietors.

BUREAU OF CUSTOMS REGULATIONS PROHIBITING IMPORTS OF COPYRIGHT INFRINGING ARTICLES. We have seen in Chapter 4, pp. 280–282 how, through recording procedures with the Bureau of Customs, imports of trademark or trade name infringing products can be stopped by the Bureau of Customs. Comparable remedies exist for registered copyright owners and the reader is invited to refer back to this discussion for background purposes.

Copyright Recording Procedures. The only copyrights eligible for the protection provided by these Bureau of Customs regulations are those that are registered in accordance with the provisions of the Copyright Act, and unregistered claims to copyright for works entitled to protection under Section 9(c) of the Act by virtue of the Universal Copyright Convention. (These unregistered claims apply only to works of foreign authors and works that were first published in foreign countries). Further, only those copyrights properly recorded with the bureau are fully protected. Applications to record copyrights must include the name and complete address of the copyright owner, the name and address of any foreign person licensed under the claim of copyright, the foreign title of the work, and in the case of protection claimed under Section 9(c) of the Copyright Act, a statement by the applicant setting forth the name of the author and his citizenship and domicile at the time of first publication, the date and country of first publication, a description of the work, including its title, and a statement that all copies bore the Universal Copyright Convention notice from the date of first publication. The application must be accompanied by an "additional certificate" of copyright registration issued by the U.S. Copyright Office when claim is made on the basis of a registered copyright. In addition, the applicant must provide 700 photographs or other likenesses of three-dimensional works or, where the application covers a book, magazine, or the like, applicant must provide 700 likenesses of a component part (title page and one page of text) of the copyrighted work. A fee of $100 is required for each copyright claim to be recorded.

Copyright Infringement Remedies. The Bureau of Customs regulations protect copyrighted works in two respects. First, they prohibit the importation of articles bearing a false notice of copyright. Second, and most importantly, they prohibit the importation of pirated copies. Pirated copies are defined as "actual copies or substantial copies of a recorded copyrighted work." The regulations require the district director to seize and institute forfeiture proceedings against an imported article that he determines to constitute a piratical copy of a recorded copyright work. The same action must be taken when there is suspicion of piratical copying and the importer does not deny an allegation to that effect.

Where it is unclear as to whether or not a particular article is a pirated copy but the district director does have reason to believe that the article is pirated, he is required to detain the articles and notify the importer that the copies are considered to be "pirated." The director also notifies the copyright owner of the suspected pirating and furnishes to the copyright owner a representative sample of the imported articles together with a notice that the imported articles will be released to the importer unless within thirty days the copyright owner files with the district director a written demand for the exclusion from entry of the detained articles, and a bond to cover any harm that might result from unwarranted detention. If the copyright owner fails to make such a filing, the articles must be released to the importer. If the copyright owner does file the demand and bond, and if the importer denies that the articles are pirated copies, the parties then have thirty days within which to submit further evidence, briefs, and other pertinent materials to substantiate the claim or denial of pirated copying. Contrary to the provision respecting trademarks and trade names, the burden of proof with respect to piratical copying is upon the party claiming that any article is in fact a pirated copy. At the close of the period specified for submission of evidence, the entire file is forwarded to the Commissioner of Customs for a decision on the disputed claim.

Although the portions of the regulations pertaining to protection of recorded copyrights do not shift the burden of proof on the question of infringement to the importer, complying with the regulations may still be important, because the questions of infringement can be resolved prior to the time that the allegedly infringing articles enter the free flow of commerce and become disbursed throughout the country. Members of the publishing and recording industry should be aware of this latter aspect of protection under the regulations, because many no doubt recognize, and probably have been confronted with, the problem of attempting to enforce a claim of copyright against pirated imports after the imports have been distributed for resale.

COSTS AND ATTORNEY'S FEES. The Copyright Act provides that the prevailing party in a statutory copyright action *must* be permitted to recover his court costs from his adversary, and the statute adds that the court may award a "reasonable attorney's fee as part of the costs." This provision does not apply, however, in actions brought against the United States or its agents.

A party's costs will usually not be great. On the other hand, his attorney's fees may be quite substantial, and some courts have awarded large amounts as reasonable attorney's fees. The majority of courts will award attorney's fees only if the losing party deserves to be penalized, as when the infringement was intentional, or when a frivolous claim or defense has been asserted, or when the court finds other conduct denoting bad faith. One survey, though now perhaps out of date, showed that attorney's fees are awarded in three out of ten copyright infringement cases.

DEFENSES TO ACTIONS FOR COPYRIGHT INFRINGEMENT

Introduction

As noted in the preceding section, the elements of plaintiff's proof in an infringement case are (1) copyright entitlement and (2) copying. Accordingly, a defendant's case initially consists in challenging the validity of plaintiff's copyright and in arguing that the two works before the court are not substantially similar. However, even if the court rules that the plaintiff has proved his case and that the defendant has infringed the plaintiff's work, there are several affirmative defenses that in appropriate circumstances may be interposed to justify or excuse infringement. These defenses are the subject of this section.

Fair Use

Although the Copyright Act purports to prohibit unauthorized copying of copyrighted works, the courts have consistently recognized that others may copy and use copyrighted material without authorization if such reproduction and use is "fair." In the lawyer's vernacular, "fair use" of copyrighted material is not actionable. No one could write an illuminating and interesting book on playwriting without extracting key quotations from many instructive plays. Similarly, an historian ideally should be able to quote from important letters and a literary critic should be permitted to describe in detail the pattern of a work; neither should be compelled to speak around his subject for fear of being charged with copying. Surely, if a copyright proprietor could absolutely restrain all copying of his work, instruction, criticism, research, and the flow of information would be measurably impeded. As the ancient Romans realized, "A dwarf standing on the shoulders of a giant can see farther than the giant himself." Thus we can see that the modern concept of fair use is based on the express purpose of the copyright laws, "to promote the progress of science and the useful arts."

That the defense of fair use is necessary is readily understood. But the application of the defense in a particular case is another matter altogether. The problem of determining when a use is fair and how much copying is permitted, has been called the most troublesome in the whole law of copyright. One reason it has proved so troublesome is that some courts have failed to comprehend that the defense of fair use is conceptually distinct from the defense of lack of copying. For example, such courts, upon finding that the defendant's work is not substantially similar to the plaintff's copyrighted materials, will state that the defendant has made a fair use of plaintiff's work. As we have seen, where there is no substantial similarity, there is no copying, for purposes of infringement. And where there is no copying, the plaintiff cannot prevail, and the defense of fair use is extraneous. The defense of fair use does not come under consideration until the plaintiff has proved his case. Similarly, some courts have confused the defense of fair use with the *de minimis* rule, also discussed earlier. Under this rule the plaintiff may not recover where the only copying he can prove is so insubstantial that the court reasonably may proceed as if no copying has been proved at all. In contrast, the affirmative defense of fair use is properly invoked only when the plaintiff has demonstrated qualitatively substantial copying. It bears repeating that the defense of fair use operates to bar a plaintiff's recovery; it applies only when the plaintiff has proved his case.

Yet the problem that makes fair use such a troublesome concept is not its definition, although some courts have found this troublesome enough, but rather its application. Many courts have attempted to articulate guidelines for determining whether the use made of a particular work is fair. Unfortunately, no workable test has been developed. Thus individual cases often are of little aid to subsequent decisions. Yet although the cases provide no immutable rule when we survey the issues that have proved dispositive in the fair use cases, we can see that most of the cases have turned on the same consideration. In nearly every case, the dispositive question has been how much the defendant's use reduces the potential demand for the plaintiff's copyrighted work. In considering whether the defendant's use tends to interfere with the sale of the copyrighted article courts will refer to the purpose and character of the use, the nature of the copyrighted work, and the substantiality of the portions used in relation to the work as a whole. Thus the defense of fair use depends on the court's evaluation of copyright policy. Those cases in which the defendant's use clearly destroys plaintiff's market for future sales, and thus is obviously unfair, are rare; ordinarily the court must carefully balance the possible effects of defendant's use against the public interest in access to defendant's work as a whole. When balancing is difficult, those materials that the court feels as a matter of policy should be widely disseminated will be given less protection than other materials.

For example, in the case of *Time, Inc.* v. *Bernard Geis Associates,* cited earlier in this chapter, the defendant, in writing a book on the murder of President Kennedy, was permitted to copy fourteen frames from the Zapruder film of the assassination. It was held that the impact of the defendant's book on the market for plaintiff's film in future motion pictures or other books was too speculative to outweigh the "public interest in having the fullest information available." The court's conclusion that the market value of the film would not be diminished and indeed might be enhanced by the defendant's book was apparently not founded on any empirical evidence; moreover, it seems quite likely that this conclusion was incorrect. Further, as the court noted, defendant could have made sketches to convey the scene depicted by the film without actually copying individual frames. Yet because the copies made defendant's book "easier to understand" and because the public was entitled to consider any serious explanation of the assassination, defendant's copying was held to constitute a fair use.

Where the defendant's use of the copyrighted materials will serve to promote the progress of knowledge and the arts, as when he has borrowed plaintiff's work for use in a textbook, or a critical review, or even a motion picture, a greater amount of borrowing will be permitted than when the use serves no such beneficial purpose. Accordingly, in one case a cigarette company included in its advertisements excerpts from plaintiff's book on the human voice in which he opined that smoking has no ill effect on the ear, nose, and throat. It was held that the purpose of such reproduction was purely commercial and that under no interpretation could defendant's work be considered to advance science or art. From this case it is apparent that in assessing the fairness of a use the court not only must assess the public's interest in dissemination of the plaintiff's materials, but must make a value judgment of the defendant's work as well. Where a court finds that the defendant's use contributes little to the progress of our culture or technology, it will be reluctant to hold that the defendant's use is fair. That the defense of fair use often involves the court in valuative criticism is most evident in the cases involving parody and satire. It is the general rule that fair use is necessary in such works in order to "conjure up the originals." Yet in a well-known case it was held that a one-half hour television show presented by comedian Jack Benny wrongfully appropiated substantial portions of the movie "Gas Light" and could not be justified under the doctrine of fair use. Although defendant's show was presented as a comedy, it closely paralleled the motion picture. The two works shared the same setting, characters, sequence of events, points of suspense, and climax, and moreover, the court noted a "detailed borrowing of much of the dialogue with some variation in wording." The humor in defendant's work was said to consist in slapstick comedy; for example, some lines were delivered by actors walking on their hands. Although the Ninth Circuit expressly held that the defendant's copying was too substantial to fall within the defense of fair use, implicitly, it in effect assessed the value of the defendant's parody, measured it against the value of the plaintiff's work, and found that the defendant's contributions were insufficient to warrant the extent to which the plaintiff's exclusive privilege to copy was usurped.

It is instructive to compare the "Gas Light" case to the case of *Berlin* v. *E. C. Publications, Inc.*, in which use of the plaintiff's work was held to be fair. In this case, the defendant, *Mad Magazine*, parodied the lyrics of twenty-five of plaintiff's songs, but did not reproduce plaintiff's music "in any form whatsoever." The court noted that in theme, content, rhyme, scheme, and style, the parodies "differed markedly" from the originals: "Thus 'the last time I saw Paris,' originally written as a nostalgic ballad . . . became in defendant's hands 'the first time I saw Maris,' a caustic commentary upon the tendency of a baseball hero to become a television pitchman. . . ." Here the value of defendant's "caustic commentary" outweighed the extent to which it reduced the demand for the plaintiff's songs. Of course, we should not lose sight of the fact that in the "Gas Light" case a very significant portion of plantiff's work was copied. It cannot be gainsaid that even where the defendant's contribution is valuable and in the public interest, he may not copy to such an extent that his work becomes a substitute for the original. Indeed, this principle was recognized by the court in *Berlin* as it noted that "Louella Schwartz

Describes Her Malady" would hardly be an acceptable substitute for a potential patron of "A Pretty Girl Is Like a Melody."

Moreover, even in the fields of scholarly works and artistic comment, where the doctrine of fair use has its most liberal application, it is well recognized that the defendant may not be permitted to copy to such an extent that the potential demand for the plaintiff's work will be reduced, even when the defendant's work as a whole perhaps contributes more to science and the arts than does the plaintiff's. For example, in *Folsom* v. *Marsh* it was ruled that a biographer who copied 391 letters of George Washington could not invoke the defense of fair use. The *Folsom* case presents an interesting contrast to the decision in *Time, Inc.* In *Folsom* the defendant's book was a simulated autobiography of our first President, the copied letters forming one third of the book and the defendant's narrative filling in the gaps. As in *Time, Inc.*, the public interest in information relating to the life of a President was clearly recognized by the court. Indeed, it was pointed out that the defendant's work was peculiarly well suited for use in school libraries. Further, in both *Time, Inc.*, in which the frames copied showed the bullets strike, and *Folsom*, in which the "most useful and interesting" letters were reproduced, the amount of copying clearly was quite substantial in a qualitative sense. Nevertheless, in *Time, Inc.*, the court held that defendant's use was fair, whereas in *Folsom* the defendant was held liable. The distinction between the two cases is instructive. In *Time, Inc.*, the court concluded (though perhaps erroneously) that sales of defendant's book would stem from the public's interest in the originality of the author's explanation of the assassination; the copies, it was felt, were used merely to support the author's theories. In *Folsom*, however, the appeal of defendant's book was held (again perhaps erroneously) to be derived largely from the copied material, and from the substance of the material itself, rather than from the manner in which it was arranged or analyzed. As Justice Story explained:

> In some cases, a considerable portion of the materials of the original work may be fused . . . into another work, so as to be undistinguishable in the mass of the latter, which has other professed and obvious objects, and cannot fairly be treated as a piracy. . . . [But] everyone must see that the work of the defendants is mainly founded upon these letters, constituting more than one-third of their work, and imparting to it its greatest, nay, its essential value. . . . It is not a case where abbreviated or select passages are taken from particular letters; but the entire letters are taken, and those of most interest and value to the public. . . .

Indeed, when the heart of a work is appropriated in the name of criticism, courts will not allow the defendant to justify his piracy in the name of fair use. Generally, critics may reproduce significant portions of a copyrighted work because their comments serve merely to supplement the original. Yet where the so-called criticism supplants the original, it cannot be deemed fair.

Accordingly, in a recent case, the defendants, the Mission Singers, representatives of a nonprofit religious organization, performed a modified version of the rock opera "Jesus Christ Superstar," in which the lyrics, score, sequence of songs, and overall pattern of the plaintiff's original production were copied. The defendants claimed that their performance represented a fair use of plaintiff's material in that their production made crucial changes in the opera's treatment of Christ's life and death. It was contended that plaintiff's script was an "unfavorable and offensive comment on Passion and Death of Jesus, and [was] offensive to long-held Christian beliefs about Him." In their production, defendants argued, Christ was portrayed as a "strong masculine individual who has no physical contact with Mary Magdalene, while the plaintiff's production reveals an effeminate, uncertain Jesus who has a 'carnal relationship' with Mary Magdalene." Further, defendants alleged that in their performance the resurrection was emphasized, whereas in plaintiff's production, Christ "merely dies." The court dismissed the defendants' argument, holding that although there are many uncertainties as to the application in individual cases of the doctrine of fair use, it is "crystal clear" that one does not have to copy a work almost in its totality in order to criticize it.

An important factor in determining whether defendant's use will reduce the demand for plaintiff's original is the presence of competition between the two works. If there is none, a surprisingly substantial amount of copying will be allowed. Thus in one case it was held that although significant portions of three 1954 *Look* magazine articles were reproduced in defendant's 1966 biography of Howard Hughes, the defense of fair use was available, for there was no showing that the biography and the articles were "in competition with each other." Accordingly, too, it has been held that no liability is incurred when a magazine article tracing the history of the Green Bay Packers reproduces eight lines of the plaintiff's song "Go Packers Go."

So far, we have seen that fair use is an affirmative defense that allows a defendant to justify copying a variable but sometimes significant amount of copyrighted material. As a corollary, it is well established that when defendant's work reproduces so much of the original, and in such a manner, that it tends to satiate the potential audience for the original, the defense of fair use is not available. Thus it would seem to follow that copying of another's work in totality can never be a fair use. Indeed, this is generally the rule. However, in one unusual case plaintiff's copyrighted puppets were used as characters and were photographed as part of a scene during the "Captain Kangaroo" television show. It was held that even if it could be said that use of the puppets in the program constituted "copying" within the meaning of the copyright laws, the defense of fair use would be applicable. Logically, the same result should follow in similar cases; therefore it should be permissible for a motion picture to reproduce copyrighted works for purposes of verisimilitude, as, for example, by depicting a copyrighted photograph hanging on a wall in the background, or by showing a copyrighted newspaper being read by an actor.

Ordinarily, however, courts have ruled that complete copying of a copyrighted work, notwithstanding a laudable motivation, cannot constitute a fair use. Thus courts have ruled that copyrighted materials may not be Xerox copied or mimeographed by a teacher and distributed to his class at large. Clearly, in such case the materials copied would serve as a substitute for the copyrighted materials. In theory, each student would buy an edition of the copyrighted book or article, but for the unauthorized reproduction. Yet what of the photocopy made by a public library at the request of one of its readers? Because the reader could check out the book, take it home, and copy those passages needed for his research or enlightenment, should he be compelled to go through the process of checking the book out and copying by hand when the time-saving shortcut of photocopying is available?

This question was confronted by the U.S. Court of Claims in the ground-breaking 1973 case of *Williams & Wilkins Co.* v. *United States.* In *Wilkins* the plaintiff corporation alleged that the National Institutes of Health and the National Library of Medicine periodically infringed its copyrights by photocopying articles in medical journals and distributing them to both readers and other libraries. The court in weighing a "multiplicity of factors" reversed a preliminary ruling and held in a 4–3 decision that the defendant's photocopying of articles for use by others in research constituted fair use. The court summarized its evaluation in the following words:

First, plaintiff has not in our view shown, and there is inadequate reason to believe, that it is being or will be harmed substantially by these specific practices of NIH and NLM; second, we are convinced that medicine and medical research will be injured by holding these particular practices to be an infringement; and, third, since the problem of accommodating the interests of science with those of the publishers (and authors) calls fundamentally for legislative solution or guidance, which has not yet been given, we should not, during the period before congressional action is forthcoming, place such a risk of harm upon science and medicine.

The court opined that it "need not enter the semantic debate over whether a photocopy supplants the original article itself" or is merely a substitute for the "library's loan of the original issue." This debate had been considered a key issue by many, for arguably, if photocopies now function as substitutes for loans and if loans are indicative of the demand for books, it would seem to follow that libraries, had they not been able to distribute photocopies, at some time in the past would have had to buy more copies of their books. Thus it would follow that the plaintiff, over the years, lost sales by reason of the defendant's Xerox copying. The court felt, however, that if photocopying were forbidden, researchers, in the interest of saving time, might very well cut down their note taking or do without certain issues altogether. Further, the court felt that the legislative history of the Act makes it arguable that the exclusive right to copy does not extend to books and journals. Moreover, it was noted, to reinforce this idea, that although photo duplication had been practiced for many years, no one had ever complained of it. Only in the last ten years, when technology has made Xerox copying widely available have copyright owners objected, but if photocopying was not a per se violation of the Act when it was passed in 1909, it has not become a per se violation by reason of technological advances. Hence, it was held that the individual facts of each case should govern, and when, as in *Wilkins*, the defendant's use is in the public interest and dimunition of the plaintiff's market is speculative, the defense of fair use should be available.

It was emphasized that if NIH were required to obtain a publisher's consent before Xerox copying his work, the publisher could withhold consent altogether or impose an unreasonable license fee. Moreover, if permission were required, it is likely that publishers would unite to create a publishing clearinghouse similar to ASCAP, through which licenses to photocopy would be sold to libraries. Such a clearinghouse no doubt would create many problems, and not the least severe of these might well be concern over anticompetitive pricing practices giving rise to antitrust problems.

The structure of such a joint association, as experience with ASCAP teaches, makes it likely that the members would sell licenses to copy at prices higher than could be obtained were each publisher competing separately. Moreover, as one legal analyst suggested prior to the *Wilkins* decision:

> We may in the next decade see the development of automatic information systems. These systems would store printed information on microfilms or microfiches. . . . The subscriber might use a computer terminal in his home or office to see relevant information; the computer would automatically contact the appropriate library and the librarian would in-

sert the appropriate microfiche in a device that would cause. its contents to appear on the subscribers' home or office viewing screen. Since microfiche is an essential ingredient in this system, a clearinghouse that allows all or most publishers to combine in setting up price for the right to make a microfiche copy may allow those publishers to extract much of the economic benefit that the development of such a system promises.

Judge Davis, writing for the court, stated that the possibility of such a licensing system "is now preeminently a problem for Congress." Implicit in this statement is the fact that under the Act a court is not empowered to impose a reasonable license fee; its remedial powers are limited to damages and injunctions. Indeed, the statutory provisions of the Act, especially the $250 statutory minimum which would have applied had photoduplicating been held to constitute an infringement per se, would have been inappropriate for resolving the *Wilkins* issues. Thus a holding favoring the plaintiff would have rewarded him undeservedly and would have impeded medical research significantly.

The dissenting judges for the most part adopted the opinion of the trial judge who had previously ruled for the plaintiff. In essence, it was the dissenters' contention that because defendant's photoduplicates were made "at the request of, and for the benefit of the very persons who constitute plaintiff's market," redistribution would "diminish plaintiff's potential market," and therefore, the majority's contention that the plaintiff had not demonstrated an injury was not accepted. Further, the majority's finding that the right to copy may not apply when the copyrighted works are books and articles was disputed. Chief Judge Cowen reiterated the trial judge's statement that "there is no case law to support the defendant's proposition that the making of a handcopy . . . of an *entire* copyrighted work is permitted by the copyright law." Clearly, then, there is no authority indicating that photocopying is permitted. Finally, the dissenters argued that the majority's fears of anticompetitive licensing practices were simply not realistic on the *Wilkins* facts, because the plaintiff had already established a fair licensing system that was operating smoothly.

It was recognized that the court had neither the authority nor the manpower to impose and regulate a licensing system, but as Judge Nichols suggested, the court had not been asked to do so. Rather, it had been asked to grant a copyright proprietor a remedy in an individual case. As Chief Judge Cowen explained:

In order to promote the progress of science, not only must authors be induced to write new works, but also publishers must be induced to disseminate those works to the public. This philosophy has guided our country, with limited exceptions, since its beginning, and I am of the opinion that if there is to be a fundamental policy change in this system, such as a blanket exception for library photocopying, it is for the Congress to determine, not for the courts. The courts simply cannot draw the distinctions so obviously necessary in this area.

We should not lose sight of the fact that the majority in *Wilkins* did not hold that all photocopying is permissible. Rather, it ruled that whether a photoduplication of a copyrighted work constitutes fair use should be determined on a case-by-case basis. It was emphasized that NIH and NLM are nonprofit institutions and that they generally offer only copies difficult to obtain elsewhere, and then only to researchers and at no charge. Thus it is doubtful that *Wilkins* will precipitate a large amount of piratical copying. However, as technologies of photocopying advance, reproduction becomes less expensive and more available; if unauthorized photocopying is a fair use when performed by a library for distribution to its readers or to other libraries, it should be no less fair for a reader to make his own copy. And because it will soon be cheaper (if it is not so already) to photoduplicate a book than to purchase it, the holding in *Wilkins* arguably is incorrect. Indeed, Judge Nichols, in his dissent, called *Wilkins* the "Dred Scott decision of copyright law." The Supreme Court has decided to hear the plaintiff's appeal in *Wilkins* and it is obvious that a high court decision that modifies or reverses the Court of Claims will have tremendous impact on the law of copyrights.

Another significant copyright problem arising from contemporary technology is whether computer software (programming) is copyrightable. If it is, it is necessary to establish standards for determining when unauthorized borrowing of copyrighted programming falls within the boundaries of fair use. The fair use problems that arise with respect to computer programming are similar to the problems discussed earlier in relation to Xerography. There are at present numerous "user groups" that share computer systems with other groups. It is customary for particular users to copy or modify elements of others' software for their personal use. If by extending copyright to programming it becomes necessary for the members of one group to obtain permission in order to use the programming devised by members of other groups, the expense may prove to be prohibitive and the procedure may become burdensome. Again, the matter is as yet unsettled, and until computer software is ruled copyrightable, more extensive comment on fair use of computer programming is unwarranted.

The Doctrines of Unclean Hands and Copyright Misuse

Whereas the defense of fair use focuses on defendant's use of the copyrighted material, there are two types of affirmative defenses in which the *plaintiff's* use of the copyrighted work is crucial. The first is called the doctrine of unclean hands and is based on the ancient principles of English courts of equity; the second is known as the defense of copyright misuse and is an offspring of the doctrine of misuse as it exists in modern patent law. Under the doctrine of unclean hands, a plaintiff's recovery may be barred when he has engaged in deception. Although this defense is as old and as time-honored as Anglo-American jurisprudence itself, in copyright cases it is rarely accepted, in part because it is considered extraneous and outmoded in view of the strong public policy favoring copyright protection. The defense of copyright misuse also is rarely accepted, but for different reasons. This defense, as in patent law, consists of a claim that the plaintiff has unfairly attempted to extend his copyright monopoly beyond statutory limits. Though misuse has been a viable defense in patent cases since 1917, in copyright cases the concept of misuse is still considered somewhat novel, and at present its ultimate scope is in doubt.

Unclean Hands.   The underlying principle of this defense is that one whose conduct has been so deceitful as to taint the subject matter of the litigation should not be allowed to recover. As noted earlier, very few courts have denied recovery upon the grounds that plaintiff had unclean hands. Generally, the defense will be recognized only when plaintiff's conduct amounts to an attempt to defraud the court, as where perjured testimony or a counterfeited court order is introduced. As a corollary, Section 18 of the Act provides that anyone who knowingly makes a false affidavit of his having complied with the manufacturing clause forfeits "all of his rights and privileges" in the copyright. Other instances of misconduct ordinarily will not bar recovery.

Copyright Misuse.   As we have seen in Chapter 2, in many cases a patentee who attempts to enlarge his patent monopoly may not maintain an infringement suit as a matter of public policy. In the *Morton Salt* case, the owner of a patent on a machine for dispensing salt tablets required those who leased the machines to use only unpatented salt tablets sold by the patent owner. When the patentee subsequently brought a patent infringement suit, the Supreme Court held that the plaintiff could not recover, notwithstanding the fact that the defendant clearly had infringed. Because both the patent and copyright statutes grant monopolies to creators of intellectual property and because both were enacted to effectuate similar public policies, it would seem logical that practices of the type involved in *Morton Salt* when engaged in with respect to copyrighted works constitute misuse of the copyright grant, and as a result would preclude recovery for infringement.

The Supreme Court, however, has never definitely stated that the misuse of copyright is a defense in an infringement action. After its decision in *United States* v. *Loew's, Inc.* it would seem possible that the court eventually may articulate such a rule. In *Loew's,* the government brought an antitrust action; at issue was the practice of block booking of copyrighted motion pictures for television. In block booking, licenses to exhibit one or a group of motion pictures are granted on the condition that the licensee must contract to show other motion pictures as well.

For such a tie-in arrangement to be illegal under the Sherman Act, the defendant must possess such economic power in the market for the tying product that by the tying arrangement he can appreciably restrain competition in the market for the tied product. The power to restrain competition is presumed when the tying product is a patented article; the key question in *Loew's* was whether the same rule applied to copyrighted works. In holding that the same rule did apply, the Court relied on a "long line of patent cases which had eventuated in the doctrine that a patentee who utilized tying arrangements would be denied all relief against infringements of his patent." Thus the Court found that patent misuse cases were applicable and persuasive in an antitrust case alleging copyright misuse. Arguably, then, these patent misuse cases should also be dispositive in a copyright infringement action wherein the defendant could show block booking or other practices that would bar recovery were a patent involved, until the misuse is purged.

Nevertheless, the lower federal courts, with one uncompelling exception, have been unanimous in rejecting the defense of copyright misuse in copyright infringement actions. It is clear that such holdings are correct insofar as they refuse to bar recovery for copyright infringement merely by reason of the fact that plaintiff has engaged in conduct violative of the antitrust statutes. Although there is a close relationship between patent and copyright misuse and the antitrust laws, not every antitrust violation constitutes misuse. Misuse, as has been noted by one commentator, is peculiarly a question of patent and copyright law and should be invoked only in situations where the patentee or the copyright proprietor has unlawfully attempted to extend his legal patent or copyright monopoly.

Supreme Court decisions subsequent to *Morton Salt* have not extended the doctrine beyond patent misuse, and for this reason in a copyright case one court held that the defense of misuse was limited to patents. On appeal this conclusion was neither restated nor expressly repudiated. Yet although courts have not been receptive to the defense of copyright misuse, it is likely that in a sophisticated court, at least in cases where the plaintiff has employed tie-in arrangements of the type struck down in *Loew's* and *Morton Salt,* the defense of copy-right misuse will bar a recovery for infringement until the misuse is purged, as with patents.

Abandonment of Copyright

Two other defenses that are grounded solely upon the plaintiff's con-duct are the defenses of forfeiture and abandonment of copyright. A copyright is forfeited when the copyright proprietor publishes his work without complying with the prescribed statutory formalities; in the usual case copyright notice is omitted. Copyright forfeiture describes those situations in which recovery is barred because of failure to comply with the necessary formalities. Upon forfeiture, by operation of law, the copy-right proprietor is divested of all rights in the copyrighted work. This is true no matter whether the publication was deliberate or inadvertent. Thus if by mistake the notice in a copyrighted work is postdated, first publica-tion actually having been made in a previous year, it is generally held that copyright protection is forfeited, although there are cases that indicate that this rule will be relaxed where the postdating was unin-tentional, was only in error by one year, and was not relied on by another to his detriment. Predating, on the other hand, does not work a forfeiture, although when the year contained in the notice is prior to the actual year of publication, copyright protection will endure only from the date given in the notice, and not from the date of first publication.

Whereas forfeiture of copyright is a matter of noncompliance with statutory formalities, the key element of abandonment of copyright is the plaintiff's intent. Any conduct that clearly manifests an intent to relinquish copyright protection will be held to constitute an abandon-ment. Typically, abandonment will consist in inaction. For example, in a recent case, suit was brought against *Mad Magazine* to restrain publication of a cartoon depicting a grinning, idiotic boy. The defen-dant, which has had the good fortune to have been the prevailing party in several significant copyright cases, had named the boy Alfred E. Neuman and had captioned the cartoon "What, Me Worry?" Plaintiff substantiated her claim that she was the copyright proprietor of the cartoon, which had been originated by her husband, but nevertheless was denied relief. The court held that in allowing many unauthorized copies of the cartoons to circulate over the years, plaintiff's husband had abandoned his copyright by failing to enforce it. At least one court, however, has indicated that inaction alone, even failure to bring suit when the infringement is notorious, will not constitute an aban-donment. Under this view, abandonment of copyright may not be inferred absent an overt act evidencing an intent to relinquish copyright protection.

The Rule in *Baker* v. *Selden*

A unique defense that may be interposed only in a few unusual cases is the rule in *Baker* v. *Selden*. As discussed earlier in this chapter, in the case of *Baker* v. *Selden,* an author created a system of bookkeeping and designed forms for its use. The author argued that his copyright in the expression of his work, including the forms, extended to cover any copying of the forms by others, even if without copying such forms his bookkeeping system could not be used. The Supreme Court rejected this contention, stating:

> The copyright of a work on mathematical science cannot give to the author an exclusive right to the methods of operation which he propounds, or to the diagrams which he employs to explain them, so as to prevent an engineer from using them whenever occasion requires. The very object of publishing a book on science or the useful arts is to communicate to the world the useful knowledge which it contains. . . . And where the art it teaches cannot be used without employing the methods and the diagrams used to illustrate the book, or such as are similar to them, such methods and diagrams are to be considered as necessary incidents to the art, and given therewith to the public, not given for the purpose of publication in other works explanatory of the art, but for the purposes of practical application.

As we see, the court distinguished copying for use from copying for purposes of explanation. If the only way the ideas embodied in a copyrighted work may be *used* by another is by copying the expression of these ideas, such copying will not constitute an infringement. However, "use" of another's ideas does not include explaining them by unauthorized copying. As a corollary to this rule, the court held that if the work in question is a work of art, the principle that one may copy for purposes of use does not apply, for presumably, one does not "use" such works as he would a system of bookkeeping; rather, "their form is their essence and their object the production of pleasure in their contemplation." Thus, one may copy bookkeeping forms for use in his business but may not reproduce lithographs to hang in his office.

Application of the rule in *Baker* v. *Selden* has had its greatest effect in cases concerning architectural plans. We have already seen that the copyright protection afforded to architectural plans covers reproductions of the plans themselves. Logically, it would seem that such protection would extend to allow recovery for infringement if a building were constructed from copyrighted plans. Such an edifice would merely be a three-dimensional reproduction of the two-dimensional plans. It has been held that a common law copyright in blueprints is infringed when a structure is built from the plans without authorization, for such construction constitutes a publication of the plans. But where the creator of architectural plans claims under a statutory copyright, publication alone is not dispositive, and it has been held that under the rule in *Baker* v. *Selden,* unauthorized construction of a building from copyrighted architectural plans is not actionable. Thus it has been held that if the defendant constructs a special traffic-reducing bridge approach copied from the plaintiff's plans, he is not liable for infringement, for by such construction defendant has copied for purposes of use.

In addition to the area of architectural plans, the rule in *Baker* v. *Selden* has had a substantial effect on the fashion industry. Under the rule, it has been consistently held that when one copyrights a drawing of a dress or an advertisement depicting a dress, he obtains only the right to prevent reproduction of the drawing or the advertisement; anyone may reproduce a substantially similar dress.

As might be expected, the rule in *Baker* v. *Selden* has often been criticized. Although much of this criticism is technical and involves fine points of the law that we need not discuss here, some of the problems arising from *Baker* merit our attention. Proper application of the rule in *Baker* v. *Selden* has proved difficult. Rarely will two courts applying *Baker* to similar facts arrive at similar results. This inconsistency has arisen primarily because the precise meaning and scope of the holding in *Baker* v. *Selden* has never been entirely clear. Although the Supreme Court took great pains to articulate its rule allowing copying for purposes of use, actually, in the beginning of its opinion before it enunciated its well-known rule, the Court found that the plaintiff had failed to demonstrate that his bookkeeping system and forms had actually been used or copied by the defendant. Thus the case could have turned on this finding alone; there was no need to confront plaintiff's claim that he alone was entitled to use his system.

Still another incongruity in the *Baker* opinion has in some ways proved the most troubling problem of all. The Court concluded its opinion in the case with the statement that "blank account-books are not the subject of copyright." If this indeed had been the case, the account forms could have been copied by anyone, whether for use or for explanation, and the rule that the court went to such great pains to articulate would have been irrelevant to the case. It is probable that in holding that the account forms were not subject to copyright, the Court meant simply that the copyright protection afforded to account forms is not infringed when a defendant copies account forms for purposes of use. Nevertheless, many courts have taken the Supreme Court's words at their face value. Accordingly, as we have noted previously, it has been held that blank forms are not copyrightable. Further, as indicated in the earlier discussion of the case of *Morrissey* v. *Procter & Gamble,* some courts have cited *Baker* v. *Selden* for the principle that certain kinds of expression are noncopyrightable, and the Copyright Office has issued regulations that withhold copyright protection to "works designed for recording information which do not in themselves convey information."

Perhaps the most cogent criticism of the rule in *Baker* v. *Selden* has been directed at the assumptions underlying the rule itself. Indeed, it is questionable whether the rule has any valid applications at all. We have noted that no one may monopolize an idea. Thus, if an idea is capable of being *explained* only in one form of expression, anyone may copy it, whether for explanation or for use. We do not need the rule in *Baker* v. *Selden* in such a case. For example, suppose a person were to develop a new system of shorthand and explain it in a copyrighted book. Clearly, he could not prevent others from using his system, for if he could, he would have a monopoly. Further, it has been held that he could not prevent others from writing a book *explaining* his system and reproducing the symbols of which it is composed. Again, if the original author could prohibit such borrowing he would have a monopoly over his idea. If the idea can be utilized without copying another's expression, the rule in *Baker* v. *Selden* is inapplicable, and if the idea can be neither used nor explained without copying the author's expression, we do not need the rule to know that copying will be allowed. We have already noted that the facts in *Baker* v. *Selden* were not within the rule. Indeed in the majority of cases in which defendants have invoked the rule, courts have refused to apply it, and instead it is usually held either that the defendant did not have to copy the plaintiff's work in order to use it or that the defendant did not actually copy the plaintiff's expression at all. Moreover, many of those courts that have applied the rule have done so needlessly, in circumstances offering the defendant many ways to borrow plaintiff's idea without copying. For example, in a leading case it was held that under *Baker* v. *Selden* a person may make verbatim copies of the contracts in another's copyrighted book of forms, because the copying was for purposes of use. The court overlooked the fact that there were many other arrangements of words by which the defendant could have used the ideas contained in plaintiff's forms. Thus one may reasonably conclude that those cases that truly fall within the rule in *Baker* v. *Selden* are extremely rare, whereas incorrect applications of the rule to situations that should be governed by other, simpler principles, are not at all uncommon. Indeed, no less an authority than Professor Nimmer has suggested that "it is factually erroneous to conclude that there is any function that can be performed by the use of only one form of written expression." If he is correct, the rule in *Baker* v. *Selden* should be overturned.

Estoppel

In infringement actions, as in most legal actions relating to rights in property, in appropriate circumstances the defendant may assert the defense of estoppel. Although each court adheres to a slightly different definition of estoppel, generally proof of an estoppel is composed of five elements: (1) the defendant is unaware of plaintiff's copyright or other crucial facts; (2) the defendant relies upon the plaintiff's conduct or assertions; (3) by reason of his reliance upon the plaintiff's conduct or assertions, the defendant commits an infringing act or otherwise prejudices his position with respect to the copyrighted materials; (4) the plaintiff knew or should have foreseen that his conduct or assertions would impel the defendant to act as he did; and (5) the plaintiff is aware of the true, material facts. Hence, as an elementary example, the plaintiff will be estopped to recover for infringement if he has inveigled the defendant into publishing his work. Although there are some similarities between the defenses of estoppel and abandonment of copyright, it is important to remember that abandonment of copyright relates solely to conduct that demonstrates to all the world an intent to relinquish copyright protection, whereas estoppel relates solely to conduct or assertions of one party that has influenced the conduct of another. Only the defendant who has relied upon plaintiff's conduct may assert an estoppel whereas abandonment of copyright may be asserted by anyone whether or not he has dealt with the plaintiff or relied upon his conduct.

The Statute of Limitations

As in other areas of the law, actions for copyright infringement must be brought within the time limit of the statute of limitations. The limitations period for infringement of a common law copyright is determined under the applicable state law. Statutory infringement actions must be filed within three years of the infringing act. Actions brought more than three years from the date of infringement are barred unless the defendant has fraudulently concealed the fact of infringement in order to take advantage of the limitations period.

Even if the copyright proprietor files suit within the limitations period, the equitable doctrine of laches may bar his recovery. Under this doctrine the court will protect an innocent infringer whose position is prejudiced by plaintiff's delay in filing suit. "[I]t is inequitable for the owner of a copyright, with full notice of the intended infringement, to stand inactive while the proposed infringer spends large sums of money . . . and to intervene only when his speculation has proved a success." However, if the infringement is intentional, laches will not apply.

Unintentional Infringement

As a final note to this section it is necessary briefly to consider the defense of unintentional infringement. Defendants in many cases have attempted to avoid liability on the grounds that they have infringed unintentionally. Where a statutory copyright is infringed, liability will be imposed regardless of the defendant's intent. This is true in all cases, and judgment will issue against a defendant who has copied from a third party without knowledge that the third party had plagiarized from the plaintiff; similarly, the defendant may not escape liability on the grounds that he has copied subconsciously.

There appears to be no valid reason why the rule should be different in cases involving infringement of common law copyrights. Nevertheless, several New York state court decisions have held that unintentional infringement of a common law copyright is not actionable. As Professor Nimmer has pointed out, these cases are of dubious lineage, and should not be considered authoritative.

Although lack of intent will not preclude liability, it may be called a defense in the sense that the scope of the remedies available against an innocent defendant is limited. For example, a few courts have implicitly held that compensatory damages may not be recovered from an innocent infringer who reasonably believed that he was not infringing, although he will be held liable for his profits. Further, as we have seen in our discussion of damages in the previous section, under the Copyright Act a broadcaster who innocently infringes a nondramatic literary work is liable for maximum damages of $100, and the same maximum applies when a film maker and his agents innocently infringe a nondramatic work. Moreover, when the maker of a film and his agents innocently infringe a dramatic or dramatico-musical work, there is a $5,000 maximum recovery for multiple infringements. In all of these statutory limitations it is expressly stated that an infringer is not innocent if he could have reasonably foreseen that he was infringing.

COPYRIGHT–ANTITRUST PROBLEMS

Introduction

Copyrights, like patents, are peculiarly subject to antitrust problems because they entail the grant of a lawful monopoly. Any device that is used to extend this monopoly beyond its lawful bounds, or to use the monopoly power coercively, may well be struck down under the antitrust laws. In the following subsections, we will explore certain of these problem areas. The reader should appreciate, however, that these areas are not the only ones in which the misuse or manipulation of copyrights can run afoul of the antitrust laws. For example, under some circumstances the mere accumulation of copyright rights may give rise to a charge of monopolization in violation of Section 2 of the Sherman Act. This is far less likely to occur in the case of copyrights than in that of patents, because by their nature copyrights do not have nearly the anticompetitive potential that patents do. Nonetheless, a famous case involving ASCAP demonstrated how the accumulation of copyright rights can amount to monopolization. In *Alden-Rochelle, Inc.* v. *ASCAP,* ASCAP was accused of numerous antitrust violations, including coercive package licensing and refusals to deal. The salient point in the case, however, was that the compositions in ASCAP's repertory constituted over 90 per cent of all copyrighted musical works in the United States. As the exclusive licensee of the performance rights in these works, ASCAP was found to wield monopoly power. This monopoly power tainted ASCAP's licensing policies, and it was found guilty of unlawful monopolization of performance rights.

Another monopolization case demonstrates how copyrights may be the vehicle for achieving an unlawful end. In *United States* v. *Paramount Pictures, Inc.,* at issue were a number of exclusionary practices of the country's five major motion picture producers. The producers were vertically integrated companies; that is, they were involved in producing, distributing, and exhibiting motion pictures. They were, of course, the owners of the copyrights in their motion pictures, and thus were able to use copyright licenses to control their exhibition. The producers owned at least 70 per cent of the country's quality motion picture theaters, which were used for "first-run" exhibition of films. And, as the Supreme Court said, the first-run field "constitutes the cream of the exhibition business." The practices engaged in by the producers involved the use of copyright licenses in their motion pictures to govern the admission price charged by exhibitors, the "run" (that is, when the film could be exhibited, first-run, second-run, and so on), and the "clearance" (that is, the delay between runs). By so manipulating price, runs, and clearances, the producers were able to give first-run exhibitors as near a monopoly of patronage as possible. And because most of the first-run theaters were owned by the major producers, the effect was to create in them a monopoly of motion picture exhibitions. This use of the motion picture copyright was condemned as violating Section 2 of the Sherman Act.

Price Fixing

Price fixing is of course illegal per se under Section 1 of the Sherman Act, whether it is the result of a horizontal agreement among competitors or a resale-price-maintenance agreement between a seller and a customer-reseller. In the case of resale-price maintenance, an exception to the per se rule exists where a state law permitting fair trading is applicable. Price-fixing cases involving copyrights have arisen in both horizontal and vertical situations.

The bundle of exclusive rights that make up copyright includes the exclusive right to vend the copyrighted work. As we have seen, this right is limited by the first-sale doctrine so that a copyright proprietor may not exercise control over his work after the first authorized sale. Prior to the first sale, however, the copyright owner may, by contract, set the price at which copies of the copyrighted work are to be sold, and such limitations are valid and enforceable. Thus an author of a copyrighted book may require the publisher to sell it to bookstores at a particular price. After this first sale, however, there may be no further control over price, and any agreement between the bookseller and the publisher to maintain a given price would be illegal. The sole exception here would be in the case of sales in a state having a fair trade statute. In such a state, resale-price-maintenance agreements will be lawful as long as the copyrighted work bears the trademark, brand, or name of its producer or distributor and as long as it is in free and open competition with other works of the same general class, not a very common situation.

Two United States Supreme Court cases, *Bobbs-Merrill Co.* v. *Straus* and *Straus* v. *American Publishers' Assoc.*, are exemplary of the application of price-fixing rules to sales of copyrighted works. In *Bobbs-Merrill*, the publisher of copyrighted books included in such books a notice that a sale at a price other than the established one would be treated as an infringement. The purchasers of the books made no agreement as to the control of future sales of the books and took upon themselves no obligation to enforce the notice printed in the book. The issue raised before the Court was whether the exclusive right to vend secured to the owner of the copyright the right to restrict future sales of the book at retail, after the sale of the book to a purchaser. The Supreme Court, in construing the issue solely as one of statutory interpretation, stated that

> the copyright statutes, while protecting the owner of the copyright in his right to multiply and sell his production, do not create the right to impose, by notice, . . . a limitation at which the book shall be sold at retail by future purchasers, with whom there is no privity of contract. . . .

To add to the right of exclusive sale the authority to control all future retail sales, by a notice that such sales must be made at a fixed sum, would give a right not included in the terms of the [copyright] statute.

In the *American Publishers* case, the American Publishers' Association composed 75 per cent of the publishers of copyrighted and uncopyrighted books in the United States. In the course of its business the association "adopted resolutions and made agreements obligating their members to sell copyrighted books only to those who would maintain the retail price of such net copyrighted books . . . ." When retailers did not conform to the agreement, they were put on a cut-off list, issued to all suppliers for the purpose of directing the suppliers to discontinue sales to such offenders. The Publishers' Association defended on the ground that the limited monopoly afforded copyright owners exempted them from the application of the antitrust laws. The Court responded:

> [N]o more than the patent statute was the copyright act intended to authorize agreements in unlawful restraint of trade and tending to monopoly, in violation of the specific terms of the Sherman law, which is broadly designed to reach all combinations in unlawful restraint of trade, and tending, because of agreements or combinations entered into, to build up and perpetuate monopolies.

In effect, the agreements entered into by the association members constituted a horizontal price-fixing conspiracy, per se illegal under the Sherman Act. As the Court noted, the fact that copyrighted subject matter was at issue could not save the illegal conspiracy.

Block Booking

Another practice that has run afoul of the antitrust laws is known as block booking. By definition, block booking is that practice whereby a licensee desiring the use of a certain film is required to take the licensor's other films as well. For example, one television network desiring to broadcast the highly acclaimed "Man Who Came to Dinner" was required to take, among others, "Gorilla Man" and "Tugboat Annie Sails Again." The reader may recognize this practice as a specie of tying arrangement. The question of the practice's validity vis-à-vis the antitrust laws was met head on in *United States* v. *Paramount Pictures, Inc.* In this case, discussed earlier in its monopolization aspects, the major producers and distributors of motion pictures engaged in block booking, requiring exhibitors to take undesirable films to get the ones they wanted. The producers had argued that a prohibition against block booking would greatly impair their ability to operate profitably. The Court observed that block booking acted to prevent competitors from bidding for single features on their individual merits. Moreover, "it 'adds to the monopoly of a single copyrighted picture that of another copyrighted picture which must be taken and exhibited in order to secure the first.'" The Court, in its condemnation of the practice engaged herein, did not, however, forbid all selling of film in blocks or groups. Rather, it held illegal only the *conditioning* of the grant of a license upon the acceptance of a license in another work.

The standard established by the *Paramount* case was expanded in *United States* v. *Loew's, Inc.* In this case six film distributors had conditioned the licensing or sale of certain films upon the acceptance by the licensee or purchaser of a package or block containing undesirable films. The Court viewed the situation as one hinging on the legality (or illegality) of such tying agreements and declared that in order to be violative of the Sherman Act, the "seller must have 'sufficient economic power with respect to the tying product to appreciably restrain free competition in the market for the tied product.' Even absent a showing of market dominance, the crucial economic power may be inferred from the tying product's desirability to consumers or from uniqueness in its attributes." The Court then concluded that the requisite economic power was presumed because the tying product was copyrighted. In holding that the block-booking practice was illegal, the Court found that not only was a substantial amount of the fees paid to defendants for the tied, or unwanted films, but that adverse effects on free competition had resulted from the block-booking contracts. "Television stations forced . . . to take unwanted films were denied access to films marketed by other distributors, who, in turn, were foreclosed from selling to the stations."

Package Licensing

Package licensing is essentially a variety of block booking. It entails the grant of a license covering the use of more than one copyright. As the reader can readily see, if in order to obtain a license under one copyright, the licensee is required to take licenses for other copyrighted works, the result is basically a tying arrangement. On the other hand, as the Supreme Court noted in the *Paramount* case, it is only when the grant of one license is *conditioned* on the acceptance of another that an illegal arrangement arises.

The reason that package licensing is treated separately here is that it weighs heavily in an evaluation of ASCAP's licensing practices. Prior to 1941, ASCAP, as the exclusive licensee of performance rights in its members' works, required that bulk or package licenses be obtained only from it. This procedure was challenged by the government in an antitrust suit, and ASCAP accepted a consent decree modifying its licensing practices. After the *Alden-Rochelle* decision involving ASCAP, the case was reopened and the consent decree modified. Subsequently the consent decree has been further modified in minor respects.

Operating under the consent decree ASCAP has certain obligations to charge nondiscriminatory license fees to similarly situated licensees. Moreover, the decree expressly provides that ASCAP cannot be the exclusive owner of performance rights, so that the individual copyright owner may grant a license for the performance of his own compositions. In practice, this right is almost worthless to the would-be licensee, because setting up a program involving numerous compositions would entail negotiating individually with each copyright owner. In the case of broadcasters, such individual negotiations would be impossible. Beyond this provision for retention of the right to license by the individual copyright owner, the consent decree contains bulk licensing provisions under which ASCAP must grant either blanket or "per program" licenses. If a potential licensee is unable to reach an agreement with ASCAP over fees, the decree provides for determination of a fair fee by the court.

Over the years there has been considerable dissatisfaction on the part of licensees with the package licensing provisions of the consent decree. On a number of occasions licensees have been unable to get ASCAP to issue a license for less than its entire repertory of compositions. This inability forces licensees to take more than they want. For example, a radio station that broadcasts only country and western music has no need for performance rights licenses in rock or jazz or show music. But under the present decree it has no real option, because negotiations with the individual copyright owners is obviously impracticable.

Confronted with this problem, a number of attempts have been made by would-be licensees to challenged ASCAP's licensing practices under the antitrust laws. Of course, the fact that ASCAP is operating under a consent decree hampers such an approach, and in one case it was held that the decree immunizes ASCAP from antitrust liability as long as ASCAP stays within its terms. The theory of illegality is based on the Supreme Court's recent decision in *Zenith* v. *Hazeltine*. This case holds that package licensing of patents, whereby the licensee pays the same royalty regardless of how many patents he actually uses, is illegal if the licensee is coerced into accepting the package license. Because the *Zenith* case was decided long after the entry of the ASCAP consent decree, it at least can be argued that the decree should not be construed to countenance now illegal activities.

In an important case that is presently pending in the courts, the Columbia Broadcasting System is challenging ASCAP's refusal to license less than its entire repertory on just such grounds. Although the case has not yet reached a decision, the court has ruled that the consent decree does not necessarily immunize ASCAP from antitrust liability. Rather, the court held that CBS should have the opportunity to show that a less restrictive licensing program could reasonably satisfy ASCAP's legitimate needs and still comply with the antitrust laws. Thus to date there has been no change in ASCAP's package licensing program. However, this program is under heavy attack and it remains to be seen if it can survive unmodified.

Rights of Privacy, Public Performances, and Publicity in Commerce

This chapter surveys the rights of public figures and other persons regarding the protection of their names, photographs, and personalities from unauthorized commercial exploitation, together with rights in public performances and communications in the entertainment and broadcast fields, principally relating to unauthorized commercial use of programming and entertainment events. The degree of available protection under state laws has varied over time and has been based upon several different theories, including the right of privacy, misappropriation, unfair competition, and the right of publicity.

RIGHT OF PRIVACY

In 1890 the concept of an individual's right to remain free from public scrutiny was adumbrated by Louis Brandeis and Samuel Warren in a famous *Harvard Law Review* article entitled "The Right to Privacy." The Brandeis–Warren thesis was that the "right of life has come to mean the right to enjoy life—the right to be let alone; the right to liberty secures the exercise of extensive civil privileges; and, the term 'property' has grown to comprise every form of possession—intangible, as well as tangible." From this premise, the authors suggested that any right of property must, by its very nature, include the right to an inviolate personality. This concept of an inviolate personality was to be protected by one's "right of privacy." The right of privacy was accepted as an independent right but was narrowly restricted. The right, as originally conceived, was not designed to deal with the mass media commercial technology that commenced with the development of radio, television, and motion pictures. An analysis of some of the decisions construing the right of privacy demonstrates its shortcomings in this area. Those cases indicate that the right of privacy was intended to be neither a property or contract right nor a remedy for breach of trust. Although possessed with some of the attributes that would normally be characteristic of those rights and remedies, the right of privacy, in its original sense, was essentially the right to peace of mind arising from the knowledge that the invasion of one's private affairs could be restricted.

The recognition and development of the right of privacy has occurred, for the most part, in New York State. One of the first cases involving the right was a 1902 New York decision, *Roberson* v. *Rochester Folding Box Co.* That case involved an action for the alleged unlawful use by defendant's flour mill of about 25,000 lithographic prints, photos, and likenesses of plaintiff for the purpose of advertising defendant's product as the "Flour of the Family." Plaintiff alleged great mental and emotional injury as the result of this use and, accordingly, sought $15,000 damages and an injunction prohibiting further use of her picture. The New York Court of Appeals refused to grant the relief requested because, in the eyes of the court, such a decision would result in an unmanageable deluge of litigation. The court held that the absence of libelous use by defendant was fatal to plaintiff's action. (The picture was, in fact, a very good likeness.) The court would not recognize a right of privacy because it viewed such a recognition as doing violence to the then settled principles of jurisprudence. The substance of the court's ruling was that the so-called right of an individual, founded on the claim that he has a right to pass through this world "without having his picture published, his business enterprises discussed, his successful experiments written up for the benefit of others, or his eccentricities commented" on in circulars, periodicals, or newspapers, "whether the comment be favorable or otherwise," did not exist in law, and was not enforceable in equity. Judge Gray, in a strong dissent, chided the majority for not recognizing that the advance of science and technology demanded the enforcement of a person's rights in his name, likeness, and personality.

As might have been expected, the court's decision was met by public dissatisfaction and indignation. As a result of this public reaction the next session of the New York State legislature enacted legislation that recognized the right of privacy. Sections 50 and 51 of the New York Civil Rights Laws provide as follows:

Section 50, which deals with criminal prohibitions:

A person, firm or corporation that uses for advertising purposes, or for the purposes of trade, the name, portrait or picture of any living person without having first obtained the written consent of such person, or if a minor of his or her parent or guardian, is guilty of a misdemeanor.

Section 51, which deals with civil actions for injunction and for damages:

Any person whose name, portrait or picture is used within this state for advertising purposes or for the purposes of trade without the written consent first obtained as above provided may maintain an equitable action in the supreme court of this state against the person, firm or corporation so using his name, portrait or picture, to prevent and restrain the use thereof; and may also sue and recover damages for any injuries sustained by reason of such use and if the defendant shall have knowingly used such person's name, portrait or picture in such manner as is forbidden or declared to be unlawful by the last section, the jury, in its discretion, may award exemplary damages.

Section 51 goes on to state exceptions where consent is involved:

But nothing contained in this act shall be so construed as to prevent any person, firm or corporation, practicing the profession of photography, from exhibiting in or about his or its establishment specimens of the work of such establishment, unless the same is continued by such person, firm or corporation after written notice objecting thereto has been given by the person portrayed; and nothing contained in this act shall be so construed as to prevent any person, firm or corporation from using the name, portrait or picture of any manufacturer or dealer in connection with the goods, wares and merchandise manufactured, produced or dealt in by him which he has sold or disposed of with such name, portrait or picture used in connection therewith; or from using the name, portrait or picture of any author, composer or artist in connection with his literary, musical or artistic productions which he has sold or disposed of with such name, portrait or picture used in connection therewith.

The purpose of these statutes is to protect an individual's freedom from the commercial intrusion in his life. The statute grants the right of action for invasion of privacy to any person whose name or picture is used, without prior consent, for purposes of advertising or trade. Such unauthorized activity may include the use of names or pictures for all types of promotional endeavors or the use of any individual's name to promote a product or company by naming it after him.

Preliminary to any action under the New York or other similar state statutes, a plaintiff must show that his name was used for "advertising purposes" or for "purposes of trade." Courts have tended to interpret those phrases liberally. For example, in a 1962 New York case, *Coleman* v. *Ted's Auto Sales, Inc.*, an established attorney sued an automobile dealer under the New York Right of Privacy statute for the unauthorized use of his name in connection with a financial investigation of the dealer's credit status by Dun & Bradstreet. An official of Ted's Auto Sales, in response to inquiries by the D & B investigators, stated that Mr. Coleman was one of its officers and directors, which was patently untrue. Holding for the attorney, the court stated that

> [s]horn of all the niceties of language, the complaint alleges that the defendants used plaintiff's name, reputation and known widespread legal talent in the automotive field for the purpose of conveying to those with whom they did business and to those from whom defendants sought credit, the notion that the plaintiff was financially connected with the firm and was responsible for its business policies, all with the view of inducing the others, on the strength of plaintiff's reputation, to impart credit to them. The granting of credit to the defendants was a means of doing business or trade; it enabled them to carry on business or trade, if the facts alleged in the complaint are deemed to be true. The circulation of the Dun & Bradstreet report, on the strength of the information imparted to Dun & Bradstreet by the defendants, is an advertisement because, based upon that circulation to those interested in the trade, the defendants sought credit.

Hence relief was granted under the New York statute.

Feeney v. *Young*, a 1920 New York decision, further illustrates the point. Katherine Feeney, in giving birth to a child, was forced to undergo a cesarean operation. She consented to the filming of the operation upon assurance from her physician, the defendant, that the picture would only be shown before medical societies and in the interest of medical science. Subsequent to its filming, the picture was exhibited in two of the leading motion picture theaters in New York City, as part of a movie entitled "Birth." The court readily found that the film exhibition was for the purpose of trade.

In those cases involving the unauthorized use of an individual's name or photo for commercial purposes, the New York courts have almost uniformly granted relief under the privacy statute, whether the individual wronged is a public figure or a private citizen. Although most of the cases normally result in the issuance of an injunction, an award of other than nominal damages is seldom granted. For example, in one case the use of an actor's picture for publicity purposes was authorized, but the court held that there was no authorization to use a composite picture that modified the original and placed the actor in an "undignified light." Use of the composite picture by the defendant was enjoined, but no damages were awarded. On the question of the actor's status as a public figure, the court stated that "[a]n actor is in public life and although subject to fair comment, his choice of profession does not entail the foreswearing of his civil rights." In another New York case an actress brought an action for the unauthorized use by the Woolworth organization of her photograph in connection with its manufactured lockets sold in the Woolworth stores. The court found that Woolworth's unauthorized use of plaintiff's picture was for advertising and trade purposes. Woolworth had voluntarily discontinued its use of the picture. The court could have awarded damages to plaintiff based upon the value accruing to defendant by virtue of its use of her picture, but it did not choose that option.

A case that provides an excellent example of the New York court's reluctance to granting monetary relief and its disinclination to protect publicity values under the privacy statutes is *Fisher* v. *Murray M. Rosenberg, Inc.,* decided in 1940. Plaintiff, a professional dancer, sued under the New York Civil Rights statute for the unlawful use of his photograph in connection with advertising defendant's line of shoes. The court refused to grant examplary damages, that is, damages granted solely in order to punish a defendant for bad behavior or to make an example of his case on the grounds that the statute requires knowing use by defendant and plaintiff had failed to meet the burden of showing such knowledge. "Exemplary damages are not to compensate plaintiff, but are to punish defendant and to deter it and others from like acts." Because plaintiff was unable to show special damages, he was awarded compensatory damages of $300, which damages were meant to compensate him for the injury sustained, the loss suffered, and nothing more. This type of decision was occasioned by the attitude, common to many courts of that day, that those who depend on publicity as a part of their career are not normally in the position to assert injured feelings.

Under interpretations of the right to privacy, a person must be clearly identified or referred to in the matter published by defendant. The person's name need not actually appear in the material in question, so long as his or her identity is readily apparent from such material. For example, in a North Carolina case a woman whose picture was published in connection with an advertisement was held to be entitled to recover for an invasion of her right to privacy, although the picture bore as a caption the name of another person. The mere existence of her picture made it possible for anyone to identify her clearly without regard to the fictitious caption appearing in the advertisement.

In a number of cases the reference to a plaintiff has been held too incidental to amount to an invasion of privacy. For example, in a 1961 New York case, the court held that no invasion of plaintiff's right of privacy occurred where a newspaper article reporting plaintiff's loss of a tennis match was partly reproduced, together with other articles, as a patchwork pattern for a fabric that defendants manufactured and sold for use in producing underwear, pajamas, and play togs. The court found that the mere incidental commercial use of a person's name or photograph was not actionable under the New York statute.

Another approach extending beyond "commercial" appropriation is taken by a tentative draft of the Restatement (Second) of Torts, which provides that "[o]ne who appropriates to his own use or benefit the name or likeness of another is subject to liability to the other for invasion of his privacy." Illustrations 9 and 10 of the Restatement provide examples of the application of these principles.

> 9. ABC is a noted millionaire philanthropist. Out of admiration for ABC, XYZ adopts the name of ABC, lists himself in the telephone book and the city directory under that name, informs all his friends and associates that he wishes to be known by it in the future and consistently makes use of it. This is not an invasion of the privacy of ABC.
>
> 10. The same facts as in illustration 9, with the addition that XYZ, representing himself to be ABC, registers under that name at an expensive summer resort hotel, where he stays for a month, incurring a large bill which he does not pay, on credit extended to him in the belief that he is ABC. This is an invasion of the privacy of ABC.

LIMITATIONS OF THE RIGHT OF PRIVACY

The right of privacy is a personal right and accordingly is not assignable. This fact of nonassignability greatly reduces the value of the right of privacy as a cause of action for misappropriation because the true publicity value of a prominent person's name or portrait is usually unattainable in the absence of such an assignment. Financial success in the exploitation of a celebrity's name or portrait is attained only when the corporation or advertising agency possesses a right to the use of that name or portrait. In those cases where an assignee has attempted to recover on the basis of violation of the right of privacy, the purported assignment is interpreted as simply releasing the assignee/purchaser from liability for his use of the celebrity's name or portrait. The purchaser is denied any right of recovery on right of privacy principles against third parties for their use of the celebrity's image, although the celebrity still has a cause of action against the third party. Thus the inability to grant an exclusive right of use reduces the publicity value that one might have in his own likeness or personality.

The limited recovery on the basis of invasion of privacy is available only in those cases involving the unauthorized use of the name or portrait of a person. Although animals, like Lassie, can develop important publicity values, the unauthorized use of those values is not protected under the right of privacy theory. For example, where a person sued for an injunction to restrain the unauthorized sale, distribution, exhibition, and publication of a photograph of her dog for advertising purposes and an accounting of all profits accruing to defendants by reason of their use of that photograph, the court pointed to the *Roberson* case (see p. 448) to support the proposition that a person does not have any rights "in an image independent of those afforded by the statutory right of privacy." The opinion stated that the "statutory right of privacy concededly does not cover the case of a dog or a photograph of a dog. Whatever rights a person may have in a photograph of his dog are dependent upon the existence of a contractual relationship between that person and the photographer." Similarly, business enterprises, whether they be partnerships or corporations, are unprotected by this particular theory.

The traditional protections afforded by the right of privacy have also been recognized as being inadequate to deal with the special problems of public figures and celebrities. Public figures and entertainment personalities are not usually interested in the complete prohibition of the use by others of their names and photographs. Rather, they have been concerned with their ability to control that use. The right of privacy does not provide methods of dealing with these needs.

Once an individual attains a status of a public figure or celebrity, he becomes ineligible to invoke all the protections normally afforded under the right of privacy. The reasoning behind this principle is that once an individual becomes a celebrity, he is deemed to have committed himself to a public life and thereby waived his right to privacy. Most courts, however, accord limited protection to those aspects of a celebrity's private life that he has chosen not to make public. For example, although the professional career of a baseball player is open to public scrutiny and hence not protected under the right of privacy, his private life off the baseball field is considered protected.

A more limited approach to the doctrine of waiver is found in the case of *Gautier* v. *Pro-Football, Inc.* In that case a producer of animal acts presented a show under contract between the halves of a football game for an audience of some 35,000 spectators. The court concluded that plaintiff's waiver of his right of privacy with respect to the individuals who were in attendance at the football game also applied to those persons who might view his performance on television. (It appears from the facts of the case that plaintiff had knowledge that the football game at which he was performing was being televised.) The same reasoning employed in the *Gautier* case was used to deny a prizefighter a preliminary injunction to restrain the broadcasting of his participation in a boxing match.

Although it is more likely that the issue of waiver will arise when the plaintiff is a "celebrity," some courts have applied the waiver theory to deny relief to "noncelebrities." For example, in the California case of *Gill* v. *Hearst Publishing Co.* the court invoked the waiver doctrine to deny recovery to plaintiffs for the alleged unauthorized use by Hearst of a picture of plaintiffs taken by a Hearst photographer. The unauthorized shot was taken while plaintiffs were seated in an affectionate pose at their place of business, a confectionery and ice cream concession, and it was used to illustrate a magazine article re-affirming the "poet's conviction that the world could not revolve without love." The court placed heavy emphasis upon the fact that the photograph was taken of plaintiffs in a pose voluntarily assumed in a public market place. This case provides still another example of the court's use of waiver as the device to deny recovery for invasion of the right to privacy.

A number of state jurisdictions have enacted statutes that, technically speaking, may be violated even though the plaintiff's name or portrait has not been used in an offensive manner, although they do generally require injury to the plaintiff in order to recover damages. For example, in a 1947 Florida case, plaintiff sought recovery for the alleged invasion of her right to privacy by the writing and publication of a book by defendant. The court recognized the existence of a cause of action on plaintiff's behalf in the absence of a showing of offensive use by defendant. However, the court refused to award damages, finding that a critical element in the determination of damages was injury resulting from mental anguish, loss of community respect, or injury to character or reputation. An extreme and technical application of this principle can be seen in *Miller* v. *Madison Square Garden*. That case involved a suit by Miller for the unauthorized use of his name and photograph in connection with a Madison Square Garden promotion of a six-day bicycle race. The court found a technical violation of the New York Civil Rights Law. However, because Miller suffered no embarrassment or ridicule as a result of the misappropriation, the court awarded nominal damages in the amount of 6 cents. This case illustrates the principle that damages for invasion of privacy are measured by the injury to plaintiff and not by the benefit flowing to defendant because of the unauthorized action.

RIGHT AGAINST COMMERCIAL MISAPPROPRIATION COMPARED TO RIGHT OF PRIVACY

Courts have also recognized that individuals possess a right to be free from the commercial exploitation of their names, likenesses, personalities, and histories. This right is considerably different from the traditional right of privacy, which is essentially the right to be let alone. Commercial exploitation involves the violation of an individual's property rights and, historically, persons seeking redress for the harm associated with this misappropriation have brought actions based on a privacy theory alleging injuries to their feelings. Courts, however, have begun to distinguish between the classic types of invasion of privacy and the appropriations and exploitations of the commercial values associated with one's name and photograph. Although most jurisdictions have recognized a common law property right in one's name or likeness, persons continue to seek damages based on the humiliation and mental anguish attendant to the use of their names or photographs, rather than damages arising out of the misappropriation of the property rights in, for example, their names. One 1907 case that did proceed on the basis of the misappropriation of one's name for commercial purposes was *Edison* v. *Edison Polyform Mfg. Co.* In that case, Thomas Edison, the famous inventor, sought an injunction to restrain the defendant from using his name as part of its corporate title or in connection with any of its product advertisements. The defendant had been selling a medicine bearing Edison's picture with the accompanying statement that Edison certified the preparation as compounded according to a formula invented and used by him. The use of Edison's picture and name was completely unauthorized. The court granted an injunction to restrain the company from fraudulently holding out in any way that Mr. Edison had any connection with the defendant's business. The court did recognize that some distinctions must be drawn between public and private figures but it did not put forth any guidelines relating to that distinction.

When seeking recovery, plaintiffs will sometimes take a double-barreled approach to the problem. *Continental Optical Co.* v. *Reed,* involved an action by Reed, an optical lens grinder, against a manufacturer of lenses for the unauthorized use of his picture for advertising purposes. Reed sought recovery on the dual theories of invasion of privacy and misappropriation of property rights. While on a tour of duty with the U.S. Army during World War II, Reed's picture had been taken by the War Department for use in a military publication and newspapers of general circulation. Continental Optical Co. appropriated Reed's picture for commercial use in its business activities without Reed's knowledge and consent and with the intent to profit thereby. Reed claimed that his property right in the picture had been invaded and, therefore, sought recovery. The defense was based on the notion that Reed's entry into active duty had made him a public figure and that any activity while on such duty was not protected. The court defined an invasion of privacy as the "unwarranted appropriation or exploitation of one's personality, the publicizing of one's private affairs with which the public has no legitimate concern, or the wrongful intrusion into one's private activities in such manner as to outrage or cause mental suffering, shame or humiliation to a person of ordinary sensibility." It also recognized the existence of a cause of action for misappropriation of property values for commercial purposes. The court did not limit damages to the injury to plaintiff's feelings. It also recognized the possibility that damages would arise simply by virtue of the loss of a property right. Continental's "public figure" defense was rejected by the court on the grounds that the use that defendant made of plaintiff's name, likeness, or personality was the true measure of recovery and not whether the plaintiff was a public figure. If the use is an appropriation for commercial purposes, then a cause of action is stated whether or not plaintiff is a public figure.

Examples are numerous of situations in which plaintiffs have confused the remedies based on injury to feelings with those awarded upon a finding of unlawful commercial appropriation. *O'Brien* v. *Pabst Sales Co.* involved a suit by a well-known football player, arising from defendant's use of his picture by placing it in a Pabst beer advertisement. The court found that O'Brien had sought and promoted wide publicity about himself and, therefore, he could show no invasion of a right of privacy. The court implied that had O'Brien pursued a cause of action based solely upon unlawful appropriation, he would have been granted a remedy. The dissenting opinions saw the difference between the right of privacy and the right to recover for unlawful commercial appropriation as follows:

> The right of privacy is distinct from the right to use one's name or picture for purposes of commercial advertisement. The latter is a property right that belongs to every one; it may have much or little, or only a nominal value; but it is a personal right which may not be violated with impunity.

UNFAIR COMPETITION AS AN ALTERNATIVE REMEDY

Having found that the right of privacy is inadequate to deal with his needs, the celebrity may turn to alternate theories in order to assure protection of his rights against the use by others of his name or portrait. An action for unfair competition may be considered. The existence of a competitive atmosphere between plaintiff and defendant generally must be shown before an action for unfair competition may be brought. In most situations involving a plaintiff celebrity and a defendant appropriator, such competition will not exist. For example, the producer of baseball picture cards bearing photographs of prominent professional baseball players is not in competition with the players themselves. It is clear that in this type of situation, although the defendant publisher is not in active competition with the ballplayer, he is certainly trading on the publicity values inherent in the ballplayer's name and photograph.

The shortcomings of the conventional theory of unfair competition —requiring a competitive relationship—to deal with the problems inherent in the misappropriation of publicity values are illustrated in a 1953 Texas decision. In that case plaintiff, the owner of an Arizona radio station, sought a permanent injunction to restrain a Texas radio station from broadcasting accounts of stock car races being held in Phoenix. Plaintiff had contracted with the South Mountain Speedway in Phoenix for the exclusive rights to broadcast the automobile races taking place at its track. The defendant stationed a correspondent within the broadcasting radius of plaintiff's station and that individual relayed the lap-by-lap description of the race by telephone back to defendant's Texas radio station. The relayed description of the race was then rebroadcast in the Texas area. The court found that because neither of the two stations could possibly operate within the other's radius, they were not in competition with each other and, accordingly, an action for unfair competition would not lie.

In order to succeed in an action for unfair competition, the plaintiff generally must show that the defendant "passed off" his goods or services as those of the plaintiff. *Passing off* is the attempted merchandising of a product by seeking to effect an unsuspecting substitution for another product. In most cases involving the misappropriation of a celebrity's name or photograph for advertising purposes, the element of passing off is not present.

As previously mentioned, most courts have traditionally required a showing of competition before a plaintiff may recover, on the theory of unfair competition, for the misappropriation of publicity values. In recent years, however, a number of courts have changed their position on this question and they no longer require this showing as a pre-requisite to recovery. Similarly, a number of courts no longer require a showing of passing off. In *Metropolitan Opera Association* v. *Wagner-Nichols Recorder Corp.* the plaintiff entered into a contract with Columbia Records that granted the latter the exclusive rights to produce and sell phonograph records of its operatic performances. Defendants, without permission, recorded the radio broadcasts of the Metropolitan Opera and produced and sold phonograph records produced from those recordings. The quality of defendant's recordings was substantially inferior to those of Columbia Records. However, it was in active competition with Columbia for the sale of those recordings. Plaintiff brought an action charging unfair competition and relief was granted even in the absence of a showing of passing off.

Sinatra v. *Goodyear Tire & Rubber Co.*, decided by the Ninth Circuit in 1970, shows in an interesting situation the limits of unfair competition relief available to performing artists in suits against advertisers who imitate the artist where third-party copyrights are involved. Nancy Sinatra recorded a song, "These Boots Are Made for Walkin'," that became quite popular. Goodyear and its advertising agency dreamed up an advertising program for "wide boots" as the theme for marketing its tires and secured a copyright license to use the song in its advertising program. Nancy Sinatra was contacted to employ her to sing "These Boots Are Made for Walkin'" in the Goodyear radio-TV commercials for "wide boots" tires, but no contract was concluded. Goodyear then developed a vocal arrangement for this song, which imitated Nancy Sinatra's recorded performance.

Nancy Sinatra sued Goodyear on the theory that the song was so popularized by her that she was identified with it, that this intentional imitation constituted passing off, and that the "secondary meaning" of the song associated with her justified relief on the theory of unfair competition. Not so, said the court. Goodyear had the right via copyright license to use the song; there was no competition between Nancy Sinatra (who is in the phonograph records business) and Goodyear (who is in the tire business). No passing off is really involved, said the court, because there was no claim in pure sound to her individual vocal characteristics, but rather to the combination of sound together with third-party copyrighted lyrics, melody and arrangement: "appellant's complaint is not that her sound is uniquely personal; it is that the sound in connection with the music, lyrics and arrangement, which made her the subject of popular identification, ought to be protected." Here the court drew a distinction between other cases that involved recovery related to a performer's readily identifiable accent (Maurice Chevalier) or range and quality (Bert Lahr or Andy Devine)—together with the fact that no copyright violation existed. Added to this was the shadow of the Supreme Court's *Sears-Compco* decisions discussed in Chapter 1 that support arm's-length copying irrespective of motive, so long as no passing off is involved and no patents or copyrights are infringed.

RIGHT OF PUBLICITY

The recognition that traditional legal remedies did not provide adequate protection for a celebrity's right in his name or photograph led to the development of a right of publicity. This change in traditional legal thinking was also brought about by a recognition of the substantial values existing in the use of a celebrity's name or photograph in connection with advertising activity. The courts began to recognize that an individual possesses a property right in his name or photograph that may be unlawfully appropriated by another. To define the right of publicity is to fill in an area previously neglected by the right of privacy. Initially, the right of publicity, in contrast to the right of privacy, must be recognized as a property right, that is, a right capable of being assigned and transferred. Recovery on the theory of infringement of the right of publicity does not require a showing that defendant used plaintiff's name or portrait in an offensive manner. The measure of damages in an action for violation of the right of publicity is not the injury to the plaintiff but rather the pecuniary gain to the defendant arising out of the unlawful appropriation. An important difference between the right of privacy and the right of publicity is that the latter is not waived simply because the individual involved is a well-known personality. As a matter of fact, actions for invasion of the right of publicity normally arise when the name or portrait of a celebrity is appropriated and used by another without the celebrity's consent. Furthermore, the right also attaches to animals, inanimate objects, and business organizations.

One situation in which the plaintiff will not be granted recovery on the grounds of infringement of his right of publicity is that case where his photograph or name is used in the dissemination of news that is broadcast in the public interest. This exception is not to be confused with the concept of waiver whereby a well-known personality voluntarily gives up his right of publicity. In the news broadcasting situation, plaintiff is not possessed of any property right that can be waived. In that case the public interest and public policy dictate the free use of names and photographs.

The leading case recognizing the right of publicity is *Haelan*

Laboratories, Inc. v. *Topps Chewing Gum, Inc.*, decided by the Second Circuit in 1953. That case stated a legal theory that had been given some scattered attention in a number of earlier decisions, such as *Gautier* v. *Pro-Football, Inc.* and *O'Brien* v. *Pabst Sales Co.* The *Haelan* case involved an action by a bubble gum manufacturer for the alleged invasion by defendant, a competitor, of plaintiff's exclusive right to use photographs of a leading baseball player in the bubble gum field. Plaintiff had contracted with a baseball player for the exclusive right to use his picture in connection with plaintiff's sale of bubble gum. Defendant induced the same ballplayer to authorize the use of their pictures in connection with defendant's sale of gum during the term of plaintiff's contract. On appeal to the United States Court of Appeals for the Second Circuit, the defendant contended that the ballplayer's contract with plaintiff was no more than a release of the liability that plaintiff would have otherwise incurred by using the photographs. Such use, without prior consent, would have violated the ballplayer's rights of privacy. Defendant further theorized that, because that right was personal and nonassignable, plaintiff's contract did not result in his acquisition of a property right that could be infringed upon. The court rejected defendant's contentions and held as follows:

> We think that in addition to and independent of that right of privacy (which in New York derives from statute), a man has a right in the publicity value of his photograph, *i.e.*, the right to grant the exclusive privilege of publishing his picture, and that such a grant may be validly made "in gross," *i.e.*, with any accompanying transfer of a business or of anything else. Whether it be labelled a "property" right is immaterial; for here, as often elsewhere, the tag "property" simply symbolizes the fact that courts enforce a claim which has pecuniary worth.
>
> This right might be called "a right of publicity." For it is common knowledge that many prominent persons (especially actors and ball players), far from having their feelings bruised through public exposure of their likenesses, would feel sorely deprived if they no longer received money for authorizing advertisements popularizing their countenances, displayed in newspapers, magazines, busses, trains and subways. This right of publicity would usually yield them no money unless it could be made the subject of an exclusive grant which barred any other advertiser from using their pictures.

This decision marked a turning point in the law concerning the protection of an individual's rights in his name, likeness, and personality. The *Haelan* case filled the vacuum created by the privacy and other related theories that had limited protection to celebrities and public figures.

In New York, the *Haelan* right to publicity has benefitted several plaintiffs. In one case although the plaintiff failed to recover for the use of her name in a review used on the book cover that had compared the author to her, the court did imply that an action would lie if the publication may be considered a blatant, selfish, commercial exploitation of the public figure's personality.

Rosemont Enterprises v. *Random House* stated that a public figure's "right of publicity" must "bow where it conflicts with the free dissemination of thoughts, ideas, newsworthy events, and matters of public interest," in holding Howard Hughes could not enjoin publication of a biography. By contrast, in *Rosemont Enterprises* v. *Urban Systems*, Howard Hughes was granted relief. The court stated that "there is no question but that a celebrity has a legitimate proprietary interest in his public personality." The court stressed that defendants, in marketing a game based on plaintiff's biographical data, "are not disseminating news. They are selling a commodity, a commercial product. . . ." And that "use for such purposes is an act of appropriation of those property rights belonging to plaintiff, Hughes."

In Pennsylvania, the status of the right to publicity is unclear, although the right was explicitly recognized and relied upon to give damages to plaintiff, in a case involving the well-known golfer, Ben Hogan. The court held that the "circumstances under which defendant published and advertised" a book containing pictures of and the name of plaintiff "constituted a misappropriation of the property right which plaintiff has in the commercial value of his name and photograph," explicitly referring to the property right protected as a "right of publicity."

New Jersey has gone far toward recognition of this right of publicity. In *Palmer* v. *Schonhorn Enterprises, Inc.* a New Jersey court held that the use of the biographical data of the well-known golfer, Arnold Palmer, for the purpose of capitalizing upon his name in connection with a commercial project other than the dissemination of news or biography constitutes an invasion of privacy. Although the court used the older term, it is clear that a right to exclusive control over the commercial publicity values of the name and reputation was what was involved.

Two federal district courts have dealt with this area: a California district court dismissed an action predicated on the right to publicity, because that right had not yet received recognition in the state of California. And a Delaware district court held that where the petition insufficiently alleged invasion of the plaintiff's right to privacy, there could be no recovery on the theory that the defendant had interfered with his property right. In this latter case, the plaintiff claimed a property right in his life story, a re-enactment of a bank robbery perpetrated by him.

MISAPPROPRIATION OF INTANGIBLES AND THE CONFLICT WITH FEDERAL LAW

A closely related line of cases orginating in the newspaper field will help to preserve a measure of conceptual confusion in this general field of law, the leading case being a 1918 Supreme Court decision called *International News Service* v. *Associated Press*. Here the Supreme Court enjoined INS from marketing on the Pacific Coast uncoyprighted AP news dispatches that were copies from AP bulletin boards and early editions of AP articles in the East Coast newspapers. The court said, "in appropriating . . . [INS] is endeavoring to reap where it has not sown. . . ." Creeping through this case is the availability of injunctive relief in situations where time, effort, and money have gone into creating the "property right"; defendant's appropriation is at little or no cost; and unless an injunction is granted, there will be a diversion of plaintiff's profits to the defendant.

The *INS* theory of appropriation has had a cloudy existence; commentators in the field have questioned whether it continues to be good law. But courts have, nevertheless, used the *INS* theory over the years to grant relief against unauthorized use.

In the well-known 1937 *Waring* case, the Supreme Court of Pennsylvania relied on *INS* in ruling an orchestra's interpretation of a musical composition to be a protectable property right. The court stated that "equity will protect an unfair appropriation of the product of another's labor or talent," and that the radio station was "in commercial competition with the orchestra itself." In interpreting this 1937 decision, the Third Circuit noted nineteen years later: "It would seem . . . that the Court's decision really went off on the ground of unfair competition damaging a property right. In other words, the Court found a property right and proceeded to protect it."

A federal court in Pennsylvania applied much the same analysis in granting a preliminary injunction to restrain a radio station from broadcasting play-by-play reports of baseball games played by the Pittsburgh Pirates, which had exclusively granted such rights to another. The court held that "[i]t is perfectly clear that the exclusive right to broadcast . . . rests in the plaintiffs, . . . [and] is a property right of the plaintiffs," noting that the Pittsburgh Pirates "has, at great expense, acquired and maintains a baseball park, pays the players who participate in the game, and have, as we view it, a legitimate right to capitalize on the news value of the games. . . ." The court concluded that the actions of the defendants "amounts to unfair competition and is a violation of the property rights of the plaintiffs." Several New York cases have applied the doctrine as well. In one case the defendant produced a motion picture showing films of the New York Rangers. The court held that the "plaintiff clearly had a property right in its good name, its reputation, its goodwill built up at considerable expense . . . ," and awarded damages, noting that "[t]here may be unfair competition by misappropriation as well as by misrepresentation. Both elements are here." However, along came the *Sears-Compco* cases in 1964, discussed in Chapter 1. It will be recalled that the Supreme Court ruled that arm's-length copying is not to be considered unlawful outside the patent and copyright field where there is no palming off by the copier of the product as coming from the copied products source. What did this mean to the *INS* case and its progeny? Some courts have distinguished between "copying" an object and "appropriating" the object itself. A New York decision, for instance, involved a charge of wrongful appropriation of a CBS news broadcast that defendant had reduced to the form of a record for sale to the general public. The court found that, unlike *Sears-Compco*, the wrong complained of amounted to an appropriation of the actual broadcast, not a copying of it. In another New York case defendant was charged with misappropriating plaintiff's records of the Beatles' hits by selling records that compiled the better selections from plaintiff's recordings. The New York court distinguished this case from *Sears-Compco* on the ground that neither opinion "stands for the proposition that this plaintiff is not entitled to protection against the unauthorized appropriation, reproduction or duplication of actual performances contained in its records." So the Supreme Court in 1973 seemed to indicate a continued vitality in the *INS* case when it held in *Goldstein* v. *California* that neither the Constitution nor federal copyright legislation pre-empts state regulation of sound recordings "fixed" prior to the time when federal copyright laws were first extended to sound recordings, notwithstanding what the Supreme Court said nine years earlier in the *Sears-Compco* cases.

Federal Tax Aspects of Intellectual Property

INTRODUCTION

The federal internal revenue laws provide basic rules governing the income tax consequences resulting from various transactions. Specific provisions concerning various types of intellectual property complement these general rules. However, such laws contain many exceptions from these general and specific rules in the case of certain transactions. For instance, certain tax consequences may result where the exploitation of property is wholly domestic while radically different consequences may result where the same transaction takes on foreign aspects. Moreover, where foreign transactions are involved, the income tax consequences discussed below may be significantly altered as the result of the existence of tax treaties which override the federal income tax laws.

Under the Internal Revenue Code of 1954, a basic distinction is drawn between the income tax consequences resulting from the exploitation of property and those resulting from the performance of services. Because of the peculiar nature of intellectual property as an intangible aggregate of its creator's efforts, there is often great difficulty in determining whether particular intellectual property constitutes property or services for federal income tax purposes. This problem is compounded where the intellectual property is embodied in tangible forms of personal property, such as the ideas of a writer being reduced to a manuscript or movie film. The ostensibly hybrid nature of many types of intellectual property raises questions as to the applicability of many federal income tax concepts, including the issue of the maximum tax and the investment credit. The complexity of these and many other problems and issues precludes them from being discussed in this chapter, and, therefore, what follows is an elementary overview of the federal income tax aspects of intellectual property. Because of the simplicity of the following discussion, professional assistance should be obtained before planning any specific transaction involving intellectual property.

ORDINARY INCOME VERSUS CAPITAL GAIN

Under the Internal Revenue Code of 1954 most owners of intellectual property are subject to an annual tax on income received during a taxable year. Included in this income subject to taxation are royalties received from the licensing or leasing of intellectual property, compensation received as payment for the performance of services rendered in developing intellectual property, and gains realized from the sale or exchange of intellectual property. Although all these types of income are subject to taxation, they are often taxed at different rates. Income characterized as long-term capital gain is taxed at rates ranging from 7 to 35 per cent in the case of individuals, and 22 to 30 per cent in the case of corporations. Income not characterized as long-term capital gain, but instead, as short-term capital gain or ordinary income is, in the case of individuals, taxed at rates varying between 14 and 70 per cent. Short-term capital gain and ordinary income earned by corporations is taxed at either a 22 or 48 per cent rate. Because income characterized as long-term capital gain is taxed at lower rates, it is usually desirable from the viewpoint of the owner of intellectual property to exploit such property in a manner that will result in income generated therefrom being characterized as long-term capital gain.

Income will generally be characterized as long-term capital gain only when resulting from the sale or exchange of intellectual property constituting either a capital or Section 1231 asset (as such terms are defined below) in the hands of the seller that was owned by the seller for at least six months prior to the transfer. Thus income generated from the leasing or licensing of property can never be taxed at long-term capital gains rates, because, by retaining ownership of the property, the licensor or lessor has not *sold or exchanged* property. (However, as discussed at page 469, certain types of *exclusive* licenses may be characterized as a sale or exchange. The terms *lease* or *license* and *sale or exchange* are used in a conclusory manner to define the nature of an actual transfer of intellectual property.) Furthermore, income received as compensation for the performance of services will always be taxed at ordinary income rates, because services do not constitute property, and thus the compensation income is not derived from the sale or exchange of *property*.

Property held by a taxpayer will be a capital asset except where it is:

1. Property held by a taxpayer primarily for sale to others in the ordinary course of his trade or business, e.g., inventory.
2. Property that is used (not held primarily for sale to others) by a taxpayer in his trade or business and that is of a character that is subject to an allowance for a federal income tax deduction for depreciation.
3. Property in the form of a copyright, a literary, musical, or artistic composition, a letter or memorandum, or similar property held by certain taxpayers (as discussed below).

Property will constitute a Section 1231 asset only when used by a taxpayer in his trade or business and when of a character giving rise to a federal income tax deduction for depreciation. Property (1) held by a taxpayer primarily for sale to others in the ordinary course of his trade or business or (2) consisting of copyrights, literary, musical or artistic compositions, letters or memoranda or similar property held by certain taxpayers (as discussed below) will not qualify as either a capital or Section 1231 asset and will therefore not give rise, except as provided in Section 1235 as discussed below, to long-term capital gain upon its disposition.

Not all transactions resulting in the sale or exchange of intellectual property qualifying as a capital or Section 1231 asset will give rise to long-term capital gain. If the property sold or exchanged by a taxpayer is a Section 1231 asset, an amount of gain realized by the seller equal to the federal income tax deductions for depreciation allowed or allowable with respect to such property in previous years will be taxed at ordinary income rates. Furthermore, sale of property with respect to which the purchaser will be able to claim a deduction for depreciation between either (1) a husband and wife, (2) a corporation and an individual, who with certain members of his family owns at least 80 per cent in value of the outstanding capital stock of such corporation, (3) a partnership and a person owning at least an 80 per cent interest in the partnership, and (4) two partnerships in which the same persons own 80 per cent or more of the interests in each partnership will result in all gain being taxed at ordinary income rates. Similar consequences will result upon sales of certain types of intellectual property to foreign corporations controlled by the seller.

Finally, certain sales or exchanges of intellectual property do not result in gain realized therefrom being subject to taxation. In such cases gain resulting from the sale or exchange is not taxed until such time as the seller transfers, in a taxable transaction, the consideration he received in exchange for the intellectual property. An example of such a nontaxable sale or exchange is when a person transfers intellectual property to a corporation, which he controls by owning more than 80 per cent of the stock immediately after the exchange, in exchange for stock in that corporation. In such a case the person transferring the intellectual property will not be taxed upon gain resulting from the transfer of property to the corporation at the time of such transfer. Instead, taxation of such gain will be deferred until the taxpayer sells or exchanges, in a taxable transaction, the stock received in exchange for the intellectual property.

Persons acquiring interests in intellectual property find that the federal income tax consequences resulting from the acquisition vary, depending upon the method by which they acquire such interest. When this interest is acquired through a lease or license, the lessee or licensee is generally entitled to a federal income tax deduction in the amount of the rent or royalties paid or accrued at such time as the rent or royalties are paid or accrued. When intellectual property is purchased, the purchaser may recoup the cost of the purchase price only through annual federal income tax deductions for depreciation either (1) pro-rated over the useful life of the property or (2) possibly where the price is dependent on income produced by the property, equal to the royalties paid. Where such property is not of a character subject to depreciation, the purchaser is not entitled to any deductions, but instead, may use the cost of acquiring the property to offset any gain taxable to the purchaser upon the subsequent resale of the property. Because taxpayers generally prefer current deductions that are usually largest where intellectual property is leased or licensed, purchasers often have interest adverse to a seller of intellectual property when structuring the method of transferring interests in property. Sellers usually prefer to sell or exchange such property as opposed to licensing or leasing it so as to have profit derived from the transfer taxed at long-term capital gain rates.

DISPOSITION OF INTELLECTUAL PROPERTY

Patents, Trade Secrets, and Related Know-how

Transfers Not Within the Scope of Section 1235. An inventor's or investor's exploitation of patents, patentable inventions for which a patent has not been obtained, nonpatentable trade secrets, or industrial know-how of a nature that is not protectable by the issuance of a patent or as a trade secret will give rise to income subject to taxation. Except as provided in Section 1235 of the Internal Revenue Code as explained below, this income will be taxed at more favorable long-term capital gain rates only where:

1. The item being exploited is characterized as property.
2. Such property constitutes a capital or Section 1231 asset in the hands of the inventor or investor.
3. Such income consists of gain realized from the sale or exchange of the property.
4. The inventor or investor owned the property for at least six months prior to its disposition.

Although patents, patentable inventions, and trade secrets are property, it is not clear whether other industrial know-how will be characterized as such. To the extent such other industrial know-how does not constitute property, income derived therefrom will be taxed at ordinary income rates.

It is reasonably easy to determine whether a patent has been owned for a period of at least six months, because the "holding period" will begin to run upon the date on which the invention has first been reduced to practice by the preparation of drawings substantially identical to those contained in the application upon which the patent may be issued. Presumably, the holding period for a trade secret will also begin to run when the process is reduced to drawings and writings in substantially final form. However, considerably more difficulty is encountered in determining whether a patent, patentable invention, trade secret, or industrial know-how constitutes either a capital or Section 1231 asset in the hands of its owner, and whether a particular disposition of such property qualifies as a sale or exchange.

These types of intellectual property will constitute either a capital or Section 1231 asset so long as they are not held by a person primarily for sale to others in the ordinary course of his business. A determination that such property is so held requires a finding that (1) the owner is engaged in the trade or business of selling these types of property and (2) the particular property being transferred is being held primarily for sale to others in the ordinary course of the owner's trade or business. If held for investment or for use (not sale) in a trade or business, such property may qualify as a capital asset or Section 1231 asset even though the taxpayer is otherwise engaged in the trade or business of selling similar types of property. The courts have generally found that a person is engaged in a trade or business of selling patents and similar types of intellectual property only when that person's business entails recurrent transactions, and in the main, these transactions are sales. A taxpayer engaged exclusively in the licensing of such property will not be regarded as being in the trade or business of selling these types of intellectual property.

Considerable difficulty arises in determining whether the method by which a person transfers his interest in inventions and secret processes qualifies as a "sale or exchange." For instance, intellectual property is sometimes transferred by the granting of an exclusive license to exploit such property for which the licensor receives royalty-type payments. Although the granting of a nonexclusive license does not normally qualify as a sale or exchange, the granting of an exclusive license may so qualify where the result is to transfer all substantial rights in the invention or secret process to the licensee.

Generally, a person is deemed to have sold or exchanged his interest in an invention or secret process where he either conveys (1) the entire interest in a patent, patentable invention, or trade secret that is defined to include the exclusive right to make, use, and sell the invention or process throughout a specified geographic area or (2) an undivided part or share of such property. In order for the granting of an exclusive license to qualify as a sale or exchange under this rule, the license must grant the *exclusive* right to make, use, and sell the invention or secret process within a specified geographic location for the remaining life of the patent or until a secret process becomes public knowledge and is no longer protectable as a trade secret. Thus the licensor may not retain (1) the right to make, use, or sell such property himself within the same geographic area, (2) the right to allow others to make, use, and sell the property within the same geographic area, or (3) the right to terminate the exclusive license at will. However, the licensor may retain the right to terminate an exclusive license upon the happening of a subsequent condition, the occurrence of which is beyond the control of the transferor, such as failure of the transferee to pay royalties when due. Furthermore, the grant may probably be limited to the right to make, use, and sell the property in a particular field or a geographic location constituting less than the entire area of a country. The method by which the amount of consideration for the transfer to be paid to the transferor is determined, whether it be a percentage of future earnings generated by the rights conveyed or a fixed purchase price, is not determinative of whether the transfer qualifies as a sale or exchange.

Whether the method of transferring the invention or secret process qualifies as a sale or exchange or constitutes a mere license is of considerable importance to the person acquiring such property. If the transferee acquires this property in a transaction qualifying as a license, he will generally be entitled to deduct royalty payments when paid or accrued, whether the property consists of patents, patentable inventions, or trade secrets. However, where the transfer constitutes a sale or exchange no such federal income tax deduction will be allowed upon the making of royalty payments. Instead, an annual deduction for depreciation will be allowed where the property acquired consists of patents. To the extent such property consists of patentable inventions for which a patent has not been issued and trade secrets, no depreciation deduction will be allowed. Instead, the cost incurred in purchasing such types of property may simply be used to reduce the amount of taxable gain realized upon a subsequent sale of the property by the purchaser.

Transfers Pursuant to Section 1235. Prior to 1954, professional inventors—persons engaged in the trade or business of inventing and selling patents—could, under the principles discussed on pp. 468–469, rarely obtain long-term capital gain treatment upon income generated from the disposition of a patent, because such patent would be regarded as property held primarily for the sale to others in the ordinary course of the inventor's business and not as a capital or Section 1231 asset. Such long-term capital gain treatment was available only to amateur inventors. In 1954, Section 1235 was enacted to eliminate this distinction between professional and amateur inventors. By increasing the opportunity for professional inventors to obtain long-term capital gain taxation rates upon income earned from their efforts in developing patentable inventions, Congress hoped to encourage the advancement of scientific work.

Where applicable, Section 1235 provides that gain realized upon the sale or exchange of patents shall be taxed at long-term capital gain rates regardless of whether (1) such property constitutes a capital or Section 1231 asset in the hands of the seller, (2) such property was owned by the seller for a period of less than six months, and (3) the purchase price is either (a) payable periodically over a period generally coterminous with the transferee's use of the patent or (b) contingent on the productivity or use of the patent.

The preferential treatment provided by Section 1235 is limited to the transfer of patents by either an individual (1) whose efforts created the invention and who would qualify as the "original and first" inventor within the meaning of the 1952 Patent Act or (2) who acquired an interest in the patent by paying full value to the original inventor prior to the time the invention covered by the patent is first reduced to practice—when the invention has been tested and operated successfully under operating conditions. This investor may be neither the (1) employer of the inventor nor (2) certain members of the family of the inventor. Although Section 1235 will not be applicable to the transfer of nonpatentable trade secrets or industrial know-how, it will apply to the transfer of patent applications and inventions not yet protected by a patent, provided a patent is subsequently obtained. It is not clear whether Section 1235 will be applicable to the transfer of inventions and patent applications for which a patent is not subsequently issued. Furthermore, the transfer of a patent by a corporation or trust will not be within the scope of Section 1235. Although the transfer of a patent by a partnership may not qualify as a transfer within the scope of Section 1235 as to the partnership, such transfer will be within the provisions of Section 1235 as to each individual partner who would qualify for Section 1235 treatment if he had transferred the patent himself.

Section 1235 permits long-term capital gain treatment only where the taxpayer transfers (other than by gift, inheritance, or devise) all substantial rights in a patent—where the transfer constitutes a sale or exchange. The granting of an exclusive license to make, use, and sell such property will qualify under the provisions of Section 1235 where such grant transfers all substantial rights in the invention.

All substantial rights in a patent will have been transferred even though the transferor retains legal title to the patent for the purpose of securing payment of the purchase price or retains the right to reacquire the patent on the happening of a subsequent condition, the occurrence of which is beyond the control of the transferor. However, the Internal Revenue Service takes the position that the granting of an exclusive license will not result in a transfer of all substantial rights in a patent for the purposes of Section 1235 where:

1. The licensor retains the right in himself, or to grant to others, the right to make, use, or sell the patent in the same geographic area in which the licensee is entitled to exploit the invention, where any of these rights are of value.
2. The grant is for a term of less than the remaining life of the patent.

3. The licensor retains the right to terminate the exclusive license at will.
4. The exclusive license grants less than all the claims or inventions covered by the patent that exist and have value at the time of the grant.
5. The exclusive license grants rights in fields of use or trades and industries that are less than all the rights covered by the patent that exist at the time of the grant and have value at the time of the grant.
6. The exclusive license is limited geographically within the country of issuance.

In several cases the United States Tax Court has invalidated the Internal Revenue Service's requirement that an exclusive license, in order to qualify as a transfer within the scope of Section 1235, must (1) grant rights in all fields of use and all trades and industries that exist at the time of the grant and have value at the time of the grant and (2) not be limited geographically within the country in which the patent is issued. However, in one of these cases the Tax Court was reversed and the United States Court of Appeals for the Sixth Circuit held that an exclusive license, in order to constitute a sale or exchange, cannot be limited to a particular field of use.

The provisions of Section 1235 will not be applicable where a patent is transferred to certain persons related to the transferor, including (1) certain members of his family, (2) corporations in which the transferor has substantial stock holdings, and (3) certain trusts and their fiduciaries, beneficiaries, and grantors.

Failure to qualify for long-term capital gains treatment under the provisions of Section 1235 does not preclude a taxpayer from obtaining such treatment if the transaction would otherwise qualify for such treatment under the rules as discussed on pp. 468–469.

Payments made by a purchaser for the acquisition of intellectual property in a transaction qualifying under the provisions of Section 1235 will not be deductible when made. Instead, the purchaser will be entitled to depreciation deductions where the property acquired consists of patents.

Transfers of Patents, Trade Secrets, and Related Know-how That Always Result in Ordinary Income.　Not all sales of capital or Section 1231 assets (1) that the seller has held for six months or (2) that come within the scope of Section 1235 will result in long-term capital gain treatment. To the extent that intellectual property, when transferred, consists of depreciable patents, an amount of gain realized upon the transfer equal to the amount of depreciation deductions previously allowed or allowable to the seller will be taxed at ordinary income rates. Where patents that are depreciable in the hands of the purchaser are transferred between either (1) a husband and wife, (2) a corporation and its controlling stockholder, (3) a partnership and its controlling partner, or (4) two partnerships controlled by the same persons, *all* gain realized will be taxed at ordinary income rates. Similarly, the transfer of patents, patentable inventions, or nonpatentable trade secrets to foreign corporations controlled by the seller will result in *all* gain being taxed at ordinary income rates.

Employee Inventors.   Finally, a brief word should be mentioned about employee inventors. Where a person is employed to invent and is contractually bound to transfer to his employer any rights he may have in inventions or secret processes that he creates during the course of his employment, payments received by the employee from the employer may never be taxed at long-term capital gain rates. Such payments are characterized as compensation received for the performance of services—the creating and inventing services—and are taxed at ordinary income rates. These payments would generally be deductible by the employer when paid or accrued.

Trademarks, Service Marks, and Franchises

Depreciation of Trademarks, Service Marks, and Franchises.   One of the major tax differences between trademarks, service marks, and franchises, on the one hand, and copyrights, on the other hand, concerns the issue of the allowance of depreciation deductions. In general, where amounts paid for the development or purchase of a copyright used by the owner in a trade or business or held for the production of income are fixed and determinable rather than dependent on income produced by the property, such amounts may be deducted over the life of the copyright, beginning from the time of the grant or acquisition of the copyright. In contrast, amounts expended for the purchase of an existing franchise may be deducted over the period of the franchise only if the franchise is not renewable. In situations where it appears that the purchaser has acquired a perpetual interest in the franchise, depreciation deductions will be denied. For example, a dancing school franchise that was subject to an automatic annual renewal after the expiration of the initial term, although revocable for cause, was found to be nondepreciable. Similarly, taxicab licenses granted by the city of Chicago were held to have indeterminable lives and, hence, were treated as being nondepreciable, despite the fact that they were granted under a municipal ordinance that could be amended after five years. Finally, a federally granted right to produce and market milk in a defined geographical area (a federal "Class 1" milk base) was held to have a useful life that was determinable only "on the basis of the nation's economy generally, and the farm economy particularly" and, hence, was deemed to be nondepreciable for tax purposes.

The issue as to whether or not a trademark or service mark (the terms are interchangeable for tax purposes) can be depreciated is quite different from the questions presented in the franchise area. With respect to marks, an initial distinction must be made between a pre-existing trademark that is purchased from a private taxpayer and a trademark that is newly registered with the government. The present position of the Internal Revenue Service is that trademarks, service marks, and trade names usually have an indefinite life so that the purchase price of such intangible property is not deductible or depreciable. Early decisions of the Supreme Court and the Tax Court were to the same effect. The apparent argument of the Revenue Service is that, even though the Lanham Act provides for an initial twenty-year registration period for trademarks, such marks may retain a value after the expiration of the initial federal registration period through continued use and protection. Furthermore, the Internal Revenue Service has noted that the Lanham Act provides for registration renewal periods and, as noted earlier in the franchise area, depreciation is not allowable with respect to an intangible asset with a renewal privilege extending for an indeterminable period.

In contrast to the situation involved where a pre-existing trademark or service mark is purchased from another taxpayer, Section 177 of the Internal Revenue Code permits certain expenditures connected with the federal registration of a mark to be treated, at the election of the taxpayer, as deferred expenses. All such expenditures that are so treated will be allowed as a deduction prorated over a period of not less than sixty months. Section 177 defines the scope of the term *trademark or trade name expenditure* to include any expenditure "which is (1) directly connected with the acquisition, protection, expansion, registration (federal, state, or foreign), or defense of a trademark or trade name; (2) is chargeable to capital account; *and* (3) is not part of the consideration paid for a trademark, trade name, or business." The Internal Revenue Service has indicated that Section 177 will usually apply to the following expenditures: (1) legal fees and other costs in connection with the acquisition of the certificate of registration of a trademark from the United States or other government, (2) artists' fees or similar expenses connected with the design of a distinctive mark of a product or service, (3) litigation expenses connected with infringement proceedings, and (4) costs in connection with the preparation and filing of an application for renewal of registration and continued use of a trademark.

An election under Section 177 is irrevocable insofar as it applies to a single trademark or trade name expenditure. Separate elections may be made, however, for other trademark or trade name expenditures, and different "write-off" periods (but not less than sixty months) may be chosen for different trademark or trade name expenditures.

Disposition of Trademarks, Service Marks, and Franchises. The characterization of taxable gain attributable to the disposition of a trademark, service mark, or franchise involves considerations that are different from those in either the patent or copyright area. Prior to 1969, questions arose as to whether the transfer of the franchise, trademark, service mark or trade name constituted a sale or license. The Tax Court took the position that the transfers of franchises were not sales and that all gains attributable to such transfers were taxable as ordinary income. There was a split among the various circuit courts on this issue. Where payments with respect to the transfer were contingent on production and payable over a period of time, a similar split of authority arose. A set of clarifying statutory rules for this area was finally adopted in the Tax Reform Act of 1969 in the form of Section 1253. It should be noted that the section does not specifically refer to service marks per se. It can be assumed, however, that the technical scope of Section 1253 includes service marks. Pursuant to Section 1253, a transfer of a franchise, trademark, or trade name shall not be treated as a sale or exchange of a capital asset if the transferor retains any significant power, right, or continuing interest with respect to the subject matter of the franchise, trademark, or trade name. This condition is similar to that involved in the patent area.

The term *significant power, right, or continuing interest* is defined as including, but not being limited to, the following rights with respect to the interest transferred:

1. A right to disapprove any assignment of such interest, or any part thereof.
2. A right to terminate at will.
3. A right to prescribe the standards of quality of products used or sold, or of services furnished, and of the equipment and facilities used to promote such products or services.
4. A right to require that the transferee sell or advertise only products or services of the transferor.
5. A right to require that the transferee purchase substantially all of his supplies and equipment from the transferor.
6. A right to payment contingent on the productivity, use, or dis-

position of the subject matter of the interest transferred, if such payments constitute a substantial element under the transfer agreement.

Any transfer pursuant to which a significant power, right, or continuing interest is retained will generate ordinary income rather than long-term capital gain to the transferor.

Section 1253 goes on to provide that the term *transfer* includes the *renewal* of a franchise, trademark, or trade name. It should also be noted that long-term capital gain treatment will not be given to a transfer of a franchise, trademark, or trade name if such property can be characterized as "property held primarily for sale [by the transferor] to customers in the ordinary course of business." This issue was discussed by the Senate Finance Committee Report that accompanied the passage of Section 1253. If the trademark, trade name, or franchise is held for only a short period of time before it is sold, the presumption arises that the property was held primarily for resale in the ordinary course of business. A large number of individual sales, as where a franchisor subdivides a franchise and transfers numerous subfranchises in the course of a year, also suggests a prior intention to hold property primarily for sale in the ordinary course of business. Section 1253 sets forth the rules governing the treatment of payments received with respect to the transfer of a franchise, trademark, or trade name from the standpoint of both the transferor and transferee.

As noted, ordinary income treatment will be accorded to the transferor of the franchise, trademark, or trade name when the amounts are "contingent payments." The term *contingent payments* has been defined as including continuing payments (other than installment payments of a definite principal sum agreed upon in the transfer contract) (1) measured by a percentage of the selling price of the products marketed or (2) based on the units manufactured or sold, or (3) based in a similar manner upon production, sale, or use or disposition of the franchise, trademark, or trade name transferred.

With respect to the tax treatment to the purchaser, a distinction must be drawn between situations wherein the payments for the trademark, trade name, or franchise are "contingent payments" and situations wherein noncontingent payments are involved. Noncontingent payments are defined as payments based upon a fixed amount, either paid in a lump sum at the time of the sale or in installments thereafter.

The tax treatment by the transferee of noncontingent payments will depend upon whether the transaction is a sale or a license. When the transaction is a sale, the purchaser may depreciate the payments if the rights he has purchased have an ascertainable useful life. If the rights do not have an ascertainable useful life, he will not be entitled to deductions for a lump sum payment or for any installment payments. When the transaction is not a sale or exchange of a capital asset by reason of the retention by the transferor of any "significant power, right or continuing interest," any noncontingent payment made in discharge of the principal sum agreed upon in the transfer agreement will be deductible by the transferee in accordance with the following rules:

1. In the case of a single payment made in discharge of the entire principal sum, equal deductions will be allowed over a period of ten taxable years or, if shorter, over the taxable years to which the agreement applies.
2. In the case of a payment that is one of a series of approximately equal payments made in discharge of the entire principal sum, and the series is payable either (a) over the period of the transfer agreement or (b) over a period of more than ten years, a deduction will be allowed for each payment for the year in which it is paid.
3. Any other payments will be governed by rules to be adopted in the future by the Internal Revenue Service.

Finally, as in the patent and copyright areas, several special types of transfers have been singled out by the Internal Revenue Code so as to create ordinary income treatment where long-term capital gain would otherwise exist. The following four situations are the most common:

1. If the property was depreciable in the hands of the *transferor,* any gain attributable to previously allowable depreciation deductions will be treated as ordinary income.
2. If the property was a Section 1231 asset in the hands of the *transferor* and the transfer is made between a husband and wife or between an individual and a "controlled" corporation, all gain will be treated as ordinary income.
3. If the property will be a Section 1231 asset in the hands of the *transferee* and the transfer is made between a partner and a "controlled" partnership or between two "commonly controlled" partnerships, all gain will be treated as ordinary income.
4. If the property was a capital asset or Section 1231 asset in the hands of the *transferor,* and the transferee is a "controlled foreign corporation," all gain will be treated as ordinary income.

Copyrights and Artistic and Literary Property

If a copyright or similar artistic or literary property is leased or licensed to another, the entire amount received by the owner of the copyright in payment for the use of such right will be characterized as a rent or royalty and will be taxable as ordinary income. Similarly, if an employee is paid to produce work that will be subsequently copyrighted and owned by his employer, the entire amount of income received by him in connection with the performance of these services will be compensation and will be taxable as ordinary income. On the other hand, if the owner of a copyright or similar property sells his rights to another, the amount of taxable income to the seller will be limited to the net gain resulting from the sale.

Certain problems exist in present tax law regarding the proper characterization of any taxable income derived from the disposition of a copyright or similar artistic or literary property for a profit. At first glance, it might appear that such gain should be taxed at ordinary income rates. Such an impression could be gleaned from the consideration that the value of a copyright is derived from the personal efforts of the creator, hence making payments for such value appear related to compensation income. Furthermore, the sales price of a copyright is often not fixed at the time of the disposition but may instead be based on a form of "earn-out," which will take into consideration the subsequent sales or use of the rights by the transferee. This factor would seem to indicate that the proper characterization of any profit realized upon the disposition of a copyright should be "royalty" income resulting in ordinary income treatment. Present law does in fact require ordinary income treatment in many situations involving the disposition of a copyright. There are, however, several significant exceptions to this general rule.

As noted in the discussion of patents, long-term capital gain treatment can be obtained when the object of the sale or exchange is either a capital asset or a Section 1231 asset. In contrast to the rather favorable attitude, noted earlier, accorded to patents, the Internal Revenue Code makes it clear that copyrights will in many cases be characterized as noncapital assets. Accordingly, the Internal Revenue Code excludes from the definition of capital asset a "copyright, a literary, musical or artistic composition, a letter or memorandum, or similar property" held by one of three types of taxpayers. The list of "prohibited" taxpayers consists of the following:

1. The taxpayer whose personal efforts created such property.
2. Any taxpayer for whom such property was prepared or produced.
3. Any taxpayer whose basis for the property is determined by reference to the basis of the property in the hands of a taxpayer described in (1) or (2). This category would generally consist of taxpayers who have received the property either as a gift

from the creator or pursuant to a taxfree exchange with the creator.

The phrase *similar property* as used in the preceding context has been given a rather broad interpretation. The Internal Revenue Service has defined *similar property* as including "such property as a theatrical production, a radio program, a newspaper cartoon strip, or any other property eligible for copyright protection (whether under statute or common law) but *does not include* a patent or an invention, or a design which may be protected only under the patent law and not under the copyright law." (Emphasis supplied.) Despite the reference by the Internal Revenue Service to "eligibility for copyright protection," case law has rejected the argument that property that is not copyrightable will automatically be included in the definition of a capital asset. For example, the Court of Claims held in *Cranford* v. *United States* that a noncopyrightable format for the radio quiz program "Take It or Leave It" was "similar property" and hence within the exclusionary scope of Section 1221(3).

In view of the seemingly all-inclusive scope of "similar property," it would appear that the only possibility for long-term capital gains treatment through the characterization of a copyright as a capital asset lies in situations wherein the seller of the copyright is not one of the three types of "prohibited" taxpayers referred to earlier.

The primary examples of taxpayers that fall outside of such three categories are the purchaser of copyrighted property and the heir or legatee of an owner of copyrighted property. Even in such situations, however, the additional requirements of the Internal Revenue Code, relating to capital assets, must be met. Accordingly, the copyright cannot be:

1. Stock in trade of the taxpayer or other property of a kind that would properly be included in the inventory of the taxpayer.
2. Property held by the taxpayer primarily for sale to customers in the ordinary course of his trade or business.
3. Depreciable property used in the taxpayer's trade or business.

As discussed in the patent area, the determination of whether intellectual property, such as a copyright, is held by its owner as inventory will depend upon whether the owner is engaged in the trade or business of selling such property and whether the particular property in question is being held primarily for sale to others in the course of the owner's trade or business. Accordingly, such property may qualify as a capital asset even though the taxpayer is otherwise engaged in the trade or business of selling copyrights or similar property if the particular copyright is held for investment.

The most frequent situation that will permit the disposition of a copyright to be characterized as a disposition of a capital asset involves an individual, other than an author or artist, who purchases a literary or artistic work and holds the same as an investment until its final disposition. As noted earlier, if the copyright is held for the production of income, it will not qualify as a capital asset because it will then be depreciable over its twenty-eight-year term and hence constitute "depreciable property used in the taxpayer's trade or business." Nevertheless, it may still qualify as a Section 1231 asset.

The definition of a Section 1231 asset excludes from its scope a "copyright, a literary, musical or artistic composition, a letter or memorandum, or similar property, held by a taxpayer described [in the capital asset area]." The effect of this exclusionary clause is to limit Section 1231 treatment to a taxpayer who is not one of the "prohibited taxpayers" in the capital asset context and whose property would otherwise qualify as a capital asset except for the fact that such property was used in such taxpayer's trade or business. Long-term capital gain treatment *may* thus be available with respect to the disposition of a copyright or similar property if it is held by a taxpayer who purchased or inherited the property from another and who either holds the property for investment or for use in his trade or business.

Some uncertainty arises from the fact that both the capital asset sections and Section 1231 require a "sale or exchange" of the property in question before long-term capital gains treatment will be allowed. The "sale or exchange" requirement creates a special problem in the copyright area because a copyright typically represents an aggregate of rights and privileges that may or may not be transferred in total in any one transaction. For example, the transfer of rights in a copyright may be restricted geographically, such as with a limit on publication rights outside the United States. Moreover, the transfer of a copyright may be subdivided into the level of individual mediums of expression: the owner may sell the stage rights to a particular work to X, the book rights to Y, and the motion picture rights to Z. The Internal Revenue Service originally took the position that an alleged disposition of a copyright that involved anything less than the title to the entire copyright was a license, rather than a "sale or exchange" and hence necessarily gave rise to ordinary income. After repeated judicial defeats, the Internal Revenue Service modified its position and acknowledged that a copyright is divisible into several components. In particular, it ruled that a copyright owner's sale of the exclusive right to exploit a copyrighted work throughout the remaining life of the copyright in a "particular medium" will effectuate a transfer of property and hence result in a "sale or exchange." The transfer of anything less, however, confers only a license, and therefore generates ordinary income. Thus long-term capital gain may be permissible in the situation where the owner of a copyright sells the motion picture rights to X and the book rights to Y.

An ambiguity exists, however, in the definition of an "entire" medium of publication. Case law has implied that the classification of rights utilized by the Copyright Act should serve as an enumeration of the number of exclusive mediums of publication accompanying any single valid copyright. The Tax Court has illustrated this principle with the following language:

> The Copyright Act segregates the various exclusive rights derived under the registration of a copyright into separately numbered paragraphs. The major rights arising under the copyright of a play are (1) the exclusive right to publish the play; (2) the exclusive right to present the play on the speaking stage; (3) the exclusive right to present the play on the radio; and (4) the exclusive right to make and exhibit motion pictures of the play. Each of these exclusive rights is enforceable by the owner against all persons. Each is substantial in itself and may be exploited independently of any of the others. Each may form the basis of a new copyright secured in the name of the holder of the exclusive right.

A crucial problem may arise when one of these categories is subdivided. For example, suppose the owner of a copyrighted work sells the right to publish the hardback book version of the work to X and subsequently sells the right to publish the paperback book version to Y.

Although the Internal Revenue Service has never publicly addressed this issue, it is conceivable that it could argue that this situation does not involve an "exclusive right to exploit the copyrighted work in a medium of publication" because the entire book rights to the copyright are not sold to any one entity. The judicial response to such an argument is uncertain. In the case of *Daniel M. Cory*, the taxpayer sold the publication rights of a copyrighted work and argued for long-term capital gain. The Internal Revenue Service contended that any profit realized on the sale should be taxed at ordinary rates because the taxpayer (1) retained the serial publication rights in their entirety, (2) retained the publication rights, in general, outside of the United States and Canada, and (3) provided for payments based upon the productivity of the property. The Court of Appeals refused to address itself to the issue of whether any one of these factors standing alone would have been sufficient to warrant ordinary income treatment. Instead it held that the combination of these factors supported the Internal Revenue

Service's contention. It is thus impossible to say with certainty whether the retention of the serial rights alone would have precluded long-term capital gains treatment. Certainly, however, the area of subdivision of rights within a single medium is uncertain for the taxpayer desiring long-term capital gains treatment.

The form of the consideration received by the taxpayer seller on the disposition of a copyright originally created some difficulties. Prior to 1960 the Internal Revenue Service argued, often unsuccessfully, that an alleged sale of a copyright providing for contingent payments of indeterminate sums was a license rather than a "sale or exchange." In 1960, however, it reversed its position and ruled that the consideration received by a proprietor of a copyright for the transfer of the exclusive right to exploit the copyrighted work in a medium of publication throughout the life of the work is to be treated as proceeds from a sale of property regardless of whether the consideration received (1) is measured by a percentage of the receipts from the sale, performance, exhibition, or publication of the copyrighted work; (2) is measured by the number of copies sold, performances given, or exhibitions made of the copyrighted work; or (3) is payable over a period generally co-terminous with the grantee's use of the copyrighted work.

Finally, as in the patent and franchise areas, there are several special types of transfers for which the Internal Revenue Code explicitly provides ordinary income treatment even if all other requirements for long-term capital gain have been met. The four most frequently encountered situations are the following:

1. If the copyright was a Section 1231 asset in the hands of the *transferor,* any gain attributable to previously allowable depreciation deductions will be treated as ordinary income.
2. If the copyright was a Section 1231 asset in the hands of the *transferor* and the transfer is made between a husband and wife or between an individual and a "controlled" corporation, all gain will be treated as ordinary income.
3. If the copyright will be a Section 1231 asset in the hands of the *transferee* and the transfer is made between a partner and a "controlled" partnership or between two "commonly controlled" partnerships, all gain will be treated as ordinary income.
4. If the copyright was a capital asset or Section 1231 asset in the hands of the *transferor,* and the transferee is a "controlled foreign corporation," all gain will be treated as ordinary income.

Appendix: Selected Bibliography

Chapter 1: Intellectual and Intangible Property Rights: The World of Ideas, Know-how, Writings, and Personalities

CASES

Compco Corp. v. *Daybright Lighting, Inc.*, 376 U.S. 234 (1964) (arm's length copying lawful outside patent and copyright field in the absence of "palming off").

Goldstein v. *California*, 412 U.S. 546 (1973) (federal copyright law does not pre-empt state regulation of sound recordings).

Kewanee Oil Co. v. *Bicron Corp.*, 416 U.S. 470 (1974) (federal patent law does not pre-empt state trade secret law).

Sears, Roebuck & Co. v. *Stiffel Co.*, 376 U.S. 225 (1964) (arm's length copying lawful outside patent and copyright field in the absence of "palming off").

Trademark Cases, 100 U.S. 82 (1879) (concurrent protection of trademarks by both federal and state law is permissible).

Chapter 2: Patents

BIBLIOGRAPHY

ABA Antitrust Section, *Antitrust Developments 1955–68,* Supplement to Report of the Attorney General's National Committee to Study the Antitrust Laws (1968).

DeSimone, Gambrell, & Gareau, *Characteristics of Interference Practice,* 45 J.P.O.S. 503 (1963).

Dunner, *Court Review of Patent Office Decisions—Comparative Analysis of C.C.P.A. and District Court Actions,* Dunner, Gambrell, & Kayton, 4 Patent Law Perspectives, Appendix 3 (New York: Matthew Bender & Co., 1972).

Federico, *Commentary on the New Patent Act,* 35 U.S.C.A. Vol. 1 (1952).

Hearings on S. 643, *A Bill for the General Revision of the Patent Laws, Title 35 of the United States Code* before the Subcommittee on Patents, Trademarks and Copyrights of U.S. Senate Committee on the Judiciary (92d Cong., 1st Sess. 1971).

Lahr, *The Federal Preemption Doctrine: Protection of Industrial Property and Its Relation to the Sherman Act,* 39 ABA Antitrust L.J. 812 (1970).

Manual of Patent Examining Procedure (Washington, D.C.: Government Printing Office, 3rd Ed., 20th Rev. 1969, 33d Rev. 1972).

Oppenheim & Weston, *Federal Antitrust Laws: Cases and Comments* (St. Paul, Minn.: West Publishing Co., 1968).

Presidential Memorandum and Statement of Government Patent Policy, 28 Fed. Reg. 10943 (1963).

Presidential Memorandum and Statement of Government Patent Policy, 36 Fed. Reg. 16887 (1971).

President's Commission on the Patent System, *To Promote the Progress of Useful Arts in an Age of Exploding Technology* (Washington, D.C.: Government Printing Office, 1966).

Report of the Commission on Government Procurement, Vol. IV, Part I: Patent, Technical Data, and Copyright (Dec. 1972).

Rich, *Infringement Under Section 271 of the Patent Act of 1952,* 21 Geo. Wash. L. Rev. 521 (1953); 35 J.P.O.S. 476 (1953).

Robinson, *The Law of Patents for Useful Inventions* (Boston: Little, Brown & Co., 1890; New York: Clark Boardman, 1971).

Smith, *Patent Law* (Ann Arbor, Mich.: Overbeck Co., 1954).

Turner, *The Patent System and Competitive Policy,* 44 N.Y.U. L. Rev. 450 (1969).

CASES

Patentable Subject Matter

Application of Tarczy-Hornoch, 397 F.2d 856 (C.C.P.A. 1968) (patentability of process claims describing the function of a machine).

Funk Bros. Seed Co. v. *Kalo Inoculant Co.*, 333 U.S. 127 (1948) (no patent on newly found plant).

Subject Matter Exempted from Patentability

American Fruit Growers, Inc. v. *Brogdex Co.*, 283 U.S. 1 (1931) (naturally occurring substances not patentable).

Ex Parte Seaborg, 131 U.S.P.Q. 202 (Pat. Off. Bd. App. 1960) (patent on synthetic production of elements not found in a natural state on earth).

Gottschalk v. *Benson*, 409 U.S. 63 (1972) (no computer program process patent for application of mathematical formula).

Hotel Security Checking Co. v. *Lorraine Co.*, 160 F. 467 (2d Cir. 1908) (account checking system not patentable).

Loew's Drive-in Theatres Inc. v. *Park-In Theatres, Inc.*, 174 F.2d 547 (1st Cir. 1949), *cert. denied*, 338 U.S. 822 (1949) (drive-in theater lay-out not patentable).

O'Reilly v. *Morse*, 56 U.S. (15 How.) 62 (1853) (patent claim so broad as to include scientific principle).

Other Statutory Hurdles for an Invention to Clear

Amerio Contact Plate Freezers, Inc. v. *Belt-Ice Corp.*, 316 F.2d 459 (9th Cir.), *cert. denied*, 375 U.S. 902 (1963) ("on sale" criteria-bar to patentability).

City of Elizabeth v. *American Nicholson Pavement Co.*, 97 U.S. 126 (1878) (experimental use v. public use).

Corona Cord Tire Co. v. *Dovan Chemical Corp.*, 276 U.S. 358 (1928) (express abandonment).

Garrett Corp. v. *United States*, 422 F.2d 874 (Ct. Cl.), *cert. denied*, 400 U.S. 931 (1970) (criteria for printed publication).

Graham v. *John Deere Co.*, 383 U.S. 1 (1966) (criteria of "obviousness" under the 1952 Act).

Philips Electronic & Pharmaceutical Industries Corp. v. *Thermal & Electronics Industries, Inc.*, 450 F.2d 1164 (3rd Cir. 1971) (sufficiency of a limited publication).

Pointer v. *Six Wheel Corp.*, 177 F.2d 153 (9th Cir. 1949), *cert. denied*, 339 U.S. 911 (1950) (joint inventorship).

Toledo Scale Corp. v. *Westinghouse Electric Corp.*, 351 F.2d 173 (6th Cir. 1965) (diligence of first inventor in an interference proceeding).

United States v. *Adams*, 383 U.S. 39 (1966) (criteria of "obviousness" under the 1952 Act).

Procedures for Obtaining a United States Patent

Anderson-Black Rock, Inc. v. *Pavement Salvage Co.*, 396 U.S. 57 (1969) (patentability of combination comprising old elements).

Englehard Industries, Inc. v. *Sel-Rex Corp.*, 253 F. Supp. 832 (D.N.J. 1966), *aff'd*, 384 F.2d 877 (3rd Cir. 1967) (need for disclosure of "best mode" of practicing the invention).

Exhibit Supply Co. v. *Ace Patents Corp.*, 315 U.S. 126 (1942) (file wrapper estoppel).

Gerhardt v. *Kinnaird*, 162 F. Supp. 858 (E.D. Ky. 1958) (intervening rights gained before reissue patent).

Ownership and Conveyancing of Patent Rights

Benger Laboratories Ltd. v. *R. K. Laros Co.*, 209 F. Supp. 639 (E.D. Pa. 1962), *aff'd per curiam*, 317 F.2d 455 (3d Cir. 1963) *cert. denied*, 375 U.S. 833 (1963) (license field-of-use limitation).

United States v. *Dubilier Condenser Corp.*, 289 U.S. 178 (1933) (shop rights).

Zenith Radio Corp. v. *Hazeltine Research Corp.*, 395 U.S. 100 (1969) (package licensing).

Royalty Arrangements

Brulotte v. *Thys Co.*, 379 U.S. 29 (1964) (postexpiration royalties).

Zenith Radio Corp. v. *Hazeltine Research, Inc.*, 395 U.S. 100 (1969) (package licensing).

Starting an Infringement Suit

City of Milwaukee v. *Activated Sludge, Inc.*, 69 F.2d 577 (7th Cir. 1934), *cert. denied*, 293 U.S. 596 (1934); 102 F.2d 972 (7th Cir. 1938) (no injunction for patent infringement if harm to public occurs).

Lear, Inc. v. *Adkins*, 395 U.S. 653 (1969) (public interest in licensee's opportunity to challenge validity).

Vitamin Technologists, Inc. v. *Wisconsin Alumni Research Foundation*, 146 F.2d 941 (9th Cir. 1944), *cert. denied*, 325 U.S. 876 (1945) (no injunction for patent infringement if harm to public occurs).

Infringement

Aro Mfg. Co. v. *Convertible Top Replacement Co.*, 377 U.S. 476 (1964) (contributory infringement under the 1952 Act).

Deepsouth Packing Co. v. *Laitram Corp.*, 406 U.S. 518 (1972) (incomplete assembly in the United States with assembly abroad—not infringement in the United States).

Graver Tank & Mfg. Co. v. *Linde Air Products Co.*, 339 U.S. 605 (1950) (direct infringement).

Nordberg Mfg. Co. v. *Jackson Vibrators, Inc.*, 153 U.S.P.Q. 777 (N.D. Ill. 1967), *rev'd*, 393 F.2d 192 (7th Cir. 1968) (active inducement to infringe).

Wilbur-Ellis Co. v. *Kuther*, 377 U.S. 422 (1964) (infringing reconstruction v. noninfringing repair).

Defending an Infringement Suit

American Securit Co. v. *Shatterproof Glass Corp.*, 268 F.2d 769 (3d Cir.), *cert. denied*, 361 U.S. 902 (1959) (coercive package licensing).

Ansul Co. v. *Uniroyal, Inc.*, 306 F. Supp. 541 (S.D.N.Y. 1969), *aff'd as modified*, 448 F.2d 872 (2d Cir. 1971), *cert. denied*, 404 U.S. 1018 (1972) (duty to license to avoid misuse of use patent).

Armstrong v. *Motorola, Inc.*, 374 F.2d 764 (7th Cir.), *cert. denied*, 389 U.S. 830 (1967) (laches).

Blonder-Tongue Laboratories, Inc. v. *University of Illinois Foundation*, 402 U.S. 313 (1971) (collateral estoppel precluding charge of infringement of patent previously adjudicated invalid).

Brulotte v. *Thys Co.*, 379 U.S. 29 (1964) (postexpiration royalties).

Carbice Corp. of America v. *American Patents Development Corp.*, 283 U.S. 27 (1931) (misuse).

Cole v. *Hughes Tool Co.*, 215 F.2d 924 (10th Cir. 1954), *cert. denied sub nom., Ford* v. *Hughes Tool Co.*, 348 U.S. 927 (1955) (no misuse in suing contributory infringers under 1952 Act).

Continental Paper Bag Co. v. *Eastern Paper Bag Co.*, 210 U.S. 405 (1908) (no duty to license).

Morton Salt Co. v. *G. S. Suppiger Co.*, 314 U.S. 488 (1942) (misuse).

Motion Picture Patent Co. v. *Universal Film Mfg. Co.*, 243 U.S. 502 (1917) (misuse).

Preformed Line Products Co. v. *Fanner Mfg. Co.*, 328 F.2d 265 (6th Cir. 1964), *cert. denied*, 379 U.S. 846 (1964) (purging patent misuse).

Patent–Antitrust

American Equipment Co. v. *Tuthill Building Material Co.*, 69 F.2d 406 (7th Cir. 1934) (licensee quantity limitations).

Automated Building Components, Inc. v. *Trueline Truss Co.*, 318 F. Supp. 1252 (D. Ore. 1970) (patents as assets under Clayton Act Section 7).

Clapper v. *Original Tractor Cab Co.*, 165 F. Supp. 565 (S.D. Ind. 1958), *rev'd in part on other grounds*, 270 F.2d 616 (7th Cir. 1959), *cert. denied*, 361 U.S. 967 (1960) (licensee veto over future licenses).

Dehydrating Process Co. v. *A. O. Smith Co.*, 292 F.2d 653 (1st Cir.), *cert. denied*, 368 U.S. 931 (1961) (permissive tie-in).

General Talking Pictures Corp. v. *Western Electric Co.*, 305 U.S. 124 (1938) (licensee field of use limitations).

IBM Corp. v. *United States*, 298 U.S. 131 (1936) (Clayton Act Section 3 tie-in).

International Salt Co. v. *United States*, 332 U.S. 392 (1947) (prohibited tie-in).

Jones Knitting Corp. v. *Morgan*, 361 F.2d 451 (3d Cir. 1966) (group boycott against patent owner).

LaPeyre v. *FTC*, 366 F.2d 117 (5th Cir. 1966) (licensing program involving unfair methods of competition under FTC Act).

Precision Instrument Mfg. Co. v. *Automotive Maintenance Machinery Co.,* 324 U.S. 806 (1945) (fraud on the Patent Office).

Standard Oil Co. (Indiana) v. *United States,* 283 U.S. 163 (1931) (lawful pool).

Transparent-Wrap Machine Corp. v. *Stokes & Smith Co.,* 329 U.S. 637 (1947) (licensee grant-backs).

United States v. *Associated Patents, Inc.,* 134 F. Supp. 74 (E.D. Mich. 1955), *aff'd per curiam,* 350 U.S. 960 (1956) (restricted pooling).

United States v. *General Electric Co.,* 272 U.S. 476 (1926) (fixing licensee's resale price).

United States v. *Glaxo Group Ltd.,* 302 F. Supp. 1 (D.D.C. 1969), *rev'd in part,* 410 U.S. 52 (1973) (bulk-sale restrictions).

United States v. *Huck Mfg. Co.,* 382 U.S. 197 (1965) (fixing licensee's resale price).

United States v. *Linde Air Products Co.,* 83 F. Supp. 978 (N.D. Ill. 1949) (economic inducement to purchase requirements).

United States v. *Line Material Co.,* 333 U.S. 287 (1948) (antitrust aspects of cross-licenses).

United States v. *Singer Mfg. Co.,* 374 U.S. 174 (1963) (restraint of trade involving interference settlement).

Walker Process Equipment Inc. v. *Food Mach. & Chem. Corp.,* 382 U.S. 172 (1965) (fraud on the Patent Office under Section 2 of the Sherman Act).

Chapter 3: Trade Secrets, Know-how, and Unsolicited Disclosures

BIBLIOGRAPHY

Bender, *Trade Secret Protection of Software,* 38 Geo. Wash. L. Rev. 909 (1970).

Blake, *Employee Agreements Not to Compete,* 73 Harv. L. Rev. 625 (1960).

Brosnahan, *Attorney's Guide to Trade Secrets* (Berkeley: The Regents of the University of California, 1971).

Callman, *Unfair Competition, Trademarks and Monopolies* (Chicago: Callaghan & Co., 1968).

Comment, *Industrial Espionage: Piracy of Secret Scientific and Technical Information,* 14 U.C.L.A. L. Rev. 911 (1967).

Developments in the Law—Competitive Torts, 77 Harv. L. Rev. 888 (1964).

Ellis, *Trade Secrets* (New York: Baker, Voorhis & Co., 1953).

Harding, *Trade Secrets and the Mobile Employee,* 22 Bus. Law. 395 (1967).

Milgrim, *Trade Secrets* (New York: Matthew Bender & Co., 1974).

Note, *Injunctions to Protect Trade Secrets,* 51 Va. L. Rev. 917 (1965).

Report of the Commission on Government Procurement, Vol. IV, Part I: Patents, Technical Data, and Copyright (Dec. 1972).

Schiller, *Trade Secrets and the Roman Law: The Actio Servi Corrupti,* 30 Colum. L. Rev. 837 (1930).

Schneider, *Protecting Trade Secrets,* 8 Trial Magazine No. 1 (January/ February 1972).

Turner, *The Law of Trade Secrets* (London: Sweet & Maxwell Limited, 1962).

CASES

Origins

Fowle v. *Park,* 131 U.S. 88 (1889) (first trade secrets Supreme Court case).

Morison v. *Moat,* 9 Hare 241, 68 Eng. Rep. 425 (1851) (English common law).

Peabody v. *Norfolk,* 98 Mass. 452 (1868) (early American trade secrets law).

The Judicial Approach to Trade Secret Cases

B. F. Goodrich Co. v. *Wohlgemuth,* 117 Oh. App. 493, 192 N.E. 2d 99 (1963) (unfairness and secrecy present).

Sarkes Tarzian, Inc. v. *Audio Devices, Inc.,* 166 F. Supp. 250 (S.D. Cal. 1958), *aff'd,* 283 F.2d 695 (9th Cir. 1960), *cert. denied,* 365 U.S. 869 (1961) (unfairness and secrecy absent).

Trade Secret Subject Matter

Arthur Murray Dance Studios of Cleveland v. *Witter,* 62 Ohio L. Abs. 17, 105 N.E. 2d 685 (C.P. 1952) (trade secret know-how not involving technology).

Bimba Manufacturing Co. v. *Starz Cylinder Co.,* 119 Ill. App. 2d 251, 256 N.E. 2d 357 (1st Dist. 1969) (general business information not a trade secret).

Hancock v. *State,* 402 S.W. 2d 906 (Tex. Crim. App. 1966), *aff'd sub. nom., Hancock* v. *Decker,* 379 F.2d 552 (5th Cir. 1967) (computer software).

K & G Oil Tool & Serv. Co. v. *G & G Fishing Tools Serv.,* 158 Tex. 594, 314 S.W. 2d 782, *cert. denied,* 359 U.S. 921 (1958) (product).

Platinum Products Corp. v. *Berthold,* 280 N.Y. 752, 21 N.E. 2d 520 (1939) (industrial formula).

Robinson Electronic Supervisory Co. v. *Johnson,* 397 Pa. 268, 154 A.2d 494 (1959) (customer information).

Sun Dial Corp. v. *Rideout,* 29 N.J. Super. 361, 102 A.2d 90 (1954), *aff'd,* 16 N.J. 252, 108 A.2d 442 (1954) (industrial process).

Town and Country House & Homes Serv., Inc. v. *Evans,* 150 Conn. 314, 189 A.2d 390 (1963) (customer list).

Water Services, Inc. v. *Tesco Chemicals, Inc.,* 410 F.2d 163 (5th Cir. 1969) (sources of supply).

Source of the Trade Secret

Wexler v. *Greenberg*, 399 Pa. 569, 160 A.2d 430 (1960) (former employee as source of the trade secret).

Secrecy

Cataphote Corp. v. *Hudson*, 444 F.2d 1313 (5th Cir. 1971) (originality).

Clark v. *Bunker*, 453 F.2d 1006 (9th Cir. 1972) (means of appropriation as an aspect of secrecy).

Drew Chemical Corp. v. *Star Chemical Co.*, 258 F. Supp. 827 (W.D. Mo. 1966) (loss of secrecy through independent efforts of others).

Ferroline Corp. v. *General Aniline & Film Corp.*, 207 F.2d 912 (7th Cir. 1953), *cert. denied*, 347 U.S. 953 (1954) (secrecy of a combination of elements).

J. T. Healy & Son, Inc. v. *James A. Murphy & Son, Inc.*, 357 Mass. 728, 260 N.E. 2d 723 (1970) (loss of secrecy through laxity).

Lowndes Products, Inc. v. *Brower*, 259 S. C. 306, 191 S.E. 2d 761 (1972) (plant security).

Mycalex Corp. of America v. *Pemco Corp.*, 64 F. Supp. 420 (D. Md. 1946), *aff'd*, 159 F.2d 907 (4th Cir. 1947) (loss of secrecy through advertising).

Servo Corp. of America v. *General Electric Co.*, 393 F.2d 551 (4th Cir. 1968) (secrecy of a combination of elements).

Vulcan Detinning Co. v. *American Can Co.*, 72 N.J. Eq. 387, 67 A. 339 (1907) (qualified secrecy).

Improper Means

American Republic Insurance Co. v. *Union Fidelity Life Insurance Co.*, 295 F. Supp. 553 (D. Ore. 1968) (appropriation by memory).

Duane Jones Co. v. *Burke*, 306 N.Y. 172, 117 N.E. 2d 237 (1954) (breach of fiduciary duty).

E. I. duPont de Nemours & Co. v. *Christopher*, 431 F.2d 1012 (5th Cir. 1970), *cert. denied*, 400 U.S. 1024 (1971) (industrial espionage by aerial photography).

Eastern Extracting Co. v. *Greater New York Extracting Co.*, 126 App. Div. 928, 110 N.Y.S. 738 (1908) (industrial espionage by misrepresentation).

Franke v. *Wiltschek*, 209 F.2d 493 (2d Cir. 1953) (industrial espionage by misrepresentation).

Metal Lubricants Co. v. *Engineered Lubricants Co.*, 284 F. Supp. 483 (E.D. Mo. 1968), *aff'd*, 411 F.2d 426 (8th Cir. 1969) (trade secret misuse after termination of employment).

Nucor Corp. v. *Tennessee Forging Steel Service, Inc.*, 476 F.2d 386 (8th Cir. 1973) (breach of fiduciary duty).

Negotiations and Unsolicited Idea Disclosures

Booth v. Stutz Motor Car Co., 56 F.2d 962 (7th Cir. 1932) (unsolicited disclosure; sufficient concreteness justifies recovery).

Desny v. Wilder, 46 Cal. 2d 715, 299 P.2d 257 (1956) (unsolicited disclosure; only written expression of ideas rather than ideas alone are protectable).

High v. Trade Union Courier Publishing Co., 69 N.Y.S. 2d 526 (Sup. Ct. 1946) (unsolicited disclosure; novelty requirement discarded in favor of terms of contract).

Smith v. Dravo Corp., 203 F.2d. 369 (7th Cir. 1953) (negotiations).

Soule v. Bon Ami Co., 195 N.Y. Supp. 574 (1922), aff'd, 139 N.E. 754, rehearing denied, 142 N.E. 281 (1923) (unsolicited disclosure; absence of novelty disallows recovery).

Bases of Trade Secret Protection

E. I. duPont de Nemours Powder Co. v. Masland, 244 U.S. 100 (1917) (property vs. confidential relationship).

In re Brandreth's Estate, 28 Misc. 468, 59 N.Y.S. 1092 (Sur. Ct. 1899), rev'd on other grounds, 58 App. Div. 575, 69 N.Y.S. 142 (1901), rev'd on other grounds, 169 N.Y. 437, 62 N.E. 563 (1902) (trade secret as taxable property).

Matarese v. Moore-McCormack Lines, 158 F.2d 631 (2d Cir. 1946) (unjust enrichment).

Monsanto Chem. Co. v. Miller, 118 U.S.P.Q. 74 (D. Utah 1958) (confidential relationship).

Motorola, Inc. v. Farichild Camera and Instrument Corp., 366 F. Supp. 1173 (D. Ariz. 1973) (hazards of general contract language).

L. M. Rabinowitz & Co., Inc., v. Dasher, 82 N.Y.S. 2d 431 (Sup. Ct. 1948) (protection by contract; covenant not to compete).

Acquisition and Conveyancing of Trade Secrets

A & E Plastik Pak Co. v. Monsanto, 396 F.2d 710 (9th Cir. 1968) (antitrust; field-of-use restrictions in license).

Kinkade v. New York Shipbuilding Corp., 21 N.J. 362, 122 A.2d 360 (1956) (shoprights).

Lear, Inc. v. Adkins, 395 U.S. 653 (1969) (duration of license).

Painton & Co. v. Bourns, Inc., 442 F.2d 216 (2d Cir. 1971) (validity of trade secret licensing).

Sperry Rand Corp. v. Rothlein, 241 F. Supp. 549 (D. Conn. 1964) (ownership).

United States v. E. I. duPont de Nemours & Co., 118 F. Supp. 41 (D. Del. 1953), aff'd, 351 U.S. 377 (1956) (antitrust; territorial limitation in license permissible).

Warner-Lambert Pharmaceutical Co. v. John J. Reynolds, Inc., 178 F. Supp.

655 (S.D.N.Y. 1959), *aff'd on opinion below*, 280 F.2d 197 (2d Cir. 1960) (duration of license).

Wireless Specialty Apparatus Co. v. *Mica Condenser Co.*, 239 Mass. 158, 131 N.E. 307 (1921) (ownership).

Government Contract Aspects of Trade Secrets

International Engineering Co. v. *Richardson*, 367 F. Supp. 640 (D.D.C. 1973) (preliminary injunctive relief available).

Remedies

Conmar Products Corp. v. *Universal Slide Fastener Co.*, 172 F.2d 150 (2d Cir. 1949) (one who destroys trade secret permitted to use it).

Harley & Lund Corporation v. *Murray Rubber Co.*, 31 F.2d 932 (2d Cir.), *cert. denied*, 279 U.S. 872 (1929) (measure of damages).

Jerrold-Stephens Co. v. *Gustaveson, Inc.*, 138 F. Supp. 11 (W. D. Mo. 1956) (injunction applies to subsequent employer).

Shellmar Products Co. v. *Allen-Qualley Co.*, 87 F.2d 104 (7th Cir. 1937), *cert. denied*, 301 U.S. 695 (1937) (one who destroys trade secret barred from use of it).

Chapter 4: Trademarks and Franchising

BIBLIOGRAPHY

Callman, *Unfair Competition, Trademarks & Monopolies* (Chicago: Callaghan & Co. 1970).

Handler & Pickett, *Trade-Marks & Trade Names–An Analysis & Synthesis*, 30 Colum. L. Rev. 168 (1930).

Isaacs, *Traffic in Trade Symbols*, 44 Harv. L. Rev. 1210 (1931).

Lunsford, *The Protection of Packages & Containers*, 56 T.M.R. 567 (1966).

Merchant, *Deceptive and Descriptive Marks*, 56 T.M.R. 141 (1966).

Nims, *The Law of Unfair Competition & Trade-Marks* (New York: Baker, Voorhis & Co., 1947).

Oppenheim, *Unfair Trade Practices* (St. Paul, Minn.: West Publishing Co., 1965).

Schechter, *The Historical Foundations of the Law Relating to Trade-Marks* (New York: Columbia University Press, 1925).

Seidel, Dubroff & Gonda, *Trademark Law & Practice* (New York: Matthew Bender & Co., 1963).

Vandenburg, *Trademark Law & Procedure* (New York: Bobbs-Merrill Co., 1968).

Weigel, *Generic Names Versus Trademarks*, 52 T.M.R. 768 (1962).

CASES

Definitions

In re *Celanese Corp. of America,* 136 U.S.P.Q. 86 (TM Bd. 1962) (function of certification mark).

Consolidated Dairy Prods. Co. v. *Gildener & Schimmel, Inc.,* 101 U.S.P.Q. 465 (Com. of Pat. 1954) (differentiate collective and certification marks).

In re *Florida Citrus Commission,* 160 U.S.P.Q. 495 (TM Bd. 1968) (no use by owner of certification mark).

Huber Baking Co. v. *Stroehmann Bros. Co.,* 252 F.2d 945 (2d Cir.), *cert. denied,* 358 U.S. 829 (1958) (function of collective mark).

Kinds of Marks

American Automobile Ass'n. v. *Spiegel,* 101 F. Supp. 185 (E.D.N.Y. 1951), *rev'd on other grounds,* 205 F.2d 771 (2d Cir. 1957) (letter trademark).

Brunswick-Balke-Collender Co. v. *American Bowling & Billiard Corp.,* 150 F.2d 69 (2d Cir.), *cert. denied,* 326 U.S. 757 (1945) (color as trademark).

Ex Parte Haig & Haig Ltd., 118 U.S.P.Q. 299 (Com. of Pat. 1958) (distinctive configuration as trademark).

In re *Hepperle,* 175 U.S.P.Q. 512 (TM Bd. 1972) (subject matter not immoral).

In re *Interstate Bakeries Corp.,* 153 U.S.P.Q. 488 (TM Bd. 1967) (package design as trademark).

Jantzen Knitting Mills v. *Spokane Knitting Mills, Inc.,* 44 F.2d 656 (E.D. Wash. 1930) (pictorial trademark).

In re *Kotzin,* 276 F.2d 411 (C.C.P.A. 1960) (statutory definition not all inclusive).

In re *Lean-To Barbecue, Inc.,* 172 U.S.P.Q. 151 (TM Bd. 1971) (building design as service mark).

Maidenform, Inc. v. *Bestform Foundations, Inc.,* 161 U.S.P.Q. 805 (TM Bd. 1969) (slogan as trademark).

McPartland, Inc. v. *Montgomery Ward & Co., Inc.,* 164 F.2d 603 (C.C.P.A. 1947), *cert. denied,* 333 U.S. 875 (1948) (phonetic equivalent of descriptive word).

In re *Minnesota Mining & Mfg. Co.,* 335 F.2d 836 (C.C.P.A. 1964) (test for registration on Supplemental Register).

Minnesota Mining & Mfg. Co. v. *3M Credit Plan, Inc.,* 172 U.S.P.Q. 626 (TM Bd. 1972) (unregistrable subject matter as falsely suggesting association).

Ex Parte *Nuodex Prods. Co., Inc.,* 107 U.S.P.Q. 300 (Com. of Pat. 1955) (secondary meaning in color).

In re *Pan Tex Hotel Corp.,* 178 U.S.P.Q. 445 (TM Bd. 1973) (foreign word for product).

In re *Runsdorf*, 171 U.S.P.Q. 443 (TM Bd. 1971) (immoral subject matter).
In re *Sociedade Agricola E. Commercal Dos Vinhos Messias, S.A.R.L.*, 159
   U.S.P.Q. 275 (TM Bd. 1968) (scandalous subject matter).
In re *Telesco Brophey Ltd.*, 170 U.S.P.Q. 427 (TM Bd. 1971) (source not
   identified by functional configuration).
Thomas J. Lipton, Inc. v. *Borden Inc.*, 72 Misc. 2d 757, 340 N.Y.S. 2d 328
   (Sup. Ct. N.Y. 1972) (similarity in package design not unfair com-
   petition).
In re *William Connors Mfg. Co.*, 27 App. D.C. 389 (1906) (prohibited sub-
   ject matter).

Limitations on Acceptable Marks

In re *Dollar-A-Day Rent-A-Car Systems, Inc.*, 173 U.S.P.Q. 435 (TM Bd.
   1972) (secondary meaning).
Nationwide Advertising Service, Inc. v. *Nation-wide Employment Agencies,
   Inc.*, 176 U.S.P.Q. 311 (C.C.P.A. 1973) (geographically descriptive).
Ex Parte *Pillsbury Flour Mills Co.*, 23 U.S.P.Q. 168 (Com. of Pat. 1934)
   (descriptiveness).
Ramada Inns, Inc. v. *Marriott Corp.*, 16 Ariz. Ct. App. 459, 494 P.2d 64
   (1972) (common words).
Ex Parte *Rivera Watch Corp.*, 106 U.S.P.Q. 145 (Com. of Pat. 1955) (pri-
   mary significance as surname).
Roselux Chemical Co., Inc. v. *Parsons Ammonia Co.*, 299 F.2d 855 (C.C.P.A.
   1962) (distinctiveness).
Singer Mfg. Co. v. *Birginal-Bigsby Corp.*, 319 F.2d 273 (C.C.P.A. 1963)
   (deceptively misdescriptive).
Weiss Noodle Co. v. *Golden Cracknel & Specialty Co.*, 290 F.2d 845
   (C.C.P.A. 1961) (generic name).

Acquiring Rights in Mark Through Use and Registration

In re *Bookbinder's Restaurant, Inc.*, 240 F.2d 365 (C.C.P.A. 1957) (commerce use).
Burger King of Florida, Inc. v. *Hoots*, 403 F.2d 904 (7th Cir. 1968) (unregistered use prior to registration).
Electronic Communications, Inc. v. *Electronic Components for Industry Co.*,
   443 F.2d 487 (8th Cir.), *cert. denied*, 404 U.S. 833 (1971) (shipping container as trademark use).
Hanover Star Milling Co. v. *Metcalf*, 240 U.S. 403 (1916) (common law
   rule).
In re *Marriot Corp.*, 459 F.2d 525 (C.C.P.A. 1972) (menu as display associated with product).
Tie Rack Enterprises, Inc. v. *Tie Rak Stores*, 168 U.S.P.Q. 441 (TM Bd.
   1970) (intrastate use as affecting registration).
United Drug Co. v. *Theodore Rectanus Co.*, 248 U.S. 90 (1918) (rights
   coextensive with use).

Van Camp Sea Food Co. v. *Universal Trading Corp.*, 138 U.S.P.Q. 323 (TM Bd. 1963) (bona fide use in commerce).

Conveyancing of Trademarks

Mishawaka Rubber & Wollen Mfg. Co. v. *S.S. Kresge Co.*, 316 U.S. 203 (1942) (trademark as advertising device).

Mister Donut of America, Inc. v. *Mr. Donut, Inc.*, 418 F.2d 838 (9th Cir. 1969) (effect of failing to assign a mark with goodwill).

Syntex Laboratories, Inc. v. *The Norwich Pharmacal Co.*, 315 F. Supp. 45 (S.D.N.Y. 1970), *aff'd.*, 437 F.2d 566 (2d Cir. 1971) (assignment of mark with goodwill).

Conflicts Between Marks, Infringement, and Unfair Competition

AMF Inc. v. *American Leisure Products, Inc.*, 474 F.2d 1403 (C.C.P.A. 1973) (family of marks).

B.H. Bunn Co. v. *AAA Replacement Parts Co.*, 451 F.2d 1254 (5th Cir. 1971) (concept of infringement).

Barton v. *Rex-Oil Co.*, 29 F.2d 474 (3d Cir. 1928) (similarity in sound).

Burger King of Florida, Inc. v. *Hoots*, 403 F.2d 904 (7th Cir. 1968) (effect of innocent use prior to first user's registration).

Carl Zeiss Stiftung v. *V.E.B. Carl Zeiss, Jena*, 298 F. Supp. 1309 (S.D.N.Y. 1969), *aff'd*, 433 F.2d 686 (2d Cir. 1970), *cert. denied*, 403 U.S. 905 (1971) (use of trademark to violate antitrust laws as defense to action for trademark infringement).

Carling Brewing Co. v. *Philip Morris, Inc.*, 297 F.Supp. 1330 (N.D. Ga. 1968) (same channels of distribution).

Carter-Wallace, Inc. v. *Procter & Gamble Co.*, 434 F.2d 794 (9th Cir. 1970) (common law protection; slogans).

Chester Barrie, Ltd. v. *Chester Laurie, Ltd.*, 189 F.Supp. 98 (S.D.N.Y. 1960) (palming off).

Coca-Cola Co. v. *Dorris*, 311 F.Supp. 287 (E.D. Ark. 1970) (palming off).

David B. Findlay, Inc. v. *Walstein C. Findlay, Jr., Inc.*, 18 N.Y. 2d 12, 218 N.E. 2d 531 (1966) (use of own name as unfair competition).

Dawn Donut Co. v. *Day*, 450 F.2d 332 (10th Cir. 1971) (similarity in meaning).

Dawn Donut Co. v. *Hart's Food Stores, Inc.*, 267 F.2d 358 (2d Cir. 1959) (no exclusive right to use by virtue of registration).

Eastman Kodak Co. v. *Royal Pioneer Paper Box Mfg. Co.*, 197 F.Supp. 132 (E.D. Pa. 1961) [Section 43(a) relief without competition].

FTC v. *Real Products Corp.*, 90 F.2d 617 (2d Cir. 1937) (FTC order prohibiting deception as to origin enforced).

Friend v *H.A. Friend & Co.*, 416 F.2d 526 (9th Cir. 1969), *cert. denied*, 397 U.S. 914 (1970) [actual deception for money damages under Section 43(a)].

Ex Parte *Galter,* 96 U.S.P.Q. 216 (Ch. Ex. 1953) (broad protection for strong mark).

Greyhound Corp. v. *Rothman,* 84 F.Supp. 233 (D. Md. 1949), *aff'd,* 175 F.2d 893 (4th Cir. 1949) (strong mark).

Geisel v. *Poynter Products, Inc.,* 283 F.Supp. 261 (E.D. Mich. 1966) [false representation of approval under Section 43(a)].

Girl Scouts of the United States of America v. *Personality Posters Mfg. Co.,* 304 F.Supp. 1228 (S.D.N.Y. 1969) (trademark dilution theory limited).

Harold F. Ritchie, Inc. v. *Chesebrough-Pond's, Inc.,* 281 F.2d 755 (2d Cir. 1960) (similarity in appearance).

Hesmer Foods, Inc. v. *Campbell Soup Co.,* 346 F.2d 356 (7th Cir. 1965) [likelihood of competitive injury standard under Section 43(a)].

Jean Patou, Inc. v. *Jacqueline Cochran, Inc.,* 312 F.2d 125 (2d Cir. 1963) (intent to infringe as evidence of likelihood of confusion).

Kiki Undies Corp. v. *Promenade Hosiery Mills, Inc.,* 308 F.Supp. 489 S.D.N.Y. 1969), *aff'd,* 411 F.2d 1097 (2d Cir. 1969), *petition for cert. dismissed,* 396 U.S. 1054 (1970) (phonetically similar marks in a common line of commerce).

King Research, Inc. v. *Shulton, Inc.,* 324 F.Supp. 631 (S.D.N.Y. 1971) (unrelated goods).

King-Seely Thermos Co. v. *Aladdin Industries, Inc.,* 418 F.2d 31 (2d Cir. 1969) (injunctive relief).

L'Aiglon Apparel, Inc. v. *Lana Lobell, Inc.,* 214 F.2d 649 (3d Cir. 1954) [deception as to origin under Section 43(a)].

Maison Prunier v. *Prunier's Restaurant & Cafe, Inc.,* 159 Misc. 551, 288 N.Y.S. 529 (Sup. Ct. 1936) (area of legitimate trade expansion).

Maternally Yours, Inc. v. *Your Maternity Shop, Inc.,* 234 F.2d 538 (2d Cir. 1956) (likelihood of confusion standard).

Mister Donut of America, Inc. v. *Mr. Donut, Inc.,* 418 F.2d 838 (9th Cir. 1969) (federal pre-emption standard).

Monsanto Chemical Co. v. *Perfect Fit Products Mfg. Co.,* 349 F.2d 389 (2d Cir. 1965), *cert. denied,* 383 U.S. 942 (1966) (judicial remedies).

Mutation Mink Breeders Association v. *Lou Nierenberg Corp.,* 23 F.R.D. 155 (S.D.N.Y. 1959) [deception as to description under Section 43(a)].

Planters Nut & Chocolate Co. v. *Crown Nut Co.,* 305 F.2d 916 (C.C.P.A. 1962) (design marks).

Polaroid Corp. v. *Polarad Electronics Corp.,* 182 F.Supp. 350 (E.D.N.Y. 1960), *aff'd,* 287 F.2d 492 (2d Cir. 1961) (laches).

Polaroid Corp. v. *Polaraid, Inc.,* 319 F.2d 830 (7th Cir. 1963) (related goods).

Sears Roebuck & Co. v. *Allstate Driving School, Inc.,* 301 F.Supp. 4 (E.D.N.Y. 1969) (descriptive word as weak mark).

Thomas J. Lipton, Inc. v. *Borden Inc.,* 72 Misc. 2d 757, 340 N.Y.S. 2d 328 (Sup. Ct. 1972) (trade dress).

Triangle Publications, Inc. v. *Rohrlich,* 167 F.2d 969 (2d Cir. 1948) (unfair competition).

Westward Coach Manufacturing Co. v. *Ford Motor Co.,* 388 F.2d 627 (7th

Cir.), *cert. denied*, 392 U.S. 927 (1968) (narrow protection for weak mark).

World Carpets, Inc. v. *Dick Littrell's New World Carpets*, 438 F.2d 482 (5th Cir. 1971) (actual confusion).

Ye Olde Tavern Cheese Products, Inc. v. *Planters Peanuts Division, Standard Brands, Inc.*, 261 F.Supp. 200 (N.D. Ill. 1966), *aff'd*, 394 F.2d 833 (7th Cir. 1967) (registration creates no additional rights).

Loss of Rights

American Home Products Corp. v. *Viviano*, 165 U.S.P.Q. 668 (TM Bd. 1970) (nonuse and failure to protect as abandonment).

American Motors Corporation v. *Action-Age, Inc.*, 178 U.S.P.Q. 377 (TM Bd. 1973) (rights not lost although product no longer manufactured).

Bayer Co., Inc. v. *United Drug Co.*, 272 F.505 (S.D.N.Y. 1921) (*Aspirin* as generic term).

Beech-Nut Packing Co. v. *P. Lorillard Co.*, 273 U.S. 629 (1927) (rights not lost although trademark not used for five years).

In re *Bridge*, 170 U.S.P.Q. 428 (TM Bd. 1972) (appearance of word in dictionary is not proof that it has become generic).

Clairol Inc. v. *Holland Hall Products, Inc.*, 165 U.S.P.Q. 214 (TM Bd. 1970) (trademark rights lost under "naked" license).

Colgate-Palmolive Co. v. *Sanford Chemical Co., Inc.*, 162 U.S.P.Q. 424 (TM Bd. 1969) (two years as prima facie abandonment).

Conwood Corp. v. *Loew's Theatres, Inc.*, 173 U.S.P.Q. 829 (TM Bd. 1972) (nominal use as abandonment).

DuPont Cellophane Co. v. *Waxed Products Co.*, 85 F.2d 75 (2d Cir. 1936), *modifying*, 6 F.Supp. 859 (1934), *cert. denied*, 299 U.S. 601 (1936) (*cellophane* as generic term).

E.I. duPont de Nemours & Co. v. *Big Bear Stores, Inc.*, 161 U.S.P.Q. 50 (TM Bd. 1969) (no abandonment where mark used on another product).

Hess's of Allentown, Inc. v. *National Bellas Hess, Inc.*, 169 U.S.P.Q. 673 (TM Bd. 1971) (slight modification of mark is not abandonment of original mark).

In re *Honeywell, Inc.*, 169 U.S.P.Q. 619 (TM Bd. 1971) (subject of patent not entitled to trademark registration after patent expires).

Ideal Toy Corp. v. *Cameo Exclusive Products Inc.*, 170 U.S.P.Q. 596 (TM Bd. 1971) (abandonment).

Izod, Ltd. v. *Liberty Hosiery Mills, Inc.*, 147 U.S.P.Q. 332 (TM Bd. 1965) (nonuse during litigation is not abandonment).

King-Seeley Thermos Co. v. *Aladdin Industries, Inc.*, 321 F.2d 577 (2d Cir. 1963) (*thermos* as generic term).

Lawyers Title Ins. Co. v. *Lawyers Title Ins. Corp.*, 109 F.2d 35 (D.C. Cir. 1939), *cert. denied*, 309 U.S. 684 (1940) (nonuse during reorganization of business not abandonment).

Lewis-Shepard Co. v. *Edera Associates Co.*, 172 U.S.P.Q. 699 (TM Bd. 1972) (advertising sufficient to preserve rights).

Mister Donut of America, Inc. v. *Mr. Donut, Inc.*, 418 F.2d 838 (9th Cir. 1969) (requirement that goodwill be transferred with assignment of trademark).

Nettie Rosenstein, Inc. v. *Princess Pat., Ltd.*, 220 F.2d 444 (C.C.P.A. 1955) (nonuse during war not abandonment).

Singer Mfg. Co. v. *Redlich*, 109 F.Supp. 623 (S.D. Cal. 1952) (trademark which has become generic reclaimed as trademark).

Sterling Brewers, Inc. v. *Schenley Industries, Inc.*, 441 F.2d 675 (C.C.P.A. 1971) (nonuse during strikes not abandonment).

Storm Waterproofing Corp. v. *L. Sonneborn Sons*, 31 F.2d 992 (D. Del. 1929) (express abandonment).

Sun Valley Co. Inc. v. *Sun Valley Mfg. Co.*, 167 U.S.P.Q. 304 (TM Bd. 1970) (presumption that rights in mark pass with sale of business).

Universal Candy Co. v. *A.G. Morse Co.*, 298 F.847 (D.C. Cir. 1924) (nonuse while raw materials scarce not abandonment).

Federal Registration of Marks

Jones & Laughlin Steel Corp. v. *Jones Engineering Co.*, 292 F.2d 294 (C.C.P.A. 1961) (rights sought to be protected by opposition are those of opposer, not third party).

Revere Paint Co. v. *Twentieth Century Chemical Co.*, 150 F.2d 135 (C.C.P.A. 1945) (challenge validity of registered trademark in cancellation proceeding).

In re *Simmons Co.*, 278 F.2d 517 (C.C.P.A. 1960) (stitching on mattress as "capable of distinguishing").

Wilson v. *Delaunay*, 245 F.2d 877 (C.C.P.A. 1957) (opposition).

Trademark–Antitrust

Albrecht v. *Herald Co.*, 390 U.S. 145 (1968) (legality of exclusive territorial franchises depends on their impact on competition).

American Motor Inns, Inc. v. *Holiday Inns, Inc.*, 365 F.Supp. 1073 (D.N.J. 1973) (territorially unlimited horizontal restrictions per se unlawful).

Anderson v. *American Automobile Association*, 454 F.2d 1240 (9th Cir. 1972) (vertically imposed territorial restrictions not per se unlawful).

Carter-Wallace, Inc. v. *United States*, 449 F.2d 1374 (Ct. Cl. 1971) (postsale restraints not illegal per se).

Dawn Donut Co. v. *Hart's Food Stores, Inc.*, 267 F.2d 358 (2d Cir. 1959) (duty of licensor to prevent misuse of trademark by licensees).

Fortner Enterprises, Inc. v. *United States Steel Corp.*, 394 U.S. 495 (1969) (market dominance not required in tying product).

Kotula v. *Ford Motor Co.*, 338 F.2d 732 (8th Cir. 1964), *cert. denied*, 380 U.S. 979 (1965) (lawful termination of franchise for failure to achieve sales quota).

Radiant Burners, Inc. v. *Peoples Gas Light & Coke Co.*, 364 U.S. 656 (1961) (group boycott).

Sandura Co. v. *FTC*, 339 F.2d 847 (6th Cir. 1964) (vertical territorial restriction questioned under FTC Act).

Siegel v. *Chicken Delight, Inc.*, 448 F.2d 43 (9th Cir. 1971), *cert. denied*, 405 U.S. 955 (1972) (tying arrangements in franchise contracts per se violations of Sherman Act).

Timken Roller Bearing Co. v. *United States*, 341 U.S. 593 (1951) (trademark licensing program secondary to central purpose of allocating trade territories).

Tripoli Co. v. *Wella Corp.*, 425 F.2d 932 (3rd Cir.), *cert. denied*, 400 U.S. 831 (1970) (rule of reason applied to post-sale restraints).

United States v. *Aluminum Company of America*, 148 F.2d 416, 429 (2d Cir. 1945) (importance of preserving an organization of industry in small units).

United States v. *Arnold, Schwinn & Co.*, 388 U.S. 365 (1967) (vertical territorial market allocation).

United States v. *Sealy, Inc.*, 388 U.S. 350 (1967) (trademark license agreement as unlawful horizontal arrangement).

United States v. *Topco Associates, Inc.*, 405 U.S. 596 (1972) (unlawful private-brand trademark purchasing cooperative).

Chapter 5: Copyrights

BIBLIOGRAPHY

Breyer, *The Uneasy Case for Copyright: A Study of Copyright in Books, Photocopies, and Computer Programs,* 84 Harv. L. Rev. 281 (1970).

Brown, *The Operation of the Damage Provisions of the Copyright Law,* Copyright Law Revision Study No. 23, U.S. Government Printing Off. 1960.

Chafee, *Reflections on the Law of Copyright,* 45 Colum. L. Rev. 503 (1945).

Comment, *Joint and Several Liability for Copyright Infringement: A New Look at Section 101(b) of the Copyright Act,* 32 U. Chi. L. Rev. 98 (1964).

Fine, *Misuse and Antitrust Defenses to Copyright Infringement Action,* 17 Hastings L. J. 315 (1965).

Gitlin & Ringer, *Copyrights* (New York: Practicing Law Institute, 1965 ed.).

Kaplan, *Publication in Copyright Law: The Question of Phonograph Records,* 103 U. Penn. L. Rev. 469 (1955).

Lorimer, *2¢ Plain, Why Pay More?,* 10 U.C.L.A. L. Rev. 561 (1963).

Miller, *Problems in the Transfer of Interests in a Copyright,* ASCAP Copyright Law Symposium No. 10 131 (1959).

Nimmer on Copyrights (New York: Matthew Bender & Co., 1973 ed.).

Note, *Monetary Recovery for Copyright Infringement,* 67 Harv. L. Rev. 1044 (1954).

Note, *Protection for the Artistic Aspects of Articles of Utility*, 72 Harv. L. Rev. 1520 (1959).
Note, *Remedies for Copyright Infringement*, 23 Ark. L. Rev. 464 (1969).
Rembar, *Xenophilia in Congress: Ad Interim Copyright and the Manufacturing Clause*, 69 Colum. L. Rev. 770 (1969).
Ringer, *Renewal of Copyright*, Copyright Law Revision Study No. 31, U.S. Gov't. Printing Off. 1960.
Treece, *American Law Analogues of the Author's "Moral Right,"* 16 Am. J. Comp. L. 487 (1968).
Yankwich, *What Is Fair Use?*, 22 U. Chi. L. Rev. 203 (1954).

CASES

Overview of the U.S. Copyright System

American Tobacco Co. v. *Werckmeister*, 207 U.S. 284 (1907) (exhibition of art work not publication).
Hemingway v. *Random House, Inc.*, 23 N.Y. 2d 341, 296 N.Y.S. 2d 771, 244 N.E. 2d 250 (1969) (common law copyright in utterances).
King v. *Mister Maestro, Inc.*, 224 F.Supp. 101 (S.D.N.Y. 1963) (oral delivery not a publication; limited publication).
White v. *Kimmell*, 193 F.2d 744 (9th Cir.), *cert. denied*, 343 U.S. 957 (1952) (limited publication).
White-Smith Music Co. v. *Apollo Co.*, 209 U.S. 1 (1908) (piano roll not copy of underlying music).

Standards of Copyrightability

Alfred Bell & Co. v. *Catalda Fine Arts*, 191 F.2d 99 (2d Cir. 1951) (mezzotint case).
Bleistein v. *Donaldson Lithographing Co.*, 188 U.S. 239 (1903) (Justice Holmes on court's reluctance to judge aesthetics).
Sheldon v. *Metro-Goldwyn Pictures Corp.*, 81 F.2d 49 (2d Cir. 1936), *aff'd.*, 309 U.S. 390 (1940) (Judge Hand on originality; Keats' Ode).
Time, Inc. v. *Bernard Geis Associates*, 293 F.Supp. 130 (S.D.N.Y. 1968) (standards of creativity; Zapruder film case).

Copyrightable Subject Matter

Amsterdam v. *Triangle Publications, Inc.*, 189 F.2d 104 (3d Cir. 1951) (map copyrightability, direct observation rule).
Berlin v. *E. C. Publications, Inc.*, 329 F.2d 541 (2d Cir.), *cert. denied*, 379 U.S. 822 (1964) (no monopoly in iambic pentameter).
Burrow-Giles Lithographic Co. v. *Sarony*, 111 U.S. 53 (1884) (copyrightability of photographs).
Capitol Records Inc. v. *Mercury Records Corp.*, 221 F.2d 657 (1st Cir.

1955) (sound recordings not copyrightable prior to 1971 amendments).

Columbia Broadcasting System, Inc. v. *DeCosta,* 377 F.2d 315 (1st Cir.), *cert. denied,* 389 U.S. 1007 (1967) ("Paladin" case; characters are copyrightable).

Goldstein v. *California,* 412 U.S. 546 (1973) (statutory "writings" narrower than constitutional "writings").

Kitchens of Sara Lee, Inc. v. *Nifty Foods Corp.,* 266 F.2d 541 (2d Cir. 1959) (copyrightability of labels; chocolate cake cases).

Mazer v. *Stein,* 347 U.S. 201 (1954) (words of applied art copyrightable).

Nichols v. *Universal Pictures Corp.,* 45 F.2d 119 (2d Cir. 1930), *cert. denied,* 282 U.S. 902 (1931) (Judge Hand on copyrightability of characters).

Warner Bros. Pictures v. *Columbia Broadcasting System,* 216 F.2d 945 (9th Cir. 1954), *cert. denied,* 348 U.S. 971 (1955) (Sam Spade case; characters not copyrightable).

Noncopyrightable Subject Matter

Baker v. *Selden,* 101 U.S. 99 (1880) (copying for purpose of use permissible).

Morrissey v. *Procter & Gamble Co.,* 379 F.2d 675 (1st Cir. 1967) (contest rules not copyrightable).

Rights Protected by Copyright

Buck v. *Jewell-LaSalle Realty Co.,* 283 U.S. 191 (1931) (multiple-performance doctrine).

Clemens v. *Press Publishing Co.,* 67 Misc. 183, 122 N.Y.S. 206 (1910) (author's right to be known as author).

Clevenger v. *Baker Voorhis & Co.,* 8 N.Y. 2d 187, 168 N.E. 2d 643 (1960) (author's right to prevent false attribution of his name).

Duchess Music Corp. v. *Stern,* 458 F.2d 1305 (9th Cir. 1972) (compulsory recording license does not permit exact duplication).

G. Ricordi & Co. v. *Paramount Pictures, Inc.,* 189 F.2d 469 (2d Cir.), *cert. denied,* 342 U.S. 849 (1951) ("Madame Butterfly" case).

Herbert v. *Shanley Co.,* 242 U.S. 591 (1917) (performance in restaurant "for profit").

Jondora Music Pub. Co. v. *Melody Recordings, Inc.,* 351 F.Supp. 572 (D.N.J. 1972) (compulsory recording license does permit exact duplication).

Platt & Munk, Inc. v. *Republic Graphics, Inc.,* 315 F.2d 847 (2d Cir. 1963) (first sale doctrine).

Rice v. *American Program Bureau,* 446 F.2d 685 (2d Cir. 1971) ("Jesus Christ Superstar" case).

United Artists Television, Inc. v. *Fortnightly Corp.,* 392 U.S. 390 (1968) (multiple-performance doctrine not applied to CATV).

Vargas v. *Esquire, Inc.,* 164 F.2d 522 (7th Cir. 1947) (moral rights not recognized in U.S.).

Who Can Obtain Copyright?

Scherr v. *Universal Match Corp.,* 297 F.Supp. 107 (S.D.N.Y. 1967), *aff'd,* 417 F.2d 497 (2d Cir. 1969), *cert. denied,* 397 U.S. 936 (1970) (governmental works).

Shapiro, Bernstein & Co. v. *Jerry Vogel Music Co.,* 221 F.2d 569 (2d Cir. 1955) (works done for hire).

Welles v. *Columbia Broadcasting System,* 308 F.2d 810 (9th Cir. 1962) (contract can permit employee to retain copyright).

Procedures for Obtaining Copyright

DeJonge & Co. v. *Breuker & Kessler Co.,* 235 U.S. 33 (1914) (inadequate notice on repeating pattern).

DeSylva v. *Ballentine,* 351 U.S. 570 (1956) (widow and children entitled to renewal right as a class; state law governs).

H. M. Kolbe Co. v. *Armgus Textile Co.,* 315 F.2d 70 (2d Cir. 1963) (notice adequate on repeating pattern).

Herbert Rosenthal Jewelry Corp. v. *Grossbardt,* 436 F.2d 315 (2d Cir. 1970) (sufficiency of short form notice).

Hervieu v. *J. S. Ogilvie Pub. Co.,* 169 F. 978 (D.C.N.Y. 1909) (dramatic work not within manufacturing clause).

Hoffenberg v. *Kaminstein,* 396 F.2d 684 (D.C. Cir), *cert. denied,* 393 U.S. 913 (1968) ("Candy" case).

Marx v. *United States,* 96 F.2d 204 (9th Cir. 1938) (copyright in unpublished work runs from date of registration).

Miller Music Corp. v. *Chas. N. Daniels, Inc.,* 362 U.S. 373 (1960) (renewal right immune from creditor's claims).

Peter Pan Fabrics, Inc. v. *Martin Weiner Corp.,* 274 F.2d 487 (2d Cir. 1960) (burden on copier to show notice would not impair work).

Washingtonian Publishing Co. v. *Pearson,* 306 U.S. 30 (1939) (delay in deposit does not invalidate copyright).

Ad Interim Copyrights and Rules Pertinent to Citizens of Foreign States

Hoffenberg v. *Kaminstein,* 396 F.2d 684 (D.C. Cir. 1968) ("Candy" case).

Ownership and Conveyancing of Copyrights

Edward B. Marks Music Corp. v. *Jerry Vogel Music Co.,* 140 F.2d 266 (2d Cir. 1944) (creation of joint authorship).

Fred Fisher Music Co. v. *M. Witmark & Sons,* 318 U.S. 643 (1943) (assignability of renewal rights).

Goodis v. *United Artists Television, Inc.,* 425 F.2d 397 (2d Cir. 1970) (doctrine of indivisibility).

Rossiter v. *Vogel,* 148 F.2d 292 (2d Cir. 1945) (assignee of renewal right may file in author's name).

Shapiro, Bernstein & Co. v. *Jerry Vogel Music Co.*, 221 F.2d 569 (2d Cir. 1955) (creation of joint authorship).

Copyright Infringement

Arnstein v. *Porter*, 154 F.2d 464 (2d Cir. 1946) (bifurcated inquiry of substantial similarity).

Dreamland Ball Room v. *Shapiro, Bernstein & Co.*, 36 F.2d 354 (7th Cir. 1929) (vicarious liability of ballroom owner for infringements of orchestra).

F. W. Woolworth Co. v. *Contemporary Arts, Inc.*, 344 U.S. 228 (1952) (infringer liable for both profits and damages; in lieu damages if damages or profits unascertainable).

Harold Lloyd Corp. v. *Witwer*, 65 F.2d 1 (9th Cir. 1933) (ordinary observer test).

L. A. Westermann Co. v. *Dispatch Printing Co.*, 249 U.S. 100 (1919) (multiple infringement).

Leon v. *Pacific Telephone and Telegraph Co.*, 91 F.2d 484 (9th Cir. 1937) (infringement found in numerically compiling phone numbers).

Nichols v. *Universal Pictures Corp.*, 45 F.2d 119 (2d Cir. 1930), *cert. denied*, 282 U.S. 902 (1931) (application of "pattern" test).

Peter Pan Fabrics, Inc. v. *Martin Weiner Corp.*, 274 F.2d 487 (2d Cir. 1960) (infringement must be determined ad hoc).

Rosemont Enterprises, Inc. v. *Random House, Inc.*, 366 F.2d 303 (2d Cir. 1966), *cert. denied*, 385 U.S. 1009 (1967) (proscription against copyright of ideas designed to present wasted effort).

Shapiro, Bernstein & Co. v. *H. L. Green Co.*, 316 F.2d 304 (2d Cir. 1963) (vicarious liability).

Sheldon v. *Metro-Goldwyn Pictures Corp.*, 309 U.S. 390 (1940) (infringer's profits should be apportioned where he has contributed his own efforts to work).

Defenses to Actions for Copyright Infringement

Baker v. *Selden*, 101 U.S. 99 (1880) (copying for use defense).

Benny v. *Loew's, Inc.*, 239 F.2d 532 (9th Cir. 1956), *aff'd by an equally divided court*, 356 U.S. 43 (1958) (unfair use; "Gas Light" case).

Berlin v. *E. C. Publications, Inc.*, 329 F.2d 541 (2d Cir.), *cert. denied*, 379 U.S. 822 (1964) fair use; parodies may "conjure up the originals").

Folsom v. *Marsh*, 9 Fed. Cas. 342 (C. C. Mass. 1841) (unfair use; extensive copying).

Henry Holt & Co. v. *Liggett & Meyers Tobacco Co.*, 23 F.Supp. 302 (E.D. Pa. 1938) (unfair use; commercial purpose).

Robert Stigwood Group Ltd. v. *O'Reilly*, 346 F.Supp. 376 (D. Conn. 1972) (unfair use; criticism does not justify wholesale copying).

Rosemont Enterprises, Inc. v. *Random House, Inc.*, 366 F.2d 303 (2d Cir. 1966) (fair use; no competition).

Stuff v. *E. C. Publications, Inc.*, 342 F. 2d 143 (2d Cir. 1965) (abandonment by failure to enforce).

Time, Inc. v. *Bernard Geis Associates*, 293 F.Supp. 130 (S.D.N.Y. 1968) (fair use; public interest).

Williams & Wilkins Co. v. *United States*, 487 F.2d 1345 (Ct. Cl. 1973) (fair use; library photocopying).

Copyright–Antitrust Problems

Alden-Rochelle, Inc. v. *ASCAP*, 80 F.Supp. 888 (S.D.N.Y. 1948) (copyright pooling).

Bobbs-Merrill Co. v. *Straus*, 210 U.S. 339 (1908) (vertical price fixing).

K-91, Inc. v. *Gershwin Publishing Corp.*, 372 F.2d 1 (9th Cir. 1967) (ASCAP immunized by consent decree).

Straus v. *American Publisher's Assoc.*, 231 U.S. 222 (1913) (horizontal price fixing).

United States v. *Loew's Inc.*, 371 U.S. 38 (1962) (block booking).

United States v. *Paramount Pictures, Inc.*, 334 U.S. 131 (1948) (copyright as vehicle for monopolizing; block booking).

Chapter 6: Rights of Privacy, Public Performances, and Publicity in Commerce

BIBLIOGRAPHY

Callmann, *Right of Personality (Right of Privacy)*, 3 Performing Arts Rev. 255 (1972).

Comment, *The Misappropriation Doctrine after Sears-Compco*, 2 U. San Fran. L. Rev. 292 (1968).

Gordon, *Right of Property in Name, Likeness, Personality and History*, 55 N.W.U.L. Rev. 553 (1960).

Nimmer, *The Right of Publicity*, 19 Law and Contemp. Prob. 202 (1954).

Note, *The Right of Publicity: A Doctrinal Innovation*, 62 Yale L. J. 1123 (1953).

Treece, *Commercial Exploitation of Names, Likenesses and Personal Histories*, 51 Texas L. Rev. 637 (1973).

Warren and Brandeis, *The Right to Privacy*, 4 Harv. L. Rev. 193 (1890).

CASES

Right of Privacy

Fisher v. *Murray M. Rosenberg, Inc.*, 175 Misc. 370, 23 N.Y.S. 2d 677 (Sup. Ct. 1940) (court's reluctance to grant monetary relief).

Roberson v. *Rochester Folding Box. Co.*, 171 N.Y. 538, 64 N.E. 442 (1902) (early case denying relief which led to enactment of New York right of privacy statute).

Limitations of the Right of Privacy

Gautier v. *Pro-Football, Inc.*, 304 N.Y. 354, 107 N.E. 2d 485 (1952) (doctrine of waiver).

Miller v. *Madison Square Garden Corp.*, 176 Misc. 714, 28 N.Y.S. 2d 811 (Sup. Ct. 1941) (damages measured by injury to plaintiff rather than benefit to defendant).

Right Against Commercial Misappropriation
Compared to Right of Privacy

Edison v. *Edison Polyform Mfg. Co.*, 73 N.J. Eq. 136, 67 A. 392 (1907) (misappropriation of one's name for commercial purposes as basis for recovery).

Unfair Competition as an Alternative Remedy

Sinatra v. *Goodyear Tire & Rubber Co.*, 435 F. 2d 711 (9th Cir. 1970), *cert. denied*, 402 U.S. 906 (1971) (absence of competitive relationship, "passing off," and copyright violation led to denial of relief sought under theory of unfair competition).

Right of Publicity

Haelan Laboratories, Inc. v. *Topps Chewing Gum, Inc.*, 202 F.2d 866 (2d Cir.), *cert. denied*, 346 U.S. 816 (1953) (leading case recognizing right of publicity).

Rosemont Enterprises, Inc. v. *Urban Systems, Inc.*, 72 Misc. 2d 788, 340 N.Y.S. 2d 144 (Sup. Ct. 1973) (celebrity has legitimate proprietary interest in his public personality).

Misappropriation of Intangibles and the Conflict with Federal Law

Compco Corp. v. *Daybright Lighting, Inc.*, 376 U.S. 234 (1964) (arm's length copying lawful outside patent and copyright field in the absence of "palming off").

Goldstein v. *California*, 412 U.S. 546 (1973) (federal copyright law does not pre-empt state regulation of sound recording).

International News Service v. *Associated Press*, 248 U.S. 215 (1918) (misappropriation doctrine).

Sears, Roebuck & Co. v. *Stiffel Co.*, 376 U.S. 225 (1964) (arm's length copying lawful outside patent and copyright field in the absence of "palming off").

Waring v. *WDAS Broadcasting Station, Inc.*, 327 Pa. 433, 194 A. 631 (1937) (performer's interpretation of a musical composition is a protectable property right).

Chapter 7: Federal Tax Aspects of Intellectual Property

BIBLIOGRAPHY

Patents, Trade Secrets and Related Know-how

Beausang, *Patent Transfers-Section 1235*, 228 *Tax Management Portfolio* (1970).

Trademarks, Service Marks, and Franchises

Reich, *A Planning Guide to Franchise Transfers in Light of Treasury's Proposed Regs*, 36 Journal of Taxation 232 (1972).

CASES

Patents, Trade Secrets, and Related Know-how

Herbert Allen, 11 TCM 1093 (1952) (holding period of patentable inventions).

Best Lock Corporation, 31 TC 1217 (1959) (royalty payments deductible).

Arthur N. Blum, 11 TC 101 (1948)(A), *aff'd*, 183 F.2d 281 (3d Cir. 1950) (royalty payments as compensation to employee).

Chu v. *Commissioner of Internal Revenue*, 486 F.2d 696 (1st Cir. 1973) (patent applications not depreciable).

Commercial Solvents Corp., 42 TC 455 (1964)(A) (sale or exchange of intellectual property).

Samuel E. Diescher, 36 BTA 732 (1937)(NA), *aff'd*, 110 F.2d 90 (3d Cir. 1940) (trade or business of selling intellectual property).

William T. Downs, 49 TC 533 (1968)(A) (royalty payments as compensation to employee).

E. I. duPont de Nemours and Co. v. *United States*, 288 F.2d 904 (Ct. Cl. 1961) (sale or exchange of intellectual property).

Thomas L. Fawick, 52 TC 104 (1969), *rev'd*, 436 F.2d 655 (6th Cir. 1971) (license limited to particular field of use).

Vincent A. Marco, 25 TC 544 (1955)(A) (license limited geographically within country).

Edward C. Myers, 6 TC 258 (1946) (NA) (sale or exchange of intellectual property).

Pickren v. *United States*, 378 F.2d 595 (5th Cir. 1967) (transfer of trade secrets).

Myron C. Poole, 46 TC 392 (1966)(A) (IRC Section 1235 exclusive).

Vincent B. Rodgers, 51 TC 927 (1969)(A) (license limited geographically within country).

Wm. S. Rouveral, 42 TC 186 (1964)(NA) (sale or exchange of intellectual property).

Taylor Winfield Corp., 57 TC 205 (1971), *aff'd,* 467 F.2d 483 (6th Cir. 1972) (sale or exchange of intellectual property).

United States v. *Carruthers,* 219 F.2d 21 (9th Cir. 1955) (exclusive license limited to particular field of use).

United States Mineral Products Co., 52 TC 177 (1969)(A) (patents are depreciable).

Wall Products, Inc., 11 TC 51 (1948)(A) (trade secrets are property).

Waterman v. *Mackenzie,* 138 U.S. 252 (1891) (transfer of patent under patent law).

Yates Industries, Inc., 58 TC 961 (1972), *aff'd,* 480 F.2d 920 (3rd Cir. 1973) (trade secrets not depreciable).

Arthur M. Young, 29 TC 850 (1958), *aff'd,* 269 F.2d 89 (2d Cir. 1959) (license terminable at will).

Trademarks, Service Marks, and Franchises

Martin V. Lawless, 25 TCM 49 (1966) (depreciation of dancing school franchise).

Norwich Pharmacal Co., 30 BTA 326 (1934) (trademark not depreciable).

Renziehausen v. *Lucas,* 280 U.S. 387 (1930) (trademark not depreciable).

Walter J. Roob, 50 TC 891 (1968) (transfer to franchise).

Triangle Publications, Inc., 54 TC 138 (1970)(A) (nondeductibility of franchise).

W. K. Co., 56 TC 434 (1971) (depreciation of taxicab license).

COPYRIGHTS, ARTISTIC, AND LITERARY PROPERTY

Joseph A. Fields, 14 TC 1202 (1950) (A), *aff'd,* 189 F.2d 950 (2d Cir. 1951) (mediums of publication).

REVENUE RULINGS

Patents, Trade Secrets, and Related Know-how

Rev. Rul. 58-353, C.B. 1958-2, 408 (sale or exchange of intellectual property).

Rev. Rul. 69-482, C.B. 1969-2, 164 (IRC Section 1235 not exclusive).

Rev. Rul. 71-564, C.B. 1971-2, 179 (length of exclusive license of trade secret).

Trademarks, Service Marks, and Franchises

Rev. Rul. 70-644, C.B. 1970-2, 167 (Federal milk base not depreciable).

Copyrights, Artistic, and Literary Property

Rev. Rul. 60-226, C.B. 1960-1, 26, modifying Rev. Rul. 54-409, C.B. 1952-2, 174 (copyrights are divisible).

Index

509

Index

expression of a narrative work than its arrangement and choice of words, as there is more to a play than merely its dialogue. To be meaningful, copyright protection of such works must extend to the very heart of the author's expression. With respect to narrative and dramatic works, one often quoted commentator has said that copyright protection should cover the *pattern* of a work as embodied in its "sequence of events, and the development and interplay of [its] characters."

However, it is one thing to describe those portions of a work that merit protection, but it is another to decide when these have been appropriated in an actual case. In practice, it has proved exceedingly difficult to determine when one work has misappropriated the protectable "pattern" of another. To this end, a court must undertake a detailed comparison of the works in question. The procedure by which courts undertake and evaluate this comparison was first set forth by Judge Learned Hand in the famous case of *Nichols v. Universal Pictures Co.* Judge Hand explained:

[W]hen the plagiarist does not take out a block in situ, but an abstract of the whole, decision is . . . troublesome. Upon any work, and especially upon a play, a great number of patterns of increasing generality will fit equally well, as more and more of the incident is left out. The last may perhaps be no more than the most general statement of what the play is about . . . but there is a point in this series of abstractions where they are no longer protected, since otherwise the playwright could prevent the use of his "ideas," to which, apart from their expression, his property is never extended [citations omitted].

Application of this formulation calls for a two-step evaluation that has since become known as the "pattern test." First, one must identify the "most detailed pattern" common to both works, and secondly, he must decide whether this pattern is protectable or is in the public domain. This two-step procedure becomes much easier to comprehend when viewed in operation. *Nichols v. Universal Pictures Co.* provides a convenient example.

In *Nichols*, the plaintiff was the author of "Abie's Irish Rose," an extraordinarily popular Broadway comedy that concerns two young lovers, one Catholic and one Jewish, whose parents are mutually hostile. Defendant was the creator of "The Cohens and the Kellys," a motion picture with a plot similar to "Abie's Irish Rose." In applying the first part of the pattern test, the court undertook a point-by-point comparison of the two works in question. When "Abie's Irish Rose" opens, the young couple has secretly married, and the young boy is concerned with preparing his prosperous orthodox Jewish parents for the shock of his mixed marriage. To this end, he convinces his alleged, the key issue is substantial similarity. Yet it is clear that the term *substantial similarity*, when used in copyright infringement cases, carries considerably different connotations than it does when used in everyday conversation; for example, we have already noted that many similar works do not evoke infringement problems. We may explain these different connotations by saying that for infringement purposes we consider only the copyrightable portions of the copyrighted work; if the similarity extends solely over noncopyrightable material, there is no infringement.

Dictionaries perhaps represent the most instructive and elementary model. Suppose someone were to copyright a dictionary purporting to contain all the new words added to the English language from 1970 to the present. Could he enjoin someone else from publishing another dictionary also purporting to define new English words of the same period? Our common sense tells us that the answer is no, and indeed, the law reaches the same result. Were the author of our hypothetical dictionary able to impound all others, he would in effect possesses a monopoly in his idea, and as we have seen, it is a rudimentary principle of both patent and copyright law that no one can monopolize ideas. Indeed, monopolization of ideas is prohibited by the First Amendment, for the "arena of public debate would be quiet indeed, if a politician could copyright his speeches . . . and thus obtain a monopoly on the ideas contained."

In our earlier discussion of the uncopyrightability of ideas, we observed that anyone can publish on Einstein's theory of relativity or produce a play concerning two lovers whose families are mutually hostile. Despite these observations, it is well established that there is a property right in a particular combination of ideas, or in the particular form in which ideas are embodied. Obviously, the line that exists between nonprotected "abstract ideas" and protected "particular combinations of ideas" or "expression" is fuzzy, if identifiable at all. Justice Story once opined that drawing a distinction between an idea and the form in which it is expressed might well be more a matter of metaphysics than jurisprudence. Not surprisingly, then, courts have often found difficulty in drawing this distinction, and insight into why this line seems so elusive is best obtained by examining how the courts have dealt with this problem in actual cases.

The area that contains most of the decisions relating to the line between ideas and expression is the field of narrative and dramatic works. Of course, where merely the dialogue or the wording of a narrative or dramatic work is allegedly infringed, it will be held that the copyrighted expression has been appropriated when the second author's paraphrasing comes too close to the original. But clearly, there is more to the

appears under a bar-by-bar comparison to be a similarity, when translated into the inscrutably abstract language of musical sound, may be
something altogether different.

Indeed, of all the different areas of copyrightable works, the one
that bears the most similarity to fictional and dramatic works, and
in which analysis of the sort required by the pattern test ought most
readily to be useful, is the area of derivative works, for in these works the
line between the protected and unprotected portions seems relatively
clear. This is particularly true of maps, compilations, and directories
that contain only public domain material. In such works, the protectable
pattern is to be found in the sequential arrangement of data, printing,
indexing, coloring, and other features of arrangement. Biography,
histories, and other similar works containing public domain materials
raise more complex problems, however, for they are composed of descriptions of fact and call for the author to exercise discretion in both his
choice of words and his choice of events. Though presented in a new
directory, a phone number will convey only one bit of information,
and no directory, no matter how arranged, would be complete without
all of the numbers. In contrast, histories of the same period may describe different events and in two works the narrative descriptions of
such events will vary. Thus such works lend themselves more readily
both to originality of composition and subtlety of appropriation than
do compilations and directories. Consequently, it is sometimes said
that the former are entitled to more protection than the latter.

But when derivative works contain new material, as well as material in the public domain, the resulting problem of separating the
ideas of the original material from their expression is essentially no
different from the same problem in cases involving works of fiction.
For example, there are numerous cases involving compilations of
court decisions wherein the compiler appended to the public domain
case reports his own analytical summary of their contents. The courts
have held that in such situations two possible categories of wrongful
copying may occur: (1) copying of the schematic organization and
pagination of the cases and (2) copying of the analytic headnotes.
As to the first, the form of arrangement is clearly divisible from the
public domain content of the cases, but as to the second, if copying
is not verbatim, a more elaborate inquiry must be made as to whether
only the ideas in the headnotes or the expression itself has been
copied. There seems to be no reason why this inquiry, in the case of
headnotes of a derivative work, should not be governed by the rules
and analysis that are determinative when the preface to a novel is at
issue. Indeed, generally, this is the case.

However, there are a special group of cases concerning nonliteral his wife's explanations, renounces her love, and abandons her. Although both works shared this pattern, the court held that the expression of the first was not copied by the second. Indeed, when such a detailed similarity between the sequence of events and the interplay of the characters of two works is held to signify merely that both authors have utilized the same "idea," it is clear that only when the "patterns" of two works are almost exactly identical down to the minutest incident will it be held that the expression rather than that idea has been duplicated. For instance, in another case, the plaintiff composed a screenplay depicting the life of Clara Barton. The plaintiff embellished the famous nurse's life considerably; for example, she created a fictional lover named Tom Maxwell, who dies, and in a letter, bequeaths Clara a legacy in gold dust. Other fictional touches were added, as well, including an imagined controversy between Clara and the New Jersey school board. The defendant's biography of Clara Barton "reproduced in substantially similar form" all of the fictional events created by the plaintiff, even the names of plaintiff's fictional characters were appropriated. Although the court went through the motions of pattern test analysis, we hardly need the pattern test to aid us in finding infringement in such a case. Indeed, in the final analysis, the pattern test, and other alternative tests that have been proposed, are ineffective guides. In the end, we must admit that Learned Hand was correct when he said, thirty years after he had conceived the pattern test in *Nichols*: "Obviously, no principle can be stated as to when an imitator has gone beyond copying the 'idea' and has borrowed its 'expression.' Decisions must therefore inevitably be *ad hoc*."

Whereas the pattern test, even with all its inadequacies, seems aptly suited to infringement cases involving narrative and dramatic works, it is an ineffective guide in many other situations. For example, where one manufacturer's statue is alleged to be an unauthorized reproduction of another's work of art, where do we look for a pattern common to both works? Indeed, in one case, involving, ironically enough, an alleged infringement of an artistic pattern, it was suggested that the pattern test is frequently ineffective. Even in those areas in which one would imagine that pattern analysis would be fruitful, it has not been productive. For example, superficially it would seem that in the field of musical compositions, pattern analysis would aid greatly. Because all such works are segmented into intervals and can contain a limited number of notes, conceivably two musical compositions could be superimposed, their common pattern becoming visible to the eye. Yet such an approach overlooks the elementary ut crucial fact that music appeals to the ear, not the eye, and what